KEEPING THE REPUBLIC

POWER AND CITIZENSHIP

IN AMERICAN POLITICS

KEEPING THE REPUBLIC

POWER AND CITIZENSHIP

IN AMERICAN POLITICS

Brief Edition

CHRISTINE BARBOUR
Indiana University

GERALD C. WRIGHT
Indiana University

Houghton Mifflin Company   Boston   New York

We dedicate this book with love to our parents,
John Barbour, Patti Barbour,
Doris Wright, and to the memory of Gerry Wright;
to our kids, Andrea and Darrin, Monica and Michael;
and to each other.

Editor-in-Chief: Jean Woy
Sponsoring Editor: Mary Dougherty
Senior Development Editor: Ann West
Senior Project Editor: Carol Newman
Senior Production/Design Coordinator: Carol Merrigan
Senior Designer: Henry Rachlin
Senior Cover Design Coordinator: Deborah Azerrad Savona
Senior Manufacturing Coordinator: Priscilla Bailey

Cover image: Barbara Cesery/SuperStocks

Printed in the U.S.A.

Library of Congress Catalog Card Number: 2001131476

ISBN: 0-618-11626-5

123456789-DOC-05 04 03 02 01

About the Authors

Professor Christine Barbour has taught political science at Indiana University in Bloomington for the past ten years. Primarily teaching large sections of *Introduction to American Politics,* she has become increasingly interested in how teachers of large classes can maximize what their students learn. At Indiana, Professor Barbour has been a Lilly Fellow, working on a project to increase student retention in large introductory courses, and she has worked with the Freshman Learning Project, a university-wide effort to improve the first-year undergraduate experience. She has served on the *New York Times* College Advisory Board for several years, working with other educators on developing ways to integrate newspaper reading into the undergraduate curriculum. Barbour believes that it is vitally important to counter college students' political apathy, and she is interested in the relationship between active learning techniques and citizenship skills. She has won several teaching awards at Indiana, but the two that mean the most to her were awarded her by students: the Indiana University Student Alumni Association Award for Outstanding Faculty (1995–96) and the Indiana University Chapter of the Society of Professional Journalists Brown Derby Award (1997). When not teaching or writing textbooks, Professor Barbour enjoys playing with her four dogs, traveling with her coauthor, gardening, cooking (and eating) good food, and playing remarkably bad golf.

Professor Gerald Wright has taught political science at Indiana University in Bloomington since 1981. He is an accomplished scholar of American politics—the author of two books, including *Statehouse Democracy: Public Opinion and Policy in the American States* with coauthors Robert S. Erikson and John P. McIver, and more than thirty articles on elections, public opinion, and state politics. He has long studied the relationship of politics to public policy, and is currently conducting research into the problems of citizenship participation and the degree to which elected officials do what voters want them to do. He has been a consultant for *Project Vote Smart* in the last several elections. Professor Wright has also become increasingly involved in the challenge of teaching large classes, spending the summer of 1998 as a member of the Freshman Learning Project at Indiana University, a university-wide effort to improve the first-year undergraduate experience by focusing on how today's college students learn and how teachers can adapt their pedagogical methods to best teach them. When not working, Professor Wright also enjoys his dogs, gardening, travel, and good food. His golf is considerably better than his coauthor's.

Contents

Preface xi

To the Student xv

1 Power and Citizenship in American Politics 1

WHAT'S AT STAKE? 1

What Is Politics? 3

Politics and Government 4   Politics and Economics 4
Rules and Institutions 7

Political Systems and the Concept of Citizenship 8

Authoritarian Systems 8   Democracy 9   Meanings
of Citizenship 10

Democracy and Citizenship in America 12

The Dangers of Democracy 12   Citizenship in America 13   Who Is a Citizen and Who Is Not? 14

What Do American Citizens Believe? 17

American Political Culture: Ideas That Unite 17
American Ideologies: Ideas That Divide 20

Themes of This Book 22

Citizenship and Politics 27

WHAT'S AT STAKE REVISITED 27

Key Terms 29   Summary 29

■ Consider the Source: Thinking Like a Political Scientist 24

2 The Politics of the American Founding 31

WHAT'S AT STAKE? 31

The Split from England 33

Revolution 35   The Declaration of Independence 36
". . . That All Men Are Created Equal" 36

■ Who, What, How 38

The Articles of Confederation 39

The Provisions of the Articles 39   Some Winners,
Some Losers 40

■ Who, What, How 41

The Constitutional Convention 41

How Strong a Central Government? 41   Large States,
Small States 42   North and South 44

■ Who, What, How 45

The Constitution 46

The Legislative Branch 46   The Executive Branch 47
The Judicial Branch 48   Separation of Powers and
Checks and Balances 50   Amendability 52

■ Who, What, How 53

Ratification 53

Federalists Versus Anti-Federalists 54   *The Federalist
Papers* 54   The Final Vote 56

■ Who, What, How 57

Citizenship and the Founding 57

WHAT'S AT STAKE REVISITED 57

Key Terms 58   Summary 59

3 Federalism 60

WHAT'S AT STAKE? 60

What Is Federalism? 62

What Does the Constitution Say? 62   Two Views of
Federalism 64   Possible Alternatives to Federalism
64   What Difference Does Federalism Make? 66

■ Who, What, How 67

**The Changing Balance: American Federalism
over Time** 67

John Marshall: Strengthening the Constitutional Powers of the National Government 69   The Civil War:
National Domination of the States 70   The New
Deal: National Power over Business 70   Civil Rights:
National Protection Against State Abuse 70

■ Who, What, How 71

Federalism Today 72

The Structure of Federalism 72   The Politics of Contemporary Federalism 72   Congressional Strategies
for Influencing State Policy 74   The Move Toward
Devolution 78

■ Who, What, How 80

Citizenship and Federalism 80

WHAT'S AT STAKE REVISITED 81

Key Terms 82   Summary 82

4 Fundamental American Liberties   83

WHAT'S AT STAKE?   83

Rights in a Democracy   86
Rights and the Power of the People 86   When Rights Conflict 87

■ **Who, What, How**   87

The Bill of Rights and the States   88
Why Is a Bill of Rights Valuable? 88   Applying the Bill of Rights to the States 89

■ **Who, What, How**   90

Freedom of Religion   91
Why Is Religious Freedom Valuable? 91   The Establishment Clause 91   The Free Exercise Clause 93

■ **Who, What, How**   94

Freedom of Expression   95
Why Is Freedom of Expression Valuable? 95   Speech That Criticizes the Government 96   Symbolic Speech 97   Freedom of Assembly 98   Obscenity and Pornography 98   Fighting Words and Offensive Speech 99   Freedom of the Press 100   Censorship on the Internet 101

■ **Who, What, How**   104

The Right to Bear Arms   104
Why Is the Right to Bear Arms Valuable? 104   Judicial Decisions 105

■ **Who, What, How**   106

The Rights of Criminal Defendants   106
Why Are the Rights of Criminal Defendants Valuable? 106   Unreasonable Searches and Seizures 107   The Right Against Self-Incrimination 108   The Right to Counsel 109   Cruel and Unusual Punishment 109

■ **Who, What, How**   110

The Right to Privacy   111
Why Is the Right to Privacy Valuable? 111   Reproductive Rights 111   Gay Rights 112   The Right to Die 113

■ **Who, What, How**   113

Citizenship and Civil Liberties   114

WHAT'S AT STAKE REVISITED   114

Key Terms 115   Summary 116

■ Consider the Source: How to Be a Savvy Web Surfer 102

5 The Struggle for Political Equality   117

WHAT'S AT STAKE?   117

The Meaning of Political Inequality   119
When Can the Law Treat People Differently? 120   Different Kinds of Equality 122

■ **Who, What, How**   122

Rights Denied on the Basis of Race: African Americans   123
The Civil War and Its Aftermath: Winner and Losers 123   The Long Battle to Overturn *Plessy:* The NAACP's Legal Strategy 125   The Civil Rights Movement 126   Blacks in Contemporary American Politics 130

■ **Who, What, How**   131

Rights Denied on the Basis of Race and Ethnicity: Native Americans, Hispanic Americans, and Asian Americans   131
Native Americans 132   Hispanic Americans 133   Asian Americans 136

■ **Who, What, How**   138

Rights Denied on the Basis of Gender: Women   139
The Birth of the Women's Rights Movement 140   The Struggle in the States 140   Winners and Losers in the Suffrage Movement 141   The Equal Rights Amendment 142   Gender Discrimination Today 142

■ **Who, What, How**   143

Rights Denied on Other Bases   144
Sexual Orientation 144   Age 145   Disability 146

■ **Who, What, How**   146

Citizenship and Civil Rights   147

WHAT'S AT STAKE REVISITED   147

Key Terms 148   Summary 149

6 Congress   150

WHAT'S AT STAKE?   150

Congress: Representation and Lawmaking   152
Four Kinds of Representation 152   National Lawmaking 153

■ **Who, What, How**   154

Congressional Powers and Responsibilities   156
Differences Between the House and the Senate 156   Congressional Checks and Balances 158

■ **Who, What, How**   159

Congressional Elections: Choosing the Members 159
Congressional Districts 160   Deciding to Run 162
The 107th Congress 165

■ Who, What, How   167

How Congress Works: Organization   167
The Central Role of Party 167   The Leadership 168
The Committee System 170   Congressional
Resources: Staff and Bureaucracy 173

■ Who, What, How   174

How Congress Works: Process and Politics   174
The Context of Congressional Policymaking 175
How a Bill Becomes Law—Some of the Time 175
The Mechanics of Congressional Decision-Making
181   How Well Does Congress Work? 182

■ Who, What, How   183

Citizenship and Congress   183

WHAT'S AT STAKE REVISITED   184

Key Terms 185   Summary 185

■ Consider the Source: How to Be a Critical Constituent 154

7 The Presidency 187

WHAT'S AT STAKE?   187

The Double Expectations Gap   188
The Gap Between Presidential Promises and the Powers
of the Office 189   The Gap Between Conflicting
Roles 190

■ Who, What, How   191

The Evolution of the American Presidency   194
The Framers' Design for a Limited Executive 194
Qualifications and Conditions of Office 194   The
Constitutional Powers of the President 195   The
Traditional Presidency 199   The Modern Presidency
200

■ Who, What, How   201

Presidential Politics: The Struggle for Power   201
The Expectations Gap and the Need for Persuasive
Power 201   Going Public 202   Working with Con-
gress 204

■ Who, What, How   207

Managing the Presidential Establishment   207
The Cabinet 207   The Executive Office of the Presi-
dent 209   The White House Office 209   The Vice
President 210   The First Lady 211   The Problem of
Control 213

■ Who, What, How   213

Presidential Character   213

■ Who, What, How   215

Citizenship and the Presidency   215

WHAT'S AT STAKE REVISITED   216

Key Terms 218   Summary 218

■ Consider the Source: How to Be a Savvy Student
of Political Cartoons 192

8 The Bureaucracy 219

WHAT'S AT STAKE?   219

What Is Bureaucracy?   221
The Spoils System 221   Bureaucracy and Democracy
222   Accountability and Rules 223

■ Who, What, How   224

The American Federal Bureaucracy   224
Evolution of the Federal Bureaucracy 224   Organization of the Federal Bureaucracy 225   Roles of the
Federal Bureaucracy 230   Who Are the Federal Bureaucrats? 231

■ Who, What, How   232

Politics Inside the Bureaucracy   232
Bureaucratic Culture 232   Presidential Appointees
and the Career Civil Service 235

■ Who, What, How   236

External Bureaucratic Politics   236
Interagency Politics 237   The Bureaucracy and the
President 238   The Bureaucracy and Congress 240
The Bureaucracy and the Courts 242

■ Who, What, How   242

Citizenship and the Bureaucracy   243

WHAT'S AT STAKE REVISITED   244

Key Terms 244   Summary 245

9 The American Legal System and the Courts 246

WHAT'S AT STAKE?   246

Law and the American Legal System   249
The Role of Law in Democratic Societies 249   The
American Legal Tradition 249   Kinds of Law 250

■ Who, What, How   252

**Constitutional Provisions and the Development
of Judicial Review**   252
The Least Dangerous Branch 253   John Marshall and
Judicial Review 253

■ Who, What, How   254

The Structure and Organization of the Dual Court System 255
Understanding Jurisdiction 255 State Courts 256 Federal Courts 257
■ **Who, What, How** 261
Politics and the Supreme Court 261
How Members of the Court Are Selected 262 How the Court Makes Decisions 264 The Political Effects of Judicial Decisions 268
■ **Who, What, How** 269
Citizenship and the Courts 270
WHAT'S AT STAKE REVISITED 271
Key Terms 272 Summary 272

10 Public Opinion 274

WHAT'S AT STAKE? 274
The Role of Public Opinion in a Democracy 275
Why We Think Public Opinion Ought to Matter 276 Why Public Opinion *Does* Matter 276
■ **Who, What, How** 277
Measuring and Tracking Public Opinion 277
The Quality of Opinion Polling Today 278 Types of Polls 280
■ **Who, What, How** 283
Citizen Values: How Do We Measure Up? 283
Political Knowledge 283 Ideology 284 Tolerance 284 Participation 286
■ **Who, What, How** 287
What Influences Our Opinions About Politics? 287
Political Socialization: Learning the Rules of the Game 287 Sources of Divisions in Public Opinion 288
■ **Who, What, How** 293
Citizenship and Public Opinion 293
Shortcuts to Political Knowledge 294 The Rational Electorate 294
WHAT'S AT STAKE REVISITED 296
Key Terms 297 Summary 297
■ Consider the Source: How to Be a Critical Poll Watcher 282

11 Parties and Interest Groups 299

WHAT'S AT STAKE? 299
The Role of Political Parties in a Democracy 301
What Are Parties? 301 The Responsible Party Model 305
■ **Who, What, How** 306

The American Party System 307
The History of Parties in America 307 What Do the American Parties Stand For? 310 Characteristics of the American Party System 317 Undisciplined Parties-in-Government 321
■ **Who, What, How** 321
The Roles, Formation, and Types of Interest Groups 322
Roles of Interest Groups 322 Why Do Interest Groups Form? 323 Types of Interest Groups 324
■ **Who, What, How** 326
Interest Group Politics 327
Direct Lobbying 328 Indirect Lobbying 330 "Astroturf" Political Campaigns and the State of Lobbying Today 331
■ **Who, What, How** 332
Interest Group Resources 332
Money 332 Leadership 335 Membership: Size and Intensity 335 Information 337
■ **Who, What, How** 337
Citizenship and Political Groups 338
WHAT'S AT STAKE REVISITED 339
Key Terms 340 Summary 340
■ Consider the Source: How to Be a Critical Reader of Political Party Platforms 314

12 Voting, Campaigns, and Elections 342

WHAT'S AT STAKE? 342
Exercising the Right to Vote in America 344
Who Votes and Who Doesn't? 344 Why Americans Don't Vote 345 Does Nonvoting Matter? 348
■ **Who, What, How** 349
How the Voter Decides 350
Partisanship 350 Issues and Policy 350 The Candidates 351
■ **Who, What, How** 352
Electing the President 352
Getting Nominated 352 The Electoral College 356 The General Election Campaign 358 Interpreting Elections 368
■ **Who, What, How** 368
Citizenship and Elections 369
WHAT'S AT STAKE REVISITED 369
Key Terms 372 Summary 372
■ Consider the Source: Interpreting Campaign Advertising 362

13 The Media   373

WHAT'S AT STAKE?   373

What Media?   375
Newspapers and Magazines 376   Radio 377   Television 377   The Internet 378   Where Do Americans Get Their News? 379

■ Who, What, How   380

History of the American Media   380
The Early American Press: Dependence on Government 381   Growing Media Independence 381   The Media Today: Concentrated Corporate Power 382   Regulation of the Broadcast Media 384

■ Who, What, How   385

Who Are the Journalists?   385
Who Chooses Journalism? 385   What Journalists Believe: Is There a Liberal Bias in the Media? 387   The Growth of the Washington Press Corps 389

■ Who, What, How   389

The Media and Politics   390
The Shaping of Public Opinion 390   The Reduction of Politics to Conflict and Image 392   Politics as Public Relations 396   A Reduction in Political Accountability 397

■ Who, What, How   398

Citizenship and the Media   399

WHAT'S AT STAKE REVISITED   400

Key Terms 401   Summary 401

■ Consider the Source: Becoming a Savvy Media Consumer 394

14 Domestic and Foreign Policy   403

WHAT'S AT STAKE?   403

Making Public Policy   404
Solving Social Problems 405   Difficulties in Solving Social Problems 406   Types of Public Policy 406   Who Makes Policy? 408   Steps in the Policymaking Process 410

■ Who, What, How   412

Foreign Policy   425
Understanding Foreign Policy 426   The Post–Cold War Setting of American Foreign Policy 426   Types of Foreign Policy 427   Who Makes Foreign Policy? 428   How Do We Define a Foreign Policy Problem? 432

■ Who, What, How   432

Citizenship and Policy   433

WHAT'S AT STAKE REVISITED   434

Key Terms 435   Summary 435

Policy Profile: Middle-Class and Corporate Welfare 413
Policy Profile: Welfare Policy 414
Policy Profile: Social Security 416
Policy Profile: Health Care 418
Policy Profile: Economic Policy 420
Policy Profile: Tax Policy 423

Appendix   A-1
Glossary   G-1
References   R-1
Credits   C-1
Index   I-1

Preface

Keeping the Republic, Brief Edition is an abridged and updated version of the first edition of *Keeping the Republic: Power and Citizenship in American Politics.* While we have streamlined the larger text's account of the American political system, we have also taken great pains to preserve the qualities of accessibility and enthusiasm already identified with that text. Our goal continues to be to share the excitement of discovering humankind's capacity to find innovative solutions to the issues of human governance. We have also focused on updating the Brief Edition to incorporate the results and drama of the 2000 elections, including the contested presidential election as well as the congressional elections and the policies of the early Bush administration.

This book aims to cover essential topics with clear explanations. It is a thematic book, to guide students through a wealth of material and to help them make sense of the content, both academically and personally. The theme is a classic in political science: politics is a struggle over limited power and resources. The rules guiding that struggle influence who will win and who will lose, so that often the struggles with the most at stake are over the rule-making itself. In short, and in the words of a very famous political scientist, politics is about who gets what and how they get it. To illustrate this theme, we begin and end every chapter with a feature called *What's at Stake?* that poses a question about what people want from politics—what they are struggling to get and how the rules affect who gets it. At the end of every major section, we stop and ask *Who, What, How?* This periodic summary helps solidify the conceptual work of the book and gives students a sturdy framework within which to organize the facts and other empirical information we want them to learn.

We unabashedly feel that a primary goal of teaching introductory politics is not only to create good scholars but to create good citizens as well. Fortunately, the skills that make good students and good academics are the same skills that make good citizens: the ability to think critically about and process new information and the ability to be actively engaged in one's subject. Accordingly, in our *Consider the Source* feature, we focus on teaching students how to examine critically the various kinds of political information they are continually bombarded with—from information in textbooks like this one, to information from the media or the Internet, to information from their congressperson or political party. In our *Points of Access* feature, we emphasize the opportunities students have to get involved in the system.

Supplements

We know how important *good* teaching resources can be in the teaching of American government, so we have collaborated with several other political scientists and teachers to develop a set of instructional materials to accompany *Keeping the Republic.* Our goal has been to create resources that not only support but also enhance the text's themes and features.

- The *Instructor's Resource Manual with Test Items,* prepared by John Kozlowicz, of the University of Wisconsin, Whitewater, provides teachers with an array of teaching resources developed around the themes and features of the book. It includes learning objectives, lecture outlines, focus questions, ideas for class, small group, and individual projects and activities, and over 1,200 test item questions.

- The *Study Guide,* written and abridged for the Brief Edition by Jim Woods, of West Virginia University, is designed to help students review and master the text material. The *Study Guide* begins with a section detailing how to use the text and do well in the course. Each chapter reviews the chapter's key concepts, with learning objectives, a chapter summary, and extensive testing review of key terms and concepts. Practice tests include both multiple-choice and short-answer questions. A final section presents critical thinking exercises based on the chapter's key themes.

- A companion web site, accessed through the Houghton Mifflin College Division home page at college.hmco.com and by selecting "Political Science," provides an exciting platform for topic review, expanded learning, and policy analysis based on current events. The web site contains a variety of book-related resources for instructors and students, including chapter outlines, practice quizzes, and a full set of downloadable PowerPoint slides. The Election 2000 portion of the site offers regular election updates and activities, an election timeline, and election-related links. A Policy Resource Center provides expanded coverage and timely updates on major U.S. policy areas, including education, social security, and campaign finance reform. The web site also provides access to Political SourceNet, Houghton Mifflin's American Government web resource site.

- A computerized test bank offers all 1,200 questions from the Test Item portion of the *Instructor's Resource Manual* in electronic format.

Acknowledgments

The Africans say that it takes a village to raise a child—it is certainly true that it takes one to write a textbook! We could not have done it without a community of family, friends, colleagues, students, reviewers, and editors, who supported us, nagged us, maddened us, and kept us on our toes. Not only is this a better book because of their help and support, but it would not have been a book at all without them.

On the family front, we thank our parents, our kids, and our siblings, who have hung in there with us even when they thought we were nuts (and even when they were right). Our friends, too, have been the very best: Bob and Kathleen, Jean and Jack, Russ and Connie, Pam and Scott, Bill and Karen, Glenn and Suzie, Dana and Pat, Fenton and Rich, Fern and Allen, Julia and Pat, Bobbi and Bill have all listened to endless progress reports (and reports of no progress at all) and cheered the small victories with us. And we are forever grateful for the unconditional love and support, not to mention occasional intellectual revelation (Hobbes was wrong: it is *not* a dog-eat-dog world after all!), offered up gladly by the menagerie at home. And we are so very thankful to Pam Stogsdill and Tammy Blunck for looking after us and keeping the whole lot in order.

Colleagues now or once in the Political Science Department at Indiana University have given us invaluable help on details beyond our ken: Yvette Alex Assensoh, Jack Bielasiak, Doris Burton, Ted Carmines, Dana Chabot, Chuck Epp, Judy Failer, Russ Hanson, Bobbi Herzberg, Virginia Hettinger, Jeff Isaac, Burt Monroe, Lin Ostrom, Rich Pacelle, Karen Rasler, Leroy Rieselbach, Pat Sellers, and John Williams. IU colleagues from other schools and departments have been terrific too: Trevor Brown, Dave Weaver, and Cleve Wilhoit from the Journalism School, Bill McGregor and Roger Parks from the School of Public and Environmental Affairs, John Patrick from the School of Education, and Pam Walters from the Sociology Department have all helped out on substantive matters. Many IU folks have made an immeasurable contribution by raising our consciousness about teaching to new levels and giving us a real kick in the pedagogical pants: Joan Middendorf, David Pace, Laura Plummer, Tine Reimers, Ray Smith, and Samuel Thompson, as well as all the Freshman Learning Project people. The computer and library support people at IU have done yeoman service for us too: Dwayne Schau, James Russell, Bob Goelhert, Fenton Martin, and all the librarians in the Government Publications section of our library. We are also grateful to colleagues from other institutions: Hugh Aprile, Shaun Bowler, Bob Brown, Tom Carsey, Kisuk Cho, E. J. Dionne, Todd Donovan, Bob Erikson, Kathleen Knight, David Lee, David McCuan, John McIver, Dick Merriman, Glenn Parker, and Dorald Stoltz. We are especially grateful to Joe Aistrup, Pat Haney, Denise Scheberle, and John Sislin, who gave us substantial research and writing help with several of the chapters. Thanks also go to Jim Woods, who took on the writing of the *Study Guide* and the *Instructor's Resource Manual,* and to John Kozlowicz, who wrote the *Test Bank.*

Special thanks to all our students, undergraduate and graduate, who inspired us to write this book in the first place. Several students have contributed in more particular ways to help us get the book out: Liz Bevers, Tom Carsey, Dave Holian, Christopher McCullough, Brian Schaffner, Rachel Hobbs Shelton, Matt Streb, Jim Trilling, Kevin Willhite, and Mike Wolf. Matt and Mike, longtime research assistants, we are especially indebted to you for your help over the years. What would we have done without you guys?

We have also benefited tremendously from the help of the folks at Project Vote Smart and the many outstanding political scientists around the country who have provided critical reviews of the manuscript at every step of the way. We'd like to thank the following people who took time away from their own work to critique and make suggestions for the improvement of ours:

Danny M. Adkison
Oklahoma State University

Sheldon Appleton
Oakland University

Kevin Bailey
Texas House of Rep., District 140

Ralph Edward Bradford
University of Central Florida

John F. Burke
University of St. Thomas

Francis Carleton
University of Wisconsin at Green Bay

Jennifer B. Clark
South Texas Community College

Christine L. Day
University of New Orleans

Robert E. DiClerico
West Virginia University

Phillip Gianos
California State University

Victoria Hammond
Austin Community College and
  University of Texas

Patrick J. Haney
Miami University

Roberta Herzberg
Utah State Logan

Ronald J. Hrebenar
University of Utah

William G. Jacoby
University of South Carolina

John D. Kay
Santa Barbara City College

Bernard D. Kolasa
University of Nebraska at Omaha

John F. Kozlowicz
University of Wisconsin–Whitewater

Lisa Langenbach
Middle Tennessee State University

Ted Lewis
Collin County Community College

Paul M. Lucko
Angelina College

Vincent N. Mancini
Delaware County Community College

Ursula G. McGraw
Coastal Bend College

Tim McKeown
University of North Carolina at
      Chapel Hill

Lauri McNown
University of Colorado at Boulder

Lawrence Miller
Collin County Community College

Maureen F. Moakley
University of Rhode Island

Theodore R. Mosch
University of Tennessee at Martin

David Nice
Washington State University

Richard Pacelle
University of Missouri at Saint Louis

George E. Pippin
Jones County Junior College

David Robinson
University of Houston—Downtown

Dario Albert Rozas
Milwaukee Area Technical College

Robert Sahr
Oregon State University

Denise Scheberle
University of Wisconsin at Green Bay

Paul Scracic
Youngstown State University

Daniel M. Shea
University of Akron

Neil Snortland
University of Arkansas at Little Rock

Michael W. Sonnleitner
Portland Community College

Robert E. Sterken, Jr.
Palomar College

Richard S. Unruh
Fresno Pacific College

Jan P. Vermeer
Nebraska Wesleyan University

Matt Wetstein
San Joaquin Delta College

Lois Duke Whitaker
Georgia Southern University

David J. Zimny
Los Medanos College

Last, but in many ways most, we thank all the folks at Houghton Mifflin. Our remarkable book rep, Mike Stull, who encouraged us to send our prospectus to HM in the first place, and who alerted his editor without delay, and Jean Woy, editor extraordinaire, who, once dispatched, did not let up, are partly responsible for the whole project. Jean has proved to be all that we had hoped for and more as an editor, and this book owes a great deal to her. Melissa Mashburn and Sandi McGuire regrettably are no longer working with us, but they contributed significantly. Mary Dougherty has been an enthusiastic, energetic, and supportive editor, and Kris Clerkin and June Smith have been gracious and encouraging publishers to work with. The following people have worked their magic and have infused the book with detailed accuracy, color, design, and dramatic imagery: Carol Newman, project editor; Carol Merrigan, production/design coordinator; Henry Rachlin, designer; Charlotte Miller, art editor; and Ann Schroeder, photo researcher. Others at Houghton Mifflin who made important contributions include Priscilla Bailey, Katherine Meisenheimer, Bonnie Melton, and Jennifer DiDomenico.

There are no words with which we can adequately thank the last person on our list. Best development editor in the world, great friend, carrier of the whole village on her back at times, Ann West has kept us going with grace, patience, good humor, and unbelievably hard work. We love her and we thank her.

Christine Barbour
Gerald C. Wright

To the Student:
Suggestions on How to Read This Textbook

1. As they say in Chicago about voting, do it **early and often.** If you open the book for the first time the night before the exam, you will not learn much from it and it won't help your grade. Start reading the chapters in conjunction with the lectures, and reread them all at least once before the exam. A minimum of two readings is necessary for a decent education and a decent grade.

2. Read the **chapter outlines!** There is a wealth of information in the outlines, and in all the chapter headings. They tell you what we think is important, what our basic argument is, and how all the material fits together. Often, chapter subheadings list elements of an argument that may show up on a quiz. Be alert to these clues.

3. **Read actively!** Constantly ask yourself: What does this mean? Why is this important? How do these different facts fit together? What are the broad arguments here? How does this material relate to class lectures? How does it relate to the broad themes of the class? When you stop asking these questions you are merely moving your eyes over the page and that is a waste of time. This is especially true of the *What's at Stake?* vignettes at the beginning of each chapter (and the follow-up at the chapter's end). Try to keep the themes and questions posed in the *What's at Stake?* vignette alive as you read the chapter so that you can make the important connections to the material being covered.

4. **Highlight or take notes.** Some people prefer highlighting because it's quicker than taking notes, but others think that writing down the most important points helps in remembering them later on. Whichever method you choose (and you must choose one), be sure you're doing it properly! The point of both methods is to make sure that you interact with the material and learn it instead of just passively watching it pass before your eyes—and that you have in some way indicated the most important points so that you do not need to read the entire chapter your second time through.

   Highlighting. Highlight with a pen or marker that enables you to read what's on the page. Do not highlight too much. An entirely yellow page will not give you any clues about what is important. Read each paragraph and ask yourself: What is the basic idea of this paragraph? Highlight that. Avoid highlighting all the examples and illustrations. You should be able to recall them on your own when you see the main idea. Beware of highlighting too little. If whole pages go by with no marking, you are probably not highlighting enough.

Outlining. Again, the key is to write down enough, but not too much. Recopying a chapter written by someone else is deadly boring—and a waste of time. Go for key ideas, terms, and arguments.

5. Don't be afraid to **write in your book.** Even if you choose to outline instead of highlight, make notes to yourself in the margins of your book, pointing out cross-references, connections, ideas, and examples. Especially note tie-ins to the lectures, or summaries of broad arguments.

6. Read and reread the *Who, What, How* summaries at the end of each chapter section. These will help you digest the material just covered and get you ready to go on to the next section.

7. Note all **key terms,** including those that appear in chapter headings. Be sure you understand the definition and significance, and write the significance in the margin of your book!

8. Do not skip **charts, graphs, pictures, or other illustrations!** These things are there for a purpose, because they convey crucial information or illustrate a point in the text. After you read a chart or graph, make a note in the margin about what it means.

9. Do not skip the *Consider the Source* boxes or other **boxed features!** They are not empty filler! The *Consider the Source* boxes provide advice on becoming a critical consumer of the many varieties of political information that come your way. They list questions to ask yourself about the articles you read, the campaign ads and movies you see, and the graphs you study, among other things. The boxed features may highlight an important trend or focus on an example of something discussed in the text. They'll often give you another angle from which to understand the chapter themes.

10. When you've finished the chapter, read the *Summary.* Like the *Who, What, How* summaries, the end-of-chapter summary will help put the chapter's information in perspective, summarizing the major points made in each chapter section.

KEEPING THE REPUBLIC

POWER AND CITIZENSHIP
IN AMERICAN POLITICS

1

What's at Stake?

What Is Politics?
• Politics and Government
• Politics and Economics
• Rules and Institutions

Political Systems and the Concept of Citizenship
• Authoritarian Systems
• Democracy
• Meanings of Citizenship

Democracy and Citizenship in America
• The Dangers of Democracy
• Citizenship in America
• Who Is a Citizen and Who Is Not?

What Do American Citizens Believe?
• American Political Culture: Ideas That Unite
• American Ideologies: Ideas That Divide

Themes of This Book
• Citizenship and Politics

What's at Stake Revisited

Power and Citizenship in American Politics

WHAT'S AT STAKE?

Welcome to American politics. Do you know who your vice president is? The Speaker of the House of Representatives? Can you name the chief justice of the U.S. Supreme Court? The father of the Constitution? Do you know how many senators there are? What the Fifth Amendment protects? If you answered no to most or all of these questions, the newspaper *USA Today* says you are in good company.[1] It reported in the fall of 1998 that among young adults, only 74 percent knew the vice president (Al Gore), 33 percent knew the Speaker (Newt Gingrich), 2 percent knew the chief justice (William Rehnquist) and the father of the Constitution (James Madison), and 25 percent knew that the Fifth Amendment protects us from having to testify against ourselves in court, among other things. On the other hand, 95 percent knew that Will Smith starred in *Fresh Prince of Bel Air*, 81 percent knew that three brothers make up the music group Hanson, and 75 percent knew that the Beverly Hills zip code is 90210. *USA Today* concluded that American democracy is in trouble. Young people are not using their brainpower to absorb political knowledge.

Since the Watergate scandal that forced the resignation of President Richard Nixon in 1974, levels of interest and trust in government have been declining. The year 1998 saw even less reason than usual for young people to pay attention to politics, with the partisan bickering and media spectacle that accompanied the impeachment of President Bill Clinton. Can democracy survive when a whole generation of young citizens and future political leaders seems to know little and care less about politics?

1

As Benjamin Franklin was leaving Philadelphia's Independence Hall in September 1787 after the signing of the Constitution, he was stopped by a woman who asked, "What have you created?" He answered, "A Republic, Madam, if you can keep it." When levels of cynicism and distrust in government run high and people tune out politics, rather than pay attention to what seems like endless partisan bickering and scandalmongering, are we keeping the republic? Just what is at stake for American government in youthful disregard for politics? We will return to this question after we introduce you to some basic facts and ideas about politics and the difference it makes in our lives. ■

Every time we open a newspaper, turn on the news, or access an electronic news network, we are bombarded with information that seems to drive home this point: politics is a dirty business. Members of Congress misuse public funds and fail to pay taxes. Presidents have affairs and lie about them, break campaign promises, and refuse to come clean about their financial dealings. Lawmakers trade favors and votes, and highly paid lobbyists buy both. Candidates run afoul of campaign finance laws and stand accused of buying, or even stealing, elections. Politicians demonize their opponents and make compromise an impossibility. Scandals are the rule of the day, and if the news-hungry media cannot dig them up, they often seem to create them from rumor and innuendo. Levels of citizen distrust and disengagement in politics rise daily.

Politics, which we would like to think of as a noble and even morally elevated activity, takes on all the worst characteristics of the business world, where we expect people to take advantage of each other and to pursue their own private interests. In the political world, however, especially in a democracy, we want the interests pursued to be ours—the public interest. We are disillusioned with the endless name-calling and finger-pointing on the nightly news. Can this really be the heritage of Thomas Jefferson and Abraham Lincoln? Can this be the "world's greatest democracy" at work? How do we square our early lessons about the proud and selfless struggle for American democracy with the seeming reality of sleaze and petty self-interests?

In this chapter, we get to the heart of what politics is and how it relates to other concepts such as power, government, rules, economics, and citizenship. Because citizens are so crucial to the success of a democracy, we investigate citizenship extra closely, looking at the ideas that have shaped the American notion of citizenship, and the ideas about government that American citizens hold.

Specifically, in this chapter, we will

- address the question of what "politics" means

- discuss the varieties of political systems and the roles they endorse for the individuals who live under them

- look at the American founders' ideas about democracy and the concept of citizenship their ideas gave rise to

- study the ideas that hold us together as a nation, and the ideas that define our political conflicts

- identify the themes of power and citizenship that will serve as our framework for understanding American politics

What Is Politics?

Consider the proposition that politics is not just a dirty business. As people who make the study of politics our life's work, we argue that politics is a fundamental and complex human activity. More than two thousand years ago, the Greek philosopher Aristotle said that we are political animals, and political animals we seem destined to remain. Politics may have its distasteful side, but it also has its exalted moments, from the dedication of a new public library to the dismantling of the Berlin Wall.

Since this book is about politics, its glory as well as its shame, we need to begin with a clear definition. One of the most famous definitions, put forth by the well-known political scientist Harold Lasswell, is still one of the best, and we will use it to frame our discussion throughout this book. Lasswell defined **politics** as "who gets what when and how."[2] Politics is a way of determining, without recourse to violence, how power and resources are distributed in society. **Power** is the ability to get other people to do what you want them to do. The resources in question here might be government jobs, public funds, laws that help you get your way, or public policies that work to your advantage. The tools of politics are compromise and cooperation, discussion and debate, and even, sometimes, bribery and deceit. Politics is the process through which we try to arrange our collective lives so that we can live without crashing into one another at every turn and to provide ourselves with goods and services that we could not obtain alone. But politics is also about getting our own way. Our own way may be a noble goal for society or pure self-interest, but the struggle we engage in, using the tools mentioned above, is a political struggle. Because politics is about power and other scarce resources, there will always be winners and losers. If everyone could always get his or her way, politics would disappear. It is because we cannot always get what we want that politics exists.

What would a world without politics be like? There would be no resolution or compromise between conflicting interests, because those are certainly political activities. There would be no agreements struck, bargains made, or alliances formed. Unless there were enough of every valued resource to go around, or unless the world were big enough that we could live our lives without coming into contact with other human beings, life would be constant conflict—what philosopher Thomas Hobbes called a "war of all against all." Individuals, unable to cooperate with one another (because cooperation is essentially political), would have no option but to resort to brute force to settle disputes and allocate resources.

Our capacity to be political saves us from that fate. We do have the ability to persuade, cajole, bargain, promise, compromise, and cooperate. We do have the ability to agree on what principles should guide our handling of power and other scarce resources and to live our collective lives according to those principles. Because there are many potential theories about how to manage power—who should have it, how it should be used, how it should be transferred—agreement on which principles are **legitimate,** or accepted as "right," can break down. When politics fails, violence takes its place. Indeed, the human history of warfare attests to the fragility of political life.

politics who gets what, when, and how; a process of determining how power and resources are distributed in a society without recourse to violence

power the ability to get other people to do what you want

legitimate accepted as "right" or proper

Politics and Government

Although the words *politics* and *government* are sometimes used interchangeably, they really refer to different things. Politics is a process or an activity through which power and resources are gained and lost. **Government,** on the other hand, is a system or organization for exercising authority over a body of people. **Authority** is power that citizens view as legitimate, or "right"—power that we have implicitly consented to. You can think of it this way: As children, we probably did as our parents told us, or submitted to their punishment if we didn't, because we recognized their authority over us. As we became adults, we started to claim that they had less authority over us, that we could do what we wanted. We no longer saw their power as wholly legitimate or appropriate. Governments exercise authority because people recognize them as legitimate, even if they often do not like doing what they are told (paying taxes, for instance). When a government ceases to be regarded as legitimate, the result may be revolution or civil war, unless the state is powerful enough to suppress all opposition.

American *politics* is what happens in the halls of Congress, on the campaign trail, at Washington cocktail parties, and in neighborhood association meetings. It is the making of promises, deals, and laws. American *government* is the Constitution and the institutions set up by the Constitution for the exercise of authority by the American people, over the American people. Other countries have governments that represent their own solutions and arrangements for the exercise of authority within their borders. Government is a product of the political process. It represents the compromises, deals, and bargains made by its founders in their quest to establish governing principles.

Politics and Economics

In addition to distinguishing between politics and government, we must also figure out where economics fits into the scheme of things. Whereas politics is concerned with the distribution of power and resources in society, **economics** is concerned specifically with the production and distribution of society's wealth—material goods and services such as bread, toothpaste, housing, medical care, education, and entertainment.

Because both politics and economics focus on the distribution of society's resources, political and economic questions often get confused in contemporary life. Once politics referred to public affairs and economy to private affairs, but today the world is more complex. Questions about how to pay for government, about government's role in the economy, or about whether government or the private sector should provide certain services all have political and economic dimensions. We'll look briefly at three different modern economic systems that arrange the public and private spheres in different ways.

Capitalism   In a **capitalist economy,** property is privately owned, and decisions about production and distribution are left to the market. The United States, like most other countries today, has a primarily capitalist economy. We do not rely on the state to decide how much of a given item to produce or how much to charge for it,

government a system or organization for exercising authority over a body of people

authority power that is recognized as legitimate

economics the production and distribution of a society's goods and services

capitalist economy an economic system in which the market determines production, distribution, and price decisions and property is privately owned

Too Big?

Surfers off Cape Canaveral, Florida, watch as astronaut–turned–U.S. senator John Glenn returns to orbit in 1998 at the age of seventy-seven. In its early stages, the exploration of space was viewed as a collective good too expensive and hazardous for private business to undertake. Today, however, the business world has increasingly assumed more of the costs of space exploration from government.

Too Small?

If the U.S. postal service had to show a profit, remote sites like this one—the smallest post office in America—would probably be shut down. Government control ensures that mail delivery is widespread and relatively inexpensive, getting your letters to icy outposts in Alaska or the swamps of Florida for less than 40 cents.

because the market—the process of supply and demand—takes care of those decisions. Take toothpaste, for example. If many people want toothpaste, it will be quite expensive until the market responds by producing lots of toothpaste, whereupon the price will drop until production evens out. In capitalist countries, people do not believe that the government is capable of making such judgments (like how much toothpaste to produce), and they want to keep such decisions out of its hands. The philosophy that corresponds with this belief is called *laissez-faire*, a French term that, loosely translated, means "let people do as they wish." However, no economic system today maintains a purely unregulated form of capitalism with the government completely uninvolved.

Although in theory the market ought to provide everything that people need and want, and should regulate itself as well, sometimes the market breaks down, or "fails," and government steps in to try to "fix" it. Our government provides many goods and services that could be produced in the private sector—that is, by nongovernmental actors—but are not because not enough people are willing to pay for them privately. Highways, streetlights, libraries, museums, schools, social security, national defense, and a clean environment are some examples of the collective goods and services that many people are unwilling or unable to pay for. Consequently, government undertakes to provide these things and, in doing so, becomes not only a political but also an economic actor. One of the many difficulties resulting from government's economic role is that we expect different sorts of behavior from our public officials than we do from businesspeople, even though they are often engaged in the same activities. In an interesting twist, sometimes governments hire private companies to provide public services, such as housing prisoners or rehabilitating juvenile offenders. How far this trend toward "privatization" should go is a matter of political debate, with some advocates claiming that even education for children and pensions for retirees should be privatized.

The line between government and economics blurs in another way as well. One of the costs of letting the market alone is that markets have cycles. Periods of growth are often followed by periods of slowdown, or recession. People and businesses look to government for protection from these cyclical effects. The most famous example of government intervention in the U.S. economy is the New Deal, which was Franklin Roosevelt's plan to get America back to work after the Great Depression of the 1930s, one of the worst market breakdowns in our history. Government also gets involved in regulating the economy to try to prevent such market disasters from taking place. Government regulation may try to ensure the safety of consumers and working people or to encourage fair business practices.

communist economy an economic system in which the state determines production, distribution, and price decisions and property is government owned

Communism   In a **communist economy,** like that of the former Soviet Union, all economic activity is considered public, and economic decisions are made not by a market but by politicians. The public and private spheres overlap, and politics controls the distribution of all resources, from political power and favors to bread and toothpaste. That is because in a communist or socialist economic system (based loosely on the ideas of German economist Karl Marx), the state (or the government) owns most of the property and runs the economy. Although there are some theoretical distinctions between communism and socialism, for our purposes both terms refer to government or collective ownership of property. According to the basic values of such a system, it is unjust for some people to own more property than others and for those who own less to be forced to work for those who own more. Consequently, the theory goes, the state or society—not corporations or individuals—should own the property. In such systems, there is no important distinction between politics and economics, between public and private. Everything is essentially political and public. Many theories hold that communism is possible only after a revolution thoroughly overthrows the old system to make way for new values and institutions. This is what happened in Russia in 1917 and later in China in the 1940s. Since the communist economies of the former Soviet Union and eastern Europe have fallen apart, communism has been left with few supporters, although the nations of China, North Korea, and Cuba still claim allegiance to it.

Social Democracy   Some countries in western Europe, especially the Scandinavian nations of Norway, Denmark, and Sweden, have developed hybrid economic systems. Primarily capitalist, they nonetheless argue that the values of equality promoted by communism are attractive. Social democrats believe, however, that the public economic system demanded by communism is unnecessary and that the revolution is undesirable. **Social democracy** claims that economic equality, the primary value of socialism, can be brought about by democratic reform—that is, by voting for change peacefully in the legislature, not by fighting in the streets. Democratic socialists have frequently headed governments or been prominent players in the governments of western Europe since World War II, although with the fall of communism the popularity of social democracy has also declined somewhat. Many countries of western Europe, having enacted policies to bring about more equality, are known for their extensive welfare states. The government guarantees citizens a comfortable standard of living, but the economy remains capitalist, essentially private, though with a good deal of public regulation. Social democrats believe that the economy does not have to be owned by the state for its effects to be controlled by the state.

social democracy
a hybrid system combining a capitalist economy and a government that supports equality

Rules and Institutions

Government is shaped by politics and economics, but it in turn provides the rules and institutions that shape the way politics (and sometimes economics) continues to operate. The rules and institutions of government have a profound effect on how power is distributed and who wins and loses in the political arena. Life is different in other countries not only because they speak different languages and eat different foods but also because their governments establish rules that cause people to live in different ways.

Rules can be thought of as the "how," in the definition "who gets what when and how." They are directives that determine how resources are allocated and how collective action takes place—that is, they determine how we try to get the things we want. We can do it violently, or we can do it politically, according to the rules. Those rules can provide for rule by a dictator, a king, God's representative on earth, the rich, a majority of the people, or any other arrangement. The point of the rules is to provide some framework for us to solve, without violence, the problems that are generated by our collective lives.

rules directives that specify how resources will be distributed or what procedures will govern collective activity

The rules we choose can influence which people will get their way most often, so understanding the rules is crucial to understanding politics. People often refer to politics as a game, which somewhat trivializes a very serious business. But consider for a moment the impact a change of rules would have on the outcome of the sport of basketball, for instance. What if the average height of the players could be no more than 5'10"? What if the baskets were lowered? What if foul shots counted for two points rather than one? Basketball would be a very different game, and the players recruited would look quite unlike the players we cheer for now. Today's winners might be tomorrow's losers. So it is with governments and politics. Change the people who are allowed to vote, or the length of time a person can serve in office, and the political process and the potential winners and losers change drastically.

We can think of **institutions** as the "where" of the political struggle, although Lasswell didn't include a "where" component in his definition. They are the organizations where government power is exercised. In the United States, our rules provide for the institutions of a representative democracy—that is, rule by elected representatives of the people—and for a federal political system. Our Constitution

institutions
organizations where governmental power is exercised

establishes the institutions of Congress, the presidency, the courts, and the bureaucracy, along with the levels of national and state politics, as a stage where the drama of politics can play itself out. Other systems might call for different institutions, perhaps an all-powerful parliament, a monarch, or even a committee of rulers.

These complicated systems of rules and institutions do not appear out of thin air. They are carefully designed by the founders of political systems to create the kinds of society they think will be stable and prosperous, but also where people like themselves are likely to be winners. Remember that not only the rules but also the institutions we choose influence who most easily and most often can get their way.

Political Systems and the Concept of Citizenship

Just as there are different kinds of economic systems, there are different sorts of political systems, based on different ideas about who should have power and how it should be used. Some ideas about politics advocate *anarchy,* a system where there is no government at all and people have the freedom to do whatever they please. Among the more practical theories of government, however, we can discern two types of political systems: those that vest authority in the state and those that vest it in the people. The first type of system potentially has total power over its subjects; the second type permits citizens to limit the state's power by claiming rights that the government must protect.

Authoritarian Systems

authoritarian government
a system in which the state holds all power

totalitarian government
a system in which absolute power is exercised over every aspect of life

Authoritarian governments give ultimate power to the state rather than to the people. Usually, by "authoritarian governments" we mean those in which the people cannot effectively claim rights against the state. Where the state chooses to exercise its power, the people have no choice but to submit to its will. Such a government may be **totalitarian**—that is, as in the former Soviet Union, it may exercise its power over every part of society, leaving little or no private realm for individuals. An authoritarian state may also limit its own power. In such cases, it may deny individuals rights in those spheres where it chooses to act, but it may leave large areas of society, such as a capitalist economy, free from government interference. Singapore is an example of this type of authoritarianism. Often authoritarian governments pay lip service to the people, but when push comes to shove, as it usually does in such states, the people have no effective power against the government.

Authoritarian governments can take various forms.

monarchy
an authoritarian government with power vested in a king or queen

theocracy an authoritarian government that claims to draw its power from divine or religious authority

- A **monarchy** vests the ultimate power in one person (the king or queen), believing either that God or some other higher power has designated that person a divine representative on earth or that the person's birth, wealth, or even knowledge entitles him or her to the supreme position. A monarchy is not necessarily authoritarian (for instance, in the British constitutional monarchy, Parliament, not the monarch, is sovereign), but it is when the king or queen holds the ultimate power.

- Some forms of authoritarian government give God or other divinities a more direct line of power. In a **theocracy,** God is the sovereign, speaking through the voice of an earthly appointee such as a priest.

fascist government
an authoritarian government in which policy is made for the ultimate glory of the state

oligarchy rule by a small group of elites

- Sometimes the state is all-powerful not because a monarch or God wills it, but for the sake of the state itself. In a **fascist government,** the state is sovereign. Nazi Germany under Adolf Hitler and Italy under Benito Mussolini are examples of states run by dictators for the greater glory not of themselves or God, but of the state.

- Finally, sovereignty may be vested in a party or group within the state, often called an **oligarchy.** The authoritarian regimes of the former Soviet Union were run by the powerful Communist Party.

Democracy

democracy
government that vests power in the people

popular sovereignty
the concept that the citizens are the ultimate source of political power

In nonauthoritarian systems, ultimate power rests with the people. The form of nonauthoritarian government that is most familiar to us is a **democracy.** Democracies are based on the principle of **popular sovereignty**—that is, there is no power higher than the people and, in the United States, the document establishing their authority, the Constitution. The central idea here is that no government is considered legitimate unless the governed consent to it, and people are not truly free unless they live under a law of their own making. The people of many Western countries have found this idea persuasive enough to found their governments on it. In recent years, especially since the mid-1980s, democracy has been spreading rapidly through the rest of the world as the preferred form of government. No longer the primary province of industrialized Western nations, attempts at democratic governance now extend into Asia, Latin America, Africa, eastern Europe, and the republics of the former Soviet Union. There are many varieties of democracy other than our own. Some democracies make the most important authority the parliament (or legislature, the representatives of the people), some retain a monarch with limited powers, and some hold referenda at the national level to get direct feedback on how the people want them to act on specific issues.

Generally, in democracies, we believe that the will of the majority should prevail. This is misleadingly simple, however. Some theories of democracy hold that all the people should agree on political decisions. This rule of unanimity makes decision-making very slow, and sometimes impossible, since everyone has to be persuaded to agree. Even when majority rule is the norm, there are many ways of calculating the majority. Is it 50 percent plus one? Two-thirds? Three-fourths? Decision-making grows increasingly difficult the greater the number of people that are required to agree. And, of course, majority rule brings with it the problem of minority rights. If the majority gets its way, what happens to the rights of those who voted against it? Democratic theorists have tried to grapple with these problems in various ways, none of them entirely satisfactory to all people.

elite democracy
a theory of democracy that limits the citizens' role to choosing among competing leaders

- Theorists of **elite democracy** propose that democracy is merely a system of choosing among competing leaders; for the average citizen, input ends after the leader is chosen.[3] Some proponents of this view believe that actual political decisions are made not by elected officials, but by the elite in business, the military, the media, and education. In this view, elections are merely symbolic, to perpetuate the illusion that citizens have consented to their government.

pluralist democracy
a theory of democracy
that holds that citizen
membership in groups
is the key to political
power

- Advocates of **pluralist democracy** argue that what is important is not so much individual participation but membership in groups that in turn participate in government decision-making on their members' behalf.[4] As a way of trying to influence a system that gives them only limited voice, citizens join groups of people with whom they share an interest, such as labor unions, professional associations, and environmental or business groups. These groups represent their members' interests and try to influence government to enact policy that carries out the group's will. Some pluralists argue that individual citizens have little effective power and that only when they are organized into groups are they truly a force for government to reckon with.

participatory democracy   a theory
of democracy that holds
that citizens should
actively and directly
control all aspects of
their lives

- Supporters of **participatory democracy** claim that more than consent or majority rule in making government decisions is needed. Individuals have the right to control all the circumstances of their lives, and direct democratic participation should take place not only in government but in industry, education, and community affairs as well.[5] For advocates of this view, democracy is more than a way to make decisions; it is a way of life, an end in itself.

Meanings of Citizenship

So far we have given a good deal of attention to the latter parts of Lasswell's definition of politics, to the "what" (power and influence), the "how" (the rules), and even the "where" (institutions). But easily as important as these factors is the "who" in Lasswell's formulation. Underlying the different political theories we have looked at are fundamental differences in the powers and opportunities possessed by everyday people.

subjects   individuals
who are obliged to
submit to a government
authority against which
they have no rights

In authoritarian systems, the people are **subjects** of their government. They possess no rights that protect them from that government; they must do whatever the government says or face the consequences, without any other recourse. They have obligations to the state, but no rights or privileges to offset those obligations. They may be winners or losers in government decisions, but they have very little control over which it may be.

citizens   members of
a political community
having both rights and
responsibilities

Everyday people in democratic systems, however, have a potentially powerful role to play. They are more than mere subjects; they are **citizens,** or members of a political community with rights as well as obligations. Democratic theory says that power is drawn from the people, that the people are sovereign, that they must consent to be governed, and that their government must respond to their will. In practical terms, this may not seem to mean much, since not consenting doesn't necessarily give us the right to disobey government. It does give us the option of leaving, however, and seeking a more congenial set of rules elsewhere. Subjects of authoritarian governments rarely have this freedom.

In democratic systems, the rules of government can provide for all sorts of different roles for citizens. At a minimum, citizens can usually vote in periodic and free elections. They may be able to run for office, subject to certain conditions, such as age or residence. They can support candidates for office, organize political groups or parties, attend meetings, write letters to officials or the press, march in protest or support of various causes, and even speak out on street corners.

Theoretically, democracies are ruled by the "people," but different democracies have at times been very selective about whom they count as citizens. Beginning with our days as colonists, Americans have excluded many groups of people from citizenship: people of the "wrong" religion, income bracket, race, ethnic group, lifestyle, and gender have all been excluded from enjoying the full rights of colonial or U.S. citizenship at different times. In fact, as we will see, American history is the story of those various groups fighting to be included as citizens. Just because a system is called a democracy is no guarantee that all or even most of its residents possess the status of citizens.

Citizens in democratic systems are said to possess certain rights, or areas where government cannot infringe on their freedom. Just what these rights are varies among democracies, but they usually include freedom of speech and the press, the right to assemble, and certain legal protections guaranteeing fair treatment in the criminal justice system. Almost all of these rights are designed to allow citizens to criticize their government openly without threat of retribution by that government.

Citizens of democracies also have obligations or responsibilities to the public realm. They have the obligation to obey the law, for instance, and they may also have the obligation to pay taxes, to serve in the military, or to sit on juries. Some theorists argue that virtuous citizens have the obligation to put community interests ahead of personal interests. A less extreme version of this view holds that while citizens may go about their own business and pursue their own interests, they must continue to pay attention to their government. Participating in its decisions is the price of maintaining their own liberty and, by extension, the liberty of the whole. Should citizens abdicate this role by tuning out to public life, the safeguards of democracy can disappear, to be replaced with the trappings of authoritarian government. There is nothing automatic about democracy. If left unattended by nonvigilant citizens, the freedoms of democracy can be lost to an all-powerful state, and citizens can become transformed into subjects of the government they failed to keep in check.

The Western notion of citizenship as conferring both rights and responsibilities first became popular in the 1700s, as Europeans emerged from the Middle Ages and began to reject notions that rulers were put on earth by God to be obeyed unconditionally. Two British philosophers, Thomas Hobbes and John Locke, led the new way of thinking about subjecthood and citizenship. Governments are born not because God ordains them, but because life without government is "solitary, poor, nasty, brutish, and short" in Hobbes's words, and "inconvenient" in Locke's. The foundation of government is reason, not faith, and reason leads people to consent to being governed because they are better off that way.

People have freedom and rights before government exists, declared Locke. When they decide they are better off with government than without it, they enter into a **social contract,** giving up some of those rights in exchange for the protection of the rest of their rights by a government established by the majority. If that government fails to protect their rights, it has broken the contract, and the people are free to form a new government or not, as they please. But the key element here is that for authority to be legitimate, citizens must consent to it.

These ideas were not exactly democratic, but they were much closer than what had come before. Nowhere did Locke suggest that all people ought to participate in politics or that people are necessarily equal. In fact, he was mostly concerned with

social contract
the notion that society is based on an agreement between government and the governed in which people agree to give up some rights in exchange for the protection of others

the preservation of private property, suggesting that only property owners would have cause to be bothered with government because only they have something concrete to lose.

Democracy and Citizenship in America

For our purposes, the most important thing about John Locke is that he was writing at the same time the American founders were thinking about how to build a new government. Locke particularly influenced the writings of James Madison, a major author of our Constitution. Madison, as we will see, was worried about a system that was too democratic.

The Dangers of Democracy

Enthusiastic popular participation under the government established by the Articles of Confederation—the document that tied the colonies together before the Constitution was drafted—almost ended the new government before it began. Like Locke, Madison thought government had a duty to protect property, and if people who didn't have property could get involved in politics, they might not care about protecting the property of others. Worse, they might form "factions," groups pursuing their own self-interests rather than the public interest, and even try to get some of that property for themselves. So Madison rejected notions of "pure democracy," in which all citizens would have direct power to control government, and opted instead for what he called a "republic."

republic
a government in which decisions are made through representatives of the people

A **republic,** according to Madison, differs from a democracy mainly in that it employs representation and can work in a large state. Most theorists agree that democracy is impossible in practice if there are a lot of citizens and all have to be heard from. But we do not march to Washington or phone our legislator every time we want to register a political preference. Instead, we choose representatives—members of the House of Representatives, senators, and the president—to represent our views for us. Madison thought this would be a safer system than direct participation (all of us crowding into town halls or the Capitol) because public passions would be cooled off by the process. You might be furious about health care costs when you vote for your senator, but he or she will represent your views with less anger. The representatives, hoped the founders, would be older, wealthier, and wiser than the average American, and they would be better able to make cool and rational decisions.

In fact, Madison's republican government has succeeded so well that many Americans today are content to leave the business of governing completely in the hands of their representatives, and they are not even particularly conscientious about participating in the election of those representatives. Although more people can participate in American politics than ever before in our history, the truth is that not very many do. Voter turnout rates (the percentages of people who go to the polls and vote on election days) are abysmally low compared to those in other Western industrialized democracies, and surveys show that many Americans are apathetic toward politics. Is such a consequence the natural result of Madison's concern to keep government slightly removed from "the people"?

Citizenship in America

The notion of citizenship that emerges from Madison's writings is not a very flattering one for the average American, and it is important to note that it is not the only ideal of citizenship in the American political tradition. Madison's low expectations of the American public were a reaction to an earlier tradition that had put great faith in the ability of democratic man to put the interests of the community ahead of his own, to act with what scholars call "republican virtue." According to this idea, a virtuous citizen could be trusted with the most serious of political decisions because if he (women were not citizens at that time, of course) were properly educated and kept from the influence of scandal and corruption, he would be willing to sacrifice his own advancement for the sake of the whole. His decisions would be guided not by his self-interest, but by his public-interested spirit. At the time of the founding, hope was strong that although the court of the British monarch had become corrupt beyond redemption, America was still a land where virtue could triumph over greed. In fact, for many people, this was a crucial argument for American independence: severing the ties would prevent that corruption from creeping across the Atlantic and would allow the new country to keep its virtuous political nature free from British taint.[6]

When democratic rules that relied on the virtue, or public interestedness, of the American citizen were put into effect, however, especially in the days immediately after independence, these expectations seemed to be doomed. Instead of acting for the good of the community, Americans seemed to be just as self-interested as the British had been. When given nearly free rein to rule themselves, they had no trouble remembering the rights of citizenship but ignored the responsibilities that come with it. They passed laws in state legislatures that canceled debts and contracts and otherwise worked to the advantage of the poor majority of farmers and debtors—and that seriously threatened the economic and political stability of the more well-to-do. It was in this context of national disappointment that Madison devised his notion of the republic. Since people had proved themselves, so he thought, not to be activated by virtue, a government must be designed that would produce virtuous results, regardless of the character of the citizens who participated in it.

Today two competing views of citizenship still exist in the United States. One, echoing Madison, sees human nature as self-interested and holds that individual participation in government should be limited, that "too much" democracy is a bad thing. A second view continues to put its faith in the citizen's ability to act virtuously, not just for his or her own good but for the common good. President John F. Kennedy movingly evoked such a view in his inaugural address in 1960, when he urged Americans to "ask not what your country can do for you—ask what you can do for your country." These views of citizenship have coexisted throughout our history. Especially in times of crisis, such as war or national tragedy, the second view of individual sacrifice for the public good has seemed more prominent. Citizens put their public obligations ahead of whatever rights they feel they have. At other times, and particularly at the national level of politics, the dominant view of citizenship has appeared to be one of self-interested actors going about their own business with little regard for the public good. When observers claim, as they often do today, that there is a crisis of American citizenship, they usually mean that civic virtue is taking second place to self-interest as a guiding principle of citizenship.

"They Shall Beat Their Swords into Ploughshares"
Public-interested citizenship can take many forms. When her small Arizona town was overrun with violent deaths—including that of her own son—Socorro Hernandez Bernasconi, inspired by the above biblical passage from Isaiah 2:4, founded a group that encourages young people to exchange their guns for a variety of rewards and services, ranging from computers to guitar lessons. The guns are then recycled into shovels, church candlesticks, or artwork.

These two notions of citizenship do not necessarily have to be at loggerheads, however. Where self-interest and public spirit meet in democratic practice is in the process of deliberation, collectively considering and evaluating goals and ideals for communal life and action. Individuals bring their own agendas and interests, but in the process of discussing them with others holding different views, parties can find common ground and turn it into a base for collective action. Conflict can erupt, too, of course, but the process of deliberation at least creates a forum from which the possibility of consensus might emerge. Scholar and journalist E. J. Dionne reflects on this possibility:

> At the heart of republicanism [remember that this is not a reference to our modern parties] is the belief that self-government is not a drab necessity but a joy to be treasured. It is the view that politics is not simply a grubby confrontation of competing interests but an arena in which citizens can learn from each other and discover an "enlightened self-interest" in common.

Despite evidence of a growing American disaffection for politics, Dionne hopes that Americans will find again the "joy" in self-governance, because, he warns, "A nation that hates politics will not long thrive as a democracy."[7]

Who Is a Citizen and Who Is Not?

Citizenship is not only a normative concept—that is, a prescription for how governments ought to treat residents and how those residents ought to act. It is also a very precise legal status. A fundamental element of democracy is not just the careful specification of the rights granted and the obligations incurred in citizenship, but also an equally careful legal description of just who is a citizen and how that status can be acquired by noncitizens. In this section, we look at the legal definition of American citizenship and the history of immigration in this country.

American Citizens   American citizens are usually born, not made. If you are born in any of the fifty states or in most of the United States' overseas territories, such as Puerto Rico or Guam, you are an American citizen, whether your parents are Americans or not. This follows the principle of international law called jus soli, which means literally "right of the soil." The exceptions to this rule in the United States are children born to foreign diplomats serving in the United States and children born on foreign ships in U.S. waters. These children are not considered U.S. citizens. According to another legal principle, jus sanguinis ("right of blood"), if you are born outside the United States to American parents, you are an American citizen (or if you are adopted by American parents, you can become one). Interestingly, if you are born in the United States but one of your parents holds citizenship in another country, depending on that country's laws, you may be able to hold dual citizenship. Most countries, including the United States, require that a child with dual citizenship declare allegiance to one country upon turning eighteen. It is worth noting that requirements for U.S. citizenship, particularly as it affects people born outside the country, have changed frequently over time.

So far, citizenship seems relatively straightforward. But as we know, the United States since its birth been a nation of **immigrants,** people who are citizens or subjects of another country but who come here to live and work. Today there are strict limitations on the numbers of immigrants who may enter the country legally. There are also strict rules governing the criteria for entry. If immigrants come here legally on permanent residence visas—that is, if they follow the rules and regulations of the U.S. Immigration and Naturalization Service (INS)—they may be eligible to apply for citizenship through a process called naturalization. **Naturalization** confers citizenship on applicants who fulfill the following requirements:

immigrants
citizens or subjects of other countries who come to the United States to live or work

naturalization
the legal process of acquiring citizenship for someone who has not acquired it by birth

- Are at least eighteen years old

- Have been permanent legal residents of the United States for at least five years (although this can be reduced under special circumstances, such as for spouses of citizens or for legal residents who have served in the U.S. military)

- Have been physically present for at least half that time

- Are of good moral character

- Show commitment to the principles of the Constitution

- Speak adequate English

- Demonstrate knowledge of U.S. history and government

- Take an oath of allegiance

Once naturalized, new citizens have all the rights and responsibilities of any other citizen, and their children become citizens as well.

Sample Citizenship Questions

Answers may be found below.

1. How many states are there in the Union?
2. What do the stripes on the flag represent?
3. What is the Constitution?
4. What did the Emancipation Proclamation do?
5. Who was the main writer of the Declaration of Independence?
6. Can the Constitution be changed?
7. Who becomes president of the United States if the president and vice president should die?
8. Who elects the president of the United States?
9. Who has the power to declare war?
10. Can you name the two senators from your state?

Answers: 1. 50; 2. the thirteen original states; 3. the supreme law of the land; 4. freed many slaves; 5. Thomas Jefferson; 6. yes; 7. Speaker of the House of Representatives; 8. the electoral college; 9. the Congress; 10. (determine by locality).

Source: U.S. Department of Justice Immigration and Naturalization Service.

asylum   protection or sanctuary, especially from political persecution

refugees   individuals who flee an area or country because of persecution on the basis of race, nationality, religion, group membership, or political opinion

Nonimmigrants   Many people who come to the United States do not come as legal permanent residents. The INS refers to these people as nonimmigrants. Some arrive seeking **asylum,** or protection. These are political **refugees,** who are allowed into the United States if they face or are threatened with persecution in their native countries because of their race, religion, nationality, membership in a particular social group, or political opinions. The INS requires that the fear of persecution be "well-founded," however, and it is itself the final judge of a well-founded fear. Refugees may become legal permanent residents after they have lived here continuously for one year (although there are annual limits on the number who may do so), at which time they can begin accumulating the in-residence time required to become a citizen, if they wish.

Other people who may come to the United States legally but without official permanent resident status include visitors, foreign government officials, students, international representatives, temporary workers, members of foreign media, and exchange visitors. These people are expected to return to their home countries and not take up permanent residence in the United States.

Illegal immigrants have arrived here by avoiding INS regulations, usually because they would not qualify for one reason or another. American laws have become increasingly harsh with respect to illegal immigrants in recent years, but people continue to come. Many illegal immigrants act like citizens, obeying the laws, paying taxes, and sending their children to school. Nonetheless, some areas of the country, particularly those near the Mexican border,

like Texas and California, often have serious problems brought on by illegal immigration. Even with border controls to regulate the number of new arrivals, communities can find themselves swamped by new residents, often poor and unskilled, looking for a better life. Because their children must be educated and they themselves may be entitled to receive social services, they can place a significant financial burden on those communities. Although many illegal immigrants pay taxes, many others work off the books, meaning they do not contribute to the tax base. Furthermore, most income taxes are federal, and federal money is distributed back to states and localities to fund social services based on the population count in the census. Since illegal immigrants are understandably reluctant to come forward and be counted, their communities are typically underfunded in that respect as well.

Just because a person is not a legal permanent resident of the United States does not mean that he or she has no rights and responsibilities here, any more than the fact that we might be traveling in another country means that we have no rights and obligations there. Immigrants enjoy some rights, primarily legal protections. Not only are they entitled to due process in the courts (guarantee of a fair trial, right to a lawyer, and so on), but the Supreme Court also has ruled that it is illegal to discriminate against immigrants in the United States.[8] Their rights are limited, however. They cannot, for instance, vote in national elections (although some localities, in the hopes of integrating immigrants into their communities, allow them to vote in local elections[9]) or decide to live here permanently without permission (which may or may not be granted). In addition, immigrants, even legal ones, are subject to the decisions of the INS, which is empowered by Congress to exercise authority in immigration matters. The 1996 Illegal Immigration Reform and Immigrant Responsibility Act has granted the INS considerable power to make nonappealable decisions at the border that can result in the deportation of an immigrant who may have quite innocently violated an INS rule and who then cannot reenter the country for five years.

What Do American Citizens Believe?

Making a single nation out of a diverse people is no easy feat. It is possible in the United States only because, despite all our differences, Americans share some fundamental attitudes and beliefs about how the world works and how it should work. These ideas that pull us together, and that, indeed, provide a framework in which we can also disagree politically, are the subject of this section.

American Political Culture: Ideas That Unite

political culture
the broad pattern of ideas, beliefs, and values about citizens and government held by a population

values central ideas, principles, or standards that most people agree are important

Our European heritage, combined with our own historical development, has produced a distinctive American political culture based on the notion of representative government. **Political culture** refers to the general political orientation or disposition of a nation—the broad pattern of ideas, beliefs, and values that most of the population holds about the proper distribution of power in public life, the relationship of individuals to government, and the role that government ought to play. **Values** are central ideas about the world that most people agree are important, even though they may disagree on exactly how a value—such as "equality" or "freedom"—ought to be defined. Keep in mind that political culture is about our public lives; it does not necessarily specify the appropriate behavior or values for private relationships. Political culture is shared, although certainly some individuals find themselves at odds with it. When we say, "Americans think . . . ," we mean that most Americans hold those views, not that there is unanimous agreement on them. Political culture is handed down from generation to generation, through families, schools, communities, literature, churches and synagogues, and so on, helping to provide stability for the nation by ensuring that a majority of citizens are well grounded in and committed to the basic values that sustain it. We will talk about the process through which values are transferred in Chapter 10, "Public Opinion."

Political cultures are complex things. They are further complicated by the fact that we often take our own culture so for granted that we aren't even aware of it, and thus we can have trouble seeing it as clearly as someone who was not raised in it. We can simplify our understanding of American political culture by characterizing it as fundamentally procedural and individualistic. By **procedural** we mean that our culture is focused on rules rather than on substantive results, or the actual outcome of the rules. By **individualistic** we mean that what is good for society as a whole is assumed to be the same as what is good individually for all the people in it. This contrasts with a collectivist point of view, which holds that what is good for society may not be the same as what is in the best interests of individuals.

procedural relating to the rules of operation, not the outcomes

individualistic believing that what is good for society derives from what is good for the individual

When we say that American political culture is procedural, we mean that Americans expect government to guarantee fair processes rather than particular results. Other political cultures, for example, those in the Scandinavian countries of Sweden, Norway, and Denmark, believe that government *should* determine certain results and produce desirable outcomes, perhaps to guarantee a certain quality of life to all citizens or to increase equality of income. Those governments can then be evaluated by how well they accomplish those substantive goals. But while American politics does set some substantive goals for public policy, Americans are generally more comfortable ensuring that things are done in a fair and proper way and trusting that the outcomes will be good ones because the rules are fair. Thus our justice system has been known to release criminals known to be guilty because their procedural rights have been violated, and the economic market, which is seen as impartial and therefore fair, is relied on to determine income levels and the distribution of property. The American government does get involved in social programs and welfare, but it aims more at helping individuals get on their feet so they can participate in the market (fair procedures) rather than at cleaning up slums or eliminating poverty (substantive goals).

The individualistic nature of American political culture means that individuals, not government or society, are responsible for their own well-being. Our politics revolves around the belief that individuals are usually the best judges of what is good for them; we assume that what is good for society will automatically follow. We don't hold that there is something good for society that is different from what is good for individuals, as collectivist cultures sometimes do. Let's look again at Sweden, a democratic capitalist country like the United States, but one with a collectivist political culture. At one time, Sweden had a policy that held down the wages of workers in more profitable firms so that the salaries of higher- and lower-paid workers would be more equal and society, according to the Swedish view, would be better off. Americans would reject this policy as violating their belief in individualism (and proceduralism as well). American government rarely asks citizens to make major economic sacrifices for the public good, although individuals often do so privately and voluntarily. A collective interest that supersedes individual interests is generally invoked in the United States only in times of war or national crisis. This echoes the two American notions of self-interested and public-interested citizenship we discussed earlier in this chapter.

We can see our American procedural and individualistic perspective when we examine the different meanings of three central American values: *democracy, freedom,* and *equality*. Democracy in America, as we have seen, is representative democracy, based on consent and majority rule. Basically, American democracy is a way to make political decisions, to choose political leaders, and to select policies for the nation. It is seen as a fundamentally just or fair way of making decisions because every individual who cares to participate is heard in the process and all interests are considered. We don't reject a democratically made decision because it is not fair; instead, we believe that it is fair precisely because it was democratically made. Democracy is not valued primarily for the way it makes citizens feel or for the effects it has on them, but for the decisions it produces. Americans see democracy as the appropriate procedure for making public decisions—that is, decisions about government—but generally not for making decisions in the private realm. Rarely do employees have a binding vote on company policy, for example.

Americans also put a very high premium on the value of freedom, defined as freedom for the individual from restraint by the state. This view of freedom is procedural in the sense that it guarantees that you won't be prevented from doing something, not that you will actually be able to accomplish it. For instance, when an American says, "You are free to go," he or she means that the door is open. By contrast, a substantive view of freedom would provide you with a bus ticket so that you could go. Americans have an extraordinary commitment to freedom, perhaps because our values were forged during a period of history when liberty was a guiding principle. This commitment can be seen nowhere so clearly as in the Bill of Rights, the first ten amendments to the U.S. Constitution, which guarantee our basic civil liberties, the areas where government cannot interfere with individual actions. Those civil liberties include freedom of speech and expression, freedom of belief, freedom of the press, and the right to assemble, to name just a few. (See Chapter 4, "Fundamental American Liberties," for a complete discussion of these rights.)

Americans also believe in economic freedom—the freedom to participate in the marketplace, to acquire money and property, and to do with those resources pretty much as we please. Americans believe that it is government's job to protect our property, not to take it away or regulate our use of it too heavily. Our commitment to individualism is apparent here, too. Even if society as a whole would be better off if we taxed people more in order to pay off the federal debt (the amount our government owes from spending more than it brings in), our individualistic view of economic freedom means that Americans have one of the lowest tax rates in the industrialized world. This reflects our national tendency in normal times to emphasize the rights of citizenship over its obligations.

A third central value in American political culture is equality. For Americans, equality is valued not because we want individuals to *be* the same, but because we want them to be *treated* the same. Of all the values we hold dear, equality is probably the one we cast most clearly in procedural versus substantive terms. Equality in America means equality of treatment, access, and opportunity, not equality of results. People should have equal access to run the race, but we don't expect them all to finish in the same place. Thus we believe in equality before the law—that the law shouldn't make unreasonable distinctions among people the basis for treating them differently—and that all people should have equal access to the legal system. One problem the courts have faced is deciding what counts as a reasonable distinction. Can the law justifiably discriminate between—that is, treat differently—men and women, minorities and white Anglo-Saxon Protestants, rich and poor, young and old? When the rules treat people differently, even if the goal is to make them more equal in the long run, many Americans get very upset. Witness how controversial affirmative action policies are in this country. The point of such policies is to allow special opportunities for members of groups that have been discriminated against in the past, in order to remedy the long-term effects of that discrimination. For many Americans, such policies violate our commitment to procedural solutions. They wonder how treating people unequally can be fair.

Another kind of equality Americans hold dear is political equality—the principle of one person, one vote. Some strenuous political battles have been fought to extend the right to vote to all Americans, as we'll see in Chapter 5, "Civil Rights." African Americans won the vote in 1870 (although even then, many were prevented from exercising that right in the South until 1965), women won suffrage rights on a national level in 1920, and the right to vote was extended to eighteen-year-olds in 1971.

American Ideologies: Ideas That Divide

Most Americans are united in their commitment to proceduralism and individualism at some level, and to the key values of democracy, freedom, and equality, but there is still a lot of room for disagreement on other ideas and issues. The sets of beliefs and opinions about politics, the economy, and society that help people make sense of their world, and that can divide them into opposing camps, are called **ideologies.** Compared with the ideological spectrum of many countries, the range of debate in the United States is fairly narrow. We have no successful communist or socialist parties here, for instance. The ideologies on which those parties are founded seem unappealing to most Americans because they violate the norms of procedural and individualistic culture.

The two main dimensions that divide contemporary ideologies are their attitudes toward government action (government can be trusted to act wisely and should intervene widely in society and economics, versus distrust of government action and a belief that it should be limited to the maintenance of social order) and their attitudes toward change (progress is almost always a good thing and should be pursued with vigor, versus change is likely to lead to trouble and should be pursued with caution). Attitudes favoring government action and change as progress tend to be labeled **liberal.** Ideas that favor limited government and traditional social order tend to be called **conservative.** We also say that liberals are on the left side of the political spectrum and that conservatives are on the right. These spatial labels come

ideologies sets of beliefs about politics and society that help people make sense of their world

liberal generally favoring government action and viewing change as progress

conservative generally favoring limited government and cautious about change

partly from the efforts of social theorists to line up ideological positions on a linear continuum, and partly from the fact that in eighteenth-century France, the liberals sat on the left side of the parliamentary chamber and the conservatives on the right. Even though revolutionary French ideologies are not relevant in twenty-first-century America, the labels have stuck.

Based on these ideological dimensions, we say that the ideologies on the far left advocate totalitarian systems, which provide no limits on what government can do. Since communist and socialist systems usually require a large role for government in running the economy and allocating resources, they are located near the left end of the spectrum. The ideologies of the far right advocate anarchy, or the absence of government altogether. Most people want something in between these extremes, although in many countries there are numerous representatives of all these ideologies. In the United States, most people identify themselves as liberals, conservatives, or something between the two. While it may seem to Americans that those two ideological camps are poles apart, from the perspective of foreign observers, Americans don't disagree all that widely.

The basic difference between conservatives and liberals is that conservatives tend to be in favor of traditional values, they are slow to advocate change, and they place a priority on the maintenance of social order. Liberals, on the other hand, emphasize the possibilities of progress and change, look for innovations as answers to social problems, and focus on the expansion of individual rights and expression. It is the nature of conservatives to conserve, or protect, the status quo, so the precise issue stances they take change over time as the status quo changes. Since the Great Depression and Roosevelt's New Deal in the 1930s, a set of government policies designed to get the economy moving and to protect citizens from the worst effects of the Depression, conservatives and liberals have also taken the following positions with respect to government and the economy: Conservatives, reflecting a belief that government is not to be trusted with too much power and is, in any case, not a competent economic actor, have reacted against the increasing role of government in the American economy. Liberals, in contrast, arguing that the economic market cannot regulate itself and, left alone, is susceptible to ailments such as depressions and recessions, have a much more positive view of government and the good it can do in addressing economic and social problems. Typically, conservatives have tended to be wealthier, upper-class Americans, whereas liberals have been more likely to be blue-collar workers, although this is beginning to change.

In the 1980s and 1990s, another dimension was added to the liberal-conservative division in the United States. Perhaps because, as some researchers have argued, most people are able to meet their basic economic needs and more people than ever identify themselves as middle-class, many Americans are focusing less on economic questions and more on issues of morality and quality of life. Growing out of the commitment to tradition, for instance, some conservatives have gone beyond the economic realm to support what they call "family values": mothers remaining in the home with their children, regular church attendance, strong family discipline, laws denying equal rights to homosexuals, and legislation outlawing abortion. Partly in reaction to the conservative stance, liberals have come to include groups left out of the traditional vision of society: working women and mothers, single parents, gays, pro-choice groups, and others who do not see themselves as part of the model family.

Across the Great Divide
In October 1998, college student Matthew Shepard was beaten to death in rural Wyoming because he was gay. His murder quickly became a symbol for both sides of the gay rights issue. Outside the courthouse on the day one of his attackers pleaded guilty, an antigay group hurls insults as a gay rights activist dressed as an angel tries to shield the Shepard family from the taunts.

Ironically, these more recent ideological positions do not necessarily fit with the original liberal and conservative orientations toward government action. An active government is required to outlaw abortions and gay rights and to otherwise legislate morality. Thus it is the liberals in this case, rather than the conservatives, who are asking government to "get off their backs" with regard to moral choices and to let individuals make their own decisions. This causes some problems, especially among more traditional economic conservatives who don't want to be associated with the new moral positions.

Libertarians, who represent a small percentage of Americans, fall to the right of conservatives on economic issues and to the left of liberals on many social issues. Although libertarians do not go as far as anarchists in advocating the absence of government, they do want the presence of government in their lives reduced to the absolute minimum. Libertarians believe that government should exist to provide security and to protect property, but within that framework they want the broadest possible sphere of unrestrained individual action. For instance, libertarians agree with many liberals who think that marijuana and other drugs should be legalized. Libertarians hold this belief because they think individuals should be able to make decisions for themselves and take responsibility for their actions without government interference. For the same reasons, however, they agree with conservatives that individuals should have the right to own handguns and other weapons.

Themes of This Book

In this book, we focus on power and citizenship in American politics. Politics, we have seen, is a way of resolving conflict over scarce resources (including power, influence, and the quality of life) that offers us an alternative to resorting to violence.

The classic definition of politics proposed by the late political scientist Harold Lasswell says that politics is "who gets what when and how." We simplify his understanding by dropping the "when" and focusing on politics as the struggle over who gets power and resources in society and how they get them. Lasswell's definition is very strong because (1) it emphasizes that politics is a method of conflict resolution and (2) it focuses our attention on questions we can ask to figure out what is going on in politics.

Lasswell's definition of politics gives us a framework of analysis for this book—that is, it outlines how we will break down politics in order to understand it. We argue, with Lasswell, that politics is a struggle over power and resources and that defining who is involved, what is at stake, and how (under what rules) the conflict is to be resolved is crucial to understanding politics. If we know these things, we have a pretty good grasp of what is going on and we will probably be able to figure out new situations, even when our days of studying American government in college are far behind us.

Accordingly, in this book we analyze American politics in terms of three questions:

- Who are the parties involved? What resources, power, and rights do they bring to the struggle?

- What do they have at stake? What do they stand to win or lose? Is it power, influence, position, policy, or values?

- How do the rules shape the outcome? Where do the rules come from? What strategies or tactics do the political actors employ to use the rules to get what they want?

We focus our analysis on these questions throughout each chapter, but we also pause several times in each chapter to provide a "Who, What, How" feature that explicitly addresses these questions and concisely summarizes what we have presented.

This theme of "who, what, how" gives us a way to interpret political events and situations. As political scientists, however, we also want to evaluate American politics—that is, we want to assess how well it works. We could choose any number of dimensions on which to do that, but the most relevant, for most of us, is the role of citizens. To assess how democratic the United States is, we look at the changing concept and practice of citizenship in this country with respect to the subject matter of each chapter. Several strands of thought about citizenship have worked their way into the rich fabric of American political thought. We can draw on them to discuss the powers, opportunities, and challenges presented to American citizens by the system of government under which they live.

Our evaluative task in each chapter is to examine some aspect of citizen involvement in government. With that in mind, each chapter ends with a section in which we ask questions such as these:

- What role do "the people" have in American politics? How has that role expanded or diminished over time?

- What kinds of political participation do the rules of American politics (formal and informal) allow, encourage, or require citizens to take? What kinds of political participation are discouraged, limited, or forbidden?

CONSIDER THE SOURCE

Thinking Like a Political Scientist

In this introduction to American politics, we will be relying on the work of political scientists. In a sense, then, this is also an introduction to political science. If you have taken government or civics classes before, you know that the typical approach is to describe our government to you, explain your rights and obligations, and otherwise prepare you to be a good citizen. The perspective of this book goes beyond those goals. We would like you to participate in what political scientists do: *critical thinking* about politics.

Political science is not exactly the same kind of science as biology or geology. Not only is it difficult to put our subjects (people and political systems) under a microscope to observe their behavior, but we are somewhat limited in our ability to test our theories. We cannot replay World War II in order to test our ideas about what caused it, for example. A further problem is our subjectivity; we *are* the phenomena under investigation, and so we may have stronger feelings about our research and our findings than we would, say, about cells and rocks.

These difficulties do not make a science of politics impossible, but they do mean we must proceed with caution. Even among political scientists there is disagreement about whether a rigorous science of the political world is a reasonable goal. What we can agree on is that it is possible to advance our understanding of politics beyond mere guessing or debates about political preferences. Although we use many methods in our work (statistical analysis, mathematical modeling, case studies, and philosophical reasoning, to name only a few), what political scientists have in common is an emphasis on critical thinking about politics.

In this book, we invite you to share the view of the researcher, looking into the microscope, as it were, and asking the kinds of questions political scientists ask. What makes citizens tick? When do they view a government as exercising legitimate authority? How do they make decisions? How do people organize themselves and express their various interests? How do they decide what role government ought to play in their lives, and what happens if they disagree on such fundamental issues? Do people make rational decisions when they vote? What does it mean to be "rational"? How do governments work? How do different sorts of institutions lead to different kinds of policy? Who *does* get what, and how do they get it? These are the kinds of questions political scientists ask about their subjects, and they construct arguments based on evidence and scientific reasoning to answer them.

What does it mean to approach these questions critically? Critical thinking means challenging the conclusions of others, asking why or why not, turning the accepted wisdom upside down and exploring alternative interpretations. It means considering the sources of information—not accepting an explanation just because someone in authority offers it, or because you have always been told that it is the true explanation, but because you have independently discovered that there are good reasons for accepting it. You may emerge from reading this textbook with the same ideas about politics that you have always had; it is not our goal to change your mind. But as a critical thinker, you will be able to back up your old ideas with new and persuasive arguments of your own, or to move beyond your current ideas to see politics in a new light.

Critical thinking can work for you in two ways. First, it provides tools to help you evaluate the arguments of others, whether it's your friend at a social gathering, a commentator on the radio, or a political scientist in this textbook. We live in an information age. In this book, we frequently ask you to "consider the source" of your information and to carefully examine its validity. Critical thinking can arm you with the tools to subject that information to a close scrutiny and prevent you from being duped by it. Second, critical thinking can also help you to construct political arguments of your own—for instance, if you were trying to convince someone that democracy is a good form of government, or that health care is better left to the private sector. When we say "argument" here, we are not referring to a fight or a dispute, but rather to a political case or contention, based on a set of assumptions, supported by evidence, and leading to a clear, well-developed conclusion. It is more than an opinion or a feeling; it is a piece of scholarly reasoning. You can refute an opinion by saying "I disagree," but you must refute an argument with another argument, again supported by evidence. Not all arguments are created equal. There are good arguments and bad arguments. Being critical is about thinking well, whether you are thinking about someone else's ideas or your own.

Critical thinking is hard work. It is much easier to sit back and let someone else do all the analyzing and interpreting and concluding. Why bother? Political scientists bother because we love our subject and because we get caught up in the excitement of creating new understanding and knowledge about politics and government. But why should *you* bother, especially if the subject doesn't capture your interest as it does ours? The main reason is that government is not an option. People besiege us with political arguments, better ideas, public policies, and ideal candidates all our lives. Our best defense against the products of the critical thinking of others is to be critical thinkers ourselves.

You can work through the process of critical thinking by asking yourself a series of questions. It may help to refer to this page as a checklist. You use the same questions whether you are evaluating someone else's argument or creating your own.

Parts of an Argument

Thesis/Hypothesis

Premises

Evidence

Logic and Clarity

Conclusions

Steps of Critical and Analytic Thinking

1. *Does the author set out a clear thesis, hypothesis, or statement about the intention of the argument?*
   Nothing is worse than reading a piece of scholarship and not understanding what point the author is making. Lack of a clear thesis may be a sign of fuzzy thinking, so beware. A hypothesis is like a thesis; it is a guess or an expectation about what the evidence will show. Arguments often look to support or disprove a hypothesis.

2. *Does the author state the basic premises, assumptions, values, and first principles on which the argument is founded?*
   We all have basic assumptions about the world, about human nature, the proper role of government, political values like freedom and equality, and so on. Are these assumptions spelled out? Often they are not, and yet they have a strong impact on the nature of the argument. Are the premises, the building blocks of the argument, clearly set out and justified or supported by evidence? In other words, if one premise of the argument that health care should be left to the private sector is that most people have private health insurance, look for ample evidence, convincing data, and scholarly citations to back up that claim.

3. *Has the author done the basic research to gather the evidence necessary to support the claims of the argument?*
   An argument cannot be based on a gut feeling, on vague beliefs, or on what you have always heard is true. Arguments are based on evidence, objective verifiable observations of the political world, or logical reasoning. Try to assess the quality of the evidence presented. Is it from reliable sources? Could others replicate the evidence if they tried? Like arguments, all evidence is not created equal. Be a strict critic.

4. *Does the author follow the rules of logic and clarity?*
   Is the argument logical? Do the conclusions follow from the premises or first principles? If someone argues that Britain has national health care and Britain has an ailing economy and *therefore* if the United States adopts national health care, its economy will decline as well, would you be convinced? We hope not. This is an example of specious reasoning; it sounds good but falls apart under close scrutiny. The author hasn't shown any causal connection between health care and lack of economic prosperity, only that they coexist in one country.
   Is the argument clear? Are all the terms defined? If someone argues that democracy is the best form of government, does he or she (or you) explain exactly what "democracy" means and what criteria are being used to determine the "best"? Worry especially about abstract terms like *democracy, equality,* and *freedom* that have lots of feelings associated with them. Don't be persuaded by someone who says he or she is for freedom, only to find out later that he or she means something very different by it than you do.

5. *How persuasive are the author's conclusions?*
   Is the argument successful? Does it convince you? Why or why not? (If you are the author, it is helpful to have a friend answer this question.) Does it change your mind about any conclusions you held previously? Does accepting this argument require you to rethink any of your other beliefs? If it is your argument, have you referred to the basic questions of politics: Who gets what and how? Who wins and who loses?

Points of Access

- **Register and vote.** This is the basic, raw power of the citizen, never to be trumped by a checkbook. Special interests may put the candidate on television, but only the voter can put that candidate in office.

- **Speak up—they can't hear you.** The power of the letter or phone call or meeting is second only to the power of the vote. Citizens can lobby; take a page from the Association of Retired Persons. A thousand postcards, or even ten, get noticed.

- **See the good.** There are many smart, dedicated people in elected office. Support them. There is a growing cadre of groups working to diffuse the power of money in politics. Join them. In Washington, Common Cause and Public Campaign are working for public financing of elections to diminish the influence of special interests.

- **Demand leadership.** Just because economic times are good doesn't mean a person can tune out. The best people should be in power in case the worst happens. Mettle-testing can't be scheduled. Voters should choose a candidate as though he or she will be given custody of their children, for in many ways that's true.

- **But don't expect perfection.** A good leader is not superhuman and will fail on occasion. Know the difference between an honest mistake and a lie. Political leaders reflect the people who elected them.

- **Raise a voter.** Instill an "I care" attitude in children and make sure their school has a strong emphasis on civics. Some do, some don't. The City on a Hill Charter School in Boston has made civics its mission. The Center for Civic Education in Calabasas, California, has made teaching the subject a national campaign.

- **Refuse to be manipulated.** See through the attack ad and turn it off. Call the attacker and promise to vote for his or her opponent.

- **Tell the press to back off.** Many news organizations have an ombudsman to hear reader complaints. If reporting seems unfair or too negative, call, write, or send a letter to the editor.

- **Understand the process.** Democracy is not pretty. It is often rough and tumble, passionate, and downright weird. It is a clash of ideas that should, if the system is working, result in the forging of a sometimes unsettling compromise, never utopia. There's a responsibility for the citizen, too: Get informed. Read. Listen. Think.

- **Don't give up.** Eastern Europe broke with communism. South Africa ended apartheid. Northern Ireland came to the table to write a peace plan. Chances are the United States can figure out how to redirect the democratic experiment and keep it boldly alive. Every American should be eager to help.

Source: "CPR for the Electorate; Democracy's Vital Signs," *Boston Globe*, Editorial, 11 May 1998, A14.

- Do citizens take advantage of the opportunities for political action that the rules provide them? How do they react to the rules that limit their participation?

- How do citizens in different times exercise their rights and responsibilities?

- What do citizens need to do to "keep the Republic"? How democratic is the United States?

To put this all in perspective—and to give you a more concrete idea of what citizen participation might mean on a more personal level—we also include a brief list of political "Points of Access" near the end of each chapter. We introduce this feature here, with some "exercises for better democratic health" that were offered in a *Boston Globe* editorial. In subsequent chapters, "Points of Access" will direct you in a briefer fashion to some specific avenues of participation that might be available to you and to others in your community as a means to achieve a political objective.

The analytic theme of this book is to ask who, what, how. That is, to understand the workings of American politics, we break it down into manageable parts and inquire who gets the power and resources and how they get them. Our evaluative framework, where we ask not how American politics works but how well it works, is to explore the role of the American citizen. The link between citizenship and the "who, what, how" framework is that we are all part of the who, we all have something at stake, the rules affect us all, and we can affect the rules. As you learn to think like a political scientist, you will also learn the techniques of evaluation and analysis that will help you become a critical citizen of democratic politics. See "Consider the Source: Thinking Like a Political Scientist" to learn the steps of **critical thinking**.

critical thinking
analysis and evaluation of ideas and arguments based on reason and evidence

Citizenship and Politics

Today's American political system, based on a set of values that favor individual rights and fair procedures, bears a pretty close resemblance to Madison's "republican government." Keeping in mind that this system was not meant to be a "pure democracy," it is interesting to note that it has grown more democratic in some ways in the past two hundred years. For one thing, more people can participate now, and, since eighteen-year-olds won the right to vote, the electorate is younger than ever. But in many ways, government remains removed from "the people," even if the definition of "the people" has expanded over time, and as we have already noted, voter turnout is low in the United States.

A growing number of educators and social scientists argue that falling levels of involvement, interest, and trust in politics are not something to be explained and dismissed with complacency, but instead signal a true civic crisis in American politics. They see a swing from the community-minded citizens of republican virtue to the self-interested citizens of Madisonian theory so severe that the fabric of American political life is threatened. These scholars argue that democracies can survive only with the support and vigilance of citizens and that American citizens are so disengaged as the new century begins as to put democracy itself in danger. They would place the responsibility for low levels of participation in the United States not just on the system but also on the citizens themselves for not availing themselves of the opportunities for engagement that do exist.

While the question of how democratic the United States is may seem to be largely an academic one—that is, one that has little or no relevance to your personal life—it is really a question of who has the power and who is likely to be a winner in the political process. Looked at this way, the question has quite a lot to do with your life, especially as government starts to make more demands on you and you on it. Are you likely to be a winner or a loser? Are you going to get what you want from the political system? How much power do people like you have to get their way in government?

WHAT'S AT STAKE REVISITED

We began this chapter by asking you what was at stake if young people paid no attention to politics or failed to learn the basic facts about their government. Since then we have covered a lot of territory, arguing that politics is fundamental to human life and in fact makes life easier for us by giving us a nonviolent way to resolve disputes. We also pointed out that politics is the method by which the valuable resources of power and influence get distributed in society: politics is who gets what and how they get it. One clear consequence of youthful disregard for politics, then, is that young people will be less likely to get what they want from the political system. In fact, that is exactly what happens.

We have also seen that democracies allow several possible roles for their citizens, ranging from merely rubber-stamping others' decisions to active participation, and that in American democracy citizenship can be both self-interested and public-spirited. When Benjamin Franklin said he was giving us a Republic, if we could keep it, he was surely hoping that the newly minted American citizens would be capable of putting their particular self-interests aside in favor of a greater public interest. This tendency toward self-sacrifice is hardly an automatic reaction, however; it comes as a result of education about citizenship and the nature of a democratic system. A less informed and interested generation of citizens is also less likely to be willing to make sacrifices for their country.

There is clearly a great deal at stake in the issue of youthful ignorance about politics. But while the recent years of scandal and partisanship have clearly taken a toll on the commitment of youth to politics, there is some reason to think that the tide may be turning. In November 1998, the month before President Clinton's impeachment in the House of Representatives, the magazine *Rolling Stone* published results of a survey it had commissioned on the political views of young people (aged eighteen to thirty-four) in general, and college students in particular.[10] Specifically, they wanted to find out if young people tuned out to politics and how they perceived the crisis over the Clinton presidency. Contrary to conventional wisdom that held that young people, sexually liberated and politically apathetic, were indifferent to the scandal, the survey instead revealed that young people are paying attention to politics and are deeply concerned about what they see. The survey showed that they have serious conflicts about politics, morality, and the role of the contemporary media.

While about 20 percent of college students said they had little or no interest in politics, 43 percent claimed to have a great deal or quite a bit of interest. About 40 percent said they were mostly or leaning toward the Democrats, 32 percent said they were mostly or leaning toward the Republicans, and 26 percent described themselves as completely independent. Like the population as a whole, young people supported the idea that Clinton should remain in office. But they were sharply split about where to lay the blame for the political circus in Washington. While 36 percent said the responsibility was Clinton's, nearly a quarter pointed at the media. And 32 percent said they most disliked the media, compared to only 24 percent who disliked Clinton. Seventy-seven percent believe that the media will be able to report on people's private lives more freely in the future.

These responses about politics and the media, though hardly cheerful, *do* provide us with some reason to be optimistic. The Clinton impeachment may have had the effect of causing young people to become more politicized, to be aware of the differences between political parties, and to recognize that their privacy is at stake and that the media, once the "watchdog of democracy," should itself be carefully watched. As we proceed through this book that introduces you to American politics, remember what you have at stake in becoming an educated citizen of the United States government. ■

key terms

asylum 16
authoritarian government 8
authority 4
capitalist economy 4
citizens 10
communist economy 6
conservative 20
critical thinking 27
democracy 9
economics 4
elite democracy 9
fascist government 9
government 4

ideologies 20
immigrants 15
individualistic 18
institutions 7
legitimate 3
liberal 20
monarchy 8
naturalization 15
oligarchy 9
participatory democracy 10
pluralist democracy 10
political culture 17
politics 3

popular sovereignty 9
power 3
procedural 18
refugees 16
republic 12
rules 7
social contract 11
social democracy 7
subjects 10
theocracy 8
totalitarian government 8
values 17

summary

■ Politics may appear to be a grubby, greedy pursuit, filled with scandal and backroom dealing. In fact, despite its shortcomings and sometimes shabby reputation, politics is an essential means for resolving differences and determining how power and resources are distributed in society. Politics is about who gets power and resources in society and how these people get them.

■ Government, a product of the political process, is the system established for exercising authority over a group of people. In America, government is embodied in the Constitution and the institutions set up by the Constitution. The Constitution represents the compromises and deals made by the founders on a number of fundamental issues, including how best to divide governing power. Government is shaped not only by poli-

tics but also by economics, which is concerned specifically with the distribution of wealth and society's resources. The United States has a capitalist economy, which means that property is owned privately and decisions about the production of goods and the distribution of wealth are left to marketplace forces.

■ Politics establishes the rules and institutions that shape ongoing political interactions. The most fundamental rules of our political system are those that define and empower our political institutions and the ways these institutions interact with each other and with individual citizens.

■ Political systems dictate how power is distributed among leaders and citizens, and they take many forms. Authoritarian systems give ultimate power to the state; nonauthoritarian systems place power largely in the hands of the people. The nonauthoritarian system most familiar to us is democracy, which is based on the principle of popular sovereignty—giving the people the ultimate power to govern. The meaning of citizenship is key to the definition of democracy, and citizens are believed to have rights protecting them from government as well as responsibilities to the public realm.

■ The meaning of American democracy can be traced to the time of the nation's founding. During that period, two competing views of citizenship emerged. The first view, articulated by James Madison, sees the citizen as fundamentally self-interested; this view led the founders to fear too much citizen participation in government. The second view puts faith in the citizen's ability to act for the common good—to put his or her obligation to the public ahead of his or her own self-interest. Both views are still alive and well, and much debated today, and we can see evidence of both at work in political life.

■ U.S. immigrants are citizens or subjects of another country who come here to live and work. To become full citizens, they must undergo naturalization by fulfilling requirements designated by the U.S. Immigration and Naturalization Service.

■ Americans share common values and beliefs about how the world should work. These values and beliefs allow us to be a nation despite our diversity.

■ The American political culture is described as both procedural and individualistic. Because we focus more on fair rules than on the outcomes of those rules, our culture has a procedural nature. In addition, our individualistic nature means that we assume individuals know what is best for themselves and that individuals, not government or society, are responsible for their own well-being.

■ Democracy, freedom, and equality are three central American values. Generally, Americans acknowledge democracy as the most appropriate way to make public decisions. We value individual freedom from government restraint and equality of opportunity rather than equality of results.

■ Ideologies are the beliefs and opinions about politics, the economy, and society that help people make sense of the world. The range of the ideological debate is fairly narrow in the United States compared to that in other countries, but there is an ideological division based largely on attitudes toward government and about change. Liberals generally favor government action and view change as progress; conservatives support limited government and a traditional social order.

■ In this book, we look at power, citizenship, and the ways in which our uniquely American rules and institutions determine who gets what in our society. We rely on two underlying themes to pursue this course. The first is the assumption that all political events and situations can be examined by looking at who the actors are, what they have to win or lose, and how the rules shape the way they engage in their struggle. This framework should provide us with a clear understanding of the issues that have dominated our political life since the founding. Examining the importance of rules in political outcomes highlights the second theme of this text: how citizens participate in political life in order to improve their own individual situations and promote the interests of the community at large. In this book, we carefully examine the exercise of citizenship as we look at each element in the political process.

■ America's growing political apathy is well documented. Many people claim that it may signal a crisis of democracy.

2

What's at Stake?

The Split from England
• Revolution
• The Declaration of Independence
• "... That All Men Are Created Equal"

The Articles of Confederation
• The Provisions of the Articles
• Some Winners, Some Losers

The Constitutional Convention
• How Strong a Central Government?
• Large States, Small States
• North and South

The Constitution
• The Legislative Branch
• The Executive Branch
• The Judicial Branch
• Separation of Powers and Checks and Balances
• Amendability

Ratification
• Federalists Versus Anti-Federalists
• The Federalist Papers
• The Final Vote

Citizenship and the Founding

What's at Stake Revisited

The Politics of the American Founding

W H A T ' S   A T   S T A K E ?

They meet in towns in nearly every state in the Union, in brightly lit public halls, in living rooms, in diners. They meet in large assemblies of several hundred and in "cells" of three or four. They are men and women, plumbers and electricians, farmers and teachers, land developers and lawyers. They say their goal is to defend and protect the Constitution. Their critics say they will destroy it. Who is right?

The Second Amendment to the Constitution reads, "A well regulated Militia, being necessary to the security of a free State, the right of the people to keep and bear Arms, shall not be infringed." The meaning of this amendment is hotly contested in America. Did the framers of the Constitution mean to protect those who took up arms against the newly formed government? Did they mean to guarantee the right to carry weapons under any and all circumstances? Members of state militias and groups like them take this amendment literally and absolutely. They liken themselves to the Sons of Liberty, who, in colonial America, rejected the authority of the British government and took it upon themselves to enforce the laws they thought were just. The Sons of Liberty instigated the Boston Massacre and the Boston Tea Party, historical events that are celebrated as patriotic but would be considered terrorist or treasonous if they took place today.

Today's militias claim that the federal government has become as tyrannical as the British government ever was, that it deprives citizens of their liberty and overregulates their everyday lives. They go so far as to claim that federal authority is illegitimate. Militia members reject a variety of federal laws, from those limiting the weapons that individual citizens can own, to those imposing taxes on income, to those requiring the registration of motor vehicles. They maintain that government should stay out of individual lives, providing security at the national level perhaps, but allowing citizens to regulate and protect their own lives.

Some militias go even further. Many militia members are convinced, for instance, that the United Nations is seeking to take over the United States and that top U.S. officials are letting this happen. Others blend their quests for individual liberty with rigid requirements about who should enjoy that liberty. White supremacist or anti-Semitic groups aim at achieving an "all-white" continent or see Jewish collaboration behind ominous plots to destroy America.

Except for the few just mentioned that practice and proclaim bigotry, these groups might not seem particularly threatening. Many of us might even agree with some of the ideas they stand for. Yet in 1995, President Bill Clinton introduced an antiterrorism bill in Congress that would have made it easier for federal agencies to monitor the activities of such groups. Although the bill was not passed, the government doesn't seem to be any fonder of militias than they are of it. What is at stake here? Why should the government react so strongly to the existence of state militias? Are these groups the embodiment of revolutionary patriotism? Do they support the Constitution or sabotage it? Think about these questions as you read this chapter on the founding of the United States. Think about the consequences and implications of revolutionary activity then and now. We will return to the question of what's at stake for American politics in the state militia movement at the end of the chapter. ■

Schoolchildren in the United States have had the story of the American founding pounded into their heads. From the moment they start coloring grateful Pilgrims and cutting out construction paper turkeys in grade school, the founding is a recurring focus of their education, and with good reason. Democratic societies, as we saw in Chapter 1, rely on the consent of their citizens to maintain lawful behavior and public order. A commitment to the rules and goals of the American system requires that we feel good about that system. What better way to stir up good feelings and patriotism than by recounting thrilling stories of bravery and derring-do on the part of selfless heroes dedicated to the cause of American liberty? We celebrate the Fourth of July with fireworks and parades, displaying publicly our commitment to American values and our belief that our country is special, in the same way that other nations celebrate their origins all over the world. Bastille Day (July 14) in France, May 17 in Norway, October 1 in China, and July 6 in Malawi all are days on which people rally together to celebrate their common past and their hopes for the future.

Of course, people feel real pride in their countries, and many nations, not only our own, do have amazing stories to tell about their earliest days. But since this is a textbook on politics, not patriotism, we need to look beyond the pride and the amazing stories. As political scientists, we must separate myth from reality. For us, the founding of the United States is central not because it inspires warm feelings of patriotism, but because it can teach us about American politics—the struggles for power that forged the political system that continues to shape our collective struggles today.

The history of the American founding has been told from many points of view. You are probably most familiar with this account: The early colonists escaped to

America to avoid religious persecution in Europe. Having arrived on the shores of the New World, they built communities that allowed them to practice their religions in peace and to govern themselves as free people. When the tyrannical British king made unreasonable demands on the colonists, they had no choice but to protect their liberty by going to war and by establishing a new government of their own.

But sound historical evidence suggests that the story is more complicated, and more interesting, than that. A closer look shows that early Americans were complex beings with economic and political agendas as well as religious and philosophical motives. After much struggle among themselves, the majority of Americans decided that those agendas could be better and more profitably carried out if they broke their ties with England.[1]

In this chapter, we talk a lot about history—the history of the American founding and the creation of the Constitution. Like all authors, we have a particular point of view that affects how we tell the story. True to the basic theme of this book, we are interested in power and citizenship. We want to understand American government in terms of who the winners and losers are likely to be. It makes sense for us to begin by looking at the founding to see who the winners and losers were then. We are also interested in how rules and institutions make it more likely that some people will win and others lose. Certainly, an examination of the early debates about rules and institutions will help us understand that. Because we are interested in winners and losers, the *who* of politics, we are interested in understanding how people come to be defined as players in the system in the first place. It was during the founding that many of the initial decisions were made about who "We, the people" would actually be. Finally, we are interested in the product of all this debate—the Constitution of the United States, the ultimate rule book for who gets what in American politics. Consequently, our discussion of American political history will focus on these issues. Specifically, we will look at

- the colonial break with England and the Revolution

- the initial attempt at American government—the Articles of Confederation

- the Constitutional Convention

- the Constitution itself

- the ratification of the Constitution

The Split from England

America was a political and military battlefield long before the Revolution. Not only did nature confront the colonists with brutal winters, harsh droughts, disease, and other unanticipated disasters, but the New World was also already inhabited before the British settlers arrived, both by Native Americans and by Spanish and French colonists (see Figure 2.1). These political actors in North America during the seventeenth and early eighteenth centuries had, perhaps, more at stake than they knew. All were trying to lay claim to the same geographical territory; none could have foreseen that that territory would one day become the strongest power in the world. Whoever

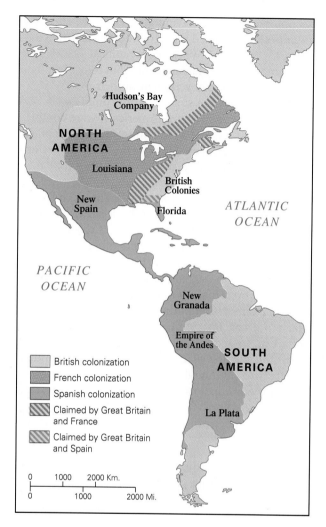

Figure 2.1
European Colonies in the New World Around 1600

won the battle for North America would put their stamp on the globe in a major way.

By the late 1700s, the eastern colonies of North America were heavily English. For many reasons, life in England had limited opportunities for freedom, for economic gain, and for political power. English settlers had arrived in America seeking, first and foremost, to find new opportunities in America. But those opportunities were not available to all. "We, the people" had been defined in various ways throughout the 1600s and 1700s, but never had it meant anything like "everybody" or even "every white male." Religious and property qualifications for the vote, and the exclusion of women and blacks from political life, meant that the colonial leaders did not feel that simply living in a place, obeying the laws, or even paying taxes carried with it the right to participate in government. Following the rigid British social hierarchy, they wanted the "right kind" of people to participate—people who could be depended on to make the kind of rules that would ensure their status and maintain the established order. The danger of expanding the vote, of course, was that the new majority might have wanted something very different from what the old majority wanted.

Those colonists who had political power in the second half of the eighteenth century gradually began to question their relationship with England. For much of the history of colonial America, England had left the colonies pretty much alone, and they had learned to live with the colonial governance that Britain exercised. Of course, they were obliged, as colonies, to make England their primary trading partner. Even goods they exported to other European countries had to pass through England, where taxes were collected on them. However, smuggling and corrupt colonial officials had made those obligations less than burdensome. It is important to remember that the colonies received many benefits by virtue of their status: they were settled by corporations and companies funded with British money, such as the Massachusetts Bay Company; they were protected by the British army and navy; and they had a secure market for their agricultural products.

Whether the British government was actually being oppressive in the years before 1776 is open to interpretation. Certainly, the colonists thought so. Britain was deeply in debt, having won the **French and Indian War,** which effectively forced the French out of North America and the Spanish to vacate Florida and retreat west of the Mississippi. The war, fought to defend the British colonies and colonists in America,

French and Indian War a war fought between France and England, and allied Indians, from 1754 to 1763; resulted in France's expulsion from the New World

turned into a major and expensive conflict across the Atlantic as well. Britain, having done its protective duty as a colonial power and having taxed British citizens at home heavily to finance the war, turned to its colonies to help pay for their defense. It chose to do that by levying taxes on the colonies and by attempting to enforce more strictly the trade laws that would increase British profits from American resources.

The series of acts passed by the British infuriated the colonists. The Sugar Act of 1764, which imposed customs taxes, or duties, on sugar, was seen as unfair and unduly burdensome in a depressed postwar economy, and the Stamp Act of 1765 incited protests and demonstrations throughout the colonies. Similar to a tax in effect in Great Britain for nearly a century, it required that a tax be paid, in scarce British currency, on every piece of printed matter in the colonies, including newspapers, legal documents, and even playing cards. The colonists claimed that the law was an infringement on their liberty and a violation of their right not to be taxed without their consent. Continued protests and political changes in England resulted in the repeal of the Stamp Act in 1766. The Townshend Acts of 1767, taxing goods imported from England such as paper, glass, and tea, and the Tea Act of 1773 were seen by the colonists as intolerable violations of their rights. To show their displeasure, they hurled 342 chests of tea into Boston Harbor in the famous Boston Tea Party. Britain responded by passing the Coercive Acts of 1774, designed to punish the citizens of Massachusetts. In the process, Parliament sowed the seeds that would blossom into revolution in just a few years.

Revolution

From the moment the unpopularly taxed tea plunged into Boston Harbor, it became apparent that Americans were not going to settle down and behave like proper and

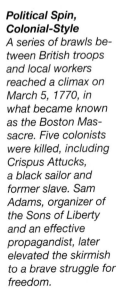

Political Spin, Colonial-Style
A series of brawls between British troops and local workers reached a climax on March 5, 1770, in what became known as the Boston Massacre. Five colonists were killed, including Crispus Attucks, a black sailor and former slave. Sam Adams, organizer of the Sons of Liberty and an effective propagandist, later elevated the skirmish to a brave struggle for freedom.

orthodox colonists. Britain was surprised by the colonial reaction, and it could not ignore it. Even before the Boston Tea Party, mobs in many towns were demonstrating and rioting against British control. Calling themselves the Sons of Liberty, and under the guidance of the eccentric and unsteady Sam Adams, cousin of the future president John Adams, they routinely caused extensive damage. In early 1770, they provoked the Boston Massacre, an attack by British soldiers that left six civilians dead and further inflamed popular sentiments.

By the time of the December 1773 Boston Tea Party, also incited by the Sons of Liberty, passions were at a fever pitch. The American patriots called a meeting in Philadelphia in September 1774. Known as the First Continental Congress, the meeting declared the Coercive Acts void, announced a plan to stop trade with England, and called for a second meeting in May 1775. Before they could meet again, in the early spring of 1775, the king's army went marching to arrest Sam Adams and another patriot, John Hancock, and to discover the hiding place of the colonists' weapons. Roused by the silversmith Paul Revere, Americans in Lexington and Concord fired the first shots of rebellion at the British, and the Revolution was truly under way.

The Declaration of Independence

In 1776, at the direction of a committee of the Continental Congress, thirty-four-year-old Thomas Jefferson sat down to write a declaration of independence from England. His training as a lawyer at the College of William and Mary and his service as a representative in the Virginia House of Burgesses helped prepare him for his task, but he had an impressive intellect in any case. President John Kennedy once announced to a group of Nobel Prize winners he was entertaining that they were "the most extraordinary collection of talents that has ever gathered at the White House, with the possible exception of when Thomas Jefferson dined alone."[2] A testimony to Jefferson's capabilities is the strategically brilliant document that he produced.

Declaration of Independence the political document that dissolved the colonial ties between the United States and Britain

The **Declaration of Independence** is first and foremost a political document. Having decided to make the break with England, the American founders had to convince themselves, their fellow colonists, and the rest of the world that they were doing the right thing. Jefferson did not have to hunt far for a good reason for his revolution. John Locke, whom we discussed in Chapter 1, had handed him one on a silver platter. Remember that Locke said that government is based on a contract between the rulers and the ruled. The ruled agree to obey the laws as long as the rulers protect their basic rights to life, liberty, and property. If the rulers fail to do that, they break the contract, and the ruled are free to set up another government. This is exactly what the second paragraph of the Declaration of Independence says, except that Jefferson changed "property" to "the pursuit of happiness," perhaps to garner the support of those Americans who didn't own enough property to worry about. The rest of the Declaration focuses on documenting the ways in which the colonists believed that England, and particularly George III, had violated their rights and broken the social contract.

"... That All Men Are Created Equal"

The Declaration of Independence begins with a proud statement of the equality of all men. Since so much of this document relies heavily on Locke, and since clearly the colonists did *not* mean that all men are created equal, it is worth turning to Locke for some help in seeing exactly what they did mean. In his most famous work, *A Second Treatise on Government,* Locke wrote,

> Though I have said above that all men are by nature equal, I cannot be supposed to understand all sorts of equality. Age or virtue may give men a just precedency. Excellency of parts and merit may place others above the common level. Birth may subject some, and alliance or benefits others, to pay an observance to those whom nature, gratitude, or other respects may have made it due.[3]

Men are equal in a natural sense, says Locke, but society quickly establishes many dimensions on which they may be unequal. A particularly sticky point for Locke's ideas on equality is his treatment of slavery. Although he hemmed and hawed about it, ultimately he failed to condemn it. Here, too, our founders would have been in agreement with him.

African Americans and the Revolution   The Revolution was a mixed blessing for American slaves. On the one hand, many slaves won their freedom during the war. Slavery was outlawed north of Maryland, and many slaves in the Upper South were also freed. The British offered freedom in exchange for service in the British army, although the conditions they provided were not always a great improvement over enslavement. The abolitionist, or antislavery, movement gathered steam in some northern cities, expressing moral and constitutional objections to the institution of slavery. Whereas before the Revolution only about 5 percent of American blacks were free, the number grew tremendously with the coming of war.[4]

In the aftermath of war, African Americans did not find their lot greatly improved, despite the ringing rhetoric of equality that fed the Revolution. The economic profitability of slave labor still existed in the South, and slaves continued to be imported from Africa in large numbers. The explanatory myth, that all men were created equal but that blacks weren't quite men and thus could be treated unequally, spread throughout the new country, making even free blacks unwelcome in many communities. By 1786 New Jersey prohibited free blacks from entering the state, and within twenty years northern states started passing laws specifically denying free blacks the right to vote.[5]

Native Americans and the Revolution   Native Americans were another group the founders did not consider to be prospective citizens. The European view of the Indians had always been that they were a simple, inferior people. Their communal property holding, their nonmonarchical political systems, and their divisions of labor between women working in the fields and men hunting for game all struck the colonists as naive and primitive. Because the colonists were continually encroaching on land traditionally hunted by the Indians, the Indians at best mistrusted them. Pushed farther and farther west by land-hungry colonists, the Indians were actively hostile to the American cause in the Revolution. Knowing this, the British hoped to gain their allegiance in the war. Fortunately for the Revolutionary effort, the colonists, having asked in vain for the Indians to stay out of what they called a "family quarrel," were able to suppress early on the Indians' attempts to get revenge for their treatment at the hands of the settlers.[6] There was certainly no suggestion that the claim of equality at the beginning of the

Declaration of Independence might include the peoples who had lived on the continent for centuries before the white man arrived.

Women and the Revolution   Neither was there any question that "all men" might somehow be a generic term for human beings that would include women. Politically, the Revolution proved to be a step backward for women: it was after the war that states began specifically to prohibit women, even those with property, from voting.[7] That doesn't mean, however, that women did not get involved in the war effort. Within the constraints of society, they contributed what they could to the American cause. They boycotted tea and other British imports, sewed flags, made bandages and clothing, nursed and housed soldiers, and collected money to support the Continental Army. Under the name Daughters of Liberty, women in many towns met publicly to discuss the events of the day, spinning and weaving to make the colonies less dependent on imported cotton and woolen goods from England, and drinking herbal tea instead of tea that was taxed by the British. Some women moved beyond such mild patriotic activities to outright political behavior, writing pamphlets urging independence, spying on enemy troops, carrying messages, and even, in isolated instances, fighting on the battlefields.[8]

Men's understanding of women's place in early American politics was nicely put by Thomas Jefferson, writing from Europe to a woman in America in 1788:

> But our good ladies, I trust, have been too wise to wrinkle their foreheads with politics. They are contented to soothe & calm the minds of their husbands returning ruffled from political debate. They have the good sense to value domestic happiness above all others. There is no part of the earth where so much of this is enjoyed as in America.[9]

Women's role with respect to politics is plain. They may be wise and prudent, but their proper sphere is the domestic, not the political, world. They are almost "too good" for politics, representing peace and serenity, moral happiness rather than political dissension, the values of the home over the values of the state. This explanation provides a flattering reason for keeping women in "their place" while allowing men to reign in the world of politics.

WHO, WHAT, HOW   By the mid-1700s, the interests of the British and the colonists were clearly beginning to separate as each developed different stakes in the political system and created, altered, and used the rules to get what they wanted.

WHO are the actors?	WHAT do they want?	HOW do they get it?
England	• To retain colonies • Money to pay war debt	• Taxation • Military power
Colonial elite	• Independence • Political power vis-à-vis other groups in the colonies	• Revolution • Restrictive voting laws

The Articles of Confederation

constitution
the rules that establish a government

Articles of Confederation
the first constitution of the United States (1777), creating an association of states with a weak central government

In 1777 the Continental Congress met to try to come up with a **constitution,** or a framework that established the rules for the new government. The **Articles of Confederation,** our first constitution, created the kind of government the founders, fresh from their colonial experience, preferred. The rules set up by the Articles of Confederation show the states' jealousy of their power. Having just won their independence from one large national power, the last thing they wanted to do was create another. They were also extremely wary of one another, and much of the debate over the Articles of Confederation reflected wide concern that the rules not give any states preferential treatment. (See the appendix for the text of the Articles of Confederation.)

The Articles established a "firm league of friendship" among the thirteen American states, but they did not empower a central government to act effectively on behalf of those states. The Articles were ultimately replaced because, without a strong central government, they were unable to provide the economic and political stability that the founders wanted. Even so, under this set of rules, some people were better off and some problems, namely the resolution of boundary disputes and the political organization of new territories, were handled extremely well.

The Provisions of the Articles

confederation
a government in which independent states unite for common purposes but retain their own sovereignty

The government set up by the Articles was called a **confederation** because it established a system in which each state would retain almost all of its own power to do what it wanted. In other words, in a confederation, each state is sovereign and the central government has the job of running only the collective business of the states. It has no independent source of power and resources for its operations. Another characteristic of a confederation is that because it is founded on state sovereignty (authority), it says nothing about individuals. It creates neither rights nor obligations for individual citizens, leaving such matters to be handled by state constitutions.

Under the Articles of Confederation, Congress had many formal powers, including the power to establish and direct the armed forces, to decide matters of war and peace, to coin money, and to enter into treaties. However, its powers were quite limited. For example, although Congress controlled the armed forces, it had no power to draft soldiers or to tax citizens to pay for its military needs. Its inability to tax put Congress—and the central government as a whole—at the mercy of the states. The government could ask for money, but it was up to the states to contribute or not as they chose. Furthermore, Congress lacked the ability to regulate commerce between states, as well as between states and foreign powers. It could not establish a common and stable monetary system. In essence, the Articles allowed the states to be thirteen independent units, printing their own currencies, setting their own tariffs, and establishing their own laws with regard to financial and political matters. In every critical case—national security, national economic prosperity, and the general welfare—the U.S. government had to rely on the voluntary good will and cooperation of the state governments. That meant that the success of the new nation depended on what went on in state legislatures around the country.

Some Winners, Some Losers

The era of American history following the Revolution was dubbed "this critical period" by John Quincy Adams, nephew of Sam, son of John, and future president of the country. During this time, while the states were under the weak union of the Articles, the future of the United States was very much up in the air. The lack of an effective central government meant that the country had difficulty conducting business with other countries and enforcing harmonious trade relations and treaties. Domestic politics was equally difficult. Economic conditions following the war were poor. Many people owed money and could not pay their debts. State taxes were high, and the economy was depressed, offering farmers few opportunities to sell their produce, for example, and hindering those with commercial interests from conducting business as they had before the war.

The radical poverty of some Americans seemed particularly unjust to those hardest hit, especially in light of the rhetoric of the Revolution about equality for all.[10] One of the places the American passion for equality manifested itself was in some of the state legislatures, where laws were passed to ease the burden of debtors and farmers. Often the focus of the laws was property, but rather than preserving property, as Lockean theory said the law should do, it frequently was designed to confiscate or redistribute property instead. The "have-nots" in society, and the people acting on their behalf, were using the law to redress what they saw as injustices in early American life. To relieve postwar suffering, they printed paper money, seized property, and suspended "the ordinary means for the recovery of debts."[11] In other words, in those states, people with debts and mortgages could legally escape or postpone paying the money they owed. With so much economic insecurity, naturally those who owned property would not continue to invest and lend money. The Articles of Confederation, in their effort to preserve power for the states, had provided for no checks or limitations on state legislatures. In fact, such actions would have been seen under the Articles as infringing on the sovereignty of the states.

popular tyranny
the unrestrained power of the people

Shays's Rebellion
a grassroots uprising (1787) by armed Massachusetts farmers protesting foreclosures

The political elite in the new country started to grumble about **popular tyranny**. In a monarchy, one feared the unrestrained power of the king, but perhaps in a republican government, one had to fear the unrestrained power of the people. The final straw was **Shays's Rebellion.** Massachusetts was a state whose legislature, dominated by wealthy and secure citizens, had not taken measures to aid the debt-ridden population. Beginning in the summer of 1787, mobs of musket-wielding farmers from western Massachusetts began marching on the Massachusetts courts and disrupting the trials of debtors in an attempt to prevent their land from being foreclosed (taken by those to whom the farmers owed money). The farmers demanded action by a state legislature they saw as biased toward the interests of the rich. Their actions against the state culminated in the January 1787 attack on the Springfield, Massachusetts, federal armory, which housed more than 450 tons of military supplies. Led by a former captain in the Continental Army, Daniel Shays, the mob, now an army of more than 1,500 farmers, stormed the armory. They were turned back, but only after a violent clash with the state militia raised to counter the uprisings. Such mob action frightened and embarrassed the leaders of the United States, who of course also were the wealthier members of society. The rebellion seemed to foreshadow the failure of their grand experiment in self-governance. In the minds of the nation's leaders, it underscored the importance of discovering what James Madison would call "a republican remedy for those diseases most incident to republican government."[12] In other words, they had to find a way to contain and limit the will of the people in a government that was to be based on that will. If the rules of government were not producing the "right" winners and losers, the rules would have to be changed before the elite lost the power to change them.

WHO, WHAT, HOW   The fledgling states had an enormous amount at stake as they forged their new government after the Revolution. Similarly, many citizens, primarily the farmers, acquired much more political clout after the war. Their gains were not without costs to other groups in society, however, who struggled to maintain their own power.

WHO are the actors?	WHAT do they want?	HOW do they get it?
States	• Independence from a strong central power	• A "firm league of friendship"
Farmers	• Political power • Relief from debt	• Easy access to state legislatures
Wealthy property owners, bankers, and merchants	• Economic stability • Political power	• A newly strong central government

The Constitutional Convention

Constitutional Convention
the assembly of fifty-five delegates in the summer of 1787 to recast the Articles of Confederation; the result was the U.S. Constitution

State delegates were assigned the task of trying to fix the Articles of Confederation, but it was clear that many of the fifty-five men who gathered in May 1787 were not interested in saving the existing framework at all. Many of the delegates represented the elite of American society—wealthy lawyers, land speculators, merchants, planters, and investors—and thus they were among those being most injured under the Articles. This impressive gathering met through a sweltering Philadelphia summer to reconstruct the foundations of American government. As the delegates had hoped, the debates at the **Constitutional Convention** produced a very different system of rules than that established by the Articles of Confederation. Many of them were compromises that emerged as conflicting interests brought by delegates to the convention were resolved.

How Strong a Central Government?

Put yourself in the founders' shoes. Imagine that you get to construct a new government from scratch. You can create all the rules and arrange all the institutions just to your liking. The only hitch is that you have other delegates to work with. Delegate

A, for instance, is a merchant with a lot of property; he has big plans for a strong government that can ensure secure conditions for conducting business and can adequately protect property. Delegate B, however, is a planter. In Delegate B's experience, big government is dangerous. Big government is removed from the people, and it is easy for corruption to take root when people can't keep a close eye on what their officials are doing. People like Delegate B think that they will do better if power is decentralized (broken up and localized) and there is no strong central government. In fact, Delegate B would prefer a government like that provided by the Articles of Confederation. How do you reconcile these two very different agendas?

The solution adopted under the Articles of Confederation basically favored Delegate B's position. The new Constitution, given the profiles of the delegates in attendance, was moving strongly in favor of Delegate A's position. Naturally, the agreement of all those who followed Delegate B would be important in ratifying, or getting approval for, the final Constitution, so their concerns could not be ignored. The compromise chosen by the founders at the Constitutional Convention is called federalism. Unlike a confederation, in which the states retain the ultimate power over the whole, **federalism** gives the central government its own source of power, in this case the Constitution of the people of the United States. But unlike a unitary system, which we will discuss in the next chapter, federalism also gives independent power to the states.

Compared to how they fared under the Articles of Confederation, the advocates of states' rights were losers under the new Constitution, but they were better off than they might have been. The states could have had *all* their power stripped away. The economic elite, people like Delegate A, were clear winners under the new rules. This proved to be one of the central issues during the ratification debates. Those who sided with the federalism alternative, who mostly resembled Delegate A, came to be known as **Federalists.** The people like Delegate B, who continued to hold on to the strong-state, weak-central-government option, were called **Anti-Federalists.** We will return to them shortly.

federalism
a political system in which power is divided between the central and regional units

Federalists
supporters of the Constitution

Anti-Federalists
opponents of the Constitution

Large States, Small States

Once the convention delegates agreed that federalism would provide the framework of the new government, they had to decide how to allot power among the states. Should all states count the same in decision-making, or should the large states have more power than the small ones? The rules chosen here would have a crucial impact on the politics of the country. If small states and large states had equal amounts of power in national government, residents of large states such as Virginia, Massachusetts, and New York would actually have less voice in the government than residents of small states like New Jersey and Rhode Island.

Picture two groups of people trying to make a joint decision, each group with one vote to cast. If the first group has fifty people in it and the second has only ten, the individuals in the second group are likely to have more influence on how their single vote is cast than the individuals in the first group. If, however, the first group has five votes to cast and the second only one, the individuals are equally represented, but the second group is effectively reduced in importance when compared to the first. This was the dilemma faced by the representatives of the large and small states at the Constitutional Convention. Each wanted to make sure that the final rules would give the advantage to states like theirs.

Two plans were offered by convention delegates to resolve this issue. The first, the **Virginia Plan,** was the creation of James Madison. Fearing that his youth and inexperience would hinder the plan's acceptance, he asked his fellow Virginian Edmund Randolph to present it to the convention. The Virginia Plan represented the preference of the large, more populous states. This plan proposed a strong national government run by two legislative houses. One house would be elected directly by the people, one indirectly by a combination of the state legislatures and the popularly elected national house. The numbers of representatives would be determined by the taxes paid by the residents of the state, which would reflect the free population in the state. In other words, large states would have more representatives in both houses of the legislature, and national law and policy would be weighted heavily in their favor. Just three large states—Virginia, Massachusetts, and Pennsylvania—would be able to form a majority and carry national legislation their way. The Virginia Plan also called for a single executive, to see that the laws were carried out, and a national judiciary, both appointed by the legislature, and it gave the national government the power to override state laws.

A different plan, presented by William Paterson of New Jersey, was designed by the small states to offer the convention an alternative that would better protect their interests. The **New Jersey Plan** amounted to a reinforcement, not a replacement, of the Articles of Confederation. It provided for a multiperson executive, so no one person could possess too much power, and for congressional acts to be the "supreme law of the land." Most significantly, however, the Congress would be much like the one that had existed under the Articles. In its one house, each state would have only one vote. The delegates would be chosen by the state legislatures. Congressional power was stronger than under the Articles, but the national government was still dependent on the states for some of its funding. The large states disliked this plan because the small states together could block what the large states wanted, even though the large states had more people and contributed more revenue.

The prospects for a new government could have foundered on this issue. The stuffy heat of the closed Convention Hall shortened the tempers of the weary delegates, and frustration made compromise difficult. Each side had too much to lose by yielding to the other's plan. The solution finally arrived at was politics at its best. The **Great Compromise** kept much of the framework of the Virginia Plan. It proposed a strong federal structure headed by a central government with sufficient power to tax its citizens, regulate commerce, conduct foreign affairs, organize the military, and exercise other central powers. It called for a single executive and a national judicial system. The compromise that allowed the small states to live with it involved the composition of the legislature. Like the Virginia Plan, it provided for two houses. The House of Representatives would be based on state population, giving the large states the extra clout they felt they deserved, but in the Senate each state would have two votes. This would give the small states much more power in the Senate than in the House of Representatives. Members of the House of Representatives would be elected directly by the people, members of the Senate by the state legislatures. Thus

Virginia Plan
a proposal at the Constitutional Convention that congressional representation be based on population, thus favoring the large states

New Jersey Plan
a proposal at the Constitutional Convention that congressional representation be equal, thus favoring the small states

Great Compromise
the constitutional solution to congressional representation: equal representation in the Senate, representation by population in the House

Table 2.1
Distribution of Powers Under the Articles of Confederation, the New Jersey and Virginia Plans, and the U.S. Constitution

Key Questions	Articles of Confederation	New Jersey Plan	Virginia Plan	The Constitution
Who is sovereign?	States	States	People	People
What law is supreme?	State law	State law	National law	National law
What kind of legislature; what is the basis for representation?	Unicameral legislature; equal votes for all states	Unicameral legislature; one vote per state	Bicameral legislature; representation in both houses based on population	Bicameral legislature; equal representation in Senate, representation by population in House
How are laws passed?	Two-thirds vote to pass important measures	Extraordinary majority to pass measures	Majority decision-making	Simple majority vote in Congress, presidential veto
What powers are given to Congress?	No congressional power to levy taxes, regulate commerce	Congressional power to regulate commerce and tax	Congressional power to regulate commerce and tax	Congressional power to regulate commerce and tax
What kind of executive is there?	No executive branch; laws executed by congressional committee	Multiple executive	No restriction on strong single executive	Strong executive
What kind of judiciary is there?	No federal court system	No federal court system	No federal court system	Federal court system
How can the document be changed?	All states required to approve amendments	Unanimous approval of amendments by states	Popular ratification	Amendment process less difficult

the government would be directly binding on the people as well as on the states. A key to the compromise is that most legislation would need the approval of both houses, so neither large states nor small states could hold the entire government hostage to their wishes. The small states were sufficiently happy with this plan that most of them voted to approve, or ratify, the Constitution quickly and easily. See Table 2.1 for a comparison of the Constitution with the Articles of Confederation and the different plans for reform.

North and South

The compromise reconciling the large and small states was not the only one crafted by the delegates. The northern and southern states, which is to say the nonslaveowning and the slaveowning states, were at odds over how population was to be determined for purposes of representation in the lower house of Congress. The southern states wanted to count slaves as part of their population when determining how many representatives they got, even though they had no intention of letting the slaves vote. Including slaves would give them more representatives and thus more power in the House of Representatives. For exactly that reason, the northern states said that if slaves could not vote, they should not be counted. The bizarre compromise, also a triumph of politics if not humanity, is known as the **Three-fifths Compromise.** It was based on a formula developed by the Confederation Congress in 1763 to allocate tax assessments among the states. According to this compromise, for representation purposes, each slave would count as three-fifths of a person—that is, every five slaves would count as three people. Interestingly, the actual language in the Constitution is a good deal cagier than this. It says that representatives and taxes shall be determined according to population, figured "by adding to the whole Number of free Persons, including those bound to Service for a Term of Years, and excluding Indians not taxed, three fifths of *all other persons.*"

Three-fifths Compromise
the formula for counting five slaves as three people for purposes of representation; reconciled northern and southern factions at the Constitutional Convention

The issue of slavery was divisive enough for the early Americans that the most politically safe approach was not to mention it explicitly at all and thus to avoid having to endorse or condemn it. Implicitly, of course, their silence had the effect of letting slavery continue. Article I, Section 9, of the Constitution, in similarly vague language, allows that

> The Migration or Importation of such Persons as any of the States now existing shall think proper to admit, shall not be prohibited by Congress prior to the Year one thousand eight hundred and eight, but a Tax or duty may be imposed on such Importation, not exceeding ten dollars for each Person.

Even more damning, Article IV, Section 2, obliquely provides for the return of runaway slaves:

> No Person held to Service or Labour in one State under the Laws thereof, escaping into another, shall, in Consequence of any Law or Regulation therein, be discharged from such Service or Labour, but shall be delivered up on Claim of the Party to whom such Service or Labour may be due.

The word *slavery* does not appear in the Constitution until it is expressly outlawed in the Thirteenth Amendment, passed in December 1865, nearly eighty years after the writing of the Constitution.

WHO, WHAT, HOW The Constitutional Convention was attended by all manner of political and economic leaders, representing all sorts of interests, who stood to gain or lose dramatically from the proceedings. They all promoted plans or schemes of government that they thought would benefit people like them.

WHO are the actors?	WHAT do they want?	HOW do they get it?
Founders	• Economic and political stability	• Limited government, with checks and balances
Representatives of large states	• Political power based on size	• Virginia Plan
Representatives of small states	• Political power based on statehood	• New Jersey Plan
Representatives of northern states	• Political power	• Representation based on population of free citizens
Representatives of southern states	• Political power	• Representation based on population of free citizens and slaves
Federalists	• Strong central government; political and economic stability	• Constitution
Anti-Federalists	• Popularly controlled government resistant to corruption	• Decentralized government; Articles of Confederation

The Constitution

The document produced as a result of these compromises was a political innovation. All governments must have the power to do three things: (1) legislate, or make the laws; (2) administer, or execute the laws; and (3) adjudicate, or interpret the laws. Because of their fear of concentrated power, however, the founders did not give all the power to one institution, but rather provided for separate branches of government to handle it, and then ensured that each branch would have the ability to check the others. In this section, we review briefly the U.S. Constitution and the principles that support it.

The Legislative Branch

legislature the body of government that makes laws

bicameral legislature a legislature with two chambers

Legislative power is lawmaking power. The body of government that makes laws is called the **legislature.** The U.S. Congress is a **bicameral legislature,** meaning that there are two chambers—the House of Representatives and the Senate. Article I, by far the lengthiest article of the Constitution, sets out the framework of the legislative branch of government. Since the founders expected the legislature to be the most important part of the new government, they spent the most time specifying its composition, the qualifications for membership, its powers, and its limitations. The best-known part of Article I is the famous Section 8, which spells out the specific powers of Congress. This list is followed by the provision that Congress can do anything "necessary and proper" to carry out its duties. The Supreme Court has interpreted this clause so broadly that there are few effective restrictions on what Congress can do.

The House of Representatives, where representation is based on population, was intended to be truly representative of all the people—the "voice of the common man," as it were. To be elected to the House, a candidate need be only twenty-five years old and a citizen for seven years. Since House terms last two years, members run for reelection often and can be ousted fairly easily, according to public whim. The founders intended this office to be accessible to and easily influenced by citizens, and to reflect frequent changes in public opinion.

The Senate is another matter. Candidates have to be at least thirty years old and citizens for nine years—older, wiser, and, the founders hoped, more stable than the representatives in the House. Because senatorial terms last for six years, senators are not so easily swayed by changes in public sentiment. In addition, senators were originally elected by members of the state legislatures, not directly by the people. (This was changed by constitutional amendment in 1913.) Election by state legislators, themselves a "refinement" of the general public, would ensure that senators were a higher caliber of citizen: older and wiser but also more in tune with "the commercial and monied interest," as Massachusetts delegate Elbridge Gerry put it at the Constitutional Convention.[13] The Senate would thus be a more aristocratic body—that is, it would look more like the British House of Lords, where members are admitted on the basis of their birth or achievement, not by election.

The Executive Branch

executive
the branch of government responsible for putting laws into effect

The **executive** is the part of government that "executes" the laws, or sees that they are carried out. Although technically executives serve in an administrative role, many end up with some decision-making or legislative power as well. National executives are the leaders of their countries, and they participate, with varying amounts of power, in making laws and policies. That role can range from the U.S. president—who, though not a part of the legislature itself, can propose, encourage, and veto legislation—to European prime ministers, who are actually part of the legislature and may have, as in the British case, the power to dissolve the entire legislature and call a new election.

The fact that the Articles of Confederation provided for no executive power at all was a testimony to the founders' conviction that such a power threatened their liberty. The chaos that resulted under the Articles, however, made it clear to founders like Alexander Hamilton that a stronger government was called for, not only a stronger legislature but a stronger executive as well. The constitutional debates reveal that many of the founders were haunted by the idea that they might inadvertently reestablish that same tyrannical power over themselves that they had only recently escaped with the Revolution.

The solution finally chosen by the founders is a complicated one, but it satisfies all the concerns raised at the convention. The president, a single executive, would serve an unlimited number of four-year terms. (A constitutional amendment in 1951 limited the president to two elected terms.) But the president would be chosen neither

electoral college
an intermediary body
that elects the president

by Congress nor directly by the people. Instead, the Constitution provides for the president's selection by an intermediary body called the **electoral college.** Citizens vote not for the presidential candidates, but for a slate of electors, who in turn cast their votes for the candidates about six weeks after the general election. The founders believed that this procedure would ensure a president elected by well-informed delegates who, having no other lawmaking power, could not be bribed or otherwise influenced by candidates. We will say more about how this works in Chapter 12, on elections.

Article II of the Constitution establishes the executive. The four sections of that article make the following provisions:

- Section 1 sets out the four-year term and the manner of election (that is, the details of the electoral college). It also provides for the qualifications for office: that the president must be a natural-born citizen of the United States, at least thirty-five years old, and a resident of the United States for at least fourteen years. The vice president serves if the president cannot, and Congress can make laws about the succession if the vice president is incapacitated.

- Section 2 establishes the powers of the chief executive. The president is commander-in-chief of the armed forces and of the state militias when they are serving the nation, and he has the power to grant pardons for offenses against the United States. With the advice and consent of two-thirds of the Senate, the president can make treaties, and with a simple majority vote of the Senate, the president can appoint ambassadors, ministers, consuls, Supreme Court justices, and other U.S. officials whose appointment is not otherwise provided for.

- Section 3 says that the president will periodically tell Congress how the country is doing (the State of the Union address given every January) and will propose to them those measures that he thinks appropriate and necessary. Under extraordinary circumstances, the president can call the Congress into session or, if the two houses of Congress cannot agree on when to end their sessions, can adjourn them. The president also receives ambassadors and public officials, executes the laws, and commissions all officers of the United States.

- Section 4 specifies that the president, vice president, and other civil officers of the United States (such as Supreme Court justices) can be impeached, tried, and convicted for "Treason, Bribery, or other high Crimes and Misdemeanors."

The Judicial Branch

judicial power
the power to interpret
laws and judge whether
a law has been broken

Judicial power is the power to interpret the laws and to judge whether they have been broken. Naturally, by establishing how a given law is to be understood, the courts (the agents of judicial power) end up making law as well. Our constitutional provisions for the establishment of the judiciary are brief and vague; much of the American federal judiciary under the Supreme Court is left to Congress to arrange. But the founders left plenty of clues about how they felt about judicial power in their debates and their writings, particularly in *The Federalist Papers,* a series of newspaper editorials written to encourage people to support and vote for the new Constitution.

For instance, the practice of judicial review is introduced through the back door,

judicial review
the power of the
Supreme Court to rule
on the constitutionality
of laws

When We Get Behind Closed Doors
*As the only government branch not subject to election,
the Supreme Court uses a certain amount of secrecy
to retain its popular and political support. The public
knows only what justices decide to reveal, and these
revelations are often chosen to reinforce an aura of
fairness, majesty, and deliberation.*

first mentioned by Hamilton in *Federalist* No. 78
and then institutionalized by the Supreme Court
itself with Chief Justice John Marshall's 1803 ruling in *Marbury* v. *Madison*, a dispute over presidential appointments. **Judicial review** allows the
Supreme Court to rule that an act of Congress or
the executive branch (or of a state or local government) is unconstitutional—that is, that it runs
afoul of constitutional principles. This review
process is not an automatic part of lawmaking; the
Court does not examine every law that Congress
passes or every executive order to be sure that it
does not violate the Constitution. Rather, if a law
is challenged as unjust or unconstitutional by an individual or group, and if it is appealed all the way to the Supreme Court, the justices may decide to rule on it.

This remarkable grant of the power to nullify legislation to what Hamilton called
the "least dangerous" branch is not in the Constitution. In *Federalist* No. 78, however, Hamilton argued that it was consistent with the Constitution. In response to
critics who objected that such a practice would place the unelected Court in a superior position to the elected representatives of the people, Hamilton wrote that, on the
contrary, it raised the people, as authors of the Constitution, over the government as
a whole. Thus judicial review enhanced democracy rather than diminished it.

In 1803 Marshall agreed. As the nation's highest law, the Constitution set the
limits on what is acceptable legislation. As the interpreter of the Constitution, the
Supreme Court must determine when laws fall outside those limits. It is interesting
to note that this gigantic grant of power to the Court was made by the Court itself
and remains unchallenged by the other branches. It is ironic that this sort of empire
building, which the founders hoped to avoid, appears in the branch that they took
the least care to safeguard. We will return to *Marbury* v. *Madison* and judicial review
in Chapter 9, on the court system.

Article III of the Constitution is very short. It says that the judicial power of the
United States is to be "vested in one Supreme Court, and in such inferior courts as
the Congress may from time to time ordain and establish," and that judges serve as
long as they demonstrate "good behavior." It also explains that the Supreme Court
has original jurisdiction in some types of cases and appellate jurisdiction in others.
That is, in some cases the Supreme Court is the only court that can rule. Much more
often, however, inferior courts try cases, but their rulings can be appealed to the
Supreme Court. Article III provides for jury trials in all criminal cases except impeachment, and it defines the practice of and punishment for acts of treason. Because

the Constitution is relatively silent on the role of the courts in America, that role has been left to the definition of Congress and, in some cases, of the courts themselves.

Separation of Powers and Checks and Balances

separation of powers a safeguard calling for legislative, executive, and judicial powers to be exercised by different people

Separation of powers means that legislative, executive, and judicial powers are not exercised by the same person or group of people, lest they abuse the considerable amount of power they hold. We are indebted to the French Enlightenment philosopher, the Baron de Montesquieu, for explaining this notion. In his massive book *The Spirit of the Laws,* Montesquieu wrote that liberty could be threatened only if the same group that enacted tyrannical laws also executed them. He said, "There would be an end of everything, were the same man or the same body, whether of nobles or of the people, to exercise those three powers, that of enacting laws, that of executing the public resolutions, and of trying the causes of individuals."[14] Putting all political power into one set of hands is like putting all our eggs in one basket. If the person or body of people entrusted with all the power becomes corrupt or dictatorial, the whole system will go bad. If, however, power is divided so that each branch is in separate hands, one may go bad while leaving the other two intact.

checks and balances

the principle that each branch of government guards against the abuse of power by the others

The principle of separation of powers gives each of the branches authority over its own domain. A complementary principle, **checks and balances,** allows each of the branches to police the others, checking any abuses and balancing the powers of government. The purpose of this additional authority is to ensure that no branch can exercise power tyrannically. In America's case, the president can veto an act of Congress; Congress can override a veto; the Supreme Court can declare a law of Congress unconstitutional; Congress can, with the help of the states, amend the Constitution itself; and so on. Figure 2.2 illustrates these relationships.

As we saw, the Constitution establishes separation of powers with articles setting up a different institution for each branch of government. Checks and balances are provided by clauses within these articles.

- Article I sets up a bicameral legislature. Because both houses must agree on all legislation, they can check each other. Article I also describes the presidential veto, with which the president can check Congress, and the override provision, by which two-thirds of Congress can check the president. Congress can also check abuses of the executive or judicial branch with impeachment.

- Article II empowers the president to execute the laws and to share some legislative function by "recommending laws." The president has some checks on the judiciary through his power to appoint judges, but his appointment power is checked by the requirement that a majority of the Senate must confirm his choices. The president can also check the judiciary by granting pardons. The president is commander-in-chief of the armed forces, but his ability to exercise his authority is checked by the Article I provision that only Congress can declare war.

- Article III creates the Supreme Court. The Court's ruling in the case of *Marbury* v. *Madison* fills in some of the gaps in this vague article by establishing judicial review, a true check on the legislative and executive branches. Congress can counter-check judicial review by amending the Constitution (with the help of the states).

LEGISLATIVE BRANCH
Makes laws

Other powers
- Controls appropriation and spending of money
- Regulates foreign and interstate commerce
- Declares war
- Approves appointments and treaties (Senate)

President's checks on the legislative branch

- Can veto legislation
- Can call special sessions of Congress
- Can propose laws to Congress
- Can issue executive agreements with foreign nations

Congress's checks on the judicial branch

- Can eliminate or refuse to create federal courts
- Can impeach and remove judges
- Can refuse to confirm judicial appointments (Senate)
- Sets number of justices on the Supreme Court

Courts' checks on the legislative branch

- Can declare laws unconstitutional

Congress's checks on the executive branch

- Can fail to pass bills president proposes
- Can override presidential veto
- Can refuse to confirm administrative and judicial appointments (Senate)
- Can impeach, try, and remove president
- Can refuse to ratify treaties (Senate)
- Can refuse to fund executive orders

JUDICIAL BRANCH
Interprets laws

President's checks on the judicial branch

- Can grant pardons
- Appoints judges

EXECUTIVE BRANCH
Implements laws

Courts' checks on the executive branch

- Can declare executive orders unconstitutional
- Judges cannot be removed by president

Other powers
- Appoints department heads and controls federal administration
- Makes treaties with foreign nations
- Is commander-in-chief of armed forces
- Issues executive orders

Figure 2.2
Separation of Powers and Checks and Balances

The Constitution wisely ensures that no branch of the government can act independently of the others, yet none is wholly dependent on the others either. This results in a structure of separation of powers and checks and balances that is distinctively American.

Amendability

amendability
the provision for the Constitution to be changed so as to adapt to new circumstances

If a constitution is a rule book, then its capacity to be changed over time is critical to its remaining a viable political document. A rigid constitution runs the risk of ceasing to seem legitimate to citizens who have no prospect of changing the rules according to shifting political realities and visions of the public good. A constitution that is too easily revised, on the other hand, can be seen as no more than a political tool in the hands of the strongest interests in society. A final feature of the U.S. Constitution that deserves mention in this chapter is its **amendability**—that is, the fact that the founders provided for a method of amendment, or change, that allows the Constitution to grow and adapt to new circumstances. In fact, they provided for two methods: the formal amendment process outlined in the Constitution, and an informal process that results from the vagueness of the document and the evolution of the role of the courts (see Figure 2.3).

In the two-hundred-plus years of its existence, almost 9,750 constitutional amendments have been introduced, but the U.S. Constitution has been amended only 27 times. By contrast, in the course of interpreting the Constitution, the Supreme Court has, for example, extended many of the Bill of Rights protections to state citizens via the Fourteenth Amendment, permitted the national government to regulate business, prohibited child labor, and extended equal protection of the laws to women. In some cases, amendments previously introduced to accomplish these goals (such as the Child Labor Amendment and the Equal Rights Amendment) were not ratified, and in other cases the Court has simply decided to interpret the Consti-

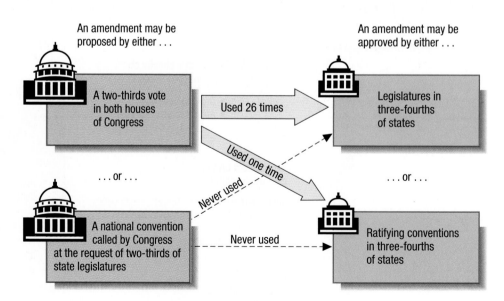

**Figure 2.3
Amending the Constitution**

tution in a new way. Judicial interpretation is at times quite controversial. Many scholars and politicians believe that the literal word of the founders should be adhered to, whereas others claim that the founders could not have anticipated all the opportunities and pitfalls of modern life and that the Constitution should be considered a flexible, or "living," document. We will return to this controversy when we look more closely at the courts in Chapter 9.

The Constitution is silent on the subject of judicial interpretation, but in part because it is silent, especially in Article III, the courts have been able to create their own role. In contrast, Article V spells out in detail the rather confusing procedures for officially amending the Constitution. These procedures are federal—that is, they require the involvement and approval of the states as well as the national government. The procedures boil down to this: Amendments may be proposed either by a two-thirds vote of the House and the Senate or when two-thirds of the states request it by a constitutional convention. Amendments must be approved either by the legislatures of three-fourths of the states or by conventions of three-fourths of the states. Two interesting qualifications are contained in Article V: no amendment affecting slavery could be made before 1808, and no amendment can deprive a state of its equal vote in the Senate without that state's consent. We can easily imagine the North-South and large-state–small-state conflicts that produced those compromises.

WHO, WHAT, HOW The founders had a stake in writing a constitution that would protect government from abuse and corruption, while citizens were concerned that the government would maintain social order while protecting their liberties.

WHO are the actors?	WHAT do they want?	HOW do they get it?
Founders	• Slow, careful lawmaking	• Bicameral legislature
Citizens	• Protection of government from human nature and abuse of power	• Presidential system
		• Independent judiciary
	• Long-term survival of American government	• Checks and balances
		• Amendment process
	• Protection of liberties	

Ratification

ratified formally approved and adopted by vote

For the Constitution to become the law of the land, it had to be **ratified,** or voted on and approved, by state conventions in at least nine states. As it happens, the Constitution was eventually ratified by all thirteen states, but not until some major political battles had been fought.

Federalists Versus Anti-Federalists

Those in favor of ratification called themselves Federalists. The Federalists, like Delegate A in our earlier hypothetical constitution-building scenario, were mostly men with a considerable economic stake in the new nation. Having fared poorly under the Articles, they were certain that if America were to grow as an economic and world power, it needed to be the kind of country people with property would want to invest in. Security and order were key values, as was popular control. The Federalists thought people like themselves should be in charge of the government, although some of them did not object to an expanded suffrage if government had enough built-in protections. Mostly they were convinced that a good government could be designed if the underlying principles of human behavior were known. If people were ambitious and tended toward corruption, then government should make use of those characteristics to produce good outcomes.

The Anti-Federalists, on the other hand, rejected the notion that ambition and corruption were inevitable parts of human nature. If government could be kept small and local, the stakes not too large and tempting, and popular scrutiny truly vigilant, then Americans could live happy and contented lives without getting involved in the seamier side of politics. America did not need sprawling urban centers of commerce and trade, nor did it need to be a world power. If it did not stray from its rural roots and values, it could permanently avoid the creeping corruption that the Anti-Federalists believed threatened the American polity. The reason the Anti-Federalists found the Articles of Confederation more attractive than the Constitution was that the Articles did not call for a strong central government that, distant from the voters' eyes, could become a hotbed of political intrigue. Instead, the Articles vested power in the state governments, which could be more easily watched and controlled.

Writing under various aliases as well as their own names, the Federalists and Anti-Federalists fired arguments back and forth in pamphlets and newspaper editorials aimed at persuading undecided Americans to come out for or against the Constitution. The Federalists were far more aggressive and organized in their "media blitz," hitting New York newspapers with a series of eloquent editorials published under the pen name Publius but really written by Alexander Hamilton, James Madison, and John Jay. These essays were bound and distributed in other states where the ratification struggle was close. Known as **The Federalist Papers,** they are one of the main texts on early American politics today. In response, the Anti-Federalists published essays under names such as Cato, Brutus, and The Federal Farmer.[15]

The Federalist Papers a series of essays written in support of the Constitution to encourage its ratification

The Federalist Papers

Eighty-five essays were written by Publius. In a contemporary introduction to the book, one scholar calls them, along with the Declaration of Independence and the Constitution, part of "the sacred writings of American political history."[16] Putting them on a par with holy things is probably a mistake. Far from being divinely inspired, *The Federalist Papers* are quintessentially the work of human beings. They are clever, well thought out, and logical, but they are also tricky and persuasive examples of the "hard sell." Three of the most important essays, numbers 10, 51, and 84, are reprinted in the appendix of this book. Their archaic language makes *The*

Federalist Papers generally difficult reading for contemporary students. However, the arguments in support of the Constitution are so beautifully laid out that it is worthwhile to take the trouble to read them. It would be a good idea to turn to them now and read them carefully.

In *Federalist* No. 10, Madison tries to convince Americans that a large country is no more likely to succumb to the effects of special interests than a small one (preferred by the Anti-Federalists). He explains that the greatest danger to a republic comes from **factions,** what we might call interest groups. Factions are groups of people motivated by a common interest, but one different from the interest of the country as a whole. Farmers, for instance, have an interest in keeping food prices high, even though that would make most Americans worse off. Businesspeople prefer high import duties on foreign goods, even though they make both foreign and domestic goods more expensive for the rest of us. Factions are not a particular problem when they constitute a minority of the population because they are offset by majority rule. They do become problematic, however, when they are a majority. Factions usually have economic roots, the most basic being a difference between the "haves" and "have-nots" in society. One of the majority factions that worried Madison was the mass of propertyless people whose behavior was so threatening to property holders under the Articles of Confederation.

To control the *causes* of factions would be to infringe on individual liberty. But Madison believed that the *effects* of factions are easily managed in a large republic. First of all, representation will dilute the effects of factions, and it is in this essay that Madison makes his famous distinction between "pure democracy" and a "republic." In addition, if the territory is sufficiently large, factions will be neutralized because there will be so many of them that no one is likely to become a majority. Furthermore, it will be difficult for people who share common interests to find one another if some live in South Carolina, for instance, and others live in Maine. (Clearly, Madison never anticipated the invention of the fax machine or electronic mail.) We discuss Madison's argument about factions again when we take up the topic of interest groups. In the meantime, however, notice how Madison relies on mechanical elements of politics (size and representation) to remedy a flaw in human nature (the tendency to form divisive factions). This is typical of the Federalists' approach to government and reflects the importance of institutions as well as rules in bringing about desired outcomes in politics.

We see the same emphasis on mechanical solutions to political problems in *Federalist* No. 51. Here Madison argues that the institutions proposed in the Constitution will lead neither to corruption nor to tyranny. The solution is the principles of checks and balances and separation of powers we have already discussed. Again building his case on a potential defect of human character, he says, "Ambition must be made to counteract ambition."[17] If men tend to be ambitious, give two ambitious men the job of watching over each other, and neither will let the other have an advantage.

The last *Federalist Paper* we talk about here was written by Hamilton. Unlike the above two by Madison, the eighty-fourth essay is interesting politically because it failed dismally. The Constitution was ratified in spite of it, not because of it. In this essay, Hamilton argues that a **Bill of Rights**—a listing of the protections against government infringement of individual rights guaranteed to citizens by government itself—is not necessary in a constitution.

faction   a group of citizens united by some common passion or interest and opposed to the rights of other citizens or to the interests of the whole community

Bill of Rights a summary of citizen rights guaranteed and protected by a government; added to the Constitution as its first ten amendments in order to achieve ratification

The original draft of the Constitution contained no Bill of Rights. Some state constitutions had them, and so the Federalists argued that a federal Bill of Rights would be redundant. Moreover, the limited government set up by the federal Constitution didn't have the power to infringe on individual rights anyway, and many of the rights that would be included in a Bill of Rights were already in the body of the text. To the Anti-Federalists, already afraid of the invasive power of the national government, this omission was more appalling than any other aspect of the Constitution.

Hamilton explains the Federalist position, that a Bill of Rights was unnecessary. Then he makes the unusual argument that a Bill of Rights would actually be dangerous. As it stands, he says, the national government doesn't have the power to interfere with citizens' lives in many ways, and any interference at all would be suspect. But if the Constitution were prefaced with a list of things government could *not* do to individuals, government would assume it had the power to do anything that wasn't expressly forbidden. Therefore government, instead of being unlikely to trespass on citizens' rights, would be more likely to do so with a Bill of Rights than without. This argument was so unpersuasive to Americans at that time that the Federalists were forced to give in to Anti-Federalist pressure during the ratification process. The price of ratification exacted by several states was the Bill of Rights, really a "Bill of Limits" on the federal government, added to the Constitution as the first ten amendments.

The Final Vote

The small states, gratified by the compromise that gave them equal representation in the Senate and believing they would be better off as part of a strong nation, ratified the Constitution quickly. The vote was unanimous in Delaware, New Jersey, and Georgia. In Connecticut (128–40) and Pennsylvania (46–23), the votes, though not unanimous, were strongly in favor of the Constitution. This may have helped to tip the balance for Massachusetts, voting much more closely to ratify (187–168). Maryland (63–11) and South Carolina (149–73) voted in favor of ratification in the spring of 1788, leaving only one more state to supply the requisite nine to make the Constitution law.

The battles in the remaining states were much fiercer. When the Virginia convention met in June 1788, the Federalists felt that it could provide the decisive vote and threw much of their effort into securing passage. Madison and his Federalist colleagues debated with Anti-Federalist advocates such as George Mason and Patrick Henry, promising as they had in Massachusetts to support a Bill of Rights. Virginia ratified the Constitution by the narrow margin of 89 to 79, preceded by a few days by New Hampshire, voting 57 to 47. Establishment of the Constitution as the law of the land was ensured with the approval of ten states. New York also narrowly passed the Constitution (30–27), but North Carolina defeated it (193–75), and Rhode Island, which had not sent delegates to the Constitutional Convention, refused to call a state convention to put it to a vote. Later both North Carolina and Rhode Island voted to ratify and join the Union, in November 1789 and May 1790, respectively.[18]

Again we can see how important rules are in determining outcomes. The Articles of Confederation had required the approval of all the states. Had the Constitutional Convention chosen a similar rule of unanimity, the Constitution may very well have been defeated. Recognizing that unanimous approval was not probable, however, the Federalists decided to require ratification by only nine of the thirteen states, making adoption of the Constitution far more likely.

WHO, WHAT, HOW The fight over ratification of the Constitution was based not only on the actual form of government but also on a deep philosophical difference about the nature of human beings.

WHO are the actors?	WHAT do they want?	HOW do they get it?
Federalists	• Government resistant to whims of popular opinion	• Ratification of Constitution
Anti-Federalists	• Government resistant to dangerous corruption of powerful elites	• Attachment of Bill of Rights to Constitution

Citizenship and the Founding

Citizenship as we know it today was a fledgling creation at the time of the founding. The British had not been citizens of the English government but subjects of the English crown. There is a world of difference between a subject and a citizen, as we pointed out in Chapter 1. The subject has a personal tie to the monarch; the citizen has a legal tie to a national territory. The subject has obligations; the citizen has both obligations and rights.

The new citizens had political power in America, but they were not entirely trusted by the leaders of American politics. They made their appearance in such episodes as Shays's Rebellion and found their voice in the business of state politics under the Articles of Confederation. They were the soldiers whose support had been vital to winning the Revolution, and they were the citizens whose power Madison feared as he wrote *Federalist* No. 10 about the danger of factions. To some extent, the writing of the Constitution was about reining in the power of the broad concept of citizenship that had been unleashed by the political freedom available under the Articles of Confederation, about checking and balancing the power of the people as well as the power of government.

Points of Access

- Get involved in student government.
- Examine the by-laws of an organization you belong to.
- Sit on a judicial board.
- Protest a school policy you disagree with.

WHAT'S AT STAKE REVISITED

Having read the history of Revolutionary America, what would you say is at stake in the modern militia movement? The existence of state militias and similar groups poses a troubling dilemma for the federal government. On the one hand, the purpose of government is to protect our rights, and the Constitution surely guarantees Americans freedom of speech and assembly. On the other hand, government must hold the monopoly on the legitimate use of force in society, or it will fall, just as the British government fell in the colonies. If groups are allowed to amass weapons and forcibly resist or even attack U.S. law enforcers, then they constitute "mini-governments," or competing centers of authority, and life for citizens becomes chaotic and dangerous.

The American system was designed to be relatively responsive to the wishes of the American public. Citizens can get involved; they can vote, run for office, change the laws, and amend the Constitution. By permitting these legitimate ways of affecting American politics, the founders hoped to prevent the rise of groups such as militias. They intended to create a society characterized by political stability, not by revolution, which is why Thomas Jefferson's Declaration of Independence is so careful to point out that revolutions should occur only when there is no alternative course of action.

Some militia members reject the idea of working through the system; they say that they consider themselves at war with the federal government. When individuals with ties to the militia movement blew up a federal building in Oklahoma City in April 1995, one supporter claimed that the blast, which killed hundreds, was unfortunate but a legitimate act of war. We call disregard for the law at the individual level "crime," at the group level "terrorism" or "insurrection," and at the majority level "revolution." It is the job of any government worth its salt to prevent all three kinds of activities.

Thus it is not the existence or beliefs but the *activities* of the militia groups that threaten legitimate government authority. When an Ohio man with a homemade license plate reading MILITIA pulled a gun on police because he didn't recognize their authority, and when a religious sect called the Branch Davidians stockpiled illegal weapons in their compound in Waco, Texas, and refused to admit federal agents with a warrant, the results were tragic. If groups of citizens can hold the government hostage in such a way, the government's authority has already begun to erode.

At stake in the militia movement are the issues of legitimate government authority and the rights of individual citizens. It is very difficult to draw the line between the protection of individual rights and the exercise of government authority. In a democracy, we want to respect the rights of all citizens, but this respect can be thwarted when a small number of individuals reject the rules of the game agreed on by the vast majority. ■

key terms

amendability   52
Anti-Federalists   42
Articles of Confederation   39
bicameral legislature   46
Bill of Rights   55
checks and balances   50
confederation   39
constitution   39
Constitutional Convention   41
Declaration of Independence   36

electoral college   48
executive   47
faction   55
federalism   42
The Federalist Papers   54
Federalists   42
French and Indian War   34
Great Compromise   43
judicial power   48
judicial review   49

legislature   46
New Jersey Plan   43
popular tyranny   40
ratified   53
separation of powers   50
Shays's Rebellion   40
Three-fifths Compromise   45
Virginia Plan   43

summary

- The politics of the American founding shaped the political compromises that are embodied in the Constitution. This in turn defines the institutions and many of the rules that do much to determine the winners and losers in political struggles today.

- The battle for America involved a number of groups, including Native Americans and Spanish, French, and British colonists. English settlers came to America for many reasons, including religious and economic ones, but then duplicated in the colonies many of the politically restrictive practices they had sought to escape in England. These included restrictions on political participation and a narrow definition of citizenship.

- The Revolution was caused by many factors, including British attempts to get the colonies to pay the costs of the wars fought to protect them.

- The pressure from Britain for additional taxes coincided with new ideas among colonial elites about the proper role of government. These ideas are embodied in Jefferson's politically masterful Declaration of Independence.

- The government under the Articles of Confederation granted too much power to the states, which in a number of cases came to serve the interests of farmers and debtors. The Constitutional Convention was called to design a government with stronger central powers that would overcome the weaknesses the elites perceived in the Articles of Confederation.

- The new Constitution was derived from a number of key compromises: federalism was set as a principle to allocate power to both the central government and the states; the Great Compromise allocated power in the new national legislature; the Three-fifths Compromise provided a political solution to the problem of counting slaves for purposes of representation in the House of Representatives.

- The Constitution established an innovative federal system, with separation of powers between executive, legislative, and judicial branches, but with checks and balances among them to keep their powers in line.

- The politics of ratification of the Constitution provides a lesson in the marriage between practical politics and political principle. *The Federalist Papers* served as political propaganda to convince citizens to favor ratification, and they serve today as a record of the reasoning behind many of the elements of our Constitution.

3

Federalism

What's at Stake?

What Is Federalism?
• What Does the
  Constitution Say?
• Two Views of Federalism
• Possible Alternatives to
  Federalism
• What Difference Does
  Federalism Make?

**The Changing Balance:
American Federalism over
Time**
• John Marshall:
  Strengthening the
  Constitutional Powers of
  the National Government
• The Civil War: National
  Domination of the States
• The New Deal: National
  Power over Business
• Civil Rights: National
  Protection Against State
  Abuse

Federalism Today
• The Structure of
  Federalism
• The Politics of
  Contemporary Federalism
• Congressional Strategies
  for Influencing State
  Policy
• The Move Toward
  Devolution

**Citizenship and
Federalism**

What's at Stake Revisited

WHAT'S AT STAKE?

On August 22, 1996, President Bill Clinton, a Democrat with faith in the power of the federal government to solve social problems but also a former Arkansas governor with considerable trust in the states to come up with innovative policy solutions, signed the Personal Responsibility and Work Opportunity Reconciliation Act. Those of us who cannot remember such a mouthful simply call the bill "welfare reform." Indeed, the bill, passed primarily with the support of congressional Republicans and over strong objections from some liberal Democrats, reformed the welfare system that had been in existence since the days of President Franklin Roosevelt, and in its present form since the Great Society days of President Lyndon Johnson. It ended a thirty-year guarantee of cash assistance to the country's poorest children.

The old welfare program was called Aid to Families with Dependent Children (AFDC). AFDC allowed Washington to set the terms for cash aid to families with children, to fund the program in conjunction with the states, and to require that the states administer the program according to federal specifications. Even supporters of welfare in general agreed that the old program needed revamping. Although established with the good intentions of relieving poverty and giving children a healthy start in life, it had many unintended consequences, not the least of which was that it did not provide incentives for welfare recipients to get off welfare and find jobs to support their children on their own. It often made more financial sense for welfare recipients to turn down jobs and stay on welfare.

Clearly, this system needed some reform, but reform can take many shapes, and Republicans and Democrats argued over how the program should be changed. With a majority in Congress, the Republicans were able to mold the new Temporary Assistance to Needy Families (TANF) program. Instead of funding the states to carry out the federal welfare program, TANF allows the states to devise their own programs within federal guidelines and gives them blocks of money to administer those programs. The federal guidelines say that the states must get half their welfare recipients into jobs by 2002 and not allow anyone to stay on welfare for more than five years. Various other provisions restrict the states' ability to give aid to many categories of legal immigrants.

Democrats argued that giving the responsibility to the states would result in an uneven provision of services for the poor, that the federal promise of aid to children would be destroyed, that state prejudices would come to the fore, that citizens would move from one state to another shopping for the best benefits, that states could not be trusted to put the interests of the poor first, and that the removal of aid to legal immigrants, many of whom had lived in this country and paid taxes for decades, was cruel and unfair. Critics in his party said that Clinton supported the bill only because he had previously promised to "end welfare as we know it" and he wanted to win reelection in 1996. Republicans defended their plan as necessary to break a disastrous dependence on federal aid among welfare recipients and to end what they called a "culture of entitlement," in which people believed that government owed them a minimal standard of living regardless of their own efforts. Ideological debate on this issue can be endless, but it was broken in this case by a moderate Democratic president who believed that the states can often come up with policy solutions that elude the federal government. Regretting only the provisions that restricted aid to legal immigrants (some of which he later succeeded in reversing), Clinton signed the bill.

Was a vote for the bill really a betrayal of America's poor? Two of Clinton's Democratic advisers felt so strongly that it was that they resigned from his administration in protest. Or was it the best answer to a welfare system clearly in need of new solutions to the problem of poverty? Who stood to win and lose by turning over responsibility for welfare from the federal government to the states? What was really at stake in the 1996 welfare reform bill? We will return to this question at the end of this chapter, when we have finished discussing the relationships among the federal, state, and local governments. ■

The Federalists and the Anti-Federalists fought intensely over the balance between national and state powers in our federal system. Debates over the Articles of Confederation and the Constitution show that the founders were well aware that the rules dividing the power between the states and the federal government were crucial to determining who would be the winners and losers in the new country. Where decisions are made—in Washington, D.C., or in the state capitals—would make a big difference in "who gets what and how." Today the same battles are being fought between defenders of state and national power. The balance of power has swung back and forth several times since the founders came to their own hard-won compromise, but over the past twenty years, there has been a movement to give more power and responsibility back to the state governments, a process known as **devolution.** In this chapter, we focus on the challenges of federalism, both today and historically. Specifically, we examine these issues:

devolution
the transfer of powers and responsibilities from the federal government to the states

- The definition of federalism and the alternatives the founders rejected when they made this compromise

- The ways the balance of power in American federalism has shifted over time

- The structure of federalism today and the ways the national government tries to secure state cooperation

What Is Federalism?

Federalism, as we said in Chapter 2, is a political system in which authority is divided between different levels of government (the national and state levels in America's case). Each level has some power independent of the other levels so that no level is entirely dependent on another for its existence. In the United States, federalism was a compromise between those who wanted stronger state governments and those who preferred a stronger national government.

The effects of federalism are all around us. We pay income taxes to the national government, which parcels out the money to the states, under certain conditions, to be spent on programs such as welfare, highways, and education. In most states, local schools are funded by local property taxes and run by local school boards (local governments are created under the authority of the state), and state universities are supported by state taxes and influenced by the state legislatures. Even so, both state and local governments are subject to national legislation, such as the requirement that schools be open to students of all races, and both can be affected by national decisions about funding various programs. Sometimes the lines of responsibility can be extremely unclear. Witness the simultaneous presence in many areas of city police, county police, state police, and, at the national level, the Federal Bureau of Investigation (FBI).

Even when a given responsibility lies at the state level, the national government frequently finds a way to enforce its will. For instance, it is up to the states to decide on the minimum drinking age for their citizens. In the 1970s, many states required people to be only eighteen or nineteen before they could legally buy alcohol; today all the states have a uniform drinking age of twenty-one. The change came about because interest groups persuaded officials in the federal, that is national, government that the higher age would lead to fewer alcohol-related highway accidents and greater public safety. The federal government couldn't pass a law setting a nationwide drinking age of twenty-one, but it could control the flow of highway money to the states. By withholding 5 percent of federal highway funds, which every state wants and needs, until a state raised the drinking age to twenty-one, Congress prevailed. This is an example of how the relations between levels of government work when neither level can directly force the other to do what it wants.

What Does the Constitution Say?

enumerated powers of Congress
congressional powers specifically named in the Constitution (Article I, Section 8)

necessary and proper clause
constitutional authorization for Congress to make any law required to carry out its powers

No single section of the Constitution deals with federalism. Instead, the provisions dividing up power between the states and the national government appear throughout the Constitution. As a state matter, local government is not mentioned in the Constitution at all. Most of the Constitution is concerned with establishing the powers of the national government. Since Congress is the main lawmaking arm of the national government, many of the powers of the national government are the powers of Congress. The strongest statement of national power is a list of the **enumerated powers of Congress** (Article I, Section 8). This list is followed by a clause that gives Congress the power to make all laws that are "necessary and proper" to carry out its powers. The **necessary and proper clause** has been used to justify giving Congress many powers

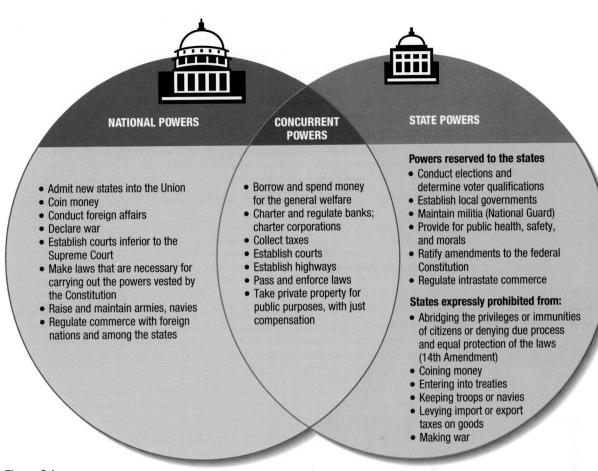

**Figure 3.1
The Constitutional Division of Powers Between the National Government and the States**

supremacy clause
constitutional declaration (Article VI) that the Constitution and laws made under its provisions are the supreme law of the land

never mentioned in the Constitution. National power is also based on the **supremacy clause** of Article VI, which says that the Constitution and laws made in accordance with it are "the supreme law of the land." This means that when national and state laws conflict, the national laws will be followed. The Constitution also sets some limitations on the national government. Article I, Section 9, lists some specific powers not granted to Congress, and the Bill of Rights (the first ten amendments to the Constitution) limits the power of the national government over individuals.

The Constitution says considerably less about the powers granted to the states. The Tenth Amendment says that all powers not given to the national government are reserved to the states, although the necessary and proper clause makes it difficult to see which powers are withheld from the national government. The states are given the power to approve the Constitution itself and any amendments to it. The Constitution also limits state powers. Article I, Section 10, denies the states certain powers, mostly the kinds that they possessed under the Articles of Confederation. The Fourteenth Amendment limits the power of the states over individual liberties, essentially a Bill of Rights that protects individuals from state action, since the first ten amendments apply only to the national government.

What these constitutional provisions mean is that the line between the national government and the state governments is not clearly drawn. We can see from Figure 3.1 that the Constitution designates specific powers as national, state, or concurrent. **Concurrent powers** are those that both levels of government may exercise. But the federal relationship is a good deal more complex than this chart would lead us to believe. The Supreme Court has become crucial to establishing the exact limits of such provisions as the necessary and proper clause, the supremacy clause, the Tenth Amendment, and the Fourteenth Amendment. This interpretation has changed over time, especially as historical demands have forced the Court to think about federalism in new ways.

concurrent powers
powers that are shared by both the federal and state governments

Two Views of Federalism

Political scientists differ in their ideas about how the balance of American federalism is to be understood. For many years, the prevailing theory was known as **dual federalism,** basically arguing that the relationship between the two levels of government was like a "layer cake." That is, the national and state governments were to be understood as two self-contained layers, each essentially separate from the other and carrying out its functions independently. In its own area of power, each level was supreme. Dual federalism reflects the formal distribution of powers in the Constitution, and perhaps it was an accurate portrayal of the judicial interpretation of the federal system for our first hundred years or so.

dual federalism
the federal system under which the national and state governments were responsible for separate policy areas

But this theory was criticized for not realistically describing the way the federal relationship was evolving in the twentieth century. It certainly did not take into account the changes brought about by the New Deal. The layer cake image was replaced by a new bakery metaphor. According to the new theory of **cooperative federalism,** rather than being two distinct layers, the national and state levels were swirled together like the chocolate and vanilla batter in a marble cake.[1] National and state powers were interdependent, and each level required the cooperation of the other to get things done. In fact, federalism came to be seen by political scientists as a partnership, but one in which the dominant partner was, more often than not, the national government.

cooperative federalism
the federal system under which the national and state governments share responsibility for most domestic policy areas

Possible Alternatives to Federalism

The federal system was not the only alternative available to our founders for organizing the relationship between the central government and the states. In fact, as we know, it wasn't even their first choice as a framework for government. The Articles of Confederation, which preceded the Constitution, handled the relationship in quite a different way. We can look at federalism as a compromise system that borrows some attributes from a unitary system and some from a confederal system, as shown in Figure 3.2. Had the founders chosen either of these alternatives, American government would look very different today.

CONFEDERAL SYSTEM

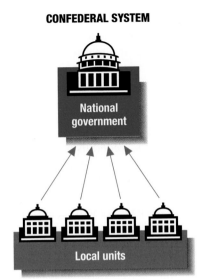

FEDERAL SYSTEM

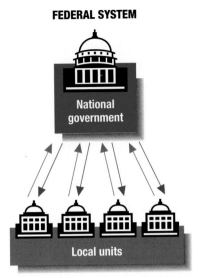

UNITARY SYSTEM

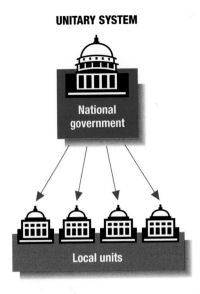

**Figure 3.2
The Division and
Flow of Power in
Confederal, Federal,
and Unitary Systems
of Government**

In a confederal system, the local units hold all the powers and the central government is dependent on those units for its existence. In a federal system, the flow of power goes in both directions: power is shared, with both the central and local governments holding some powers independent of the other. In a unitary system, the central government ultimately has all the power, and the local units are dependent on it.

unitary system
government in which all power is centralized

confederal system
government in which local units hold all the power

Unitary Systems   In a **unitary system,** the central government ultimately has all the power. Local units (states or counties) may have some power at some times, but basically they are dependent on the central unit, which can alter or even abolish them. Many contemporary countries have unitary systems, among them Britain, France, Japan, Denmark, Norway, Sweden, Hungary, and the Philippines.

Politics in Britain, for example, works very differently than politics in the United States, partly due to the different rules that organize central and local government. Most important decisions are made in London, from foreign policy to housing policy—even the details of what ought to be included in the school curriculum. Even local taxes are determined centrally. When Margaret Thatcher, the former British prime minister, believed that some municipal units in London were not supportive of her government's policies, she simply dissolved the administrative units. Similarly, in 1972, when the legislature in Northern Ireland (a part of Great Britain) could not resolve its religious conflicts, the central government suspended the local lawmaking body and ruled Northern Ireland from London. These actions are tantamount to a Republican president dissolving a Democratic state that disagreed with his policies, or the national government deciding to suspend the state legislature in Alabama during the days of segregation and run the state from Washington. Such an arrangement has been impossible in the United States except during the chaotic state of emergency following the Civil War. What is commonplace under a unitary system is unimaginable under our federal rules.

Confederal Systems   Confederal systems provide an equally sharp contrast to federal systems, even though the names sound quite similar. In **confederal systems,** the local units hold all the power, and the central government is dependent on them for its existence. The local units remain sovereign, and the central government has only as much power as they allow it to have. Examples of confederal systems include America under the Articles of Confederation and associations such as the United

Nations and the European Union, fifteen European nations that have joined economic and political forces. The European Union has been experiencing problems much like ours after the Revolutionary War, debating whether it ought to move in a federal direction. Most of the nations involved, jealous of their sovereignty, say no.

What Difference Does Federalism Make?

That our founders settled on federalism, rather than a unitary or a confederal system, makes a great deal of difference to American politics. Federalism gave the founders a government that could take effective action, restore economic stability, and regulate disputes among the states, while still allowing the states considerable autonomy.

However, not only units of government but also citizens have something at stake in the relationship between local and national government. Federalism provides real power at levels of government that are close to the citizens. Citizens can thus have access to officials and processes of government that they could not have if there were just one distant, effective unit. Federalism allows government to preserve local standards and to respond to local needs—that is, to solve problems at the levels where they occur. Examples include local traffic laws, community school policies, and city and county housing codes. Finally, federalism allows experimentation with public policy. If all laws and policies need not be uniform across the country, different states may try different solutions to common problems and share the results of their experiments.

For instance, in 1994 the state of Oregon began a controversial experiment in the financing of health care by adding many uninsured people to the Medicaid program and paying for the additional number of services covered. Although the plan has suffered some setbacks, it has been politically popular. More time is needed to determine just how successful such a program can be, but Oregon's opportunity to experiment may provide valuable lessons about health care policy for other states and for the national government.[2]

Federalism is not a perfect system, however, and there are some disadvantages. Where policies are made and enforced locally, all economies of scale are lost. Many functions are also repeated across the country as states locally administer national programs. Most problematic is the fact that federalism permits, even encourages, local prejudices to find their way into law. Until the national government took enforcement of civil rights legislation into its own hands in the 1960s, federalism allowed southern states to practice segregation. Before the passage of the Nineteenth Amendment, women could vote in some states but not others. Gay Americans do not have the same rights in all localities of the United States today. To the degree that states have more rather than less power, the uniform enforcement of civil rights cannot be guaranteed.

Overall, federalism has proved to be a flexible and effective compromise for American government. The United States is not the only nation with a federal system, although other countries may distribute power among their various units differently than we do. Germany, Canada, Mexico, Australia, and Switzerland are all examples of federal systems.

WHO, WHAT, HOW   Federalism has proved to be an institutional arrangement that allows the nation, the states, and the citizens of America to get political benefits that would not be available under a unitary or confederal system.

WHO are the actors?	WHAT do they want?	HOW do they get it?
National government	• Stability and control	• Federalism
States	• State autonomy • Responsiveness to local needs • Policy experimentation • Preservation of local values, standards, and prejudices	• Federalism
Citizens	• Access at nonnational levels • Local solutions to local problems • National authority to combat local prejudices	• Federalism

The Changing Balance: American Federalism over Time

Although the Constitution provides for both national powers and state powers (as well as some shared powers), several factors have caused the balance between the two to change considerably since it was written. First, because of the founders' disagreement over how power should be distributed in the new country, the final wording about national and state powers was intentionally kept vague, which probably helped the Constitution get ratified. Because it wasn't clear how much power the different levels held, it has been possible ever since for both ardent Federalists and states' rights advocates to find support for their positions in the document.

A second factor that has caused the balance of national and state power to shift over time has to do with the role given to the Supreme Court to step in and interpret what it thinks the Constitution really means when there is some conflict about which level of government should have the final say on a given issue. Those interpretations have varied along with the people sitting on the Court and with historical circumstances. As the context of American life has been transformed through events such as the end of slavery and the Civil War, the process of industrialization and the growth of big business, the economic collapse of the Great Depression in the 1930s and the relative prosperity of the late 1900s, the demands made on the different levels of government have shifted, too. When we talk about federalism in the United

States, we are talking about specific constitutional rules and provisions, but we are also talking about a fairly continuous evolution of how those rules are understood.

Two trends are apparent when we examine American federalism throughout our history. One is that American government in general is growing in size, at both the state and national levels. We make many more demands of government than did, say, the citizens of George Washington's time, or Abraham Lincoln's, and the apparatus to satisfy those demands has grown accordingly. But within that overall growth, a second trend has been the gradual strengthening of the national government at the expense of the states.

The increase in the size of government shouldn't surprise us. One indisputable truth about the United States is that over the years, it has gotten bigger, more industrialized, more urban, and more technical. As the country has grown, so have our expectations of what the government will do for us. We want to be protected from the fluctuations of the market, from natural disasters, from unfair business practices, and from unsafe foods and drugs. We want government to protect our "rights," but our concept of those rights has expanded beyond the first ten amendments to include things like economic security in old age, a minimum standard of living for all citizens, a safe interstate highway system, and crime-free neighborhoods. These new demands and expectations create larger government at all levels, but particularly at the national level, where the resources and will to accomplish such broad policy goals are more likely to exist.

The national government has grown so large, so quickly that the proper balance of power between the national and state governments is a central and controversial political issue today, and one that divides the liberals and conservatives we spoke of in Chapter 1. Liberals feel the need for a strong central government to solve society's

Heightened Expectations
Once, the aftermath of acts of God, like the tornado that wiped out Spencer, South Dakota, in 1998, was not considered government's responsibility. Today victims are eligible to receive aid if the national government declares the region a disaster area. Only hours after this tornado struck, Federal Emergency Management Agency teams arrived to offer help.

problems, and conservatives believe that "big government" causes more problems than it solves. People in the latter category, like the Anti-Federalists at the founding, would prefer to see power and the distribution of government services located at the state or local level, closer to the people being governed. So, for example, although they might support increased federal funding for education, they want local school districts to decide whether the money should be spent on upgrading science labs or hiring more teachers.

The growth of the national government's power over the states can be traced by looking at four moments in our national history: the early judicial decisions of Chief Justice John Marshall, the Civil War, the New Deal, and the civil rights movement and the expanded use of the Fourteenth Amendment from the 1950s through the 1970s. Since the late 1970s, we have seen increasing opposition to the growth of what is called "big government" on the part of citizens and officials alike, but most of the efforts to cut it back in size and to restore power to the states have been unsuccessful.

John Marshall: Strengthening the Constitutional Powers of the National Government

McCulloch v. Maryland
Supreme Court ruling (1819) confirming the supremacy of national over state government

John Marshall, the third chief justice of the Supreme Court (1801–1835), was a man of decidedly Federalist views. His rulings did much to strengthen the power of the national government both during his lifetime and after. The 1819 case of **McCulloch v. Maryland** set the tone. In resolving this dispute about whether Congress had the power to charter a bank and whether the state of Maryland had the power to tax that bank, Marshall had plenty of scope for exercising his preference for a strong national government. Congress did have the power, he ruled, even though the Constitution didn't spell it out, because Congress was empowered to do whatever was necessary and proper to fulfill its constitutional obligations. Marshall did not interpret the word *necessary* to mean "absolutely essential," but rather he took a looser view, holding that Congress had the power to do whatever was "appropriate" to execute its powers. If that meant chartering a bank, then the necessary and proper clause could be stretched to include chartering a bank. Furthermore, Maryland could not tax the federal bank because "the power to tax involves the power to destroy."[3] If Maryland could tax the federal bank, that would imply it had the power to destroy it, making Maryland supreme over the national government and violating the Constitution's supremacy clause, which makes the national government supreme.

Gibbons v. Ogden
Supreme Court ruling (1824) establishing national authority over interstate business

Marshall continued this theme in **Gibbons v. Ogden**[4] in 1824. In deciding that New York did not have the right to create a steamboat monopoly on the Hudson River, Marshall focused on the part of Article I, Section 8, that allows Congress to regulate commerce "among the several states." He interpreted commerce very broadly to include almost any kind of business, creating a justification for a national government that could freely regulate business and that was dominant over the states.

Gibbons v. *Ogden* did not immediately establish national authority over business. Business interests were far too strong to meekly accept government authority, and subsequent Court decisions recognized that strength and a prevailing public philosophy of *laissez-faire*. The national government's power in general was limited by cases such as *Cooley* v. *Board of Wardens of Port of Philadelphia* (1851),[5] which gave the states greater power to regulate commerce if local interests outweigh national interests, and *Dred Scott* v. *Sanford* (1857),[6] which held that Congress did not have the power to outlaw slavery in the territories.

The Civil War: National Domination of the States

The Civil War represented a giant step in the direction of a stronger national government. The war itself was fought for a variety of reasons. Besides the issue of slavery and the conflicting economic and cultural interests of the North and South, the war was fought to resolve the question of national versus state supremacy. When the national government, dominated by the northern states, passed legislation that would have furthered northern interests, the southern states tried to invoke the doctrine of nullification. **Nullification** was the idea that states could render national laws null if they disagreed with them, but the national government never recognized this doctrine. The southern states also seceded, or withdrew from the United States, as a way of rejecting national authority, but the victory of the Union in the ensuing war decisively showed that states did not retain their sovereignty under the Constitution.

nullification
declaration by a state that a federal law is void within its borders

The New Deal: National Power over Business

The Civil War did not settle the question of the proper balance of power between national government and business interests. In the years following the war, the courts struck down both state and national laws regulating business. In 1895 *Pollock* v. *Farmer's Loan and Trust Co.*[7] held that the federal income tax was unconstitutional (until it was legalized by the Sixteenth Amendment to the Constitution in 1913). *Lochner* v. *New York* (1905)[8] said that states could not regulate working hours for bakers. This ruling was used as the basis for rejecting state and national regulation of business until the middle of the New Deal in the 1930s. *Hammer* v. *Dagenhart* (1918)[9] said that national laws prohibiting child labor were outside Congress's power to regulate commerce and therefore were unconstitutional.

Throughout the early years of Franklin Roosevelt's New Deal, designed amid the devastation of the Great Depression of the 1930s to recapture economic stability through economic regulations, the Supreme Court maintained its antiregulation stance. But the president berated the Court for striking down his programs, and public opinion backed the New Deal and Roosevelt himself against the interests of big business. Eventually, the Court had a change of heart. Once established as constitutional, New Deal policies redefined the purpose of American government, and thus the scope of both national and state powers. The relationship between nation and state became more cooperative as the government became employer, provider, and insurer of millions of Americans in times of hardship. Our social security system was born during the New Deal, as were many other national programs designed to get America back to work and back on its feet. A sharper contrast to the *laissez-faire* policies of the turn of the century can hardly be imagined.

Civil Rights: National Protection Against State Abuse

The national government picked up a host of new roles as American society became more complex, including that of guarantor of individual rights against state abuse.

Selling a New Deal
This highly partisan contemporary cartoon shows President Franklin Roosevelt cheerfully steering the American ship of state toward economic recovery, unswayed by selfish big-business barons. New Deal programs ushered in a greatly expanded role for the national government.

The Fourteenth Amendment to the Constitution was passed after the Civil War to make sure southern states extended all the protections of the Constitution to the newly freed slaves. In the 1950s and 1960s, it was used by the Supreme Court to strike down a variety of state laws that maintained segregated, or separate, facilities for whites and African Americans, from railway cars to classrooms. By the 1970s, the Court's interpretation of the Fourteenth Amendment had expanded, allowing it to declare unconstitutional many state laws that it said deprived state citizens of their rights as U.S. citizens. For instance, the Court ruled that states had to guarantee those accused of state crimes the same protections that the Bill of Rights guaranteed those accused of federal crimes. As we will see in more detail in the next chapter, the Fourteenth Amendment has come to be a means for severely limiting the states' powers over their own citizens, sometimes very much against their will.

The trend toward increased national power has not put an end to the debate over federalism, however. In the 1970s and 1980s, Presidents Richard Nixon and Ronald Reagan tried hard to return some responsibilities to the states, mainly by giving them more control over how they spend federal money. In the following section, we look at recent efforts to alter the balance of federal power in favor of the states.

WHO, WHAT, HOW Historically, the balance of power between nation and states has swung back and forth, although the national government has gained more power overall.

WHO are the actors?	WHAT do they want?	HOW do they get it?
Nation	• More power	• Ambiguity in Constitution
		• Supreme Court rulings
States		• Increasing citizen demands

Federalism Today

Clearly, federalism is a continually renegotiated compromise between advocates of strong national government on the one hand and advocates of state power on the other. From the 1970s through the end of the century, however, frustration over the size of the national government's deficit (the result of spending more money than it brings in) and ideological changes, particularly the election of Republican majorities in Congress, brought demands for an expanding role for the states. How far this movement toward devolution will go is not yet clear, but naturally, as the state-federal relationship changes, so do the arenas in which citizens and their leaders make the decisions that become government policy. Such a fundamental shift usually means changes in the probable winners and losers of American politics.

The Structure of Federalism

As we noted earlier, contemporary federalism is best characterized as the marble cake of cooperative federalism. The national government tends to provide the money and direction for policies, which are then carried out, to a large extent, by employees of the states and cities. Thus the two levels of government are jointly carrying out functions that, most likely, would not have even been assigned to government seventy years ago.

The Medicaid program is an excellent example. Medicaid is a federally funded program to provide health care to the poorest segment of society. Before the New Deal, the idea that government should provide health care to any of its citizens would have seemed like an illegitimate use of its power. Now the federal government supplies the money and establishes the basic requirements and the base amounts that the states will provide for health care. States can build on that amount or apply for a waiver to provide innovative health services, as Oregon has done. Although the money comes from the federal government, which continually audits the states, Medicaid is administered by state and local employees.

The Politics of Contemporary Federalism

Beginning with *Marbury* v. *Madison,* the Supreme Court has gradually interpreted the Constitution in ways that give the national government more and more power relative to the states. This means that when Congress decides to expand federal policy into new areas, the Supreme Court is unlikely to step in to protect the states. This was highlighted in the 1985 case of *Garcia* v. *San Antonio Metropolitan Transit Authority,*[10] which involved the constitutionality of allowing the federal government to dictate minimum wage standards to municipal governments. (A municipality is a unit of government providing local services for a city or town.) The Court ruled that Congress could regulate municipal salaries and that the Court would not get involved in disputes between the federal government and state and local governments.[11] In other words, the Court would allow the federal government to decide how far to involve itself in state and local matters.

In subsequent decisions, however, the Court has argued that there are some limits to federal encroachment, and most recently a majority on the Court has moved to adopt a much stronger states' rights position. In 1995, for example, the Court ruled that Congress took its constitutional authority to regulate interstate commerce too far when it made laws about how far from a schoolyard a person carrying a gun had to stay.[12] In *Printz* v. *United States* (1997), the Court struck down part of the Brady bill, a federal gun control law that required state law enforcement officers to conduct background checks of prospective gun purchasers, because it compelled state employees to administer a federal program, essentially making them agents of the federal government.[13]

The Supreme Court's decisions give the federal government great latitude in exercising its powers, but the states are still responsible for the policies that most affect our lives. For instance, the states retain primary responsibility for everything from education to regulation of funeral parlors, from licensing physicians to building roads and telling us how fast we can drive on them. Most questions of contemporary federalism involve the national government trying to influence how the states and localities go about providing the goods and services and regulating the behaviors that have traditionally been within their jurisdictions.

Why should the national government care so much about what the states do? Congress wants to make policies that influence or control the states for several reasons. First, from a member of Congress's perspective, it is easier to solve many social and economic problems at the national level. Pervasive problems such as race discrimination or air and water pollution do not affect just the populations of individual states. When a political problem does not stop at the state border, it can be easier to conceive of solutions that cross the border as well; such solutions require national coordination. In some instances, national problem solving involves redistributing resources from one state or region to another, which individual states, on their own, would be unwilling or unable to do.

A second reason members of Congress frequently want to control policymakers in their states is so that their constituents will see them as the deliverers of resources and good things and will reward their generosity and political skill at the polls. After the expansion of the federal government's role during the New Deal, the Democratic Party maintained a majority in Congress by becoming known as the party that delivered economic benefits to various socioeconomic groups and geographic areas of the country.[14] Since the 1970s, as Americans have identified less strongly with political parties, politicians have used the promise of local benefits to convince voters to support them. Incumbents have embraced their roles as representatives who can deliver highways, parks, welfare benefits, urban renewal, and assistance to farmers, ranchers, miners, educators, and just about everyone else. Doing well by constituents gets incumbents reelected.[15]

Third, sometimes members of Congress prefer to adopt national legislation to preempt what states may be doing or planning to do. In some cases, they might object to state laws, as Congress did when it passed civil rights legislation against the strong preferences of the southern states. In other cases, they might enact legislation to prevent states from making fifty different regulatory laws for the same product. Here they are being sensitive to the wishes of corporations and businesses—generally large contributors to politicians—to have a single set of laws governing their activities. If Congress makes a set of nationally binding regulations, a business does not have to incur the expense of altering its product (or service) to meet different state standards.

To deliver on their promises, national politicians must have the cooperation of the states. Although some policies, such as social security, can be administered easily at the national level, others, such as changing educational policy or altering the drinking age, remain under state authority and cannot be legislated in Washington. It is here that federal policymakers face one of their biggest challenges: how to get the states to do what federal officials have decided they should do.

Let's take the question of mathematics education as an example. Assume that members of Congress have decided that we face a "math crisis" and that more math training needs to take place in our high schools for the nation to remain competitive in the world economy of the twenty-first century. How will they get the education policymakers—that is, the states—to go along with them? One sure way to influence math education would be for the federal government to build and staff a system of "federal schools." Then it could have any kind of a curriculum it wanted. But doing so would be enormously expensive and wasteful, since the states and localities already have schools and already teach math in them. The more efficient alternative would be to try to influence how the states and localities teach math. Here Congress would face the same challenges it does with respect to other policy areas such as health, occupational safety, transportation, and welfare. When Congress wants to act in these areas, it has to find ways to work with the states and localities.

Congressional Strategies for Influencing State Policy

Congress has essentially two resources to work with when it comes to influencing the states to do what it wants: authority and money. As we can see in Table 3.1, this combination yields four possibilities, all of which Congress has practiced: (1) the federal government can give the states no orders and no money, in which case it exerts no influence on the states; (2) the federal government can tell the states what to do and pay for the administration of the policy, which allows Congress to get its way but limits the states' options; (3) the federal government can tell the states only the broad outline of what it wants and provide money to them, which the states like because it preserves their autonomy while helping them financially; or (4) the federal government can tell the states what to do but provide no funds, and even reserve the option of taking away funds given for other purposes if the states don't cooperate. This last is the states' least favorite option, for obvious reasons. As we'll see, the winners and losers in the political process will change depending on which option Congress chooses.

Option One: No Federal Influence   In the period of dual federalism, the federal government left most domestic policy decisions to the states. Precollege education is a good example: the federal government did not provide instructions to the states about curriculum goals (let alone math training), nor did it provide the funds for education. The combination of no instructions and no funding (first row in Table 3.1) yields the outcome of no federal influence. This means the states organized education as they wished. To follow our math example, the outcome of no federal influence would be that some states might concentrate on math, while others might emphasize

Table 3.1
How the Federal Government Influences the States

Option	Rules	Federal Funds?	Character of the National/State Relationship
Option One: No Federal Influence	Few or no rules	No	States have autonomy and pay for their own programs. Results in high diversity of policies, including inequality. Promotes state competition and its outcomes. Calls for congressional and presidential restraint in exercising their powers.
Option Two: Categorical Grants	Strict rules and regulations	Yes	Good for congressional credit taking. Ensures state compliance and policy uniformity. Heavy federal regulatory burden ("red tape"). National policy requirements may not be appropriate for local conditions.
Option Three: Block Grants	Broad grants of power within program areas	Yes	Greater state flexibility, program economy. State politicians love money without "strings." Greater program innovation. Undermines congressional credit taking. Grants become highly vulnerable to federal budget cuts. Leads to policy diversity and inequality, meeting state rather than national goals.
Option Four: Unfunded Mandates	Specific rules and compliance obligations	No	Very cheap for the federal government. Easy way for members of Congress to garner favor. States complain about unfairness and burdensome regulations. Undermines state cooperation.

a different educational issue. Such policy differences are a natural outcome of a situation in which the states, rather than the federal government, have more power.

Option Two: Categorical Grants   In our example, Congress might decide that the nation's long-run economic health depends on massive improvements in high school mathematics education. "No federal influence" is clearly not an option here. Congress could pass a resolution declaring its desire for better math education in high school, but if it wants results, it would have to put some teeth in its "request." If Congress really wants to effect a change, it would have to provide instructions and an incentive for the states to improve math education.

categorical grant
federal funds provided for a specific purpose, restricted by detailed instructions, regulations, and compliance standards

The most popular tool Congress has devised for this purpose is the **categorical grant,** (see the second row in Table 3.1) which provides very detailed instructions, regulations, and compliance requirements for the states (and sometimes for local governments as well) in specific policy areas. If a state complies with the requirements, federal money is released for those specified purposes. If a state doesn't comply with the detailed provisions of the categorical grant, it doesn't get the money. In many cases, the states have to provide some funding themselves. They might, for instance, have to match the amount contributed by the federal government.

Using our example, the federal government could pass a math education act that would provide funds on a per pupil basis for math education in the high schools. The bill might set standards for certain performance or testing levels, requirements for teacher certification in advanced math education training, and perhaps specific goals for decreasing the gender and racial gaps in math performance. School districts and state school boards would have to document their compliance in order to receive their funds.

The states, like most governments, never have enough money to meet all their citizens' demands, so categorical grants can look very attractive, at least on the surface. The grants can be refused, but most of the time they are welcomed. In fact, over time state and local governments have become so dependent on federal subsidies that these subsidies now make up about 24 percent of all state and local spending.[16] Thus the categorical grant has become a powerful tool of the federal government in getting the states to do what it wants.

Categorical grants are responsible for the large growth in federal influence on the states. Use of the grants blossomed in the 1960s and 1970s, primarily because they are very attractive to Congress. Members of Congress receive credit for sponsoring specific grant programs, which in turn help establish members as national policy leaders, building their reputations with their constituents for bringing "home" federal money. Also, because senators and House members are backed by coalitions of various interest groups, specific program requirements are a way to ensure that a policy actually does what members (and their backers) want—even in states where local political leaders prefer a different course. By contrast, state politicians hate the requirements and all the paperwork that goes with reporting compliance with federal regulations. States and localities also frequently argue that federal regulations prevent them from doing a good job. They want the money, but they also want more flexibility.

Option Three: Block Grants   Conservatives and Republicans have long chafed at the detailed, Washington-centered nature of categorical grants. State politicians understandably want the maximum amount of freedom possible. They want to control their own destinies, not just carry out political deals made in Washington, and they want to please the coalitions of interests and voters that put them in power in the states. Thus they argue for maintaining federal funding, but with fewer regulations. Their preferred policy tool, the **block grant,** (seen in the third row of Table 3.1), combines broad (rather than detailed) program requirements and regulations with funding from the federal treasury. Block grants give the states considerable freedom in using the funds in broad policy areas.

block grant
federal funds provided for a broad purpose, unrestricted by detailed requirements and regulations

Continuing our math education example, the federal government might provide the states with a lump-sum block grant and instructions to spend it on education as each state sees fit. If Congress demanded that the money be spent on math education and insisted on other conditions, the grant would start to look more like a categorical grant and less like a block grant. With an education block grant, members of Congress could not count on their math education problem being solved on a national basis unless it coincidentally resulted from the individual decisions in fifty states and innumerable localities.

One extreme and short-lived form of the block grant was President Richard Nixon's proposal to give money to the states and localities with no strings attached—not in place of categorical grants, but largely in addition to existing programs. Beginning in the 1970s, under General Revenue Sharing (GRS) the federal government turned over money to all units of lower government automatically. GRS was immensely popular with the governors and mayors, but it never had great congressional backing because members of Congress could neither take credit for nor control how lower governments were spending these federal funds. In practice, GRS never replaced categorical grants; it was just one set of no-strings grants to the subgovernments. Congress did not object when, in 1986, President Ronald Reagan suggested abolishing GRS as a way of reducing the deficit.[17]

Less extreme versions of the block grant were pushed by Republican presidents Nixon, Reagan, and Gerald Ford. However, the largest and most significant block grant was instituted under Democratic president Bill Clinton in 1996 with the passage of the welfare reform act discussed earlier. This reform changed the categorical grant program of Aid to Families with Dependent Children (AFDC) to a welfare block grant to the states, Temporary Assistance to Needy Families (TANF). Under TANF, the states have greater leeway in defining many of the rules of their welfare programs, such as qualifications and work requirements. The states do not get a blank check, however; they must continue to spend at certain levels and to adopt some federal provisions, such as the limits on how long a person can stay on welfare. TANF has ended welfare as an entitlement. Under AFDC, all families who qualified were guaranteed benefits—just as people who qualify for social security are assured coverage. This guarantee is not part of TANF. If the states run short of money—for example, if the economy slows down—families that might otherwise qualify may not receive welfare benefits. Such decisions, and their repercussions, are left to the individual states.

Congress has generally resisted the block grant approach for both policy and political reasons. In policy terms, many members of Congress fear that the states will do what they want instead of what Congress intends. One member characterized the idea of putting federal money into block grants as "pouring money down a rat hole."[18] That is, members are concerned that the states will not do a good job without regulations. And since it is impossible to control how the states deal with particular problems under block grants, there are a number of important differences, or inequalities, in how the state programs are run.

Congress also has political objections to block grants, and these may be even more important to its members than their policy concerns. When federal funds are not attached to specific programs, they lose their electoral appeal for members of Congress, as the members can no longer take credit for the programs. From a representative's standpoint, it does not make political sense to take the heat for taxing people's income, only to turn those funds over in block grants so that governors and mayors get the credit for how the money is spent. In addition, interest groups contribute millions of dollars to congressional campaigns when members of Congress have control over program specifics. If Congress allows the states to assume that control, interest groups have less incentive to make congressional campaign contributions. As a result, the tendency has been to place more conditions on block grants with each annual congressional appropriation.[19]

Categorical grants remain the predominant form of federal aid, amounting to about 80 percent of all aid to state and local governments. The change from AFDC to TANF was an important milestone in welfare policy, but it remains to be seen whether Congress will continue this approach in other policy areas.

Option Four: Unfunded Mandates   The politics of federalism yields one more strategy, which is shown in the bottom row of Table 3.1. When the federal government issues an **unfunded mandate,** it imposes specific policy requirements on the states but does not provide a way to pay for those activities. Here Congress either threatens criminal or civil penalties or promises to cut off other, often unrelated, federal funds if the states do not comply with its directions. A good example of an unfunded mandate that achieved its goal was the legislation passed by Congress in 1984 ordering the secretary of transportation to withhold 5 percent of federal highway funds from states that did not adopt a minimum drinking age of twenty-one. This resulted in all fifty states raising the drinking age to twenty-one.

In terms of our math education example, the national government might say to the states that at least 45 percent of the students enrolled in advanced high school math courses be female, and if that quota is not met, the states stand to lose 5 percent of their sewage treatment funds. This requirement could be set with no new federal funding for education at all.

Unfunded mandates became more attractive to members of Congress in the era of the ballooning national deficit.[20] Whereas Congress passed unfunded mandates only eleven times from 1931 through the 1960s, it passed fifty-two such mandates in the 1970s and 1980s, a trend that continued into the 1990s.[21] Congress can please interest groups and particular citizen groups by passing such laws, but the laws infuriate state politicians, who have to come up with the money to pay for them. In 1987 South Dakota challenged the law tying federal highway funds to a minimum drinking age, arguing that Congress had exceeded its spending powers. The Supreme Court ruled in favor of the federal government.[22]

President Clinton, working with the Republican majorities in Congress, pushed through the Unfunded Mandate Act of 1995, which promises to reimburse the states for expensive unfunded mandates or to pass a separate law acknowledging the cost of an unfunded mandate. This act, however, may not be enough to dissuade Congress from passing "good laws" with no cost to the U.S. Treasury. What the states see as an unfunded mandate can be defined by Congress in several different ways—as no more than a "clarification of legislative intent," for example.[23]

The Move Toward Devolution

As we mentioned in the introduction to this chapter, there has been a movement since the 1980s toward giving power back to the states, or devolution. The states have shown a new enthusiasm for charting their own course with respect to policy initiatives. Congress has watched this enthusiasm with mixed feelings. Federal budget difficulties present a significant pressure to economize, and this belt-tightening, combined with conservative sentiments in the Republican-controlled Congress, has pushed

unfunded mandate
a federal order that states operate and pay for a program created at the national level

Washington in the direction of less federal control and more block grants. Ideologically, Republicans favor devolution, but congressional Republicans lose some of their enthusiasm in practice because more devolution means less power for members of Congress, whose reelection efforts are strengthened if they can point to accomplishments that voters value.

The current practice seems to be a contradictory mix of rhetoric about returning power to the states and new congressional initiatives (and program requirements) in areas such as Medicaid, welfare, and law enforcement. Although Congress talks about devolution, it often gives in to electoral pressure to try new national solutions to salient problems. Even the 1996 welfare reform bill, with its enormous block grant, was accompanied by new federal restrictions on who could receive aid and for how long.

One odd halfway strategy that has unfolded is for the national government to create national policy but to grant "waivers" from federal regulations so that the states can experiment with different policies. The Oregon Medicaid policy we discussed earlier is one example, as is the old welfare policy that existed before 1996. Notice, however, that with waivers, the federal government retains all the power; the conditional leeway it gives the states should not be confused with real power at the state level. The federal government is just letting the states wander around the policy landscape on a longer leash with less food. The advantage is that some of the states may develop new programs that work better than the old federal programs. If this happens and it serves congressional interests, the federal government may pressure the rest of the states to adopt the successful program. Indeed, state innovations are one of the prime justifications for federalism. Justice Louis Brandeis called the states our "laboratories of democracy," in which many different solutions to societal problems can be tried. A question for the new century is whether this spirit of devolution will continue or whether congressional ambivalence will reel it back in.

Advocates for the national government and advocates for the states are engaged in a constant struggle for more power, and have been since the days of the Articles of Confederation. To get more power for the national government, advocates have relied on cooperative federalism, which gives the federal government a role in domestic policy, and on the rules of categorical grants and unfunded mandates, which maximize national power with minimal

Experiments in Welfare
Since the early 1980s, the movement of power from the national government to state governments has spurred hope that the states can find innovative solutions to seemingly intractable problems. Here, alongside then Governor Tommy G. Thompson, Michelle Crawford explains how a welfare program devised by the state of Wisconsin led to her new job as a machine operator.

state input. States, by contrast, benefited more from dual federalism, under which the federal role was largely confined to foreign affairs. Since the advent of cooperative federalism, the states have favored policies in which the power of the federal government is limited. The process of devolution has meant more block grants and fewer categorical grants and unfunded mandates.

WHO, WHAT, HOW   Advocates for the national government and advocates for the states continue to be engaged in a constant struggle for power.

WHO are the actors?	WHAT do they want?	HOW do they get it?
National government	• More power	• Cooperative federalism • Categorical grants • Unfunded mandates
State governments	• More power	• Dual federalism • Block grants • No federal influence on policy • Devolution

Citizenship and Federalism

State and local governments are closer to their citizens than the federal government is. Whereas the federal government may seem to take the form of an elite democracy, run by people far removed from everyday citizens, state and local governments allow far more opportunities for participatory governance, if citizens choose to get involved. Citizens may vote for initiatives and referenda, run for local office, sit on school boards and other advisory boards, or even take part in citizen judicial boards and community-run probation programs.[24]

But there is another way that citizens can shape state and local policies as surely as when they vote at the polls, and that is by voting with their feet. In a kind of political pressure that the federal government almost never has to confront, citizens can move from a state or locality they don't like to one that suits them better. Consider this: few Americans ever think seriously about changing countries. Other nations may be nice to visit, but most of us, for better or worse, will continue to live under the U.S. government. At the same time, far fewer of us will live in the same state or city throughout our lives. We may move for jobs, for climate, or for a better quality of life. When we relocate, we can often choose where we want to go. Businesses also move—for better facilities, better tax rates, a better labor force, and so on—and they are also in a position to choose where they want to go. This mobility of people and businesses creates incentives for competition and cooperation among states and localities that influence how they operate in important ways. Although we do not con-

Points of Access

- Serve on your town/city citizen advisory board.
- Vote in town/municipal elections.
- Attend your town/city open meetings bringing together citizens and elected officials.
- Run for city council.
- Talk to your city councilor or county commissioner about local concerns.
- Write a letter to the editor of your local newspaper about problems in your town.

ventionally consider the decision to move to be a political act, it affects policy just as much as more traditional forms of citizen participation.

WHAT'S AT STAKE REVISITED

As we have seen in this chapter, state governments are different political arenas than the federal government, with different rules that lead to different sorts of outcomes. Moving welfare policy to the states, as was done in the Personal Responsibility and Work Opportunity Reconciliation Act that President Clinton signed on August 22, 1996, has clear consequences for who wins and who loses in terms of welfare. Although there is much debate over the immediate effects of this act on immigrants, the wages of the working poor, and other issues, our focus here is on the more general question of what's at stake when responsibility for welfare devolves from the federal government to the states.

In many ways, the arguments over what's at stake in this welfare reform echo all the arguments for and against other block grants that entail more state responsibility and less federal control. From the perspective of many liberal Democrats, including the two who resigned in protest from Clinton's administration, the losers in moving the policy responsibility to the states will be the poor. Since only the federal government can guarantee that no child in America will live in poverty, that guarantee had to go when the states took over. Individual states might make that commitment for their own citizens, but they can't make it for the nation. An advantage of centralized policy is that a single goal can be enforced in all the states, regardless of each state's wishes. With decentralized policies such as welfare reform, there can be fifty separate goals. As long as the economy is strong, critics argue, all the states may be able to afford generous welfare policies, but when state finances become tighter, welfare benefits will be among the first things to go.

But there are also potential benefits in the transfer of policy from the federal government to the states. With responsibility clearly located at the state level rather than several levels of government, it will be easier to know whom to hold accountable for glitches or problems.[25] The law retains some federal restrictions, but the states still have considerable latitude to experiment. Since they are closer to the people, they may have a better understanding of their needs. Many states have developed innovative programs that are far more creative and potentially rewarding than anything the more unwieldy federal government could have attempted. Some of the innovations include using welfare money to subsidize wages, housing, and even, in the case of Texas and Virginia (which currently have welfare surpluses), cars for welfare recipients to drive to work. States may dock welfare benefits to penalize recipients who don't get a job quickly enough, or raise benefits so that recipients can get a job and still keep some benefits, such as health care and child care.

Some of these state experiments will undoubtedly fail. What is useful about allowing the states to live up to their potential as "laboratories of democracy" is that those experiments that are successful can be adopted by other states or even used as models by the federal government for national policy. ∎

key terms

block grant   76

categorical grant   75

concurrent powers   64

confederal system   65

cooperative federalism   64

devolution   61

dual federalism   64

enumerated powers of
    Congress   62

Gibbons v. *Ogden*   69

McCulloch v. *Maryland*   69

necessary and proper clause   62

nullification   70

supremacy clause   63

unfunded mandate   78

unitary system   65

summary

- The Constitution is the rule book of American politics. The great decisions and compromises of the founding were really about the allocation of power among the branches of the government, between the national and state governments, and between government and citizens.

- The Constitution is ambiguous in defining federalism, giving "reserved powers" to the states but providing the "necessary and proper clause," which has allowed tremendous growth of national power.

- The growth of national power can be traced to the early decisions of Chief Justice John Marshall, the constitutional consequences of the Civil War, the establishment of national supremacy in economics with the New Deal, and the new national responsibilities in protecting citizens' rights that have been associated with the civil rights movement.

- Our understanding of federalism in the United States has evolved from a belief in dual federalism, with distinct policy responsibilities for the national and state governments, to the more realistic cooperative federalism, in which the different levels share responsibility in most domestic policy areas.

- Alternatives to our federal arrangement are unitary systems, which give all effective power to the central government, and confederal systems, in which the individual states (or other subunits) have primary power. The balance of power that is adopted between central and subnational governments directly affects the national government's ability to act on large policy problems and the subnational units' flexibility in responding to local preferences.

- Federalism reflects a continually changing compromise between advocates of a strong national government and advocates of strong state governments.

- Under dual federalism, national and state governments were thought to be responsible for separate policy areas. With cooperative federalism (our current arrangement), state and national governments share responsibility for most domestic policy areas. Congress can use authority and money to encourage state cooperation with its agenda in four ways: it can exercise no influence, or it can issue categorical grants, block grants, or unfunded mandates.

- State and local governments provide citizens with many opportunities for participation should they choose to get involved. Even if they don't participate in the usual ways, citizens can exert power over their states and localities by moving away, or "voting with their feet."

4

What's at Stake?

Rights in à Democracy
- *Rights and the Power of the People*
- *When Rights Conflict*

The Bill of Rights and the States
- *Applying the Bill of Rights*

Freedom of Religion
- *The Establishment Clause*
- *The Free Exercise Clause*

Freedom of Expression
- *Speech That Criticizes the Government*
- *Symbolic Speech*
- *Freedom of Assembly*
- *Obscenity and Pornography*
- *Freedom of the Press*
- *Censorship on the Internet*

The Right to Bear Arms
- *Judicial Decisions*

The Rights of Criminal Defendants
- *Unreasonable Searches and Seizures*
- *The Right Against Self-Incrimination*
- *The Right to Counsel*
- *Cruel and Unusual Punishment*

The Right to Privacy
- *Reproductive Rights*
- *Gay Rights*
- *The Right to Die*

Citizenship and Civil Liberties

What's at Stake Revisited

Fundamental American Liberties

It's night. You are studying in your dorm room, writing an English paper, when you are disturbed by raucous noise outside. Sorority members are singing and celebrating outside your window, and it really bugs you. You yell, "Please be quiet." Twenty minutes later, intensely irritated, you yell again. This time, less polite, you use an English translation of a word that, in your family's ethnic tradition, means "fool" or "jerk." "Shut up, you water buffalo!" you bellow out the window. "If you want a party, there's a zoo a mile from here."[1] What kind of reaction would you expect your words to arouse?

For University of Pennsylvania freshman Eden Jacobowitz, on January 13, 1993, the use of the words *water buffalo* launched him into a legal nightmare. The university's speech code forbids the use of any verbal or symbolic behavior that insults or demeans an identifiable person on the basis of race, color, ethnicity, or national origin and that is intended to inflict injury on the person or is so demeaning that a reasonable observer would conclude that such an intention exists.[2] The sorority women outside Jacobowitz's window were African Americans, and students other than Jacobowitz had also yelled at them, using the term *black bitches.* The sorority women accused the perpetrators of violating the speech code. Only Jacobowitz admitted yelling out the window, however, and only Jacobowitz was accused of racial harassment.

The words *water buffalo* were taken by the university to be a racial slur by virtue of the fact that water buffalo are "primitive dark animals that live in Africa." Jacobowitz, an Orthodox Jew who had attended a religious Jewish high school in which Hebrew was spoken, was used to referring to rowdy classmates as *behema,* a Hebrew word best translated as "water buffalo." Besides, his many defenders claimed, water buffalo don't even live in Africa, but in Asia. White and African American scholars alike came forward to testify that *water buffalo* was not a racial slur that anyone had ever heard of. Still, the University of Pennsylvania persisted. The only way Jacobowitz could settle the case short of a hearing, the university said, was to acknowledge his inappropriate behavior, devise a diversity program for his dormitory, be on residential probation while living in a university residence, and have his transcript marked for several years with the notation "Violation of the Code of Conduct and Racial Harassment Policy."

Though willing to apologize and explain, Jacobowitz refused to settle. The American Civil Liberties Union, a legal interest group that defends what it sees as intolerable restrictions on civil liberties, including freedom of speech, took up his defense, and the national media swarmed onto the Penn campus. Finally, four months later, the initial complaint was withdrawn, essentially because the adverse publicity was affecting the university politically. The publicity stemmed from two issues. One was the almost humorous question about whether *water buffalo* was indeed a racial slur, and the other, far broader, was whether the use of even undeniable racial, ethnic, gender, and other slurs ought to be banned from American college campuses.

Proponents of speech codes claim that they increase public awareness of the power relationships and oppressions that exist in society, and that they create a comfortable and nonthreatening environment of diversity in which everyone can learn. Opponents argue not only that speech codes can lead to absurdities like the water buffalo case but also that the entire effort constitutes a restriction of freedom of speech that is most inappropriate on college campuses, where the exchange of ideas should flourish. Just what is at stake in college speech codes? ■

"Give me liberty," declared Patrick Henry, "or give me death." "Live Free or Die," proudly proclaims the New Hampshire license plate. Americans have always put a lot of stock in their freedom. Certain that they live in the least restrictive country in the world, Americans celebrate their freedom and are proud of the Constitution, the laws, and the traditions that preserve them.

And yet, living collectively under a government means that we aren't free to do whatever we want. There are limits on our freedom that allow us to live peacefully with our fellows, minimizing the conflict that would result if we all did exactly what we pleased. John Locke said that liberty does not equal license—that is, the freedom to do some things doesn't mean the freedom to do everything. Deciding what rights we give up to join civilized society and what rights we retain is one of the great challenges of democratic government.

What are these things called "rights" or "liberties," so precious that some Americans are willing to lay down their lives to preserve them? On the one hand, the answer is very simple. *Rights* and *liberties* are synonyms; they mean freedoms or privileges that one has a claim to. In that respect, we use the words more or less interchangeably. On the other hand, when prefaced by the word *civil*, both *rights* and *liberties* take on a more specific meaning, and they no longer mean quite the same thing.

civil liberties
individual freedoms
guaranteed to the
people primarily by
the Bill of Rights

Our **civil liberties** are individual freedoms that place limitations on the power of government. In general, civil liberties protect our right to think and act without government interference. Some of these rights are spelled out in the Constitution, particularly in the Bill of Rights. These include the rights to express ourselves and to choose our own religious beliefs. Others, like the right to privacy, rest on the shakier ground of judicial decision-making. Although government is prevented from limiting these freedoms per se, we will see that sometimes one person's freedom to speak or act in a certain way may be limited by another person's rights. Government does play a role in resolving the conflicts between individuals' rights.

civil rights
citizenship rights
guaranteed to the
people (primarily in the
Thirteenth, Fourteenth,
Fifteenth, and Nine-
teenth Amendments)
and protected by
government

While civil liberties relate to restrictions on government action, **civil rights** refer to the extension of government action to secure citizenship rights for all members of society. When we speak of civil rights, we most often mean that the government must treat all citizens equally, apply laws fairly, and not discriminate unjustly against certain groups of people. Most of the rights we consider civil rights are guaranteed by the Thirteenth, Fourteenth, Fifteenth, Nineteenth, and Twenty-sixth Amendments. These amendments lay out the fundamental rights of citizenship, most notably the right to vote but also the right to equal treatment before the law and the right to due process of the law. They forbid government from making laws that treat people differently on the basis of race, and they ensure that the right to vote cannot be denied on the basis of race or gender.

Not all people live under governments whose rules guarantee them fundamental liberties. In fact, we argued earlier that one way of distinguishing between authoritarian and nonauthoritarian governments is that nonauthoritarian governments, including democracies, give citizens the power to challenge government if they believe that it has denied their basic rights. When we consider our definition of politics as "who gets what and how," we see that rights are crucial in democratic politics, where a central tension is the power of the individual pitted against the power of the government. What's at stake in a democracy is the resolution of that tension. In fact, democracies depend on the existence of rights in at least two ways. First, civil liberties provide rules that keep government limited, so that it cannot become too powerful. Second, civil rights help define who "We, the people" are in a democracy, and they give those people the power necessary to put some controls on their government.

We will take two chapters to explore the issues of civil liberties and civil rights in depth. In this chapter, we begin with a general discussion of the meaning of rights or liberties in a democracy and the problem of conflicting rights. Then we look at the traditional civil liberties that provide a check on the power of government. In Chapter 5, we focus on civil rights and the continuing struggle of groups of Americans—like women, African Americans, and other minorities—for the right to be fully counted and empowered in American politics.

Specifically, in this chapter we examine

- the meaning of rights in a democratic society
- the Bill of Rights as part of the federal Constitution and its relationship to the states
- freedom of religion in the United States
- freedom of speech and of the press

- the right to bear arms as necessary for maintaining a well-regulated militia
- the rights of people accused of crimes in the United States
- the right to privacy

Rights in a Democracy

The freedoms we consider indispensable in a democracy are part of the everyday language of politics in America. We take many of them for granted: we speak confidently of our freedom of speech, of the press, and of religion, as well as of our rights to bear arms, to a fair trial, and to privacy. There is nothing inevitable about these freedoms, however.

In fact, there is nothing inevitable about the idea of rights at all. Until the writings of philosophers such as John Locke, it was rare for individuals to talk about claiming rights against government. Government was assumed to have all the power, and subjects had only such privileges as government was willing to bestow. Locke argued that the rights to life, liberty, and the pursuit of property were conferred on individuals by nature and that those individuals did not have to obey a government that failed to guarantee their natural rights. Rights, he claimed, existed before government did, and one of the primary purposes of a government was to preserve the natural rights of its citizens.

This notion of natural rights and limited government was central to the founders of the American system. In the Declaration of Independence, Thomas Jefferson wrote that men are "endowed by their Creator with certain inalienable rights; that among these are life, liberty, and the pursuit of happiness; that, to secure these rights, governments are instituted among men." John Locke could not have said it better himself.

Practically speaking, of course, any government can make its citizens do anything it wishes, regardless of their rights, as long as it is in charge of the military and the police. But in nonauthoritarian governments, the public is usually outraged at the invasion of individual rights. Unless the government is willing to dispense with its reputation as a democracy, it must respond in some way to pacify public opinion. In a democracy, public opinion can be a powerful guardian of citizens' rights.

Rights and the Power of the People

Just as rights limit government, they also empower citizens. A person who can successfully claim that he or she has rights that must be respected by government is a citizen of that government. A person who is under the authority of a government but cannot claim rights is merely a subject, bound by the laws but without any power to challenge or change them. This does not mean, as we will see, that citizens can always have things their own way. Nor does it mean that noncitizens have no rights in a democracy. It does mean that citizens have special protections and powers that allow them to stand up to government and plead their case when they believe an injustice has been done.

Lilies of the Field
In 1999 the San Francisco Catholic Archdiocese tried to postpone the annual Easter block party hosted by the Sisters of Perpetual Indulgence, a flamboyant, largely gay street theater troupe whose members wear mock religious outfits and go by names such as Sister Reyna Terror and Sister Ann R. Key. Catholic fathers found fault with the celebration's "extraordinary insensitivity to people of all faiths" and criticized the city of San Francisco's Board of Supervisors for having granted the group a permit to close one block of Castro Street for the Easter performance. The board's president, Tom Ammiano, refused to change the permit, arguing that just because "the actions of one group are not popular with another group is no reason to deny anyone their rights."

When Rights Conflict

Because rights represent power, they are, like all forms of power, subject to conflict and controversy. It would be great if all people could have all the rights they wanted, but we have already seen that power is a scarce resource and that there is not enough to go around. Often for one person to get his or her own way, someone else must lose out.

People clash over rights in two ways. First, individuals' rights conflict with each other; for instance, one person's right to share a prayer with classmates at the start of the school day conflicts with another student's right not to be subjected to a religious practice against his or her will. Second, individuals' rights conflict with society's needs; for example, an individual's right to decide whether or not to wear a motorcycle helmet conflicts with society's need to protect its citizens. Although sometimes conflicts over rights lead to violence, usually they are resolved in the United States through politics—through the process of arguing, bargaining, and compromising over who gets what and how. All this wrangling takes place within the institutions of American politics, primarily in Congress and the courts, but also in the White House, at the state and local levels, and throughout our daily lives.

WHO, WHAT, HOW Citizens of democracies have a vital interest in this issue of fundamental rights. What they stand to gain is more power for themselves and less power for government.

WHO are the actors?	WHAT do they want?	HOW do they get it?
Citizens	• Limited government • Power as citizens • Resolution of rights conflicts	• Rights of citizenship • Politics

The Bill of Rights and the States

The Bill of Rights looms large in any discussion of American civil liberties, but the document that today seems so inseparable from American citizenship had a stormy birth. Controversy raged over whether a bill of rights was necessary in the first place, deepening the split between Federalists and Anti-Federalists during the founding. More than a century passed before the Supreme Court agreed that at least some of the restrictions imposed on the national government by the Bill of Rights should be applied to the states as well.

Why Is a Bill of Rights Valuable?

Recall from Chapter 2 that we came very close to not having a Bill of Rights in the Constitution. The Federalists had argued that the Constitution itself was a bill of rights, that individual rights were already protected by many of the state constitutions, and that to list the powers that the national government did not have was dangerous, as it implied that it did have every other power.

habeas corpus
the right of an accused person to be brought before a judge and informed of the charges and evidence against him or her

bills of attainder
laws under which persons or groups are detained and sentenced without trial

ex post facto laws
laws that criminalize an action after it occurs

To some extent, they were correct in calling the Constitution a bill of rights in itself. Protection of some very specific rights is contained in the text of that document. The national government may not suspend writs of **habeas corpus,** which means that it cannot fail to bring prisoners, at their request, before a judge and inform the court why they are being held and what evidence it has against them. This protects people from being imprisoned solely for political reasons. Both the national and the state governments are forbidden to pass **bills of attainder,** which are laws that single out a person or group as guilty and impose punishment without a trial. Neither can they pass **ex post facto laws,** which are laws that make an action a crime after the fact, even though it was legal when it was committed. States may not impair or negate the obligation of contracts; here the founders obviously had the failings of the Articles of Confederation in mind. And the citizens of each state are entitled to "the privileges and immunities of the several states," which prevents any state from discriminating against citizens of other states. This protects a nonresident's right to travel freely, conduct business, and have access to state courts while visiting another state.[3] Of course, nonresidents are discriminated against when they have to pay a higher nonresident tuition to attend a state college or university, but the Supreme Court has ruled that this type of "discrimination" is not a violation of the privileges and immunities clause.

Some Federalists, however, including James Madison, came to agree with such Anti-Federalists as Thomas Jefferson, who wrote, "A bill of rights is what the people are entitled to against every government on earth."[4] Even though, as the Federalists argued, the national government was limited in principle by popular sovereignty (the concept that ultimate authority rests with the people), it could not hurt to limit it in practice as well. A specific list of the rights held by the people would give the judiciary a more effective check on the other branches.

Applying the Bill of Rights to the States

If you look closely at the Bill of Rights, you'll see that most of the limitations on government action are directed toward Congress. "Congress shall make no law . . . ," begins the First Amendment. Until about the turn of the twentieth century, the Supreme Court clearly stipulated that the Bill of Rights applied only to the national government and not to the states.[5]

Not until the passage of the Fourteenth Amendment in 1868 did the Constitution make it possible for the Court to require that states protect their citizens' basic liberties. That post–Civil War amendment was specifically designed to force southern states to extend the rights of citizenship to African Americans, but its wording left it open to other interpretations. The amendment says, in part,

> No State shall make or enforce any law which shall abridge the privileges and immunities of citizens of the United States; nor shall any State

Amendment	Addresses . . .	Case	Year
Fifth	Just compensation	*Chicago, Burlington & Quincy* v. *Chicago*	1897
First	Freedom of speech	*Gilbert* v. *Minnesota*	1920
		Gitlow v. *New York*	1925
		Fiske v. *Kansas*	1927
	Freedom of the press	*Near* v. *Minnesota*	1931
Sixth	Counsel in capital cases	*Powell* v. *Alabama*	1932
First	Religious freedom (generally)	*Hamilton* v. *Regents of California*	1934
	Freedom of assembly	*DeJonge* v. *Oregon*	1937
	Free exercise	*Cantwell* v. *Connecticut*	1940
	Religious establishment	*Everson* v. *Board of Education*	1947
Sixth	Public trial	In re *Oliver*	1948
Fourth	Unreasonable search and seizure	*Wolf* v. *Colorado*	1949
	Exclusionary rule	*Mapp* v. *Ohio*	1961
Eighth	Cruel and unusual punishment	*Robinson* v. *California*	1962
Sixth	Counsel in felony cases	*Gideon* v. *Wainwright*	1963
Fifth	Self-incrimination	*Malloy* v. *Hogan*	1964
Sixth	Impartial jury	*Parker* v. *Gladden*	1966
	Speedy trial	*Klopfer* v. *North Carolina*	1967
	Jury trial in serious crimes	*Duncan* v. *Louisiana*	1968
Fifth	Double jeopardy	*Benton* v. *Maryland*	1969

Figure 4.1
Applying the Bill of Rights to the States

deprive any person of life, liberty, or property, without due process of law; nor deny to any person within its jurisdiction the equal protection of the laws.

incorporation

Supreme Court action making the protections of the Bill of Rights applicable to the states

In 1897 the Supreme Court tentatively began the process of nationalization, or **incorporation,** of most (but not all) of the protections of the Bill of Rights into the states' Fourteenth Amendment obligations to guarantee their citizens due process of the law.[6] Through the process of incorporation, the Bill of Rights was gradually made applicable to the states.

It was not until the case of *Gitlow* v. *New York* (1920), however, that the Court began to articulate a clear theory of incorporation. In *Gitlow,* Justice Edward Sanford wrote, "We may and do assume that freedom of speech and of the press . . . are among the fundamental rights and liberties protected . . . from impairment by the states."[7] Without any great fanfare, the Court reversed almost a century of ruling by assuming that some rights are so fundamental that they deserve protection by the states as well as the federal government. This approach meant that all rights did not necessarily qualify for incorporation; the Court had to consider each on a case-by-case basis to see how fundamental it was. This was a tactic that Justice Benjamin Cardozo called **selective incorporation.** Over the years, the Court has switched between a theory of selective incorporation and total incorporation. As a result, almost all of the rights in the first ten amendments have been incorporated, with some notable exceptions, such as the Second Amendment (see Figure 4.1).

selective incorporation

incorporation of rights on a case-by-case basis

Keep in mind that since incorporation is a matter of interpretation rather than an absolute constitutional principle, it is a judicial creation. What justices create they can also uncreate if they change their minds or if the composition of the Court changes. Like all judicial creations, the process of incorporation is subject to reversal, and it is possible that such a reversal may currently be under way as today's more conservative Court narrows its understanding of the rights that states must protect.

WHO, WHAT, HOW   Because rights are so central to a democracy, citizens clearly have a stake in seeing that their rights are guaranteed at every level of government. The Supreme Court also has a stake in this process, which considerably expands its power over the states and within the federal government.

WHO are the actors?	WHAT do they want?	HOW do they get it?
Citizens	• Protection of their rights from abuse by the federal and state governments	• National Bill of Rights • State Bills of Rights • Incorporation
Supreme Court	• National control over which rights states must protect	• Fourteenth Amendment and selective incorporation

Freedom of Religion

The First Amendment reads, "Congress shall make no law respecting an establishment of religion, or prohibiting the free exercise thereof; or abridging the freedom of speech, or of the press; or the right of the people peaceably to assemble, and to petition the Government for a redress of grievances." These are the "democratic freedoms"—the liberties that the founders believed to be necessary to maintain a representative democracy by ensuring a free and unfettered people. For all that, none of these liberties has escaped controversy, and none has been interpreted by the Supreme Court to be absolute or unlimited.

Why Is Religious Freedom Valuable?

The briefest look around the world tells us what happens when politics and religion are allowed to mix: the Catholics and the Protestants battle in Northern Ireland; the Muslims and the Christians fight in Bosnia; the Jews and the Muslims go to war over land in Israel. When it comes to conflicts over religion—over our fundamental beliefs about the world and the way life should be lived—the stakes are enormous. Passions run deep, and compromise is difficult. In the United States, religious battles tend to take place in the courts, under the guidelines set out by the First Amendment.

While not all the founders endorsed religious freedom for everyone, some of them, notably Thomas Jefferson and James Madison, cherished the notion of a universal freedom of conscience—the right of all individuals to believe as they pleased. Jefferson wrote that the First Amendment built "a wall of separation between church and State."[8] The founders based their view of religious freedom on three main arguments. First, history has shown, from the Holy Roman Empire to the Church of England, that when church and state are linked, all individual freedoms are in jeopardy. After all, if government is merely the arm of God, what power of government cannot be justified? A second argument for practicing religious freedom is based on the effect that politics can have on religious concerns. Early champions of a separation between politics and religion worried that the spiritual purity and sanctity of religion would be ruined if it was mixed with the worldly realm of politics, with its emphasis on power and influence.[9] Finally, as politics can have negative effects on religion, so religion can have negative effects on politics, dividing society into the factions that Madison saw as the primary threat to republican government.

The Establishment Clause

establishment clause the First Amendment guarantee that the government will not create and support an official state church

separationists supporters of a "wall of separation" between church and state

accommodationists supporters of government nonpreferential accommodation of religions

The beginning of the First Amendment, forbidding Congress to make laws that would establish an official religion, is known as the **establishment clause.** Americans have fought over the meaning of the establishment clause almost since its inception. Although founders such as Jefferson and Madison were clear on their position that church and state should be separate realms, other early Americans were not.

A similar division continues today between **separationists,** who believe that a "wall" should exist between church and state, and nonpreferentialists, or **accommodationists,** who contend that the state should not be separate from religion but rather should accommodate it, without showing a preference for one religion over another. Accommodationists argue that the First Amendment should not prevent government aid to religious groups, prayer in school or during public ceremonies, public aid to parochial schools, the posting of religious documents such as the Ten Commandments in public places, or the teaching of the Bible's story of creation along with evolution in public schools. Adherents of this position claim that a rigid interpretation of separation of church and state amounts to intolerance of their religious rights or, in the words of Supreme Court Justice Anthony Kennedy, to "unjustified hostility to religion."[10] President Ronald Reagan, both Presidents Bush, and many other Republicans share this view, as have powerful interest groups, including the Moral Majority and the Christian Coalition.

There is clearly a lot at stake in the battle between the separationists and the accommodationists. On one side of the dispute is the separationists' image of a society in which all citizens' rights, including minorities', receive equal protection by the law. In this society, private religions abound, but they remain private, not matters for public action or support. Very different is the view of the accommodationists, which emphasizes the sharing of community values, determined by the majority and built into the fabric of society and political life.

Recent Rulings on the Establishment Clause

Today U.S. practice stands somewhere between these two images. Sessions of Congress open with prayers, for instance, but a school child's day does not. Religion is not kept completely out of our public lives, but the Supreme Court has generally leaned toward a separationist stance. In the 1960s, the Court tried to cement this stance, refining a test that made it unconstitutional for the government to pass laws that affect religion unless the laws have what the Court has called a "secular intent" (that is, a nonreligious intent) and "a primary effect that neither advances nor inhibits religion."[11] The Court struck down state laws requiring that the Bible be read at the start of the day in public schools,[12] that the school day begin with the Lord's Prayer,[13] and that nondenominational prayers be required of public school children.[14] It also struck down a law that prohibited the teaching of evolution in public schools.[15] With these rulings, the Court was aligning itself firmly with the separationist interpretation of the establishment clause.

The Lemon Test

As the more conservative appointments of Republican presidents Richard Nixon and Ronald Reagan began to shape the Supreme Court, its rulings moved in a more accommodationist direction. In *Lemon* v. *Kurtzman* (1971), the Court added to the old test a third provision that a law not foster "an excessive government entanglement with religion."[16] Under the new **Lemon test,** the justices had to decide how much entanglement there was between politics and religion, leaving much to their own discretion.

Lemon test
three-pronged rule used by the courts to determine whether the establishment clause has been violated

As the current rule in deciding establishment cases, the *Lemon* test is not as useful as it could be, primarily because the justices really have not settled among themselves the underlying issues of whether religion and politics should be separate or whether state support of religion is permissible. Although the justices still lean in a separationist direction, their rulings are divided, with their vote being split on a number of cases since the mid-1980s.[17]

The Free Exercise Clause

Another fundamental question that divides the public and justices alike is what to do when religious beliefs and practices conflict with state goals. The second part of the First Amendment grant of religious freedom guarantees that Congress shall make no law prohibiting the free exercise of religion. The **free exercise clause,** as it is called, has generated as much controversy as the establishment clause. When is the state justified in regulating religion? While Americans have an absolute right to believe whatever they want, their freedom to act is subject to government regulation.[18] The state's **police power** allows it to regulate behavior in order to protect its citizens and to provide social order and security. These two valued goods of religious freedom and social order are bound to conflict, and the Court has had an uneasy time trying to draw the line between them.

The Court's ambivalence can be seen in two cases, three years apart, concerning the obligation to salute the flag. In *Minersville School District* v. *Gobitis* (1940), two children of a Jehovah's Witness family, whose religion forbids the worshiping of graven images, were expelled from school for violating a rule that required them to salute the flag each day.[19] The Court rejected their father's claim that the rule violated his children's religious freedom, arguing that children are required to salute the flag to promote national unity, which in turn fosters national security. Within three years, however, the composition of the Court had changed, and several members had changed their minds. *West Virginia State Board of Education* v. *Barnette* (1943) again dealt with children of Jehovah's Witnesses who were expelled for refusing to salute the flag, but this time the Court overturned the school board's rule requiring the salute.[20] In his opinion for the majority, Justice Robert Jackson said that the one certain thing in American constitutional law is that no official can tell anyone what to think about politics or religion or force them to confess what they believe.

While *Barnette* still holds, the Court has gone back and forth on other religious freedom issues as it has struggled to define what actions the state might legitimately seek to regulate. Under their police power, states have been allowed to require that businesses close on Sundays or that certain merchandise not be sold then. Such laws have forced people whose religions require them to hold Saturday as the Sabbath either to take two days off and lose business or to violate their religious beliefs. In *The Blue Law Cases,* the Court argued that the states are within their rights to require Sunday closings as a provision for a day of rest and that the Sunday closing laws, while religious in origin, no longer contain religious intent.[21] In *Sherbert* v. *Verner* (1963), however, the Court seemed to contradict itself. A Seventh-Day Adventist, for whom Saturday is the Sabbath, was fired from a company for refusing to work on Saturday and was denied unemployment compensation when she refused to take other jobs with compulsory Saturday hours. The Supreme Court found in favor of Sherbert, finding the denial of benefits was a clear violation of her constitutional rights. The Court wrote that any incidental burden placed on religious freedom must be justified by a **compelling state interest**—that is, the state must show that it is absolutely necessary for some fundamental state purpose that religious freedom be limited.[22] Requiring that the state have a compelling interest in regulating behavior provides considerable protection to religious freedom.

The Court later rejected this compelling state interest test, however, in *Employment*

free exercise clause the First Amendment guarantee that citizens may freely engage in the religious activities of their choice

police power the ability of a government to protect its citizens and maintain social order

compelling state interest a fundamental state purpose, which must be shown before the law can limit some freedoms or treat some groups of people differently

Division, Department of Human Resources v. *Smith,* where it upheld a law denying state unemployment benefits to employees of a drug rehabilitation organization who were fired for using peyote, a hallucinogenic drug, for sacramental purposes in religious ceremonies.[23] Here the Court held that if the infringement on religion is not intentional but is rather the by-product of a general law prohibiting socially harmful conduct, applied equally to all religions, it is not unconstitutional. It found that the compelling state interest test, though necessary in cases dealing with matters of race and free speech, was inappropriate for religious freedom issues.

Religious groups consider the *Smith* ruling a major blow to religious freedom because it places the burden of proof on the individual or church to show that its religious practices should not be punished, rather than on the state to show that the interference with religious practices is absolutely necessary. In response to the *Smith* decision, Congress in 1993 passed the Religious Freedom Restoration Act (RFRA). This act, supported by a coalition of ninety religious groups, restored the compelling state interest test for state action limiting religious practices and required that when a state did restrict religious practices, the restrictions must be carried out in the least burdensome way. The Supreme Court, however, did not allow the law to stand. In the 1997 case of *Boerne* v. *Flores,*[24] the Court held that the RFRA was an unconstitutional exercise of congressional power and that it constituted too great an intrusion on government power. Religious groups have declared the *Boerne* ruling an assault on religious freedom and have called for the passage of RFRA legislation at the state level. Some even support an amendment to the U.S. Constitution to restore the protection of the former interpretation of the First Amendment.

WHO, WHAT, HOW   Religious freedom has proved to be a battleground on which citizens fight fiercely because such fundamental principles are at stake.

WHO are the actors?	WHAT do they want?	HOW do they get it?
Citizens	• No established religion • Freedom to practice religion	• First Amendment establishment and free exercise clauses
Separationists	• Separation of church and state	• *Smith/Boerne,* overturning compelling state interest test
Accommodationists	• Accommodation of religion	• RFRA • State law, constitutional amendment, reversal of court rulings

Freedom of Expression

Among the most cherished of American values is our right to free speech. The First Amendment says that "Congress shall make no law . . . abridging the freedom of speech, or of the press," and, at least theoretically, most Americans agree.[25] When it comes to actually practicing free speech, however, our national record is not impressive. In fact, time and again, Congress has made laws abridging freedom of expression, often with the enthusiastic support of much of the American public. As a nation, we have never had a great deal of difficulty restricting speech we don't like, admire, or respect. The challenge of the First Amendment has always been to protect the speech we despise.

Why Is Freedom of Expression Valuable?

Freedom of expression is valuable in a democratic society for several important reasons. First, free speech is important because citizens are responsible for participating in their government's decisions and they need information provided by a free and independent press to protect them from government manipulation. A second, and related, reason to value free speech is that it can limit government corruption. By being free to voice criticism of government, to investigate its actions, and to debate its decisions, both citizens and journalists are able to exercise an additional check on government that supplements our valued principle of checks and balances.

A third reason for allowing free speech—even (or especially) speech of which we do not approve—is the danger of setting a precedent of censorship. Censorship in a democracy usually allows the voice of the majority to prevail. One of the reasons to support minority rights as well as majority rule, however, is that we never know when we may fall into the minority on an issue.

A fourth reason that free speech is valuable comes from the nineteenth-century English philosopher John Stuart Mill, who argued that there should be no limits on speech because only by allowing the free traffic of all ideas—those known to be true as well as those suspected to be false—can we ensure the vigorous protection of the truth. By allowing the expression of all speech, we discover truths we had previously believed to be false (the earth is not flat after all), and we develop strong defenses against known falsehoods like racist and sexist ideas.

Freedom of speech, it can thus be argued, is important for making democracy function well, for preventing corruption and tyranny in government, for preserving minorities against the power of majorities, and for strengthening and defending the truth. Why, then, is it so controversial? Like freedom of religion, free speech requires tolerance of ideas and beliefs other than our own, even ideas and beliefs that we find personally repugnant. Those who are convinced that their views are eternally true often see no real reason to practice tolerance. Many people believe that in a democracy, the majority should determine the prevailing views and the minority, having lost the vote, so to speak, should shut up. In this section, we look at the way the Supreme Court has handled the American dilemma over free speech.

Speech That Criticizes the Government

sedition   speech that criticizes the government

Speech that criticizes the government, called **sedition,** has long been a target of restrictive legislation, and most of the founders were quite content that it should be so. Of course, all of the founders had engaged daily in the practice of criticizing their government when they were in the process of inciting their countrymen to revolution against England, so they were well aware of the potential consequences of seditious activity. Now that the shoe was on the other foot and they were the government, many were far less willing to encourage dissent. Especially during wartime, it was felt, criticism of the government undermined authority and destroyed patriotism.

It didn't take long for American "revolutionaries" to pass the Alien and Sedition Act of 1798, which outlawed "any false, scandalous writing against the government of the United States." Throughout the 1800s and into the next century, all levels of government, with the support and encouragement of public opinion, squashed the views of radical political groups, labor activists, religious sects, and other minorities. By the end of World War I, thirty-two of forty-eight states had laws against sedition, which essentially prohibited the advocacy of the use of violence or force to bring about industrial or political change. In 1917 the U.S. Congress passed the Espionage Act, which made it a crime to "willfully obstruct the recruiting or enlistment service of the United States," and a 1918 amendment to the act spelled out what that meant. It became a crime to engage in "any disloyal . . . scurrilous, or abusive language about the form of government of the United States, . . . or any language intended to bring the form of government of the United States . . . into contempt, scorn, contumely, or disrepute."[26] Such sweeping prohibitions made it possible to arrest people on the flimsiest of pretexts.

Those arrested and imprisoned under the new sedition laws looked to the Supreme Court to protect their freedom to criticize the government, but they were doomed to disappointment. The Court did not dispute the idea that speech criticizing the government could be punished. The question it dealt with was just how bad the speech had to be before it could be prohibited. The history of freedom of speech cases is a history of the Court devising tests for itself to determine whether certain speech should be protected or could be legitimately outlawed.

clear and present danger test   rule used by the Court in which language can be regulated only if it presents an immediate and urgent danger

In two cases upholding the Espionage Act, *Schenck* v. *United States* (1919) and *Abrams* v. *United States* (1919), Justice Oliver Wendell Holmes began to articulate what he called the **clear and present danger test.**[27] This test, as Holmes conceived it, focused on the circumstances under which language was used. If there were no immediately threatening circumstances, the language in question would be protected, and Congress could not regulate it. But Holmes's views did not represent the majority opinion of the Court, and the clear and present danger test was slow to catch on.

With the tensions that led to World War II, Congress again began to fear the power of foreign ideas, especially communism. The Smith Act of 1940 made it illegal to advocate the violent overthrow of the government or to belong to an organization that did so. The McCarran Act of 1950 required members of the Communist Party to register with the U.S. attorney general. At the same time, Senator Joseph McCarthy was conducting investigations of American citizens to search out communists, and the House Un-American Activities Committee was doing the same thing. The suspicion or accusation of being involved in communism was enough to stain a person's reputation irreparably, even if there were no evidence to back up the claim. Many careers and lives were ruined in the process.

Again the Supreme Court did not weigh in on the side of civil liberties. Convictions under the Smith and McCarran Acts were upheld. The Court had used the clear and present danger test intermittently in the years since 1919, but usually not as Holmes and Brandeis intended, to limit speech only in the rarest and most dire circumstances. Instead, the clear and present danger test had come to be seen as a kind of balancing test in which the interests of society in prohibiting the speech were weighed against the value of free speech. The emphasis on an obvious and immediate danger was lost.

The Court's record as a supporter of sedition laws finally ended with the personnel changes that brought Earl Warren to the position of chief justice in 1953. In 1969 the Court ruled that abstract teaching of violence is not the same as incitement to violence. In a concurring opinion, Justice William O. Douglas pointed out that it was time to get rid of the clear and present danger test because it was so subject to misuse and manipulation. Speech, except when linked with action, he said, should be immune from prosecution.[28]

Symbolic Speech

The question of what to do when speech is linked to action remained. Many forms of expression go beyond mere speech or writing. No one disputes that government has the right to regulate actions and behavior if it believes it has sufficient cause, but what happens when that behavior is also expression? Is burning a draft card, wearing an arm band to protest a war, or torching the American flag an action or an expression? The Supreme Court, generally speaking, has been more willing to allow regulation of symbolic speech than of speech alone, especially if such regulation is not a direct attempt to curtail the speech.

We already saw, under freedom of religion, that the Court has decided that the Constitution protects some symbolic expression, such as saluting or not saluting the American flag. But drawing the line between what is and is not protected has been extremely difficult for the Court. In *United States* v. *O'Brien* (1968), the Court held that burning a draft card at a rally protesting the Vietnam War was not protected speech because the law against burning draft cards was not aimed at restricting expression and fulfilled an important government interest.[29] Following that reasoning, in 1969 the Court struck down a school rule forbidding students to wear black arm bands as an expression of their opposition to the Vietnam War, arguing that the fear of a disturbance was not a sufficient state interest to warrant the suppression.[30]

One of the most divisive issues of symbolic speech that has confronted the Supreme Court, and indeed the American public, concerns that ultimate symbol of our country, the American flag. There is probably no more effective way of showing one's dissatisfaction with the United States or its policies than burning the Stars and Stripes. Emotions ride high on this issue. In 1969 the Court split five to four when it overturned the conviction of a person who had broken a New York law making it illegal to deface or show disrespect for the flag (he had burned it).[31] Twenty years later, with a more conservative Court in place, the issue was raised again. Again the Court divided five to four, voting to protect the burning of the flag as symbolic expression.[32] Because the patriotic feelings of so many Americans were fired up by this ruling, Congress passed the federal Flag Protection Act in 1989, making it a crime to desecrate the flag. In *United States* v. *Eichman,* the Court declared the federal law unconstitutional for the same reasons it had overturned the state laws earlier: all were aimed specifically at "suppressing expression."[33] The only way to get around a Supreme Court ruling of unconstitutionality is to amend the Constitution. Efforts to pass an amendment have failed in the House and Senate, meaning that despite the strong feeling of the majority to the contrary, flag burning is still considered protected speech in the United States.

Freedom of Assembly

freedom of assembly   the right of people to gather peacefully and to petition government

Closely related to symbolic speech is an additional First Amendment guarantee, **freedom of assembly,** or "the right of the people peaceably to assemble, and to petition the Government for a redress of grievances." The courts have interpreted this to mean not only that people can meet and express their views collectively but also that their very association is protected as a form of political expression. So, for instance, they have ruled that groups such as the National Association for the Advancement of Colored People (NAACP) cannot be required to make their membership lists public[34] (although groups deemed to have unlawful purposes do not have such protection) and that teachers do not have to reveal what associations they belong to.[35] In addition, the Court has basically upheld people's right to associate with whomever they please, although it has held that public[36] and, in some circumstances, private groups cannot discriminate on the basis of race or sex.[37]

Obscenity and Pornography

Of all the forms of expression, obscenity has probably presented the Court with its biggest headaches. In attempting to define it, Justice Potter Stewart could only conclude, "I know it when I see it."[38] The Court has used a variety of tests for determining whether material is obscene, but until the early 1970s, only the most hard-core pornography was regulated.

Miller test   rule used by the courts in which the definition of *obscenity* must be based on local standards

Coming into office in 1969, however, President Richard Nixon made it one of his administration's goals to control pornography in America. Once the Court began to reflect the ideological change that came with Nixon's appointees, rulings became more restrictive. In 1973 the Court developed the **Miller test,** which returned more control over the definition of obscenity to state legislatures and local standards. Under the *Miller* test, the Court asks "whether the work depicts or describes, in a patently offensive way, sexual conduct specifically defined by state law" and "whether the work, taken as a whole, lacks serious literary, artistic, political or scientific value" (called the SLAPS test).[39] These provisions have also been open to interpretation, and the Court has tried to refine them over time. The emphasis on local standards has meant that pornographers can look for those places with the most lenient definitions of obscenity in which to produce and market their work, and the Court has let this practice go on.

The issue of whether obscenity should be protected speech raises some fundamental issues and has created some unlikely alliances. Justice John Marshall Harlan was quite right when he wrote that "one man's vulgarity is another man's lyric."[40] People offended by what they consider to be obscenity believe that their values should be represented in their communities. If that means banning adult bookstores, nude dancing in bars, and naked women on magazine covers at the supermarket, then so be it. But opponents argue that what is obscene to one person may be art or enjoyment to another. The problem of majorities enforcing decisions on minorities is inescapable here. A second issue that has generated debate over these cases is the feminist critique that pornography represents aggression toward women and should be banned primarily because it perpetuates stereotypes and breeds violence. Thus radical feminists, usually on the left end of the political spectrum, have found themselves in alliance with conservatives on the right. There is a real contradiction here for feminists, who are more often likely to argue for the expansion of rights, particularly as they apply to women. Feminists advocating restrictions on pornography reconcile the contradiction by arguing that the proliferation of pornography ultimately limits women's rights by making life more threatening and fundamentally unequal.

Fighting Words and Offensive Speech

fighting words
speech intended to incite violence

Among the categories of speech the Court has ruled may be regulated is one called **fighting words,** words whose express purpose is to create a disturbance and incite violence in the person who hears the speech.[41] However, the Court rarely upholds legislation designed to limit fighting words unless the law is written very carefully and specifically. Consequently, it has held that threatening and provocative language is protected unless it is likely to "produce a clear and present danger of serious substantive evil that rises far above public inconvenience, annoyance, or unrest."[42] It has also ruled that offensive language, though not protected by the First Amendment, may occasionally contain a political message, in which case constitutional protection applies.[43]

political correctness
the idea that language shapes behavior and therefore should be regulated to control its social effects

These rulings have taken on modern-day significance in the wake of the **political correctness** movement that swept the country in the late 1980s and 1990s, especially on college campuses. Political correctness refers to an ideology, held primarily by some liberals, including some civil rights activists and feminists, that language shapes society in critical ways, and therefore that racist, sexist, homophobic, or any other language that demeans any group of individuals should be silenced to minimize its social effects. An outgrowth of the political correctness movement was the passing of speech codes on college campuses that ban speech that might be offensive to women or ethnic and other minorities. Critics of speech codes, and of political correctness in general, argue that such practices unfairly repress free speech, which should flourish on, of all places, college campuses. In 1989 and 1991, federal district court judges agreed, finding speech codes on two campuses, the University of Michigan and the University of Wisconsin, in violation of students' First Amendment rights.[44] Neither school appealed. The Supreme Court spoke on a related issue in 1992 when it struck down a Minnesota "hate crime law." The Court held that it is unconstitutional to outlaw broad categories of speech based on its content. The prohibition against activities that "arouse anger, alarm or resentment in others on the basis of race, color, creed, religion or gender" was too sweeping and thus unconstitutional.[45]

Freedom of the Press

The First Amendment covers not only freedom of speech but also freedom of the press. Many of the controversial issues we have already covered apply to both of these areas, but some problems are confronted exclusively, or primarily, by the press. Among these are the issue of prior restraint, libel restrictions, the conflict between a free press and a fair trial, and the issue of censorship on the Internet.

prior restraint punishment for expression of ideas before the ideas are spoken or printed

Prior Restraint   **Prior restraint,** a restriction on the press before its message is actually published, was the primary target of the founders when they drew up the First Amendment. The Supreme Court has shared the founders' concern that prior restraint is a particularly dangerous form of censorship and has almost never permitted it. Two classic judgments illustrate their view. In *Near* v. *Minnesota,* Jay Near's newspaper, the *Saturday Press,* was critical of African Americans, Jews, Catholics, and organized labor. His paper was shut down in 1927 under a Minnesota law that prohibited any publication of "malicious, scandalous and defamatory" material. If he had continued to publish the paper, he would have been subject to a $1,000 fine or a year in jail. The Court held that the Minnesota law infringed on Near's freedom of the press. Although an extreme emergency, such as war, might justify previous restraint on the press, wrote Justice Charles Evans Hughes, the purpose of the First Amendment is to limit it to those rare circumstances.[46] Similarly and more recently, in *New York Times Company* v. *United States,* the Court prevented the Nixon administration from stopping the publication by the *New York Times* and the *Washington Post* of a "top-secret" document about U.S. involvement in Vietnam. The so-called Pentagon Papers were claimed by the government to be too sensitive to national security to be published. The Court held that "security" is too vague to be allowed to excuse the violation of the First Amendment. To grant such power to the president, it ruled, would be to run the risk of destroying the liberty that the government is trying to secure.[47]

libel written defamation of character

Libel   Freedom of the press also collides with the issue of **libel,** the written defamation of character (verbal defamation is called *slander*). Obviously, it is crucial to the watchdog and information-providing roles of the press that journalists be able to speak freely about the character and actions of those in public service. But at the same time, because careers and reputations are easily ruined by rumors and innuendoes, journalists ought to be required to "speak" responsibly. The Supreme Court addressed this issue in *New York Times* v. *Sullivan,* where it ruled that public officials, as opposed to private individuals, when suing for libel, must show that a publication acted with "actual malice," which means not that the paper had an evil intent but that it acted with "knowledge that [what it printed] was false or with reckless disregard for whether it was false or not."[48] Shortly thereafter, the Court extended the ruling to include public figures other than officials. Public figures might include movie or television stars, sports celebrities, or musicians, as well as other people whose actions put them in a public position—a candidate running for office, an author promoting her book, or the host of a radio talk show.

The Court's rulings attempt to give the press some leeway in its actions. Without *Sullivan*, investigative journalism would never have been able to uncover the United States' role in Vietnam, for instance, or the Watergate cover-up. Freedom of the press, and thus the public's interest in keeping a critical eye on government, are clearly the winners here. The Court's view is that when individuals put themselves in the public domain, the public's interest in the truth outweighs the protection of their privacy.

The Right to a Fair Trial   Freedom of the press also confronts head-on another Bill of Rights guarantee, the right to a fair trial. Media coverage of a crime can make it very difficult to find an "impartial jury," as required by the Sixth Amendment. Publicity during a trial can arguably violate the privacy rights of both defendant and victim. On the other side of this conflict, however, is the "public's right to know." The Sixth Amendment promises a "speedy and public trial," and many journalists interpret this to mean that the proceedings ought to be open. The courts, however, have usually held that this amendment protects the rights of the accused, not of the public. But while the Supreme Court has overturned a murder verdict because a judge failed to control the media circus in his courtroom,[49] on the whole it has ruled in favor of media access to most stages of legal proceedings. Likewise, courts have been extremely reluctant to uphold gag orders, which would impose prior restraint on the press during those proceedings.[50]

Censorship on the Internet

Lawmakers do not always know how to deal with new outlets for expression as they become available. Modern technology has presented the judiciary with a host of free speech issues the founders never anticipated. The latest to make it to the courts is the question of censorship on the Internet, a vast electronic network linking computers worldwide and permitting individuals to set up sites that can be visited by anyone with access to the World Wide Web. Some of these sites contain explicit sexual material, obscene language, and other content that many people find objectionable. Since children often find their way onto the Net on their own, parents and groups of other concerned citizens have clamored for regulation of this medium. Congress obliged in 1996 with the Communications Decency Act (CDA), which made it illegal to knowingly send or display indecent material on the Internet. In 1997 the Supreme Court ruled that such provisions constituted a violation of free speech and that communication via the Internet, which it called a modern "town crier," is subject to the same protections as nonelectronic expression. Arguing that the CDA prohibitions were so broad as to even exclude e-mail between a parent and a child, the Court quoted itself in a former case: "Regardless of the strength of the government's interest in protecting children, 'the level of discourse reaching a mailbox cannot be limited to that which would be suitable for a sandbox.' "[51] (For some tips on how to evaluate what *you* find on the Internet, see Consider the Source: How to be a Savvy Web Surfer.)

CONSIDER THE SOURCE

How to Be a Savvy Web Surfer

P. T. Barnum said there's a sucker born every minute—and that was decades *before* the advent of the Internet. He would have rubbed his hands in glee over the gullibility of the electronic age. While freedom of speech is a powerful liberty, as we have seen in this chapter, one consequence is that it makes it very difficult to tell people to keep their mouths shut. We regulate radio and TV, of course, but that is because these media were originally (before the days of cable and satellites) held to be scarce resources that belonged to the public. Private publishers can enforce standards of excellence, or accuracy, or style, on what they publish but when a medium is quasi public, like the Internet, and access to it is easy and cheap, it is impossible to restrict the views and ideas that are published without also doing some serious damage to freedom of speech. Consequently anything goes, and it is up to us as consumers to sort the grain from the chaff.

Today we have access to more information than we could ever have imagined, but we are not trained to use it critically and competently. Recently, a father and son traveled six hours from Canada to Mankato, Minnesota, lured by a web site singing the praises of Mankato's sunny beaches and whale watching opportunities.[1] The site turned out to be a spoof perpetrated by winter-weary Mankato residents. Confronted with the reality of more of the frozen north they had just left, the disillusioned dad was angry, but a reasonable target of his anger might have been his own eagerness and willingness to believe unquestioningly what he read on the Web.

All of us, of course—professors, students, politicians, journalists, doctors, lawyers, CEOs, and anyone else with access to the Web—are potential suckers when it comes to the Web. The Internet is merely an electronic link between those who have information to give, and those who want information—much like the telephone. Anyone who has the small amount of money needed to set up a web page can get on the Web and disseminate information. Discussing the curious willingness of Pierre Salinger, former press secretary to President Kennedy, to believe an Internet report that the 1996 crash of TWA flight 800 was due to "friendly fire" from American military aircraft, one author likens it to the conviction that something is true just because we heard it on the phone, or found it on a document "blowing across a busy city street."[2]

The fact that some piece of information appears on a computer screen does not confer any special distinction on it, or make it more reliable than any other rumor we may happen to hear. This is not to disparage everything that you find on the Internet. Some of it is terrific, and our ability to surf the Web in search of new information expands our intellectual horizons like nothing has since the invention of the printing press. What allows us to rely on what we find on the Internet is our own hard work and careful scrutiny. Here are some tips to help you become a savvy surfer of the World Wide Web.

1. **Find out the source of the web site.** Examine the web address, or URL, for clues. Web addresses end with .com, .org, .gov, .net, or .edu, to indicate commercial, nonprofit, government, network, or educational sites. Sites from other countries end with abbreviations of the nation. For example, ".kr" indicates the site is from Korea and ".fr" indicates France. If a tilde (~) appears in the address, it is likely to be a personal home page, rather than an official site.[3] Remember, however, that anyone can purchase rights to a web address; an official looking address does not necessarily confer legitimacy on a site.

2. **Check out the author of the site.** Sometimes it is not who it seems to be—many authors try to disguise the source of their sites to gain respectability for their ideas or to lure users further into a site. Amnesty International, a global human rights organization, maintains a site at www.amnesty.org/tunisia to refute what it says are false claims by the Tunisian government, posted at www.amnesty-tunisia.org. The Tunisian government's address is deliberately designed to encourage users to think they are reading the Amnesty International point of view, and that Amnesty International approves of Tunisian policy, which it does not.[4] Similarly, some members of hate groups in the United States and elsewhere create sites that seem to support groups or individuals who turn out to be their targets. A site that at first appears to be a tribute to Martin Luther King accuses him

several links later of being "just a degenerate, an America-hating Communist."[5]

3. **If something about a site does not look right (what one author calls the "J.D.L.R." or the Just Doesn't Look Right, test), investigate more closely.**[6] Be suspicious if, for example, you notice lots of misspellings or grammatical errors, or if the site has an odd design. Analyze the site's tone and approach. A very shrill or combative tone could signal a lack of objectivity. When a familiar site doesn't look the way you expect it to, consider the possibility that hackers have broken into it and changed its content. Users of the C-SPAN site looking up television scheduling in September 1999 were greeted by a hacker's screen displaying song lyrics, but no schedules. The next day CNN apologized for the glitch, saying that someone outside CSPAN had invaded their site. Sometimes hackers go for more subtle alterations that are not immediately obvious. Ultimately, remember this: anyone can put up a web site—even you. Are you a reliable enough source to be quoted in a college student's research paper?

4. **Find out who is footing the bill.** Whoever said there is no such thing as a free lunch might have been speaking of the Internet. Ultimately our access to the glorious world of cyberspace must be paid for, and since we as consumers seem to be singularly unwilling to pay for the information we find, providers of that information are increasingly looking to advertisers to pick up the bill.[7] Commercial interests can shape the content of what we find on the Web in any number of ways; links to sponsors' pages may appear prominently on a web page, web sites may promote the products of their advertisers as if they were objectively recommending them without making the financial relationship clear, or the commercial bias may be even more subtle. Amazon.com, an online bookseller that provides reviews of the books it sells, admitted in early 1999 that it showcased the reviews of books whose publishers paid for this special treatment. Such behavior, while perfectly legal, is misleading to the consumer, who has no way of knowing whether he or she is getting straight advice or a paid advertisement. Even the search engines you use to find the sites, such as Yahoo or Lycos, are supported by advertisers, and may give preference to their sponsors' sites when you think you are conducting an impartial search. One author says that "trusting an Internet site to navigate the World Wide Web . . . is like following a helpful stranger in Morocco who offers to take you to the best rug store. You may very well find what you are looking for, but your guide will get a piece of whatever you spend."[8]

5. **Use the Internet to evaluate the Internet.** You can find out who runs a site by going to rs.internic.net and using the "whois" search function. This will give you names and contact information but is not, warns Tina Kelly of the *New York Times,* conclusive. Similarly, she suggests running authors' names through a search engine or Dejanews.com, which searches newsgroups, to see what you can find out about them. Some browsers will tell you when a site was last updated. On Netscape, for instance, you can get this information by clicking on the View option and going to Page Info or Document Info. And remember that you can always e-mail authors of a site and ask for their credentials.[9] If there is no contact information for the author in the site itself, that alone can tell you something about its reliability. For more information on how to evaluate various types of web sites, check out the Widener University Wolfgram Memorial Library's "Evaluating Web Pages" at http://www2.widener.edu/ Wolfgram-Memorial-Library/webeval.htm.

6. **Note the other kinds of information the site directs you to.** If you are in doubt about a site's legitimacy, check some of its links to external sites. Are they up-to-date and well maintained? Do they help you identify the ideological, commercial, or other bias the site may contain? If there are no links to other sites, ask yourself what this might mean.

---

[1]Tina Kelly, "Whales in the Minnesota River? Only on the Web, Where Skepticism is a Required Navigational Aid," *New York Times,* 4 March 1999, D1.

[2]David Sieg, "The Internet as an Information Source," posted on the Web, 12/17/96. http://www.tricon.net/Features/infosources.html

[3]Kelly, D9.

[4]Kelly, D9.

[5]Michel Marriot, "Rising Tide: Sites Born of Hate," *New York Times,* 18 March 1999, G1.

[6]Kelly, D1.

[7]Saul Hansell and Amy Harmon, "Caveat Emptor on the Web: Ad and Editorial Lines Blur," *New York Times* on the Web, 26 February 1999.

[8]Hansell and Harmon.   [9]Kelly, D9.

WHO, WHAT, HOW   No less than the success of free democratic government is at stake in the issue of freedom of expression.

WHO are the actors?	WHAT do they want?	HOW do they get it?
Citizens	• Information about government	• Free speech and press
	• Limited corruption	• Clear and present danger
	• Protection of minority rights	• *Miller* test
	• Vigorous defense of the truth	• Revised libel laws
	• Political, social, and moral order	

The Right to Bear Arms

The Second Amendment to the Constitution reads, "A well regulated Militia, being necessary to the security of a free State, the right of the people to keep and bear Arms, shall not be infringed." This amendment has been the subject of some of the fiercest debates in American politics. Originally, it was a seemingly straightforward effort by opponents of the Constitution to keep the federal government in check by limiting the power of standing, or permanent, armies. Over time, it has become a rallying point for those who want to engage in sporting activities involving guns, those who believe that firearms are necessary for self-defense, those who oppose contemporary American policy and want to use revolution to return to what they think were the goals of the founders, and those who simply don't believe that it is government's business to make decisions about who can own guns.

While various kinds of gun control legislation have been passed at the state and local levels, powerful interest groups like the National Rifle Association (NRA) have kept it to a minimum at the national level. The 1990s, however, saw the passage of three federal bills that affect the right to bear arms: the 1993 Brady Bill, requiring background checks on potential handgun purchasers; the 1994 Crime Bill, barring semiautomatic assault weapons; and a 1995 bill making it illegal to carry a gun near a school. The 1995 law and the interim provisions of the Brady Bill, which imposed a five-day waiting period for all gun sales, with local background checks until a national background check system could be established, were struck down by the Supreme Court on the grounds that they were unconstitutional infringements of the national government on state power.[52] In the wake of the school shooting in Littleton, Colorado, in the spring of 1999, new gun control measures were proposed in Congress, and the issue was once again on the federal agenda.

Why Is the Right to Bear Arms Valuable?

During the earliest days of American independence, the chief source of national stability was the state militia system—armies of able-bodied men who could be counted

Go Ahead, Make My Day
The pistol this woman is checking out at a National Rifle Association (NRA) convention wasn't designed for shooting squirrels. NRA supporters believe the freedoms ensured by the Second Amendment are as relevant as ever. Opponents cite sobering statistics: for instance, in 1996 handguns were used in over 80 percent of armed robberies and accounted for more than eight thousand murders.

on to assemble, with their own guns, to defend their country from external and internal threats, whether from the British, Native Americans, or local insurrection. Local militias were seen as far less dangerous to the fledgling republic than a standing army under national leadership. Such an army could seize control and create a military dictatorship, depriving citizens of their hard-won rights.

The restructuring of the U.S. military and the growing evidence that under civilian control it did not pose a threat to the liberties of American citizens caused many people to view the Second Amendment as obsolete. But although the militia system that gave rise to the amendment is now defunct, supporters of rights for gun owners, such as the NRA, argue that the amendment is as relevant as ever because hunting and other leisure activities involving guns do not hurt anybody (except, of course, the hunted) and are an important part of American culture; because possession of guns is necessary for self-defense; because citizens should have the right to arm themselves to protect their families and property from a potentially tyrannical government; and because the federal government does not have the power to regulate gun use.

Opponents of these views, such as Handgun Control and the Coalition to Stop Gun Violence, counter that none of these claims has anything to do with the Second Amendment, which refers only to the use and ownership of guns by state militia members; that countries with stricter gun control laws have less violence and fewer gun deaths; that none of the rights of Americans, even such fundamental ones as freedom of speech and the press, is absolute; and that it is ironic to claim the protection of the Constitution to own weapons that could be used to overturn the government based on that Constitution.[53]

Judicial Decisions

The Supreme Court has ruled on only six cases that have an impact on gun rights and the Second Amendment. Because federal gun control legislation has been scarce until recently, most of the cases dealt with gun control efforts at the state and local levels. In these cases, the Court has kept a narrow definition of the Second Amendment as intending to arm state militias, and it has let state gun-related legislation stand.[54] The Court did strike down the legislation concerning possession of guns near schools and reversed one provision of the Brady Bill on federalism, not Second Amendment, grounds. In the close Brady case, four dissenters argued that the burden put on the localities by the bill was not disproportionate to the good done by addressing what they called an "epidemic of gun violence."[55] Federalism has been a divisive issue in the Court, but the Second Amendment has not, and the Court's interpretation has given little encouragement to gun rights supporters.

WHO, WHAT, HOW American citizens are divided between those who want no restrictions on gun ownership and those who believe that some regulation of guns is necessary for social order.

WHO are the actors?	WHAT do they want?	HOW do they get it?
Citizens	• Unfettered gun ownership • Gun control	• Second Amendment interpretations • Federalism tensions • National and state legislation

The Rights of Criminal Defendants

Half of the amendments in the Bill of Rights and several clauses in the Constitution itself are devoted to protecting the rights of people who are suspected or accused of committing crimes. The Fourth through Eighth Amendments protect people against unreasonable searches and seizures, self-incrimination, and cruel and unusual punishment, and they guarantee people accused of a crime the right to legal advice, the right to a speedy and public trial, and various other procedural protections.

Why Are the Rights of Criminal Defendants Valuable?

The primary reason for protecting the rights of the accused is to limit government power. One way government can stop criticism of its actions is by jailing critics. The guarantees in the Bill of Rights provide checks on government's ability to prosecute its enemies.

Another reason for guaranteeing rights to those accused of crimes is the strong tradition in American culture, coming from our English roots, that a person is innocent until proven guilty. An innocent person, naturally, still has the full protection of the Constitution, and even a guilty person is protected to some degree—for instance, against cruel and unusual punishment. All Americans are entitled to what the Fifth and Fourteenth Amendments call due process of the law. **Due process of the law** means that laws must be reasonable and fair and that those accused of breaking the law, and who stand to lose life, liberty, or property as a consequence, have the right to appear before their judges to hear the charges and evidence against them, to have legal counsel, and to present any contradictory evidence in their defense. Due process means essentially that those accused of a crime have a right to a fair trial.

During the 1960s and 1970s, the Supreme Court expanded the protection of the rights of the accused and incorporated them so that the states had to protect them as well. And yet the more conservative 1980s and 1990s witnessed a considerable backlash against a legal system perceived as having gone soft on crime—a system over-concerned with the rights of criminals at the expense of safe streets, neighborhoods, and cities, and deaf to the claims of victims of violent crimes. We want to protect the

due process of the law guarantee that laws will be fair and reasonable and that citizens suspected of breaking the law will be fairly treated

innocent, but when the seemingly guilty go free because of a "technicality," the public is often incensed. The Supreme Court has had the heavy responsibility of drawing the line between the rights of defendants and the rights of society. We can look at the Court's deliberations on these matters in four main areas: the protection against unreasonable searches and seizures, the protection against self-incrimination, the right to counsel, and the protection against cruel and unusual punishment.

Unreasonable Searches and Seizures

The Fourth Amendment says,

> The right of the people to be secure in their persons, houses, papers, and effects, against unreasonable searches and seizures, shall not be violated, and no warrants shall issue but upon probable cause, supported by oath or affirmation, and particularly describing the place to be searched, and the persons or things to be seized.

The founders were particularly sensitive on this question because the king of England had the right to order the homes of his subjects searched without cause, looking for any evidence of criminal activity. For the most part, this amendment has been interpreted by the Court to mean that a person's home is private and cannot be invaded by police without a warrant, obtainable only if they have very good reason to think that criminal evidence lies within.

What's Reasonable?   Under the Fourth Amendment, there are few exceptions to the rule that searches require warrants. Cars present a special case, for example, since by their nature they are likely to be gone by the time an officer appears with a warrant. Cars can be searched without a warrant if the officer has probable cause to think that a law has been broken, and the Court has gradually widened the scope of the search so that it can include luggage or closed containers in cars. Modern innovations like wiretapping and electronic surveillance have presented more difficult problems for the Court, since previous laws did not allow for them. It was not until 1967 that the Court required that a warrant be obtained before phones could be tapped.[56]

Yet another modern area in which the Court has had to determine the legality of searches is mandatory random testing for drug or alcohol use, usually by urine or blood tests. These are arguably a very unreasonable kind of search, but the Court has tended to allow them where the violation of privacy is outweighed by a good purpose, for instance discovering the cause of a train accident,[57] preventing drug use in schools,[58] or preserving the public safety by requiring drug tests of train conductors and airline pilots.

exclusionary rule
rule created by the Supreme Court holding that evidence illegally seized may not be used to obtain a conviction

The Exclusionary Rule   By far the most controversial part of the Fourth Amendment rulings has been the exclusionary rule. In a 1914 case, *Weeks* v. *United States,* the Court confronted the question of what to do with evidence that had been illegally obtained. It decided that such evidence should be excluded from use in a defendant's trial.[59] This **exclusionary rule,** as it came to be known, meant that even though the police might have concrete evidence of criminal activity, if that evidence was obtained unlawfully, it could not be used to gain a conviction of the culprit. Obviously guilty people could go free as a result of sloppy, inept, or criminal police behavior.

The exclusionary rule has been controversial from the start. Although it does serve as a deterrent to police, it can also help criminals avoid punishment. The Court itself has occasionally seemed uneasy about the rule. The Warren Court (1953–1969) continued to uphold it, but the Burger and Rehnquist Courts (1969–present) have cut back on the protections it offers. In 1974 the Court ruled that the exclusionary rule was meant to be a deterrent to abuse by the police, not a constitutional right of the accused.[60] The Court subsequently ruled that illegally seized evidence could be used in civil trials[61] and came to carve out what it called the *good faith exception,* whereby evidence is admitted to a criminal trial, even if it was obtained illegally, if the police were relying on a warrant that appeared to be valid at the time or a law that appeared to be constitutional (although either basis may turn out to be defective).[62] The Court's more conservative turn on this issue has not silenced the debate, however. Some observers are appalled at the reduction in the protection of individual rights, whereas others do not believe that the Court has gone far enough in protecting society against criminals.

The Right Against Self-Incrimination

No less controversial than the rulings on illegally seized evidence are the Court's decisions on unconstitutionally obtained confessions. The Fifth Amendment provides for a number of protections for individuals, among them that no person "shall be compelled in any criminal case to be a witness against himself." The Supreme Court has expanded the scope of the protection against self-incrimination from criminal trials, as the amendment dictates, to grand jury proceedings, legislative investigations, and even police interrogations. It was this last extension that proved most controversial.

In 1966 the Warren Court ruled, in *Miranda* v. *Arizona,* that police had to inform suspects of their rights to remain silent and to have a lawyer present during questioning to prevent them from incriminating themselves. The *Miranda* rights are familiar to watchers of TV police shows: "You have the right to remain silent. Anything you say can and will be used against you. . . ." If a lawyer could show that a defendant had not been "read" his or her rights, information gained in the police interrogation would not be admissible in court. Like the exclusionary rule, the *Miranda* ruling could and did result in criminals going free even though evidence existed to convict them.

Reacting to public and political accusations that the Warren Court was soft on crime, Congress passed the Crime Control and Safe Streets Act of 1968, which allowed confessions to be used in federal courts not according to the *Miranda* ruling, but according to the "totality of the circumstances" surrounding the confession. In 2000, despite the fact that some justices had been highly critical of the *Miranda* ruling over the years, the Court upheld the 1966 decision, claiming that it had become an established part of the culture, and held the 1968 Crime Control and Safe Streets Act to be unconstitutional.[63]

The Right to Counsel

Closely related to the *Miranda* decision, which upholds the right to a lawyer during police questioning, is the Sixth Amendment declaration that the accused shall "have the assistance of counsel for his defense." The founders' intentions are fairly clear from the 1790 Federal Crimes Act, which required courts to provide counsel for poor defendants only in capital cases—that is, those punishable by death. Defendants in other trials had a right to counsel, but the government had no obligation to provide it. The Supreme Court's decisions were in line with that act until 1938, when, in *Johnson* v. *Zerbst,* it extended the government's obligation to provide counsel to impoverished defendants in all criminal proceedings in federal courts. Only federal crimes carried that obligation until 1963. Then, in one of the most dramatic tales of courtroom appeals (so exciting that it was made into both a book and a movie called *Gideon's Trumpet*), a poor man named Clarence Earl Gideon was convicted of breaking and entering a pool hall and stealing money from the vending machine. Gideon asked the judge for a lawyer, but the judge told him that the state of Florida was not obligated to give him one. He tried to defend the case himself but lost to the far more skilled and knowledgeable prosecutor. Serving five years in prison for a crime he swore he did not commit, he filed a handwritten appeal with the Supreme Court. In a landmark decision, *Gideon* v. *Wainwright,* the Court incorporated the Sixth Amendment right to counsel.[64]

The *Gideon* decision was a tremendous financial and administrative burden for the states, who had to retry or release many prisoners. Conservatives believed that *Gideon* went far beyond the founders' intentions. Both the Burger and Rehnquist Courts succeeded in rolling back some of the protections won by *Gideon,* ruling, for instance, that the right to a court-appointed attorney does not extend beyond the filing of one round of appeals, even if the convicted indigent person is on death row.[65]

Cruel and Unusual Punishment

The final guarantee we will look at in this section also has generated some major political controversies. The Eighth Amendment says, in part, that "cruel and unusual punishments" shall not be inflicted. Like some of the earlier amendments, this reflects a concern of English law, which sought to protect British subjects from torture and inhumane treatment by the king. It is easy to see why it would be controversial, however. What is "cruel," and what is "unusual"? Despite intense lobbying on the part of impassioned interest groups, the Supreme Court has not ruled that the death penalty itself is cruel or unusual, and most of the states have death penalty laws.

The strongest attack on the death penalty began in the 1970s, when the NAACP Legal Defense Fund joined with the American Civil Liberties Union and the American Bar Association to argue that the death penalty was disproportionately given to African Americans, especially those convicted of rape. They argued that this was a violation of the Eighth Amendment and of the Fourteenth Amendment guarantee of equal protection of the law. Part of the problem was that state laws differed about what constituted

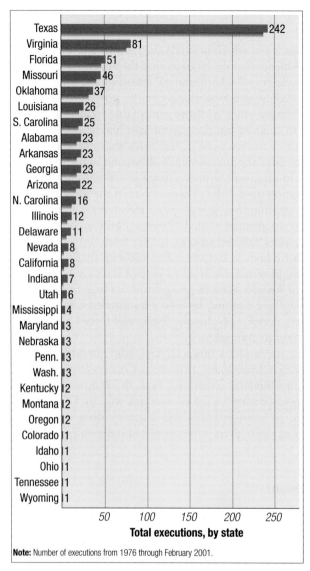

Total executions, by state

Texas	242
Virginia	81
Florida	51
Missouri	46
Oklahoma	37
Louisiana	26
S. Carolina	25
Alabama	23
Arkansas	23
Georgia	23
Arizona	22
N. Carolina	16
Illinois	12
Delaware	11
Nevada	8
California	8
Indiana	7
Utah	6
Mississippi	4
Maryland	3
Nebraska	3
Penn.	3
Wash.	3
Kentucky	2
Montana	2
Oregon	2
Colorado	1
Idaho	1
Ohio	1
Tennessee	1
Wyoming	1

Note: Number of executions from 1976 through February 2001.

Figure 4.2
Executions Since 1976

Source: Death Penalty Information Center *www.deathpenaltyinf.org/ dpicreg.html*

grounds for imposing the death penalty, and juries had no uniform standards to rely on. Consequently, unequal patterns of application of the penalty developed.

In *Furman* v. *Georgia* (1972) and two related cases, the Court ruled that Georgia's and Texas's capital punishment laws were unconstitutional, but the justices were so far from agreement that they all filed separate opinions, totaling 231 pages.[66] Thirty-five states passed new laws trying to meet the Court's objections and to clarify the standards for capital punishment. By 1976 six hundred inmates waited on death row for the Court to approve the new laws. That year the Court ruled in several cases that the death penalty is not unconstitutional, although it struck down laws requiring the death penalty for certain crimes.[67] The Court remained divided over the issue. In 1977 Gary Gilmore became the first person executed after a ten-year break. Executions by state from 1976 to May 1999 are listed in Figure 4.2.

In 1987 *McClesky* v. *Kemp* raised the race issue again, but by then the Court was growing more conservative. It voted five to four that statistics showing that blacks who murdered whites received the death penalty more frequently than whites who murdered blacks did not prove a racial bias in the law or in how it was being applied.[68] The Rehnquist Court has continued to knock down procedural barriers to imposing the death penalty.

WHO, WHAT, HOW Even those of us who have never been arrested and who intend to keep it that way have a huge stake in the protection of the rights of criminal defendants.

WHO are the actors?	WHAT do they want?	HOW do they get it?
Citizens	• Guarantees that government won't use the legal system for political purposes	• Due process of law (including Fourth through Eighth Amendments)

The Right to Privacy

One of the most controversial rights in America is not even mentioned in the Constitution or the Bill of Rights: the right to privacy. This right is at the heart of one of the deepest divisions in American politics, the split over abortion rights, and is fundamental to two other areas of civil liberties that will be central in the politics of the early twenty-first century, gay rights and the right to die.

Why Is the Right to Privacy Valuable?

Although the right to privacy is not spelled out in the Bill of Rights, it goes hand in hand with the founders' insistence on limited government. Their goal was to keep government from getting too powerful and interfering with the lives and affairs of individual citizens. They certainly implied a right to privacy, and perhaps even assumed such a right, but they did not make it explicit.

The right to privacy, to be left alone to do what we want, is so clearly desirable that it scarcely needs a defense. The problem, of course, is that a right to privacy without any limits is anarchy, the absence of government altogether. Clearly, government has an interest in preventing some kinds of individual behavior—murder, theft, and rape, for example. But what about other, more subtle behaviors that do not directly affect the public safety but arguably have serious consequences for the public good—such as prostitution, drug use, and gambling? Should these behaviors fall under the right to privacy, or should the state be able to regulate them? The specific issues related to this topic that the Court has dealt with are contraception use and abortion, laws restricting the behavior of homosexuals, and laws preventing terminally ill patients from ending their lives.

Reproductive Rights

Throughout the 1940s, people tried to challenge state laws that made it a crime to use birth control, or even to give out information about how to prevent pregnancy. The Supreme Court routinely refused to hear these challenges until the 1965 case of *Griswold* v. *Connecticut*. Connecticut had a law on its books making it illegal to use contraceptive devices or to distribute information about them. Under that law, Griswold, the Connecticut director of Planned Parenthood, was convicted and fined $100 for counseling married couples about birth control.

The Court held that although the right to privacy is not explicit in the Constitution, a number of other rights, notably those in the First, Third, Fourth, Fifth, and Ninth Amendments, create a "zone of privacy" in which lie marriage and the decision to use contraception. The Fourteenth Amendment applies that right to the states, and so Connecticut's law was unconstitutional.[69] In 1973 the Court extended the ruling to cover the rights of unmarried people to use contraception as well.[70]

Because of the Court's insistence that reproductive matters are not the concern of the government, abortion rights advocates saw an opportunity to use the *Griswold* ruling to strike down state laws prohibiting or limiting abortion. The Court had tried to avoid ruling on the abortion issue, but by 1973 it had become hard to escape. In *Roe* v. *Wade,* the justices held that the right to privacy does indeed encompass the right to abortion. But it tried to balance a woman's right to privacy in reproductive matters with the state's interest in protecting human life by treating the three trimesters of pregnancy differently. In the first three months of pregnancy, it held, there can be no compelling state interest that offsets a woman's privacy rights. In the second three months, the state can regulate access to abortions if it does so reasonably. In the last trimester, the state's interest becomes far more compelling, and the state can limit or even prohibit abortions as long as the mother's life is not in danger.[71]

The *Roe* decision launched the United States into an intense and divisive battle over abortion. States continued to try to limit abortions by requiring the consent of husbands or parents, outlawing clinic advertising, imposing waiting periods, and erecting other roadblocks. The Court struck down most of these, at least until 1977, when it allowed some state limitations. But the battle was not confined to statehouses. Congress, having failed to pass a constitutional amendment banning abortions, passed more than thirty laws restricting access to abortions in various ways.

The balance on the Supreme Court was crucial. *Roe* had been decided by a 7–2 vote, but many in the majority were facing retirement. When Chief Justice Warren Burger retired in 1986, President Ronald Reagan elevated William Rehnquist, one of the two dissenters, to chief justice, and appointed conservative Antonin Scalia in his place. Reagan's appointees finally turned the Court in a more conservative direction, but even these justices have not been willing to overturn *Roe*. The 1973 ruling has been limited in some ways, but Rehnquist has not succeeded in gathering a majority to strike it down.[72]

The debate over abortion in this country is certainly not finished. It has become a rallying point for the Christian Right, organized since 1989 as the Christian Coalition, which has become a powerful part of the Republican Party. Since 1980 the Republicans have included a commitment to a constitutional amendment banning abortion in their presidential party platform. But because a majority of Americans support at least some rights to abortion, the issue has proved damaging to the electoral fortunes of some Republican candidates. Heeding this, Republican President George W. Bush downplayed the issue in the 2000 campaign so successfully that some voters were unaware that he was not, in fact, pro-choice.

Gay Rights

The *Griswold* and *Roe* rulings have opened up a variety of difficult issues for the Supreme Court. If there is a right to privacy, what might be included under it? On the whole, the Court has been very restrictive in expanding that right beyond the reproductive rights of the original cases. Most controversial was its ruling in *Bowers* v. *Hardwick* (1986).

Michael Hardwick was arrested under a Georgia law outlawing heterosexual and homosexual sodomy. Hardwick challenged the law (although he wasn't prosecuted under it), claiming that it violated his right to privacy. The Court disagreed. Looking at the case from the perspective of whether there was a constitutional right to engage in sodomy, rather than from the dissenting view that what took place between consenting adults was none of their business, the Court held five to four that the state of Georgia had a legitimate interest in regulating such behavior. Justice Lewis Powell, who provided the fifth vote for the majority, said after his retirement that he regretted his vote in the *Bowers* decision, but by then, of course, it was too late. Several states have also been critical of the Court's ruling. The Georgia Supreme Court struck down Georgia's sodomy law in 1998 on privacy grounds, but in a case involving heterosexual rather than homosexual activity. The issue has not gone back to the U.S. Supreme Court, but in striking down a Colorado law in 1996 that would have made it difficult for gays to use the Colorado courts to fight discrimination, the Court upheld gay rights under the equal protection clause of the Fourteenth Amendment.[73] Whether it will change its mind on the right to privacy remains to be seen.

The Right to Die

A final right to privacy issue that has stirred up controversy in the Court is the so-called right to die. In 1990 the Court ruled on the case of Nancy Cruzan, a woman who had been unconscious and on life-support systems since a car accident in 1983. Her parents asked the doctors to withdraw the life support and allow her to die, but the state of Missouri, claiming an interest in protecting the "sanctity of human life," blocked their request. The Cruzans argued that the right to privacy included the right to die without state interference, but the Court upheld Missouri's position, saying it was unclear that Nancy's wishes in the matter could be known for sure. The Court did add, however, that when such wishes were made clear, either in person or via a living will, a person's right to terminate medical treatment was protected under the Fourteenth Amendment's due process clause.[74]

As on the issue of gay rights, the public is divided on the legal questions surrounding a person's right to suspend medical treatment, to have assistance with suicide, and to otherwise end his or her life when terminally ill and in severe pain. Proponents of this right argue that such patients should have the right to decide whether to continue living, and that since they are frequently incapacitated or lack the means to end their lives painlessly, they are entitled to help. Opponents say that a patient's right to die may require a doctor to violate the Hippocratic oath and that granting this right opens the door to abuse. Patients, especially those whose illnesses are chronic and costly, might feel obligated to end their lives out of concern for family or financial matters. In 1997 the Court heard arguments on whether Americans possess a right to have assistance with suicide when they face a terminal illness. The Court's answer was that each state must decide and that there is no barrier to state legislation in this area. The Court did not rule out the possibility, however, that dying patients might not be able to make a claim to a constitutional right to die in the future.[75]

WHO, WHAT, HOW   What's at stake in the right to privacy seems amazingly simple, given the intensity of the debate about it. In short, the issue is whether citizens have the right to control their own bodies in fundamentally intimate matters such as birth, death, and sex, or whether such matters should be regulated according to moral principles.

WHO are the actors?	WHAT do they want?	HOW do they get it?
Citizens	• Control over their bodies in matters of birth, sex, and death • Promotion of religious or moral principles	• Right to privacy created by Supreme Court based on other rights • Legal fights, constitutional amendment, legislative battles to eliminate undesirable behavior

Citizenship and Civil Liberties

In the United States, we are accustomed to thinking about citizenship as a status that confers on us certain rights. But although obligation without rights is an authoritarian dictatorship, rights without obligation leads to a state of nature, or anarchy, with no government at all. Plainly, the status of a citizen in a democracy requires both rights and duties in order to "keep the Republic."

The final section of a chapter on civil liberties is an interesting place to speculate about the duties attached to American citizenship. We have explored the Bill of Rights; what might a "bill of obligations" look like? The Constitution itself suggests the basics. Obligations are very much the flip side of rights: for every right guaranteed, there is a corresponding duty to use it. For example:

- The provisions for elected office and the right to vote imply a duty to vote.

- Congress is authorized to collect taxes, duties, and excises, including an income tax. Citizens are obligated to pay those taxes.

- Congress can raise and support armies, provide and maintain navies, and provide for and govern militias. Americans have a duty to serve in the military.

- The Fifth and Sixth Amendments guarantee grand juries and jury trials to those accused of crimes. Citizens must serve on those juries.

But Americans are notoriously lax in fulfilling some of these obligations. We turn out to vote in low numbers, we like to avoid paying taxes, and the draft, like jury duty, is an obligation many Americans have actively sought to escape. It might be worthwhile considering what the political consequences are for a democratic republic when the emphasis on preserving civil liberties is not balanced by a corresponding commitment to fulfilling political obligations.

Points of Access

- Read your school's code of ethics and compare your rights with your responsibilities.

- Serve on a student disciplinary board.

- Go to the web site of the American Civil Liberties Union (ACLU) "http://www.aclu.org" and access information on "Students' Rights" or any other issues that interest you.

WHAT'S AT STAKE REVISITED

Eden Jacobowitz's run-in with the University of Pennsylvania speech code illustrates some of the complexities of American civil liberties that we have seen in this chapter. No rights are absolute, but drawing limits on any right is fraught with difficulty. The questions raised here are not just legal issues, about what the Constitution and other laws actually mean, but also political issues, about who has power and what rules determine how they get it. What is at stake in campus speech codes is both legal and political. Given the history of Supreme Court rulings on freedom of speech and the Court's tendency to limit censorship, it is hard to make a case that speech codes are constitutional. In fact, federal courts have held exactly that, resulting in watered-down codes on many campuses.

But the political issues involved are more difficult to resolve. Those who favor speech codes argue that the rules have favored certain groups in society all along, notably white Anglo-Saxon Protestant males. They see the codes as an attempt to change the rules and to create a new distribution of winners and losers in politics and society, one in which women and minorities would stand as good a chance of winning as males traditionally have had. Since fighting oppression—real or imagined—is their primary goal, some loss of freedom is reasonable to justify their long-term ends.

For those who oppose speech codes, something different is at stake. While there are undeniably those who object because they benefit from the power structure that was supported by the former rules of speech and don't want change, others take a different view. Even if diversity and a change in power structures are worthy goals, they argue, they are not worth the resulting loss of freedom. Freedom of speech is a fundamental value, and once we start cutting it back for political reasons, especially at universities—the sanctuaries of truth and open debate—it will be difficult to draw the line. Their argument is that ultimately everyone would be a loser from a change in rules that allows the suppression of speech to avoid offense.

The debate between these two points of view, which goes beyond campus speech codes to self-censorship and political correctness in general, reflects some of the fundamental divisions in American politics today—ones that do not fall along traditional liberal-conservative lines. Proponents of liberalism, traditionally an ideology that endorses broader interpretations of rights, find themselves divided between those who believe that speech codes increase the freedom of disadvantaged groups and those who believe that only the exercise of free speech can bring about the fundamental rule changes that make all groups equal. ■

key terms

accommodationists   91
bills of attainder   88
civil liberties   85
civil rights   85
clear and present danger test   96
compelling state interest   93
due process of the law   106
establishment clause   91

exclusionary rule   107
ex post facto laws   88
fighting words   99
freedom of assembly   98
free exercise clause   93
habeas corpus   88
incorporation   90
Lemon test   92

libel   100
Miller test   98
police power   93
political correctness   99
prior restraint   100
sedition   96
selective incorporation   90
separationists   91

summary

■ Our civil liberties are individual freedoms that place limitations on the power of government. Most of these rights are spelled out in the text of the Constitution or in its first ten amendments, the Bill of Rights, but some have developed over the years through judicial decision-making.

■ Sometimes rights conflict, and when they do, government, guided by the Constitution and through the institutions of Congress, the executive, and the actions of citizens themselves, is called upon to resolve these conflicts.

■ According to the establishment and free exercise clauses of the First Amendment, citizens of the United States have the right not to be coerced to practice a religion in which they do not believe, as well as the right not to be prevented from practicing the religion they do espouse. Because these rights can conflict, religious freedom has been a battleground ever since the founding of the country. The courts have played a significant role in navigating the stormy waters of religious expression.

■ Freedom of expression, also provided for in the First Amendment, is often considered the hallmark of our democratic government. Freedom of expression produces information about government, limits corruption, protects minorities, and helps maintain a vigorous defense of the truth. But this right may also at times conflict with the preservation of social order and the protection of

civility, decency, and reputation. Again, it has been left to the courts to balance freedom of expression with social and moral order.

■ The right to bear arms, supported by the Second Amendment, has been hotly debated—more so in recent years than in the past, as federal gun control legislation has only recently been enacted. Most often the debate over gun laws is carried out in the state legislatures.

■ The founders believed that to limit government power, people needed to retain certain rights throughout the process of being accused, tried, and punished for criminal activities. Thus they devoted some of the Constitution itself and the Bill of Rights to a variety of procedural protections, including the right to a speedy and public trial, protection from unreasonable search and seizure, and the right to legal advice.

■ The right to privacy is not mentioned in either the Constitution or the Bill of Rights, and did not even enter the American legal system until the late 1800s, but it has become a fiercely debated right on a number of different issues, including reproductive rights, gay rights, and the right to die. In the absence of constitutional protection, a series of court cases on these matters has determined how they are to be resolved. Many of these issues are still controversial, as the states create new legislation and the courts hand down new rulings.

5

What's at Stake?

The Meaning of Political Inequality
- When Can the Law Treat People Differently?
- Different Kinds of Equality

Rights Denied on the Basis of Race
- The Civil War and Its Aftermath
- The Long Battle to Overturn Plessy
- The Civil Rights Movement
- Blacks in Contemporary American Politics

Rights Denied on the Basis of Race and Ethnicity
- Native Americans
- Hispanic Americans
- Asian Americans

Rights Denied on the Basis of Gender
- The Birth of the Women's Rights Movement
- The Struggle in the States
- Winners and Losers in the Suffrage Movement
- The Equal Rights Amendment
- Gender Discrimination Today

Rights Denied on Other Bases
- Sexual Orientation
- Age
- Disability

Citizenship and Civil Rights

What's at Stake Revisited

The Struggle for Political Equality

WHAT'S AT STAKE?

Four Fort Wayne, Indiana, high school students—two black and two white—who are bused from their neighborhoods to attend racially integrated North Side High School, are asked by a newspaper reporter how they feel about the possibility that Fort Wayne might join a national trend in which students return to their more racially separate neighborhood schools. "No way. We'd strike. We'd rebel. We wouldn't come to school anymore. It wouldn't work. We'd miss each other," the four quickly reply.[1] These are amazing responses, considering how slowly Fort Wayne came to school integration and what a controversial issue busing remains in American politics.

In 1954–1955, the Supreme Court ruled unanimously in *Brown* v. *Board of Education* that the segregation of schools violates the equal protection clause of the Fourteenth Amendment to the Constitution. Separate schools for white and black children are, decided the justices, by their very nature unequal. The Court ordered schools across the nation to desegregate "with all deliberate speed." Thirty years after *Brown,* however, the U.S. Department of Education's Office of Civil Rights declared that twenty-two of thirty-six elementary schools in Fort Wayne were "seriously imbalanced" in terms of racial composition. Yet only eight years later, in 1992, all Fort Wayne elementary schools were racially balanced, and in 1998 Katrina, Mylshia, Amber, and Shawn are declaring their allegiance to their school system and to one another.

Not only has Fort Wayne achieved racial balance in the schools, but statistics demonstrate that the "experiment" has been a success in terms of student achievement. In 1997–1998, 91 percent of all high school students in Fort Wayne graduated, up from 74 percent in 1993–1994 (the first year records were kept). The dropout rate was only 2.6 percent in

117

1998, down from 7.5 percent in 1988. State test scores have not risen, but they haven't dropped either, as can happen in the flurry of activity that usually surrounds desegregation efforts. How did Fort Wayne achieve these results in just fourteen years?

The short answer is busing. For reasons of past discrimination, economics, and preference, among others, residential patterns themselves tend to be segregated. Therefore, if students go to school in their own neighborhoods, the schools are also likely to be segregated. Busing involves driving white and black children from the neighborhoods in which they live to schools in other neighborhoods so the schools will have a mix of races, or be integrated. Busing has been the predominant method of achieving school integration throughout the United States, but it has always been controversial. From the start, newspaper headlines have recorded the strong and sometimes violent reactions of people who feel they have more to lose than to gain by instituting busing.

Opponents of busing charge that it moves children away from their friends, breaks up neighborhoods and communities, deprives parents of choice and control, and intrudes unreasonably into family life. They see busing as fundamentally unfair as well. Because schools are funded in large part by the property taxes of the localities in which they exist, parents may move to a more expensive neighborhood, where more money is spent on education, only to see their children bused back to the neighborhood from which they moved.

Advocates of busing concede that busing may have some drawbacks and may inconvenience some families, but they insist that the benefits are worth the hardships. Children who go to integrated schools are more likely to live in integrated areas afterward, creating a more integrated society generally. Poor students get a better education under busing because a district's resources are more evenly shared among all its schools. All children are winners when they can learn about and appreciate the differences among people. Most important, say proponents, in an "equal opportunity" society where education is the ticket to success, busing levels the playing field for all children.

Clearly, busing is controversial, but just as clearly, the students in Fort Wayne don't share the negative views of it. How did the school system in Fort Wayne avoid the pitfalls that many other schools in the nation have fallen into? The answer lies in Fort Wayne's ability to bridge competing visions of fairness and equality and to create new rules of access to school programs so that all the participants are able to see themselves as winners. At the end of this chapter, we will return to the question of what exactly is at stake for families, and the country, when busing is used to desegregate schools. ■

The opening ceremonies of the 1996 Summer Olympic Games in Atlanta, Georgia, were spectacular. Amid sparkling pomp and pageantry, musicians, dancers, and singers celebrated the American South, acting out a metaphor for the devastation that the region had suffered during and after the Civil War and the glory of its rebirth. Prominent among the many participants were African Americans. As recently as fifty years ago, their participation would have been unwelcome, if not illegal, but in 1996 they were crucial to the success of the show.

Still, the social, political, and economic change reflected in the Atlanta Olympic Games is in some ways only superficial. Racial inequality, while technically at an end legally and politically, continues to be reflected in economic and social statistics. On average, blacks are less educated and much poorer than whites, they experience higher crime rates, they live disproportionately in poverty-stricken areas, they score lower on standardized tests, and they rank at the bottom of most social measurements. Life expectancy is lower for African American men and women as compared to their white counterparts, and a greater percentage of African American children live in single-parent homes than do white or Hispanic children. During the Olympic Games, the human rights group Amnesty International (AI) released a report claiming that in Georgia, the death penalty, which AI opposes, is implemented in a "racist, arbitrary and unfair manner."[2] The statistics illustrate what we suggested in Chapter 4—that rights equal power and the long-term deprivation of rights results in powerlessness. Unfortunately, the restoration of formal **civil rights** does not immediately bring about a change in social and economic status.

civil rights
citizenship rights guaranteed to the people (primarily in the Thirteenth, Fourteenth, Fifteenth, and Nineteenth Amendments) and protected by government

African Americans are not the only group of people who show the effects of having been deprived of their civil rights. Native Americans, Hispanic Americans, and Asian Americans, often marked by their appearance, names, or language as "different" from white Anglo-Saxon Protestants, have all faced or do face unequal treatment in the legal system, the job market, and schools. Women, who account for more than half of the U.S. population, have long struggled to gain economic parity with men. People in America are denied rights, and consequently power, on the basis of sexual orientation, age, and physical abilities. A country once praised by the French observer Alexis de Tocqueville as a place of extraordinary equality, the United States today is haunted by traditions of unequal treatment and intolerance that it cannot entirely shake.

In this chapter, we look at the struggles of various groups to gain equal rights and the power to enforce those rights. The struggles differ because the groups themselves, and the political avenues open to them, vary in important ways. Studying these battles for rights will help us to see how groups can use different political strategies to change the rules and win power.

Specifically, we look at

- the meaning of political inequality

- the struggle of African Americans to claim rights denied to them because of race

- the struggle of Native Americans, Hispanic Americans, and Asian Americans to claim rights denied to them because of race or ethnicity

- women's battle for rights denied to them on the basis of gender

- the fight by other groups in society to claim rights denied to them on a variety of bases

The Meaning of Political Inequality

Despite the deeply held American expectation that the law should treat all people equally, laws by nature must treat some people differently than others. Not only are laws designed to discriminate between those who abide by society's rules and those who don't,[3] but they can legally treat criminals differently once they are convicted. For instance, in forty-six states and the District of Columbia, convicted felons are denied the right to vote while in prison, and in fourteen of those states, convicts lose the right to vote for life.[4] But when particular groups are treated differently because of some characteristic like skin color, gender, sexual orientation, age, or wealth, we say that the law discriminates against them, that they are denied the equal protection of the laws. Throughout our history, legislatures, both state and national, have passed laws treating groups differently based on characteristics such as these. Sometimes those laws have seemed just and reasonable, but often they have not. Deciding which characteristics may fairly be the basis of unequal treatment and which may not is the job of all three branches of our government, but especially of our court system.

The Supreme Court has expended considerable energy and ink on this problem, and its answers have changed over time as various groups have waged the battle for equal rights against a backdrop of ever-changing American values, public opinion, and politics. Before we look at the struggles those groups have endured in their pursuit of equal treatment by the law, we will look briefly at the Court's formula for determining what sorts of discrimination need what sorts of legal remedies. This formula, like the clear and present danger test and the *Lemon* test, which we explained in Chapter 4, allows the Court to reduce the enormous complexity of its caseload to manageable proportions and ensures that it is focusing on the legal merits of the cases and not the individual details. The product of a painful national evolution in the way Americans think about equal rights, the Court's formula reflects the way that discrimination cases are handled today.

When Can the Law Treat People Differently?

The Supreme Court has divided the laws that treat people differently into three tiers (see Table 5.1). The top tier refers to those ways of classifying people that are so rarely constitutional that they are immediately "suspect." **Suspect classifications** require that the government have a compelling state interest for treating people differently. Race is a suspect classification. To determine whether laws making suspect classifications are constitutional, the Court subjects them to a heightened standard of review called **strict scrutiny.** Strict scrutiny means that the Court looks very carefully at the law and the government interest involved.

The next tier refers to "quasi-suspect" classifications, which the Court views as less potentially dangerous and which may or may not be legitimate grounds for treating people differently. These classifications are subject not to strict scrutiny, but to an **intermediate standard of review.** That is, the Court looks to see whether the law requiring different treatment of people bears a substantial relationship to an important state interest. An "important interest" test is not as hard to meet as a "compelling interest" test. Laws that treat women differently than men fall into this category.

Finally, the least scrutinized tier consists of "nonsuspect" classifications; these are subject to the **minimum rationality test.** The Court asks whether the government had a rational basis for making a law that treats a given class of people differently.

suspect classification classification, such as race, for which any discriminatory law must be justified by a compelling state interest

strict scrutiny a heightened standard of review used by the Supreme Court to assess the constitutionality of laws that limit some freedoms or that make a suspect classification

intermediate standard of review standard of review used by the Supreme Court to evaluate laws that make a quasi-suspect classification

minimum rationality test standard of review used by the Supreme Court to evaluate laws that make a nonsuspect classification

Table 5.1
When Can the Law Treat People Differently?

Legal Classification	When Laws Treat People Differently Because of . . .	The Court Applies . . .	The Court Asks . . .
Suspect	Race (or legislation that infringes on some fundamental rights)	Strict scrutiny standard of review	Is there a *compelling state interest* in this classification?
Quasi-suspect	Gender	Intermediate standard of review	Is there an *important state purpose* for this classification, and are the means used by the law substantially related to the ends?
Nonsuspect	Age, wealth, sexual orientation	Minimum rationality standard of review	Is there a *rational basis* for this classification?

A law that discriminates on the basis of age, such as a curfew for young people, or on the basis of economic level, such as a higher tax rate for a certain income bracket, need not stem from compelling or important government interests. The government must merely have had a rational basis for making the law, which is fairly easy for a legislature to show.

The significance of the three tiers of classifications and the three review standards is that all groups who feel discriminated against want the Court to view them as a suspect class so that they will be treated as a protected group. Civil rights laws might cover them anyway, and the Fourteenth Amendment, which guarantees equal protection of the law, may formally protect them. However, once a group is designated as a suspect class, the Supreme Court is very unlikely to permit any laws to treat them differently. Thus gaining suspect status is crucial in the struggle for equal rights.

The current Supreme Court has been reluctant to expand its definition of which classes are suspect. After more than a hundred years of decisions that effectively allowed people to be treated differently because of their race, the Court finally agreed in the 1950s that race is a suspect class. Women's groups, however, have failed to convince the Court or to amend the Constitution to make gender a suspect classification. The intermediate standard of review was devised by the Court to express its view that it is a little more dangerous to classify people by gender than by age or wealth, but not as dangerous as classifying them by race or religion. Some groups in America—homosexuals, for instance—have not managed to get the Court to consider them in the quasi-suspect category. Although some states and localities have passed legislation to prevent discrimination on the basis of sexual orientation, gays can be treated differently by law as long as the state can demonstrate a rational basis for doing so.

These standards of review make a real difference in American politics. Remember that the rules of politics determine society's winners and losers. Americans who are treated unequally by the law consequently have less power to use the democratic system to get what they need and want (like legislation to protect and further their interests), to secure the resources available through the system (like education and other government benefits), and to gain new resources (like jobs and material goods). People who cannot claim their political rights have little if any standing in a democratic society.

Different Kinds of Equality

The notion of equality is very controversial in America. Disputes arise in part because we often think that *equal* must mean "identical" or "the same." Thus equality can seem very threatening to the American value system, which prizes people's freedom to be different, to be unique individuals. We can better understand the controversies over the attempts to create political equality in this country if we return briefly to a distinction we made in Chapter 1 between substantive and procedural equality.

In American political culture, we prefer to rely on government to guarantee fair treatment and equal opportunity (a procedural view) rather than to manipulate fair and equal outcomes (a substantive view). We want government to treat everyone the same, and we want people to be free to be different, but we do not want government to treat people differently in order to make them equal at the end. This distinction, as we will see, has posed a problem for the civil rights movement in America—the effort to achieve equal treatment by the law for all Americans.

WHO, WHAT, HOW   In the struggle for political equality, the people with the most at stake are members of groups that, because of some characteristic beyond their control, have been denied their civil rights. What they seek is equal treatment under the law.

WHO are the actors?	WHAT do they want?	HOW do they get it?
Groups in society who are discriminated against	• Equal treatment by the law	• Court action; different standards of review

Rights Denied on the Basis of Race: African Americans

We cannot separate the history of our race relations from the history of the United States. Americans have struggled for centuries to come to terms with the fact that citizens of African nations were kidnapped, packed into sailing vessels, exported to America, and sold, often at great profit, into a life that destroyed their families, their spirit, and their human dignity. The stories of white supremacy and black inferiority, told to numb the sensibilities of European Americans to the horror of their own behavior, have been almost as damaging as slavery itself and have lived on in the American psyche much longer than the institution they justified. Racism is not a "southern problem" or a "black problem"; it is an American problem, and one that we have not yet managed to eradicate from our national culture.

Not only has racism had a decisive influence on American culture, but it also has been central to American politics. From the start, those with power in America have been torn by the issue of race. The framers of the Constitution were so ambivalent that they would not use the word *slavery*, even while that document legalized its existence. The Northwest Ordinance of 1787, which prohibited slavery in the northwestern territories, contained the concession to the South that fugitive slaves could legally be seized and returned to their owners. The accumulated tensions associated with slavery exploded in the American Civil War.

The Civil War and Its Aftermath: Winners and Losers

We can't begin to speculate here on all the causes of the American War Between the States. Suffice to say that the war was not fought simply over the moral evil of slavery. Slavery was an economic and political issue as well as an ethical one. The southern economy depended on slavery, and when, in an effort to hold the Union together in 1863, President Abraham Lincoln issued the Emancipation Proclamation, he was not simply taking a moral stand; he was trying to use economic pressure to keep the country intact. The proclamation, in fact, did not free all slaves, only those in states rebelling against the Union.[5]

It is hard to find any real "winners" in the American Civil War, which took such a toll on North and South that neither world war in the twentieth century would claim as many American casualties. The North "won" the war, in that the Union was restored, but the costs would be paid for decades afterward. Politically, the northern Republicans, the party of Lincoln, were in their ascendance, controlling both the House and the Senate, but their will was often thwarted by President Andrew Johnson, a Democrat from Tennessee who was sympathetic toward the South.

black codes a series of laws in the post–Civil War South designed to restrict the rights of former slaves before the passage of the Fourteenth and Fifteenth Amendments

The Thirteenth Amendment, banning slavery, was passed and ratified in 1865. In retaliation, and to ensure that white political and social dominance of southern society would continue, the southern state governments legislated black codes. **Black codes** were laws that essentially sought to keep blacks in a subservient economic and political position by restoring as many of the conditions of slavery as possible. "Freedom" did not make a great deal of difference in the lives of most former slaves after the war.

Reconstruction and Its Reversal   Congress, led by northern Republicans, tried to check southern obstruction of its will by instituting a period of federal control of southern politics called **Reconstruction.** In an attempt to make the black codes unconstitutional, the Fourteenth Amendment was passed, guaranteeing all people born or naturalized in the United States the rights of citizenship. Further, no state could deprive any person of life, liberty, or property without due process of the law, or deny any person equal protection of the law. As we saw in Chapter 4, the Supreme Court has made varied use of this amendment, but its original intent was to bring some semblance of civil rights to southern blacks. The Fifteenth Amendment followed in 1870, effectively extending the right to vote to all adult males.

At first Reconstruction worked as the North had hoped. Under northern supervision, southern life began to change. Blacks voted, were elected to some local posts, and cemented Republican dominance with their support. But soon southern whites responded with violence. Groups like the Ku Klux Klan terrorized blacks in the South and made them reluctant to claim the rights they were legally entitled to for fear of reprisals. Lynchings, arson, assaults, and beatings made claiming one's rights or associating with Republicans a risky business. Congress fought back vigorously and suppressed the reign of terror for a while, but its efforts earned accusations of military tyranny, and the Reconstruction project began to run out of steam. Plagued by political problems of their own, the Republicans were losing electoral strength and seats in Congress. Meanwhile, the Democrats were gradually reasserting their power in the southern states. By 1876 Reconstruction was effectively over, and shortly after that, southern whites set about the business of disenfranchising blacks, or taking away their newfound political power.

The End of Reconstruction and the Era of Jim Crow   Without the opposition of northern Republicans, disenfranchisement turned out to be easy to accomplish. The strategy chosen by the Democrats, who now controlled the southern state governments, was a sly one. Under the Fifteenth Amendment, the vote could not be denied on the basis of race, color, or previous condition of servitude, so they set out to deny it on other, legal bases that would have the primary effect of targeting blacks. **Poll taxes,** which required the payment of a small tax before voters could cast their votes, effectively took the right to vote away from the many blacks who were too poor to pay. **Literacy tests,** which required potential voters to demonstrate some reading skills, excluded most blacks, who had been denied an education and could not read. To permit illiterate whites to vote, literacy tests were combined with **grandfather clauses,** which required a literacy test for only those prospective voters whose grandfathers had not been allowed to vote before 1867. Thus, unlike the black codes, these new laws, called **Jim Crow laws,** obeyed the letter of the Fifteenth Amendment, never explicitly saying that they were denying blacks the right to vote because of their race, color or previous condition of servitude. This strategy proved devastatingly effective, and by 1910 the registration of black voters had dropped dramatically, and the registration of poor, illiterate whites had fallen as well.[6] The southern Democrats were back in power and had eliminated the possibility of competition.

Jim Crow laws were not just about voting but concerned many other dimensions of southern life as well. This was an era of **segregation** in the South—of separate fa-

---

Reconstruction
the period following the Civil War during which the federal government took action to rebuild the South

poll tax   a tax levied as a qualification for voting

literacy test   the requirement of reading or comprehension skills as a qualification for voting

grandfather clause
a provision exempting from voting restrictions the descendants of those able to vote in 1867

Jim Crow laws
southern laws designed to circumvent the Thirteenth, Fourteenth, and Fifteenth Amendments and to deny blacks rights on bases other than race

segregation   the practice and policy of separating races

cilities for blacks and whites for leisure, business, travel, education, and other activities. The whites-only facilities were invariably superior to those intended for blacks; they were newer, cleaner, and more comfortable. Before long, the laws were challenged by blacks, who asked why equal protection of the law shouldn't translate into some real equality in their lives.

One Jim Crow law, a Louisiana statute passed in 1890, required separate accommodations in all trains passing through the state. Homer Plessy, traveling through Louisiana, chose to sit in the white section. Although Plessy often passed as a white person, he was in fact one-eighth black, which made him a black man according to Louisiana law. When he refused to sit in the "coloreds-only" section, Plessy was arrested. He appealed his conviction all the way to the Supreme Court, which ruled against him in 1896. In *Plessy* v. *Ferguson,* the Court held that enforced separation of the races did not mean that one race was inferior to the other. As long as the facilities provided were equal, states were within their rights to require them to be separate. Rejecting the majority view, Justice John Marshall Harlan wrote in a famous dissent, "Our Constitution is color-blind, and neither knows nor tolerates classes among citizens."[7] It would be more than fifty years before a majority of the Court shared his view. In the meantime, everyone immediately embraced the "separate" and forgot the "equal" part of the ruling. Segregated facilities for whites and blacks had received the Supreme Court's seal of approval.

The Long Battle to Overturn Plessy: The NAACP's Legal Strategy

The years following the *Plessy* decision were bleak ones for African American civil rights. The formal rules of politics giving blacks their rights had been enacted at the national level, but no branch of government at any level was willing to enforce them. The Supreme Court had rejected attempts to give the Fourteenth Amendment more teeth. Congress was not inclined to help, since the Republican fervor for reform had worn off. Nor were the southern state governments likely to support black rights.

National Association for the Advancement of Colored People (NAACP) an interest group founded in 1910 to promote civil rights for African Americans

The **National Association for the Advancement of Colored People (NAACP),** founded in 1910, aimed to help individual blacks, to raise white society's awareness of the atrocities of contemporary race relations, and to change laws and court rulings that kept blacks from true equality. The NAACP, over time, was able to develop a legal strategy that was finally the undoing of Jim Crow and the segregated South.

Beginning with a challenge to segregation in law schools, a form of discrimination that Supreme Court justices would be most likely to see as dangerous, NAACP lawyers made the case that separate could not be equal in education. A series of victories over legal education set the stage for tackling the issue of education more broadly.

The NAACP had four cases pending that concerned the segregation of educational facilities in the South and the Midwest. In 1954 the Court ruled on all of them under the case name *Brown* v. *Board of Education of Topeka.* In their now-familiar arguments, NAACP lawyers emphasized the intangible aspects of education, including how it made black students feel to be made to go to a separate school. They cited sociological evidence of the low self-esteem of black schoolchildren, and they argued that it resulted from a system that made black children feel inferior by treating them differently.

Under the new leadership of Chief Justice Earl Warren, the Court ruled unanimously in favor of Linda Brown and the other black students. Without explicitly denouncing segregation or overturning *Plessy*, lest the South erupt in violent outrage again, the Warren Court held that separate schools, by their very definition, could never be equal because it was the fact of separation itself that made black children feel unequal. Segregation in education was inherently unconstitutional.[8] The principle of "separate but equal" was not yet dead, but it had suffered serious injury.

The *Brown* decision did not bring instant relief to the southern school system. The Court, in a 1955 follow-up to *Brown*, ruled that school desegregation had to take place "with all deliberate speed."[9] Such an ambiguous direction was asking for school districts to drag their feet. The most public and blatant attempt to avoid compliance took place in Little Rock, Arkansas, in September 1957, when Governor Orval Faubus posted the National Guard at the local high school to prevent the attendance of nine African American children. Rioting white parents, filmed for the nightly news, showed the rest of the country the faces of southern bigotry. Finally, President Dwight Eisenhower sent one thousand federal troops to guarantee the safe passage of the nine black children through the angry mob of white parents who threatened to lynch them rather than let them enter the school. The *Brown* case and the attempts to enforce it proved to be catalysts for a civil rights movement that would change the whole country.

The Civil Rights Movement

In the same year that the Supreme Court ordered school desegregation to proceed "with all deliberate speed," a woman named Rosa Parks sat down on a bus and started a chain of events that would end with a Court order to stop segregation in all aspects of southern life. Parks was a former NAACP secretary living in Montgomery, Alabama, where, as in the rest of the South, the public transportation system was segregated. Riding the bus on December 1, 1955, she refused to vacate her seat for a white person. She was arrested and sent to jail. Overnight, black citizens organized a boycott of the Montgomery bus system. A **boycott** seeks to put economic pressure on a business to do something by encouraging people to stop purchasing its goods or services. Montgomery blacks wanted the bus company to lose so much money that it would force the local government to change the bus laws. Against all expectations, the bus boycott continued for more than a year. In the meantime, the case wound its way through the legal system, and a little over a year after the boycott began, the Supreme Court affirmed a lower court's judgment that Montgomery's law was unconstitutional.[10] Separate bus accommodations were not equal.

boycott the refusal to buy certain goods or services as a way to protest policy or force political reform

Two Kinds of Discrimination   The civil rights movement that was launched by the Montgomery bus boycott confronted two different types of discrimination. **De jure discrimination** (discrimination by law) is created by laws that treat people differently based on some characteristic like race. This is the sort of discrimination that most blacks in the South faced. Especially in rural areas, blacks and whites lived and worked side by side, but by law they used separate facilities. Although the process of

de jure discrimination discrimination arising from or supported by the law

changing the laws was excruciating, once the laws were changed and the new laws were enforced, the result was integration.

The second sort of discrimination, called **de facto discrimination** (discrimination in fact), produces a kind of segregation that is much more difficult to eliminate. Segregation in the North was of this type, because blacks and whites did not live and work in the same places to begin with. It was not the law that kept them apart, but past discrimination, tradition, custom, economic status, and residential patterns. The reason this kind of segregation is so hard to remedy is that there are no laws to change; the segregation is woven more intricately into the fabric of society.

We can look at the civil rights movement in America as having two stages. The initial stage involved the battle to change the laws so that blacks and whites would be equally protected by the law, as the Fourteenth Amendment guarantees. The second stage, which is still ongoing today, is the fight against the aftereffects of those laws, and of centuries of discrimination, which leave many blacks and whites still living in communities that are worlds apart.

Changing the Rules: Fighting De Jure Discrimination

Rosa Parks and the Montgomery bus boycott launched a new strategy in blacks' fight for equal rights. Although it took the power of a court judgment to move the city officials, blacks themselves had exercised considerable power through peaceful protests and massive resistance to the will of whites. One of the leaders of the boycott was a young Baptist minister named Martin Luther King, Jr. A founding member of the Southern Christian Leadership Conference (SCLC), a group of black clergy committed to expanding civil rights, King became known for his nonviolent approach to political protest.

This philosophy of peacefully resisting the enforcement of laws perceived to be unjust and of marching or "sitting in" to express political views captured the imagination of supporters of black civil rights in both the South and the North. Black college students, occasionally joined by whites, staged peaceful demonstrations called "sit-ins" to desegregate lunch counters in southern department stores and other facilities. Although the sit-ins frequently resulted in violence, the violence was on the part of southern whites, not the protesters. The protest movement was important for the practices it challenged directly—such as segregation in motels and restaurants, beaches and other recreational facilities—but also for the pressure it brought to bear on elected officials and the effect it had on public opinion, particularly in the North, which had been largely unaware of southern problems.

The nonviolent resistance movement, in conjunction with the growing political power of northern blacks, brought about remarkable social and political change in the 1960s. The administration of Democratic

de facto discrimination
discrimination that is not the result of the law but rather of tradition and habit

A Picture Worth a Thousand Words
National magazines and a relatively new medium, television, brought stark images like this one—an Alabama policeman using dogs against a nonviolent protester— into the homes of white Americans, forcing them to recognize the injustices of de jure segregation.

president John F. Kennedy, not wanting to alienate the support of southern Democrats, tried at first to limit its active involvement in civil rights work. But the political pressure of black interest groups forced Kennedy to take a more visible stand. The Reverend Martin Luther King, Jr., was using his tactics of nonviolent protest to great advantage in the spring of 1963. Kennedy responded to the political pressure, so deftly orchestrated by King, by sending to Birmingham federal mediators to negotiate an end to segregation, and then by sending to Congress a massive package of civil rights legislation.

Kennedy did not live to see his proposals become law, but they became the top priority of his successor, President Lyndon Johnson. During the Johnson years, the president, majorities in Congress, and the Supreme Court were in agreement on civil rights issues, and their joint legacy is impressive. The Kennedy-initiated Civil Rights Bill of 1964 reinforced the voting laws, allowed the attorney general to bring school desegregation suits, permitted the president to deny federal money to state and local programs that practiced discrimination, prohibited discrimination in public accommodations and in employment, and set up the Equal Employment Opportunity Commission (EEOC) to investigate complaints about job discrimination. Johnson also sent Congress the Voting Rights Act of 1965, which, when passed, disallowed discriminatory tests, such as literacy tests, and provided for federal examiners to register voters throughout much of the South. In addition, the Twenty-fourth Amendment, outlawing poll taxes in federal elections, was ratified in 1964.

The Supreme Court, still the liberal Warren Court that had ruled in *Brown*, backed up this new legislation.[11, 12] Because of the unusual cooperation among the three branches of government, by the end of the 1960s life in the South was radically different for blacks. In 1968, 18 percent of southern black students went to schools with a majority of white students; in 1970 the percentage rose to 39 percent and in 1972 to 46 percent. The comparable figure for black students in the North was only 28 percent in 1972.[13] Voter registration had also improved dramatically. From 1964 to 1969, black voter registration in the South nearly doubled, from 36 percent to 65 percent of adult blacks.[14]

Changing the Outcomes: Fighting De Facto Discrimination

Political and educational advances did not translate into substantial economic gains for blacks. They remained, as a group, at the bottom of the economic hierarchy, and ironically the problem was most severe not in the rural South but in the industrialized North. Many southern blacks who had migrated to the North in search of jobs and a better quality of life found conditions not much different from those they had left behind. Abject poverty, discrimination in employment, and segregated schools and housing led to frustration and inflamed tempers. In the summers of 1966 and 1967, race riots flashed across the northern urban landscape. Impatient with the passive resistance of the nonviolent protest movement in the South, many blacks became more militant in their insistence on social and economic change. The Black Muslims, led by Malcolm X until his assassination in 1965, the Black Panthers, and the Student Nonviolent Coordinating Committee (SNCC) all demanded "black power" and radical change. These activists rejected the King philosophy of peacefully working through existing political institutions to bring about gradual change.

Northern whites who had applauded the desegregation of the South grew increasingly nervous as angry African Americans began to target segregation in the North. The de facto segregation there meant that black inner-city schools and white suburban schools were often as segregated as if the hand of Jim Crow had been at work.

In the 1970s, the courts and some politicians, believing that they had a duty not only to end segregation laws in education but also to integrate the schools, instituted a policy of **busing** in some northern cities. Students in majority white schools would be bused to mostly black schools, and vice versa. The policy was immediately controversial; riots in South Boston in 1974 resembled those in Little Rock seventeen years earlier.

As we indicated in What's at Stake, not all opponents of busing were reacting from racist motives. Busing students from their homes to a distant school strikes many Americans as fundamentally unjust. Parents seek to move to better neighborhoods so that they can send their children to better schools, only to see those children bused back to the old schools. Parents want their children to be part of a local community and its activities, which is hard when the children must leave the community for the better part of each day. And they fear for the safety of their children when they are bused into poverty-stricken areas with high crime rates.

The Supreme Court has shared America's ambivalence about busing. Although it endorsed busing as a remedy for segregated schools in 1971,[15] three years later it ruled that busing plans could not merge inner-city and suburban districts unless officials could prove that the district lines had been drawn in a racially discriminatory manner.[16] Since many whites were moving out of the cities, that meant that there were fewer white students to bus, and consequently busing did not really succeed in integrating schools in many urban areas. By the late 1980s, most urban schools were more segregated than they had been in the 1960s.[17]

The example of busing highlights a problem faced by civil rights workers and policymakers: deciding whether the Fourteenth Amendment guarantee of equal protection simply requires that the states not sanction discrimination or imposes an active obligation on them to integrate blacks and whites. As the northern experience shows, the absence of legal discrimination does not mean equality. In 1965 President Johnson issued Executive Order 11246, which not only prohibited discrimination in firms doing business with the government but also ordered them to take **affirmative action** to compensate for past discrimination. In other words, if a firm had no black employees, it wasn't enough not to have a policy against hiring them; the firm now had to actively recruit and hire blacks. The test would not be federal law or company policy, but the actual racial mix of employees.

Johnson's call for affirmative action was taken seriously not only in employment situations but also in university decisions. Patterns of discrimination in employment and higher education showed the results of decades of decisions by white males to hire or admit other white males. Blacks, as well as other minorities and women, were relegated to low-paying, low-status jobs. After Johnson's executive order, the EEOC decided that the percentage of blacks working in firms should reflect the percentage of blacks in the labor force. Many colleges and universities reserved space on their admissions lists for minorities, sometimes accepting minority applicants with lower grades and test scores than whites.

We have talked about the tension in American politics between procedural and

busing achieving racial balance by transporting students to schools across neighborhood boundaries

affirmative action a policy of creating opportunities for members of certain groups as a substantive remedy for past discrimination

substantive equality, between equality of treatment and equality of results. That is precisely the tension that arises when Americans are faced with policies of busing and affirmative action, both of which are instances of American policy attempting to bring about substantive equality. The end results seem attractive, but the means to get there—treating people differently—seems inherently unfair in the American value system. The Supreme Court reflected the public's unease with affirmative action policies but did not reject the idea, holding in 1978 that schools can have a legitimate interest in having a diversified student body and that they can take race into account in admissions decisions, just as they can consider geographic location, for instance.[18]

Few of the presidents after Kennedy and Johnson took strong pro–civil rights positions, but none effected a real reversal in policy until Ronald Reagan. Reagan's strong conservatism led him to regret the power that had been taken from the states by the Supreme Court's broad interpretation of the Fourteenth Amendment, and he particularly disliked race-based remedies for discrimination, like busing and affirmative action. The Reagan administration lobbied the Court strenuously to get it to change its rulings on the constitutionality of those policies, but it wasn't until the end of Reagan's second term, when the effect of his conservative appointments to the Court kicked in, that a true change in policy occurred.

In 1989 the Court fulfilled civil rights advocates' most pessimistic expectations. In a series of rulings, it held that the Fourteenth Amendment did not protect workers from racial harassment on the job,[19] that the burden of proof in claims of employment discrimination was on the worker,[20] and that affirmative action was on shaky constitutional ground.[21] The Democratic-led Congress sought to undo some of the Court's late-1980s rulings by passing the Civil Rights Bill of 1991, which made it easier for workers to seek redress against employers who discriminate.

Blacks in Contemporary American Politics

Racism in America is not over. The Supreme Court's use of strict scrutiny on laws that discriminate on the basis of race has put an end to most de jure discrimination, but de facto discrimination remains. We began the chapter noting that blacks fall behind whites on most socioeconomic indicators, although we should not disregard the existence of a growing black middle class. Still, although blacks accounted for 11 percent of the U.S. population in 1992, they owned only 4 percent of U.S. businesses. And in recent years, the average pay of college-educated African Americans has been falling compared to that of similarly educated whites. This growing gap is blamed, in part, on lack of enforcement of antidiscrimination laws, showing that even when laws change, society may not.[22]

The United States remains in many respects a segregated country. Urban schools are resegregating as the practice of busing falls off. In 1996 voters in California declared affirmative action illegal in their state, and in 1998 voters in Washington did the same. With the judicial elimination of affirmative action policies in Texas and elsewhere, professional schools and colleges are also resegregating. In 1998 the percentage of African Americans graduating from high school finally equaled the percentage of whites (87 percent), but the percentage of those completing college is only 14 percent, compared to 29 percent for whites.[23]

But African Americans have made some real political gains since the civil rights movement began. By 1999 there were nearly 9,000 black elected officials in the

United States, in posts ranging from local education and law enforcement to the U.S. Congress. In the 107th Congress, elected in 2000, 39 of 435 members of the House of Representatives were black, although there were no black senators. In 1999 there were 450 black mayors, although only one black governor. In 1996 the one Republican who was thought to have a chance to beat Democrat Bill Clinton was an African American, the former head of the Joint Chiefs of Staff, General Colin Powell. Though Powell declined to run for president, he became the first black secretary of state in 2001, one of the two African Americans in President George W. Bush's cabinet. Public opinion polls have indicated that more than 135 years after the end of the Civil War, Americans may very well be ready to elect a black president.[24]

WHO, WHAT, HOW   All Americans have a great deal at stake in the civil rights movement. Blacks have fought to be recognized as American citizens. The recognition of their rights has inevitably upset the traditional power structure of the South, and southerners have fought hard to keep that from happening. Northerners, practicing a more subtle and less intentional discrimination, also have a stake in preserving the status quo.

WHO are the actors?	WHAT do they want?	HOW do they get it?
African Americans	• Recognition and realization of civil rights • Economic and social equality	• Constitutional amendments • Interest groups • Court action • Nonviolent resistance • Affirmative action
Southerners	• Maintenance of power and the status quo	• Black codes • Jim Crow laws • De jure discrimination • Intimidation and violence
Northerners	• Maintenance of power and the status quo	• De facto discrimination • Resistance to substantive remedies • Intimidation and violence

Rights Denied on the Basis of Race and Ethnicity: Native Americans, Hispanic Americans, and Asian Americans

African Americans are by no means the only Americans whose civil rights have been denied on racial or ethnic grounds. Native Americans, Hispanics, and Asian Americans have all faced discrimination. For historical and cultural reasons, these groups have had different political resources available to them, and thus their struggles have taken shape in different ways.

Native Americans

Native Americans inhabited the so-called New World for centuries before it was discovered by European Americans. The relationship between the original inhabitants of this continent and the European colonists and their governments was difficult, marked by the new arrivals' clear intent to settle and develop Native Americans' ancestral lands, and complicated by their failure to understand the Indians' cultural, spiritual, and political heritage. The lingering effects of these centuries-old conflicts continue to color the political, social, and economic experience of Native Americans today.

The precise status of Native American tribes in American politics and in constitutional law is somewhat hazy. The Indians always saw themselves as sovereign independent nations, making treaties, waging war, and otherwise dealing with the early Americans from a position of strength and equality. But that sovereignty has not consistently been recognized by the U.S. government, and many of the treaties that the government made with Indian tribes were broken as the tribes were forced off their native lands. The commerce clause of the Constitution (Article I, Section 8) gives Congress the power to regulate trade "with foreign nations, among the several states, and with the Indian tribes," but it also has been interpreted as giving Congress guardianship over Indian affairs. The creation of the Bureau of Indian Affairs (BIA) in 1824 as part of the Department of War (moved to the Department of the Interior in 1849) institutionalized that guardian role.

Government policy toward Native Americans has alternated between trying to assimilate them into the broader, European-based culture, largely through education and missionary efforts, and encouraging them to forgo their dependence on federal assistance and develop economic independence and self-government. The combination of these two strategies—stripping them of their native lands and the culture that gave them their identity, and reducing their federal funding to encourage more independence—has resulted in tremendous social and economic dislocation in Indian communities. Poverty, joblessness, and alcoholism have created conditions of despair and frustration for many Native Americans. Their situation has been aggravated as Congress has denied them many of the rights promised in their treaties, in order to exploit the natural resources so abundant on the western lands the Indians had been forced onto, or as they have been forced to sell their rights to those resources in order to survive.

The political environment in which Native Americans found themselves in the mid-twentieth century was very different from the one faced by African Americans. What was denied them was not simply formal rights, or their enforcement, but the fulfillment of old promises and the preservation of a culture that did not easily coexist with modern American economic and political beliefs and practices. State politics did not provide any remedies, not merely because of local prejudice, but because Indian reservations are separate legal entities under the federal government. Because Congress itself was largely responsible for the plight of Native Americans, it was not a likely source of support for the expansion of their rights. Nor were the courts anxious to extend rights to Native Americans.

Like many other groups shut out from access to political institutions, Native Americans took their political fate into their own hands. In the 1960s and after, they focused on working outside the system to change public opinion and to persuade Congress to alter public policy. Not unlike the black protest movement of the sixties, but without its foundation of judicial victories, Indians formed groups such as the National Indian Youth Council, which organized "fish-ins" in 1964 to defend fishing rights lost in a state court decision, AMERIND, the Indian Land Rights Association, and the American Indian Civil Rights Council. The most well known of these groups was the American Indian Movement (AIM), founded in 1968.

But for all the militant activism of the 1960s and 1970s, Native Americans have made no great strides in redressing the centuries of dominance by white people. They remain at the bottom of the income scale in America, earning less than African Americans on average, and their living conditions are often poor. Only 65.6 percent of Native Americans are high school graduates, compared to 75 percent of the nation overall. Consider, for example, the Navajos living on and off the reservation in Montezuma Creek, Utah. Sixty percent have no electricity or running water, half don't have jobs, fewer than half have graduated from high school, and 90 percent receive some kind of government support.[25]

Since the 1980s, an ironic twist of legal interpretation has enabled some Native Americans to parlay their status as semisovereign nations into a foundation for economic prosperity. At least twenty states now allow gambling on Indian reservations, and in 1992 Americans spent three times as much at Indian-run casinos as they did on movie tickets, with the amount expected to double before 2002.[26] Casino gambling is controversial on several counts among Native Americans themselves, some of whom see it as their economic salvation and others as spiritually ruinous, and among other Americans, many of whom object for economic reasons. Regardless of the moral and economic questions unleashed by the casino boom, Native Americans argue that it is a way to recoup at least some of the resources that have been taken from them in the past.

Politically, there has been some improvement as well. In 1996 President Bill Clinton issued an executive order that requires federal agencies to protect and provide access to sacred religious sites of American Indians, which has been a major point of contention in Indian-government relations. And in national politics, people such as Senator Ben Nighthorse Campbell have been changing stereotypes of Native Americans and working to benefit Indian communities.

Hispanic Americans

Hispanic Americans, also called Latinos, are a diverse group with yet another story of discrimination in the United States. Among the reasons the Hispanic experience is different from that of other groups we discuss are the diversity within the Hispanic population, the language barrier that many face, and the political reaction to immigration, particularly illegal immigration, from Mexico into the United States.

Hispanics are one of the fastest-growing ethnic groups in America. The 2000 U.S. census counted 32 million Latinos/Hispanics, up from 22.5 million ten years earlier, and projected to hit 100 million by 2050. This growing population is strikingly diverse, as Figure 5.1 shows, consisting of people whose roots are in Mexico,

U.S. HISPANIC POPULATION IS GROWING

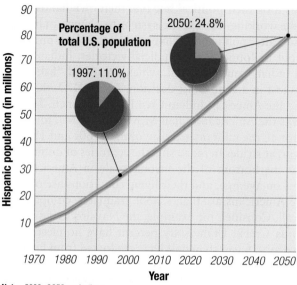

Note: 2000–2050: projections.

**Figure 5.1
America's Hispanic Population**

America's Hispanic population is diverse and growing. Hispanics account for about 11 percent of the total population today, and they are expected to make up almost one-quarter of the population by 2050.

U.S. HISPANIC POPULATION IS DIVERSE

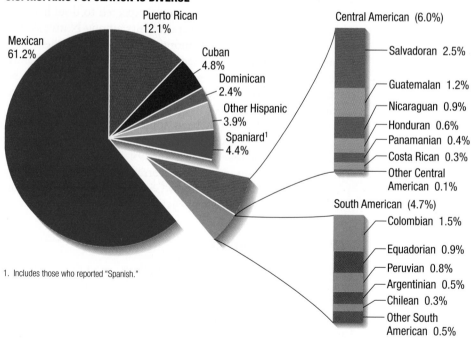

1. Includes those who reported "Spanish."

Puerto Rico, Cuba, Central and South America, and other Spanish-speaking parts of the world. These groups have settled in different parts of the country as well. Mexican Americans are largely located in California, Texas, Arizona, and New Mexico. Puerto Ricans live primarily in New York, New Jersey, and other northern cities. Cubans tend to be clustered in South Florida.

These groups differ in more than places of origin and settlement. Cubans are much more likely to be political refugees, whereas those from other countries tend to be economic refugees looking for a better life. Because primarily educated, professional Cubans fled their native country, they have largely gained a higher socioeconomic status in the United States as well. For instance, almost 20 percent of Cuban Americans are college educated, roughly the same percentage as for Americans as a whole, but only 6 percent of Mexican Americans and 9 percent of Puerto Ricans have graduated from college. Although the numbers suggest that if Hispanics acted together, they would wield considerable clout, their diversity has led to fragmentation and powerlessness.

Language has presented a special challenge to Hispanics. The United States today ranks sixth in the world in the number of people who consider Spanish a first language, with active and influential Spanish-language media (radio, television, and print). This preponderance of Spanish-speakers is probably due less to a refusal on the part of Hispanics to learn English than to the fact that new immigrants are continually streaming into this country.[27] Nonetheless, especially in areas with large Hispanic populations, white Anglos feel threatened by what they see as the encroachment of the Spanish language, and many communities have launched movements to make English the official language, which would preclude foreign languages from appearing on ballots and other official documents.

A final challenge to Hispanics is the American reaction against immigration, particularly illegal immigration from Mexico. A backlash against illegal immigration has some serious consequences for Hispanic American citizens, who may be indistinguishable in appearance, name, and language from recent immigrants. All of these things make acceptance into American society more difficult for Hispanics, encourage segregation, and make the subtle denial of equal rights in employment, housing, and education, for instance, easier to carry out.

Although the barriers to assimilation that Hispanics face are formidable, their political position is improving. Cesar Chavez, as leader of the United Farm Workers in the 1960s, drew national attention to the conditions under which Hispanic farm workers labored. Following the principles of the civil rights movement, he highlighted concerns of social justice in his call for a nationwide boycott of grapes and lettuce picked by nonunion labor, and in the process he became a symbol of the Hispanic struggle for equal rights. Groups such as the Mexican American Legal Defense and Education Fund (MALDEF), the Puerto Rican Legal Defense and Education Fund, and the League of United Latin American Citizens (LULAC) continue to lobby to end discrimination against Hispanic Americans.

There are currently twenty-one Hispanics in the 107th Congress, and President George W. Bush has named one Hispanic American to his cabinet (earlier Bill Clinton had appointed three). There are also high-level Hispanics in many other state offices. The voter turnout rate for Hispanics has traditionally been low, because they are disproportionately poor and poor people are less likely to vote, but this situation

Waking the Sleeping Giant *Although Hispanics are one of the fastest-growing ethnic groups in the United States, they remain one of the least mobilized groups in American politics. In 1996 less than 27 percent of voting-age Hispanics went to the polls. Here Dolores Huerta, cofounder of the United Farm Workers of America, leads a 1998 rally urging Latinos to vote for Gray Davis, the successful Democratic candidate for governor of California.*

is changing. Where the socioeconomic status of Hispanics is high and where their numbers are concentrated, as in South Florida, their political clout is considerable. Presidential candidates, mindful of Florida's twenty-five electoral votes, regularly make pilgrimages to South Florida to denounce Cuba's communist policies, a popular position among Cuban American voters there. Grassroots political organization has also paid off for Hispanic communities. In Texas, for instance, local groups called Communities Organized for Public Service (COPS) bring politicians to Hispanic neighborhoods so that poor citizens can meet their representatives and voice their concerns. They also organize voter registration drives that boost Hispanic participation. Similarly, the Southwest Voter Registration Project (SWVRP) has led more than a thousand voter registration drives in such states as California, Texas, and New Mexico. Groups like Latino Vote USA have targeted Hispanics in recent elections, to encourage them to register to vote and to turn out on election day. Such movements have increased Hispanic voter registration by more than 50 percent.

Asian Americans

Asian Americans share some of the experiences of Hispanics, facing cultural prejudice as well as racism and absorbing some of the public backlash against immigration. Yet the history of Asian American immigration, the explosive events of World War II, and the impressive educational and economic success of many Asian Americans mean that the Asian experience is in many ways different.

Like Hispanics, Asian Americans are a diverse population (see Figure 5.2), including people with roots in China, Japan, Korea, the Philippines, India, Vietnam, Laos, and Cambodia, to name just a few. There are Chinese Americans and Japanese Americans whose families have lived here since the 1800s, having arrived with the waves of immigrants who came to work in the frontier West, as well as much more recent immigrants from all over Asia.

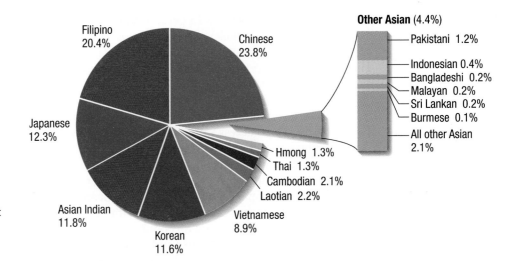

Figure 5.2
America's Asian
Population
The 1990 census counted nearly 7 million Asians, a nearly 100 percent increase over the 1980 count. As shown in this pie chart, they come from many different countries.
Source: U.S. Census Bureau.

Asian Americans live in every region of the United States. They make up the majority of the population of Hawaii, and 11 percent of the population of California. New York City has the largest Chinese community outside China. The more recent immigrants are spread throughout the country. The South is experiencing an especially fast-growing Asian population. From 1980 to 1990, the Asian and Pacific Islander population increased 146 percent in the South, compared to 103 percent in the rest of the country.[28]

Asians have faced discrimination in the United States since their arrival. The fact that they are identifiable by their appearance has made assimilation into the larger European American population difficult. While most immigrants dream of becoming citizens in their new contry, and eventually gaining political influence through the right to vote, that option was not open to Asians. The Naturalization Act of 1790 provided only for white immigrants to become naturalized citizens, and with few exceptions—for Filipino soldiers in the U.S. Army during World War II, for example—the act was in force until 1952. Exclusionary immigration reflected this country's long-standing hostility toward Asians, but anti-Asian sentiment was especially evident in the white American reaction to Japanese Americans during World War II. In 1942 the U.S. government rounded up Japanese Americans, forced them to abandon or sell their property, and put them in detention camps for purposes of "national security." The government was worried about security threats posed by people with Japanese sympathies, but two-thirds of the 120,000 people incarcerated were American citizens. Perhaps the greatest insult was the Supreme Court's approval of curfews and detention camps for Japanese Americans.[29] Although the government later reversed its policy and, in 1988, paid $1.25 billion in reparations to survivors of the ordeal, Japanese American internment is an ugly scar on America's civil rights record.

One unusual feature of the Asian American experience is their overall academic success and corresponding economic prosperity. Asian Americans graduate from high school and college at higher rates than other ethnic groups, and at least as high, and in some places higher, than whites. In 1999, 12 percent of the students at

Harvard were Asian, as were 23 percent at Stanford, and 33 percent at the University of California at Berkeley.[30] Median household incomes in the United States in 1998 were $51,205 for Asian and Pacific Islanders, $44,366 for whites, $30,735 for Hispanics, and $27,910 for blacks. Probably a number of factors account for this success. Forced out of wage labor in the West by resentful white workers in the 1880s, many Asian immigrants developed entrepreneurial skills and started their own businesses. A cultural emphasis on hard work and high achievement lent itself particularly well to success in the American education system. Furthermore, many Asian immigrants were highly skilled workers in their own countries and passed on the values of their achievements to their children.

According to our conventional understanding of what makes people vote in the United States, participation among Asian Americans ought to be quite high. But although voter turnout usually rises along with education and income levels, Asian American voter registration and turnout rates have been among the lowest in the nation. Particularly in states such as California, where Asian Americans constitute 11 percent of the population, their political representation and influence do not reflect their numbers.

Political observers account for this lack of participation in several ways. Until after World War II, immigration laws restricted the citizenship rights of Asian Americans. In addition, the political systems that many Asian immigrants left behind did not have traditions of democratic political participation. Finally, many Asian Americans came to the United States for economic reasons and have focused their attention on building economic security rather than learning to navigate an unfamiliar political system.[31]

There is some evidence, however, that this trend of nonparticipation is changing. Researchers have found that where Asian Americans do register to vote, they tend to do so at rates higher than those of other groups.[32] In the 1996 election, a national coalition of Asian American interest groups seeking to maximize their impact at the polls made a concerted effort to register and turn out Asian American voters. Partially as a result, Gary Locke was elected the first Asian American governor of a mainland state (Washington), and in 1998 there were two thousand elected U.S. officials of Asian and Pacific Islander descent—up 10 percent from 1996.[33] In 1996 about 33 percent of the Asian American voters in California were first-time voters.[34] Asian Americans made up only 6 percent of the California electorate in 1998 and 2000, despite projections that that percentage would increase.[35]

When Asian Americans do vote, they tend to split their support more or less equally between Democrats and Republicans as they did in 2000, giving 48 percent of their support to Gore and 47 percent to Bush.[36] While African Americans vote for Democrats over Republicans at a ratio of eight to one and Hispanic Americans at a ratio of two to one, Asian Americans favor Democrats only slightly, and 20 percent claim no party affiliation at all.[37]

WHO, WHAT, HOW   Native Americans, Hispanic Americans, and Asian Americans, like African Americans, all want their rights as citizens to be recognized, and they want to have their interests represented in the political system and to gain economic and social equality. And also like African Americans, they have faced strong opposition in their quest for equal rights.

WHO are the actors?	WHAT do they want?	HOW do they get it?
Native Americans	• Recognition and protection of civil rights • Economic and social equality	• Political activism • Establishment of casinos • Commerce clause
Hispanic Americans	• Recognition and protection of civil rights • Economic and social equality	• Boycotts • Voter education
Asian Americans	• Recognition and protection of civil rights • Economic and social equality	• Academic and economic success
Opponents of extended rights	• Maintenance of status quo	• Court action • Discriminatory legislation • General hostility and intimidation

Rights Denied on the Basis of Gender: Women

Of all the battles fought for equal rights in the American political system, women's struggle has perhaps been the most peculiar. Women, though certainly denied most civil and economic rights, were never outside the system in the same way racial and ethnic groups have been. In early America, most women lived with their husbands or fathers, and many shared their view that men, not women, should have power in the political world. Women's realm, after all, was the home, and the prevailing belief was that women were too good, too pure, too chaste to deal with the sordid world outside. As a New Jersey senator argued in the late 1800s, women should not be allowed to vote because they have "a higher and holier mission. . . . Their mission is at home."[38] Today there are still some women, as well as men, who agree with the gist of this sentiment. That means that the struggle for women's rights has not only failed to win the support of all women, but it has also been actively opposed by some of them, as well as by men whose power, standing, and worldview it has threatened.

The legal and economic position of women in the early nineteenth century, though not exactly "slavery," in some ways was not far different. According to English common law, on which our legal system is based, when a woman married, she merged her legal identity with her husband's, which is to say that in practical terms, she no longer had one. Once married, she could not be a party to a contract, bring a lawsuit, own or inherit property, earn wages for any service, gain custody of her children in case of divorce, or initiate divorce from an abusive husband. If her husband were not a U.S. citizen, she lost her own citizenship. Neither married nor unmarried women could vote. In exchange for the legal identity his wife gave up, a husband was expected to provide security for her, and if he died without a will, she was entitled to one-third of his estate. If he made a will and left her out of it, however, she had no legal recourse to protect herself and her children.[39]

The Birth of the Women's Rights Movement

The women's movement is commonly dated from an 1848 convention on women's rights held in Seneca Falls, New York. At the convention, propositions that were enthusiastically and unanimously approved included calls for the right to own property, to have access to higher education, and to receive custody of children after divorce. The only resolution not to receive unanimous support, even among the supporters of women's rights at the convention, was one calling for women's right to vote.

The women's movement picked up steam after Seneca Falls, but it had yet to settle on a political strategy. The courts were closed to women, since they had no independent legal identity. For a long time, women's rights advocates worked closely with the antislavery movement, assuming that when blacks received their rights, they and the Republican Party would rally to the women's cause. Not only did that fail to happen, but the passage of the Fourteenth Amendment marked the first time the word *male* appeared in the Constitution, causing a bitter split between the two movements.

Regularly, from 1878 to 1896 and again after 1913, a federal woman suffrage amendment called the Susan B. Anthony Amendment, named after an early advocate of women's rights, was introduced into Congress but failed to pass. Other women's rights advocates focused efforts at the state level, taking on the more practical task of changing state electoral laws. It was this state strategy that would finally create the conditions under which the Nineteenth Amendment would be passed and ratified in 1920.

The Struggle in the States

The state strategy was a smart one for women. Unlike the situation blacks faced after the war, the national government was not behind their cause. It was possible for women to have an impact on state governments, however, even those where discrimination was a problem. Different states have different cultures and traditions, and the Constitution allows them to decide who may legally vote. Women were able to target states that were sympathetic to them, then gradually gain enough political clout that their demands were listened to on the national level.

Women were able to vote beginning in 1869 in the Territory of Wyoming, and when Wyoming was admitted to the Union in 1890, it was the first state to give women the vote. Wyoming's experience did not prove contagious, however. From 1870 to 1910, women waged 480 suffrage campaigns in thirty-three states, caused seventeen referenda to be held in eleven states, and won in only two of them—Colorado (1893) and Idaho (1896). In 1910 women began to refine their state strategy and were soon able to win two more referenda, in Washington (1910) and California (1911). By 1912, with the addition of Arizona, Kansas, Oregon, and Illinois, women could vote in states that controlled 74 of the 483 electoral college votes that decided the presidency.

In 1914 an impatient, militant offshoot of the women's movement began to work at the national level again, picketing the White House and targeting the presidential party, contributing to the defeat of twenty-three of forty-three Democratic candidates in the western states where women could vote. The appearance of political power lent momentum to the state efforts. In 1917 North Dakota gave women presidential suffrage. Ohio, Indiana, Rhode Island, Nebraska, and Michigan soon followed suit. Arkansas and New York joined the list later that year. A major women's rights group issued a statement to Congress that if it would not pass the Susan B. Anthony Amendment, its members would work to defeat every legislator who opposed it. The amendment passed in the House but not the Senate, and the group targeted four senators. Two were defeated, and two held on to their seats by a narrow margin. Nine more states gave women the right to vote in presidential elections.

In 1919 the Susan B. Anthony Amendment was reintroduced into Congress with the support of President Woodrow Wilson and passed by the necessary two-thirds majority in both houses. When, in August 1920, Tennessee became the thirty-sixth state to ratify the Nineteenth Amendment, women finally had the vote nationwide. Unlike the situation faced by African Americans after the passage of the Fifteenth Amendment, the legal victory ended the woman suffrage battle. Although many women were not inclined to use their newly won right, enforcement of woman suffrage was not as difficult as enforcement of black suffrage. But right to the end, opposition to woman suffrage had been petty and virulent, and the victory was only narrowly won.

Winners and Losers in the Suffrage Movement

The debate over woman suffrage, like the fight over black civil rights, was bitter because so much was at stake. If women were to acquire political rights, opponents feared, an entire way of life would end. In many ways, of course, they were right.

The opposition to woman suffrage came from a number of different directions. In the South, white men rejected it for fear that women would encourage enforcement of the Civil War amendments, giving political power to blacks. And if women could vote, then of course black women could vote, further weakening the white male position. In the West, and especially the Midwest, brewing interests fought suffrage, believing that women would force temperance on the nation. Liquor interests fought the women's campaign vigorously, stuffing ballot boxes and pouring huge sums of money into antisuffrage efforts. In the East, women's opponents were industrial and business interests, who were concerned that voting women would pass enlightened labor legislation and would organize for higher wages and better working conditions. Antisuffrage women's groups, usually representing upper-class women, claimed that women's duties at home were more than enough for them to handle and that suffrage was unnecessary because men represented and watched out for women's interests.[40] For well-to-do women, the status quo was comfortable, and changing expectations about women's roles could only threaten that security.

Eventually, everything these opponents feared came to pass, though not necessarily as a result of women voting. Although women's rights advocates were clear winners in the suffrage fight, it took a long time for all the benefits of victory to materialize. As the battle over the Equal Rights Amendment would show, attitudes toward women were changing at a glacial pace.

The Equal Rights Amendment

The Nineteenth Amendment gave women the right to vote, but it did not ensure the constitutional protection against discrimination that the Fourteenth Amendment had provided for African Americans. It was unconstitutional to treat people differently on account of race but not on account of gender. Following ratification of the Nineteenth Amendment in 1920, some women's groups turned their attention to the passage of an **Equal Rights Amendment (ERA),** which would ban discrimination on the basis of gender and guarantee women equal protection of the law. Objections to the proposed amendment again came from many different directions. Traditionalists, both men and women, opposed changing the status quo and giving more power to the federal government. But even some supporters of women's rights feared that requiring laws to treat men and women the same would actually make women worse off by nullifying legislation that sought to protect women. Many social reformers, for instance, had worked for laws that limited working hours or established minimum wages for women, and these laws would now be in jeopardy. Opponents also feared that the ERA would strike down laws preventing women from being drafted and sent into combat. Many laws in American society treated men and women differently, and few, would survive under the ERA.

In the early 1970s, several pieces of legislation signaling that public opinion was favorable to the idea of expanding women's rights were passed. Among these was Title IX of the Education Amendments, which in 1972 banned gender discrimination in schools receiving federal funds. This meant, among other things, that schools had to provide girls with an equal opportunity and equal support to play sports. The ERA was, however, less successful.

The House of Representatives finally passed the ERA in 1970, but the Senate spent the next two years refining the language of the amendment. Finally, on March 22, 1972, the Senate passed the amendment, and the process of getting the approval of three-quarters of the state legislatures began. By early 1973, thirty states had ratified the amendment, but over the next four years, only five more states voted for ratification, bringing the total to thirty-five states, three short of the necessary thirty-eight. Despite the extension of the ratification deadline from 1979 to 1982, the amendment died unratified.

There are several reasons the ERA failed to pass. First, although most people supported the idea of women's rights in the abstract, they weren't sure what the consequences of such an amendment would be, and they feared the possibility of radical social change. Second, the ERA came to be identified in the public's mind with the 1973 Supreme Court ruling in *Roe* v. *Wade,* ensuring women's abortion rights in the first trimester of a pregnancy, a ruling that remains controversial today.[41] Finally, the Supreme Court had been striking down some (though not all) laws that treated women differently from men, using the equal protection clause of the Fourteenth Amendment., According to some opponents, this made the ERA unnecessary.[42]

Gender Discrimination Today

Despite the failure of the ERA, most of the legal barriers to women's equality in this country have been eliminated. But because the ERA did not pass and there is no constitutional amendment specifically guaranteeing equal protection of the law regard-

Equal Rights Amendment (ERA) constitutional amendment, passed by Congress but never ratified, that would have banned discrimination on the basis of gender

World-Class Women
The 1999 World Cup champions celebrate their victory at the Rose Bowl in California. Many people credit Title IX of the Higher Education Act (aimed at ending discrimination in athletic programs at federally funded institutions) with giving female athletes in the United States the opportunities they needed to make this victory possible.

less of gender, the Supreme Court has not been willing to treat gender as a suspect classification, although it has come close at times. Laws that treat men and women differently are subject only to the intermediate standard of review, not the strict scrutiny test.

Having achieved formal equality, women still face some striking discrimination in the workplace. They earn only seventy cents for every dollar earned by men, and the National Committee on Pay Equity, a nonprofit group in Washington, calculates that the pay gap may cost some women almost half a million dollars over their work lives.[43] In addition, women are tremendously underrepresented at the upper levels of corporate management and academic administration, as well as in other positions of power. Some people argue that the reason women earn less than men and wield less power is that many women leave and enter the job market several times or put their careers on hold to have children. Such interruptions prevent them from accruing the kind of seniority that pays dividends for men. The so-called mommy track has been blamed for much of the disparity between men's and women's positions in the world. Others argue that there is an enduring difference in the hiring and salary patterns of women that has nothing to do with childbearing or that reflects male inflexibility when it comes to integrating motherhood and corporate responsibility. These critics claim that there is a "glass ceiling" in the corporate world, invisible to the eye but impenetrable, which prevents women from realizing their full potential. The Civil Rights Act of 1991 created the Glass Ceiling Commission to study this phenomenon, and among the commission's conclusions was the observation that business is depriving itself of a large pool of talent by denying leadership positions to women.

Some analysts have argued that the glass ceiling is a phenomenon that affects relatively few women. Most women today are less preoccupied with moving up the corporate ladder than with making a decent living, or getting off what one observer has called the "sticky floor" of low-paying jobs.[44] Although the wage gap between men and women with advanced education is narrowing, women still tend to be excluded from the more lucrative blue-collar positions in manufacturing, construction, communication, and transportation.[45]

WHO, WHAT, HOW   Supporters and opponents of the women's movement struggled mightily over the extension of rights to women.

WHO are the actors?	WHAT do they want?	HOW do they get it?
Women	• Civil rights • Strict scrutiny of discriminatory laws	• State politics • Gains in electoral power • ERA (failed)
Opponents of women's rights	• Maintenance of power and the status quo • Protection of business interests	• Rules that denied access to courts and Congress • Encouraging public resistance to change

Rights Denied on Other Bases

Race, gender, and ethnicity are not the only grounds on which the laws treat people differently in the United States. Three more classifications that provide interesting insights into the politics of rights in America are sexual orientation, age, and disability.

Sexual Orientation

Gays and lesbians have faced two kinds of legal discrimination in this country. First, certain laws in some states make it illegal for them to engage in homosexual activities (sodomy), to join the military, or teach in public schools, for instance. This is overt discrimination. But a more subtle kind of discrimination doesn't forbid their actions or behavior; it simply fails to recognize them legally. Thus gays cannot marry or claim the rights that married people share, such as collecting their partner's social security, being covered by their partner's insurance plan, being each other's next of kin, or having a family. Some of these rights can be mimicked with complicated and expensive legal arrangements, and some are possible because of the good will of some companies toward their employees. But others are out of reach under the current laws. Being gay, unlike being black or female or Asian American, is something that can be hidden from public view, and until the 1970s many gays escaped overt discrimination by denying or concealing who they were. Many argue that that, too, is a serious deprivation of civil rights.

The legal status of gays in America was spelled out in the case of *Bowers* v. *Hardwick*, discussed in Chapter 4.[46] Here the Supreme Court argued that there was no constitutionally protected right to engage in homosexual behavior, nor any reason why the states could not regulate or outlaw it. The Court did not require that a law that treated people differently on the basis of sexual orientation fulfill either a compelling or an important state purpose; it merely had to be a reasonable use of state power. The *Bowers* judgment remained more or less intact until 1996, when a bitterly split Court struck down an amendment to the Colorado constitution that would have prevented gays from suing for discrimination in housing and employment. The Court ruled that gays could not be singled out and denied the fundamental protection of the law—that "a state cannot deem a class of persons a stranger to its laws." Although the majority on the Court did not rule that sexual orientation was a suspect classification, it did hint at greater protection than the minimum rationality test would warrant.[47] For the first time, it treated gay rights as a civil rights issue.

The courts are not the only political avenue open to gays in their struggle for equal rights. Gays began to organize politically in 1969, after riots following police harassment at a gay bar in New York City called the Stonewall Inn. Because, on average, gays tend to be well educated and economically well-off, and because they are well organized politically and make a point of voting, they have, as a group, more influence than their numbers would indicate. A 1994 survey found that only 6 percent of the population identify themselves as gay, but the average household income for gays was estimated in 1995 to be $72,440, as opposed to $35,695 for the general population.[48] In the past, gays have primarily supported the Democratic Party, but a group of conservative gays calling themselves the Log Cabin Republicans have now become active on the political right. Openly gay congressmen have been elected from both sides of the partisan divide.

The issue of gay rights has come to the forefront of the American political agenda not only because of gays' increasing political power but also because of the fierce opposition of the Christian Right. Their determination to banish what they see as an unnatural and sinful lifestyle, and their conviction that protection of the basic rights of homosexuals means that they will be given "special privileges," has focused tremendous public attention on issues that most of the public would prefer remained private. Controversial political issues in the 1990s have included gays in the military, gay marriages, and funding for AIDS research. Public opinion remains mixed on the subject, but tolerance is increasing. In 1996, 56 percent of Americans disapproved of same-sex relationships, down from 75 percent in 1987. Americans oppose job discrimination against gays in higher numbers, however. In 1996, 84 percent supported equal rights to job opportunities, up from 56 percent in 1977.[49] This civil rights struggle will certainly continue to be on the political agenda in the twenty-first century.

Age

In 1976 the Supreme Court ruled that age is not a suspect classification.[50] That means that if government has rational reasons for doing so, it may pass laws that treat younger or older people differently from the rest of the population, and courts do not have to use strict scrutiny when reviewing those laws. Young people are often not granted the full array of rights of adult citizens, being subject to curfews or locker searches at school, nor are they subject to the laws of adult justice if they commit a crime. Some people have argued that children should have expanded rights to protect them in dealing with their parents.

Older people face discrimination most often in the area of employment. Compulsory retirement at a certain age, regardless of an individual's capabilities or health, may be said to violate basic civil rights. The Court has generally upheld mandatory retirement requirements.[51] Congress, however, has sought to prevent age discrimination with the Age Discrimination Act of 1967, outlawing discrimination against people up to seventy years of age in employment or in the provision of benefits unless age can be shown to be relevant to the job in question. In 1978 the act was amended to prohibit mandatory retirement before age seventy, and in 1986 all mandatory retirement policies were banned except in special occupations.

Unlike younger people, who can't vote until they are eighteen and don't vote in great numbers after that, older people defend their interests very effectively. Voter participation rates rise with age, and older Americans are also extremely well organized politically. The American Association of Retired Persons (AARP), a powerful interest group with more than 30 million members, has been active in pressuring government to preserve policies that benefit elderly people. The AARP is very much present in debates about cutting government services, and in light of their advice and voting power, programs such as social security and Medicare (health care for older Americans) have remained virtually untouched.

Disability

People with physical and mental disabilities have also organized politically to fight for their civil rights. Advocates for people with disabilities include disabled people themselves, those who work in social services catering to the disabled, and veterans groups. Even though laws do not prevent disabled people from voting, staying in hotels, or using public telephones, circumstances often do. Inaccessible buildings, public transportation, and other facilities can pose barriers as insurmountable as the law, as can public attitudes toward and discomfort around disabled people.

The 1990 Americans with Disabilities Act (ADA), modeled on the civil rights legislation that empowers racial and gender groups, protects the rights of the more than 44 million mentally and physically disabled people in this country. Disabilities covered under the act need not be as dramatic or obvious as confinement to a wheelchair or blindness. People with AIDS, recovering drug and alcohol addicts, and heart disease and diabetes patients are among those covered. The act provides detailed guidelines for access to buildings, mass transit, public facilities, and communications systems. It also guarantees protection from bias in employment. The Equal Employment Opportunity Commission (EEOC) is authorized to handle cases of job discrimination because of disabilities, as well as race and gender. The ADA was controversial because many of the required changes in physical accommodations, such as ramps and elevators, are extremely expensive. Advocates for the disabled respond that these expenses will be offset by increased business from disabled people and by the added productivity and skills that people with disabilities bring to the workplace.

WHO, WHAT, HOW   This section has looked at what is at stake in the rights struggles of groups who already enjoy the most fundamental civil rights, including the right to vote. Nonetheless, these groups continue to face considerable discrimination in other parts of their lives.

WHO are the actors?	WHAT do they want?	HOW do they get it?
Gays and lesbians Youth and elderly People with disabilities	• Protection of civil rights	• Court action • Interest group formation • Lobbying Congress • Supporting presidential candidates • Electoral power
Opponents of extended rights	• Particular moral vision of society • Cost efficiency • Maintenance of power and status quo	• Court action • Interest group formation • Lobbying Congress • Supporting presidential candidates • Electoral power

Citizenship and Civil Rights

It should be clear that the stories of America's civil rights struggles are the stories of citizen action. Of the three models of democratic participation that we discussed in Chapter 1—elite, pluralist, and participatory—the pluralist model best describes the actions citizens have taken to gain protection of their civil rights from government. Pluralism emphasizes the ways that citizens can increase their individual power by organizing into groups. The civil rights movements in the United States have been group movements. Groups succeeded in gaining rights where individual action and pleas for government action were unavailing. To the extent that groups in America have been unable to organize effectively to advance their interests, their civil rights progress has been correspondingly slowed.

Points of Access

- Attend a rally to protect the rights of a campus group (for example, a Martin Luther King Day rally or a Take Back the Night march).

- Join a campus organization devoted to protecting the rights of a group claiming discrimination.

- Volunteer to work in a service organization that serves a disadvantaged community population.

- Teach English to immigrants.

WHAT'S AT STAKE REVISITED

In this chapter, we have explored the history and politics of discrimination in the United States and the efforts that have been made to counteract the effects of discrimination that linger after it has been made illegal. One such method is busing. Busing, like its policy cousin affirmative action, long under attack for unfairly discriminating against whites, has fallen into disrepute. But we opened this chapter with a busing success story—the story of desegregation in Fort Wayne, Indiana, which does not seem to fit the national pattern. We asked what really is at stake in busing and how Fort Wayne managed to reassure those who saw themselves as having a great deal to lose.

The stakes in busing should be clearer to us now. On one side, what is at stake are values of neighborhood and community, combined with the right of parental choice and the American dream of improving the quality of one's life and one's family life. On the other side, what is at stake is a vision of an integrated society, where valued goods such as education are distributed equally, so that all children have a truly fair start in society. These goals are usually assumed to be on opposite sides of the debate, but they are not mutually exclusive. Opponents of busing may also value integration, and busing advocates may certainly cherish family and community. At the heart of the division is an underlying difference over the meaning of equality, a commitment to fair rules (procedural equality) or to fair outcomes (substantive equality), and a difference of opinion on whether America has done enough to end its race problem.

Given these very deep and serious stakes, how did Fort Wayne desegregate its schools in such a short time with such a seemingly positive reaction? The city drew on the techniques of procedural equality to achieve the results of substantive equality, thereby gaining the acceptance of citizens on both sides of the divide—even though 323 buses transport 18,000 students more than 16,600 miles to school each day.[52] The Fort Wayne plan involved voluntary school choice. Instead of busing students willy-nilly from one neighborhood school to another, administrators let parents choose the school their kids would attend. To make the schools in the black neighborhoods more attractive, inner-city schools were renovated and modernized. Magnet schools— five elementary schools and a middle school with attractive programs such as fine arts, Spanish immersion, and Montessori instruction—were developed to draw students away from their neighboorhood schools. Admissions to these schools were determined by lottery, but high school and middle school students were allowed to apply to schools outside their neighborhoods, where they could maintain friendships made in elementary school. The staffs of the schools also were integrated; thirty-one principals in Fort Wayne's schools are black. Fort Wayne's schools were integrated by busing, but it was not *forced* busing, and therein lies much of the difference.

It should be noted that school integration in Fort Wayne was not without strife. Initially, almost everyone opposed it, and parents who favored integration filed a lawsuit to force the district to deal with the issue. What is worth paying attention to, however, is that Fort Wayne found a way to bridge two seemingly incompatible visions of equality in America by using means that were seen as procedurally fair to achieve substantive ends. If solutions to inequality such as affirmative action and busing are not palatable to the majority of Americans because they seem to violate fundamental norms of American culture, then innovative and creative remedies like Fort Wayne's may be our only alternatives. ■

key terms

affirmative action   129
black codes   123
boycott   126
busing   129
civil rights   119
de facto discrimination   127
de jure discrimination   126
Equal Rights Amendment
  (ERA)   142

grandfather clause   124
intermediate standard of
  review   120
Jim Crow laws   124
literacy test   124
minimum rationality test   120
National Association for the
  Advancement of Colored
  People (NAACP)   125

poll tax   124
Reconstruction   124
segregation   124
strict scrutiny   120
suspect classification   120

summary

- Throughout U.S. history, various groups, because of some characteristic beyond their control, have been denied their civil rights and have fought for equal treatment under the law.

- Groups that are discriminated against may seek procedural remedies, such as changing the law to guarantee *equality of opportunity,* or substantive remedies, such as the institution of affirmative action programs, to achieve *equality of outcome.*

- African Americans have experienced both *de jure discrimination,* created by laws that treat people differently, and *de facto discrimination,* which occurs when societal tradition and habit lead to social segregation.

- African Americans led the first civil rights movement in the United States. By forming interest groups such as the NAACP and developing strategies such as nonviolent resistance, African Americans eventually defeated de jure discrimination.

- Native Americans, Hispanics, and Asian Americans also have fought to gain economic and social equality. Congressional control over Native Americans' land has led them to assert economic power through the development of casinos. Using boycotts and voter education drives, Hispanic Americans have worked to stem the tide of English-only movements and anti-immigration efforts. Despite their smaller numbers, Asian Americans aim for equal political clout, but it is mainly through their cultural emphasis on education that they have gained considerable economic power.

- The women's rights movement has represented challenges to power, the traditional way of life, and economic profit. Early activists were restricted by the courts and Congress and instead found success through state politics. Present efforts focus on the courts to give women greater protection of the law.

- Gays, youth, the elderly, and people with disabilities enjoy the most fundamental civil rights, but they still face de jure and de facto discrimination. Whereas moral concerns motivate opposition to gays, social order and cost efficiency inspire restrictions on youth, the elderly, and disabled Americans.

6

Congress

What's at Stake?

Congress: Representation and Lawmaking
- Four Kinds of Representation
- National Lawmaking

Congressional Powers and Responsibilities
- Differences Between the House and the Senate
- Congressional Checks and Balances

Congressional Elections: Choosing the Members
- Congressional Districts
- Deciding to Run

How Congress Works: Organization
- The Central Role of Party
- The Leadership
- The Committee System
- Congressional Resources: Staff and Bureaucracy

How Congress Works: Process and Politics
- The Context of Congressional Policymaking
- How a Bill Becomes Law—Some of the Time
- The Mechanics of Congressional Decision-Making
- How Well Does Congress Work?

Citizenship and Congress

What's at Stake Revisited

WHAT'S AT STAKE?

Marjorie Margolies-Mezvinsky was not supposed to win her 1992 congressional election. A Democrat running in a Pennsylvania district that had not elected a Democratic representative since 1916, she went to her campaign headquarters on election night with her concession speech to opponent Jon D. Fox in hand. To her surprise, the same voters in her district who chose Bill Clinton for president elected her as well by a margin of almost fourteen hundred votes—a narrow victory that meant reelection two years down the line could be difficult. It was. Swept into office with Bill Clinton, she was swept out of office just two years later by virtue of her association with him.

The reason for Margolies-Mezvinsky's brief tenure in Congress was what commentators and politicians have come to call "The Vote." Margolies-Mezvinsky had convinced her constituents that, though a Democrat, she was economically conservative, meaning above all that she was against raising taxes. President Clinton's budget, submitted to Congress in 1993, represented what observers called "Clintonomics"—a policy to eliminate the budget deficit by raising taxes and cutting spending. Margolies-Mezvinsky vowed to vote against it, and in a preliminary vote she did, declaring that "there was an overriding principle that was more important than calls from the president and vice-president. That was to keep my promise to the voters."[1]

But Clinton's budget was the centerpiece of his new administration. Already facing criticism for political missteps and misjudgments, the president needed a budget victory to keep his administration afloat. He did what all presidents do, canvassing his party members for votes, sending out staffers to plead his case, calling in favors, and making promises and personal calls to get the needed votes.

Margolies-Mezvinsky's call came after 9:00 P.M. on Thursday, August 5, 1993, the day of the final budget vote. She had already prepared a statement explaining the vote she had promised her constituents she would make—the "no" vote she expected to cast. Unbeknownst to her constituents, however, she had made another promise as well. In reply to an earlier plea for support from the president, Margolies-Mezvinsky had told him that she did not want to vote for the budget but that she would

Representative Marjorie Margolies-Mezvinsky (D-PA) promised constituents she wouldn't raise taxes. Still, when President Bill Clinton pleaded for her support, she voted for his 1993 budget bill. It was an agonizing decision. Costly, too: despite attempts to explain her vote, she wasn't reelected the following year.

not be the one "to sink his administration."[2] Thursday night Clinton asked her to make good on that pledge. He needed 218 House votes to pass the budget; he had only 217. He pulled out all the stops: "Without your vote I can't win. I think my administration will grind to a halt without the passage of this budget. The entire rest of our agenda depends on getting this behind us. What would it take?"[3]

What it would take, a torn Margolies-Mezvinsky told the president, was his presence at a conference to be held in her district on the perils of entitlement spending (welfare, social security, and so on), issues that she thought had not been adequately addressed in the budget. He agreed. Telling herself, "You're not one-tenth as important as a president,"[4] Margolies-Mezvinsky went down to the floor of the House with an escort of senior Democrats and cast the 218th vote to pass Clinton's budget. Around her, knowing the political cost of what she was doing, Republicans on the floor called out, "Goodbye, Marjorie," and waved farewell. Was her seat actually at stake because of this vote? Was Clinton's administration at stake as he claimed? How could Margolies-Mezvinsky evaluate the rival claims of her constituents, on the one hand, and what she believed to be the national interest, and her party's, on the other? ■

The U.S. Congress is the longest-running and most powerful democratic legislature in the world. The Capitol in Washington, D.C., home to both the House of Representatives and the Senate, is as much a symbol of America's democracy as the Stars and Stripes or the White House. We might expect Americans to express considerable pride in their national legislature, with its long tradition of serving democratic government. But if we did, we would be wrong. Congress is generally distrusted, seen by the American public as incompetent, corrupt, torn by partisanship, and at the beck and call of special interests.[5] And yet, despite their contempt for the institution of Congress as a whole, Americans typically revere their representatives and senators and reelect them so often that critics have long been calling for term limits to get new people into office. How can we understand this bizarre paradox?[6]

If politics is about who gets what and how, then Congress is arguably the center of American national politics. Not only does it often decide exactly who gets what, but it also has the power to alter many of the rules (or the how) that determine who wins and who loses in American political life. Within this context, there are two main reasons for America's love-hate relationship with Congress. The first is that citizens have conflicting goals when it comes to the operation of their national legislature. On the one hand, they want an advocate in Washington to take care of their local or state interests and to ensure that their home district gets a fair share of national resources such as highway funds, military expenditures, and agricultural support. On the other hand, citizens also want Congress to take care of the nation's business. This can pose a quandary for legislators, because what is good for the home district, like price supports for tobacco farmers or keeping a redundant military base open, might not be good for the nation as a whole. The second reason for citizens' love-hate relationship with Congress is that the rules that determine how Congress works were designed by the founders to produce slow, careful lawmaking that can seem motionless to an impatient public. When citizens are looking to Congress to produce policies that they favor or to distribute national resources, the built-in slowness can look like intentional foot-dragging and partisan bickering.

These twin themes, Congress's conflicting goals and its institutionalized slowness, will take us a long way toward understanding our mixed feelings about our national legislature. In this chapter, we focus on who—including citizens, other politicians, and members of Congress themselves—gets the results they want from Congress, and how the rules of legislative politics help or hinder them. We look at

- the clash between representation and lawmaking
- the powers and responsibilities of Congress
- congressional membership and elections
- the organization of Congress and the rules of congressional operation

Congress: Representation and Lawmaking

representation
the efforts of elected officials to look out for the interests of those who elect them

constituency
the voters in a state or district

We count on our elected representatives in both the House and the Senate to perform two major functions: representation and lawmaking. These two functions, as we shall see, are often in conflict, making the job of legislator a potentially very difficult one.

Four Kinds of Representation

By **representation,** we mean that those we elect should represent, or look out for, our local interests and carry out our will. We usually elect people who we believe would do what we would do if we were in Congress ourselves. Representation means working on behalf of one's **constituency**—the folks back home in the district who voted for the member, as well as those who voted for someone else. Most members of Congress try to excel at four different types of representation so that their constituents will rate them highly and return them to Washington.[7]

policy representation congressional work to advance the issues and ideological preferences of constituents

- **Policy representation** refers to congressional work for laws that advance the economic and social interests of the constituency or, more rarely, the nation. House members and senators from petroleum-producing states, for instance, can be safely predicted to vote in ways favorable to the profitability of the oil companies, members from the plains states try to protect subsidies for wheat farmers, and so on.

allocative representation congressional work to secure projects, services, and funds for the represented district

pork barrel public works projects and grants for specific districts paid for by general revenues

- Voters have also come to expect a certain amount of **allocative representation,** in which the congressperson gets projects and grants for the district. Such perks are called **pork barrel** benefits, paid for by all the taxpayers but enjoyed by just a few. Representatives who are good at getting pork barrel projects for their districts (for example, highway construction or the establishment of a research institution) are said to "bring home the bacon."

casework legislative work on behalf of individual constituents to solve their problems with government agencies and programs

- Senators and representatives also represent their states or districts through **casework,** or constituency service, taking care of the individual problems of constituents, especially problems that involve the federal bureaucracy. Casework can cover things such as finding out why a constituent's social security check has not shown up, sending a flag that has flown over the nation's Capitol to a high school in the district, or helping with immigration and naturalization problems.

symbolic representation the efforts of members of Congress to stand for American ideals or to identify with common constituency values

- Finally, members of Congress engage in **symbolic representation,** projecting many of the positive values Americans associate with public life and government. Thus members are glad to serve as commencement speakers at high school graduations or to attend town meetings to explain what is happening in Washington.

National Lawmaking

lawmaking the creation of policy to address national problems

At the same time that we expect our legislators to represent their constituents' interests, we also believe that they should address the country's social and economic problems by **lawmaking**—passing laws that serve the national, not the local, interest. A variety of factors go into a representative's calculation of how to vote on matters of national interest. He or she might be guided by conscience or ideology, by what opinion polls say the local constituents want, or by party position.

The functions of representation and lawmaking often conflict. What is good for us and our local community may not serve the national good. If we are a dairy-farming district, higher milk prices might suit us just fine, but the rest of the nation will be worse off. By the same token, our particular community might suffer when policy is made to solve a national problem. Losing an expensive military installation might hurt our community even though it will help to balance our national budget. One of the chief lessons of this chapter is that the rules under which Congress operates make it likely that when these primary functions do conflict, members of Congress will favor their jobs as representatives—that is, they usually do what the local district wants. Thus national problems go unaddressed while local problems get

CONSIDER THE SOURCE

How to Be a Critical Constituent

As an American, you are often urged to write to your congressperson, but it is actually far more likely that your congressperson will write to you! Members of Congress want to tell you what a great job they are doing on your behalf, and they take every opportunity to highlight the programs they have sponsored or the good deeds they have done—especially when they are running for reelection. Similarly, members of Congress maintain spiffy web sites that allow you to review your legislators' accomplishments and even respond by e-mail (see http://www.house.gov/ for the House of Representatives and http://www.senate.gov/ for the Senate). These kinds of member-provided public relations materials are easy to get, but they are not completely reliable if you are looking for balanced information on the performance of your elected representatives—information you need if you are going to be a critical constituent.

Being a critical constituent means more than sitting around the dinner table griping about Congress. Being a critical constituent means knowing what your representatives are doing and evaluating how well they are representing your interests to determine whether or not you should vote for them again or look around for another choice. Being a critical constituent means being a savvy citizen. How can you learn about your rep-

resentative's or senators' performance in Congress? There is an abundance of information out there, but it is not all equally reliable or equally easy to find. Here we give you a guide to sources that can help you discover and evaluate what your elected representatives are up to.

1. One of the very best sources of information for the average citizen about members of Congress comes from a nonpartisan organization called Project Vote Smart (PVS). PVS collects information on the background, issue positions, campaign finances, and voting records of more than thirteen thousand officeholders and candidates for president, governor, Congress, and the state legislatures. They also track performance evaluations for members of Congress from all special-interest groups that provide them. These evaluations represent the frequency with which the member of Congress voted with that organization's preferred position on a number of votes that it has identified as key to its issue area. One big advantage of PVS is that it attempts to provide data on all the candidates, not just incumbents, and makes its information available during the campaign. All the information is free and on-line at http://www.vote-smart.org. And if you're not sure who your elected representatives (two senators and one House member) are, PVS can help you get that information, too. Another helpful web site providing congressional vital statistics is CapWeb, "The Internet Guide to the U.S. Congress," at http://www.voxpop.org.

2. For an overview of the debates going on in Congress, you can find the detailed proceedings of past sessions in the *Congressional Record,* which is available in print at many university libraries and on-

attention, resources, and solutions. No wonder we love our individual representatives but think poorly of the job done by Congress as a national policymaking institution.

WHO, WHAT, HOW   Both citizens and their representatives have something serious at stake in the tension between representation and lawmaking. Constitutional provisions and the rules of electoral politics mean that the tension is likely to be a lasting one.

line (http://www.thomas.loc.gov/) for the last few sessions. Though informative, the *Congressional Record* can be tedious to read, and it is not an exact transcript of congressional proceedings. Members are regularly given permission, by unanimous consent, to "extend and revise" their remarks even to the extent of adding whole speeches they never gave. So take this source with a grain of salt.

3. There are a number of media sources, both local and national, that track congressional action. Your own local paper should cover the activities of your state's senators and representatives through articles and editorials and may report on how each representative votes on various bills. Try to figure out from the tone of the editorials, or from what you know about the paper's political endorsements, how the editorial board feels about your congressional members so you can fairly evaluate what they have to say. The national media may cover your representatives as well. A quick search on Lexis Nexis, if your library provides it, can help you out here. You can also go to the highly readable biennial almanacs that provide detailed portraits of members of Congress and their districts and states. These are *The Almanac of American Politics,* published by National Journal, and *Politics in America,* published by Congressional Quarterly (CQ). Professionals who need regular and in-depth information on Congress consult *Congressional Quarterly Weekly* and *National Journal* (most college libraries will have these publications). Expensive on-line services such as CQ's "On Congress" and National Journal's "Cloakroom" cater to the needs of professionals who require up-to-the-minute information on the comings and goings of Congress. Both have extensive databases that can be used to develop a detailed political biography of a member of Congress. Some colleges and universities maintain subscriptions to these services.

4. Many lobbyists, professional campaign consultants, and others with big appetites for congressional information spend handily for insider newsletters, such as *Roll Call* and *Hotline,* that cover Congress and campaigns in great detail. You can read about some of the inner workings of Congress yourself by going to Roll Call Online (http://www.rollcall.com), which is devoted to "the people, politics, and process of Congress," or to the on-line version of *The Hill,* a nonpartisan, nonideological weekly newspaper (http://www.hillnews.com).

5. Finally, take the opportunity to get to know your elected representatives. Members regularly come home for long weekends in part to maintain contact with constituents. Send an e-mail message or letter to your congressperson asking when he or she will be nearby. He or she will be happy to tell you of upcoming town meetings or visits to district offices. This is harder to arrange for a senator from a large state, but most citizens can meet with their representative with just a bit of effort.

What do you do with all this information? Getting the facts is only part of the job of being a critical constituent. Evaluating them is no less important. Anytime you engage in evaluation, you need a clear yardstick against which to measure the thing you are evaluating. Here it may be helpful to remember the twin pressures on a member of Congress to be both a representative and a national lawmaker. Which do you think is more important? What kind of balance should be struck between them? How does your congressperson measure up?

WHO are the actors?	WHAT do they want?	HOW do they get it?
Citizens	• Local interests protected • National interests protected	• Four kinds of representation • National lawmaking
Senators and representatives	• Influence on national policy • Reelection	• Rules of electoral politics • Constitutional rules of lawmaking

Congressional Powers and Responsibilities

Even though the process of policymaking it establishes is slow and incremental, the Constitution gives the U.S. Congress enormous powers. It is safe to say that the founders could not have imagined the scope of contemporary congressional power, since they never anticipated the growth of the federal government to today's size. As we will see, they were less concerned with a conflict between the representation of local versus national interests than they were with one between the representation of short-term public opinion versus long-term national interests. The basic powers of Congress are laid out in Article I, Section 8, of the Constitution. They include the power to tax, to pay debts, and to provide for the common defense and welfare of the United States, among many other things.

Differences Between the House and the Senate

The term *Congress* refers to the institution that is formally made up of the House of Representatives and the Senate. Congresses are numbered so that we can talk about them over time in a coherent way. Each Congress covers a two-year election cycle. The 107th Congress was elected in November 2000, and its term runs from January 2001 through the end of 2002. The **bicameral** (two-house) **legislature** is laid out in the Constitution. The founders wanted two chambers so that they could serve as a restraint on each other, strengthening the principle of checks and balances. The framers' hope was that the smaller, more elite Senate would "cool the passions" of the people represented in the House. Accordingly, while the two houses are equal in their overall power—both can initiate legislation (although tax bills must originate in the House), and both must pass every bill in identical form before it can be signed by the president to become law—there are also some key differences, particularly in the extra responsibilities assigned to the Senate. In addition, the two chambers operate differently, and they have distinct histories and norms of conduct (informal rules and expectations of behavior).[8] Some of the major differences are outlined in Table 6.1.

bicameral legislature
a legislature with two chambers

The single biggest factor determining differences between the House and the Senate is size. With 100 members, the Senate is less formal; the 435-person House needs more rules and hierarchy in order to function efficiently. The Constitution also provides for differences in terms: two years for the House, six for the Senate (on a staggered basis—all senators do not come up for reelection at the same time). In the modern context, this means that House members never stop campaigning. Senators, in contrast, can suspend their preoccupation with the next campaign for the first four or five years of their terms and thus, at least in theory, have more time to spend on the affairs of the nation. The minimum age of the candidates is different as well: members of the House must be at least twenty-five years old, senators thirty. This again reflects the founders' expectation that the Senate would be older, wiser, and better able to deal with national lawmaking. This distinction was reinforced in the constitutional provision that senators be elected not directly by the people, as are members of the House, but by state legislatures. Although this provision was

Table 6.1
Differences Between the House and the Senate

	House	Senate
Constitutional Differences		
Term length	2 years	6 years
Minimum age	25	30
Citizenship required	7 years	9 years
Residency	In state	In state
Apportionment	Changes with population	Fixed; entire state
Impeachment	Impeaches official	Tries the impeached official
Treaty-making power	No authority	2/3 approval
Presidential appointments	No authority	Majority approval
Organizational Differences		
Size	435 members	100 members
Number of standing committees	19	18
Committee assignments per member	Approx. 5	Approx. 7
Rules Committee	Yes	No
Limits on floor debate	Yes	No (filibuster possible)
Electoral Differences		
Costs of Elections		
Incumbents	$678,556	$4.2 million
Challengers	$286,582	$3.1 million
Incumbency Advantage	94% reelected	90% reelected

Sources: N. Ornstein, T. Mann, and M. Malbin, *Vital Statistics on Congress 1997–1998* (Washington, DC: AEI, 1998); R. Davidson and W. Oleszak, *Congress and Its Members*, 6th ed. (Washington, DC: Congressional Quarterly Press, 1998), 201.

changed by constitutional amendment in 1913, its presence in the original Constitution reflects the convictions of its authors that the Senate was a special chamber, one step removed from the people.

Budget bills are initiated in the House of Representatives. In practice, this is not particularly significant, since the Senate has to pass budget bills as well, and most of the time differences are negotiated between the two houses. The budget process has gotten quite complicated, as demonstrated by congressional struggles in the 1980s and 1990s to deal with the federal deficit, which called for reductions in spending at the same time that constituencies and interest groups were pleading for expensive new programs. The budget process illustrates once again the constant tension for members of Congress between being responsive to local or particular interests and at the same time trying to make laws in the interest of the nation as a whole.

Other differences between the House and the Senate include the division of power in the impeachment of public figures such as presidents and Supreme Court justices. The House impeaches, or charges an official with "Treason, Bribery, or other high Crimes and Misdemeanors," and the Senate tries the official. Presidents Andrew Johnson and Bill Clinton were impeached by the House, but in both cases the Senate failed to find the president guilty of the charges. In addition, only the

Senate is given the responsibility of confirming appointments to the executive and judicial branches and of sharing the treaty-making power with the president, responsibilities we explore in more detail in the following section.

Congressional Checks and Balances

The founders were concerned generally about the abuse of power, but since they were most anxious to avoid executive tyranny, they granted Congress an impressive array of powers. Keeping Congress at the center of national policymaking are the power to regulate commerce; the exclusive power to raise and to spend money for the national government; the power to provide for economic infrastructure (roads, postal service, money, patents); and significant power in foreign policy, including the power to declare war, to ratify treaties, and to raise and support armed forces. But the Constitution also limits congressional power through the protection of individual rights and the watchful eye of the other two branches of government, with whom Congress shares power.

Congress and the President   Our system of checks and balances means that to exercise its powers, each branch has to have the cooperation of the others. Thus Congress has the responsibility for passing bills, but the bills do not become law unless (a) the president signs them or, more passively, refrains from vetoing them or (b) both houses of Congress are able to muster a full two-thirds majority to override a presidential veto. While he cannot vote on legislation or introduce bills, the Constitution gives the president a powerful policy formulation role in calling for his annual State of the Union address and in inviting him to recommend to Congress "such Measures as he shall judge necessary and expedient."

Cooperation between Congress and the president is also necessitated by the requirement that major presidential appointments—for instance, to cabinet posts, ambassadorships, and the Supreme Court—must be confirmed by the Senate. Historically, most presidential appointments have proceeded without incident, but in recent administrations appointments have increasingly set off huge clashes. Senators sometimes use their confirmation powers to do more than "advise and consent" on the appointment at hand. They may tie up appointments, either because they oppose the candidate or to extract promises and commitments from the president.

A continuing source of institutional conflict between Congress and the president is the difference in their constituencies. The president looks at each policy in terms of a national constituency and his own policy program, whereas members of Congress necessarily take a narrower view. For example, the president may decide that clean air should be a national priority, while for some members of Congress, a clean air bill might mean closing factories in their districts.

Congress and the Courts   The constitutional relationship between the federal courts and Congress is simple in principle. Congress makes the laws, and the courts interpret them. The Supreme Court also has the lofty job of deciding whether laws and procedures are consistent with the Constitution, although this power of judicial review is not actually contained in the Constitution.

We think of the judiciary as independent of the other branches, but this self-

Fresh Faces
Every new Congress sees some turnover as older members retire or are defeated. Some "freshman classes" arrive with a distinct identity. The very conservative Class of '94 allowed the Republican party to take control of Congress in what has often been referred to as the "Republican Revolution." By contrast, the freshman class of 2000 is diverse and likely to go their individual ways. The especially close presidential race meant that there were no presidential coattails which might make freshman members beholden to the administration.

sufficiency is only a matter of degree. Congress, for example, is charged with setting up the lower federal courts and determining the salaries for judges, with the interesting constitutional provision that a judge's salary cannot be cut. Congress also has considerable powers in establishing some issues of jurisdiction—that is, in deciding which courts hear which cases (Article III, Section 2). And in accepting or rejecting the president's Supreme Court and federal court nominees, the Senate can influence the long-term operation of the courts.[9]

WHO, WHAT, HOW   The Constitution gives great power to both the House and the Senate, but it does so in the curiously backhanded way known as checks and balances, leaving the two houses of Congress to share power with each other and with the other institutions, and to resort to negotiation, compromise, and cooperation to get what they want.

WHO are the actors?	WHAT do they want?	HOW do they get it?
Congress	• Power	• Constitutional rules
President		• Checks and balances
Courts		• Political tactics

Congressional Elections: Choosing the Members

The first set of rules a future congressperson has to contend with are those that govern congressional elections. These, more than any others, are the rules that determine the winners and losers in congressional politics. No matter what a member of Congress might hope to accomplish, he or she cannot achieve it as a legislator without winning and keeping the support of voters. With House elections every two years and Senate elections every six years, much of the legislator's life is spent running for reelection.

Congressional Districts

reapportionment
a reallocation of congressional seats among the states every ten years, following the census

As a result of the Great Compromise of 1787, the Constitution provides that each state will have two senators and that seats in the House of Representatives will be allocated on the basis of population. Two important political processes regulate the way House seats are awarded. One is **reapportionment,** in which the 435 House seats are reallocated among the states after each ten-year census, the official count of the nation's population. States whose populations grow gain seats, which are taken from those whose populations decline or remain steady. Table 6.2 shows the states that gained and lost representation in 2000. The winners these days are mostly in the rapidly growing Sun Belt states of the South and Southwest; the losers are largely in the Northeast and Midwest. Since little political discretion is involved, the process of reapportionment has always been fairly straightforward.

Far more political, however, is the second process, which regulates the way districts are drawn. Until the 1960s, the states often suffered from **malapportionment,** the unequal distribution of population among the districts, so that some had many fewer residents than others. This, in effect, gave greater representation to those living in lower-population districts. This difference is built into the Constitution in the case of the U.S. Senate, but the Supreme Court decided in 1964 that for the U.S. House of Representatives, as well as for both houses of the state legislatures, Americans should be represented under the principle of "one person, one vote" and that the districts therefore must have equal populations.[10] The population per House district in the year 2000 was 632,184.[11] Districts are equalized through a political process called redistricting. **Redistricting** is the re-

malapportionment
the unequal distribution of population among districts

redistricting
the process of dividing states into legislative districts

Table 6.2
Changes in Representation with the 1990 and 2000 Reapportionments

State	Net Change from 1980 to 1990	Change for 2000
Winners		
Arizona	+1	+2
California	+7	+1
Colorado	—	+1
Florida	+4	+2
Georgia	+1	+2
Nevada	—	+1
North Carolina	+1	+1
Texas	+3	+2
Virginia	+1	—
Washington	+1	—
Losers		
Connecticut	—	−1
Illinois	−2	−1
Indiana	—	−1
Iowa	−1	—
Kansas	−1	—
Kentucky	−1	—
Louisiana	−1	—
Massachusetts	−1	—
Michigan	−2	−1
Mississippi	—	−1
Montana	−1	—
New Jersey	−1	—
New York	−3	−2
Ohio	−2	−1
Oklahoma	—	−1
Pennsylvania	−2	−2
West Virginia	−1	—
Wisconsin	—	−1

Source: U.S. Bureau of the Census.

drawing of district lines in states with more than one representative. This procedure, which is carried out by the state legislatures (or by commissions they empower), is frequently a bitter political battle because how district lines are drawn has a lot to do with who has, gets, and keeps power in the state.

gerrymandering
redistricting to benefit a particular group

Gerrymandering is the process of drawing district lines to benefit one group or another, and it can result in some extremely strange shapes by the time the state politicians are through. One type of gerrymandering is partisan, with the party controlling the redistricting process, drawing lines to maximize the number of seats it wins. A Democratic legislature, for instance, might draw a district so that it splits a conservative town or community, reducing its ability to elect a Republican representative.

racial gerrymandering
redistricting to enhance or reduce the chances that a racial or ethnic group will elect members to the legislature

Racial gerrymandering occurs when district lines are drawn to favor or disadvantage an ethnic or racial group. For many years, states in the Deep South drew district lines to ensure that black voters would not constitute a majority that could elect an African American to Congress. Since the 1982 Voting Rights Act, the drawing of such districts has been used to maximize the likelihood that African Americans *will* be elected to Congress. Both Republicans and African American political activists have backed the formation of "majority minority" districts, in which African Americans or Hispanic Americans constitute a majority. This has the effect of concentrating enough minority citizens in one district to elect one of their own, but at the same time it takes these (usually Democratic) voters out of other districts, thus making it easier for Republicans to win nonminority districts.[12] Some very strange looking districts have resulted from gerrymandering. For instance, when the boundaries of the First and Twelfth Districts in North Carolina were redrawn after the 1990 census to consolidate the state's African American population, the Twelfth District was particularly odd-shaped, snaking for more than 160 miles along a narrow stretch of Interstate 85 (see Figure 6.1). The gerrymandering did accomplish its purpose, however. Two African Americans—the first since 1889—were elected to represent North Carolina in Congress in 1992.[13]

Racial gerrymandering is highly controversial. While politicians and racial and ethnic group leaders continue to jockey for the best district boundaries to satisfy their interests, the courts struggle to find a fair set of rules for

After the 1990 census (1992)

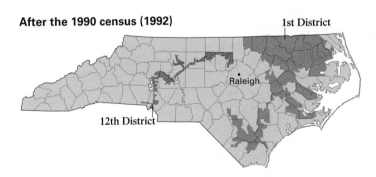

1st District

Raleigh

12th District

After the Supreme Court decision (1997)

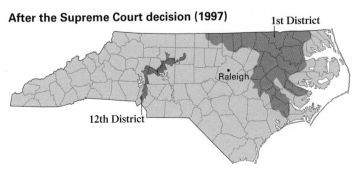

1st District

Raleigh

12th District

Figure 6.1
Gerrymandering in the 1990s
The First and Twelfth Districts of North Carolina were redrawn in 1992 (based on the 1990 census) to consolidate African American communities. The Supreme Court invalidated the gerrymandered districts, and they were redrawn again in 1997.

drawing district lines. In two cases decided in 1993 and 1995, the Supreme Court declared that race cannot be the predominant factor in drawing congressional districts. It can be taken into account, but so must other factors, such as neighborhood and community preservation. Since race is a suspect classification (see Chapter 5), it is subject to strict scrutiny whenever the law uses it to treat citizens differently, and the law must fulfill a compelling state purpose, whether it penalizes them or, in these cases, benefits them.[14] Two more cases decided in 1996 affirmed the Court's view that gerrymandering is unconstitutional when race is the main factor in drawing new district lines. The Court ruled that North Carolina's Twelfth District and three new districts in Texas were unconstitutional and ordered the states to draw new lines.[15]

Deciding to Run

Imagine that your interest in politics is piqued as a result of your American politics class. You decide that the representative from your district is out of touch with the people and too wrapped up in Washington politics, and you start thinking about running for office. What sorts of things should you consider? What would you have to do to win?

Who Can Run?   The formal qualifications for Congress are not difficult to meet. In addition to the age and citizenship requirements listed in Table 6.1, the Constitution requires that you live in the state you want to represent, although state laws vary on how long or when you have to have lived there (New York, for instance, requires that a U.S. senator elected from that state live there only at the time of the election, hence former First Lady Hillary Clinton's unusual run for the Senate in 2000). Custom also dictates that if you run for the House, you live in the district you want to represent. There are no educational requirements for Congress.

While constitutionally the qualifications for Congress are looser than those for many other jobs you may apply for when you graduate, in fact, most members of Congress have gone to college, two-thirds have graduate degrees, many are lawyers and businesspeople, and quite a few are millionaires. In many ways, Congress is an educational, occupational, and economic elite.

Congress is also an overwhelmingly white male institution. White males make up 40 percent of the U.S. population, but they account for 80 percent of the U.S. Congress.[16] Congress is, however, more representative today than it has been through most of our history. Figure 6.2 shows changes in the numbers of African Americans, Hispanics, and women in the House of Representatives and the Senate from 1901 to 2001.

Why Would Anyone Want This Job?   Perhaps you want to run for Congress because you want to serve your country. Many people run from a sense of duty to country or party or on a wish to realize certain ideals. But you may also think that the job of a representative is very attractive in its own right. First, there is all the fun of being in Washington and living a life that is undeniably exciting and powerful. The salary, $141,300 in 2000, puts representatives and senators among the top wage earners in the nation, and the "perks" of office are rather nice as well. These perks include prestige and reputation, as well as more tangible rewards: generous travel al-

Figure 6.2
Number of African Americans, Hispanics, and Women of all Races Serving in Congress, 1901–2001

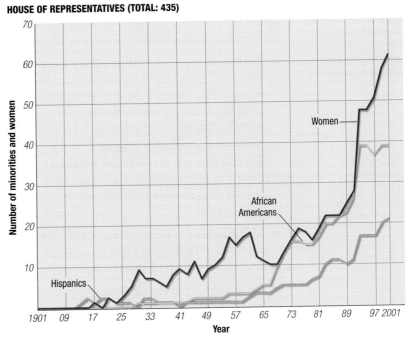

HOUSE OF REPRESENTATIVES (TOTAL: 435)

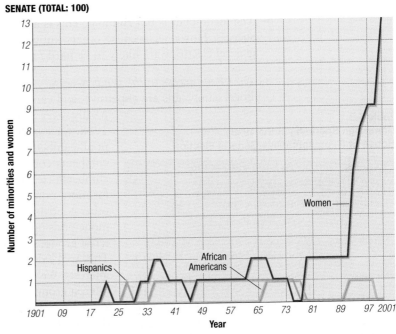

SENATE (TOTAL: 100)

franking

the privilege of free mail service provided to members of Congress

lowances, ample staff, and **franking,** the privilege of free mail service provided to members of Congress.

Offsetting these enviable aspects of serving in Congress are the facts that the work is awfully hard, it is expensive to maintain two households (one in Washington and one back home), the pressure can be intense, and the job security is nonexistent.

strategic politician
an office seeker who bases the decision to run on a rational calculation that he or she will be successful

How Can I Win?   **Strategic politicians** act rationally and carefully in deciding when to run for Congress and what office to run for. As a strategic candidate yourself, consider these four questions:

1. *Is this the right district or state for me?* People want to vote for and be represented by people like themselves, so determine whether you and the district are compatible. Liberals do not do well in conservative parts of the South, African Americans have great difficulty getting elected in predominantly white districts, Republicans have a hard time in areas that are mostly Democratic, and so forth.

2. *What is the strategic situation in the district?* The strategic situation is largely governed by the **incumbency advantage**, which refers to the edge in visibility, experience, organization, and fundraising ability possessed by incumbents—those people who already hold the job. It can make them hard to defeat. Three possibilities exist:

incumbency advantage
the electoral edge afforded to those already in office

- An incumbent of your party already holds the seat. If so, winning the nomination is a long shot. Only forty-eight incumbents, or 1.3 percent of all those seeking reelection, lost in primary battles to determine a party's nominee between 1982 and 2000.

- An incumbent of the opposite party holds the seat. If so, winning the primary to get your party's nomination will probably be easier, but the odds are against winning the general election. More than 94 percent of incumbents have won their general election contests over the past twenty years.

- The incumbent is not running. This is an "open seat" and is your best chance of success. However, because others know this as well, both the primary and the general elections are likely to be hard fought by high-quality candidates.

3. *Do I have access to the funds necessary to run a vigorous campaign?* Modern political campaigns are expensive, and campaigns run on a budget and a prayer are hardly ever successful. Winning nonincumbents in 1998, for example, spent over three times as much as nonincumbents who did not win, and even then nonincumbents could not keep up with the spending of incumbents (see Table 6.3). Incumbents have access to a lot more political action committee (PAC) money and other contributions than do nonincumbents. (PACs are money-raising organizations devoted to a particular interest group, such as a labor union or trade association. They make donations to candidates that represent their interests. We'll hear more about PACs in Chapter 11, on interest groups.) A nonincumbent must raise on average about two-thirds of a million dollars to have even a chance of winning in the House. Senate contests, with their much larger constituencies, cost much more.

Table 6.3
Campaign Spending in the 1998 House of Representatives General Election

Average Campaign Expenditures by Type of Candidate		
Incumbents	Winners ($N = 395$)	$629,330
	Losers ($N = 6$)	$1,285,030
Challengers	Winners ($N = 6$)	$1,148,979
	Losers ($N = 246$)	$283,770
Open seats	Winners ($N = 34$)	$996,650
	Losers ($N = 32$)	$545,115

Note: Expenditures reported to the FEC 1997–1998 as of September 2000 [http://www.fec.gov/finance/state97.htm].

4. *How are the national tides running?* Some years are good for Democrats, some for Republicans. These tides are a result of such things as presidential popularity, the state of the economy, and military engagements abroad. If it is a presidential election year, a popular presidential candidate of your party might sweep you to

**Figure 6.3
Party Control in
Congress,
1928–2000**

After a long period of uninterrupted dominance by the Democratic Party, the House of Representatives came under Republican control in the "Republican Revolution" of 1994. The Republicans held control of the House in the 2000 election, but their small edge in seats guarantees intense competition as they struggle for control of the House in the 2002 election and beyond.

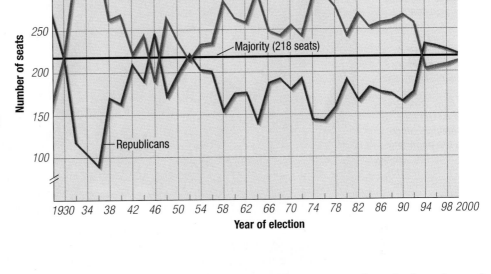

coattail effect

the added votes received by congressional candidates of a winning presidential party

midterm loss

the tendency for the presidential party to lose congressional seats in off-year elections

victory on his or her coattails. The **coattail effect,** less significant in these times of declining party ties, refers to the added votes congressional candidates of the winning presidential party receive in a presidential election year as voters generalize their enthusiasm for the national candidate to the whole party.

While the strength of coattails might be declining, until 1998 there was no arguing with the phenomenon of the **midterm loss.** This is the striking regularity with which the presidential party loses seats in Congress in midterm, or off-year, elections, which fall between presidential election years. The presidential party lost seats in the House of Representatives in every midterm election in the twentieth century except those in 1934—an election that took place during the New Deal, amid the massive growth of the Democratic Party in national politics—and 1998, when, under unusual circumstances, President Clinton's party, the Democrats, picked up five House seats. The 1994 election, which brought Republicans to power in Congress for the first time in forty years (see Figure 6.3), was a striking example of the midterm loss: fifty-three seats changed from Democratic to Republican control, making it the largest change of this sort in fifty years.[17] In general, the biggest factors that determine how many seats the presidential party will lose in a midterm election are the president's standing with the public and the state of the economy. An unpopular president and a sour economy spell bad news for congressional candidates of the presidential party in an off-year election.[18]

The 107th Congress

While the drama of the 2000 presidential election dominated post-election discussion, the Congressional elections in 2000 provided their own excitement and may come to be remembered for a number of interesting outcomes. One, certainly will be

Some Are Asked to Stay, Some Aren't . . . *Election 2000 provided for a lot of changes, including some significant "firsts" captured in this picture of Vice President Al Gore swearing in Hillary Rodham Clinton as the new U.S. senator from New York. She is the first First Lady to hold elective office, while the departing president, Bill Clinton, was the first Democratic president to complete two full terms of office since Franklin D. Roosevelt.*

the precedent-breaking election which moved Hillary Rodham Clinton from her role as First Lady in the White House to junior Senator in Congress representing the state of New York. The electoral Senate victory of deceased Democratic Missouri governor Mel Carnahan over Republican incumbent Senator John Ashcroft, also proved to be one of the stranger twists of the election. Carnahan had died in a tragic airplane accident three weeks before the election, and Carnahan's widow agreed to accept appointment to the Senate in her husband's stead. Jean Carnahan and Hillary Clinton join a Senate that will include a record number of women.

But a more far-ranging feature of Election 2000 in Congress was how close the American electorate came to achieving an almost perfect partisan stand-off. The presidential race ended in a virtual dead heat and both the House and the Senate moved from tiny Republican majorities to razor-thin Republican control of both chambers, resulting in the most narrowly divided Congress in almost half a century.

This high level of partisan balance in Congress was not matched, interestingly, in the competitiveness of the 2000 congressional elections. As usual, incumbents were returned by generally large margins with not much more than token resistance from the other party. Over 97 percent of the House incumbents and 80 percent of the Senate incumbents running for reelection were successful.

The Democrats and Republicans running and getting elected to both the House and the Senate continued the trend of polarizing debate, with the Democrats ranging from moderately to extremely liberal viewpoints and Republicans ranging from moderately to extremely conservative. As members work to fulfill their many campaign promises, high levels of conflict between the parties are almost inevitable. It will take exceedingly effective leadership and, perhaps, good luck, for the 107th to bridge the considerable differences between the parties and pull off the often acclaimed but hard to attain "bipartisan solutions" to our nation's problems.

WHO, WHAT, HOW Congressional elections are the meeting ground for citizens and their representatives, where each side brings its own goals and its own stakes in the process.

WHO are the actors?	WHAT do they want?	HOW do they get it?
Citizens	• Representation of local interest • National lawmaking	• Constitutional provisions for representation in the House and the Senate
Members of Congress	• Election and reelection	• Electoral politics • Incumbency advantage • Perks of office

How Congress Works: Organization

In spite of the imperatives of reelection and the demands of constituency service, the primary business of Congress is making laws. Lawmaking is influenced a great deal by the organization of Congress—that is, the rules of the institution that determine where the power is and who can exercise it. In this section, we describe how Congress organizes itself and how this structure is influenced by members' goals.

The Central Role of Party

majority party
the party with the most seats in a house of Congress

Political parties are central to how Congress functions for several reasons. First, Congress is organized along party lines. In each chamber, the party with the most members—the **majority party**—decides the rules for each chamber and gets the top leadership posts, such as Speaker of the House, majority leader of the Senate, and the chairmanships of all the committees and subcommittees.

Party is also important in Congress because it is the mechanism for members' advancement. Because all positions are determined by the parties, members have to advance within their party to achieve positions of power in the House or Senate, whether as a committee chair or in the party leadership.

Finally, party control of Congress matters because the parties stand for very different things. Across a wide range of issues, Democrats embrace more liberal policies and Republicans advocate more conservative ones. On issues from abortion to term limits to foreign affairs, Democratic members of Congress are more liberal and Republicans more conservative. Thus, although Americans like to downplay the importance of parties in their own lives, political parties are fundamental to the operation of Congress and hence what the national government does.

The Leadership

The majority and minority parties in each house elect their own leaders, who are, in turn, the leaders of Congress. Strong centralized leadership allows Congress to be more efficient in enacting party or presidential programs, but it gives less independence to members to take care of their own constituencies or to pursue their own policy preferences.[19] Although the nature of leadership in the House of Representatives has varied over time, the current era is one of considerable centralization of power. Because the Senate is a smaller chamber and thus easier to manage, its power is more decentralized.

Leadership Structure   The Constitution provides for the election of some specific congressional officers, but Congress itself determines how much power the leaders of each chamber will have. The main leadership offices in the House of Representatives are Speaker of the House, majority leader, minority leader, and the whips. The **Speaker of the House** is elected by the full membership, but this vote is a technicality: members always vote with their parties in this case, and the Speaker is therefore always the leader of the majority party. The real political choice about who the party leader should be occurs within the party groupings in each chamber. These are called the **party caucuses**. The Speaker of the House (or his designee) presides over floor deliberations and is the most powerful House member. The House majority leader, second in command, is given wide-ranging responsibilities to assist the Speaker. Figure 6.4 shows the structure of leadership for the two houses in the 107th Congress.

The leadership organization in the Senate is similar but not as elaborate. The presiding officer of the Senate is the vice president of the United States, who can cast a tie-breaking vote when necessary but otherwise does not vote. When the vice president is not present, which is almost always the case, the president pro tempore of the Senate officially presides, although the role is usually performed by a junior senator. Because of the Senate's much freer rules for deliberation on the floor, the presiding officer in the Senate has less power than the presiding officer in the House, where debate is generally tightly controlled. The locus of real leadership in the Senate is in the majority leader and the minority leader. Each is advised by party committees on both policy and personnel matters, such as committee appointments.

In both chambers, Democratic and Republican leaders are assisted by party whips. (The term *whip* comes from an old English hunting expression. The "whipper in" was charged with keeping the dogs together in pursuit of the fox.) Elected by party members, the whips find out how people intend to vote on important bills so that the leaders can adjust the legislation, negotiate acceptable amendments, or employ favors (or occasionally threats) to line up support. The whips work to persuade party members to support the party on key bills, and they are active in making sure favorable members are available to vote when needed.

Leadership Powers   Leaders can exercise only the powers that their party members give them. From the members' standpoint, the advantage of a strong leader is that he or she can move legislation along, get the party program passed, do favors for the members, and improve the standing of the party. The disadvantage is that a

Speaker of the House   the leader of the majority party, who serves as the presiding officer of the House of Representatives

party caucuses   party groupings in each legislative chamber

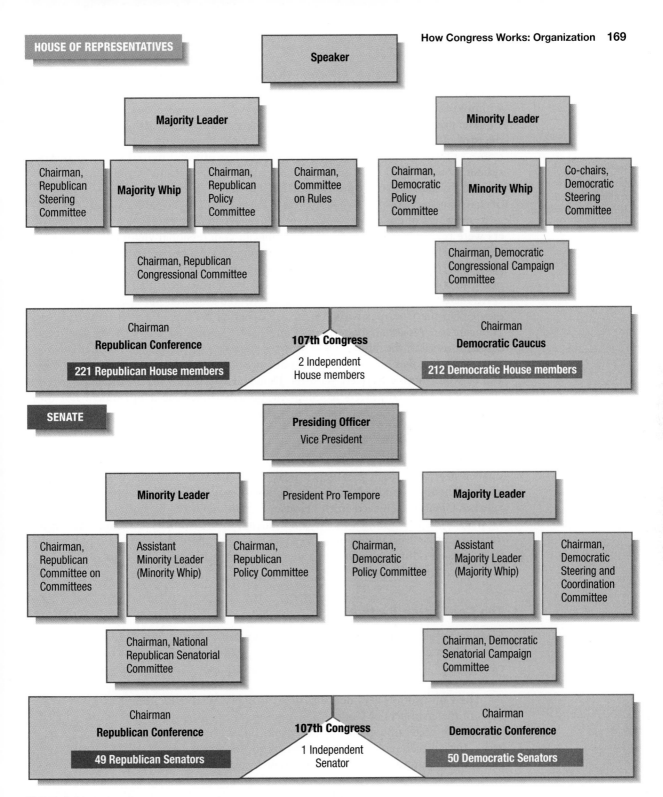

Figure 6.4
Structure of the House and Senate Leadership in the 107th Congress

strong party leader can pursue national party (or presidential) goals at the expense of members' pet projects and idiosyncratic constituency interests, and he or she can withhold favors.

The power of the Speaker of the House has changed dramatically over time. At the turn of the century, the strong "boss rule" of Speaker Joe Cannon greatly centralized power in the House. Members rebelled at this and moved to the **seniority system,** which vested great power in committee chairs instead of the Speaker. The seniority system was reformed in the 1970s by a movement that weakened the grip of chairs and gave some power back to the Speaker and to the party caucuses, as well as to members of committees and, especially, subcommittees.[20] The Speaker's powers were further enhanced with the Republican congressional victories in the 1994 election, when Representative Newt Gingrich (R-GA) became Speaker. Gingrich quickly became the most powerful Speaker since the era of boss rule. His House Republican colleagues were willing to give him new powers because his leadership enabled them to take control of the House and to enact the well-publicized agenda that they called the Contract with America.[21] Gingrich continued as the powerful Republican congressional spokesperson and leader until the party's almost unprecedented reversal of the midterm loss in 1998. Gingrich's replacement, Speaker Dennis Hastert (R-IL), was a compromise candidate chosen to bring Republicans together and to work more effectively with the Democrats in the House. Although Hastert has the same formal powers as Gingrich, he has neither the temperament nor the support of his party members to achieve the remarkable centralization of power realized under Gingrich.[22]

The leaders of the Senate have never had as much formal authority as those in the House, and that remains true today. The traditions of the Senate, with its much smaller size, allow each senator to speak or to offer amendments when he or she wishes. The highly individualistic Senate would not accept the kind of control that Speaker Gingrich achieved in the House. But although the Senate majority leader cannot control senators, he or she can influence the scheduling of legislation, a factor that can be crucial to a bill's success. The majority leader may even pull a bill from consideration—a convenient exercise of authority when defeat would embarrass the leadership.

seniority system
the accumulation of power and authority in conjunction with the length of time spent in office

The Committee System

Meeting as full bodies, it would be impossible for the House and Senate to consider and deliberate on all of the 12,000 bills and 100,000 nominations it receives every two years.[23] Thus the work is broken up and handled by smaller groups called committees.

The Constitution says nothing about congressional committees; they are creatures of the chambers of Congress they serve. The committee system has developed to meet the needs of a growing nation and the evolving goals of members of Congress. Initially, congressional committees formed to consider specific issues and pieces of legislation. After they made their recommendations to the full body, they dispersed. As the nation grew, and with it the number of bills to be considered, this ad hoc system became unwieldy, so beginning in the early nineteenth century, Congress formed a system of more permanent committees. Longer service on a committee permits members to develop expertise and specialization in a particular policy area, and thus bills can be considered more efficiently. Committees also provide members with a principal source of institutional power and the primary position from which they can influence national policy.

What Committees Do   It is at the committee, and, even more, the subcommittee, stage that the nitty-gritty details of legislation are worked out. Committees and subcommittees do the hard work of considering alternatives and drafting legislation. Committees are the primary information gatherers for Congress. Through hearings, staff reports, and investigations, members gather information on policy alternatives and discover who will support different policy options. Thus committees act as the eyes, ears, and workhorses of Congress in considering, drafting, and redrafting proposed legislation.

legislative oversight
a committee's ·
investigation of
government agencies to
ensure they are acting
as Congress intends

Committees do more, however, than write laws. Committees also undertake **legislative oversight**—that is, they check to see that executive agencies are carrying out the laws as Congress intended them to. Committee members gather information about agencies from the media, constituents, interest groups, staff, and special investigations. A lot of what is learned in oversight is reflected in changes to the laws giving agencies their powers and operating funds.

Members and the general public all strongly agree on the importance of congressional oversight. It is part of the "continuous watchfulness" that Congress mandated for itself in the Legislative Reorganization Act of 1946 and reiterated in the Legislative Reorganization Act of 1970. Nevertheless, oversight tends to be slighted in the congressional process. The reasons are not hard to find. Oversight takes a lot of time, and the rewards to individual members are less certain than from other activities, like fundraising or grabbing a headline in the district with a new pork barrel project. Consequently, oversight most often takes the form of "fire alarm" oversight, in which some scandal or upsurge of public interest directs congressional attention to a problem in the bureaucracy, rather than careful and systematic reviews of agencies' implementation of congressional policies.[24]

standing committee
a permanent committee
responsible for
legislation in a
particular policy area

Types of Committees   There are four types of committees in Congress: standing, select, joint, and conference. The vast majority of work is done by the **standing committees.** These are permanent committees, created by statute, that carry over from one session of Congress to the next. They review most pieces of legislation that are introduced to Congress. So powerful are the standing committees that they scrutinize, hold hearings on, amend, and, frequently, kill legislation before the full Congress ever gets the chance to discuss it.

Standing committee membership is relatively stable, as seniority on each committee is a major factor in gaining a subcommittee or committee chair. The chair wields considerable power and is a coveted position. Standing committees deal primarily with issues in specific policy areas, such as agriculture, foreign affairs, or justice. There are 19 standing committees and 85 subcommittees in the House. The Senate has 16 standing committees and 69 subcommittees. Committee size ranges from 8 to 74 members in the House and from 12 to 28 members in the Senate. The size of the committees and the ratio of majority to minority party members on each committee are determined at the start of each Congress by the majority leadership in the House and by negotiations between the majority and minority leaders in the Senate.

The policy areas represented by the standing committees of the two houses roughly parallel each other, but the Senate has no committee with the same powers as the House Rules Committee. The **House Rules Committee** provides a "rule" for each bill that specifies when it will be debated, how long debate can last, how it can be amended, and so on. Because the House is so large, debate would quickly become chaotic without the organization and structure provided by the Rules Committee. Such structure is not neutral in its effects on legislation, however. Since the committees are controlled by the majority party in the House, the rule that structures a given debate will reflect the priorities of the majority party.

When a problem before Congress does not fall into the jurisdiction of a standing committee, a **select committee** may be appointed. These are temporary and do not recommend legislation. They are used to gather information on specific issues, as did the Special Committee on the Year 2000 Technology Problem, or to conduct an investigation, like the Senate Select Committee on Whitewater, which in 1995 investigated the allegations concerning President and Mrs. Clinton's financial dealings in Arkansas.

Joint committees are made up of members of both houses of Congress. While each house generally considers bills independently (making for a lot of duplication of effort and staff), in some areas they have coordinated activities to expedite consideration of legislation. Examples of the joint committees in the 107th Congress included economics, the Library of Congress, and taxation.

Before a bill can become law, it must be passed by both houses of Congress in exactly the same form. But because the legislative process in each house often subjects bills to different pressures, they may be very different by the time they are debated and passed. **Conference committees** are temporary committees made up of members of both houses of Congress commissioned to resolve these differences, after which the bills go back to each house for a final vote. Members of the conference committees are appointed by the presiding officer of each chamber, who usually taps the senior members, especially the chairs, of the committees that considered the bill. Most often the conferees are members of those committees.

In the past, conference committees have tended to be small (five to ten members). In recent years, however, as Congress has tried to work within severe budget restrictions, it has taken to passing huge "megabills" that collect many proposals into one. Conference committees have expanded in turn, sometimes ballooning into gigantic affairs with many "subconferences."[25]

Getting on the Right Committees

Getting on the right committees is vital for members of Congress because so much of what they want to accomplish is realized through their work on committees. Because members are concerned with reelection, they try to get on committees that deal with issues of concern to constituents or that enhance their ability to get campaign contributions. Members who seek to maximize national lawmaking goals go after such committee assignments as Foreign Affairs or the highly sought House Ways and Means Committee and the Senate Finance Committee. Those who want to build a power base within Congress might pursue as-

---

House Rules Committee
the committee that determines how and when debate on a bill will take place

select committee
a committee appointed to deal with an issue or problem not suited to a standing committee

joint committee
a combined House-Senate committee formed to coordinate activities and expedite legislation in a certain area

conference committee
a temporary committee formed to reconcile differences in the House and Senate versions of a bill

signments on the House Rules Committee or the Senate Appropriations, Armed Services, Finance, and Foreign Relations Committee.[26]

Decisions on who gets on what committee vary by party and chamber. Generally, a newly elected member (or an incumbent who wants to receive a different and perhaps more prestigious assignment) makes his or her preference clear to the party leadership and then campaigns for that slot. Both the Democrats and the Republicans accommodate their members when they can, since both parties' goal is to support their ranks and help them be successful. Under Speaker Gingrich, the leadership of the House was especially dominant in the committee assignment process, and in both parties in the House, the selection committees have paid some attention to members' loyalty to the party in assigning them to committees.

Committee Chairs   For much of the twentieth century, congressional power rested with the chairmen and chairwomen of the committees of Congress; their power was unquestioned under the seniority system. Today seniority remains important, but chairs serve at the pleasure of their party caucuses and the party leadership. The committees are expected to reflect more faithfully the preferences of the average party member rather than just those of the committee chair or current committee members.[27]

Congressional Resources: Staff and Bureaucracy

In order for Congress to make policy, it needs expertise and information. Members find, however, that alone they are no match for the enormous amount of information generated by the executive branch, on the one hand, or the sheer informational demands of the policy process—economic, social, military, and foreign affairs—on the other. The need for independent, expert information, along with the ever-present reelection imperative, has led to a big growth in what we call the congressional bureaucracy. Congress has more than 26,000 employees, paid for by the federal government. This makes it the largest-staffed legislature in the world by far. Figure 6.5 shows the tremendous growth over time in the number of people working for Congress.

The vast majority of congressional staff—secretaries, computer personnel, clerical workers, and professionals—work for individual members or committees. The staff handle mailings; meet visiting constituents; answer mail, phone calls, faxes, and e-mail messages; create and maintain member web sites; and contact the executive agencies on behalf of constituents. They arrange meetings for members in their constituencies, and they set up local media events. The committees' staff (about 2,200 in the House and 1,200 in the Senate) do much of the committee work, from honing ideas, suggesting policy options to members, scheduling hearings, and recruiting witnesses, to actually drafting legislation.[28]

Congress also has its own agencies to facilitate its work. Unlike personal or committee staff, these are strictly nonpartisan, providing different kinds of expert advice and technical assistance. The Congressional Research Service (CRS), a unit of the Library of Congress, employs more than 800 people to do research for members of Congress. The Government Accounting Office (GAO), with its 5,000 employees, audits the books of executive departments and conducts policy evaluation and analysis. The Congressional Budget Office (CBO) is Congress's economic adviser, providing members with economic estimates about the budget, the deficit or surplus, and the national debt, and forecasts of how they will be influenced by different tax

**Figure 6.5
Growth in
Congressional Staff,
1891–1997**

Source: Norman J.
Ornstein, Thomas E.
Mann, and Michael J.
Malbin, *Vital Statistics on
Congress, 1997–1998,*
133–139. Copyright ©
1998 Congressional
Quarterly Press. Reprinted
with permission.

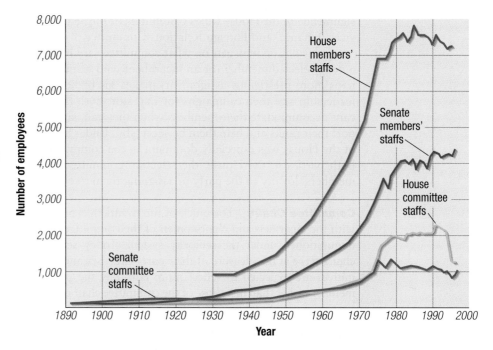

and spending policies. Congress has a stronger and more independent role in the policy process when it is not completely dependent on the executive branch for information and expertise.

WHO, WHAT, HOW   When it comes to the organization of Congress, the members all have a great deal at stake, as do the congressional leaders and the parties.

WHO are the actors?	WHAT do they want?	HOW do they get it?
Members of Congress	• Autonomy • Choice committee assignments	• Party and leadership cooperation
Congressional leaders	• Strong rules to promote leadership control	• Internal party rules • House and Senate rules

How Congress Works: Process and Politics

The policies passed by Congress are a result of both external and internal forces. The external environment includes the problems that are important to citizens at any given time—the economy, foreign affairs, crime, the federal deficit, the plight of the homeless, and so forth. The policy preferences of the president loom large in this external environment as well, as do parties and organized interests.

The Context of Congressional Policymaking

Congress also has a distinct internal institutional environment that shapes the way it carries out its business. Three characteristics of this environment are especially important. First, Congress is bicameral. Almost all congressional policy has to be passed, in identical form, by both houses. This requirement, laid out by the founders in the Constitution, makes the policy process difficult because the two houses serve different constituencies and operate under different decision-making procedures. The House, for example, because of its size and traditions, is much more hierarchically organized. The leadership has a good deal of influence over committees and particularly over how legislation is considered. The Senate is more egalitarian and its debate wide-open; the leadership has less control and fewer powers.

Because the houses are different, getting legislation through both is difficult. Interests that oppose a bill and lose in one chamber can often be successful at defeating the bill in the other. The opposition only has to stop a bill in one place to win, but the proponents of a bill have to win in both houses. In Congress, it is much easier to play defense than offense.

The second overriding feature of the institutional environment of Congress as a policymaking institution is its fragmentation. As you read the next section on how a bill becomes a law, think about how piecemeal the policy process is in Congress. Legislation is broken into bits, each considered individually in committees. It is very difficult to coordinate a bill with those laws that are already on the books or with what another committee might be doing in a closely related area. Thus Congress does such seemingly nonsensical things as subsidizing both tobacco growers and antismoking campaigns. This fragmentation increases opportunities for constituencies and individual members, as well as well-organized groups, to influence policy on issues they really care about. It also makes it very hard for national policymakers—the president or congressional leaders—to take a large-scale, coordinated approach to major policy problems.

norms informal rules that govern behavior in Congress

The third institutional influence on Congress are congressional **norms**—informal rules of procedure that are quickly learned by newcomers whenthey enter Congress. Norms include the idea that members should work hard, develop a specialization, treat other members with the utmost courtesy, reciprocate favors, and take pride in their respective chambers and in Congress as a whole. The purpose of congressional norms is to constrain conflict and personal animosity in an arena where disagreements are inevitable, but they also aid in getting business done. Although congressional norms continue to be important, they are less constraining on members today than they were in the 1950s and 1960s.[29] The current norms allow for more individualistic, media-oriented, and conflictual behavior than in the past.

How a Bill Becomes Law—Some of the Time

This section briefly considers how demands for solutions to our public problems become laws. Very few proposed policies, as it turns out, actually make it into law. We will consider two aspects of congressional policy: (1) the agenda, the source of ideas for new policies, and (2) the legislative process, the steps a bill goes through to become law.

legislative agenda
the slate of proposals and issues that representatives think it worthwhile to consider and act on

Setting the Agenda   Before a law can be passed, it must be on the **legislative agenda.** Potential new laws can get on Congress's agenda in several ways. First, because public attention is focused most closely on presidential elections and campaigns, new presidents are especially effective at setting the congressional agenda. Their proposals may be efforts to fulfill campaign promises, to pay political debts, or to realize ideological commitments.

A second way an issue gets on the legislative agenda is when it is triggered by a well-publicized event. When there were several highly publicized shootings on school grounds in the late 1990s, Congress took up the issue of gun control, even though the National Rifle Association had previously been relatively successful at keeping it off the agenda. The media are often key players in getting issues and problems onto the congressional agenda.

A third way an idea gets on the agenda is for one or more members to find it in their own interests, either political or ideological, to invest time and political resources in pushing the policy. Many members of Congress want to prove their legislative skills to their constituents, key supporters, the media, and fellow lawmakers. The search for the right issue to push at the right time is called **policy entrepreneurship.** Policy entrepreneurship by members is important in setting the congressional policy agenda, and it can reap considerable political benefits for those associated with important initiatives.

policy entrepreneurship
the practice of legislators becoming experts and taking leadership roles in specific policy areas

Legislative Process: Beginning the Long Journey   Bills, even those widely recognized as representing the president's legislative program, must be introduced by members of Congress. The formal introduction is done in the House by putting a bill in the *hopper* (a wooden box), where it goes to the clerk of the House, or in the Senate by giving it to the presiding officer. The bill is then given a number (for example, HR932 in the House or S953 in the Senate) and begins the long journey that might result in its becoming law. The actual details can get messy, (as Figure 6.6 on page 178 shows), but the following diagram shows the general route for a bill once it is introduced in either the House or the Senate. A bill introduced in the House normally goes first through the House and then on to the Senate, and vice versa. However, bills may be considered simultaneously in both houses.

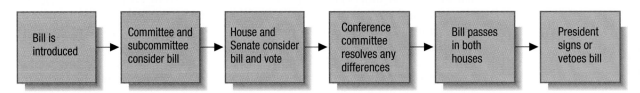

Bill is introduced → Committee and subcommittee consider bill → House and Senate consider bill and vote → Conference committee resolves any differences → Bill passes in both houses → President signs or vetoes bill

How a Bill Becomes Law: Short Version

The initial stages of committee consideration are similar for the House and the Senate. The bill first has to be referred to committee. This is largely automatic for most bills; they go to the standing committee with jurisdiction over the content of the bill. A bill to change the way agricultural subsidies for cotton are considered, for example, would start with the House Committee on Agriculture. In some cases, a bill might logically fall under more than one committee's jurisdiction, and here the Speaker exercises a good deal of power. He can choose the committee that will consider the bill or even refer the same bill to more than one committee. This gives the Speaker important leverage in the House because he often knows which committees are likely to be more or less favorable to different bills. Senators do not worry quite as much about where bills are referred because they have much greater opportunity to make changes later in the process than representatives do. We'll see why when we discuss floor consideration.

Bills then move on to subcommittees, where they may or may not get serious consideration. Most bills just die in committee because the committee members either don't care about the issue (it isn't on their agenda) or they actively want to block it. Even if a bill's life is brief, the member who introduced it can still campaign as its champion. In fact, a motivation for the introduction of many bills is not that the member seriously believes that the bill has a chance of passing but that he or she wants to be seen back home as taking some action on the issue.

When a subcommittee decides to consider a bill it holds hearings—testimony from experts, interest groups, executive department secretaries and undersecretaries, and even other members of Congress. In each case, the subcommittee deliberates and votes the bill back to the full committee. There, the committee considers the bill further and makes changes and revisions in a process called *markup*. If the committee votes in favor of the final version of the bill, it goes forward to the floor. Here, however, there is a crucial difference between the House and the Senate.

In the House, bills go from the standing committee to the Rules Committee. This committee, highly responsive to the Speaker of the House, gives each bill a *rule,* which includes when and how the bill will be considered. Some bills go out under an *open rule,* which means that any amendments can be proposed and added. More typically, especially for important bills, the House leadership gains more control by imposing a *restrictive rule,* which limits the time for debate and restricts the amendments that can be offered. For example, if the leadership knows that there is a lot of sentiment in favor of a tax cut, it can control the form of the tax cut by having a restrictive rule that prohibits any amendments to the committee's bill. Thus even members who would like to vote for a different kind of tax cut face pressure to go along with the bill because they can't amend it; it is either this tax cut or none at all, and they don't want to vote against a tax cut altogether. Thus, in some cases, the Rules Committee can not only make or break the bill, but it can also influence its final content.

The Senate generally guarantees all bills an open rule by default. Any senator can introduce any proposal as an amendment to any bill, sometimes called a *rider,* and get a vote on it. Thus senators have access to the floor in a way that is denied to representatives. Furthermore, whereas in the House the rule for each bill stipulates how long a member can debate, under the Senate's tradition of unlimited debate, a member can talk indefinitely. Senators opposed to a bill can engage in a **filibuster,** which is an effort to tie up the floor of the Senate in debate to stop the members from voting on a bill. A filibuster can be stopped only by cloture. **Cloture,** a vote to cut off debate and end a filibuster, requires an extraordinary three-fifths majority, or sixty votes. A dramatic example of a filibuster occurred when southern senators temporarily derailed Minnesota senator Hubert Humphrey's efforts to pass the Civil

filibuster
the practice of unlimited debate in the Senate to prevent or delay a vote on a bill

cloture   a vote to end a Senate filibuster; requires a three-fifths majority, or sixty votes

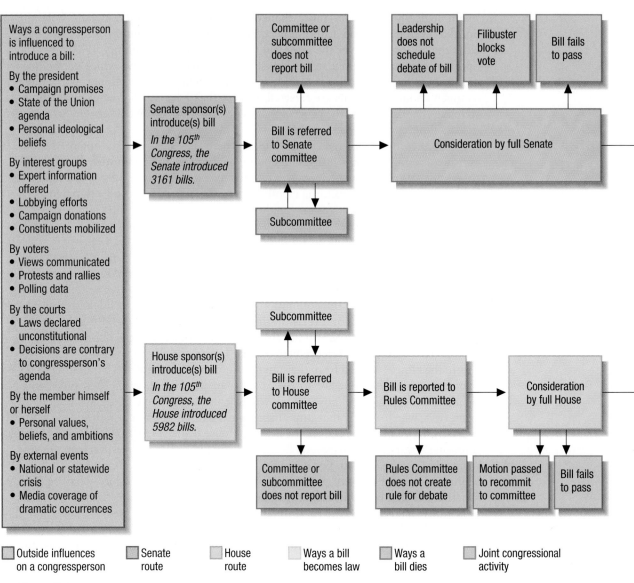

Figure 6.6
How a Bill Becomes Law:
Long Version

Rights Act of 1964. First, they filibustered Humphrey's attempt to bypass the Judiciary Committee, whose chair, a southern Democrat, opposed the bill. This was known as the "minibuster," and it stopped Senate business for sixteen days.[30] It was considered "mini" because from March 30 to June 30, 1964, these same southern Democrats filibustered the Civil Rights Act and created a twenty-week backlog of legislation.[31] These senators often resorted to reading the telephone book in order to adhere to the rules of constant debate. The consequence of a filibuster, as this exam-

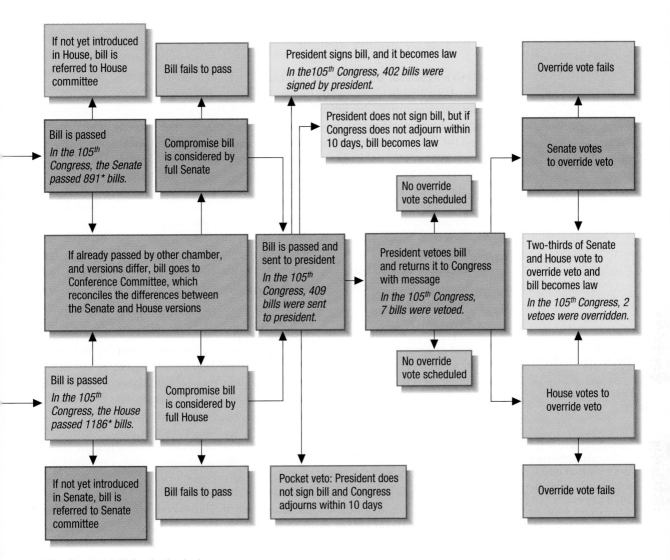

If not yet introduced in House, bill is referred to House committee

Bill fails to pass

President signs bill, and it becomes law
In the 105th Congress, 402 bills were signed by president.

Override vote fails

Bill is passed
In the 105th Congress, the Senate passed 891 bills.*

Compromise bill is considered by full Senate

President does not sign bill, but if Congress does not adjourn within 10 days, bill becomes law

Senate votes to override veto

If already passed by other chamber, and versions differ, bill goes to Conference Committee, which reconciles the differences between the Senate and House versions

Bill is passed and sent to president
In the 105th Congress, 409 bills were sent to president.

No override vote scheduled

President vetoes bill and returns it to Congress with message
In the 105th Congress, 7 bills were vetoed.

Two-thirds of Senate and House vote to override veto and bill becomes law
In the 105th Congress, 2 vetoes were overridden.

Bill is passed
In the 105th Congress, the House passed 1186 bills.*

Compromise bill is considered by full House

No override vote scheduled

House votes to override veto

If not yet introduced in Senate, bill is referred to Senate committee

Bill fails to pass

Pocket veto: President does not sign bill and Congress adjourns within 10 days

Override vote fails

*These figures include bills from the other chamber.

ple suggests, is that a minority in the Senate is able to thwart the will of the majority, often in a more permanent fashion.

Recent sessions have seen a striking increase in the use of the filibuster. Rarely used until the 1960s, it has become increasingly popular, with Congresses now averaging around forty attempts at cloture. Only about a third of these attempts are successful, in the rest of the cases a minority has prevailed over the majority. The filibuster is considered "hardball politics," and its increasing use reflects growing partisan ideological conflicts in Congress. For a political party to have effective control of the Senate, it now needs to have sixty seats, rather than the fifty-one seats necessary for a simple majority, so that it can invoke cloture and break filibusters.

Legislative Process: Overcoming Obstacles

It is clear that a bill must survive a number of challenges to get out of Congress alive. A bill can be killed, or just left to die, in a subcommittee, the full committee, the Rules Committee in the House, or any of the corresponding committees in the Senate, and, of course, it has to pass votes on the floors of both houses. If it emerges from both houses relatively intact, it goes to the president, unless the chambers pass different versions. If the bills differ, the two versions go to a conference committee made up of members of both houses, usually the senior members of the standing committees that reported the bills. If the conferees can reach an agreement, the bill goes back to each house to be voted up or down; no amendments are permitted at this point. If the bill is rejected, that chamber sends it back to the conference committee for a second try.

Finally, any bill still alive at this point moves on to the president's desk. He has several choices of action. The simplest choice is to sign the bill, which then becomes law. If the president doesn't like the bill, he can veto it. In that case, he sends it back to the originating house of Congress with a short explanation of what he does not like. Congress can then attempt a **veto override,** which requires a two-thirds vote of both houses. Because the president can usually count on the support of at least one-third of one house, the veto is a powerful negative tool; it is hard for Congress to accomplish legislative goals that the president opposes. Congress can, however, send the president bills in legislative packages that are difficult to veto. Representative Robert S. Walker (R-PA) noted this strategy: "The president is probably going to veto a pork bill, but if we put the crime package in there, it has got a better chance of getting enacted into law."[32] To get around this problem, Congress passed in 1996 a **line-item veto** bill, which would have allowed presidents to strike out spending provisions they didn't like. President Bill Clinton exercised his line-item veto authority in 1997 by canceling one provision of the Balanced Budget Act of 1997 and two provisions of the Taxpayer Relief Act of 1997. Those who stood to lose funding from these cuts challenged the law's constitutionality, and in June 1998 the Supreme Court ruled that the line-item veto was unconstitutional. Had it survived, the line-item veto would have made for a subtle shift in power in the Washington budget process, making it easier for the White House to control spending.[33]

The president can also kill a bill with the **pocket veto,** which occurs when Congress sends a bill to the president within ten days of the end of a session and the president does not sign it. The bill fails because Congress is not in session to consider a veto override. The president might choose this option when he wants to veto a bill without drawing much public attention to it. Similarly, the president can do nothing, and if Congress remains in session, the bill will automatically becomes law in ten days, excluding Sundays. This seldom-used option signals presidential dislike for a bill, but not enough dislike for him to use his veto power.

The striking aspect of our legislative process is how many factors have to fall into place for a bill to become law. At every step, there are ways to kill a bill, and a well-organized group of members in the relatively decentralized Congress has a good chance, in most cases, of blocking a bill that it strongly opposes. In terms of procedures, Con-

---

veto override
the reversal of a presidential veto by a two-thirds vote in both houses of Congress

line-item veto
presidential authority to strike out individual spending provisions in a budget; passed by Congress but ruled unconstitutional by the Supreme Court

pocket veto
presidential authority to kill a bill submitted within ten days of the end of a legislative session by not signing it

gress is better set up to ensure that bills do not impinge on organized interests than it is to facilitate coherent, well-coordinated attacks on the nation's problems.

The Mechanics of Congressional Decision-Making

The formal procedures that a bill must go through to become law are complex. Congressional politics is the art of using these procedures and rules to get a bill passed or killed. The best way to get a feel for what congressional politics is like is to read a firsthand account, such as Eric Redman's *Dance of Legislation*, or a biography of one of the masters of congressional politics, like former president Lyndon Baines Johnson during his years as majority leader of the Senate.

How a Member Decides   The congressional decision-making process really begins with the individual member's decision on how to vote. With an array of complex choices, how does the member decide? Congressional voting is called **roll call voting,** and all votes are a matter of public record, open to one's party, one's constituency, the president, the interest groups that made substantial campaign contributions, and the interest groups that lobbied on the other side. All this openness serves to make the member accountable for his or her vote, but it also means that the decision on how to vote must be carefully made.

roll call voting
publicly recorded votes on bills and amendments on the floor of the House or Senate

Studies have long shown that party affiliation is the most important factor in determining roll call voting. Indeed, in recent years party has become even more important. Constituency also plays a big role in roll call voting. When a member's constituents have an interest in or care about an issue, the member will usually follow their wishes. The president can also play a role in congressional decision-making. If the president takes a clear public stand, presidential politics get tied up with a roll call vote. Other members are an important source of information on how a particular member will vote on a bill. Representatives and senators have to vote on hundreds of bills each year, but they have time to study only a handful of them carefully. Thus they take cues from other members whom they respect and generally agree with.[34] They also consult with their staff, some of whom may be very knowledgeable about certain legislation. Finally, interest groups have an effect on how a member of Congress votes, but studies suggest that their impact is much less than we usually imagine. Lobbying and campaign contributions buy access to members so that the lobbyists can try to make their case, but they do not actually buy votes.[35]

Political Strategies   The congressperson who is committed to passing or defeating a particular bill cannot do so alone, however, and he or she looks to find like-minded members for political support. Once a representative or senator knows where he or she stands on a bill, there are a variety of methods for influencing the fate of that bill, many of them effective long before the floor vote takes place. Congressional politics—using the rules to get what one wants—can entail many complex strategies, including controlling the agenda (whether a bill ever reaches the floor), proposing amendments to a bill, influencing its timing, and forming coalitions with other members to pass or block a bill. Knowing how to use the rules makes a huge difference in congressional politics.

How Well Does Congress Work?

Some critics see Congress as too powerful and advocate reforms that would clip its wings. Term limits would put the brakes on professional politicians, campaign finance reform would curb special interests' cozy relationship with lawmakers, and cutting privileges and perks would bring the high and mighty members of Congress closer to the level of the people they represent. Other critics, however, see continual congressional inaction on social security reform and, on the needs of the cities, the underclass, or small businesses, and decry Congress's lack of progress. From this perspective Congress needs the power to get something done and not just to engage in partisan bickering. Does Congress have too much or too little power? The answer is that it has a tremendous amount of power and that it can only occasionally use this power effectively.

When it is unified, Congress is a powerful and effective institution. It has passed many landmark pieces of legislation that have shaped American history. These laws include the federal responses to the Great Depression (the Work Projects Administration, Social Security Act, and Civilian Conservation Corps, among others) and to civil rights violations (the Civil Rights Act of 1964 and Voting Rights Act of 1965). But these spurts of legislative activity to meet national problems came at times of perceived national emergency and large partisan majorities in Congress.

Congress has also been effective, when united, in protecting its own powers. During the Cold War, beginning in 1945, observers worried frequently about the "imperial presidency," under which Congress was taking a back seat to the president. Although the presidency did capture more public attention during the 1960s and early 1970s, the events of the unpopular Vietnam War and Watergate led to a series of congressional reassertions of its powers, including the 1973 War Powers Act, which theoretically gave Congress a greater say in the use of American armed forces overseas, and the 1974 Congressional Budget and Impoundment Act, which gave Congress more power over the budget process and the expenditure of funds it had appropriated. When congressional power wanes compared to other institutions, particularly the presidency, Congress is fully capable of using its constitutionally delegated powers to reassert itself.

In summary, Congress does have the power to act, and when it is unified

***A Rare Moment of
Unanimous Acclaim***
Making laws usually means making someone unhappy, but occasionally a significant piece of legislation is just about universally applauded. Such was the case when President Franklin D. Roosevelt signed the G.I. Bill of Rights on June 22, 1944. The bill, designed to ease the reentry of American military personnel into civilian life after World War II, provided for subsidized loans and paid for hundreds of thousands to attend college.

and sufficiently motivated, it actually does so. More often, though, its power remains "potential," largely because it has more incentives on a daily basis to be a representative institution rather than a national lawmaking body. It is important to remember, too, that the founders intended to create a legislature that would not move hastily or without deliberation. The irony is that the founders' mixed bag of incentives works so well that today Congress often does not move very much at all.

WHO, WHAT, HOW   All American political actors, those in Washington and those outside, have something important at stake in the legislative process. This is, after all, the heart of democratic lawmaking.

WHO are the actors?	WHAT do they want?	HOW do they get it?
Citizens and interest groups	• Representation • Promotion of national public good	• Grassroots techniques • Lobbying
President	• Success for presidential agenda	• Influence on legislative agenda • Influence on public opinion • Veto
Members of Congress	• Reputation as policy entrepreneurs • Reputation as skilled and effective legislators	• Legislative strategies • Veto override

Citizenship and Congress

From 1974 through the early 2000s, periodic Gallup polls showed that from half to less than a third of the public "approves of the way Congress is handling its job." At least four factors help to explain why citizens are not always very happy with Congress. First, some candidates encourage a negative image of the institution they want to join—running for Congress by running against it, and declaring their intention to fight against special interests, bureaucrats, and the general incompetence of Washington.[36] Second, in the post-Watergate wave of investigative reporting, media coverage of Congress has gotten more negative, even though impartial observers say that Congress is probably less corrupt than ever before. Third, since the 1970s, the law requires that information about how much campaigns cost and who contributes to them must be made public, casting a shadow of suspicion on the entire process and raising the concern that congressional influence can be bought. Finally, citizens are turned off by what they see as the incessant bickering and partisanship in Congress.[37]

Given the reasons why many Americans are unhappy with Congress, many of the reforms currently on the agenda are not likely to change their minds. One of the most popular reforms being advocated is term limits. The specific proposals vary, but the intent is to limit the number of terms a member of Congress can serve, usually

Points of Access

- Write a bill sugges-
  tion to your state or
  national represen-
  tative.

- Join a campaign
  staff.

- Apply to be a
  legislative aide.

- Join the Young
  Democrats or Young
  Republicans at your
  school.

- Organize a debate
  at your school
  between two rival
  candidates.

- Support your con-
  gressional candi-
  date by putting a
  sign on your lawn
  or in your window
  or by wearing a pin.

- Write to your
  representative or
  senator—or attend
  a public hearing—
  on a policy issue of
  importance to you.

to somewhere between eight and twelve years. Term limits might work if there were evidence that serving in Congress corrupts good people, but there is no evidence of this at all. It just puts them in the public eye.

Other reforms, however, might make a difference in public support for Congress. Campaign finance reform, for instance, could have a significant impact. Institutional reforms might be able to speed up congressional lawmaking and reduce the need to compromise on details. Such reforms, however, probably will not fundamentally change how the public feels about Congress. When Congress is cohesive and acts with reasonable dispatch, the public seems to applaud. But Congress often has a hard time acting because, as a representative institution, it reflects a sharply divided society.

The truth is that democracy is messy. Bickering arises in Congress because members represent many different Americans with varied interests and goals. It is precisely our bickering, our inefficiency, and our willingness to compromise, to give and take, that preserve the freedoms Americans hold dear. It is the nature of representative government.[38]

We conclude where we began. Congress has the dual goals of lawmaking and representation. These goals often and necessarily conflict. The practice of congressional politics is fascinating to many close-up observers but looks less appealing to average citizens, watching the nightly news and of following political campaigns from afar. It is important to understand that this view of Congress stems from the conflicting expectations we place on the body more than the failings of the people we send to Washington.

WHAT'S AT STAKE REVISITED

Did Marjorie Margolies-Mezvinsky's vote on the side of the president cost her her seat? After the August 5, 1993, budget vote, early signs from her district confirmed Margolies-Mezvinsky's guess that she had jeopardized her congressional seat by breaking her promise and voting for Clinton's budget. Enraged constituents tied up her phone lines with angry calls. The *Independent and Montgomery Transcript* called her "just another run-of-the-mill, cheap, soiled, ward-heeling politician whose word was not worth a spit stain in the street."[39] Elected in a heavily Republican district by a narrow margin, she would have faced a difficult reelection campaign in any case, especially as 1994 saw Democratic incumbents across the country swept out of office. Although she raised and spent far more money than her opponent (once again Jon D. Fox) in the 1994 campaign, she lost by more than eight thousand votes. (Ironically, four years later Fox would in turn lose to a Democratic challenger.)

What happened to Marjorie Margolies-Mezvinsky? Was she merely an inexperienced and inept freshman congresswoman? Was she overly gullible when she responded to Clinton's plea for help? Should a representative put her district's wishes first, no matter what her conscience says? In this chapter, we have learned that the primary challenge a member of Congress faces is to balance the representation claims of his or her constituency with the lawmaking claims of the national interest. In Margolies-Mezvinsky's case, she was convinced that her support of the budget mattered to the nation, where important legislation would have been hanstrung were the president's administration seriously weakened. She pointed out that she had voted against many aspects of Clinton's economic program but had voted for the budget "not because I liked it but because I wanted to break through gridlock, so we could move on to crime, health care, and other major issues.[40] Her constituents saw her vote as a betrayal, a sign that she could not be trusted. She gambled that she could regain that trust before the next election, and she lost.

Knowing what's at stake makes the representation versus lawmaking dilemma more difficult for members of Congress. It is often the national interest, or at least the members' perception of the national interest, that is sacrificed, with members rationalizing that they must comply with their constituents' wishes because if they do not get reelected, they can do no good at all. The ultimate losers are the U.S. citizens, who, although their local interests are taken care of, must live with the resulting gridlock and inattention to national problems. The irony is that it is the voters who are also ultimately responsible for this sacrifice by putting their own short-term local interests first at the ballot box. ∎

key terms

allocative representation   153
bicameral legislature   156
casework   153
cloture   177
coattail effect   165
conference committee   172
constituency   152
filibuster   177
franking   163
gerrymandering   161
House Rules Committee   172
incumbency advantage   164
joint committee   172

lawmaking   153
legislative agenda   176
legislative oversight   171
line-item veto   180
majority party   167
malapportionment   160
midterm loss   165
norms   175
party caucuses   168
pocket veto   180
policy entrepreneurship   176
policy representation   153
pork barrel   153

racial gerrymandering   161
reapportionment   160
redistricting   160
representation   152
roll call voting   181
select committee   172
seniority system   170
Speaker of the House   168
standing committee   171
strategic politician   164
symbolic representation   153
veto override   180

summary

■ Members of Congress are responsible for both representation and lawmaking. These two duties are often at odds because what is good for a local district may not be beneficial for the country as a whole.

■ Representation style takes four different forms—policy, allocative, casework, and symbolic—and congresspersons attempt to excel at all four.

However, since the legislative process designed by the founders is meant to be very slow, representatives have fewer incentives to concentrate on national lawmaking when reelection interests, and therefore local interests, are more pressing.

■ The founders created our government with a structure of checks and balances. In addition to checking each other, the House and Senate may be checked by either the president or the courts. Congress is very powerful but must demonstrate unusual strength and consensus to override presidential vetoes and to amend the Constitution.

- Citizens and representatives interact in congressional elections. The incumbency effect is very powerful in American politics because those in office often create legislation that makes it difficult for challengers to succeed.

- Representatives want autonomy and choice committee assignments to satisfy constituent concerns. They achieve these goals by joining together into political parties and obeying their leadership and party rules. House and Senate members make their own organizational rules, which means that the dominant party in each house has great power over the internal rules of Congress and what laws are made.

- Citizens, interest groups, the president, and members of Congress all have a stake in the legislative process. Voters organized into interest groups may have a greater impact on legislative outcomes than would the individual. Yet Congress, with various legislative tools and strategies, holds the most sway over the fate of legislation.

7

What's at Stake?

The Double Expectations Gap
- *The Gap Between Presidential Promises and the Powers of the Office*
- *The Gap Between Conflicting Roles*

The Evolution of the American Presidency
- *The Framers' Design for a Limited Executive*
- *Qualifications and Conditions of Office*
- *The Constitutional Powers of the President*
- *The Traditional Presidency*
- *The Modern Presidency*

Presidential Politics: The Struggle for Power
- *The Expectations Gap and the Need for Persuasive Power*
- *Going Public*
- *Working with Congress*

Managing the Presidential Establishment
- *The Cabinet*
- *The Executive Office of the President*
- *The White House Office*
- *The Vice President*
- *The First Lady*
- *The Problem of Control*

Presidential Character

Citizenship and the Presidency

What's at Stake Revisited

The Presidency

WHAT'S AT STAKE?

Political observers and the American public were astonished when the House of Representatives voted to impeach President Bill Clinton on December 19, 1998. Indeed, as late as the day before the House vote, more than half of the American people had been telling pollsters that they did not think the House would or should impeach the president.

Impeachment is not the actual removal of a president from office, but it is the first step in that process. If the House of Representatives votes to send articles of impeachment to the Senate, the Senate must hold a trial on those charges, with the chief justice of the Supreme Court presiding over the proceedings. Only twice before had the nation faced the prospect of impeachment: once more than 130 years ago in the case of President Andrew Johnson, who was impeached by the House of Representatives but not convicted by the Senate, and again in the mid-1970s, when President Richard Nixon resigned on hearing that there were sufficient votes in both the House and the Senate to impeach and convict him.

When Republican opponents of President Clinton began talking about impeachment in the mid-1990s, most people dismissed it as so much partisan bickering. As it slowly became evident that Clinton would indeed be impeached, in a vote that split almost exactly along party lines (meaning that Democrats voted against the impeachment of a Democratic president, and Republicans voted for it), scholars, lawyers, politicians, and the public themselves scrambled to figure out what would happen next. What does impeachment mean to the functioning of the system as a whole? Who would win and who would lose as Clinton was impeached by the House and faced a trial in the Senate? This was uncharted territory for Americans, and it was with some trepidation that they asked themselves and each other, "What is at stake when we impeach a president?" ■

Ask just about anyone who the most powerful person in the world is and the answer would probably be the president of the United States. He, or perhaps some day soon, she, is the elected leader of the nation that has one of the most powerful economies, one of the greatest military forces, and the longest-running representative government that the world has seen. Media coverage enforces this belief in the importance of the U.S. president. The television networks and news services all have full-time reporters assigned to the White House. The evening news tells us what the president has been doing that day, even if he only went to church or played a round of golf. This attention is what one scholar calls the president's "monopolization of the public space."[1] It means that the president is the first person the citizens and the media think of when anything of significance happens, whether it is an earthquake, a war, or a big drop in the stock market. We look to the president to solve our problems and to represent our nation in times of struggle, tragedy, and triumph. Given that the U.S. Constitution provides for a relatively weak chief executive, people's expectations, both here and abroad, constitute a major challenge for modern presidents.

Meeting these expectations is all the more difficult because so many political actors have something at stake in the office of the presidency. Obviously, the president himself wants to widen his authority to act so that he can deliver on campaign promises and extend the base of support for himself and his party. Although the formal rules of American politics create only limited presidential powers, informal rules help the president expand them. Citizens, both individually and in groups, often have high expectations of what the president will do for them and for the country, and they may be willing to allow a popular president to expand his powers to act. An unpopular president, however, will face a public eager to limit his options and ready to complain about any perceived steps beyond the restrictive constitutional bounds. Congress, too, stands to gain or lose based on the president's success. Members of the president's party share some of his popularity, but in general the more power the president has, the less Congress has. This is especially true if the majority party in Congress is different from the president's. So Congress has a stake in limiting what the president may do.

This chapter tells the story of who gets what from the American presidency and how they get it. We focus on the following points:

- The double gap between what we expect of the president and what he can deliver, in terms of the actual power he can exercise and the roles he has to play

- The evolution of the American presidency, from its constitutional origins to the present

- The president's struggle for power

- The organization and functioning of the executive office

- Presidential character

The Double Expectations Gap

Presidential scholars note that one of the most remarkable things about the modern presidency is how much the office has become intertwined with public expectations and perceptions. The implication, of course, is that we expect one thing and get something less—that there is a gap between our expectations and reality. In fact, we can identify two different expectations gaps when it comes to popular perceptions of the presidency. One is between the very great promises that presidents make, and that we want them to keep, on the one hand, and the president's limited constitutional powers to fulfill those promises on the other. The second gap is between two conflicting roles that the president is expected to play—the formal and largely symbolic role of head of state and the far more political head of government. These two expectations gaps form a framework for much of our discussion of the American presidency.

The Gap Between Presidential Promises and the Powers of the Office

The problem of the modern presidency that concerns many scholars is that what today's public expects from the president is seriously out of line with what any president can reasonably do. This expectations gap is of relatively recent vintage. Through the 1930s, the presidency was pretty much the office the founders had planned—an administrative position dwarfed by the extensive legislative powers of Congress. During Franklin Roosevelt's New Deal, however, public expectations of the president changed. Roosevelt did not act like an administrator with limited powers; he acted like a leader whose strength and imagination could be relied on by an entire nation of citizens to rescue them from the crisis of the Great Depression. Over the course of FDR's four terms in office, the public became used to seeing the president in just this light, and future presidential candidates promised similarly grand visions of policy in their efforts to win supporters.

Rather than strengthening the office to allow presidents to deliver on such promises, however, the only constitutional change in the presidency weakened it. In reaction to FDR's four elections, the Twenty-second Amendment, limiting the number of terms a president can serve to two, was passed.

Today's presidents suffer the consequences of this history. On the one hand, we voters demand that they woo us with promises to change the course of the country, to solve our problems, and to enact visionary policy. On the other hand, we have not increased the powers of the office to meet this greatly expanded job description. Thus, to meet our expectations, the president must wheel, deal, bargain, and otherwise gather the support he needs to overcome his constitutional limitations. And if

Table 7.1
Length of Time in Office for the Last Eight Presidents

President	Terms Served
Kennedy	Assassinated in the third year of his first term.
Johnson	Served out Kennedy's term, elected to one term of his own. Chose not to run for reelection, knowing he would lose.
Nixon	Served one full term, reelected, resigned halfway through second term.
Ford	Served out Nixon's term. Ran for reelection and lost.
Carter	Served one full term. Ran for reelection and lost.
Reagan	Served two full terms.
Bush	Served one full term. Ran for reelection and lost.
Clinton	Served two full terms. Impeached halfway through second term but acquitted.

the president doesn't meet our expectations, or if the country doesn't thrive the way we think it should, even if it isn't his fault and there's nothing he could have done to change things, we hold him accountable and vote him out of office. Some evidence of this can be seen in the fates of the last nine presidents. Only two, Ronald Reagan and Bill Clinton, were reelected and served two full terms, and Clinton was impeached in the process. The inability of some of our most skilled politicians to survive for even two terms of office (see Table 7.1) suggests that our expectations of what can be done outstrip the resources and powers of the position.

The Gap Between Conflicting Roles

The second expectations gap that presidents face is in part a product of the first. Since we now expect our presidents to perform as high-level legislators as well as administrators, holders of this office need to be adept politicians. That is, today's presidents need to be able to get their hands dirty in the day-to-day political activities of the nation or, as we just said, to wheel, deal, and bargain. As **head of government,** the president is supposed to run the government and function as leader of his political party. These functions have expanded greatly since FDR's time.

head of government the political role of the president as leader of a political party and chief arbiter of who gets what resources

head of state the apolitical, unifying role of the president as symbolic representative of the whole country

Even so, the image of their president as a politician—an occupational class not held in high esteem by most Americans—often doesn't sit well with citizens who also want their president to be **head of state,** a role above politics in which he serves as a unifying symbol of all that is good and noble about America. In this capacity, the president performs functions such as greeting other heads of state, attending state funerals, tossing out the first baseball of the season, hosting the annual Easter egg hunt on the White House lawn, and consoling survivors of national tragedies. Some countries, like Britain, separate the head of state (the queen) from the head of government (the prime minister), allowing each to do his or her job untarnished by comparisons with the other, but in the U.S. we expect the president to juggle both roles.

Thus not only must the president contend with a job in which he is required to do far more than he is given the power to do, but he also must cultivate the talents to perform two very contradictory roles: the essentially political head of government, who makes decisions about who will get scarce resources, and the elevated and apolitical

Sticking to His Campaign Promises . . .
President George W. Bush promised a huge tax cut throughout his election 2000 campaigning. In the early days of his administration, he made a point of announcing his plans to pursue the tax cut to a group of families in the White House. As head of government, the president uses his access to the media to set the policy agenda for the nation and sell the policy initiatives that will define his administration.

head of state, who should unify rather than divide the public. Few presidents are skilled enough to carry off both roles with aplomb; the very talents that make someone adept in one role often disqualify him from being good in the other.

WHO, WHAT, HOW The person with the most at stake in the conflicting expectations and rules that govern the American presidency is undoubtedly the president himself, although the American voters also stand to gain or lose quite a lot depending on whether their expectations of the presidency are fulfilled.

WHO are the actors?	WHAT do they want?	HOW do they get it?
The president	• Historical legacy	• Battling the expectations gap created by popular enthusiasm for campaign promises and constitutional limitations on executive power • Battling the expectations gap created by the requirement that the president be both head of state and head of government.
Citizens	• Fulfilled expectations	• Voting and public opinion

How to Be a Savvy Student of Political Cartoons

Political cartoons are not just for laughs. Although they may often use humor as a way of making a political point, that point is likely to be sharp and aimed with uncanny accuracy at their political targets. In fact, noted cartoonist Jeff MacNelly, who won a Pulitzer Prize for his work, once said that if cartoonists couldn't draw, most of them would probably have become hired assassins.[1]

Since the first days of our Republic, Americans have been using drawings and sketches to say what mere words cannot. Benjamin Franklin and Paul Revere, among others, used pen, ink, and engraving tools to express pointed political views.[2] And cartoonists' hapless targets have been acutely aware of the presence of these "annoying little pups, nipping at the heels."[3] On the one hand, politicians crave the attention, knowing they have arrived when a cartoonist can draw them without having to indicate their names. On the other hand, they dread the sharp sting of the cartoonist's pen. In the 1870s, "Boss" Tweed of Tammany Hall (a New York City political machine) reportedly offered cartoonist Thomas Nast $100,000 to stop drawing cartoons about him,[4] saying, "Stop them damn pictures. I don't care so much what the papers write about me. My constituents can't read. . . . But, damn it, they can see pictures."[5]

By the early 1900s, legislatures in four states—Pennsylvania, California, Indiana, and Alabama—had introduced anti–cartoon censorship bills to protect the First Amendment freedoms of the political cartoonist.[6]

Political cartoons do more than elicit a laugh or a chuckle. Frequently, they avoid humor altogether, going for outrage, indignation, ridicule, or scathing contempt. Their goal is to provoke a reaction from their audience, and they use the tools of irony, sarcasm, symbolism, and shock as well as humor. With this barrage of weapons aimed at you, your critical skills are crucial. The next time you are confronted with a political cartoon, ask yourself these questions:[7]

1. **What is the event or issue that inspired the cartoon?** Political cartoonists do not attempt to inform you about current events; they assume that you already know what has happened. Their job is to comment on the news, so your first step in savvy cartoon readership is to be up on what's happening

in the world. The Clinton/Nixon cartoon makes the assumptions that (1) you know that Nixon and Clinton were the only two modern presidents to face impeachment, and (2) you are familiar enough with the scandal-ridden history of the Clinton administration to know that much of the action centered on Clinton's alleged prevarication and his insistence that he wasn't really lying when he said he did not have sexual relations with "that woman" (Monica Lewinsky). The cartoonist here suggests that Clinton might have believed he wasn't lying because he had his fingers crossed when he spoke. One might also interpret Clinton's crossed fingers as his wish that the good luck responsible for saving him from several close calls in the past might stay with him during the impeachment process.

2. **Are there any real people in the cartoon? Who are they?** Cartoonists develop caricatures of prominent politicians that exaggerate some gesture or facial feature (often the nose, the ears, or the eyebrows, although cartoonists had a field day with Reagan's hair) that makes them immediately identifiable.[8] Richard Nixon's ski jump nose and swarthy complexion were frequently lampooned, as was his habit of raising his hands over his head in a victory salute. In the cartoon here, a sheepish, pudgy-cheeked, round-nosed Clinton is shown side by side with Nixon, with his fingers crossed rather than spread wide in triumph.

Many cartoonists do not confine their art to real people. Some will use an anonymous person labeled to represent a group (big business, U.S. Senate, environmentalists). Others increasingly draw stereotypical middle-class citizens, talking television sets, or multipaneled "talking head" cartoons to get their views across.[9]

3. **Are there symbols in the cartoon? What do they represent?** Without a key to the symbols cartoonists use, their art can be incomprehensible. Uncle Sam stands for the United States, donkeys are Democrats, and elephants are Republicans. Tammany Hall frequently appeared in political cartoons of the time as a tiger. Often these symbols are combined in unique ways. (See the cartoon on page 316, which casts elephants—Republicans—as Pilgrims and labels them the "Religious Right.") The cartoon on page 189 symbolizes presidential power as a giant, complicated, and frightening-looking machine, in front of which the president stands, awestruck. However, as politics has fo-

cused more on image and personality, symbols, while still important, have taken a back seat to personal caricature.[10]

4. **What is the cartoonist's opinion about the topic of the cartoon? Do you agree with it or not? Why?** A cartoon is an editorial as surely as are the printed opinion pieces we focus on in Chapter 10. The cartoon has no more claim to objective status than someone else's opinion, and you need to evaluate it critically before you take what it says to be an accurate reflection of the world. Often this is harder in a cartoon than in print, because the medium can be so much more effective in provoking a reaction from us, whether it is shock, laughter, or scorn, and often there can be multiple interpretations of a single cartoon.

In the drawing here, the artist might be trying to say that both Nixon and Clinton were very good at fooling themselves into thinking they were in the right when they got into presidential hot water. Many people remember that Nixon gave the "victory" sign even as he left the White House in disgrace. Similarly, Clinton's boyish grin and use of a child's ploy to shade the truth ("it didn't count, my fingers were crossed") suggests that, like a child, he truly felt he had not broken any rules. Another reading is that Nixon's "dark side" got him into legal troubles, whereas Clinton's travails were more like the shenanigans of a mischievous little boy, and good luck would see him through.

[1] Kirkus Reviews, Review of *Them Damned Pictures: Explorations in American Political Cartoon Art,* by Roger A. Fischer, 15 January 1996.

[2] Richard E. Marschall, "The Century in Political Cartoons," *Columbia Journalism Review,* May–June 1999, 54.

[3] Richard Ruelas, "Editorial Cartoonists Nip at the Heels of Society," *Arizona Republic,* 9 June 1996, A1.

[4] Marschall.

[5] Ira F. Grant, "Cartoonists Put the Salt in the Stew," *Southland Times,* Southland, New Zealand, 20 February 1999, 7.

[6] Marschall.

[7] Questions are from the Teacher's Guide, http://politicalcartoons.com/teacher/middle/analysis.html.

[8] Robert W. Duffy, "Art of Politics: Media with a Message," *Saint Louis Post Dispatch Magazine,* 2 September 1992, 3D.

[9] Marschall.

[10] Marschall.

The Evolution of the American Presidency

The framers designed a much more limited presidency than the one we have today. The constitutional provisions give most of the policymaking powers to Congress, or at least require power sharing and cooperation. For most of our history, this arrangement was not a problem. As leaders of a rural nation with a relatively restrained government apparatus, presidents through the nineteenth century were largely content with a limited authority that rested on the powers granted by the Constitution. But the presidency of Franklin Delano Roosevelt, beginning in 1933, ushered in a new era in presidential politics.

The Framers' Design for a Limited Executive

The presidency was not a preoccupation of the framers when they met in Philadelphia in 1787 since the legislature was presumed by all to be the real engine of the national political system. The breakdown of the national government under the Articles of Confederation demonstrated the need for some form of a central executive, however. Nervous about trusting the general public to choose the executive, the founders provided for an electoral college, a group of people who would be chosen by the states for the sole purpose of electing the president. The assumption was that this body would be made up of leading citizens who would exercise care and good judgment in casting their ballots and who would not make postelection claims on him. Because of their experience with King George III, the founders also wished to avoid the concentration of power that could be abused by a strong executive. Their compromise was a relatively limited scope of presidential authority as laid out in the Constitution.

Qualifications and Conditions of Office

The framers' conception of a limited presidency can be seen in the brief attention the office receives in the Constitution. Article II is short and not very precise. It provides some basic details on the office of the presidency:

- The president is chosen by the electoral college to serve four-year terms. The number of terms was unlimited until 1951, when, in reaction to FDR's unprecedented four terms in office, the Constitution was amended to limit the president to two terms.

- The president must be a natural-born citizen of the United States, at least thirty-five years old, and a resident for at least fourteen years.

- The president is succeeded by the vice president if he dies or is removed from office. The Constitution does not specify who becomes president in the event that the vice president is unable to serve. In 1947 Congress passed the Presidential Succession Act, which established the following order of succession after the vice president: Speaker of the House, president pro tempore of the Senate, and the cabinet secretaries in the order in which their offices were established.

- The president can be removed from office by impeachment and conviction by the House of Representatives and the Senate for "Treason, Bribery, or other high Crimes and Misdemeanors." The process of removal involves two steps: first, after an in-depth investigation, the House votes to impeach by a simple majority vote, which charges the president with a crime; second, the Senate tries the president on the articles of impeachment and can convict by a two-thirds majority vote. Only two American presidents, Andrew Johnson and Bill Clinton, have been impeached (in 1868 and 1998), but so far, none has been convicted. The Senate failed, by one vote, to convict Johnson and could not assemble a majority against Clinton.

The Constitutional Powers of the President

The Constitution uses vague language to discuss some presidential powers and is silent on the range and limits of others. It is precisely this ambiguity that allowed the Constitution to be ratified by both those who wanted a strong executive and those who did not. In addition, it is this vagueness that has allowed the powers of the president to expand over time without constitutional amendment. We can think of the president's constitutional powers as falling into three categories: executive authority to administer government and legislative and judicial authority to check the other two branches.

chief administrator
the president's executive role as the head of federal agencies and the person responsible for the implementation of national policy

cabinet
a presidential advisory group selected by the president and made up of the vice president, the heads of the fourteen federal executive departments, and other high officials to whom the president elects to give cabinet status

commander-in-chief
the president's role as the top officer of the country's military establishment

Executive Powers   Article II, Section 1, of the Constitution begins, "The executive Power shall be vested in a President of the United States of America." However, the document does not explain exactly what "executive Power" entails, and scholars and presidents through much of our history have debated the extent of these powers.[2] Section 3 states that the president "shall take Care that the Laws be faithfully executed." Herein lies much of the executive authority: the president is the **chief administrator** of the nation's laws. This means that he is the chief executive officer (CEO) of the country—the person who, more than anyone else, is held responsible for the agencies of the national government and the implementation of national policy.

The Constitution also specifies that the president, with the approval of the majority of the Senate, will appoint the heads of departments, who will oversee the implementation of policy. These heads, who have come to be known collectively as the **cabinet,** report to the president. Today the president is responsible for the appointment of more than four thousand federal employees—cabinet and lower administrative officers, federal judges, military officers, and members of the diplomatic corp. His responsibilities place him at the top of a vast federal bureaucracy. But his control of this bureaucracy is limited, as we will see in Chapter 8, by the fact that although he can make a large number of appointments, he is not able to fire many of the people he hires.

Other constitutional powers place the president, as **commander-in-chief,** at the head of the command structure for the entire military establishment. The Constitution gives Congress the power to declare war, but as the commander-in-chief, the

The President as Peace Broker
One of the most important roles of the president is that of statesman, and U.S. presidents have had many opportunities in recent years to help other countries work toward peaceful solutions to their conflicts. On October 1, 1996, President Clinton hosted Middle East leaders at the White House for peace talks. Left to right are Palestine Liberation Organization (PLO) leader Yasser Arafat, King Hussein of Jordan, Clinton, and Israeli prime minister Benjamin Netanyahu.

chief foreign policy maker
the president's executive role as the primary shaper of relations with other nations

treaties formal agreements with other countries; negotiated by the president and requiring two-thirds Senate approval

executive agreement
a presidential arrangement with another country that creates foreign policy without the need for Senate approval

president has the practical ability to wage war. These two powers, meant to check each other, instead provide for a battleground on which Congress and the president struggle for the power to control military operations. After the controversial Vietnam War, which was waged by Presidents Lyndon Johnson and Richard Nixon but never officially declared by Congress, Congress passed the War Powers Act of 1973, which was intended to limit the president's power to send troops abroad without congressional approval. Most presidents have ignored the act, however, when they wished to engage in military action abroad, and since public opinion tends to rally around the president at such times, Congress has declined to challenge popular presidential actions. The War Powers Act remains more powerful on paper than in reality.

Finally, under his executive powers, the president is the **chief foreign policy maker.** This role is not spelled out in the Constitution, but the foundation for it is laid in the provision that the president negotiates **treaties**—formal international agreements with other nations—with the approval of two-thirds of the Senate. The president also appoints ambassadors and receives ambassadors of other nations, a power that essentially amounts to determining which nations the United States will recognize.

The requirement of Senate approval for treaties is meant to check the president's foreign policy power, but the president can get around the senatorial check by issuing an executive agreement directly with the heads of state of other nations. The **executive agreement** allows the president the flexibility of negotiating, often in secret, to set important international policy without creating controversy or stirring up opposition. For example, U.S. military bases set up in Egypt, Saudi Arabia, Kuwait, and other Persian Gulf states are the result of executive agreements made between the president and the leaders of those countries.

Legislative Powers   Even though the president is the head of the executive branch of government, the Constitution gives him some legislative powers to check Congress. "He shall from time to time give to the Congress Information of the State of the Union, and recommend to their Consideration such Measures as he shall judge necessary and expedient." Although the framers' vision of this activity was quite limited, today the president's **State of the Union address,** delivered before the full Congress every January, is a major statement of the president's policy agenda.

State of the Union address   a speech given annually by the president to a joint session of Congress and to the nation announcing the president's agenda

The Constitution gives the president the nominal power to convene Congress and, when there is a dispute about when to disband, to adjourn it as well. Before Congress met regularly, this power, though limited, actually meant something. Today we rarely see it invoked. Some executives, such as the British prime minister, who can dissolve Parliament and call new elections, have a much more formidable convening power than that available to the U.S. president.

presidential veto   a president's authority to reject a bill passed by Congress; may be overridden only by a two-thirds majority in both houses

The principal legislative power of the president in the Constitution is the **presidential veto.** If the president objects to a bill passed by the House and Senate, he can veto it, sending it back to Congress with a message indicating his reasons. Congress can override a veto with a two-thirds vote in each house, but because mustering the two-thirds support is quite difficult, the presidential veto is a substantial power. Even the threat of a presidential veto can have a major impact on getting congressional legislation to fall in line with the administration's preferences.[3] Table 7.2 shows the number of bills vetoed by recent presidents and the number of successful veto overrides by Congress. President George Bush (1989–1993) was particularly successful in using the veto against a Democratic Congress and was overridden only once. Pres-

Table 7.2
Presidential Vetoes, Roosevelt to Clinton

Years	President	Total Vetoes	Regular Vetoes	Pocket Vetoes	Vetoes Overridden	Veto Success Rate
1933–1945	Franklin D. Roosevelt	635	372	263	9	97.6%
1945–1953	Harry S. Truman	250	180	70	12	93.3
1953–1961	Dwight D. Eisenhower	181	73	108	2	97.3
1961–1963	John F. Kennedy	21	12	9	0	100.0
1963–1969	Lyndon B. Johnson	30	16	14	0	100.0
1969–1974	Richard M. Nixon	43	26	17	7	73.1
1974–1977	Gerald R. Ford	66	48	18	12	75.0
1977–1981	Jimmy Carter	31	13	18	2	84.6
1981–1989	Ronald Reagan	78	39	39	9	76.9
1989–1993	George Bush	46	27	19*	1	96.3
1993–2000	Bill Clinton	37	37	0	2	94.6

*Two pocket vetoes were not recognized by Congress, which passed subsequent legislation that did not encounter vetoes.

Sources: Gary L. Galemore, "The Presidential Veto and Congressional Procedure" in *CRS Report for Congress,* updated 16 October 1996 (http://www.house.gov/rules/95-1195.htm). Calculated by the author from *Presidential Vetoes, 1789–1976* (Washington, DC: Government Printing Office, 1978) and *Presidential Vetoes, 1977–1984* (Washington, DC: Government Printing Office, 1985); updated from successive volumes of *Congressional Quarterly Almanac* (Washington, DC: Congressional Quarterly) and "Résumé of Congressional Activity, 105th Congress" from the *Congressional Record Daily Digest,* 19 January 1999, D29. Victoria Allred, "Versatility with the Veto," *CQ Weekly* (January 20, 2001), pp. 175–177.

ident Bill Clinton never used the veto in 1993 and 1994, when he had Democratic majorities in Congress. Over the next four years, however, when he faced a mostly Republican Congress, he attempted to stop twenty-five bills. Congress was able to override him only twice.

Congress has regularly sought to get around the obstacle of presidential vetoes by packaging a number of items together in a bill. Traditionally, presidents have had to sign a complete bill or reject the whole thing. Thus, for example, Congress regularly adds things such as a building project or a tax break for a state industry onto, say, a military appropriations bill that the president wants. Often presidents calculate that it is better to accept such add-ons, even if they think them unjustified or wasteful, in order to get what they judge to be important legislation.

Before it was ruled unconstitutional by the Supreme Court in 1998, the short-lived *line-item veto* promised to provide an important new tool for presidents. Favored by conservatives and by President Clinton, the 1996 line-item veto was supposed to save money by allowing the president to cut some items, such as pork barrel projects, from spending bills without vetoing the entire package. The Supreme Court declared the law unconstitutional because the Constitution says that all legislation is to be passed by both houses and then presented as a whole to the president for his approval. The line-item veto essentially allowed the president, by cutting out the parts he didn't like, to create a different law from that passed by Congress; bills would become law without having been approved in their final form by the legislature.

executive order
a clarification of congressional policy issued by the president and having the full force of law

Although the Constitution does not grant the president the power to make law, his power to do so has grown over time and now is generally accepted. Presidents can issue **executive orders** (not to be confused with the executive agreements he can make with other nations), which are supposed to be clarifications of how laws passed by Congress are to be implemented by specific agencies. One of the most famous executive orders in American history was President Harry Truman's Executive Order 9381 integrating the U.S. military and requiring equal treatment and opportunity for all people in the armed forces.[4]

Judicial Powers   Presidents can have a tremendous long-term impact on the judiciary, but in the short run their powers over the courts are meager. Their continuing impact comes from nominating judges to the federal courts, including the Supreme Court. The political philosophies of individual judges significantly influence how they interpret the law, and this is especially important for Supreme Court justices, who are the final arbitrators of constitutional meaning. Since judges serve for life, presidential appointments have a long-lasting effect. For instance, today's Supreme Court is considered to be distinctly more conservative than its immediate predecessors due to the appointments made by Presidents Ronald Reagan and George Bush in the 1980s and early 1990s. Moreover, President Reagan is credited by many for having ushered in a "judicial revolution" because he, together with his successor, Bush, appointed 550 federal judges (out of a total of 837), most of them conservatives. Although the Senate was slow to hold hearings on many of President Clinton's nominations, his more moderate appointees to the federal bench temporarily halted the conservative trend, which is likely to begin again with George W. Bush as president.

The presidential power to appoint is limited to an extent by the constitutional requirement for Senate approval of federal judges. Traditionally, most nominees have been approved, with occasional exceptions. Sometimes rejection stems from questions about the candidate's competence, but in other instances rejection is based more on style and judicial philosophy. The Democratic-led Senate's rejection of President Reagan's very conservative Supreme Court nominee Robert Bork in 1987 is the most recent and obvious case.[5] Some observers believe that the battle over the Bork nomination signaled the end of deference to the president and opened up the approval process to endless challenges and partisan bickering.[6]

A president's choice of judges for the federal district courts is also limited by the tradition of **senatorial courtesy,** whereby senior senators of the president's party from the states in which the appointees reside have what amounts to a veto power over the president's choices. If the president ignores the custom of senatorial courtesy and pushes a nomination that is unpopular with one of these senators, the rest of that senator's colleagues will generally refuse to confirm the appointee.

The least controversial way a president can try to influence a court decision is to have the Justice Department invest resources in arguing a case. The third-ranking member of the Justice Department, the **solicitor general,** is a presidential appointee whose job it is to argue cases for the government before the Supreme Court. The solicitor general is thus a bridge between the executive and the judiciary, not only deciding which cases the government will appeal to the High Court but also filing petitions stating the government's (usually the president's) position on cases to which the government is not even a party. These petitions, called *amicus curiae* ("friend of the court") briefs, are taken very seriously by the Court.

One additional judicial power of the president granted by the Constitution is the **pardoning power,** which allows a president to exempt a person, convicted or not, from punishment for a crime. This power descends from a traditional power of kings as the court of last resort and thus a check on the courts. Pardons are usually not controversial, although they have occasionally backfired in dramatic ways. After President Gerald Ford pardoned Richard Nixon in the hopes that the nation would heal from its Watergate wounds more quickly if it didn't have to endure the spectacle of its former president on trial, Ford experienced a tremendous backlash that may have contributed to his 1976 reelection loss to Jimmy Carter. More recently, controversy surrounding Bill Clinton's pardons as he left office in 2001 dogged his footsteps into private life.

senatorial courtesy
the tradition of granting senior senators of the president's party considerable power over federal judicial appointments in their home states

solicitor general
the Justice Department officer who argues the government's cases before the Supreme Court

pardoning power
the president's authority to release or excuse a person from the legal penalties of a crime

The Traditional Presidency

The presidency that the founders created and outlined in the Constitution is not the presidency of today. In fact, so clearly have the effective rules governing the presidency changed that scholars speak of the era of the traditional presidency, from the founding to the 1930s, and the era of the modern presidency, from the thirties to the present. Although the constitutional powers of the president have been identical in both eras, the interpretation of how far the president can go beyond his constitutional powers has changed dramatically.

The founders' limited vision of the office survived more or less intact for a little over one hundred years, although several early presidents exceeded the powers granted in the Constitution. George Washington expanded the president's foreign policy powers, for instance; Thomas Jefferson entered into the Louisiana Purchase; Andrew Jackson developed the role of president as popular leader; and Abraham Lincoln, during the emergency conditions of the Civil War, stepped outside his constitutional role to try to save the Union.

inherent powers
presidential powers implied but not explicitly stated in the Constitution

These presidents believed that they had what modern scholars call **inherent powers** to fulfill their constitutional duty to "take Care that the Laws be faithfully executed." Some presidents, like Lincoln, claimed that national security required a broader presidential role. Others held that the president, as our sole representative in foreign affairs, needs a stronger hand abroad than at home. Inherent powers are not explicitly listed in the Constitution but are implied by the powers that are granted, and they have been supported, to some extent, by the Supreme Court.[7] But most nineteenth- and early-twentieth-century presidents, conforming to the founders' expectations, took a more retiring role, causing one observer to claim that "twenty of the twenty-five presidents of the nineteenth century were lords of passivity."[8] The job of the presidency was seen as a primarily administrative office, in which presidential will was clearly subordinate to the will of Congress.

The Modern Presidency

The rural nature of life in the United States changed rapidly in the century and a half after the founding. Government in the nineteenth century sought bit by bit to respond to the new challenges of its changing people and economy, and as it responded, it grew beyond the bounds of the rudimentary administrative structure supervised by George Washington. The crisis of the Great Depression and Franklin Roosevelt's New Deal solution exploded the size of government and changed popular ideas of what government was all about.

Nothing in their prior experience had prepared Americans for the calamity of the Great Depression. Following the stock market crash of October 1929, the economy went into a tailspin. Unemployment soared to 25 percent, and the gross national product (GNP) plunged from around $100 billion in 1928 to less than $60 biilion in 1932.[9] President Herbert Hoover held that the U.S. government had only limited powers and responsibility to deal with what was, he believed, a private economic crisis. There was no widespread presumption, as there is today, that the government was responsible for the state of the economy or for alleviating the suffering of its citizens.

The election of Franklin Roosevelt in 1932, and his three reelections, initiated an entirely new level of government activism. For the first time, the national government assumed responsibility for the economic well-being of its citizens on a substantial scale. Relying on the theory mentioned earlier, that foreign affairs are thought to justify greater presidential powers than domestic affairs, Roosevelt portrayed himself as waging war against the Depression and sought from Congress the powers "that would be given to me if we were in fact invaded by a foreign foe."[10] The New Deal programs he put in place tremendously increased the size of the federal establishment and its budget. The number of civilians (nonmilitary personnel) working for the federal government increased by more than 50 percent during Roosevelt's first two terms (1933–1939). The crisis of the Great Depression created the conditions for extraordinary action, and the leadership of FDR created new responsibilities and opportunities for the federal government. Congress delegated a vast amount of discretionary power to FDR so that he could implement his New Deal programs.

The legacy of the New Deal is that Americans now look to their president and their government to regulate their economy, solve their social problems, and provide political inspiration. FDR's New Deal was followed by Truman's Fair Deal. Eisenhower's presidency was less activist, but it was followed by Kennedy's New Frontier and Johnson's Great Society. All of these comprehensive policy programs did less than they promised, but they reinforced Americans' belief that it is the government's, and in particular the president's, job to make ambitious promises. While presidents from Carter to Reagan to Clinton to George W. Bush have enthusiastically promoted plans for cutting back the size of the government, few efforts have been successful. Not even Reagan, the most conservative and therefore the most hostile to "big government," was able to significantly reduce government size and popular expectations of government action.

WHO, WHAT, HOW The founders feared a powerful executive, but presidents have worked to expand the powers of the office, aided, since FDR's days, by a public that looks to the president to solve many social and problems.

WHO are the actors?	WHAT do they want?	HOW do they get it?
Founders	• Limited presidential powers	• Constitution
President	• Inherent (expanded) powers	• Supreme Court rulings
Citizens	• Leadership in a complex world	• Popular approval of and consent to expanded powers

Presidential Politics: The Struggle for Power

Presidential responsibilities and the public's expectations of what the president can accomplish have increased greatly in this century, but as we have discussed, the Constitution has not been altered to give the president more power. To avoid failure, presidents have to seek power beyond that which is explicitly granted by the Constitution, and even beyond what they can claim as part of their inherent powers.

The Expectations Gap and the Need for Persuasive Power

Even those presidents who have drawn enthusiastically on their inherent powers to protect national security or conduct foreign policy cannot summon the official clout to ensure that their legislation gets through Congress, that the Senate approves their appointments, and that other aspects of their campaign promises are fulfilled. Some scholars believe that presidents should be given the power necessary to do the job correctly. Others argue that no one can do the job; it is not a lack of power that is the problem, but rather that no human being is up to the task of solving everyone's problems on all fronts. The solution, according to this view, is to lower expectations and return the presidency to a position of less prominence.[11]

New presidents quickly face the dilemma of high visibility and status and limited constitutional authority. Yet people continue to run for and serve as president. How do they deal with the expectations gap? The answer is that they attempt to augment their power. In addition to the inherent powers we have already discussed, the primary extraconstitutional power the president tries to use is, in one scholar's phrase, the **power to persuade**.[12] To achieve what is expected of them, presidents must persuade others—most often members of Congress, but also the courts, the media, state and local officials, bureaucrats, foreign leaders, and even the American people—to cooperate with their agendas.

Going Public

One central strategy presidents follow in their efforts to persuade people "inside the Beltway" (that is, Washington insiders) to go along with their agendas is to reach out and appeal to the public directly for support. This strategy of **going public** is based on the expectation that public support will in turn put pressure on other politicians to give the president what he wants.[13] Presidents use their powers as both head of government and head of state to appeal to the public.[14] A president's efforts to go public can include a trip to an international summit, a town meeting–style debate on a controversial issue, or even the president's annual State of the Union address or other nationally televised speeches.

The Presidency and the Media   At the simplest level of the going public strategy, the president just takes his case to the people. Consequently, presidential public appearances have greatly increased in the era of the modern presidency. Recent presidents have had some sort of public appearance almost every day of the week, all year round. Knowing that the White House press corps will almost always get some airtime on the network news, presidents want that coverage to be favorable. Shaping news coverage so that it generates favorable public opinion for the president is now standard operating procedure.[15]

The Ratings Game   Naturally, only a popular president can effectively use the strategy of going public, so popularity ratings become crucial to how successful a president can be. Since the 1930s, the Gallup organization has been asking people, "Do you approve

power to persuade
a president's ability to convince Congress, other political actors, and the public to cooperate with the administration's agenda

going public
a president's strategy of appealing to the public on an issue, expecting that public pressure will be brought to bear on other political actors

Press on the Potomac
President George Bush holds an impromptu press conference outside the White House in December 1990 during the Persian Gulf Crisis.

or disapprove of the way [the current president] is handling his job as president?" The public's rating of the president—that is, the percentage saying they approve of how the president is handling his job—varies from one president to the next and typically rises and falls within any presidential term. The president's ratings are a kind of political barometer: the higher they are, the more effective the president is with other political and economic actors; the lower they are, the harder he finds it to get people to go along. In the modern presidency, the all-important power to persuade is intimately tied to presidential popularity.

Three factors in particular can affect a president's popularity: the cycle effect, the economy, and unifying or divisive current events.[16]

- The **cycle effect** refers to the tendency for presidents to begin their terms of office with relatively high popularity ratings, which decline as they move through their four-year terms (see Figure 7.1). During the very early months of this cycle, often called the **honeymoon period,** presidents are frequently most effective with Congress. Often, but not always, presidential ratings rise going into their second terms, but this seldom approaches the popularity they had immediately after being elected the first time. The posthoneymoon drop in approval demonstrated in Figure 7.1 may be explained by the fact that by then presidents have begun to try to fulfill the handsome promises on which they campaigned. Fulfilling promises requires political action, and as presidents exercise their head-of-government responsibilities, they lose the head-of-state glow they bring with them from the election. Political change seldom favors everyone equally, and when someone wins, someone else usually loses. The cycle effect means that presidents need to present their programs early, while they enjoy popular support. Unfortunately, much op-

cycle effect
the predictable rise and fall of a president's popularity at different stages of a term in office

honeymoon period
the time following an election when a president's popularity is high and congressional relations are likely to be productive

Figure 7.1 Average Quarterly Presidential Approval Ratings, Eisenhower to Clinton
Notice the cyclical effect from the beginning to the end of each president's term.
Source: Data provided by Robert S. Erikson; developed for Robert S. Erikson, James A. Stimson, and Michael B. MacKuen, *The Macro Polity* (Cambridge, UK: Cambridge University Press, forthcoming); data from http://www.gallup.com.

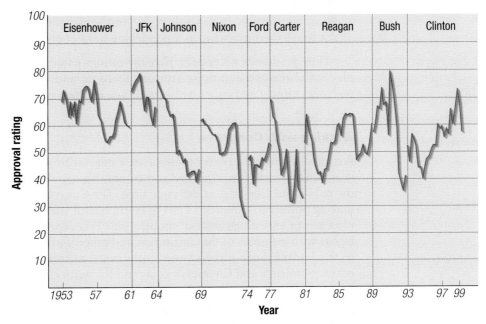

Note: Respondents were asked, "Do you approve or disapprove of the way [the current president] is handling his job as president?" Because results have been averaged to show quarterly ratings, the curve shown here for Clinton does not exactly match that shown in Figure 7.5.

portunity available during the honeymoon period can be squandered because of inexperience, as it was for Bill Clinton. George W. Bush avoided the pitfalls of the early Clinton administration by bringing an experienced staff, including vice president Dick Cheney, to the White House with him.

- The second important factor that consistently influences presidential approval is the state of the economy. At least since FDR, the government has taken an active role in regulating the national economy, and every president promises economic prosperity. In practice, presidential power over the economy is quite limited, but we nevertheless hold our presidents accountable for economic performance. President Bush lost the presidency in 1992 in large measure because of the prolonged recession in the latter part of his presidency. The theme of the successful Clinton campaign that year is effectively summarized by the sign that hung in Democratic campaign headquarters: "It's the economy, stupid!" President Clinton presided over the nation's longest postwar period of economic growth, and this was a big factor in both his relatively easy reelection in 1996 and his healthy approval ratings even in the face of the string of embarrassing, and headline grabbing allegations of wrongdoing that led to his impeachment.[17]

- Third, newsworthy events can influence presidential approval. In general, unifying events help, and divisive events hurt. Unifying events tend to be those that focus attention on the president's head-of-state role. Television footage of the president signing agreements with other heads of state is guaranteed to make the incumbent "look presidential." The same effect usually occurs when the United States confronts or makes war on other nations. The elder Bush's ratings soared to an all-time high during the Persian Gulf War. Notice in Figure 7.1 that President Bush achieved the highest rating of any president at that time.[18] Other events tend to be divisive; these usually sink approval ratings. Presidential vetoes and political controversy in general erode presidential stature[19] because people prefer not to see their executive as a politicking head of government.

Thus presidents necessarily play the ratings game.[20] Those who choose not to play suffer the consequences: Truman, Johnson, and Ford tended not to heed the polls very closely and either had a hard time in office or were not reelected.[21]

Working with Congress

Presidents do not always try to influence Congress by going public. Sometimes they deal directly with Congress, and sometimes they combine strategies and deal with the public and Congress at the same time. The Constitution gives the primary lawmaking powers to Congress. Thus to be successful with his policy agenda, the president has to have congressional cooperation. This depends in part on the reputation he has with members of that institution and other Washington elites for being an effective leader.[22] Such success varies with several factors, including the compatibility of the president's and Congress's goals and the party composition of Congress.

Shared Powers and Conflicting Policy Goals   Presidents usually conflict with Congress in defining the nation's problems and their solutions. In addition to the philosophical and partisan differences that may exist between the president and

members of Congress, each has different constituencies to please. The president, as the one leader elected by the whole nation, needs to take a wider, more encompassing view of the national interest. Members of Congress have relatively narrow constituencies and tend to represent their particular interests. Thus in many cases, members of Congress do not want the same things the president does.

What can the president do to get his legislation through a Congress made up of members whose primary concern is with their individual constituencies? For one thing, the president has a staff of assistants to work with Congress. The **legislative liaison** office specializes in determining what members of Congress are most concerned about, what they need, and how legislation can be tailored to get their support. In some cases, members just want their views to be heard; they do not want to be taken for granted. In other cases, the details of the president's program have to be adequately explained. It is electorally useful for members to have the president do this in person, complete with photo opportunities for release to the papers back home.

legislative liaison
executive personnel who work with members of Congress to secure their support in getting a president's legislation passed

Partisanship and Divided Government   When the president and the majority of Congress are of the same party, the president is more successful at getting his programs passed. When the president faces **divided government**—that is, when he is of a different party than the majority in one or both houses—he does not do as well.[23] The problem is not just that members of one party act to spite a president of the other party, although that does occur at times. Rather, members of different parties tend to stand for different approaches and solutions to the nation's problems. Democratic presidents and members of Congress tend to be more liberal than the average citizen, and Republican presidents and members of Congress tend to be more conservative.

divided government
political rule split between two parties, one controlling the White House and the other controlling one or both houses of Congress

Figure 7.2 shows a hypothetical example of the positions that President George W. Bush might take in dealing with a Republican-led Congress as opposed to a Democratic-led one. When the same party controls the presidency and Congress, the two institutions can cooperate relatively easily on ideological issues, because the majority party wants to go in the same direction as the president. The president prefers his own position, but he would be happy to cooperate with the Republican majority on proposal A because this is much closer to what he wants than is the status quo or the opposition party's proposal. This reflects the situation in 2001 and 2002, when the Republicans controlled the presidency and both houses of Congress. Consider how drastically the situation could change if the Democrats won either or both houses in 2002. Whenever the president sent in a bill like proposal A, Congress would ignore it or amend it to something more palatable, such as proposal B. Notice, however, that if the Democratic Congress then sent a bill like proposal B to the president, he would veto it because he prefers the alternative of no bill, the status quo, to what Congress might pass. Thus, under divided government, Congress tends to ignore what the president wants, and the president tends to veto what the majority party in Congress offers. Presidential success is likely to falter under divided government.

This pattern stands out rather clearly when we compare how successful presidents are in getting their bills passed in Congress. Figure 7.3 on page 207 shows the percentage of bills passed that were supported by each president since Eisenhower.

**Figure 7.2
Hypothetical Policy
Alternatives Under
Unified and Divided
Government**
It is much easier to
pass legislation under
unified government,
where the president's
position and that of
Congress start out
relatively close
together, than under
divided government,
where there is a large
gap between the
initial positions of the
president and Con-
gress. Presidential
success in getting
bills passed is much
higher under unified
government than it is
when the opposition
party has a majority
in Congress (see
Figure 7.3).

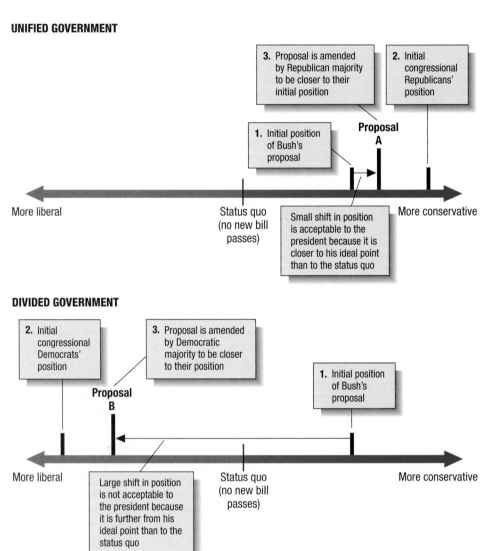

Notice that the success rate has been consistently higher under unified government.
A dramatic example of the impact of divided government can be seen in the Clinton
administration. During his first two years in office, Clinton worked with a Democratic majority in both houses, and Congress passed 86 percent of the bills he supported. During the next two years (1995–1996), the Republicans had a majority in
both houses, and Clinton's success rate dropped to 46 percent.[24]

Divided government, however, does not doom Washington to inaction. When
national needs are pressing or the public mood seems to demand action, the president and opposition majorities have managed to pass important legislation.[25] For
example, the government was divided with a Democrat in the White House and Republicans in control of both houses of Congress when a major welfare reform bill,
the Personal Responsibility and Work Opportunity Act, was passed in 1996.

Figure 7.3
Presidential Success Under Unified and Divided Government, Eisenhower to Clinton
Source: Data from Norman J. Ornstein, Thomas E. Mann, and Michael J. Malbin, *Vital Statistics on Congress, 1997–1998* (Washington, DC: Congressional Quarterly Press, 1998), Table 8-1; *CQ Weekly,* 59, (Jan. 6, 2001), pp. 61–63.

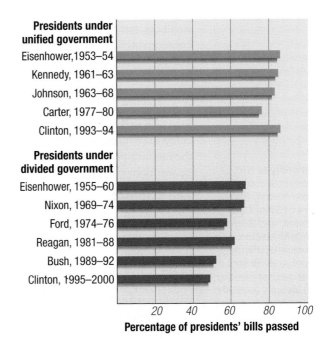

WHO, WHAT, HOW   In this section, we have discussed how the president struggles with the public and with Congress to pass his legislative agenda. The several actors in this struggle all have something important at stake.

WHO are the actors?	WHAT do they want?	HOW do they get it?
The president	• Presidential legislation passed • Public approval • Congressional approval	• Constitutional powers • Maintaining reputation • Going public • Using the media • Maintaining economic health
Citizens	• Fulfilled campaign promises • Positive national direction	• Ability to withhold approval
Congress	• Congressional agenda passed • Satisfied constituents	• Cooperation with the president

Managing the Presidential Establishment

The modern president is one individual at the top of a large and complex organization called the presidency, which itself heads the even larger executive branch of government. George Washington got by with no staff to speak of and consulted with his small cabinet of just three departments, but citizens' expectations of government, and consequently the sheer size of the government, have grown considerably since then, and so has the machinery designed to manage that government. Today the executive branch includes the cabinet with its fourteen departments, the Executive Office of the President, and the White House staff, amounting altogether to hundreds of agencies and almost 3 million employees. The modern president requires a vast bureaucracy to help him make the complex decisions he faces daily, but at the same time the bureaucracy itself presents a major management challenge for the president. The reality of the modern presidency is that the president is limited in his ability to accomplish what he wants by the necessity of dealing with this complex bureaucracy.

The Cabinet

Diversity Is "In"
Interior Secretary Gale Norton, Secretary of State Colin Powell, and Secretary of Defense Donald Rumsfeld attend George W. Bush's first cabinet meeting on January 31, 2001. Part of the balancing act in putting together a cabinet is concern for the many different constituencies represented. George W. Bush's initial cabinet appointments included two African Americans, four women, one Hispanic American, one Lebanese American, two Asian Americans, and one Italian American.

Each department in the executive branch is headed by a presidential appointee; collectively, these appointees form the president's cabinet. Today the cabinet consists of fourteen people heading up fourteen departments. The cabinet is not explicitly set up by the Constitution, although that document does make various references to the executive departments, indicating that the founders were well aware that the president would need specialty advisers in certain areas. Whereas once the president appointed close advisers to his cabinet, today he considers the demands of organized interests and political groups and the stature of his administration in putting his cabinet together. The number of departments has grown as various interest groups (farmers, veterans, workers) have pressed for cabinet-level representation. Appointments to the cabinet have come to serve presidential political goals coming out of the election rather than the goal of helping him run the government. The president also seeks balance in the overall makeup of his cabinet so that the various constituencies that elected him can see "their person" or "their people" among the highest appointees. In addition, the president chooses cabinet members who have a certain stature and reputation independent of their appointment. The president's sense of legitimacy is underscored by having top-quality people working in his administration.

The combination of these factors in making cabinet choices—political payoffs

to organized interests and the legitimacy provided by top people in the area—often results in a team that may not necessarily be focused on carrying out the president's agenda. Their independence and attachment to their own agencies and the groups their departments serve mean that cabinet members often have their own ideas, agendas, and careers to worry about. They come to presidential meetings as advocates for their departments, not servants of the chief executive. The president tends to rely more on those in the Executive Office of the President for advice he can trust.

The Executive Office of the President

Executive Office of the President collection of nine organizations that help the president with his policy and political objectives

Office of Management and Budget organization within the Executive Office of the President that oversees the budgets of departments and agencies

Council of Economic Advisers organization within the Executive Office of the President that advises the president on economic matters

National Security Council organization within the Executive Office of the President that provides foreign policy advice to the president

White House Office the approximately five hundred employees within the Executive Office of the President who work most closely and directly with the president

chief of staff the person who oversees the operations of all White House staff and controls access to the president

The **Executive Office of the President** (EOP) is a collection of organizations that form the president's own bureaucracy. Instituted by Franklin Roosevelt in 1939, the EOP was designed specifically to serve the president's interests—to supply information and provide expert advice.[26] Among the organizations established in the EOP is the **Office of Management and Budget** (OMB), which helps the president exert control over the departments and agencies of the federal bureaucracy by overseeing all their budgets. The director of the OMB works to ensure that the president's budget reflects his own policy agenda. Potential regulations created by the agencies of the national government must be approved by the OMB before going into effect. This provides the president with an additional measure of control over what the bureaucracy does.

Because modern presidents are held responsible for the performance of the economy, all presidents attempt to bring about healthy economic conditions. The job of the **Council of Economic Advisers** is to predict for the president where the economy is going and to suggest ways to achieve economic growth without much inflation.

Another department in the EOP is the **National Security Council** (NSC), which provides the president with daily updates about events around the world. The NSC's job is to give the president information and advice about foreign affairs, although the position has expanded at times into actually carrying out policy.

The White House Office

Closest to the president, both personally and politically, are the members of the **White House Office,** which is included as a separate unit of the EOP. White House staffers have offices in the White House, and they do not have to be confirmed by the Senate. Just as the public focus on the presidency has grown, so has the size of the president's staff, currently at about five hundred people.

Central to the White House Office is the president's **chief of staff,** who is responsible for overseeing all White House personnel. Depending on how much power the president delegates, the chief of staff may decide who gets appointments with the president and whose memoranda he reads. The chief of staff also has a big hand in hiring and firing decisions at the White House. Critics claim that the chief of staff isolates the president by removing him from the day-to-day control of his administration, but demands on the president have grown to the point that a chief of staff is now considered a necessity. Presidents Carter and Ford tried to get by without one, but each appointed a chief of staff in the middle of his term to make his political life more manageable.[27]

The chief of staff and the other top assistants to the president have to be his eyes and ears, and they act on his behalf every day. The criteria for a good staffer are very different from those for a cabinet head. First and foremost, the president demands loyalty. This loyalty is developed from men and women who have hitched their careers to the president's. That is why presidents typically bring along old friends and close campaign staff as personal assistants.

Emphasizing intense loyalty in his top staff can lead the president to sacrifice Washington experience and the vision needed to help him in all situations. After his loyal but inexperienced staff got Bill Clinton into a series of embarrassing situations by not fully vetting appointments, advising ill-timed decisions (such as an early move to liberalize the policy on gays in the military), and engaging in some ethically questionable behavior (possibly moving files of Whitewater material and firing White House travel office personnel), Clinton saw the wisdom of bringing in more experienced people such as Leon Panetta, a respected former congressman and Clinton's director of the OMB, and Republican adviser David Gergen.

The different backgrounds and perspectives of the White House staff and the cabinet mean that the two groups are often at odds. The cabinet secretaries, dedicated to large departmental missions, want presidential attention to those efforts; the staff want the departments to put the president's immediate political goals ahead of their departmental interests. As a result, the last several decades have seen more centralization of important policymaking in the White House and more decisions being taken away from the departments.[28]

The Vice President

For most of our history, vice presidents have not been important actors in presidential administrations. Custom for most of the twentieth century put a premium on balancing the ticket in terms of regional, ideological, or political interests, which meant that the person in the second spot was typically not close to the president. In fact, the vice president has sometimes been a rival even in modern times, as when John Kennedy named Lyndon Johnson, the Senate majority leader from Texas, as his vice president in 1960 in an effort to gain support from the southern states.

More than a Master of Ceremonies
Vice presidents have traditionally been relegated to ceremonial duties, but that trend has changed significantly in recent administrations. Former Vice President Al Gore was a key advisor in the Clinton administration, and Vice President Dick Cheney, shown here with President George W. Bush during a staff meeting, brought a record of service, experience, and connections that made him one of the principal forces in the early Bush administration.

Since the Constitution provides only that the vice president act as president of the Senate—a position that carries no power unless there is a tie vote—most vice presidents have tried to make small, largely insignificant jobs seem important, often admitting that theirs is not an enviable post. Thomas Marshall, Woodrow Wilson's vice president, observed in his inaugural address, "I believe I'm entitled to make a few remarks because I'm about to enter a four-year period of silence."[29] FDR's first vice president, John Nance Garner, expressed his disdain for the office even more forcefully, saying that the job "is not worth a pitcher of warm piss."[30]

Ultimately, however, the job of vice president is what the president wants it to be. Ronald Reagan largely ignored Vice President George Bush, for instance, while Jimmy Carter created a significant policy advisory role for Walter Mondale, who brought to the job considerable Washington expertise, which Carter lacked. Former Tennessee senator Al Gore, serving under Bill Clinton, had an even more central advisory role and headed up the National Performance Review, which streamlined the bureaucracy and cut government personnel and costs.

Dick Cheney has a good deal of Washington experience for George W. Bush to draw on, leading many observers to speculate that the Texas governor selected him for that very reason. Once a congressman from Wyoming, chief of staff in the Ford White House, and secretary of defense under the elder Bush, Cheney has a much stronger résumé than many presidents bring to office.

Thus even though the office of the vice-presidency is not a powerful one, a vice president who establishes a relationship of trust with the president can have a significant impact on public policy. The office is important as well, of course, because it is the vice president who assumes the presidency if the president dies, is incapacitated, resigns, or is impeached. Many vice presidents also find the office a good launching pad for a bid for the presidency. Four of the last ten presidents—Lyndon Johnson, Richard Nixon, Gerald Ford, and the elder George Bush—ended up in the Oval Office, although Al Gore did not enjoy similar success in 2000.

The First Lady

The office of the first lady (even the term seems strangely antiquated) is undergoing immense changes that reflect the tremendous flux in Americans' perceptions of the appropriate roles of men and women in our society. But the position of first lady has always contained controversial elements, partly the result of conflict over the role of women in politics, but also because the intimate relationship between husband and wife gives the presidential spouse unique insight into and access to the president's mind and decision-making process. For all the checks and balances in the American system, there is no way to check the influence of the first spouse. Even though the president is free to appoint other trusted friends as advisers, the presence of the first lady as an unelected political consultant in the White House has been viewed with suspicion by some. It will be interesting to see whether "first gentlemen" become as controversial as their female counterparts.

Since the 1960s and the advent of the women's movement, the role of the first lady has served as something of a surrogate for our cultural confusion over what role women should play. Jacqueline Kennedy brought grace, sophistication, and a good deal of public attention to the office. She created an almost fantasy "first family,"

Fulfilling Public Expectations
The First Lady is expected to be a role model, but carving out a role in controversial policy areas can be risky, as demonstrated by the intense public reaction to former First Lady Hillary Rodham Clinton's efforts to participate in health care policymaking early in her husband's first term. The safer path seems to be to take a stand on an issue with which most Americans can agree. Lady Bird Johnson touted beautification of America, Nancy Reagan told us to "Just Say No!" to drugs, and First Lady Laura Bush, shown here during a visit to the Seaton Elementary School in Washington, D.C., signaled early on that much of her public policy activities would be oriented toward promoting literacy, an important—and relatively safe—issue.

sometimes referred to as Camelot, after the legendary medieval court of King Arthur. This public image certainly contributed to JFK's effectiveness as head of state. Barbara Bush's autobiography portrays the traditional role of first lady perfectly: the totally supportive wife of a president and the self-sacrificing mother of a future president, whose ambitions were centered on her family.[31]

Offsetting this traditional vision was the more directly involved and equally supportive Rosalynn Carter. Public objections to her activities and her position as informal presidential adviser showed that the role of the first lady was controversial even in the late 1970s. Far more in the Carter than the Bush mode, Hillary Rodham Clinton did the most to shake up public expectations of the first lady's role. A successful lawyer who essentially earned the family income while husband Bill served four low-paid terms as governor of Arkansas, Hillary Rodham Clinton has been the target of both public acclaim and public hatred. Her nontraditional tenure as first lady was capped, at the end of her husband's second term, by her election to the U.S. Senate from New York.

The politically safest strategy for a first lady appears to be to stick with a noncontroversial moral issue and ask people to do what we all agree they ought to do. Lady Bird Johnson beseeched us, rather successfully, to support highway beautification; Rosalynn Carter called for more attention to mental health; and Nancy Reagan suggested, less successfully, that we "Just Say NO!" to drugs. Laura Bush, a former teacher and school librarian, focuses on education and literacy. Far closer to the tradition of her mother-in-law, Barbara, than to Hillary Rodham Clinton, she went out of her way during her husband's campaign to say that she would not sit in on cabinet meetings and that she considered herself a wife, not an adviser.[32]

The Problem of Control

President Harry Truman once lamented that he was responsible for hundreds of employees in the executive branch and yet he didn't even have time to meet with them, much less actually see that they did their jobs.[33] Since the government is much larger today, the problem of presidential control of the executive branch is even more of a challenge. The president's difficulty is not so much rules that limit his power as it is the different incentives that drive the bureaucracy and the unwieldy nature of bureaucratic organization. But the president must control the bureaucracy if he wants to use it to advance his political interests.

The president confronts not only the problem of overeager and inexperienced staffers, as mentioned earlier, but also appointed officials who have their own agendas and constituencies, leading to clashes of interests among his advisers and managers. This presents him with a real challenge in deciding whose counsel to heed.

WHO, WHAT, HOW   The executive branch can both help and hinder the president as he seeks to fulfill his campaign promises and promote his policy agenda.

WHO are the actors?	WHAT do they want?	HOW do they get it?
The president	• Fulfillment of goals • Control of the bureaucracy	• Executive bureaucracy • Choice of advisers who will follow presidential agenda • Management of executive staff
Executive bureaucracy	• Autonomy • Ability to further own interests	• Cooperation with president • Attempts to persuade president • Clashes with president
First lady, vice president	• Noncontroversial public roles • Support for future ambitions	• Cooperation with president

Presidential Character

Effective management of the executive branch is one feature of a successful presidency, but there are many others. Historians and presidential observers regularly evaluate presidential success and failure, even to the point of actually rating presidential greatness.[34] In this section, we look at the personal resources of a president that lead to his success or failure.

Most presidents share some personality characteristics—giant ambition and large egos, for instance—but this does not mean that they are carbon copies of one another. They clearly differ in fundamental ways. A number of scholars have developed classification schemes of presidential personalities. Each of these is based on

The Great Communicator
This was the label many people applied to President Ronald Reagan because of his ability to connect with the American public. His effectiveness as a communicator had little to do with explaining complex policy decisions. Rather, he conveyed a sense of confidence, trustworthiness, and warmth. He made people feel good.

the expectation that knowing key dimensions of individual presidential personalities will help explain, or even predict, how presidents will behave in certain circumstances. The most famous of these schemes was developed by James David Barber, who classifies presidents on two dimensions: their energy level (passive or active) and their orientation toward life (positive or negative).[35] This yields four types of presidents: active-positive, active-negative, passive-positive, and passive-negative (see Figure 7.4).

Some of our best and most popular presidents have been active-positives. They have had great energy and a very positive orientation toward the job of being president. Franklin Roosevelt, John Kennedy, and Bill Clinton represent this type. Others have had less energy (passives) or have been burdened by the job of being president (negatives). They have acted out their roles, according to Barber, as they thought they should, out of duty or obligation. George W. Bush is likely to fit the model of the passive-positive president. He likes being a leader but believes that his job is one of delegating and setting the tone rather than of taking an active policymaking role. Some scholars use Barber's classification scheme to explain political success and failure. Richard Nixon is usually offered as one of the clearest examples of an active-negative president; he had lots of energy but could not enjoy the job of being president. According to this theory, Nixon's personality caused him to make unwise decisions that led to the Watergate scandal and, eventually, to his political ruin.

Assessing individual personalities is a fascinating enterprise, but it is fraught with danger. Few politicians fit neatly into Barber's boxes (or the categories of other personality theorists) in an unambiguous way. Although some scholars find that personality analysis adds greatly to their understanding of the differences between presidencies, others discount it altogether, claiming that it leads one to overlook the ways rules and external forces have shaped the modern presidency.[36]

Figure 7.4
Classification of Presidents

	Passive	Active
Positive	• Likable • Agreeable • Cooperative *William Taft* *Warren Harding* *Ronald Reagan* *George W. Bush*	• Highly energetic • Self-confident • Flexible • Dynamic *Franklin D. Roosevelt* *John F. Kennedy* *Bill Clinton*
Negative	• Virtuous • Principled *Calvin Coolidge* *Dwight D. Eisenhower*	• Ambitious • Aggressive • Inflexible • Eager for power *Herbert Hoover* *Richard Nixon*

WHO, WHAT, HOW In the matter of presidential personality, the person with the most at stake is clearly the president himself.

WHO are the actors?	WHAT do they want?	HOW do they get it?
The president	• Popularity • Political success • Legacy	• Ambition, ego, ability to make hard decisions • Enjoyment of office • Energy in office

Citizenship and the Presidency

Although the Constitution does not say so, the citizens of the United States have the ultimate power over the president. We elect him (and someday her), it is true, but our power goes beyond a once-every-four-years vote of approval or disapproval. Modern polling techniques, as we have seen, allow us to conduct a "rolling election," as the media and the politicians themselves track popular approval of the president throughout his term. The presidential strategy of going public is made possible by the fact that all Americans—citizens, president, and members of Congress—know just where the president stands with the public and how much political capital he has to spend.

In 1998 and 1999, we saw perhaps the clearest example of the power that citizens' support can give to a president, in the fate of Bill Clinton's imperiled presidency. As we have indicated, President Clinton had the same problems with the polls in his early years as every other president (see the early Clinton polls in Figure 7.1). By 1996, however, he had hit his political stride and was reelected with 49 percent of the vote. His approval ratings were at normal levels through the first year of his second term, fluctuating between 54 and 62 percent (see Figure 7.5). Once he was under threat of removal from office, however, his ratings soared, hitting a peak of 73 percent on December 19, 1998, the day the House voted to impeach him. Questioned on specifics, people said they disapproved of Clinton's moral character and found his behavior repellent, but that they thought the impeachment movement was politically motivated and that his private behavior had no impact on his ability to do his job. Of course, we know the end of the story. Clinton went on to be acquitted in the Senate. Once he was no longer under threat, Clinton's ratings dropped to the more normal levels of a popular president near the end of his second term.

It is arguable that these polls saved Clinton's political life. Had they fallen during the impeachment process, it would have been much harder for his supporters to defend him, especially if Democrats and moderates in the House and Senate felt that they were risking their own political futures to do so. It is safe to say that if his approval ratings had fallen, the president may well have lost his job. The institution of the American presidency, like most of the government designed by the framers, was meant to be insulated from the whims of the public. It is an irony that in contempo-

Points of Access

• Volunteer to help in a presidential election campaign.

• Write a letter to the president on a policy issue of importance to you.

• Host a viewing of the presidential debate.

• Solicit the president to be a commencement speaker.

• Visit the White House.

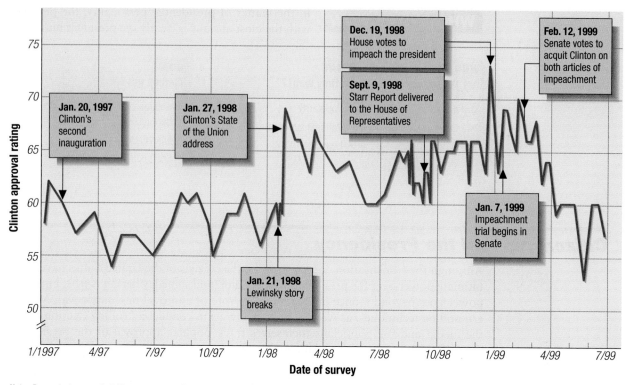

Jan. 20, 1997
Clinton's second
inauguration

Jan. 27, 1998
Clinton's State
of the Union
address

Jan. 21, 1998
Lewinsky story
breaks

Dec. 19, 1998
House votes to
impeach the president

Sept. 9, 1998
Starr Report delivered
to the House of
Representatives

Jan. 7, 1999
Impeachment
trial begins in
Senate

Feb. 12, 1999
Senate votes to
acquit Clinton on
both articles of
impeachment

Note: Respondents were asked, "Do you approve or disapprove of the way Bill Clinton is handling his job as president?"

**Figure 7.5
Clinton Approval
Ratings, January
1997–July 1999**
Source: The Gallup web
page: http://gallup.com.

rary American politics, the president is more indebted to the citizens for his power than to the electoral college, Congress, the courts, or any of the political elites the founders trusted to stabilize American government.

WHAT'S AT STAKE REVISITED

What is at stake in impeaching a president has become increasingly clear for the nation. There are the obvious consequences of the time spent on House hearings and a Senate trial, tying up representatives, senators, and the chief justice for the duration and putting the nation's business on hold. Less obvious is the toll that impeachment takes on separation of powers and checks and balances, as well as on political trust and civility in America.

Parliamentary systems, as we have seen, combine the executive (the prime minister) and the legislature in one body. They are not based on the principle of separation of powers, since powers are fused, and the executive serves at the will not directly of the people, but of the legislators. When the legislators do not like what the prime minister is doing, they can force him or her out of office. Our founders explicitly rejected this kind of system, wanting the president to be removed not when he displeased Congress but when he committed crimes against the state. For more than two hundred years, legislators have mostly restrained themselves from calling for the impeachment of a president they didn't like or disagreed with, reserving impeachment for crimes involving the abuse of presidential power so heinous that until 1998 the bar had been crossed only twice (Andrew Johnson and Richard Nixon). By impeaching President Clinton for causes that most agree were criminal, but far lower on the scale than Johnson's or Nixon's offenses, Congress "lowered the bar," which is to say it lowered the standards sufficiently that future presidents will be far more likely to be impeached if they alienate a majority of Congress. This act has moved the United States closer to the fused powers of the parliamentary system and means that the presidency is considerably weakened, as future presidents will have to weigh the consequences of jeopardizing their jobs if they choose to alienate Congress.

A second consequence of Clinton's impeachment is that, because many see the charges against Clinton as being primarily private, in that they stemmed from alleged perjury about a private and consensual sexual affair, new norms about the privacy of public officials have been set. Some members of the media took the exposure of Clinton's private life as a challenge to uncover private misbehavior on the part of other public figures. Speaker of the House designate Robert Livingston, for instance, resigned his post before he had even officially taken it because *Hustler* magazine threatened to report on his extramarital affairs. Public officials were being vetted for their ability to hold public office on the basis of their private sexual behavior.

A third major consequence of the Clinton impeachment is that the action was seen by the public and by many politicians to be a matter of partisan politics rather than a determination that the president had committed high crimes or misdemeanors. The founders foresaw this possibility. The process of impeachment that they crafted is a tricky one, relying as it does on the House and the Senate to determine the proper grounds for impeachment. Recognizing the potential danger of this solution, Alexander Hamilton noted that the issue was not fundamentally legal but *political.* And, he warned, the popular passions stirred up by impeachment would reignite existing factions, "enlisting all their animosities, partialities, influence, and interest on one side or the other."[37] If care were not taken, he warned, the outcome would be a victory for the strongest party rather than a determination of the president's innocence or guilt.

In the aftermath of Clinton's impeachment, many people felt that Hamilton's words had proved to be prophetic. Because the impeachment was seen to be partisan, many people had less confidence in the process and in government generally. Republican public approval ratings plummeted as Clinton's rose and as the public in large numbers continued to insist that he should stay in office. Relations between House Democrats and Republicans, already strained, soured further in light of what Democrats perceived to be an unfair process intent on getting Clinton at any cost. The Clinton impeachment highlighted the growing division between Democrats and Republicans in Congress and between moderates and conservatives in the Republican Party itself.   ■

key terms

cabinet   195

chief administrator   195

chief foreign policy maker   196

chief of staff   209

commander-in-chief   195

Council of Economic Advisers   209

cycle effect   203

divided government   205

executive agreement   196

Executive Office of the President   209

executive order   198

going public   202

head of government   190

head of state   190

honeymoon period   203

inherent powers   200

legislative liaison   205

National Security Council   209

Office of Management and Budget   209

pardoning power   199

power to persuade   202

presidential veto   197

senatorial courtesy   199

solicitor general   199

State of the Union address   197

treaties   196

White House Office   209

summary

■ Presidents face two expectations gaps when it comes to their relationship with the American public. The first gap is between what the president must promise in order to gain office and the limitations put on the president by the actual powers granted by the Constitution. The second gap occurs between conflicting roles. The American president must function both as the political head of government and the apolitical head of state, and often these two roles conflict.

■ When it came to defining the functions and powers of the president, the founders devised rules that both empower and limit the president. Whereas some of the founders argued for a strong leader with far-reaching powers, others argued for several executives who would check one another's powers. The constitutional compromise gives us an executive who has certain powers and independence but is checked by congressional and judicial powers.

■ We have seen two periods of presidential leadership so far. The first period, called the traditional presidency, lasted until the 1930s and included chief executives who mainly lived within the limits of their constitutional powers. Since then,

presidents have entered into a more complex relationship with American citizens, branching out to use more informal powers yet remaining indebted to public approval for this expansion.

■ The president is in a constant struggle with Congress and the public for the furthering of his legislative agenda. The president needs both congressional cooperation and public approval to fulfill his campaign promises. The chief executive uses several strategies to achieve these goals, including going public and building coalitions in Congress.

■ The presidential establishment includes the cabinet, the Executive Office of the President, and the White House Office—a huge bureaucracy that has grown considerably since the days of George Washington's presidency. Although the resources are vast, managing such a large and complex organization presents its own problems. The president's closest advisers are generally focused on his interests, but other staff members and agency heads—often with their own agendas and difficult to control—can make life challenging for the chief executive.

8

What's at Stake?

What Is Bureaucracy?
- The Spoils System
- Bureaucracy and Democracy
- Accountability and Rules

The American Federal Bureaucracy
- Evolution of the Federal Bureaucracy
- Organization of the Federal Bureaucracy
- Roles of the Federal Bureaucracy
- Who Are the Federal Bureaucrats?

Politics Inside the Bureaucracy
- Bureaucratic Culture
- Presidential Appointees and the Career Civil Service

External Bureaucratic Politics
- Interagency Politics
- The Bureaucracy and the President
- The Bureaucracy and Congress
- The Bureaucracy and the Courts

What's at Stake Revisited

The Bureaucracy

WHAT'S AT STAKE?

What did the chicken who laid your breakfast egg have for *its* breakfast? Was your hamburger once on drugs? And just what is the pedigree of the french fries you ate at lunch? Do you care? Some people do. Those who worry about eating vegetables that were grown with the aid of chemicals or animals that were treated with hormones or antibiotics, or who are concerned about the environmental effects of such practices, form part of a growing number of consumers who look for the label "organic" before they buy food. One estimate says that Americans spend about $5 billion a year on organic foods.[1]

What does it mean to be organic? There is no standardized definition, so states, localities, and private agencies are free to define it as they wish. Usually the standards are stringent. For example, many groups require organic farmers to use land on which no artificial or synthetic fertilizers, pesticides, or herbicides have been used for five years. Such farming techniques favor the small, committed organic farmer and are difficult for large agribusinesses to apply.[2]

In an effort to eliminate the patchwork of local regulations and to assure consumers that organic foods purchased anywhere in the country were equally safe, the organic food industry repeatedly asked the U.S. Department of Agriculture (USDA) to nationalize standards. When the USDA revealed its standardized definition of *organic,* however, it was a definition that traditional organic farmers and consumers didn't recognize. USDA standards proposed in December 1997 would allow the use of genetic engineering, irradiation, antibiotics and hormones, and sewer sludge—techniques that run directly counter to the values of organic farming—to be labeled "organic." Though strongly supported by the conventional food manufacturers and the developers of biotechnology, these standards were bitterly opposed by the organic food industry and consumers.

Before federal agencies issue new regulations, they must give interested parties and the public the opportunity to be heard. In the battle to win USDA support, the conventional food industry and the food preparers associations had all the resources of big business; the organic food industry had none. Searching for another strategy for influencing the enormous bureaucracy of the USDA, they began a grassroots campaign, encouraging consumers to write to the USDA objecting to the new standards. Natural food stores posted information and distributed fliers on the proposed regulation, and Horizon Organic Dairy used the back panels of its milk cartons to pass on the information and urge consumer action.[3]

The campaign was successful. The USDA received nearly 300,000 letters and e-mail messages opposing the proposal. Even Congress went on record against it.[4] The result was that then Secretary of Agriculture Dan Glickman eliminated the provision allowing genetic engineering, crop irradiation, and the use of sewage sludge as fertilizer, and the proposal is undergoing revision. Glickman said, "Democracy will work. We will listen to the comments and will, I am sure, make modifications to the rule."[5]

Depending on where you stand, the moral of this story varies. It might be a David and Goliath success story or just a quirky tale about a handful of food fanatics. What is really at stake in the issue of whether the organic food industry should be regulated by the USDA? ■

Kids have dramatic aspirations for their futures. They want to be adventurers or sports stars, doctors or lawyers, even president of the United States. Almost no one aspires to be the bureaucrats that so many of us become. But bureaucrats are the people who make national, state, and local government work for us. They are the people who give us our driving tests and renew our licenses, who deliver our mail, who maintain our parks, and who order books for our libraries. Bureaucrats send us our social security checks, find us jobs in the unemployment office, process our student loans, and ensure that we get our military benefits. In fact, bureaucrats defend our country from foreign enemies, chase our crooks at home, and get us aid in times of natural disasters. We know them as individuals. We greet them, make small talk, laugh with them. They may be our neighbors or friends. But as a profession, civil servants are seldom much admired or esteemed in this country. Indeed, they are often the targets of scorn or jokes, and the people who work in the organizations we call bureaucracies are derided as lazy, incompetent, power hungry, and uncaring.

Such a jaded view, like most negative stereotypes, is based on a few well-publicized bureaucratic snafus and the frustrating experiences we all have with the bureaucracy at times. Waiting in endless lines at the post office or department of motor vehicles, expecting a government check in the mail that never arrives, filling out tax forms that seem to be written in another language—all of these things can irritate us to screaming level. In addition, the bureaucracy is the source of many of the rules that can help us get what we want from government but that often aggravate us with their seeming arbitrariness and rigidity. Although bureaucrats aren't elected, they can have a great deal of power over our lives.

Bureaucracies are essential to running a government. Bureaucracy, in fact, is often the only ground on which citizens and politics meet, the only contact many Americans have with government except for their periodic trips to the voting booth. Bureaucrats are often called civil servants, because ultimately their job is to serve the civil society in which we all live. In this chapter, we give bureaucracy a closer look, focusing on the following points:

- The definition of bureaucracy

- The evolution, organization, and roles of the federal bureaucracy

- Politics inside the bureaucracy

- The relationship between the federal bureaucracy and the branches of the federal government

What Is Bureaucracy?

bureaucracy
an organization characterized by hierarchical structure, worker specialization, explicit rules, and advancement by merit

In simplest terms, a **bureaucracy** is any organization that is hierarchically structured—that is, in which orders are given at the top by those with responsibility for the success of the organization and are followed by those on the bottom. The classic definition comes to us from German sociologist Max Weber. Weber's model of bureaucracy features the following four characteristics:[6]

- *Hierarchy.* There is a clear chain of command, with all employees knowing who their bosses or supervisors are, as well as who they in turn are responsible for.

- *Specialization.* The effectiveness of the bureaucracy is accomplished by having tasks divided and handled by expert and experienced full-time professional staffs.

- *Explicit rules.* Bureaucratic jobs are governed by rules rather than by bureaucrats' own feelings or judgments about how the job should be done. Thus bureaucrats are limited in the discretion they have, and one person in a given job is expected to make pretty much the same decisions as another. This leads to standardization and predictability.

- *Merit.* Hiring and promotions are often based on examinations, but also on experience or other objective criteria. Politics, in the form of political loyalty, party affiliation, or dating the boss's son or daughter, is not supposed to play a part.

neutral competence
the principle that bureaucracy should be depoliticized by making it more professional

As governments make their bureaucracies look more like Weber's model, we say they are closer to achieving neutral competence.[7] **Neutral competence** represents the effort to depoliticize the bureaucracy, or to take politics out of administration, by having the work of government done expertly, according to explicit standards, rather than according to personal preferences or party loyalties. The bureaucracy in this view should not be a political arm of the president or of Congress, but rather it should be neutral, administering the laws of the land in a fair, evenhanded, efficient, and professional way.

The Spoils System

spoils system
the nineteenth-century practice of rewarding political supporters with public office

Americans have not always been so concerned with the norm of neutral competence in the bureaucracy. Under a form of bureaucratic organization called the **spoils system,** practiced through most of the nineteenth century, elected executives—the president, governors, and mayors—were given wide latitude to hire their friends, family, and

patronage   a system in which successful party candidates reward supporters with jobs or favors

civil service
nonmilitary employees of the government who are appointed through the merit system

Pendleton Act   civil service reform (1883) that required the hiring and promoting of civil servants to be based on merit, not patronage

Hatch Act   a 1939 law limiting the political involvement of civil servants to protect them from political pressure and keep politics out of the bureaucracy

political supporters to work in their administrations (a practice known as **patronage**). The spoils system is often said to have begun with the administration of President Andrew Jackson and gets its name from the adage "To the victor belong the spoils of the enemy." But Jackson was neither the first nor the last politician to see the acquisition of public office as a means of feathering his cronies' nests.

Filling the bureaucracy with political appointees almost guarantees incompetence, because those who get jobs for political reasons are more likely to be politically motivated than genuinely skilled in a specific area. America's disgust with the corruption and inefficiency of the spoils system, as well as our collective distrust of placing too much power in the hands of any one person, led Congress to institute various reforms of the American **civil service,** as it is sometimes called, aimed at achieving a very different sort of organization.

One of the first reforms, and certainly one of the most significant, was the Civil Service Reform Act of 1883. This act, usually referred to as the **Pendleton Act,** created the initial Civil Service Commission, under which federal employees would be hired and promoted on the basis of merit rather than patronage. It prohibited firing employees for failure to contribute to political parties or candidates.

Protection of the civil service from partisan politicians got another boost in 1939 with the passage of the **Hatch Act,** designed to take the pressure off civil servants to work for the election of parties and candidates. They cannot run for federal political office, head up an election campaign, or make contributions or public speeches on behalf of candidates, although they can get involved in election activities that do not focus on just one candidate or party. The Hatch Act was an attempt to neutralize the political effects of the bureaucracy, but in doing so, it denies federal employees a number of activities that are open to other citizens.

Bureaucracy and Democracy

Much of the world is organized bureaucratically. Large tasks require organization and specialization. While the Wright brothers were able to construct a rudimentary airplane, no two people or small group could put together a Boeing 747. Similarly, although we idolize individual American heroes, we know that military undertakings like the D-day invasion of Europe or the mobilization of forces for the Persian Gulf War take enormous coordination and planning. Less glamorous, but still necessary, are routine tasks like delivering the mail, evaluating welfare applications, ensuring that social security recipients get their checks, and processing student loans.

Obviously, many bureaucracies are public, like those that form part of our government. But the private sector has the same demand for efficient expertise to manage large organizations. Corporations and businesses are bureaucracies, as are universities and hospitals. It is not being public or private that distinguishes a bureaucracy; rather it is the need for a structure of hierarchical, expert decision-making. Naturally, in this chapter we focus on public bureaucracies.

The existence of bureaucratic decision-making, where hierarchy and specialization count and decisions are often made behind closed doors, may seem like a real puzzle in a country that prides itself on its democratic traditions. Consider, however, that democracy may not be the best way to make every kind of decision. If we want to ensure that many voices are heard, democracy is an appropriate way to make decisions. But those decisions will be made slowly (it takes a long time to poll many people on what they want to do), and although they are likely to be popular, they are not necessarily made by people who know what they are doing. When we're deciding whether to have open-heart surgery, we don't want to poll the American people, or even the hospital employees. Instead, we want an expert, a heart surgeon, who can make the "right" decision, not the popular decision, and make it quickly.

Democracy could not have designed the rocket ships that formed the basis of America's space program, decided the level of toxic emissions allowable from a factory smokestack, or determined the temperature at which beef must be cooked in restaurants to prevent food poisoning. Bureaucratic decision-making, by which decisions are made at upper levels of an organization and carried out at lower levels, is essential when we require expertise and dispatch.

Accountability and Rules

accountability
the principle that bureaucratic employees should be answerable for their performance to supervisors, all the way up the chain of command

Bureaucratic decision-making does leave open the problem of **accountability:** who is in charge, and to whom does that person answer? Where does the buck stop? Unlike private bureaucracies, where the need to turn a profit usually keeps bureaucrats relatively accountable, the lines of accountability are less clear in public bureaucracies. Because the Constitution does not provide specific rules for the operation of the bureaucracy, Congress has filled in a piecemeal framework for the bureaucracy that, generally speaking, ends up promoting the goals of members of Congress and the interests they represent.[8] The president of the United States, nominally the head of the executive branch of government, also has goals and objectives he would like the bureaucracy to serve. Thus at the very highest level, the public bureaucracy must answer to several bosses, who often have conflicting goals.

The problem of accountability exists at a lower level as well. Even if the lines of authority from the bureaucracy to the executive and legislative branches were crystal clear, no president or congressional committee has the interest or time to supervise the day-to-day details of bureaucratic workings. To solve the problem of accountability within the bureaucracy and to prevent the abuse of public power at all levels, we again resort to rules. If the rules of bureaucratic policy are clearly defined and well publicized, it is easier to tell if a given bureaucrat is doing his or her job and not taking advantage of the power that comes with it.

There can also be negative consequences associated with the bureaucratic reliance on rules. Bureaucrats' jobs can quickly become rule-bound—that is, deviations from the rules become unacceptable, and individuality and creativity are stifled. Sometimes the rules that bind bureaucrats do not seem relevant to the immediate task at hand, and the workers are rewarded for following the rules, not for fulfilling the goals of the organization. Furthermore, compliance with rules has to be monitored, and the best way we have developed to guarantee compliance is to generate a paper record of what has been done—thus the endless forms for which the bureaucracy is so famous.

red tape   the complex procedures and regulations surrounding bureaucratic activity

For the individual citizen applying for a driver's license, a student loan, or food stamps, the process can become a morass of seemingly unnecessary rules, regulations, constraints, forms, and hearings. We call these bureaucratic hurdles **red tape,** after the red tape that seventeenth-century English officials used to bind legal documents. Citizens may feel that they are treated as little more than numbers, that the system is impersonal and alienating. These excessive and anonymous procedures cause citizens to think poorly of the bureaucracy, even while they value many of the services that it provides.

Rules thus generate one of the great tradeoffs of bureaucratic life. If we want strict fairness and accountability, we must tie the bureaucrat to a tight set of rules. If we allow the bureaucrat discretion to try to reach goals with a looser set of rules or to waive a rule when doing so seems appropriate, we may gain some efficiency but lose accountability. Given the vast numbers of people who work for the federal government, we have opted for accountability, even while we howl with frustration at the inconvenience of the rules.

WHO, WHAT, HOW   The American public is strongly committed to democratic governance, but sometimes decisions need to be made that do not lend themselves to democracy.

WHO are the actors?	WHAT do they want?	HOW do they get it?
Citizens	• Decisions responsive to the public will • Complex technical decisions • Accountability and fairness	• Democratic decision-making • Hierarchy and specialization • Strict adherence to the rules and principle of merit • Red tape

The American Federal Bureaucracy

About 3 million civilians work for the federal government, with another million and a half or so in the armed forces. Only a handful of federal employees (2 percent) work in the legislative branch (37,889) or the judiciary (27,918). The rest—98 percent of federal workers[9]—are in the executive branch, home of the federal bureaucracy. In this section, we look at the evolution of the federal bureaucracy, its present-day organization, and its basic functions.

Evolution of the Federal Bureaucracy

The central characteristic of the federal bureaucracy is that most of its parts developed independently of the others in a piecemeal and political fashion, rather than emerging from a coherent plan. The picture that emerges is more like a patchwork quilt than the streamlined, efficient government structure we would like to have.[10] We can understand federal agencies as falling into three categories:[11]

- *Some government departments deal with fundamental activities.* For example, the Departments of State, War, and the Treasury were the first cabinet offices because the activities they handle are essential to the smooth functioning of government. The Department of State exists to handle diplomatic relations with other nations. The Department of Defense (formerly War) supervises the air force, army, navy, marines, and, in time of war, coast guard. The Department of the

Time to Make the Money
Not many people have seen millions of dollars, yet workers at the Bureau of Engraving and Printing see that much every day. Congress often cuts the funding of government departments it views as nonessential. Few members, however, would question the necessity of this particular operation.

clientele groups groups of citizens whose interests are affected by an agency or department and who work to influence its policies

A Helping Hand from Uncle Sam
During the Great Depression, anxious Americans needed a financial safety net. The Social Security Act, featured in this 1935 poster, was written and ratified in response.

Treasury, which oversees the Internal Revenue Service, performs the key tax collection function, prints the money we use, and oversees the horrendous job of managing the national debt.

- *Other government departments developed in response to national problems* and to meet the changing needs of the country as it industrialized and evolved into an urban society. For instance, the Department of the Interior was created in 1848 to deal with some of the unforeseen effects of westward expansion. The Interstate Commerce Commission, Federal Trade Commission, Federal Reserve System, and other agencies were created to regulate the burgeoning American marketplace. The Social Security Administration was designed to supplement inadequate and failed old-age pensions during a time of economic hardship. The Office of Economic Opportunity (1964) and the Department of Housing and Urban Development (1965) were intended to cope with the poverty that continued to exist as America prospered after the New Deal. The National Science Foundation and the National Aeronautics and Space Administration were crafted to help America respond to the intellectual challenges of the Cold War.

- *Still other government departments develop in response to different* **clientele groups,** which want government to do something for them. These may include interest groups—groups of citizens, businesses, or industry members who are affected by the regulatory action of the government and who organize to try to influence policy. Or they may include unorganized groups, such as poor people, to which the government has decided to respond. Departments in these areas are sensitive to the concerns of specific groups rather than focusing on what is good for the nation as a whole. The Department of Agriculture, among the first of these departments, was set up in 1862 to assist U.S. agricultural interests. It began by providing research information to farmers and later arranged subsidies and developed markets for agricultural products. Politicians in today's budget-cutting climate talk about cutting back on agricultural subsidies, but no one expects the Department of Agriculture to change its focus of looking out, first and foremost, for the farmer. Other agencies that have been created in response to the demands of clientele groups include the Departments of Commerce (businesspeople), Labor (workers), Education (teachers), and Veterans Affairs (veterans).

Organization of the Federal Bureaucracy

The federal bureaucracy consists of four types of organizations: (1) cabinet-level departments, (2) independent agencies, (3) regulatory agencies, and (4) government corporations. As you might suspect, some organizations fit into more than one classification. The difficulty in classifying an agency as one type or another stems partly from Congress's habit of creating hybrids—agencies that act like government corporations, for instance, or cabinet-level departments that regulate. Even experts have difficulty determining the exact number of organizations in the federal government, but the total is approximately four hundred.[12] The overall organizational chart of the U.S. government (see Figure 8.1) makes this complex bureaucracy look reasonably orderly. To a large extent, however, the impression of order is an illusion.

Figure 8.1
Organizational Chart of the United States Government

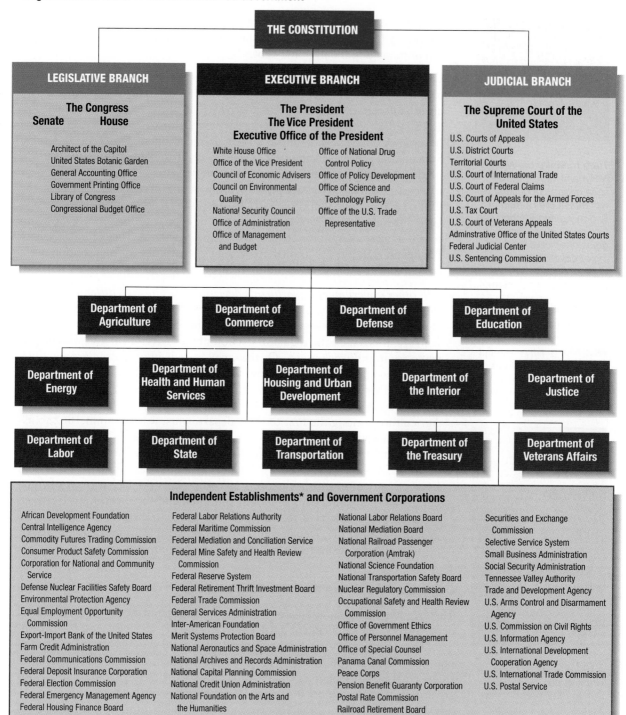

THE CONSTITUTION

LEGISLATIVE BRANCH

The Congress
Senate   House

Architect of the Capitol
United States Botanic Garden
General Accounting Office
Government Printing Office
Library of Congress
Congressional Budget Office

EXECUTIVE BRANCH

The President
The Vice President
Executive Office of the President

White House Office
Office of the Vice President
Council of Economic Advisers
Council on Environmental
  Quality
National Security Council
Office of Administration
Office of Management
  and Budget

Office of National Drug
  Control Policy
Office of Policy Development
Office of Science and
  Technology Policy
Office of the U.S. Trade
  Representative

JUDICIAL BRANCH

**The Supreme Court of the
United States**

U.S. Courts of Appeals
U.S. District Courts
Territorial Courts
U.S. Court of International Trade
U.S. Court of Federal Claims
U.S. Court of Appeals for the Armed Forces
U.S. Tax Court
U.S. Court of Veterans Appeals
Adminstrative Office of the United States Courts
Federal Judicial Center
U.S. Sentencing Commission

Department of Agriculture

Department of Commerce

Department of Defense

Department of Education

Department of Energy

Department of Health and Human Services

Department of Housing and Urban Development

Department of the Interior

Department of Justice

Department of Labor

Department of State

Department of Transportation

Department of the Treasury

Department of Veterans Affairs

Independent Establishments* and Government Corporations

African Development Foundation
Central Intelligence Agency
Commodity Futures Trading Commission
Consumer Product Safety Commission
Corporation for National and Community
  Service
Defense Nuclear Facilities Safety Board
Environmental Protection Agency
Equal Employment Opportunity
  Commission
Export-Import Bank of the United States
Farm Credit Administration
Federal Communications Commission
Federal Deposit Insurance Corporation
Federal Election Commission
Federal Emergency Management Agency
Federal Housing Finance Board

Federal Labor Relations Authority
Federal Maritime Commission
Federal Mediation and Conciliation Service
Federal Mine Safety and Health Review
  Commission
Federal Reserve System
Federal Retirement Thrift Investment Board
Federal Trade Commission
General Services Administration
Inter-American Foundation
Merit Systems Protection Board
National Aeronautics and Space Administration
National Archives and Records Administration
National Capital Planning Commission
National Credit Union Administration
National Foundation on the Arts and
  the Humanities

National Labor Relations Board
National Mediation Board
National Railroad Passenger
  Corporation (Amtrak)
National Science Foundation
National Transportation Safety Board
Nuclear Regulatory Commission
Occupational Safety and Health Review
  Commission
Office of Government Ethics
Office of Personnel Management
Office of Special Counsel
Panama Canal Commission
Peace Corps
Pension Benefit Guaranty Corporation
Postal Rate Commission
Railroad Retirement Board

Securities and Exchange
  Commission
Selective Service System
Small Business Administration
Social Security Administration
Tennessee Valley Authority
Trade and Development Agency
U.S. Arms Control and Disarmament
  Agency
U.S. Commission on Civil Rights
U.S. Information Agency
U.S. International Development
  Cooperation Agency
U.S. International Trade Commission
U.S. Postal Service

* Includes independent agencies and regulatory commissions.

Table 8.1
Departments of the United States Government

Department	Year Formed	Budget 1998 (billions)	Function and History
Agriculture	1862	$15.8	Administers federal programs related to food production and rural life, including price support programs and soil conservation
Commerce	1903	$4.2	Responsible for economic and technological development; includes Census Bureau; was Commerce and Labor until 1913, when Labor split off
Defense	1789	$259.8	Manages U.S. Army, Air Force, Navy; created as War Department in 1789; changed to Defense in 1949
Education	1979	$29.8	Provides federal aid to local school districts and colleges and student college loans; until 1979 was part of Health, Education, and Welfare
Energy	1977	$16.8	Oversees national activities relating to the production, regulation, marketing, and conservation of energy
Health and Human Services	1953	$37.1	Administers government health and security programs; includes Centers for Disease Control and Food and Drug Administration; formerly Health, Education, and Welfare
Housing and Urban Development	1965	$22.4	Administers housing and community development programs
Interior	1849	$8.1	Manages the nation's natural resources through its eight bureaus, including the Bureau of Land Management and the National Park Service
Justice	1870	$17.6	Legal arm of executive branch responsible for enforcement of federal laws, including civil rights and antitrust laws
Labor	1903	$10.7	Responsible for work force safety and employment standards; originated in Interior in 1884, moved to Commerce and Labor in 1903, split from Commerce in 1913
State	1789	$5.6	Responsible for foreign policy and diplomatic relations
Transportation	1966	$15.0	Coordinates and administers overall transportation policy, including highways, urban mass transit, railroads, aviation, and waterways
Treasury	1789	$11.5	Government's financial agent, responsible for money coming in and going out (including tax collection); advises president on fiscal policy
Veterans Affairs	1989	$18.9	Administers programs to help veterans and their families, including pensions, medical care, disability, and death benefits

Sources: *U.S. Government Manual 1997/1998* (Washington, DC: Office of the Federal Register, National Archives and Records Administration, 1997–1998), "Summaries by Agency: Table S-10 Discretionary Budget Authority by Agency." *Budget of the United States* (OMB home page: http://www.access.gpo.gov/usbudget/fy2000/maindown.html). White House home page (www.whitehouse.gov) has links to each department's home page.

department
one of fourteen major subdivisions of the federal government, represented in the president's cabinet

Departments There are currently fourteen **departments** of the federal government. Table 8.1 lists these departments and their dates of creation, budgets (as of 1998), and functions. The heads of departments are known as secretaries—for example, the secretary of state or the secretary of defense—except for the head of the Department of Justice, who is called the attorney general. These department heads

Table 8.2
Selected Federal Independent Agencies, Regulatory Commissions and Boards, and Government Corporations

Independent Agencies	Regulatory Commissions and Boards	Government Corporations
Central Intelligence Agency	Federal Communications Commission	Commodity Credit Corporation
National Aeronautics and Space Administration	Federal Home Loan Bank Board	Export-Import Bank
National Foundation on the Arts and Humanities	Federal Labor Relations Authority	Federal Crop Insurance Corporation
	Federal Trade Commission (FTC)	
	Food and Drug Administration	Federal Deposit Insurance Corporation (FDIC)
National Science Foundation	National Labor Relations Board	
Office of Personnel Management	Occupational Safety and Health Review Commission (OSHA)	National Railroad Passenger Corporation (Amtrak)
Peace Corps		
Small Business Administration	Securities and Exchange Commission	Tennessee Valley Authority
U.S. Information Agency		U.S. Postal Service

collectively make up the president's cabinet. They are appointed by the president, with the consent of the Senate, to provide advice on critical areas of government affairs, such as foreign relations, agriculture, and education. These areas are not fixed, and presidents may propose different cabinet offices. Although the secretaries are political appointees who usually change when the administration changes (or even more frequently), they head the large, more or less permanent bureaucracies we call departments. Cabinet heads may not have any more actual power than other agency leaders, but their posts do carry more status and prestige.

Independent Agencies   Congress has established a host of agencies outside the cabinet departments. Some of these are listed in Table 8.2. The **independent agencies** are structured like the cabinet departments, with a single head appointed by the president. Their areas of jurisdiction tend to be narrower than those of the cabinet departments. Congress does not follow a blueprint about how to make an independent agency or a department. Instead, it expands the bureaucracy to fit the case at hand, given the mix of political forces of the moment—that is, given what groups are demanding what action and with what resources. As a result, the independent agencies vary tremendously in size, from 300 employees in the Federal Election Commission to more than 18,000 in the Environmental Protection Agency. Agencies are called "independent" because of their independence from cabinet departments, but they vary in their independence from the president. Some agency heads serve at the president's discretion and can be fired at any time. Others serve fixed terms, and the president can appoint a new head or commissioner only when a vacancy occurs. Independent agencies also vary in their freedom from judicial review. Congress has established that some agencies' rulings cannot be challenged in the courts, but others' can.[13]

independent agency   a government organization independent of the departments but with a narrower policy focus

independent regulatory boards and commissions   government organizations that regulate various businesses, industries, or economic sectors

regulations   limitations or restrictions on the activities of a business or individual

Independent Regulatory Boards and Commissions   Independent **regulatory boards and commissions** make regulations for various industries, businesses, and sectors of the economy. **Regulations** are simply limitations or restrictions on the behavior of an individual or business; they are bureaucratically determined prescriptions for how business is to take place. Regulations usually seek to protect the public from some industrial or economic danger or uncertainty. The Securities and Exchange Commission, for example, regulates the trading of stocks and bonds on the nation's stock markets, while the Food and Drug Administration regulates things such as how drugs must be tested before they can be marketed and what information must appear on the labels of processed foods and beverages sold throughout the country. Regulations are extremely controversial in a society such as ours that prides itself on both its freedoms and its citizens' health and safety, pitting an individual's freedom to do what he or she wants or a business's drive to make a profit against some vision of what is good for the public.

There are thirty-eight agencies of the federal government whose principal job is to issue and enforce regulations about what citizens and businesses can do and how they have to do it. This effort employs nearly 185,000 people and takes up about 5 percent of the federal budget.[14] Given the size of the enterprise, it is not surprising that regulation occasionally gets out of hand. If an agency exists to regulate, regulate it probably will, whether a clear case for restricting action can be made or not. The average cheeseburger in America, for instance, is the subject of more than forty thousand federal and state regulations, specifying everything from the vitamin content of the flour in the bun, to the age and fat content of the cheese, to the temperature at which it must be cooked, to the speed at which the ketchup must flow to be certified Grade A Fancy.[15] Some of these rules are undoubtedly crucial; we all want to be able to buy a cheeseburger without risking food poisoning and possible death. Others are informative; those of us on restrictive diets need to know what we are eating, and none of us likes to be ripped off by not getting what we think we are paying for. Still others seem silly; when we consider that adult federal employees are paid to measure the speed of ketchup, we readily sympathize with those who claim that the regulatory function is getting out of hand in American government.

The regulatory agencies are set up to be largely independent of political influence, although some are bureaus within cabinet departments. The Food and Drug Administration, for example, is located in the Department of Health and Human Services. Most independent regulatory agencies are run by a commission of three or more people who serve overlapping terms, and the terms of office, usually between three and fourteen years, are set so that they do not coincide with presidential terms. Commission members are nominated by the president and confirmed by Congress, often with a bipartisan vote. Unlike the cabinet secretaries and some agency leaders, the heads of the regulatory boards and commissions cannot be fired by the president. All of these aspects of their organization are intended to insulate them from political pressure so that they can regulate in the public interest and not in the interests of those they hope will reappoint them.

government corporation

a company created by Congress to provide a good or service to the public that private enterprise cannot or will not profitably provide

Government Corporations   Congress created publicly owned **government corporations** primarily to provide a good or service that a private business cannot profitably provide. The U.S. Postal Service (ensuring that mail is delivered to even the most remote areas) is one of the larger businesses in the nation in terms of sales and personnel. The Tennessee Valley Authority and the Bonneville Power Administration are both in the business of generating electricity and selling it to citizens throughout their regions. If you ride the rails as a passenger, you travel by Amtrak, a government-owned corporation (technically called the National Railroad Passenger Corporation). All of these corporations are set up to be largely independent of both congressional and presidential influence. This independence is not insignificant. Consider, for example, how angry citizens are when postal rates go up. Because the Postal Rate Commission is independent, both the president and Congress avoid the political heat for such unpopular decisions. Examples of some of the businesses run by the federal government are listed in Table 8.2.

Roles of the Federal Bureaucracy

Federal bureaucrats at the broadest level are responsible for helping the president to administer the laws, policies, and regulations of government. Bureaucrats are not confined to administering the laws, however. Although the principle of separation of powers—by which the functions of making, administering, and interpreting the laws are carried out by the executive, legislative, and judicial branches—applies at the highest level of government, it tends to dissolve at the level of the bureaucracy. In practice, the bureaucracy is an all-in-one policymaker. It administers the laws, but it effectively makes and judges compliance with the laws as well.

Bureaucracy as Administrator   We expect the agencies of the federal government to implement the laws passed by Congress and signed by the president. Operating under the ideal of neutral competence, a public bureaucracy should serve the political branches of government in a professional, unbiased, and efficient manner. In many cases, this is exactly what happens, and with admirable ability and dedication. The rangers in the national parks help citizens enjoy our natural resources, police officers enforce the statutes of criminal law, social workers check for compliance with welfare regulations, and postal workers deliver letters and packages in a timely way. All these bureaucrats are simply carrying out the laws that have been made elsewhere in government.

The Bureaucracy as Rule Maker   The picture of the bureaucrat as an impartial administrator removed from political decision-making is a partial and unrealistic one. The bureaucracy has a great deal of latitude in administering national policy. Because Congress often lacks the time, technical expertise, and political coherence and leverage to write clear and detailed legislation, it frequently passes laws that are vague, contradictory, and overly general. To carry out or administer the laws, the bureaucracy must first fill in the gaps. Congress has essentially delegated some of its legislative power to the bureaucracy, whose role here is called **bureaucratic discretion.** Top bureaucrats must use their own judgment, which under the ideal of neutral competence should remain minimal, to carry out the laws enacted by Congress. Congress does not say how many park rangers should be assigned to Yosemite versus Yellowstone, for instance; the National Park Service has to interpret the broad intent of the laws and make decisions on this and thousands of other specifics. Bureaucratic discretion is not limited to allocating personnel and other "minor" administrative details. Congress cannot make decisions on specifications for military aircraft, dictate the advice that agricultural extension agents should give to farmers, or determine whether the latest sugar substitute is safe for our soft drinks. The appropriate bureaucracy must fill in all those details.

bureaucratic discretion
top bureaucrats' authority to use their own judgment in interpreting and carrying out the laws of Congress

The procedures of administrative rule making are not completely insulated from the outside world. Before they become effective, all new regulations must be publicized in the **Federal Register,** which is a primary source of information for thousands of interests affected by decisions in Washington. Before adopting the rules, agencies must give outsiders—the public and interest groups—a chance to be heard.

Federal Register
publication containing all federal regulations and notifications of regulatory agency hearings

The Bureaucracy as Judge   The third major function of government is adjudication, or the process of interpreting the laws in specific cases for potential violations and deciding the appropriate penalties when violations are found. This is what the courts do. However, a great deal of adjudication in America is carried out by the bureaucracy. For example, regulatory agencies not only make many of the rules that govern the conduct of business, but they are also responsible for seeing that individuals and, more often, businesses comply with their regulations. Tax courts under the Internal Revenue Service, for instance, handle violations of the tax codes, and their decisions have the full force of law.

Who Are the Federal Bureaucrats?

The full civilian work force of the federal bureaucracy fairly accurately reflects the general population. For example, 51.1 percent of the U.S. population is female, and

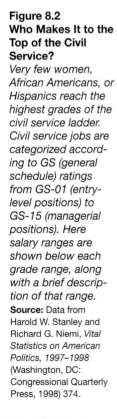

Figure 8.2
Who Makes It to the Top of the Civil Service?
Very few women, African Americans, or Hispanics reach the highest grades of the civil service ladder. Civil service jobs are categorized according to GS (general schedule) ratings from GS-01 (entry-level positions) to GS-15 (managerial positions). Here salary ranges are shown below each grade range, along with a brief description of that range.
Source: Data from Harold W. Stanley and Richard G. Niemi, *Vital Statistics on American Politics, 1997–1998* (Washington, DC: Congressional Quarterly Press, 1998) 374.

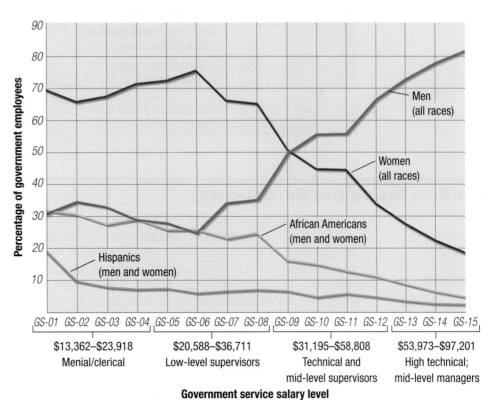

Note: Pay rates were effective as of January 1999. The ranges of salaries indicated are from the lowest step in the lower grade to the highest step in the upper grade of each bracket.

48.7 percent of the civil service is female. African Americans make up 12.1 percent of the population and 16.5 percent of the civil service. The distributions are similar for other demographic characteristics such as ethnic origin and level of education. This representative picture is disturbed, however, by the fact that not all bureaucratic positions are equal. Policymaking is done primarily at the highest levels, and the upper grades are predominantly staffed by well-educated white males. As we can see in Figure 8.2, women and minorities are distinctly underrepresented in the policymaking (and higher-paying) levels of the bureaucracy.[16]

WHO, WHAT, HOW   Government exists, among other reasons, to solve citizens' common problems and to provide goods and services that the market cannot or does not provide. Citizens or groups of citizens who want something from government must deal with the bureaucracy. But bureaucrats, with their own largely unchecked powers, are a formidable part of the federal government to contend with.

WHO are the actors?	WHAT do they want?	HOW do they get it?
Citizens Clientele groups, interest groups, regulated industries	• Provision of basic government services • Solutions to national problems • Goods and services businesses have no incentive to produce • Protection from business and economic hazards	• Growth of bureaucracy
Bureaucrats	• The necessary powers to do their jobs	• Administrative, legislative, and judicial powers

Politics Inside the Bureaucracy

Politicians and bureaucrats alike are wary about the effects of politics on decision-making. They act as if fairness and efficiency could always be achieved if only the struggle over competing interests could be set aside through an emphasis on strict rules and hierarchical organization. We know, of course, that the struggle can't be set aside. As a fundamental human activity, politics is always with us, and it is always shaped by the particular rules and institutions in which it is played out. Politics within bureaucracies is a subset of politics generally, but it takes on its own cast according to the context in which it takes place.

Bureaucratic Culture

bureaucratic culture the accepted values and procedures of an organization

The particular context in which internal bureaucratic politics is shaped is called **bureaucratic culture**—the accepted values and procedures of an organization. Consider any place you may have been employed. When you first began your job, the accepted standards of behavior may not have been clear, but over time you figured out who had power, what your role was, which rules could be bent and which had to be followed strictly, and what the goals of the enterprise were. Chances are you came to share some of the values of your colleagues, at least with respect to your work. Those things add up to the culture of the workplace. Bureaucratic culture is just a specific instance of workplace culture.

Knowing the four main elements of bureaucratic culture will take us a long way toward understanding why bureaucrats and bureaucracies behave the way they do. Essentially, these elements define what is at stake within a bureaucracy and what bureaucrats need to do to ensure that they are winners and not losers in the bureaucratic world. To explore bureaucratic culture, let's imagine that you have landed a job working in the Department of Agriculture. Over time, if you are successful in your job, you will come to share the values and beliefs of others working in your department—that is, you will come to share their bureaucratic culture.

Policy Commitment   As a good bureaucrat-in-training, the first thing you will do is develop a commitment to the policy issues of agriculture. No matter if you've never thought much about farming before. As an employee of the Department of Agriculture, you will eventually come to believe that agricultural issues are among the most important facing the country, just as those working at the National Aeronautics and Space Administration place a priority on investigating outer space and bureaucrats at the National Institutes of Health believe fervently in health research. You share a commitment to your policy area not only because your job depends on it but also because all the people around you believe in it.

Adoption of Bureaucratic Behavior   Not long after you join your department, you will start to see the logic of doing things bureaucratically; you may even start to sound like a bureaucrat. **Bureaucratese,** the formal and often (to outsiders) amusing way that bureaucrats sometimes speak in their effort to convey information without controversy, may become your second tongue. The elaborate rule structure that defines the bureaucracy will come to seem quite normal to you. You will even depend on it, because relying on the rules relieves you of the responsibility of relying on your own judgment.

The hierarchical organization of authority will also make a good deal of sense, and you will, in fact, find yourself spending a lot of time helping to make your superiors look good to their superiors, even as the people working under you will be helping you to look good to your bosses. As you become committed to the bureaucratic structure, you will learn that conformity to the rules and norms of the enterprise is the name of the game. Free spirits are not likely to thrive in a bureaucratic environment, where deference, cooperation, and obedience are emphasized and rewarded, and the relentless rule orientation and hierarchy can wear down all but the most committed independent souls.

Specialization and Expertise   Early on in your career, you will realize that departments, agencies, and bureaus have specific areas of responsibility. There is not a great deal of interagency hopping; most bureaucrats spend their whole professional lives working in the same area, often in the same department. The lawyers in the Justice Department, scientists at the National Science Foundation, physicians at the

bureaucratese
the often unintelligible language used by bureaucrats to avoid controversy and lend weight to their words

National Institutes of Health, and even you as a soybean expert at the Department of Agriculture all have specialized knowledge as the base of their power.

Identification with the Agency   All three of the characteristics of bureaucratic culture discussed so far lead to the fourth: identification with and protection of the agency. As you become attached to the interests of agriculture, committed to the rules and structures of the bureaucracy, concerned with the fortunes of your superiors, and appreciative of your own and your colleagues' specialized knowledge, your estimation of the Department of Agriculture will rise. You begin to think that what is good for Agriculture is good for you, and threats to the department's well-being become threats to you as well. You identify with the department, not just because your job depends on it but because you believe in what it does.

Consequences of the Bureaucratic Culture   This pervasive bureaucratic culture breeds a number of political consequences. On the plus side, it holds the bureaucracy together, fostering values of commitment and loyalty to what could otherwise be seen as an impersonal and alienating work environment. It means that the people who work in the federal government for the most part really believe in what they do.

On the negative side, sometimes the customs and expectations of the bureaucratic culture can lead to devastating mistakes. The tragic explosion of the space shuttle *Challenger* in 1986 resulted, in part, from an entrenched bureaucratic culture at the National Aeronautics and Space Administration (NASA) that had a fierce commitment to its goal of space flight and confidence in its ability to perform. Employees at NASA, convinced of the superiority of their engineering and management expertise, had developed a strong can-do attitude. This led them to accept increasingly more ambitious technical projects. They placed enormous emphasis on keeping to their flight schedules, and they scorned the role of intuition in evaluating prospects for a flight's success. After the disaster, one engineer testified to the investigating commission that although he and others had had reservations about the reliability of the shuttle rockets, especially the fittings that joined sections of the fuel tanks (which were later found to be related to the disaster), he did not speak up:

> I have been personally chastised in flight readiness reviews . . . for using the words 'I feel' or 'I think,' and I have been crucified . . . because 'I feel' and 'I think' are not engineering-supported statements, but they are just judgmental. . . . And for that reason, nobody [raises objections] without a complete, fully documented, verifiable set of data.[17]

A Tragedy Surrounded by an Enigma
The aftermath of the explosion that destroyed the space shuttle Challenger in 1986 is often pointed to as a textbook example of the drawbacks of bureaucracy. Bureaucratic culture, with its inflexible rules and dispersed authority, frequently inhibits efforts to uncover policy errors or hold specific people accountable.

A host of factors led to the accident, but NASA's culture, emphasizing a reliance on solid engineering data rather than subjective judgments, coupled with a compulsion to meet a schedule even if it required shortcuts, contributed to the agency's failure to find the fatal flaw in time.

When an agency is charged with making the rules, enforcing them, and even adjudicating them, it is relatively easy to cover up less catastrophic agency blunders. If Congress, the media, or the public had sufficient information and the expertise to interpret it, this would not be as big a problem. However, specialization necessarily concentrates the expertise and information in the hands of the agencies. Congress and the media are generalists. They could tell something had gone wrong when *Challenger* blew up, but they could not evaluate the hundreds of less obvious problems that only an expert would even recognize.

whistle blowers
individuals who publicize instances of fraud, corruption, or other wrongdoing in the bureaucracy

Congress has tried to check the temptation for bureaucrats to cover up their mistakes by offering protection to whistle blowers. **Whistle blowers** are employees who expose instances or patterns of error, corruption, or waste in their agencies. The Whistleblower Protection Act of 1989 established an independent agency to protect employees from being fired, demoted, or otherwise punished for exposing wrongdoing. Protecting whistle blowers is certainly a step in the direction of counteracting a negative tendency of organizational behavior, but it does very little to offset the pervasive pressure to protect the programs and the agencies from harm, embarrassment, and budget cuts.

Presidential Appointees and the Career Civil Service

Another aspect of internal bureaucratic politics worth noting is the giant gulf between those at the very top of the department or agency, who are appointed by the president, and those in the lower ranks, who are long-term civil service employees. Of the 3 million civilian employees in the federal bureaucracy, the president or his immediate subordinates appoint about 6,000. Political appointees, though generally quite experienced in the agency's policy area, have their own careers or the president's agenda as their primary objective, rather than the long-established mission of the agency. In contrast, rank-and-file civil service employees, thoroughly imbued with the bureaucratic norms we have just discussed, are wholly committed to the agency. Minor clashes are frequent, but they can intensify into major rifts when the ideology of a newly elected president varies sharply from the central values of the operating agency.

The political appointees and the professionals also have different time perspectives. Political appointees have short-term outlooks. Typically, they are brought in at the highest levels of the department or agency, but their time is limited. The average tenure for political appointees is just under two years, although they can conceivably last as long as the president who appointed them is in office.[18] The professionals, in contrast, serve long tenures in their positions. The average upper-level civil servant has worked in his or her agency for more than seventeen years and expects to remain there.[19] Chances are the professionals were there before the current president was elected, and they will be there after he leaves office. Not surprisingly, the bureaucrat's best strategy when the political appointee presses for a new but unpopular policy direction is to stall, knowing that the political appointee may soon be gone.

"Ask What You Can Do for Your Country"
One of President John F. Kennedy's long-standing achievements was the 1961 creation of the Peace Corps, an independent agency that recruits and trains Americans for volunteer work in impoverished parts of the world. This Peace Corps worker is teaching English in the former Soviet republic of Kyrgyz-stan, in a classroom without a working heating system.

Given the difficulty that presidents and their appointees can have in dealing with the entrenched bureaucracy, presidents who want to institute an innovative program are better off starting a new agency than trying to get an old one to adapt to new tasks. In the 1960s, when President John Kennedy wanted to start the Peace Corps, a largely volunteer organization that would provide assistance to third world countries by working at the grassroots level with the people themselves, he could have added it to any number of existing departments. The problem was that these existing agencies were either unlikely to accept the idea that nonprofessional volunteers could do anything useful, or they were likely to subvert them to their own purposes, such as spying or managing aid. Thus President Kennedy was easily persuaded to have the Peace Corps set up as an independent agency, an all-too-common occurrence in the change-resistant world of bureaucratic politics.[20]

WHO, WHAT, HOW   Life inside the bureaucracy is clearly as political as life outside. Many actors attempt to use the rules to advance themselves and the interests of their agency or clientele group, but the bureaucracy has its own culture in which the rules are played out.

WHO are the actors?	WHAT do they want?	HOW do they get it?
Bureaucrats	• Job advancement • Protection of agency from threat or change	• Norms of bureaucratic culture • Time
Whistle blowers	• To correct perceived injustices	• Whistleblower Protection Act
President President's political appointees	• To shape the direction of bureaucratic politics	• Appointing agency heads with interest

External Bureaucratic Politics

Politics affects relationships not only within bureaucratic agencies but also between those agencies and other institutions. Although the bureaucracy is not one of the official branches of government, since it falls technically within the executive branch, it is often called the fourth branch of government because it wields so much power.

It can be checked by other agencies, by the executive, by Congress, or even by the public, but it is not wholly under the authority of any of those entities. In this section, we examine the political relationships that exist between the bureaucracy and the other main actors in American politics.

Interagency Politics

As we have seen, agencies are fiercely committed to their policy areas, their rules and norms, and their own continued existence. The government consists of a host of agencies, all competing intensely for a limited amount of federal resources and political support. They all want to protect themselves and their programs, and they want to grow, or at least to avoid cuts in personnel and budgets.

To appreciate the agencies' political plight, we need to see their situation as they see it. Bureaucrats tend to feel unappreciated and vulnerable. They are a favorite target of the media and elected officials. Their budgets are periodically up for review by congressional budget, authorization, and appropriations committees. And the Office of Management and Budget, the president's budget department, frequently trims agency requests before budgets even get to Congress. Agencies then are compelled to work for their survival and growth. They have to act positively in an uncertain and changing political environment to keep their programs and their jobs.

Constituency Building   One way agencies compete against each other is by building groups of supporters. Members of Congress are sensitive to voters' wishes, and because of this, the support of the general public as well as interest groups is important for agencies. Congress would not want to cut an agency's budget, for instance, if doing so would anger a substantial number of voters.

Consequently, agencies try to control some services or products that are crucial to important groups. In most cases, the groups are obvious, as with the clientele groups of, say, the Department of Agriculture. Department of Agriculture employees work hard for farming interests, not just because they believe in the programs but also because they need strong support from agricultural clienteles to survive. Agencies whose work does not earn them a lot of fans, like the Internal Revenue Service (IRS), whose mission is tax collection, have few groups to support them. When Congress decided to reform the IRS in 1998, there were no defenders to halt the changes.[21] Most agencies have a very clear conception of their constituencies, and they work with those constituencies on a regular basis to maintain their support.

Even independent regulatory commissions run into this problem. Numerous observers have noted how commissions tend to be captured by the very interests they are supposed to regulate. In other words, as the regulatory bureaucrats become more and more immersed in a policy area, they come to share the views of the regulated industries. The larger public's preferences tend to be less well formed and certainly less well expressed because the general public does not hire teams of lawyers, consultants, and lobbyists to represent its interests. The regulated industries have a tremendous amount at stake. Over time, some regulatory agencies' actions have become so favorable to regulated industries that the industries themselves have fought deregulation, as did the airlines when Congress and the Civil Aeronautics Board deregulated air travel in the 1980s.[22]

Guarding the Turf   Agencies want to survive, and one way to stay alive is to offer services that no other agency offers. Departments and agencies are set up to deal with the problems of fairly specific areas. They do not want to overlap with other agencies, because duplication of services might indicate that one of them was unnecessary, inviting congressional cuts. This turf jealousy can undermine good public policy. Take, for example, the military. For years, the armed services successfully resisted a unified weapons procurement, command, and control system. Each branch wanted to maintain its traditional independence in weapons development, logistics, and communications technologies, which meant production of a jet for both the air force and the navy, costing taxpayers millions of dollars. Getting the branches to give up control of their turf was politically difficult, although it was eventually accomplished.

The Bureaucracy and the President

As we discussed in Chapter 7, one of the president's jobs is that of chief administrator. In fact, organizational charts of departments and agencies suggest a clear chain of command, with the cabinet secretary at the top reporting directly to the president. But in this case, being "the boss" does not mean that the president always, or even usually, gets his way. The long history of the relationship between the president and the bureaucracy is largely one of presidential frustration. President John F. Kennedy voiced this exasperation when he said that dealing with the bureaucracy "is like trying to nail jelly to the wall." The reasons for presidential frustration lie in the fact that although the president has some authority over the bureaucracy, the bureaucracy's different perspectives and goals often thwart the chief administrator's plans.

Appointment Power   Presidents have some substantial powers at their disposal for controlling the bureaucracy. The first is the power of appointment. For the departments, and for quite a few of the independent agencies, presidents appoint the heads and the next layer or two of undersecretaries and deputy secretaries. The president's formal power, though quite significant, is often watered down by the political realities of the appointment and policymaking processes, chiefly the need to gain Senate approval of his appointments.

The appointment process begins at the start of the president's administration, when he is working to gain support for his overall program, so he doesn't want his choices to be too controversial. This desire for early widespread support means that presidents tend to play it safe and nominate individuals with extensive experience in the policy areas they will oversee. This expertise means that the president's men and women are only partially his. They arrive on the job with some sympathy for the special interests and agencies they will supervise, as well as loyalty to the president. And, as we have seen, political appointees face their own leadership challenges within their departments and agencies.

The Budget Proposal   The president's second major power in dealing with the bureaucracy is his key role in the budget process. About fifteen months before a budget request goes to Congress, the agencies send their preferred budget requests to the Office of Management and Budget (OMB). The OMB is a White House agency serving the preferences of the president. It can lower or raise departmental budget requests. Thus the president's budget, which is sent to Congress, is a good statement of the president's overall program for the national government. It reflects his priorities, new initiatives, and intended cutbacks. His political appointees and the civil servants who testify before Congress are expected to defend his budget, and they do, at least in their prepared statements.

However, civil servants have contacts with interest group leaders, congressional staff, the media, and members of Congress. Regardless of what the president wants, the agencies' real preferences are made known to sympathetic members of the key authorization and appropriations committees. Thus the president's budget is a beginning bargaining point, but Congress can freely add to or cut back presidential requests, and most of the time it does so. The president's budget powers, while not insignificant, are no match for an agency with strong interest group and congressional support. Presidential influence over the bureaucratic budget is generally more effective in terminating an activity that the president opposes than in implementing a program that the agency opposes.[23]

The Presidential Veto The third major power of the president is the veto, but it is only a blunt tool for influencing the bureaucracy. For instance, the president may want a different set of funding priorities for, say, mass transit systems, but he is unable to veto a congressional bill because such funding is buried in a multibillion-dollar, multiagency appropriation. He may not like everything in the bill, but he does not want to risk shutting down the government or starting a public battle. Without a line-item veto, his veto can be used only as a threat in political bargaining. By itself, it does not guarantee the president what he wants.

Government Reorganization In addition to his other efforts, the president can try to reorganize the bureaucracy, combining some agencies, eliminating others, and generally restructuring the way government responsibilities are handled. Such reorganization efforts have become a passion with some presidents, but the chief executive is limited in his attempts by the need for congressional approval.[24]

The most recent major effort at reorganizing the bureaucracy was undertaken by President Clinton's National Performance Review (NPR), which later became the National Partnership for Reinventing Government, headed by Vice President Al Gore. The goal of the NPR—to reduce the size of the federal government while also making it work better—was to be accomplished by decentralizing, deregulating, and freeing government employees to show more initiative in getting their jobs done. In fact, as of January 2000, the federal government had more than 375,000 fewer employees than it had when Clinton took office, a 17 percent reduction in the civilian work force. A survey of federal agency customers at the end of 2000 showed that the federal government was nearly as well regarded as the private sector in terms of customer satisfaction.[25]

Efforts such as these, though effective, do have some limitations. Greater discretion available to bureaucrats at lower levels, for instance, opens up the opportunity for arbitrary decisions based on racial, gender, family, or personal preferences. This latitude has the potential to make the public just as angry as does the atmosphere of suffocating red tape, delay, and seemingly irrelevant rules. Although the results of the NPR look promising, we need to be cautious in our expectations of what it or any other reform effort can accomplish.

Powers of Persuasion   The final major power of the president over the bureaucracy is an informal one—the prestige of the office itself. The office of the President impresses just about everyone. If the president is intent on change in an agency, his powers of persuasion and the sheer weight of his office can produce results. Few bureaucrats could stand face-to-face with the president of the United States and ignore a legal order. But the president's time is limited, his political pressures are many, and he needs to choose his priorities carefully. The temptation for a bureaucracy that does not want to cooperate with a presidential initiative is to wait it out, to take the matter under study, to be "able" to accomplish only a minor part of the president's agenda. The agency or department can then begin the process of regaining whatever ground it lost. It, after all, will be there long after the current president is gone.

The Bureaucracy and Congress

Relationships between the bureaucracy and Congress are not any more clear-cut than those between the bureaucracy and the president, but in the long run individual members of Congress, if not the whole institution itself, have more control over what the agencies do than does the executive branch. This is not because of any particular grant of power by the Constitution, but rather because of informal policymaking relationships that have grown up over time and are now all but institutionalized.

iron triangle
the phenomenon of a clientele group, congressional committee, and bureaucratic agency cooperating to make mutually beneficial policy

Iron Triangles   Much of the effective power in making policy in Washington is lodged in what political scientists call iron triangles. An **iron triangle** is a tight alliance between congressional committees, interest groups or representatives of regulated industries, and bureaucratic agencies, in which policy comes to be made for the benefit of the shared interests of all three, not for the benefit of the greater public (see Figure 8.3). Politicians are themselves quite aware of the pervasive triangular monopoly of power. Former secretary of health, education, and welfare John Gardner once declared before the Senate Government Operations Committee,

> As everyone in this room knows but few people outside of Washington understand, questions of public policy nominally lodged with the Secretary are often decided far beyond the Secretary's reach by a trinity—not exactly a holy trinity—consisting of (1) representatives of an outside lobby, (2) middle-level bureaucrats, and (3) selected members of Congress.[26]

A good example of the iron triangle is the tobacco policymakers, as shown in Figure 8.3. The Department of Agriculture has long subsidized tobacco growers. Not surprisingly, many of the key congressional leaders on the agriculture committees in the House and Senate come from tobacco-growing states. The department wants Congress to continue to authorize its budget, and the tobacco farmer constituents of the committee members appreciate the financial and scientific assistance

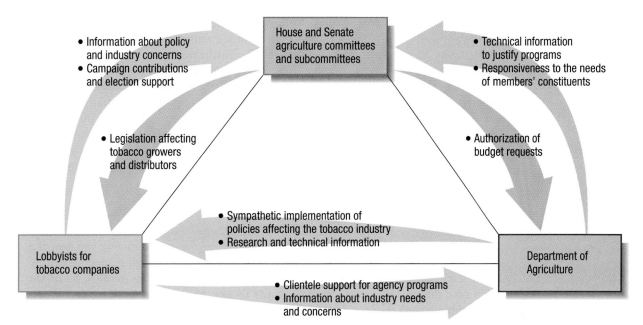

Figure 8.3
The Tobacco-Agriculture Iron Triangle

Iron triangles (involving Congress, the bureaucracy, and special-interest groups) exist on nearly every subgovernment level. In this example, you can see how the Department of Agriculture (which depends on the House and Senate for its budget) influences and is influenced by tobacco company lobbyists, who in turn influence and are influenced by House and Senate committees and subcommittees. This interdependence represents a monopoly of power.

they receive from the department as a result. The third portion of the triangle, the tobacco interests, are also very involved. The large U.S. tobacco companies have worked together to promote the interests of their industry through groups such as the Tobacco Institute. By giving enormous amounts of money to congressional candidates, these companies have ensured that their interests are heard on key congressional committees and in intense debates about the industry. They benefit from subsidies to tobacco farmers by receiving more cheaply produced tobacco, which allows them to keep the price of cigarettes and other tobacco products low.

The metaphor of the iron triangle has been refined by scholars, who speak instead of *issue networks*.[27] The iron triangle suggests a particular relationship among a fixed interest group, fixed agencies, and fixed subcommittees. The network idea suggests that the relationships are more complex than a simple triangle. There are really clusters of interest groups, policy specialists, consultants, and research institutes (think tanks) that are influential in the policy areas. To continue with the tobacco example, antismoking interest groups such as the American Lung Association have begun to weaken the dominance of the tobacco iron triangle. Working with members of Congress sympathetic to their cause, such as Representative Henry Waxman of California, they have supported laws to reduce teen smoking and to increase the taxes on cigarettes. These interests have also had support from friends in the executive department. Former surgeon general C. Everett Koop used his position to battle the negative health effects of tobacco, and former Food and Drug Administration chair David Kessler attempted to declare nicotine a drug that could be regulated by his administration. This shows that even though iron triangles exist, they do not necessarily incorporate all the actors in a particular policy area.

Congressional Control of the Bureaucracy   Congressional control of the bureaucracy is found more in the impact of congressional committees and subcommittees that we just discussed, than in the actions of the institution as a whole. Congress, of course, passes the laws that create the agencies, assigns them their responsibilities, and funds their operations. Furthermore, Congress can, and frequently does, change the laws under which the agencies operate. Thus Congress clearly has the formal power to control the bureaucracy. It also has access to a good deal of information that helps members monitor the bureaucracy. But Congress is itself often divided about what it wants to do and is unable to set clear guidelines for agencies. Only where there is a congressional consensus on what an agency should be doing is congressional control fully effective.

The Bureaucracy and the Courts

Agencies can be sued by individuals and businesses for not following the law. If a citizen disagrees with an agency ruling on welfare eligibility or the adequacy of inspections of poultry processing plants, or even with a ruling by the IRS, he or she can take the case to the courts. The ability to use the courts to ensure that policies are administered fairly and in accordance with the intent of the law would seem to be an important tool for controlling and influencing the bureaucracy. And in some cases, the courts have been important. A highly controversial example occurred when environmentalists sued the Department of the Interior and the U.S. Forest Service to prevent logging in some of the old-growth forests of the Pacific Northwest. They sought protection for the spotted owl under the terms of the Endangered Species Act. Since 1992, after a decade-long struggle, logging has been greatly restricted in the area, despite opposition by the economically important timber interests in the region.

More often, though, the courts play only a modest role in controlling the bureaucracy. One of the reasons is that since the Administrative Procedures Act of 1946, the courts have tended to defer to the expertise of the bureaucrats when agency decisions are appealed. That is, unless a clear principle of law is violated, the courts usually support administrative rulings.[28]

A second reason for the limited role of the courts in bureaucratic politics is that Congress explicitly puts the decisions of numerous agencies, such as the Department of Veterans Affairs, beyond the reach of the courts. They do this, of course, when members expect that they will agree with the decisions of an agency but are uncertain about what the courts might do.

Finally, even without these restrictions, the courts' time is extremely limited. The departments and independent agencies make thousands of important decisions each year. The courts act only on those that someone feels sufficiently aggrieved about to file a lawsuit. Court proceedings can drag on for years, and meanwhile the agencies go about their business making new decisions. In short, the courts can, in specific instances, decide cases that influence how the bureaucracy operates, but such instances are the exception rather than the rule.

WHO, WHAT, HOW   As we have seen, all of Washington and beyond has something at stake in bureaucratic politics.

WHO are the actors?	WHAT do they want?	HOW do they get it?
Bureaucratic agencies	• Largest possible share of limited resources	• Constituency building • Separating functions
The president	• Control of the bureaucracy	• Appointment power • Budget proposals • Presidential veto • Government reorganization • Persuasion
Congress	• Control of the bureaucracy	• Legislation • Iron triangles
Interest groups and regulated industries	• Control of the bureaucracy	• Iron triangles

Citizenship and the Bureaucracy

citizen advisory council a citizen group that considers the policy decisions of an agency; a way to make the bureaucracy responsive to the general public

sunshine laws legislation opening the process of bureaucratic policymaking to the public

Freedom of Information Act a 1966 law that allows citizens to obtain copies of most public records

Privacy Act of 1974 a law that gives citizens access to the government's files on them

To help increase bureaucratic responsiveness and sensitivity to the public, Congress has made citizen participation a central feature of the policymaking of many agencies. This frequently takes the form of **citizen advisory councils** that, by statute, subject key policy decisions of agencies to outside consideration by members of the public. There are more than twelve hundred such committees and councils in the executive branch. The people who serve on these councils are not representative of the general public. Rather, they are typically chosen by the agency and have special credentials or interests relevant to the agency's work.

Other reforms have attempted to make the bureaucracy more accessible to the public. Citizen access has been enhanced by the passage of **sunshine laws,** which require that meetings of policymakers be open to the public. However, most national security and personnel meetings, as well as many criminal investigation meetings, are exempt. The right to attend a meeting is of little use if one doesn't know that it is being held in the first place. The Administrative Procedures Act requires advance published notice of all hearings, proposed rules, and new regulations so that the public can attend and comment on decisions that might affect them. These announcements appear in a regularly published document called the *Federal Register*.

A related point of access is the **Freedom of Information Act** (FOIA), which was passed in 1966 and has been amended several times since. This act provides citizens with the right to copies of most public records held by federal agencies. Citizens also receive protection under the **Privacy Act of 1974,** which gives them the right to find out what information government agencies have about them. It also sets up procedures so that erroneous information can be corrected and ensures the confidentiality of social security, tax, and related records.

These reforms may provide little practical access for most citizens, however. Few of us have the time, the knowledge, or the energy to plow through the *Federal Register* and to attend meetings regularly. Similarly, while many citizens no doubt feel that they are not getting the full story from government agencies, they do not have much of an idea of what it is they don't know. Hence few of us ever use the FOIA.

WHAT'S AT STAKE REVISITED

Let's go back to the question of what's at stake in the dispute over the USDA's organic food regulation. Remember that regulations are a form of rules, and rules determine who the winners and losers are likely to be. Regulations can serve a variety of interests. In this case, they could serve the public interest, simply making it easier for consumers to buy organic foods by standardizing what it means to be organic. But regulations can also serve other interests. Here there were competing business interests as well. Agribusiness and the food preparation industry wanted to use regulations to break into a lucrative market previously closed to them because of the labor-intensive nature of organic farming. For the traditional organic farmers, the new regulations spelled disaster.

As far as big business was concerned, this case was like many others. Businesses in the United States are able to lobby the government to try to get rules and regulations passed that will enhance their positions and to try to stop those that will hurt them. As we will see in Chapter 11, the larger sums of money that big business can bring to the lobbying effort usually give them an edge in influencing government. If the larger businesses were allowed to compete as organic food producers, the small businesses would lose the only advantage they had, and they would be forced out of business. They were aided in this case by citizen action. This example shows that it is possible to energize a public audience to respond to the bureaucracy. Because consumers who eat organic foods were a focused, committed, and assertive segment of the population, they were able to follow through with political action. ■

key terms

accountability   223
bureaucracy   221
bureaucratese   233
bureaucratic culture   232
bureaucratic discretion   230
citizen advisory council   243
civil service   222
clientele groups   225
department   227

Federal Register   231
Freedom of Information Act   243
government corporation   229
Hatch Act   222
independent agency   228
independent regulatory boards and commissions   228
iron triangle   240

neutral competence   221
patronage   222
Pendleton Act   222
Privacy Act of 1974   243
red tape   223
regulations   228
spoils system   221
sunshine laws   243
whistle blowers   235

summary

■ Bureaucracies are everywhere today, in the private as well as the public sphere. They create a special problem for democratic politics because the desire for democratic accountability often conflicts with the desire to take politics out of the bureaucracy. We moved from the spoils system of the nineteenth century to a civil service merit system with a more professionalized bureaucracy in the twentieth century.

■ The U.S. bureaucracy has grown from just three cabinet departments at the founding to a gigantic apparatus of fourteen cabinet-level departments and hundreds of independent agencies, regulatory commissions, and government corporations. This growth has been in response to the expansion of the nation, the politics of special economic and social groups, and the emergence of new problems.

■ Many people believe that the bureaucracy should simply administer the laws that the political branches have enacted. In reality, the agencies of the bureaucracy make government policy, and they play the roles of judge and jury in enforcing those policies. These activities are in part an unavoidable consequence of the tremendous technical expertise of the agencies because Congress and the president simply cannot perform many technical tasks.

■ The culture of bureaucracy refers to how agencies operate—their assumptions, values, and habits. The bureaucratic culture increases employees' belief in the programs they administer, their commitment to the survival and growth of their agencies, and the tendency to rely on rules and procedures rather than goals.

■ Agencies work actively for their political survival. They attempt to establish strong support outside the agency, to avoid direct competition with other agencies, and to jealously guard their own policy jurisdictions. Presidential powers are only modestly effective in controlling the bureaucracy. The affected clientele groups working in close cooperation with the agencies and the congressional committees that oversee them form powerful iron triangles.

■ Regardless of what the public may think, the U.S. bureaucracy is actually quite responsive and competent when compared with the bureaucracies of other countries. Citizens can increase this responsiveness by taking advantage of opportunities for gaining access to bureaucratic decision-making.

9

What's at Stake?

Law and the American Legal System
- *The Role of Law in Democratic Societies*
- *The American Legal Tradition*
- *Kinds of Law*

Constitutional Provisions and the Development of Judicial Review
- *The Least Dangerous Branch*
- *John Marshall and Judicial Review*

The Structure and Organization of the Dual Court System
- *Understanding Jurisdiction*
- *State Courts*
- *Federal Courts*

Politics and the Supreme Court
- *How Members of the Court Are Selected*
- *How the Court Makes Decisions*
- *The Political Effects of Judicial Decisions*

Citizenship and the Courts

What's at Stake Revisited

The American Legal System and the Courts

WHAT'S AT STAKE?

The Supreme Court was a thorn in Franklin Delano Roosevelt's side. Faced with the massive unemployment and economic stagnation that characterized the Great Depression of the 1930s, FDR knew he would have to use the powers of government creatively. He was hampered by a Court that was not only ideologically opposed to his efforts to regulate business and industry but also skeptical of his constitutional power to do so. In response to FDR's National Industrial Recovery Act (NIRA), the Supreme Court ruled in *Schechter Poultry Corporation* v. *United States* (also known as the "sick chicken case") that the NIRA delegated too much legislative power to the president and put no limits on his ability to regulate.[1]

Many parts of the NIRA were reenacted more carefully by Congress, but still the Supreme Court haunted FDR's efforts at national recovery. In 1936 it overturned the Agricultural Adjustment Act designed to help farmers, legislation regulating the coal industry, and a New York State minimum wage law for women. In FDR's view, he and Congress had been elected by the people, and public opinion favored his New Deal policies. But the "nine old men," as they were called, on the Supreme Court, or at least a majority of them, consistently stood in his and the public's way. Six of the justices were over seventy, and FDR had appointed none of them. Determined to block what they saw as his excesses of power and his unconstitutional infringement on the rights of business, those justices who might otherwise have retired tried to hang on.

FDR accused the Court of setting itself up as a third house of Congress—a superlegislature striking down laws its members didn't like—and of believing that the Constitution meant whatever they said it did. In a radio broadcast in March 1937, he said,

We have, therefore, reached the point as a nation where we must take action to save the Constitution from the Court and the Court from itself. We must find a way to take an appeal from the Supreme Court to the Constitution it-self. We want a Supreme Court which will do justice under the Constitution— not over it. In our courts we want a government of laws and not of men. . . . [W]e cannot yield our constitutional destiny to the personal judgment of a few men who, being fearful of the future, would deny us the necessary means of dealing with the present.[2]

Thus FDR proposed to change the Court that continually thwarted him. His broad view of the powers of his office led him to see the machinery of government as exist-ing to enable him to execute his political will. The Constitution allows Congress to set the number of justices on the Supreme Court, and indeed the number has ranged from six to ten at various times in our history. FDR's answer to the recalcitrant Court was to ask Congress to allow him to appoint a new justice for every justice over seventy who refused to retire, up to a possible total of fifteen. Thus he would create a Court whose majority he had chosen and which he confidently believed would support his New Deal programs.

The country was outraged by Roosevelt's Court-packing proposal. Although his policies were popular, his plan to make them law was not. If Americans didn't object to FDR's New Deal programs, which gave unprecedented power to Congress and the president and dramatically enlarged the size of government, why were they so in-censed at his attempts to create a Court that would stop obstructing those policies? What did they think was at stake in FDR's plan to pack the Court?   ■

Imagine a world without laws. You careen down the road in your car at any speed that takes your fancy. You park where you please and enter a drugstore that sells drugs of all sorts, including prescription drugs (of course, there would be no need for prescriptions), but other drugs as well: nicotine, alcohol, marijuana, cocaine, and LSD. You purchase what you like. No one asks your age. There are no restrictions on how much you can buy or on what day of the week or what hours of the day you can make your purchase. There are no rules governing the production or use of cur-rency either, so you hope that the drugstore will accept what you have to offer in trade, although you never know about these things in advance.

Life is looking pretty good as you head back out to the street, only to see that your car is no longer there. Theft is not an uncommon occurrence, since it is not il-legal, and you curse yourself for forgetting to set the car alarm and for not using your wheel lock. There are no police to call, and even if there were, tracking down your car would be tough, since there are no vehicle registration laws to help anyone find it or to assist you in identifying it.

The street you are standing on looks unlike the streets in a world with laws. Churches rise up next to bars and strip joints, and buildings are of varying and un-regulated heights, bringing skyscrapers into residential neighborhoods. In the ab-sence of construction codes and inspections, some buildings are falling apart. You keep your hand on your wallet as you walk down the street because anything any-one can grab is fair game.

As you tire of walking, you look for a likely car to get you home. Appropriating a car, you have to wrestle with the previous occupant, who manages to clout you over the head before you drive away. It isn't much of a prize, covered with dents and nicks from innumerable crashes with other cars jockeying for position at intersec-tions, where there are neither stop signs nor lights and the right of the faster prevails. Arriving home to enjoy your beer (or whatever) in peace and to gain a respite from the war zone you call your local community, you find that another family has moved in while you were shopping. Groaning with frustration, you think that surely there must be a better way.

And there is. As often as we might rail against restrictions on our freedom, such as not being able to buy beer if we are under twenty-one, having to wear a motorcycle helmet, or not being able to speed down an empty highway, laws actually do us much more good than harm. The British philosophers Thomas Hobbes and John Locke, whom we discussed in Chapter 1, imagined a "prepolitical" world without laws. Inhabitants of Hobbes's state of nature found life without laws to be dismal, or, as he put it, "solitary, poor, nasty, brutish, and short." Although residents of Locke's state of nature found the lawless life to be merely "inconvenient," they had to mount a constant defense of their possessions and their lives. One of the reasons both Hobbes and Locke thought people would be willing to leave the state of nature for civil society and to give up their freedom to do whatever they wanted, was so that they could gain security, order, and predictability in life. Because we tend to focus on the laws that stop us from doing the things we want to do or that require us to do things we don't want to do, we often forget the full array of laws that make it possi-ble for us to live together in relative peace and to leave behind the brutishness of Hobbes's state of nature and the inconveniences of Locke's.

Laws occupy a central position in any political society, but especially in a democracy, where the rule is ultimately by law and not the whim of a tyrant. Laws are the "how" in the formulation of politics as "who gets what when and how." They dictate how our collective lives are to be organized, what rights we can claim, what principles we should live by, and how we can use the system to get what we want. Laws also can be the "what" in the formulation, as citizens and political ac-tors use the existing rules to create new rules that produce even more favorable out-comes.

In this chapter, we examine the following aspects of law:

- The notion of law and the role that it plays in democratic society in general and in the American legal system in particular

- The constitutional basis for the American judicial system

- The dual system of state and federal courts in the United States

- The Supreme Court and the politics that surround and support it

- The relationship of citizens to the courts in America

Law and the American Legal System

Thinking about the law can be confusing. On the one hand, laws are the sorts of rules we have been discussing: limits and restrictions that get in our way or that make life a little easier. On the other hand, we would like to think that our legal system is founded on rules that represent basic and enduring principles of justice, that create for us a higher level of civilization. Laws are products of the political process, created by political human beings to help them get valuable resources. Those resources may be civil peace and security, a particular moral order, power and influence, or even goods or entitlements. Thus for security, we have laws that eliminate traffic chaos, enforce contracts, and ban violence. For moral order (and for security as well), we have laws against murder, incest, and rape. And for political advantage, we have laws like those that give large states greater power in the process of electing a president and that allow electoral districts to be drawn by the majority party. Laws dealing with more concrete resources give tax breaks to homeowners or subsidize dairy farmers, for example.

The Role of Law in Democratic Societies

For the purpose of understanding the role of law in democratic political systems, we can focus on five important functions of laws.[3]

- The first, and most obvious, function follows directly from Hobbes and Locke: laws *provide security* (for people and their property) so that we may go about our daily lives in relative harmony.

- Laws *provide predictability,* allowing us to plan our activities and go about our business without fearing a random judgment that tells us we have broken a law we didn't know existed.

- The fact that laws are known in advance and identify punishable behaviors leads to the third function of laws in a democracy, that of *conflict resolution,* through neutral third parties known as **courts.**

- A fourth function of laws in a democratic society is *to reflect and enforce conformity to society's values*—for instance, that murder is wrong or that parents should not be allowed to abuse their children.

- A fifth function of laws in a democracy is *to distribute the benefits and rewards society has to offer and to allocate the costs of those good things,* whether they are welfare benefits, civil rights protection, or tax breaks.

courts institutions that sit as neutral third parties to resolve conflicts according to the law

The American Legal Tradition

common law tradition a legal system based on the accumulated rulings of judges over time, applied uniformly— judge-made law

The U.S. legal system, and that of all fifty states except Louisiana, is based on common law, which developed in Great Britain and the countries that once formed the British Empire. The **common law tradition** relied on royal judges making decisions based on their own judgment and on previous legal decisions, which were applied

precedent
a previous decision or ruling that, in common law tradition, is binding on subsequent decisions

civil law tradition
a legal system based on a detailed, comprehensive legal code, usually created by the legislature

uniformly, or *commonly,* across the land. The emphasis was on preserving the decisions that had been made before, what is called relying on **precedent,** or *stare decisis* (Latin for "let the decision stand"). Judges in such a system have far more power in determining what the law is than do judges in the **civil law tradition,** where laws are codified by a legislature and leave little discretion to judges.

The legal system in the United States, however, is not a pure common law system. Legislatures do make laws, and attempts have been made to codify, or organize, them into a coherent body. But American legislators are less concerned with creating such a coherent body of laws than with responding to the various needs and demands of their constituents. As a result, American laws have a somewhat haphazard and hodgepodge character. The common law nature of the legal system is reinforced, however, by the fact that American judges still use their considerable discretion to decide what the laws mean, and they rely heavily on precedent and the principle of *stare decisis.* Thus when a judge decides a case, he or she will not only look at the relevant law but will also consult previous rulings on the issue before making a ruling of his or her own.

Kinds of Law

Laws are not all of the same type, and distinguishing among them can be very difficult. It's not important that we understand all the shades of legal meaning; in fact, it often seems that lawyers speak a language all their own. Nevertheless, most of us will have several encounters with the law in our lifetimes, and it's important that we know what laws regulate what sorts of behavior.

substantive law
law whose content, or substance, defines what we can or cannot do

procedural law
law that establishes how laws are applied and enforced—how legal proceedings take place

procedural due process   procedural laws that protect the rights of individuals who must deal with the legal system

criminal law
law prohibiting behavior the government has determined is harmful to society; a violation of a criminal law is called a crime

Substantive and Procedural   We have used the terms *substantive* and *procedural* elsewhere in this book, and although the meanings we use here are related to the earlier ones, these are precise legal terms that describe specific kinds of laws. **Substantive laws** are those whose actual content, or substance, defines what we can and cannot do legally. **Procedural laws** establish the procedures used to conduct the law—that is, how the law is used, or applied, and enforced. Thus a substantive law spells out what behaviors are restricted—for instance driving over a certain speed or killing someone. A procedural law refers to how legal proceedings are to take place: how evidence will be gathered and used, how defendants will be treated, and what juries can be told during a trial. Because our founders were very concerned about limiting the power of government in order to prevent tyranny, our laws are filled with procedural protections for those who must deal with the legal system—what we call guarantees of **procedural due process.** Given their different purposes, these two types of laws sometimes clash. For instance, someone guilty of breaking a substantive law might be spared punishment if procedural laws meant to protect him or her were violated: because, for example, the police failed to read the accused his or her rights or searched the accused's home without a warrant. Such situations are complicated by the fact that not all judges interpret procedural guarantees the same way.

Criminal and Civil Law   **Criminal laws** prohibit specific behaviors that the government (state, federal, or both) has determined are not conducive to the public peace—behaviors as heinous as murder or as relatively innocuous (harmless) as stealing an apple. Since these laws refer to crimes against the state, it is the government that prosecutes these cases rather than the family of the murder victim or the owner of the apple. The penalty, if the person is found guilty, will be some form of payment to the public, either community service, jail time, or even death, depending on the severity of the crime and the provisions of the law. In fact, we speak of criminals having to pay their "debt to society," because in a real sense, their actions are seen as a harm to society. *Felonies* and *misdemeanors* are examples of criminal laws.

civil law
law regulating interactions between individuals; a violation of a civil law is called a tort

Civil laws regulate interactions between individuals. If one person sues another for damaging his or her property, causing physical harm, or failing to fulfill the terms of a contract, it is not a crime against the state that is alleged, but rather an injury to a specific individual. A violation of a civil law is called a *tort* instead of a crime. The government's purpose here is not to prosecute a harm to society, but to provide individuals with a forum in which they can peacefully resolve their differences. Apart from peaceful conflict resolution, government has no stake in the outcome.

Sometimes a person will face both criminal charges and a civil lawsuit for the same action. An example might be a person who drives while drunk and causes an accident that seriously injures someone in another car. The drunk driver would face criminal charges for breaking a law against driving while intoxicated and might also be sued by the injured party to receive compensation for medical expenses, missed income, and pain and suffering. Such damages are called *compensatory damages*. The injured person might also sue the bar that served the alcohol to the drunk driver; this is because people suing for compensation often target the involved party who has the best ability to pay. A civil suit may include a fine intended to punish the individual for causing the injury. Such damages are called *punitive damages*.

constitutional law
law stated in the Constitution and the body of judicial decisions about the meaning of the Constitution handed down in the courts

Constitutional Law　One kind of law we have discussed often in this book is **constitutional law.** This, of course, refers to the laws that are in the Constitution, that establish the basic powers of and limitations on government institutions and their interrelationships, and that guarantee the basic rights of citizens. But in addition, constitutional law refers to all the many decisions that have been made by lower court judges in America, as well as by the justices on the Supreme Court, in their attempts to decide precisely what the Constitution means and how it should be interpreted. Because of our common law tradition, these decisions, once made, become part of the vast foundation of American constitutional law. All of the cases discussed in the chapters on civil liberties and equal rights are part of the constitutional law of this country. As we saw in those chapters, constitutional law evolves over time as circumstances change, justices are replaced, cases are overturned, and precedent is reversed.

statutory law
law passed by a state or the federal legislature

Statutory Law, Administrative Law, and Executive Orders　Most laws in the country are made by Congress and the state legislatures, by the bureaucracy under the authority of Congress, and even by the president. **Statutory laws** are laws that legislatures make at either the state or the national level. Statutes reflect the will of the bodies elected to represent the people, and they can address virtually any behavior. Statutes tell us to wear seat belts, pay taxes, and stay home from work on Memorial Day. The only limits on what statutes may do are found in the Constitution. According to the principle of judicial review, judges may declare statutes unconstitutional if they conflict with the basic principles of government or the rights of citizens established in that document.

Because legislatures cannot be experts on all matters, they frequently delegate some of their lawmaking power to bureaucratic agencies and departments. When these bureaucratic actors exercise their lawmaking power on behalf of Congress, they are making **administrative law.** Administrative laws include all those thousands of regulations that agencies make concerning how much food coloring and other additives can be in food, how airports will monitor air traffic, what kind of material baby pajamas can be made of, and what deductions can be legally taken when figuring your taxable income. These laws, although made under the authority of elected representatives, are not made by people who are accountable to the citizens of America. The implications of the undemocratic nature of bureaucratic decision-making were discussed in Chapter 8.

Finally, some laws, called **executive orders,** are made by the president. These laws, as we explained in the chapter on the presidency, are made without any participation by Congress and need be binding only during the issuing president's administration. Famous executive orders include President Harry Truman's desegregation of the armed forces in 1948 and President Lyndon Johnson's initiation of affirmative action programs for companies doing business with the federal government in 1967.

administrative law
law established by the bureaucracy, on behalf of Congress

executive order
a clarification of congressional policy issued by the president and having the full force of law

| **WHO, WHAT, HOW** | All citizens (even lawbreakers) have a broad stake in a lawful society. |

WHO are the actors?	**WHAT** do they want?	**HOW** do they get it?
Citizens	• Security • Predictability • Conflict resolution • Enforcement of social norms • Distribution of social benefits and costs	• Common law tradition • Criminal and civil law • Constitutional law • Statutes, regulations, executive orders

Constitutional Provisions and the Development of Judicial Review

Americans may owe much of our philosophy of law (called *jurisprudence*) to the British, but the court system we set up to administer that law is uniquely our own. Like every other part of the Constitution, the nature of the judiciary was the subject of hot debate during the nation's founding. Large states were comfortable with a strong court system as part of the strong national government they advocated. Small states, cringing at the prospect of national dominance, preferred a weak judiciary. Choosing a typically astute way out of their quandary, the authors of the Constitution simply postponed it, leaving it to Congress to settle later.

Article III, Section 1, of the Constitution says simply this about the establishment of the court system: "The judicial Power of the United States, shall be vested in one supreme Court, and in such inferior Courts as Congress may from time to time ordain and establish." It goes on to say that judges will hold their jobs as long as they demonstrate "good Behaviour"—that is, they are appointed for life—and that they will be paid regularly and cannot have their pay reduced while they are in office. The Constitution does not spell out the powers of the Supreme Court. It only specifies which cases must come directly to the Court (cases affecting ambassadors, public ministers and consuls, and states); all other cases come to it only on appeal. It was left to Congress to say how. By dropping the issue of court structure and power into the lap of Congress, the writers of the Constitution neatly sidestepped the brewing controversy. It would require an act of Congress, the Federal Judiciary Act of 1789, to begin to fill in the gaps on how the court system would be organized. We will turn to that act and its provisions shortly. First we will look at the controversy surrounding the birth of the one court that Article III does establish, the U.S. Supreme Court.

The Least Dangerous Branch

The idea of an independent judiciary headed by a supreme court was a new one to the founders. No other country had one, not even England. Britain's highest court was also its Parliament, or legislature. To those who put their faith in the ideas of separation of powers and checks and balances, an independent judiciary was an ideal way to check the power of the president and Congress. But to others it represented an unknown threat. To put those fears to rest, Alexander Hamilton penned *Federalist* No. 78, arguing that the judiciary was the least dangerous branch of government. It lacked the teeth of both the other branches; it had neither the power of the sword (the executive power) nor the power of the purse (the legislative budget power), and consequently it could exercise "neither force nor will, but merely judgment."[4]

John Marshall and Judicial Review

The low prestige of the Supreme Court was not to last for long, however, and its elevation was due almost single-handedly to the work of one man. John Marshall was the third chief justice of the Court and an enthusiastic Federalist. During his tenure in office, he found several ways to strengthen the Court's power, the most important of which was having the Court create the power of **judicial review**. This is the power that allows the Court to review acts of the other branches of government and to invalidate them if they are found to run counter to the principles in the Constitution.

judicial review
the power of the courts to determine the constitutionality of laws

The Constitution does not give the power of judicial review to the Court, but it doesn't forbid the Court to have that power either, and Hamilton had supported the idea in *Federalist* No. 78. Chief Justice Marshall shrewdly engineered the adoption of the power of judicial review in *Marbury* v. *Madison* in 1803. This case involved a series of judicial appointments to federal courts made by President John Adams in the final hours of his administration. Most of those appointments were executed by Adams's secretary of state, but the letter appointing William Marbury to be justice of the peace for the District of Columbia was overlooked and not delivered. (In an interesting twist, John Marshall, who was finishing up his job as Adams' secretary of state, had just been sworn in as chief justice of the Supreme Court; he would later hear the case that developed over his own incomplete appointment of Marbury.) These "midnight" (last-minute) appointments irritated the new president, Thomas Jefferson, who wanted to appoint his own candidates, so he had his secretary of state, James Madison, throw out the letter, along with several other appointment letters. According to the Judiciary Act of 1789, it was up to the Supreme Court to decide whether Marbury got his appointment, which put Marshall in a fix. If he exercised his power under the act and Jefferson ignored him, the Court's already low prestige would be severely damaged. If he failed to order the appointment, the Court would still look weak.

From a legal point of view, Marshall's solution was breathtaking. Instead of ruling on the question of Marbury's appointment, which was a no-win situation for him, he focused on the part of the act that gave the Court the authority to make the decision. This he found to go beyond what the Constitution had intended. That is, according to the Constitution, Congress didn't have the power to give the Court that authority. So Marshall ruled that although he thought Marbury should get the appointment (he had originally made it, after all), he could not enforce it because the relevant part of the Judiciary Act of 1789 was unconstitutional and therefore void. He justified the Court's power to decide what the Constitution meant by saying "it is emphatically the province of the judicial department to say what the law is."[5]

In making this ruling, Marshall chose to lose a small battle in order to win a very large war. By creating the power of judicial review, he vastly expanded the potential influence of the Court and set it on the road to being the powerful institution it is today. While Congress and the president still have some checks on the judiciary through the powers to appoint, to change the number of members and the jurisdiction of the Court, to impeach justices, and to amend the Constitution, the Court now has the ultimate check over the other two branches: the power to declare what they do to be null and void. What is especially striking about the gain of this enormous power is that the Court gave it to itself. What would have been the public reaction if Congress had voted to make itself the final judge of what is constitutional?

Aware of just how substantially their power was increased by the addition of judicial review, justices have tended to use it sparingly. The power was not used from its inception in 1803 until 1857, when the Court struck down the Missouri Compromise.[6] Since then, it has been used only about 140 times to strike down acts of Congress, although much more frequently (1,200 times) to invalidate acts of state legislatures.

WHO, WHAT, HOW   With the ratification of the Constitution at stake, the founders did not wish to jeopardize the success of the new government by creating a controversial court system. They were instead deliberately vague on the subject, leaving the controversy to less cautious politicians, like John Marshall.

WHO are the actors?	WHAT do they want?	HOW do they get it?
Founders	• Ratification of the Constitution	• Ambiguity about court system
John Marshall	• Vastly strengthened Court	• Judicial review and common law principles

The Structure and Organization of the Dual Court System

In response to the Constitution's open invitation to design a federal court system, Congress immediately got busy putting together the Federal Judiciary Act of 1789. The system created by this act was too simple to handle the complex legal needs and the growing number of cases in the new nation, however, and it was gradually crafted by Congress into the very complex network of federal courts we have today. It is not enough that we understand the federal court system, however. Our federal system of government requires that we have two separate court systems, state and national, and, in fact, most of the legal actions in this country take place at the state level. Because of the diversity that exists among the state courts, some people argue that in truth we have fifty-one court systems. Since we cannot look into each of the fifty state court systems, we will take the "two-system" perspective and consider the state court system as a whole (see Figure 9.1).

Understanding Jurisdiction

jurisdiction
a court's authority to hear certain cases

A key concept in understanding our dual court system is the issue of **jurisdiction,** the courts' authority to hear particular cases. Not all courts can hear all cases. In fact, the rules regulating which courts have jurisdiction over which cases are very specific.

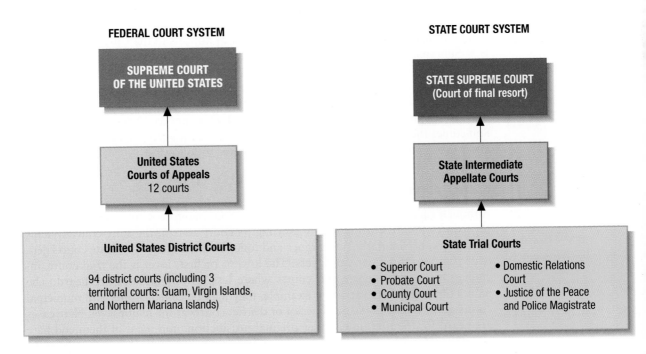

Figure 9.1
The Dual Court System

Most cases in the United States fall under the jurisdiction of state courts. As we will see, cases go to federal courts only if they qualify by virtue of the kind of question raised or the parties involved.

The choice of a court, though dictated in large part by constitutional rule and statutory law (both state and federal), still leaves room for political maneuvering. Four basic characteristics of a case help determine which court has jurisdiction over it: the involvement of the federal government or the Constitution, the parties to the case, where the case arose, and how serious an offense it involves.[7]

Once a case is in either the state court system or the federal court system, it almost always remains within that system. It is extremely rare for a case to start out in one system and end up in the other. Just about the only time this occurs is when a case in the highest state court is appealed to the U.S. Supreme Court, and this can happen only for cases involving a question of federal law.

Cases come to state and federal courts under either their original jurisdiction or their appellate jurisdiction. A court's **original jurisdiction** refers to those cases that can come straight to it without being heard by any other court first. The rules and factors just discussed refer to original jurisdiction. **Appellate jurisdiction** refers to those cases that a court can hear on **appeal**—that is, when one of the parties to a case believes that some point of law was not applied properly at a lower court and asks a higher court to review it. Almost all the cases heard by the U.S. Supreme Court come to it on appeal. The Court's original jurisdiction is limited to cases that concern ambassadors and public ministers and to cases in which a state is a party—usually amounting to no more than two or three cases a year.

All parties in U.S. lawsuits are entitled to an appeal, although more than 90 percent of losers in federal cases accept their verdicts without appeal. After the first appeal, further appeals are at the discretion of the higher court; that is, the court can choose to hear them or not. The highest court of appeals in the United States is the U.S. Supreme Court, but its appellate jurisdiction is also discretionary. When the Court refuses to hear a case, it may mean, among other things, that the Court regards the case as frivolous or that it agrees with the lower court's judgment. Just because the Court agrees to hear a case, though, does not mean that it is going to overturn the lower court's ruling, although it does so about 70 percent of the time. Sometimes the Court hears a case in order to rule that it agrees with the lower court and to set a precedent that other courts will have to follow.

original jurisdiction
the authority of a court to hear a case first

appellate jurisdiction
the authority of a court to review decisions made by lower courts

appeal   a rehearing of a case because the losing party in the original trial argues that a point of law was not applied properly

State Courts

Although each state has its own constitution, and therefore its own set of rules and procedures for structuring and organizing its court system, the state court systems are remarkably similar in appearance and function (see Figure 9.1). State courts generally fall into three tiers, or layers. The lowest, or first, layer is the trial court, including major trial courts and courts where less serious offenses are heard. The names of these courts vary—for example, they may be called county and municipal courts at the minor level and superior or district courts at the major level. Here cases are heard for the first time, under original jurisdiction, and most of them end here as well.

Occasionally, however, a case is appealed to a higher decision-making body. In

A Many-Paneled System

The American judiciary is divided into federal, state, and local courts, each with very different jurisdictions, organizations, and operations. Especially at the state level, both judicial structure and the methods used to select judges vary widely from state to state. The panel shown here is the Texas Court of Criminal Appeals.

about three-fourths of the states, intermediate courts of appeals hear cases appealed from the lower trial courts. In terms of geographic organization, subject matter jurisdiction, and number of judges, courts of appeals vary greatly from state to state. The one constant is that these courts all hear appeals directly from the major trial courts and, on very rare occasions, directly from the minor courts as well.

Each of the fifty states has a state supreme court, although again the names vary. Since they are appeals courts, no questions of fact can arise, and there are no juries. Rather, a panel of five to nine *justices,* as supreme court judges are called, meet to discuss the case, make a decision, and issue an opinion. As the name suggests, a state's supreme court is the court of last resort, or the final court of appeals, in the state. All decisions rendered by these courts are final unless a case involves a federal question and can be heard on further appeal in the federal court system.

Judges in state courts are chosen through a variety of procedures specified in the individual state constitutions. The procedures range from appointment by the governor or election by the state legislature to the more democratic method of election by the state population as a whole.

Federal Courts

The federal system is also three-tiered. There is an entry-level tier, called the district courts, an appellate level, and the Supreme Court at the very top (see Figure 9.1). In this section, we discuss the lower two tiers and how the judges for those courts are chosen. Given the importance of the Supreme Court in the American political system, we discuss it separately in the following section.

District Courts   The lowest level of the federal judiciary hierarchy consists of ninety-four U.S. federal district courts. These courts are distributed so that each state has at least one and the largest states each have four. The district courts have original jurisdiction over all cases involving any question of a federal nature or any issue that involves the Constitution, Congress, or any other aspect of the federal government. Such issues are wide-ranging but might include, for example, criminal charges resulting from a violation of the federal anti-car-jacking statute or a lawsuit against the Environmental Protection Agency.

     The district courts hear both criminal and civil law cases. In trials at the district level, evidence is presented, and witnesses are called to testify and are questioned and cross-examined by the attorneys representing both sides, one of whom is a U.S. attorney. U.S. attorneys, one per district, are appointed by the president, with the consent of the Senate. In district courts, juries are responsible for returning the final verdict.

U.S. Courts of Appeals   Any case appealed beyond the district court level is slated to appear in one of the U.S. courts of appeals. These courts are arranged in twelve circuits, essentially large superdistricts that encompass several of the district court territories, except for the twelfth, which covers just Washington, D.C. (see Figure 9.2). This twelfth circuit court hears all appeals involving government agencies, and so its caseload is quite large even though its territory is small. Cases are heard in the circuit that includes the district court where the case was originally heard. Therefore,

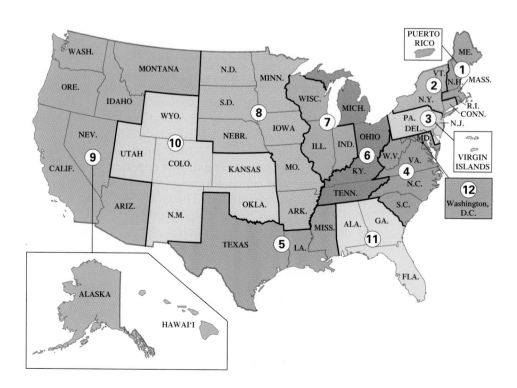

Figure 9.2
The Federal Judicial Circuits
Source: Administrative Office of the United States Courts.

a case that was initially tried in Miami, in the southern district in Florida, would be appealed to the court of appeals in the eleventh circuit, located in Atlanta, Georgia.

The jurisdiction of the courts of appeals, as their name suggests, is entirely appellate in nature. The sole function of these courts is to hear appeals from the lower federal district courts and to review the legal reasoning behind the decisions reached there. As a result, the proceedings involved in the appeals process differ markedly from those at the district court level. No evidence is presented, no new witnesses called, and no jury impaneled. Instead, the lawyers for both sides present written briefs summarizing their arguments and make oral arguments as well. The legal reasoning used to reach the decision in the district court is scrutinized, but the facts of the case are assumed to be the truth and are not debated.

The decisions in the courts of appeals are made by a rotating panel of three judges who sit to hear the case. Although many more than three judges are assigned to each federal appeals circuit (the Court of Appeals for the Ninth Circuit, based in San Francisco, has twenty-eight), the judges rotate in order to provide a decision-making body that is as unbiased as possible. In rare cases where a decision is of crucial social importance, all the judges in a circuit will meet together, or *en banc,* to render a decision. Having all the judges present, not just three, gives a decision more legitimacy and sends a message that the decision was made carefully.

Selection of Federal Judges   The Constitution is silent about the qualifications of federal judges. It specifies only that they shall be appointed by the president, with the advice and consent of the Senate, and that they shall serve lifetime terms under good behavior. They can be removed from office only if impeached and convicted by the House of Representatives and the Senate, a process that has resulted in only thirteen impeachments and seven convictions in more than two hundred years.

Traditionally, federal judgeships have been awarded on the basis of several criteria, not the least of which has been to reward political friendship and support and to cultivate future political support, whether of a particular politician or an entire gender or ethnic or racial group. An increasingly important qualification for the job of federal judge is the ideological or policy position of the appointee. In the past thirty years or so, politicians have become more aware of the political influence of these courts.

Consequently, politicians can have quite an impact in shaping the U.S. judicial system by the appointments they make. Together, Republican presidents Ronald Reagan and the elder George Bush appointed more than 60 percent of all federal judges, and they made a conscious effort to redirect what they saw as the liberal tenor of court appointments in the years since the New Deal. Even though democratic president Bill Clinton appointed many judges as well, the moderate ideology of most of his appointees means that the courts have not swung back in a radically liberal direction.[8] He renewed a commitment made by President Carter to create diversity on the federal bench, as can be seen by Table 9.1. Nearly half of Clinton's appointees were women and minorities, compared to 35 percent under Carter, 14 percent under Reagan, and 27 percent under Bush.[9] Clinton's appointees also were what one observer called "militantly moderate"—more liberal than Reagan's and Bush's, but less liberal than Carter's, and similar ideologically to the appointments of Republican president Gerald Ford.[10]

Table 9.1
Characteristics of Presidential Appointees to U.S. District Court Judgeships
(by presidential administration, 1963–1996*)

	President Johnson's Appointees 1963–1968 (N=122)	President Nixon's Appointees 1969–1974 (N=179)	President Ford's Appointees 1974–1977 (N=52)	President Carter's Appointees 1977–1980 (N=202)	President Reagan's First-Term Appointees 1981–1984 (N=129)	President Reagan's Second-Term Appointees 1985–1988 (N=161)[†]	President Bush's Appointees 1989–1992 (N=148)	President Clinton's Appointees 1993–2000 (N=169)
Sex								
Male	98.4%	99.4%	98.1%	85.6%	90.7%	92.5%	80.4%	69.8%
Female	1.6	0.6	1.9	14.4	9.3	7.4	19.6	28.2
Ethnicity								
White	93.4	95.5	88.5	78.7	93.0	91.9	89.2	73.8
Black	4.1	3.4	5.8	13.9	0.8	3.1	6.8	19.0
Hispanic	2.5	1.1	1.9	6.9	5.4	4.3	4.0	5.2
Asian	0	0	3.9	0.5	0.8	0.6	0	1.6
Native American	NA	NA	NA	0	0	0	0	0.4
Religion								
Protestant	58.2	73.2	73.1	60.4	58.9	60.9	64.2	NA
Catholic	31.1	18.4	17.3	27.7	34.1	27.3	28.4	NA
Jewish	10.7	8.4	9.6	11.9	7.0	11.2	7.4	NA
Political Party								
Democrat	94.3	7.3	21.2	92.6	3.1	6.2	5.4	89.1
Republican	5.7	92.7	78.8	4.4	96.9	90.7	88.5	4.8
Independent or none	0	0	0	3.0	0	3.1	6.1	6.1
Other	NA	NA	NA	0	0	0	0	0.6
American Bar Association Rating								
Exceptionally well/ well qualified	48.4	45.3	46.1	50.9	50.4	57.1	57.4	63.9
Qualified	49.2	54.8	53.8	47.5	49.6	42.9	42.6	34.3
Not qualified	2.5	0	0	1.5	0	0	0	1.8

*Percents may not add to 100 because of rounding.
[†]One appointee classified as nondenominational.

Source: Sheldon Goldman, "Reagan's Judicial Legacy: Completing the Puzzle and Summing Up," *Judicature* 72 (April–May 1989), pp. 320, 321, Table 1; and Sheldon Goldman and Elliot Slotnick, "Clinton's First Term Judiciary: Many Bridges to Cross," *Judicature* 80 (May–June 1997), p. 261. Table adapted by Sourcebook staff, Bureau of Justice Statistics, Sourcebook of Criminal Justice Statistics, 1996, U.S. Dept. of Justice, Table 1.77, p. 62; Harold W. Stanley and Richard G. Niemi, *Vital Statistics on American Politics, 1999–2000*, Washington: CA Press, 2000, p. 276.

senatorial courtesy
the tradition of granting senior senators of the president's party considerable power over federal judicial appointments in their home states

Another influence on the appointment of federal judges is the principle of **senatorial courtesy,** which we discussed in Chapter 7, on the presidency. In reality, senators do most of the nominating of district court judges, often aided by applications made by lawyers and state judges. Should the president nominate a candidate who fails to meet with the approval of the state's senior senator, it is highly unlikely that the Senate will vote to confirm the candidate, if the president is lucky enough even to get the Senate Judiciary Committee to hold a hearing on the nomination.

The growing influence of politics in the selection of federal judges does not mean that merit is unimportant. As the nation's largest legal professional association, the American Bar Association (ABA) has had the informal role since 1946 of evaluating the legal qualifications of potential nominees. While poorly rated candidates are occasionally nominated and confirmed, perhaps because of the pressure of a senator or a president, most federal judges receive the ABA's professional blessing.

WHO, WHAT, HOW   The dual court system in America is shaped by rules that ultimately determine who will win and lose in legal disputes.

WHO are the actors?	WHAT do they want?	HOW do they get it?
Citizens, attorneys	• Resolution of legal conflict	• Rules of jurisdiction • State courts • Federal courts
President Senators	• Appointees to the federal courts who favor their views or political ambitions	• Nomination and confirmation processes

Politics and the Supreme Court

At the very top of the nation's judicial system reigns the U.S. Supreme Court. While the nine justices do not wear the elaborate wigs of their British colleagues in the House of Lords, the highest court of appeals in Britain, they do don long black robes to hear their cases and sit against a majestic background of red silk, perhaps the closest thing to the pomp and circumstance of royalty that we have in American government. Polls show that the Court gets higher ratings from the public than does Congress or the president and that it doesn't suffer from the popular cynicism about government that afflicts the other branches. This might, however, change in the wake of the Court's unusual ruling deciding the outcome of the 2000 presidential election.[11]

The American public seems to believe that the Supreme Court is indeed above politics, as the founders wished it to be. Such a view, while gratifying to those who want to believe in the purity and wisdom of at least one aspect of their government, is not strictly accurate. The members of the Court are preserved, by the rule of lifetime tenure, from continually having to seek reelection or reappointment, but as the 2000 election decision makes clear, they are not removed from the political world around them. It is more useful, and closer to reality, to regard the Supreme Court as an intensely political institution. In at least three critical areas—how its members are chosen, how those members make decisions, and the effect of the decisions they make—the Court is a decisive allocator of "who gets what when and how."

How Members of the Court Are Selected

In a perfect world, the wisest and most intelligent jurists in the country would be appointed to make the all-important constitutional decisions daily faced by members of the Supreme Court. In a political world, however, the need for wise and intelligent justices needs to be balanced against the demands of a system that makes those justices the choice of an elected president, confirmed by elected senators. The need of these elected officials to be responsive to their constituencies means that the nomination process for Supreme Court justices is often a battleground of competing views of the public good. Merit is certainly important, but it is tempered by other considerations resulting from a democratic selection process.

On paper, the process of choosing justices for the Supreme Court is not a great deal different from the selection of other federal judges, though no tradition of senatorial courtesy exists at the High Court level. Far too much is at stake in Supreme Court appointments to grant any individual senator veto power. The Constitution, silent on so much concerning the Supreme Court, does not give the president any handy list of criteria for making these critical appointments. But the demands of his job suggest that merit, shared ideology, political reward, and demographic representation all play a role in this choice.[12]

Merit   The president will certainly want to appoint the most qualified person and the person with the highest ethical standards who also meets the other prerequisites. Scholars agree that most of the people who have served on the Court over the years have been among the best legal minds available, but they also know that sometimes presidents have nominated people whose reputations have proved questionable.[13] The ABA passes judgment on candidates for the Court, as it does on those for the lower courts, issuing verdicts of "well qualified," "qualified," and "not qualified." The Federal Bureau of Investigation (FBI) also checks out each nominee's background.

Political Ideology   Although a president wants to appoint a well-qualified candidate to the Court, he is constrained by the desire to find a candidate who shares his views on politics and the law. Political ideology here involves a couple of dimensions. One is the traditional liberal-conservative dimension. Supreme Court justices, like all human beings, have views on the role of government, the rights of individuals, and the relationship between the two. Presidents want to appoint justices who look at the world the same way they do, although they are occasionally surprised when a nominee's ideological stripes turn out to be different than they had anticipated. Republican president Dwight Eisenhower called the appointment of Chief Justice Earl Warren, who turned out to be quite liberal in his legal judgments, "the biggest damn fool mistake I ever made."[14]

strict constructionism
a judicial approach holding that the Constitution should be read literally with the framers' intentions uppermost in mind

But ideology has another dimension when it refers to the law. Justices can take the view that the Constitution means exactly what it says it means and that all interpretations of it must be informed by the founders' intentions. This approach, called **strict constructionism,** holds that if the meaning of the Constitution is to be changed, it must be done by amendment, not by judicial interpretation. Judge Robert Bork, a Reagan nominee who failed to be confirmed by the Senate, is a strict constructionist. During his confirmation hearings, when he was asked about the famous reapportionment ruling in *Baker* v. *Carr* that the Constitution effectively guarantees every citizen one vote, Bork replied that if the people of the United States wanted their Constitution to guarantee "one man one vote," they were free to amend the document to say so. In Bork's judgment, without that amendment, the principle was simply the result of justices rewriting the Constitution. When the senators asked him about the right to privacy, another right enforced by the Court but not specified in the Constitution, Bork simply laughed.[15] The opposite position to strict constructionism, what might be called **judicial interpretivism,** holds that the Constitution is a living document, that the founders could not possibly have anticipated all possible future circumstances, and that justices should interpret the Constitution in light of social changes. When the Court, in *Griswold* v. *Connecticut,* ruled that although there is no right to privacy in the Constitution, the Bill of Rights can be understood to imply such a right, it was engaging in judicial interpretation. Strict constructionists would deny that there is a constitutional right to privacy.

judicial interpretivism
a judicial approach holding that the Constitution is a living document and that judges should interpret it according to changing times and values

While interpretivism tends to be a liberal position because of its emphasis on change, and strict constructionism tends to be a conservative position because of its adherence to the status quo, the two ideological scales do not necessarily go hand in hand. It is entirely possible to be a conservative who believes that the Constitution should be broadly interpreted, at least on some issues. For instance, even though the Second Amendment refers to the right to bear arms in the context of militia membership, many conservatives would argue that this needs to be understood to protect the right to bear arms in a modern context, when militias are no longer necessary or practical—not a strict constructionist reading of the Constitution. Liberals, on the other hand, tend to rely on a strict reading of the Second Amendment to support their calls for tighter gun control.

Reward More than half of the people who have been nominated to the Supreme Court have been personally acquainted with the president.[16] Often nominees are either friends of the president or his political allies or are people he wishes to reward in an impressive fashion. Harry Truman knew and had worked with all four of the men he appointed to the Court, Franklin Roosevelt appointed people he knew (and who were loyal to his New Deal), John Kennedy appointed his longtime friend and associate Byron White, and Lyndon Johnson appointed his good friend Abe Fortas.[17]

Welcome to the Fraternity
Concerned about weak support among women voters, President Ronald Reagan in 1981 heeded calls to diversify the Supreme Court, which had always been composed entirely of men. He appointed Sandra Day O'Connor, an Arizona Court of Appeals judge, shown here with Reagan and Chief Justice Warren Burger.

Representation Finally, the president wants to appoint people who represent groups he feels should be included in the political process or whose support he wants to gain. As we will see, this does not necessarily mean that the Court should reflect U.S. demographics. When Ronald Reagan's polls showed that his support was weak among women, a promise to appoint the first woman to the Supreme Court helped to change his image as a person unconcerned with women's issues. He fulfilled that promise with the appointment of Sandra Day O'Connor. Similarly, Lyndon Johnson's appointment of Thurgood Marshall was at least in part because he wanted to appoint an African American to the Court. After Marshall retired, President George Bush appointed Clarence Thomas to fill his seat. Although Bush said that he was making the appointment because Thomas was the person best qualified for the job, and not because he was black, few people believed him. In earlier years, presidents also felt compelled to ensure that there was at least one Catholic and one Jew on the Court. This necessity has lost much of its force today as interest groups seem more concerned with the political than the religious views of appointees.

Different presidents put different weights on these four considerations when they choose a nominee for Supreme Court justice. And, of course, these four are not the only influences. Campaigning by a potential candidate, recommendations from people the president respects or whose support he needs, and expectations about the Senate's response to the candidate all affect the president's decision.

The current composition of the Supreme Court does not reflect the population of the United States, although it can certainly be argued that it comes closer than it ever has. There are seven men on the Court and two women (the only two ever appointed). Three justices are Catholic, four Protestant, and two Jewish; only Judeo-Christian religions have been represented on the Court so far. Seven of the current justices are Republicans, primarily a reflection of appointments by Reagan and Bush, and two, appointed by Clinton, are Democrats. They have attended an elite array of undergraduate institutions and law schools. In 2001 their ages ranged from fifty-three to eighty-one, with an average of sixty-seven. There have never been any Hispanic Americans, Native Americans, or Asian Americans on the Court, and there have been only two African Americans, whose terms did not overlap. The overwhelmingly elite white male Christian character of the Court raises the interesting question of whether the nation's highest court should represent demographically the people whose Constitution it guards.

Confirmation by the Senate   As with the lower courts, the Senate must approve presidential appointments to the Supreme Court. Here again, the Senate Judiciary Committee plays the largest role, holding hearings and inviting the nominee, colleagues, and concerned interest groups to testify. Sometimes the hearings, and the subsequent vote in the Senate, are mere formalities, but increasingly, as the appointments have become more ideological and when the Senate majority party is not the party of the president, they have the potential to become political battlefields. The hearings over the nominations of Robert Bork and Clarence Thomas are excellent examples of what can happen when interest groups and public opinion get heavily involved in a controversial confirmation battle. These grueling political litmus tests can leave the candidate bitter and angry, as happened with both candidates.

How the Court Makes Decisions

The introduction of political concerns into the selection process makes it almost inevitable that political considerations will arise as the justices make their decisions. The justices arrive on the Court aware of the great responsibility they bear as members of the nation's highest court, but also possessed of ideas and values that they believe are right and that they know were significant in their nomination and confir-

Figure 9.3
Pathway to and Through the Supreme Court
Source: Administrative Office of the United States Courts.

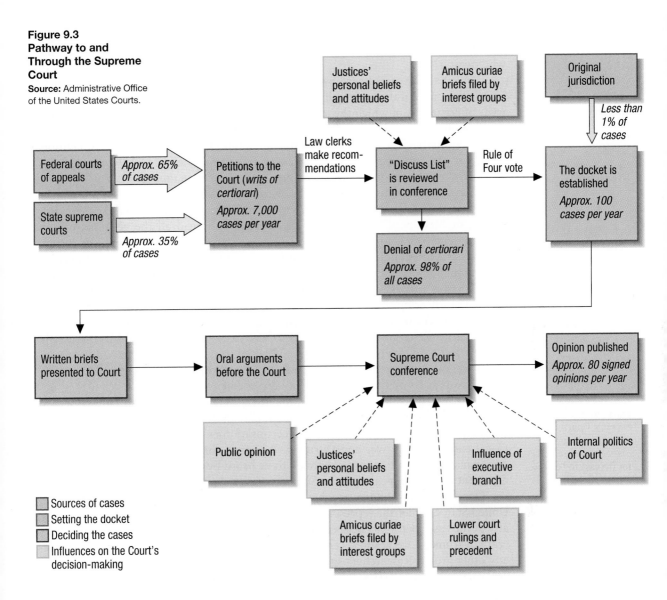

mation. Few of them are able to abandon, or even see the need to abandon, those values and beliefs when they start making decisions. And so there are struggles among the justices as each tries to promote his or her view of what the Constitution means and what is right for American society. There are three points in the decision-making process where politics makes an appearance: in the selection of the cases to be heard, in the actual decision- making on the cases, and in writing the opinions on the cases. As we look at each of these in turn, refer to Figure 9.3, which summarizes the steps in the process.

Choosing Which Cases to Hear The Supreme Court could not possibly hear the almost 7,000 petitions it receives each year.[18] Intensive screening is necessary to reduce the number to the more manageable 90 to 120 that the Court finally hears. This screening process is a political one; having one's case heard by the Supreme Court is a scarce resource. What rules and which people determine who gets this resource and who doesn't?

Almost all the cases heard by the Court come from its appellate, not its original, jurisdiction, and of these virtually all arrive at the Court in the form of petitions for **writs of certiorari,** in which the losing party in a lower court case explains in writing why the Supreme Court should hear its case. The Court can either grant or deny a writ of certiorari. Those too poor to pay the $200 filing fee are allowed to petition the Court *in forma pauperis,* which exempts them from the fee. In 1997 nearly two-thirds of the petitions filed with the Court were *in forma pauperis.*[19]

writ of certiorari
formal request by the U.S. Supreme Court to call up the lower court case it decides to hear on appeal

Law clerks, usually recent law school graduates who have served for one year as clerks to judges on lower courts, have tremendous responsibility over certiorari petitions, or "cert pets," as they call them. They must read all the petitions (thirty pages in length plus appendices) and summarize each in a two-to-five-page memo that includes a recommendation to the justices on whether or not to hear the case, all with minimal guidance or counsel from the justices.[20] The memos are circulated to the justices' offices, where clerks read them again and make comments on the advisability of hearing the cases. The memos, with the clerks' comments, go on to the justices, who decide which cases they think should be granted cert and which denied. The chief justice circulates a weekly list of the cases he thinks should be discussed, which is known unimaginatively as the Discuss List. Other justices can add cases to the list that they think should be discussed in their Friday afternoon meetings.

Rule of Four
requirement that four Supreme Court justices must agree to grant a case certiorari in order for the case to be heard

Once a case is on the Discuss List, it takes a vote of four justices to agree to grant it certiorari. This **Rule of Four** means that it takes fewer people to decide to hear a case than it will eventually take to decide the case itself, and thus it gives some power to a minority on the Court. A denial of certiorari does not necessarily mean that the Court endorses the lower court's ruling. Rather, it simply means that the case was not seen as important or special enough to be heard by the highest court. Fewer than 5 percent of cases appealed to the Supreme Court survive this screening process.

solicitor general
the Justice Department officer who argues the government's cases before the Supreme Court

One factor that influences whether a case is heard by the Court is whether the United States, under the representation of its lawyer, the **solicitor general,** is party to any of the cases before it. Between 70 and 80 percent of the appeals filed by the federal government are granted cert by the justices, a far greater proportion than for any other group. Researchers speculate that this is because of the stature of the federal government's interests, the justices' trust in the solicitor general's ability to weed out frivolous lawsuits, and the experience the solicitor general brings to the job.[21] Justices are also influenced by **amicus curiae briefs,** or "friend of the court" documents that are filed in support of about 8 percent of petitions for certiorari by interest groups that want to encourage the Court to grant or deny cert. As we will see, amicus curiae briefs are also used later on in the process.

amicus curiae brief
a "friend of the court" document filed by interested parties to encourage the court to grant or deny certiorari or to urge it to decide a case in a particular way

Deciding Cases   Once a case is on the docket, the parties are notified, and they prepare written briefs and oral arguments. Lawyers for each side get only a half-hour to make their case verbally in front of the Court, and they are often interrupted by justices who seek clarification, criticize points, or offer supportive arguments. The actual decision-making process occurs before and during the Supreme Court conference meeting. Conference debates and discussions take place in private, although justices have often made revealing comments in their letters and memoirs that give insight into the dynamics of conference decision-making. A variety of factors affect the justices as they make decisions on the cases they hear. Some of those factors come from within the justices—their attitudes, values, and beliefs—and some are external.

Justices' attitudes toward the Constitution and how literally it is to be taken are clearly important, as we saw earlier in our discussion of strict constructionism and interpretivism. Judges are also influenced by the view they hold of the role of the Court: whether it should be an active lawmaker and policymaker or should keep its rulings narrow and leave lawmaking to the elected branches of government. Those who adhere to **judicial activism** are quite comfortable with the idea of overturning precedents, exercising judicial review, and otherwise making decisions that shape government policy. In contrast, practitioners of **judicial restraint** believe more strongly in the principle of *stare decisis* and reject any active lawmaking by the Court as unconstitutional.

judicial activism
view that the courts should be lawmaking, policymaking bodies

judicial restraint
view that the courts should reject any active lawmaking functions and stick to judicial interpretations of the past

These positions seem at first to line up with the positions of interpretivism and strict constructionism, and often they do. But exceptions exist, as when liberal justice Thurgood Marshall, who had once used the Constitution in activist and interpretivist ways to change civil rights laws, pleaded for restraint among his newer and more conservative colleagues who were eager to roll back some of the earlier decisions by overturning precedent and creating more conservative laws.[22] Activism is not necessarily a liberal stance, and restraint is not necessarily conservative. It depends on what status quo the justice is seeking to change or maintain. A justice seeking to overturn the *Roe* v. *Wade* ruling allowing a woman to have an abortion during the first trimester of pregnancy would be an activist conservative justice. In contrast, Justice Thurgood Marshall ended his term on the Court as a liberal restraintist. Researchers have also found that justices are influenced in their decision-making by their background (region of residence, profession, place of education, and the like), party affiliation, and political attitudes, all of which the president and the Senate consider in selecting future justices.[23]

Justices are also influenced by external factors.[24] Despite the founders' efforts to make justices immune to politics and the pressures of public opinion by giving them lifetime tenure, political scientists have found that they usually tend to make decisions that are consistent with majority opinion in the United States. Of course, this doesn't mean that justices are reading public opinion polls over breakfast and incorporating their findings into judicial decisions by afternoon. Rather, the same forces that shape public opinion also shape the justices' opinions, and people who are elected by the public choose the justices they hope will help them carry out their agendas, which are usually responsive to what the public wants.

Other political forces also exert an influence on the Court. The influence of the executive branch, discussed earlier, contributes to the high success rate of the solicitor general, who generally wins 70 to 80 percent of the cases he or she brings to the Court.[25] Interest groups put enormous pressure on the Supreme Court, although with varying success. Interest groups are influential in the nomination and confirmation process, they file amicus curiae briefs to try to shape the decisions on the certiorari petitions, and they file an increasingly large number of briefs in support of one or the other side when a case is actually reviewed by the Court. One study showed that in 1987, 80 percent of cases had at least one amicus curiae brief and that sixteen hundred interest groups, both public and private, participated in cases before the Supreme Court. One 1989 abortion case, *Webster* v. *Reproductive Services*,[26] had forty-eight briefs filed in connection with it. Interest groups also have a role in sponsoring cases when individual petitioners do not have the resources to bring a case before the Supreme Court.

A final influence on the justices worth discussing here is the justices themselves. While they usually (at least in recent years) arrive at the conference meetings with their minds already made up, they cannot afford to ignore each other. It takes five votes to decide a case, and the justices need each other as allies. One scholar who has looked at the disputes among justices over decisions, and who has evaluated the characterization of the Court as "nine scorpions in a bottle," says that the number of disagreements is not noteworthy. On the contrary, what is truly remarkable is how well the justices tend to cooperate, given their close working relationship, the seriousness of their undertaking, and the varied and strong personalities and ideologies that go into the mix.

opinion written decision of the court that states the judgment of the majority

Writing Opinions   Once a decision is reached, or sometimes as it is being reached, the writing of the opinion is assigned. The **opinion** is the written part of the decision that states the judgment of the majority of the Court. It is the lasting part of the process, read by law students, lawyers, judges, and future justices. The opinion is the living legacy of the case, and how the opinion explains the decision is vitally important for how the nation will understand what the decision actually means. If, for instance, it is written by the least enthusiastic member of the majority, it will be weaker and less authoritative than if it is written by the most passionate member. The same decision can be portrayed in different ways; for instance, it can be stated broadly or narrowly, with implications for many future cases or for only a few.

It is the job of the chief justice to assign the opinion-writing job if he or she is in the majority. If not, the senior member in the majority assigns the opinion. So important is this task that chief justices have been known to vote with a majority they do not agree with just so that they could assign the opinion to the justice who would write the weakest version of the majority's conclusion.[27] Justices who agree with the general decision, but for reasons other than or in addition to those stated in the majority opinion, may write **concurring opinions,** and those who disagree may write **dissenting opinions.** These opinions often have lasting impact as well, especially if the Court changes its mind, as it often does over time and as its composition changes. When such a reversal occurs, the reasons for the about-face are sometimes to be found in the dissent or the concurrence.

concurring opinions documents written by justices expressing agreement with the majority ruling but describing different or additional reasons for the ruling

dissenting opinions documents written by justices expressing disagreement with the majority ruling

The Political Effects of Judicial Decisions

The last area in which we can see the Supreme Court as a political actor is in the effects of the decisions it makes. These decisions, despite the best intentions of those who adhere to the philosophy of judicial restraint, often amount to the creation of public policies as surely as do acts of Congress. The chapters on civil liberties and the struggle for equal rights make clear that the Supreme Court, at certain points in its history, has taken an active lawmaking role. The history of the Supreme Court's policymaking role is the history of the United States, and we cannot possibly recount it here, but a few examples should show that rulings of the Court have had the effect of distributing scarce and valued resources among people, affecting decisively who gets what when and how.[28]

It was the Court, for instance, under the early leadership of John Marshall, that greatly enhanced the power of the federal government over the states by declaring that the Court has the power to invalidate state laws (and acts of Congress as well) if they conflict with the Constitution,[29] that state law is invalid if it conflicts with national law,[30] that Congress's powers go beyond those listed in Article I, Section 8, of the Constitution,[31] and that the federal government can regulate interstate commerce.[32] In the early years of the twentieth century, the Supreme Court was an ardent defender of the right of business not to be regulated by the federal government, striking down laws providing for maximum working hours,[33] regulation of child labor,[34] and minimum wages.[35] The role of the Court in making civil rights policy is well known. In 1857 it decided that slaves, even freed slaves, could never be citizens;[36] in 1896 it decided that separate accommodations for whites and blacks were constitutional;[37] and in 1954 it reversed itself, declaring separate but equal to be unconstitutional.[38] It is the Supreme Court that has been responsible for the expansion of due process protection for criminal defendants;[39] for instituting the principle of one person, one vote in drawing legislative districts;[40] and for creating the right of a woman to have an abortion in the first trimester of pregnancy.[41] Each of these actions has altered the distribution of power in American society in ways that some would argue should be done only by an elected body.

WHO, WHAT, HOW The Supreme Court is a powerful institution, and a number of people—from citizens to senators to the president himself—have a great stake in what it does.

WHO are the actors?	WHAT do they want?	HOW do they get it?
Citizens	• View of the Court as above politics	• Lack of critical thinking about judicial politics
The president	• Legacy • Justices on the Court who reflect president's views • Influence on the Court's decisions	• Selection criteria • Action by solicitor general
The Senate	• Justices on the Court who reflect senators' views	• Confirmation hearings
Interest groups	• Justices on the Court who reflect group members' views • Influence on the Court's decisions	• Lobbying Senate during confirmation hearings • Writing amicus curiae briefs
Justices	• Manageable caseload • Significant and respected decisions • Legacy	• Rules of procedure • Decision-making criteria • Careful opinion writing

Citizenship and the Courts

In this chapter, we have argued that the legal system and the American courts are central to the maintenance of social order and conflict resolution and are also a fundamental component of American politics—who gets what and how they get it. This means that a crucial question for American democracy is, Who uses the courts? Who takes advantage of this powerful system for allocating resources and values in society? An important component of American political culture is the principle of equality before the law, which we commonly take to mean that all citizens should be treated equally by the law, but which also implies that all citizens should have equal access to the law.

In Chapter 5, on equal rights, we examined in depth the issue of equality before the law in a constitutional sense. But what about the day-to-day treatment of citizens by the law enforcement and legal systems? Citizens are treated differently by these systems according to their race, their income level, and the kinds of crimes they commit. African Americans and white Americans do not experience our criminal justice system in the same ways, beginning with what is often the initial contact with the system, the police. Blacks are often harassed by police or treated with suspicion simply because they are black, and they tend to perceive the police as persecutors rather than protectors. In fact, blacks are more likely to be arrested than whites, and they are more likely to go to jail, where they serve harsher sentences. Blacks do commit more crimes than whites. They are more likely to be poor and urban and to belong to a socioeconomic class in which crime not only doesn't carry the popular sanctions that it does for the middle class but it also may provide some of the only opportunities for economic advancement. But studies show that racial bias and stereotyping also play a role in the racial disparities in the criminal justice system.[42]

Race is not the only factor that divides American citizens in their experience of the criminal justice system. Income also creates a barrier to equal treatment under the law, and because blacks and some other minorities are disproportionately represented in the ranks of the poor, this only increases the racial divide. More than half of those accused of felonies in the United States have court-appointed lawyers. These lawyers are likely to be less than enthusiastic about these assignments, as pay is modest and sometimes irregular. Consequently, the quality of the legal representation available to the poor is not the same as that available to those who can afford to pay well. Yale law professor John H. Langbein is scathing on the role of money in determining the legal fate of Americans. He says, "Money is the defining element of our modern American criminal-justice system." The wealthy can afford crackerjack lawyers, but

> if you are not a person of means, if you cannot afford to engage the elite defense-lawyer industry—and that means most of us—you will be cast into a different system, in which the financial advantages of the state will overpower you and leave you effectively at the mercy of prosecutorial whim.[43]

Whereas the issue with respect to the criminal justice system is equal treatment, the issue for the civil justice system is equal access. The Supreme Court has ruled that

Points of Access

- Serve on a campus judicial board.
- Volunteer to work as a Court Appointed Special Advocate (CASA) or a translator in a family or juvenile court.
- Participate in a college mock trial.
- Serve on a jury, if called.

low-income defendants must be provided with legal assistance in state and federal criminal cases, but there is no such guarantee in civil cases. That doesn't mean, however, that less affluent citizens have no recourse for their legal problems. Both public and private legal aid programs exist. For example, in 1974 Congress created the Legal Services Corporation (LSC), a nonprofit organization that provides resources to more than 260 legal aid programs around the country. The LSC helps citizens and some immigrants with legal problems, such as those concerning housing, employment, family issues, finances, and immigration. This program has been controversial, as conservatives fear that it has a left-wing agenda. President Reagan tried to phase it out but was rebuffed by Congress. More recently Congress, under Republican control, has acted to limit eligibility for LSC aid for immigrants and prisoners.

These arguments do not mean that the United States has made no progress toward a more equal dispensation of justice. Without a doubt, we have made enormous strides since the days of Dred Scott, when the Supreme Court ruled that blacks did not have the standing to bring cases to court, and since the days when lynch mobs dispensed their brand of vigilante justice in the South. Still, the goal of equal treatment by and equal access to the legal system in America is some way off.

WHAT'S AT STAKE REVISITED

When a president tries to fill up the Supreme Court with justices who share his ideas and support his policies, it is called Court packing. We have seen in this chapter that most presidents try to pack the Court, building their own legacies with appointees who they hope will perpetuate their vision of government and politics. We have also seen that it often fails for the simple reason that justices do not reliably vote as their nominating presidents think they will. Eisenhower was seriously disappointed in the opinions of his appointees, Earl Warren and William Brennan. Reagan found that Sandra Day O'Connor was not the predictable conservative, antiabortion voice on the Court he had hoped she would be.

But no president has attempted to pack the Court as blatantly as Franklin Roosevelt, and none has failed so ignominiously. Public opinion may have backed his New Deal policies, but it turned on him when he tried to pack the Court. The backlash may have contributed to the slowing down of the New Deal and to the Republican victories in 1938 that left him with a weakened Democratic majority in Congress.

FDR himself was reelected two more times. The Court, ironically, did an about-face. One justice changed his mind and started voting with the Roosevelt supporters; another retired. Eventually, FDR made eight appointments to the Court, putting his own stamp on it more effectively than any president since Washington. The Court was, in essence, packed by Roosevelt after all.

Still, his proposal to enlarge the Court was not a neutral one. Not only did he risk his presidency and perhaps hamper its possibilities for future success, but he also put the constitutional balance of power in the country at stake. As the public realized, even a popular president has to be held in check, for the potential for abuse of power is enormous. Had FDR succeeded in his plan, the Court would have essentially moved from independence to subordination. Judicial review would have ceased to be a meaningful check on the legislature and could instead have become a presidential weapon against Congress. Both separation of powers and checks and balances would have been seriously damaged. FDR would have made Hamilton's claim that the judiciary was the least dangerous branch of government into a truism, while raising the power of the presidency to a height even Hamilton had not imagined. ■

key terms

administrative law   252
amicus curiae brief   266
appeal   256
appellate jurisdiction   256
civil law   251
civil law tradition   250
common law tradition   249
concurring opinions   268
constitutional law   251
courts   249

criminal law   250
dissenting opinions   268
executive order   252
judicial activism   267
judicial interpretivism   263
judicial restraint   267
judicial review   253
jurisdiction   255
opinion   268
original jurisdiction   256

precedent   250
procedural due process   250
procedural law   250
Rule of Four   266
senatorial courtesy   260
solicitor general   266
statutory law   251
strict constructionism   262
substantive law   250
writ of certiorari   266

summary

■ Laws serve five main functions in a democratic society. They offer security, supply predictability, provide for conflict resolution, reinforce society's values, and provide for the distribution of social costs and benefits.

■ American law is based on legislation, but its practice has evolved from a tradition of common law and the use of precedent by judges.

■ Laws serve many purposes and are classified in different ways. Substantive laws cover what we can or cannot do, while procedural laws establish the procedures used to enforce laws generally. Criminal laws concern specific behaviors considered undesirable by the government, while civil laws cover interactions between individuals. Constitutional law refers to laws included in the Constitution, as well as the precedents that have

been established over time by decisions relating to those laws. Statutory, administrative, and executive laws are established by Congress and the state legislatures, the bureaucracy, and the president, respectively.

■ The founders were deliberately vague in setting up a court system so as to avoid controversy during the ratification process. The details of design were left to Congress, which established a layering of district, state, and federal courts with differing rules of procedure.

■ The Constitution does not state that courts can decide the constitutionality of legislation. The courts gained the extraconstitutional power of judicial review when Chief Justice John Marshall adopted it in *Marbury* v. *Madison*.

■ The political views of a judge and the jurisdiction of a case can have great impact on the verdict. The rules of the courtroom may vary from one district to another, and the American dual court system often leads to more than one court with the authority to deliberate.

■ The U.S. Supreme Court reigns at the top of the American court system. It is a powerful institution, revered by the American public, but it is also as political an institution as the other two branches of government. Politics is involved in how the Court is chosen, how it decides a case, and the effects of its decisions.

■ Although the U.S. criminal justice system has made progress toward a more equal dispensation of justice, minorities and poor Americans have not always experienced equal treatment by the courts or had equal access to them.

10

Public Opinion

What's at Stake?

The Role of Public Opinion in a Democracy
- Why We Think Public Opinion Ought to Matter
- Why Public Opinion Does Matter

Measuring and Tracking Public Opinion
- The Quality of Opinion Polling Today
- Types of Polls

Citizen Values: How Do We Measure Up?
- Political Knowledge
- Ideology
- Tolerance
- Participation

What Influences Our Opinions About Politics?
- Political Socialization: Learning the Rules of the Game
- Sources of Divisions in Public Opinion

Citizenship and Public Opinion
- Shortcuts to Political Knowledge
- The Rational Electorate

What's at Stake Revisited

WHAT'S AT STAKE?

How much responsibility do you want to take for the way you are governed? Most of us are pretty comfortable with the idea that we should vote for our *rulers* (although we don't all jump at the chance to do it), but how about voting on the *rules?* Citizens of some states—California, for instance—have become used to being asked for their votes on new state laws. But what about national politics—do you know enough or care enough to vote on laws for the country as a whole, just as if you were a member of Congress or a senator? Should we be governed more by public opinion than by the opinions of our elected leaders? This is the question that drives the debate about whether U.S. citizens should be able to participate in such forms of direct democracy as the national referendum or initiative.

Not only do many states (twenty-four out of fifty) employ some form of direct democracy, but many other countries do as well. In the past ten years, voters in Ireland were asked to decide about the legality of divorce, in Bermuda about national independence, in Norway and Sweden about joining the European Union, in Iraq about supporting Saddam Hussein (there was no real freedom of choice in this vote), and in Bosnia about peace.

In 1995 former senator Mike Gravel (D-AK) proposed that the United States join many of the world's nations in adopting a national *plebiscite,* or popular vote on policy. He argued that Americans should support a national initiative he called "Philadelphia II" (to evoke "Philadelphia I," which was, of course, the Constitutional Convention), which would set up procedures for direct popular participation in national lawmaking.[1] Such participation could take place through the ballot box (the Swiss go to the polls four times a year to vote on national policy) or even electronically, as some have suggested, with people voting on issues by computer at home. Experts agree that the technology exists for at-home participation in government. And public opinion is overwhelmingly in favor of proposals to let Americans vote for or against major national issues before they become law.[2]

Do you agree with Gravel and the roughly three-quarters of Americans who support more direct democracy at the national level? Should we have rule by public opinion in the United States? How would the founders have responded to this proposal? And what would be the consequences for American government if a national plebiscite were passed? Just what is at stake in the issue of direct democracy at the national level? ■

I t is fashionable these days to denounce the public opinion polls that claim to tell us what the American people think about this or that political issue. Politicians accuse one another of pandering to public opinion when one of them changes his or her mind in response to what the public thinks. During the Clinton impeachment hearings in Congress, when public opinion polls were giving the president a 66 percent approval rating and well over a majority of Americans were telling pollsters that they wanted him to remain in office, members of the House Judiciary Committee (where the initial hearings were being held) asserted that either (a) the polls were wrong or (b) they would not be ruled by public opinion but rather by what they perceived to be right. On the floor of the House of Representatives, Representative Ed Bryant (R-TN) declared, "We cannot govern this country by polls."[3]

These reactions to public opinion raise an interesting question. What is so bad about being ruled by the polls in a democracy, which, after all, is supposed to be ruled by the people? If politics is about who gets what and how they get it, shouldn't we care about what the "who" thinks? **Public opinion** is just what the public thinks. It is the aggregation, or collection, of individual attitudes and beliefs on one or more issues at any given time. **Public opinion polls** are nothing more than scientific efforts to measure that opinion—to estimate what an entire group of people thinks about an issue by asking a smaller sample of the group for their opinions. If the sample is large enough and chosen properly, we have every reason to believe that it will provide a reliable estimate of the whole. Today's technology gives us the ability to keep a constant finger on the pulse of America and to know what its citizens are thinking at almost any given time. And yet at least some Americans seem torn about the role of public opinion in government today. On the one hand, we want to believe that what we think matters, but on the other, we'd like to think that our elected officials are guided by unwavering standards and principles.

In this chapter, we argue that public opinion is important for the proper functioning of democracy, that the expression of what citizens think and what they want is a prerequisite for their ability to use the system and its rules to get what they want from it. But the quality of the public's opinion on politics, and the ways that it actually influences policy, may surprise you. Specifically, in this chapter we look at

- the role of public opinion in a democracy
- how public opinion can be measured
- what our opinions are (Do we think like the "ideal democratic citizen"?)
- where our opinions come from
- the relationship of citizenship to public opinion

public opinion
the collective attitudes and beliefs of individuals on one or more issues

public opinion polls
scientific efforts to estimate what an entire group thinks about an issue by asking a smaller sample of the group for its opinion

The Role of Public Opinion in a Democracy

Public opinion is important in a democracy for at least two reasons. The first reason is normative: we believe that public opinion *should* influence what government does. The second is empirical: a lot of people actually behave as though public opinion *does* matter, and to the degree that they measure, record, and react to it, it does indeed become a factor in American politics.

Why We Think Public Opinion Ought to Matter

The presence of "the people" is pervasive in the documents that created and support the American government. In the Declaration of Independence, Thomas Jefferson wrote that a just government must get its powers from "the consent of the governed." Our Constitution begins "We the People. . . ." And Abraham Lincoln's Gettysburg Address hails our nation as "government of the people, by the people, for the people." What all of this tells us is that the very legitimacy of the U.S. government, like that of all democracies, rests on the idea that government exists to serve the interests of its citizens. As political scientist V. O. Key, Jr., observed, "Unless mass views have some place in shaping of policy, all talk about democracy is nonsense."[4]

But how to determine whose views should be heard? As we saw in Chapter 1, different theories of democracy prescribe different roles for "the people," in part because they disagree about how competent the citizens of a country are to govern themselves. Elitists suspect that citizens are too ignorant or ill-informed to be trusted with major political decisions; pluralists trust groups of citizens to be competent on those issues in which they have a stake, but they think that individuals may be too busy to gather all the information they need to make informed decisions; and proponents of participatory democracy have faith that the people are both smart enough and able to gather enough information to be effective decision-makers.

As Americans, we are also somewhat confused about what we think the role of the democratic citizen should be. We introduced these conflicting notions of citizenship in Chapter 1. One view, which describes what we might call the *ideal democratic citizen,* is founded on the vision of a virtuous citizen activated by concern for the common good, who recognizes that democracy carries obligations as well as rights. In this familiar model, a citizen should be attentive to and informed about politics; have reasonably formed, stable opinions on the issues; exhibit political tolerance and a willingness to compromise; and practice high levels of participation in civic activities.

A competing view of American citizenship holds that Americans are *apolitical, self-interested actors.* According to this view, Americans are almost the opposite of the ideal citizen: inattentive and ill-informed, easily manipulated, politically intolerant and rigid, and unlikely to get involved in political life.

We argue in this chapter, as we have earlier, that the American public displays both of these visions of citizenship. But we also argue that there are mechanisms in American politics that buffer the impact of apolitical, self-interested behavior, so that government by public opinion does not have disastrous effects on the American polity. Although it may seem like some kind of magician's act, we show that Americans as a *group* often behave as ideal citizens, even though as *individuals* they do not.

Why Public Opinion Does Matter

Politicians and media leaders act as though they agree with Key's conclusion, which is the practical reason public opinion matters in American politics. Elected politicians, for example, overwhelmingly believe that the public is keeping tabs on them. When voting on major bills, members of Congress worry quite a lot about public opinion in their districts.[5] Presidents, too, pay close attention to public opinion. In fact, recent presidents have invested major resources in having an in-house public opinion expert whose regular polls are used as an important of presidential political strategies. And, indeed, the belief that the public is paying attention is not totally unfounded. Although the public does not often act as if it pays attention or cares very much about politics, it can change its mind and act decisively if the provocation is sufficient. Witness the Republican losses in the 1998 midterm election after Republicans repeatedly ignored public opinion polls and proceeded with plans to impeach President Clinton.

Politicians are not alone in their tendency to monitor public opinion as they do their jobs. Leaders of the media also focus on public opinion, making huge investments in polls and devoting considerable coverage to reporting what the public is thinking. Polls are used to measure public attitudes toward all sorts of things. Of course, we are familiar with "horse race" polls that ask about people's voting intentions and lend drama to media coverage of electoral races. Sometimes these polls themselves become the story the media covers. With the availability of a twenty-four-hour news cycle and the need to find something to report on all the time, it is not surprising that the media have fastened on their own polling as a newsworthy subject. Public opinion, or talk about it, seems to pervade the modern political arena.

WHO, WHAT, HOW Public opinion is important in theory—in our views about how citizens and politicians should behave—and in practice—how they actually do behave.

WHO are the actors?	WHAT do they want?	HOW do they get it?
Founders and citizens	• Government legitimated by popular consent • Government responsive to public opinion but protected from public ignorance	• Constitutional protections • Constitutional amendment and informal change
Politicians	• Job security	• Public opinion polls
The media	• Higher ratings, enough content to fill news cycle	• Media coverage of its own polls

Measuring and Tracking Public Opinion

Long before the beginning of modern scientific polling, politicians gauged what their constituents wanted through talking and listening to them. They still learn about constituent opinion from the letters, phone calls, and e-mail messages they receive. They visit constituents, make speeches, attend meetings, and talk with community leaders and interest group representatives. Direct contact with people puts politicians in touch with concerns that could be missed entirely by a scientifically designed public opinion poll. That poll might focus on issues of national news that are on the

**Figure 10.1
Congressional
Sources of Public
Opinion Informa-
tion**
Source: Data from the
Pew Research Center
for the People and the
Press, Trust in Govern-
ment Study, October
1997 and February
1998.

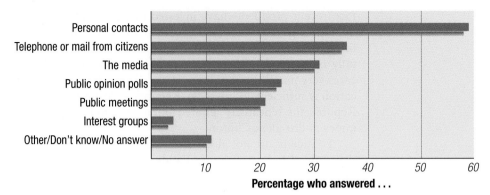

Note: 81 members of Congress were asked, "What is your principal source of information about the way the public feels about issues?"

minds of national politicians or pollsters, while citizens may be far more concerned about the building of a dam upriver from their city or teacher layoffs in their school district. A survey of members of Congress found that they use a mix of sources to learn about public opinion, with opinion polls being fairly far down the list (see Figure 10.1).

Although public opinion polls are sometimes discounted by politicians who don't like their results, the truth is that most social scientists and political pollsters conduct public opinion surveys according to the highest standards of scientific accuracy, and their results are for the most part reliable. Informal soundings of public opinion may be useful to a politician for some purposes, but they are not very reliable for gauging how everyone in a given population thinks, because they are subject to sampling problems. A **sample** is the portion of the population a politician or pollster surveys on an issue. Based on what that sample says, the surveyor then makes an estimation of what everyone else thinks. This may sound like hocus-pocus, but if the sample is scientifically chosen to be representative of the whole population, sampling actually works very well. Pollsters are trained in how to select a truly random sample—that is, one that does not overrepresent any portion of the population and whose responses can therefore be safely generalized to the whole. When a sample is not chosen scientifically and has too many people from one portion of the population, we say it has a problem of **sample bias.** When trying to judge public opinion from what they hear among their supporters and friendly interest groups, politicians must allow for the bias of their own sampling. If they are not effective in knowing how those they meet differ from the full public, they will get a misleading idea of public opinion.

sample   the portion
of the population that is
selected to participate in
a poll

sample bias
the effect of having a
sample that does not
represent all segments
of the population

The Quality of Opinion Polling Today

The quality of public opinion polling today is vastly improved compared to its early days in the 1930s. Today polling is big business—and a relatively precise science. Political polls are actually a small portion of the marketing business, which tries to gauge what people want and are willing to buy. Many local governments also conduct surveys to find out what their citizens want and how satisfied they are with various municipal services. All polls face the same two challenges: (1) getting a good sample, which entails both sampling the right number of people and eliminating sample bias, and (2) asking questions that yield valid results.

How Big Does a Sample Need to Be?   No sample is perfect in matching the population from which it is drawn, but it should be close. Confronted with a critic who did not trust the notion of sampling, George Gallup is said to have responded, "Okay, if you do not like the idea of a sample, then the next time you go for a blood test, tell them to take it all!" Although it might seem counterintuitive, statisticians have determined that a sample of only 1,000 to 2,000 people can be very representative of the entire 275 million residents of the United States.

sampling error
a number that indicates within what range the results of a poll are accurate

Sampling error is a number that indicates how reliable a poll is. Based on the size of the sample, it tells within what range the opinion of the whole population would fall. Typically, a report of a poll will say that its "margin of error" is plus or minus 3 percent. That means that, based on sampling theory, there is a 95 percent chance that the real figure for the whole population is within 3 percent of that reported. For instance, when a poll reports a presidential approval rating of 60 percent and a 3 percent margin of error, this means that there is a 95 percent chance that between 57 and 63 percent of the population approves of the president's job performance. A poll that shows one candidate leading another by 2 percent of the projected vote reflects a race that is really too close to call, since the 2 percent might be due to sampling error. The larger the sample, the smaller the sampling error, but samples larger than 2,000 add very little in the way of reliability. Surveying more people, say 5,000, is much more expensive and time-consuming but does not substantially reduce the sampling error. Because reputable survey firms use scientific sampling strategies, sampling bias is not generally a problem that plagues modern pollsters.

The Importance of Asking the Right Questions   Asking the right questions in surveys is a surprisingly tricky business. Researchers have emphasized several concerns with respect to constructing survey questions. For instance, respondents should be asked about things they know and have thought about. Otherwise, they will often try to be helpful but will give responses based on whatever cues they can

pick up from the context of the interview or the particular question. Questions should not be ambiguous and should not use words that evoke strong emotional responses, like *affirmative action* or *welfare*. In addition, studies have shown that the order in which questions are asked can change the results, as can even such a simple factor as the number of choices offered for responses.

Types of Polls

Many people and organizations report the results of what they claim are measures of public opinion. To make sense of this welter of claims, it is useful to know some basic polling terminology and the characteristics of different types of polls.

National Polls   National polls are efforts to measure public opinion within a limited period of time using a national representative sample. The time period of interviewing may be as short as a few hours, with the results reported the next day, or extended over a period of weeks, as in academic polls. The underlying goal, however, is the same: to achieve scientifically valid measures of the knowledge, beliefs, or attitudes of the adult population. Many national polls are conducted by the media in conjunction with a professional polling organization.

Campaign Polls   A lot of polling is done for candidates in their efforts to win election or reelection. Most well-funded campaigns begin with a benchmark poll, taken of a sample of the population, or perhaps just of the voters, in a state or district to gather baseline information on how well the candidate is known, what issues people associate with the candidate, what issues people are concerned about, and assessments of the opposition, especially if the opponent is an incumbent. Benchmark polls are instrumental in designing campaign strategy.

tracking poll
an ongoing series of surveys that follow changes in public opinion over time

Presidential candidates and those running for a few of the better-funded statewide races (for example, governor or U.S. senator) commission **tracking polls.** These polls follow changes in attitudes toward the candidates through ongoing sets of interviews. The oldest interviews are dropped as newer ones are added, providing a dynamic view of changes in voters' preferences and perceptions. The news media undertake tracking polls as part of their election coverage. The Gallup/CNN/*USA Today* polls in 2000 were extensive tracking polls of the presidential contest and showed just how close the race was, right up through election day.

On election night, media commentators often "call" a race, declaring one candidate the winner, sometimes as soon as the voting booths in a state close but well before the official vote count has been reported. These predictions are made on the basis of **exit polls,** which are short questionnaires administered to samples of voters in selected precincts after they vote.

exit poll   election-related questions asked of voters right after they vote

Exit polls are expensive to conduct because polling has to be done in person at a number of voting sites and because the media want sufficient samples to enable them to make predictions on every state's races. Consequently, in recent years the media organizations have banded together to share the costs of conducting national exit polls. The data are gathered and distributed to the media by an umbrella organization called the Voter News Service (VNS).[6]

It is important to note that exit polls, like national polls, can be wrong. The biggest challenge, of course, is sample bias. Many people refuse to cooperate in exit polls. The pollsters try to correct for this by "weighting" the sample based on the gender, race, and age characteristics of those who refuse, but such tactics don't always work. Unfortunately, pollsters often know about polling problems only after the fact. For instance, it was the VNS that provided the faulty data that led several networks to prematurely call Florida for Al Gore, and then for George W. Bush, in the 2000 election, causing both the pollsters and the media to establish new standards for their election night behavior.

Polls That Aren't Polls   A number of opinion studies are wrongly presented as polls. More deceptive than helpful, these pseudo-polls range from potentially misleading entertainment to outright fraud. Among them are viewer or listener call-in polls and Internet polls. These polls tell only how a portion of the audience (self-selected in the first place by their choice of a particular media outlet) who care enough to call in or click a mouse (self-selected in the second place by their willingness to expend effort) feel about an issue.

push poll a poll that asks for reactions to hypothetical, often false, information in order to manipulate public opinion

A second and increasingly common kind of pseudo-poll is the **push poll,** which poses as a legitimate information-seeking effort, but which is usually a shady campaign trick to change people's attitudes. Push polls present false information about a candidate, often in a hypothetical form, and ask respondents to react to it. The false information, presented as if true or at least possible, can raise doubts about a candidate and even change a person's opinion about him or her. Such polls are often conducted without any acknowledgment of who is sponsoring them (usually the opponent of the person being asked about) and at the last minute so the candidate cannot rebut the charges being circulated. Legislation against push polling has been introduced in several state legislatures, and the practice has been condemned by the American Association of Political Consultants.[7] There is a real question, however, about whether efforts to regulate push polls can survive a First Amendment test before the Supreme Court.

How Accurate Are Polls?   For many issues, such as attitudes toward the environment or presidential approval, we have no objective measure against which to judge the accuracy of public opinion polls. With elections, however, polls do make predictions, and we can tell by the vote count whether the polls are correct.

The record of the polls is, in general, quite good. For example, all of the major polls have predicted the winner of presidential elections correctly since 1980. They are not correct to the percentage point, nor would we expect them to be, given the known levels of sampling error, preelection momentum shifts, and the usual 15 percent of voters who claim to remain "undecided" up to the last minute. Polls taken closer to election day typically become more accurate as they catch more of the late deciders.[8] Even in the unusually close 2000 presidential election, most of the polls did a fairly good job of predicting the tightness of the race, although none could have foretold the contested outcome.

CONSIDER THE SOURCE

How to Be a Critical Poll Watcher

In the heat of the Clinton impeachment hearings, angry conservative Republicans could not believe the polls: over 65 percent of Americans still approved of the job the president was doing and did not want to see him removed from office. Their conclusion? The polls were simply wrong. "The polls are targeted to get a certain answer," said one Floridian. "There are even T-shirts in South Florida that say 'I haven't been polled.'"[1]

Do we need to know people personally who have been polled in order to trust poll results? Of course not. But there are lots of polls out there, not only those done carefully and responsibly by reputable polling organizations but also polls done for marketing and overtly political purposes—polls with an agenda, we might say. How are we, as good scholars and citizens, to know which results are reliable indications of what the public thinks and which are not? One thing we can do is bring our critical thinking skills to bear by asking some questions about the polls reported in the media. Try these.[2]

1. **Who is the poll's sponsor?** Even if the poll was conducted by a professional polling company, it may still have been commissioned on behalf of a candidate or company. Does the sponsor have an agenda? How might that agenda influence the poll, the question wording, or the sponsor's interpretation of events?

2. **Is the sample representative?** That is, were proper sampling techniques followed? What is the margin of error?

3. **From what population was the sample taken?** There is a big difference, for instance, between the preference of the *general public* for a presidential candidate and the preference of *likely voters,* especially if one is interested in predicting the election's outcome. Read the fine print. Sometimes a polling organization will weight responses according to the likelihood that the respondent will

actually vote in order to come up with a better prediction of the election result. Some polls survey only the members of one party, the readers of a particular magazine, or people of a certain age, depending on the information they are seeking to discover. Be sure the sample is not self-selected. Always check the population being sampled, and do not assume it is the general public.

4. **How are the questions worded?** Are loaded, problematic, or vague terms used? Could the questions be confusing to the average citizen? Are the questions available with the poll results? If not, why not? Do the questions seem to lead you to respond one way or the other? Do they oversimplify issues or complicate them? If the survey claims to have detected change over time, be sure the same questions were used consistently. All these things could change the way people respond.

5. **Are the survey topics ones that people are likely to have information and opinions about?** Respondents rarely admit that they don't know how to answer a question, so responses on obscure or technical topics are likely to be more suspect than others.

6. **What is the poll's response rate?** A lot of "don't knows," "no opinions," or refusals to answer can have a decided effect on the results.

7. **If the poll results differ from those in other polls, ask why.** Don't necessarily assume that public opinion has changed. What about this poll might have caused the discrepancy?

8. **What do the results mean?** Who is doing the interpreting? What are that person's motives? For instance, pollsters who work for the Democratic Party will have an interpretation of the results that is favorable to Democrats, and a Republican interpretation will favor Republicans. Try interpreting the results yourself.

[1]Melinda Henneberger, "Where G.O.P. Gathers, Frustration Does Too," *New York Times,* 1 February 1999, 3 (web version).

[2]Some of these questions are based in part on similar advice given to poll watchers in Herbert Asher, *Polling and the Public: What Every Citizen Should Know,* 3rd ed. (Washington, D.C.: Congressional Quarterly Press, 1995), 164–168.

WHO, WHAT, HOW   Citizens, politicians and their staffs, the media, and professional polling organizations are all interested in the business of measuring and tracking public opinion.

WHO are the actors?	WHAT do they want?	HOW do they get it?
Citizens	• Accurate information • Sense of where other Americans stand on the issues	• Media polls and stories based on polls
Politicians and their staffs	• Information on what voters want • Information on campaign progress	• Direct contact with constituents • Public opinion polls • Tracking polls
Media organizations	• Accurate information for reporting purposes • Wider audiences	• Public opinion polls • Tracking polls • Polls that seek to entertain
Professional pollsters	• Accurate results for clients	• Scientific polling techniques

Citizen Values: How Do We Measure Up?

At the beginning of this chapter, we reminded you of the two competing visions of citizenship in America: (1) the ideal democratic citizen, who is attentive and informed, holds reasoned and stable opinions, is tolerant, and participates in politics; and (2) the apolitical, self-interested actor, who does not meet this ideal. As we might expect, our behavior falls somewhere in between the two. For instance, some citizens tune out political news but are tolerant of others and vote regularly. Many activist citizens are informed, opinionated, and participatory but are intolerant of others' views, which can make the give-and-take of democratic politics difficult. Here we look at how we measure up on the key dimensions of political knowledge, ideological consistency, tolerance, and political participation.

Political Knowledge

The ideal democratic citizen understands how government works, who the main actors are, and what major principles underlie the operation of the political system. Public opinion pollsters periodically take readings on what the public actually knows about politics, and the conclusion is always the same: Americans are not very well informed about their political system.[9] For instance, while virtually everyone (99 percent of Americans) can name the president, knowledge falls sharply for less central offices.[10] Only about one-quarter of the public can name both senators of their state, and only 8 percent can name the Supreme Court chief justice. American citizens have a reasonable understanding of the most prominent aspects of the government system and the most visible leaders, but they are ignorant about other central actors and key principles of American political life.

Ideology

Ideologies are the sets of ideas about politics, the economy, and society that help us deal with the political world. They provide citizens with an organizational framework for analyzing the political world and directing their actions. In Chapter 1, we pointed out that for some people, liberalism and conservatism represent fundamental philosophical positions, but few of us walk around with whole political philosophies in our heads. For many Americans today, liberalism stands for faith in government action and social tolerance, conservatism for the belief that government should be limited and that its policies should emphasize "family values." A whole host of other issue positions follow from these central tenets.

To determine people's political ideologies, pollsters ask their respondents to "self-identify"—that is, to place themselves on a liberal-conservative scale. In the United States for the past thirty years, there have been more self-identified conservatives than liberals, but more people call themselves moderate than either liberal or conservative. Over this time period, the percentage of liberals has declined modestly, while the number of self-proclaimed moderates has increased.[11] More than one-fifth of Americans, when given the option, say that they do not know where or how to locate themselves ideologically.[12] Although it is possible, and in fact logical, to be liberal on some issues and conservative on others, scholars have found that the most politically informed and active citizens tend to be liberal on most issues or conservative on most issues.[13] Such ideological consistency fits with the reasoned and stable opinion holding of the ideal democratic citizen and is comparatively rare among the American public.

Tolerance

A key democratic value is tolerance. In a democracy, with many people jockeying for position and many competing visions of the common good, tolerance for ideas different from one's own and respect for the rights of others are the oil that keeps the demo-

Freedom Isn't Always Pretty
A Ku Klux Klan rally in Gainesville, Georgia, sparked a counterdemonstration by residents who did not want their community associated with KKK views. Extending First Amendment rights to all groups regardless of belief is a necessary cost of living in a democracy.

cratic machinery running smoothly. Tolerance is also a prerequisite for compromise—an essential component of politics generally and democratic politics particularly.

How do Americans measure up on the important democratic requirement of respect for others' rights? The record is mixed. As we saw in Chapters 4 and 5, America has a history of denying basic civil rights to some groups, but clearly tolerance is on the increase since the civil rights movement of the 1960s. Small pockets of intolerance persist, primarily among such extremist groups as those who advocate violence against doctors who perform abortions, the burning of black churches in the South, or terrorist acts like the Oklahoma City bombing in 1995. Such extremism, however, is the exception rather than the rule in contemporary American politics.

In terms of general principles, almost all Americans support the values of freedom of speech, religion, and political equality. For instance, 90 percent of respondents told researchers that they believed in "free speech for all, no matter what their views might be." However, when citizens are asked to apply these principles to particular situations in which specific groups have to be tolerated (especially unpopular groups

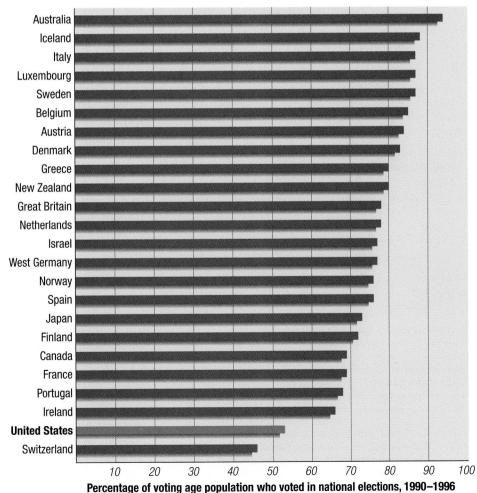

Figure 10.2 Comparison of Voter Turnout Among Industrialized Nations

Source: Data from Russell Dalton, *Citizen Politics,* 2nd Ed., Chatham House, 1996.

Percentage of voting age population who voted in national elections, 1990–1996

like the American Nazi Party preaching race hatred or atheists preaching against God and religion), the levels of political tolerance drop dramatically.[14]

In studies of political tolerance, the least politically tolerant are consistently the less educated and less politically sophisticated. For example, one study found that on a civil liberties scale designed to measure overall support for First Amendment rights, only 24 percent of high school graduates earned high scores, compared with 52 percent of college graduates.[15]

Many such findings have led some observers to argue that elites are the protectors of our democratic values. Critics of this theory, however, say that educated people simply know what the politically correct responses to polls are and so can hide their intolerance better. In practice, the mass public's record has not been bad, and some of the worst offenses of intolerance in our history, from slavery to the incarceration of Japanese Americans during World War II, have been led by elites, not the mass public. Nevertheless, the weight of the evidence does indicate that democratic political tolerance increases with education.

Participation

One of the most consistent criticisms of Americans by those concerned with the democratic health of the nation is that we do not participate enough. And indeed, as participation is usually measured, the critics are right. Figure 10.2 shows that the United States ranks next to last among industrialized nations in voter turnout for national elections. Explanations for low voter turnout include the failure of parties to work to mobilize turnout and obstacles to participation, such as restrictive registration laws, limited voting hours, and the frequency of elections.

Political participation in the United States is also unusual in other ways. For example, unlike in many European countries, political participation in the United States is quite highly correlated with education and measures of socioeconomic achievement. This means that there is a much higher class bias to political participation in the United States, with greater portions of the middle and upper classes participating compared with the working and lower classes.[16] Table 10.1 shows that turnout

Table 10.1
Percent Reporting Voting in the 1992 and 1996 Presidential Elections

	1992	1996
Total[a]	61.3%	54.2%
18 to 20 years old	38.5	31.2
21 to 24 years old	45.7	33.4
25 to 44 years old	58.3	49.2
45 to 64 years old	70.0	64.4
65 years old and over	70.1	67.0
Male	60.2	52.8
Female	62.3	55.5
White	63.6	56.0
Black	54.0	50.6
Hispanic[b]	28.9	26.7
School years completed		
8 years or less	35.1	29.9
High school:		
1 to 3 years[c]	41.2	33.8
4 years[d]	57.5	49.1
College:		
1 to 3 years[e]	68.7	60.5
4 years or more[f]	81.0	72.6
Employed	63.8	55.2
Unemployed	46.2	37.2
Not in labor force	58.7	54.1

[a]Includes other races not shown separately.
[b]Hispanic persons may be of any race.
[c]Represents those who completed grades 9–12 but have no high school diploma.
[d]High school graduate.
[e]Some college or associate's degree.
[f]Bachelor's or advanced degree.

Source: U.S. Bureau of the Census, Current Population Reports, P20-453 and P20-466; and unpublished data: http://www.census.gov/mp/www/pub/pop/mspop.html#CPR; Roll Call OnLine, "The Turnout File: Voting and Registration, 1992–1996."

varies greatly with education, employment status, race, and age. In part because of lower education levels, minorities have lower participation rates than whites.

WHO, WHAT, HOW In a nation that claims to be ruled by the people, all American citizens have a stake in ensuring that "the people" are as close to being public-spirited, ideal democratic citizens as they can be.

WHO are the actors?	WHAT do they want?	HOW do they get it?
American citizens	• Civility in public life • Rule by ideal democratic citizens • Survival of democratic system	• Political education • Consistent ideology • Tolerance • Political participation

What Influences Our Opinions About Politics?

So far, we have learned that many, but by no means all, Americans exhibit the characteristics of our so-called ideal democratic citizen, and we have discovered that the traits of ideal citizenship are not distributed equally across the population. In this section, we look at several sources of our opinions about politics: political socialization, economic self-interest, religion, age, race, gender, and geographic region. All of these things affect the way we come to see the political world, what we believe we have at stake in the political process, and the kind of citizenship we practice.

Political Socialization: Learning the Rules of the Game

Democracies, and indeed all political systems, depend for their survival on each new generation picking up the values and allegiances of previous generations—beliefs in the legitimacy of the political system and its leaders, along with a willingness to obey the laws and the commands of those leaders. You can well imagine the chaos that would result if each new generation of citizens, freshly arrived at adulthood, had to be convinced from scratch to respect the system and obey its laws. In fact, that doesn't happen, because we all learn from the cradle to value and support our political system, which is why the children in Saddam Hussein's Iraq support their leaders as surely as the children of the United States support theirs. The process by which we learn our political orientations and allegiances is called **political socialization.**

political socialization
the process by which we learn our political orientations and allegiances

Political socialization works through a variety of agents. Chief among these is the family, which has a tremendous opportunity to influence the political development of children. Preschool-age children are highly receptive to messages from parents and older siblings, and learning about government begins at an early age. Studies show that the greatest impact of the family is on party identification. Children tend to choose the same political party as their parents.[17] The family has a weaker effect on attitudes about social and political issues such as race relations and welfare.[18]

Little Patriots
*Early political social-
ization can happen
unintentionally. Par-
ents take youngsters
to parades to enjoy
the music and the
colorful pageantry.
Once there, children
begin to develop an
emotional response
to political celebra-
tions (like the Fourth
of July) and national
symbols (like the
American flag).*

Schools, where many children begin their day with the Pledge of Allegiance and where an emphasis is placed on getting along with the group, are also important agents of political learning and the development of citizen orientations. Most school districts include as part of their explicit missions that the schools should foster good citizenship,[19] and many require the teaching of American government or civics.

Churches, neighborhoods, and workplaces can be central in the development of political beliefs. This can be traced in part to the ways people select themselves into groups, but beliefs are reinforced by social contacts. The processes of talking, working, and worshiping together lead people to see the world similarly.[20] Peer groups in general have a lot of influence on individuals' social and political attitudes through the simple and familiar process of peer pressure. Most people want to be like their fellows, and few of us like to stand out as different.

The major political and social events we live through can also have a profound impact on our political orientations. Some examples include the New Deal realignment that came out of the Great Depression, the political optimism following World War II and the prosperity of the 1950s, the political activism surrounding the civil rights movement and the unpopular Vietnam War in the 1960s and 1970s, and the drop in political trust that resulted from the Watergate scandal and the resignation of President Richard Nixon.[21]

Sources of Divisions in Public Opinion

Political socialization produces a citizenry that largely agrees with the rules of the game and accepts the outcomes of the national political process as legitimate. That does not mean, however, that we are a nation in agreement on most or even very many things. There is a considerable range of disagreement in the policy preferences of Americans, and those disagreements stem in part from citizens' interests, education, age, race, gender, and religion—even the area of the country in which they live.

Self-Interest   People's political preferences often come from an assessment of what is best for them economically, from asking "What's in it for me?" So, for instance, as Figure 10.3 shows, the wealthy are more likely to say that their taxes are too high or that too much money is spent on programs for the poor, while the poor are more likely to say the opposite. These patterns are only tendencies, however. Some wealthy people favor the redistribution of wealth and more spending on welfare; some people living in poverty oppose these policies. Even on these straightforward economic questions, other factors are at work.

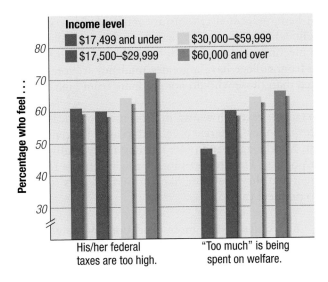

Figure 10.3
Attitudes Toward Taxes and Welfare Spending by Income
Source: Data from General Social Survey, 1990–1996.

Education   As we suggested earlier in our discussion of the ideal democratic citizen, a number of political orientations change as a person attains more education. Researchers have found that political tolerance, knowledge of democratic principles, and knowledge of current political facts increase with higher levels of education.[22] In

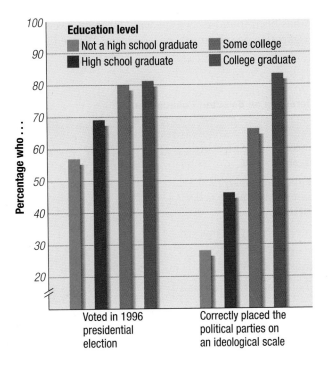

Figure 10.4
The Effect of Education on Voter Turnout and Political Knowledge
Source: Data from National Election Study, 1996.

addition, better-educated citizens are more likely to vote, be attentive to politics, know political leaders, and participate in other, demanding political activities like going to meetings and working for candidates. Figure 10.4 shows that those who graduate from college have a greater tendency to vote and are more politically so-phisticated than those who do not graduate from high school.[23]

Age   Extensive research shows that on most political issues, there are only small differences in policy preferences related to age,[24] except with respect to political en-gagement. Middle-aged and older citizens are typically more attentive to and more active in politics. They report more frequent efforts to persuade others, they vote more often, and they are more likely to write letters to public officials and to con-tribute to political campaigns.

Gender   As women gained more education and entered the work force in greater numbers, they also increased their level of participation in politics. Whereas in the 1950s women trailed men in voter turnout by more than 12 percent, by 1996 women voted at slightly higher rates than men (see Table 10.1). Interestingly, in the last quarter of the twentieth century, as men and women approached equality in their levels of electoral participation, their attitudes on issues diverged. This ten-dency for men and women to take different issue positions or to evaluate political figures differently is called the **gender gap.** In almost all cases, it means that women are more liberal than men. The ideological stances of women overall have not changed significantly since the 1970s, but those of men have shifted steadily, as more call themselves conservatives. The gap is substantial (10 percent or larger) on the death penalty and spending on space exploration (see Table 10.2). In general, the gender gap has been found to be especially large on issues that deal with violence.[25] The gender gap also has electoral consequences. Women are more likely than men to

gender gap
the tendency of men and women to differ in their political views on some issues

Table 10.2
Gender Differences on Selected Political Items

Item	Men	Women	Gap*
Favor women's right to an abortion for any reason	41%	38%	−3%
Strongly agree that employers should hire and promote women to make up for past discrimination	54	59	5
Favor the death penalty for murder	81	71	10
Say government spends "too much" on space exploration	42	57	15
Voted for Bill Clinton for president, 1996	39	51	12

*A positive gender gap mirrors the expectation of a more liberal response among women. A negative gender gap indicates that the difference is contrary to the expectation of a more liberal response among women.

Source: General Social Survey, 1990–1996; National Election Study, 1996.

vote for Democratic candidates. In fact, had it not been for women voters, President Bill Clinton would have lost the presidency to Senator Robert Dole in 1996.[26]

The differences between men and women might be explained by their different socialization experiences and by the different life situations they face. The impact of one's life situation has recently emerged in what observers are calling the **marriage gap.** This refers to the tendency for different opinions to be expressed by those who are married or widowed versus those who have never been married. "Marrieds" tend toward more traditional and conservative values; "never marrieds" tend to have a more liberal perspective. The "never marrieds" are now sufficiently numerous that in many localities, they constitute an important group that politicians must heed in deciding which issues to support.

marriage gap
the tendency for married people to hold different political opinions than people who have never been married

Race   Race has been a perennial cleavage in American politics. Only in recent decades have blacks achieved the same political rights as the white majority, and yet disparity in income between whites and blacks continues. Differences in opinion follow. For instance, African Americans are more favorable than whites to the idea of spending federal money to improve the condition of blacks. On issues of economic policy and race in general, African Americans also are substantially more liberal than whites. However, on social issues like abortion and prayer in schools, the racial differences are more muted.

The root of the differences in the political attitudes of blacks and whites most certainly lies in the racial discrimination historically experienced by African Americans. Blacks tend to see much higher levels of discrimination and racial bias in the criminal justice system, in education, and in the job market. There is undeniably a very large gulf between the races in their perceptions about the continuing frequency and severity of racial discrimination.[27]

Reflecting the very different stands on racial and economic issues the parties have taken, African Americans are the most solidly Democratic group in terms of both party identification and voting. Interestingly, as income and other status indicators rise for whites, they become more conservative and Republican. This does not happen among African Americans. Better-educated and higher-income blacks actually have a stronger racial identification, which results in distinctly liberal positions on economic and racial issues and solid support for Democratic candidates.[28] In recent years, however, the increasing numbers of black conservatives, exemplified perhaps by Supreme Court justice Clarence Thomas, and opponents of affirmative action, like California Board of Regents member Ward Connerly, show that the assumptions once made about African Americans and the Democratic Party may be changing.

Religion   Following the New Deal realignment, there were major political differences in the preferences of religious groups, with nonsouthern Protestants being predominantly Republican, and Catholics and Jews tending to be Democrats and to call themselves liberals. Over the years, those differences have softened quite a bit, but today Catholics are still more Democratic and liberal than Protestants, and Jews are even more so (see Figure 10.5).

Specific religious affiliations may no longer be the most important religious cleavage for understanding citizen opinions on social issues. Since the 1970s, a new

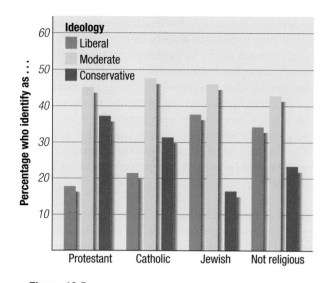

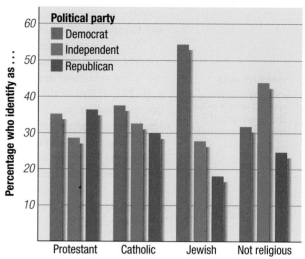

**Figure 10.5
Ideological and
Party Identification
by Major Religious
Denomination**
Source: Data from CBS/
New York Times Polls.

political distinction has emerged between those who say that traditional religion plays a central role in their lives and those who say that it is less important. In this alignment, those who adhere to traditional religious beliefs and practices tend to take conservative positions on an array of social issues; those who may be called "seculars" take more liberal positions. This is suggested in Figure 10.5: among those who say they are not religious, Democrats outnumber Republicans and liberals outnumber conservatives.

Geographic Region   Where we live matters in terms of our political beliefs. People in the Farm Belt talk about different things than do New Englanders. Southerners appreciate subtle assumptions that are not shared by plains dwellers. Politicians

**Table 10.3
Where We Live Makes a Difference: Size of Place and Public Opinion**

	Central Cities	Suburbs	Other Urban	Rural
Party identification				
Democratic	48	35	38	37
Republican	20	28	27	29
Ideology				
Liberal	35	27	23	21
Conservative	36	36	41	43
Policy (percent taking liberal response)				
Affirmative action for blacks	21	16	14	19
Spending on education	69	63	61	53
Spending on the environment	67	63	58	51
Allowing homosexuals to make public speeches	79	82	71	54
Permit abortions if a woman is too poor to support additional children	53	55	44	37

Source: General Social Survey, 1990–1996. For party identification and ideology, the middle categories—Independent and Moderate—have been omitted.

who come from these areas represent people with different preferences, and much of the politics in Congress is about being responsive to different geography-based opinions.[29] Our opinions are affected not only by geographic region but also by whether we live in the city, the suburbs, or the country. For instance, big-city dwellers tend to be more liberal in their policy preferences and more Democratic in their political preferences (see Table 10.3).

WHO, WHAT, HOW Political socialization helps to fuel and maintain the political system by transferring fundamental democratic values from one generation to the next. More specific values come from demographic characteristics—age, race, and gender—and from our life experiences—education, religious affiliation, and where we live.

WHO are the actors?	WHAT do they want?	HOW do they get it?
American citizens	• Political stability and continuity • Opinions that represent their interests and circumstances	• Political socialization • Economic self-interest • Race, gender, age, education, religion, geographic region

Citizenship and Public Opinion

We have seen ample evidence that although politicians may act as if citizens are informed and attentive, many citizens do not measure up to the ideal we defined. In fact, only some Americans live up to our model of good citizenship, and those who do often belong disproportionately to the ranks of the well-educated, the well-off, and the older portions of the population. This disparity between our ideal citizen and reality raises some provocative questions about the relationship between citizens, public opinion, and democracy. Were the founders right to limit the influence of the masses on government? Do we want less informed and coherent opinions represented in politics? Can democracy survive if it is run only by an educated elite?

Earlier in this chapter, we suggested that all would not be lost for American democracy if only some of us turned out to be ideal citizens, and that it was possible to argue that although Americans as individuals might not fit the ideal, Americans as a group might behave as that ideal would predict. How is such a trick possible? The argument goes like this.

It may not be rational for all people to be deeply immersed in the minutiae of day-to-day politics. Our jobs, families, hobbies, and other interests leave us little time for in-depth study of political issues, and unless we get tremendous satisfaction from keeping up with politics (and some of us certainly do), it might be rational for us to leave the political information gathering to others. Social scientists call this idea **rational ignorance.**

rational ignorance the state of being uninformed about politics because of the cost in time and energy

This does not mean that we are condemned to make only ignorant or mistaken political decisions. Citizens are generally pretty smart. In fact, studies show that voters can behave much more intelligently than we could ever guess from their answers to surveys about politics. A great many of us use shortcuts to getting political information that serve us quite well, in the sense that they help us make the same decisions we might have made had we invested considerable time and energy in collecting that political information ourselves.

Shortcuts to Political Knowledge

on-line processing
the ability to receive and evaluate information as events happen, allowing us to remember our evaluation even if we have forgotten the specific events that caused it

two-step flow of information
the process by which citizens take their political cues from more well-informed opinion leaders

opinion leaders
people who know more about certain topics than we do and whose advice we trust, seek out, and follow

One shortcut is the **on-line processing** of information.[30] (On-line here does not refer to time spent on the Internet, as you will see.) Many of the evaluations we make of people, places, and things in our lives (including political figures and ideas) are made on the fly. We assemble impressions and reactions while we are busy leading our lives. When queried, we might not be able to explain why we like or dislike a thing or a person, and we might sound quite ignorant in the sense of not seeming to have reasons for our beliefs. But we do have reasons, and they may make a good deal of sense, even if we can't identify what they are.

A second important mental shortcut that most of us use is the **two-step flow of information.** Politicians and the media send out massive amounts of information. We can absorb only a fraction of it, and even then it is sometimes hard to know how to interpret it. In these circumstances, we tend to rely on **opinion leaders,** who are more or less like ourselves but who know more about the subject than we do.[31] Opinion leaders and followers can be identified in all sorts of realms besides politics. When we make an important purchase, say a computer or car, most of us do not research all the scientific data and technical specifications. We ask people who are like us, who we think should know, and whom we can trust. We compile their advice, consult our own intuition, and buy. The result is that we get pretty close to making an optimal purchase without having become experts ourselves. The two-step flow allows us to behave as though we were very well informed without requiring us to expend all the resources that actually being informed entails.

The Rational Electorate

Politicians deal with citizens mostly in groups and only rarely as individuals. Elected officials think about constituents as whole electorates ("the people of the great state of Texas") or as members of groups (women, environmentalists, developers, workers, and so forth). Groups, it turns out, appear to be better behaved, more rational, and better informed than the individuals who make up the group, precisely because of the sorts of shortcuts we discussed in the previous section. This doesn't seem to make sense, so perhaps a nonpolitical example will clarify what we mean.

Consider the behavior of fans at a football game. People seem to cheer at the appropriate times; they know pretty much when to boo the referees; they oooh and aaaah more or less in unison. We would say that the crowd understands the game and participates effectively in it. However, what do the individual spectators know? If we were to do a football survey, we might ask about the players' names, the teams' win-loss records, the different offensive and defensive positions, the meaning of the referees' signals, and so forth. Some fans would do well, but many would probably get only a few questions right. From the survey, we might conclude that many people in this crowd do not know football at all. But because they take their cues from others, following the behavior of those who cheer for the same team, they can act as if they know what they are doing. Despite its share of football-ignorant individuals, in the aggregate—that is, as a group—the crowd acts remarkably football-intelligent.

Singularly, if we were to ask people when national elections are held, for instance, only a handful would be able to say it is the Tuesday after the first Monday in November of evenly numbered years. Some people would guess that they occur in November, others might say in the fall sometime, and others would admit they don't know. Based on the level of individual ignorance in this matter, it would be surprising if many people ever voted at all, since you can't vote if you don't know when election day is. But somehow, as a group, the electorate sorts it out, and almost everyone who is registered and wants to vote finds his or her way to the polling booth on the right day. By using shortcuts and taking cues from others, the electorate behaves just as if it knew all along when the election was. More substantively, even though many voters may be confused about which candidates stand where on specific issues, groups of voters do a great job of sorting out which party or candidate best represents their interests. Members of the religious right vote for Republicans, and members of labor unions vote for Democrats, for instance. Even though there are undoubtedly quite a few confused voters in the electorate in any particular election, they tend to cancel each other out in the larger scheme of things. As a whole, from the politician's point of view, the electorate appears to be responsive to issues and quite rational in evaluating an incumbent's performance in office.[32]

So even though citizens do not spend a lot of time learning about politics, politicians are smart to assume that the electorate is attentive and informed. In fact, this is precisely what most of them do. For example, studies have shown that state legislators vote in accordance with the ideological preferences of their citizens, just as if the citizens were instructing them on their wishes.[33] The states with the most liberal citizens—for example, New York, Massachusetts, and California—have the most liberal policies. And the most conservative states, those in the South and the Rocky Mountains, have the most conservative policies. Other studies confirm a similar pattern in national elections.[34]

We began this chapter by asking why polling is routinely disparaged by politicians. Why don't we have more confidence in being ruled by public opinion? After all, in a democracy where the people's will is supposed to weigh heavily with our elected officials, we have uncovered some conflicting evidence. Many Americans do not model the characteristics of the ideal democratic citizen, but remember that the United States has two traditions of citizenship—one much more apolitical and self-interested than the public-spirited ideal. The reality in America is that the ideal citizen marches side by side with the more self-interested citizen, who, faced with many demands, does not put politics ahead of other daily responsibilities. But we have also argued that there are mechanisms and shortcuts that allow even some of the more apolitical and self-interested citizens to cast intelligent votes and to have their views represented in public policy. This tells us that at least one element of democracy—responsiveness of policies to public preferences—is in good working order.

We should not forget that political influence goes hand in hand with opinion formation. Those who are opinion leaders have much more relative clout than their more passive followers. And opinion leaders are not distributed equally throughout

Points of Access

- If you are selected, participate in a survey or a poll.
- Respond to an Internet poll and compare the results to a scientific poll.
- Work as a poll taker for the local party of your choice.

the population. They are drawn predominantly from the ranks of the well-educated and the well-off. Similarly, even though the shortcuts we have discussed allow many people to vote intelligently without taking the time to make a personally informed decision, many people never vote at all. Voters are also drawn from the more privileged ranks of American society. The poor, the young, and minorities—all the groups who are underrepresented at the voting booth—are also underrepresented in policymaking. There cannot help but be biases in such a system.

WHAT'S AT STAKE REVISITED

We have argued in this chapter that public opinion is important in policymaking and that politicians respond to it in a variety of ways. But what would happen if we more or less bypassed elected officials altogether and allowed people to participate directly in national lawmaking through the use of national referenda or initiatives? What is at stake in rule by public opinion?

On the one hand, voters would seem to have something real to gain in such lawmaking. It would give new meaning to government "by the people," and decisions would have more legitimacy with the public. Certainly, it would be harder to point the finger at Washington as responsible for bad laws. In addition, as has been the case in states with initiatives, citizens might succeed in getting legislation passed that legislators themselves refuse to vote for. Prime examples are term limits and balanced-budget amendments. Term limits would cut short many congressional careers, and balanced-budget amendments would force politicians to make hard choices about taxing and spending cuts that they would prefer to avoid.

On the other hand, voters might actually be worse off. While policies like the two mentioned above clearly threaten the jobs of politicians, they also carry unintended consequences that might not be very good for the nation as a whole. Who should decide—politicians who make a career out of understanding government, or people who pay little attention to politics and current events and who vote from instinct and outrage? Politicians who have a vested interest in keeping their jobs, or people who can provide a check on political greed and self-interest? The answer changes with the way you phrase the question, but the public might well suffer if left to its own devices on questions of policy it does not thoroughly understand.

There is no doubt that the writers of the Constitution, with their limited faith in the people, would have rejected such referenda wholeheartedly. Not only would having referenda bring government closer to the people, but it would wreak havoc with the system of separation of powers and checks and balances. Popular opinion was supposed to be checked by the House and the Senate, which were in turn to be checked by the other two branches of government. Bringing public opinion to the fore would upset this delicate balance.

In addition, many scholars warn that the hallmark of democracy is not just hearing what the people want but also allowing the people to discuss and deliberate over their political choices. Home-computer voting or trips to the ballot box do not necessarily permit such key interaction.[35] Majority rule without the tempering influence of debate and discussion can quickly deteriorate into majority tyranny, with a sacrifice of minority rights.

The flip side may also be true. Since voters tend to be those who care more intensely about political issues, supporters of national referenda also leave themselves open to the opposite of majority tyranny: the tyranny of an intense minority who care enough to campaign and vote against an issue that a majority prefer, but only tepidly. Similarly, as we will see in Chapter 11, special-interest groups with sufficient resources can wage public relations campaigns and gain support for policies benefiting a minority that would not be able to pass muster with the legislature.

Finally, there are political stakes for politicians in such a reform. First, as we have already seen, the passage of laws they would not have supported would make it harder for politicians to get things done. But on the positive side, national referenda would allow politicians to avoid taking the heat for decisions that are bound to be intensely unpopular with some segment of the population. One of the reasons national referenda are often used in other countries is to diffuse the political consequences for leaders of unpopular or controversial decisions.

Clearly, direct democracy at the national level would have a major impact on American politics, but it is not clear who the winners and losers would be, or even if there would be any consistent winners. The new rules would benefit different groups at different times. The American people believe that they would enjoy the power, and various groups are confident that they would profit. But in the long run, the public interest might be damaged in terms of the quality of American democracy and the protections available to minorities. Politicians have very little to gain. If such a reform ever does come about, it will be generated not by the elite, but by public interest groups, special-interest groups, and reformers from outside Washington. ■

key terms

exit poll   280
gender gap   290
marriage gap   291
on-line processing   294
opinion leaders   294
political socialization   287

public opinion   275
public opinion polls   275
push poll   281
rational ignorance   293
sample   278
sample bias   278

sampling error   279
tracking poll   280
two-step flow of
   information   294

summary

■ Although polling is often scorned by politicians and the public alike, Americans believe that public opinion ought to matter in a democracy, and politicians and the media both watch public opinion very closely. Elected officials look for job

security by responding to immediate public desires or by skillfully predicting future requests. The media make large investments in polls, sometimes covering public attitudes on a candidate or issue as a story in itself.

- Most politicians pay attention to their own informal sampling of opinion, but they also have come to rely on professional polling. Such polls are based on scientific polling methods that focus on getting a good sample and asking questions that yield valid results.

- There are two competing visions of citizenship in America. One is the ideal democratic citizen, who demonstrates political knowledge, possesses an ideology (usually liberal or conservative), tolerates different ideas, and votes consistently. The other is the apolitical, self-interested citizen. Most Americans fall somewhere between these extremes, but factors such as increased age, education, and socioeconomic status seem to contribute to behavior that is closer to the ideal.

- We get our political opinions through the process of political socialization—the transfer of fundamental democratic values from one generation to the next. But our political beliefs are also affected by demographic characteristics, such as race and gender, and by life experiences, such as education and religion.

- Even though Americans do not measure up to the ideal of the democratic citizen, there is much evidence to support the idea that public opinion does play a large role in government policy. Although some citizens may seem apolitical and uninterested, many use rational information shortcuts to make their voting decisions. Policymakers have responded by staying generally responsive to public preferences.

11

What's at Stake?

The Role of Political Parties in a Democracy
• What Are Parties?
• The Responsible Party Model

The American Party System
• The History of Parties in America
• What Do the American Parties Stand For?
• Characteristics of the American Party System
• Undisciplined Parties-in-Government

The Roles, Formation, and Types of Interest Groups
• Roles of Interest Groups
• Why Do Interest Groups Form?
• Types of Interest Groups

Interest Group Politics
• Direct Lobbying
• Indirect Lobbying
• "Astroturf" Political Campaigns and the State of Lobbying Today

Interest Group Resources
• Money
• Leadership
• Membership: Size and Intensity
• Information

Citizenship and Political Groups

What's at Stake Revisited

Parties and Interest Groups

WHAT'S AT STAKE?

In late September 1998, Berkeley, California, software entrepreneurs Wes Boyd and Joan Blades were "angry and disgusted" by the Monica Lewinsky sex scandal and the talk of impeaching President Bill Clinton. Together they spearheaded the formation of a bipartisan group called Censure and Move On, which promoted the "speedy resolution of the Lewinsky sex scandal" by censuring President Clinton for his wrongdoings and avoiding lengthy impeachment hearings.

Like other citizen groups in the past that have formed to influence Congress, Censure and Move On encouraged signing petitions and writing letters to Congress. However, unlike other groups in the past, Censure and Move On used the Internet and the World Wide Web to mobilize hundreds of thousands of citizens. For the price of an $89.50 web site, Censure and Move On was able to gather names via a "cyberpetition" instead of collecting signatures in malls, churches, and other public gathering places. In its first week, it amassed 100,000 signatures on its one-sentence petition: "The Congress must immediately censure President Clinton and move on to pressing issues facing the country." Censure and Move On set up a web site to get the message to Capitol Hill. A concerned citizen needed only to type in his or her name, address, zip code, and comments, and a letter was automatically sent to the e-mail addresses of his or her U.S. representative and senators.

By October 15, 1998, MoveOn.org (Censure and Move On's web site) had delivered more than 250,000 e-mail messages and 20,000 pages of citizen comments to House members and the president. The group also channeled more than 30,000 phone calls to congressional offices. Just as impressive was Censure and Move On's network of more

299

than 2,000 volunteers, in 50 states and 402 congressional districts, dedicated to local campaigns favoring censure of the president.[1]

As the House of Representatives moved toward an impeachment vote, Censure and Move On's activities became more intense. Teaming up with the liberal public interest group People for the American Way and the long-distance telephone provider Working Assets, Censure and Move On set up a toll-free hotline to Congress. By December 15, 1998, more than 94,000 calls had been directed to House members' offices.[2] By Saturday, December 19, 1998, the day the U.S. House of Representatives voted to impeach President Clinton, the effort had yielded more than 450,000 electronic petitioners.

After losing its fight in the House, Censure and Move On immediately began to collect donations for a new cause: removing members of the House who had voted in favor of impeachment. MoveOn.org sent e-mail messages to its more than 450,000 petitioners asking them to contribute to the "We Will Remember" campaign. Its web site stated,

> With disregard for the will of the people, Congress has impeached the President. Impeachment has become a partisan political tool. The President must now face a trial in the Senate, throwing our nation into crisis and uncertainty. To correct this abuse of our Constitutional system, there must be consequences. We are asking you to join us and make the following pledge: In the 2000 election, I will work to defeat Members of Congress who voted for impeachment or removal. I hereby pledge to give contributions to ten congressional campaigns, ($25, $50, $100, $250, $500, $1000) for each campaign.[3]

On December 22, 1998, just three days after the House impeached President Clinton, Censure and Move On had collected $7.7 million in pledges. By February 1999, pledges totaled $13 million and 650,000 volunteer hours.[4] Pollster Bruce Merrill of Arizona State University's Walter Cronkite School of Journalism said, "This is a watershed moment in national politics. For years, people have talked about the potential of the Internet to someday revolutionize political organizing. Based on the efficiency, power, and sheer numbers shown by MoveOn.org, that someday appears to have arrived."[5]

If that day has indeed arrived, what will it mean for American politics? James Madison feared the impact of an easily roused and organized public, and he sought to create a government that would reduce the ability of groups to organize and act. Technology, from printing press to telegraph to telephone to Internet, has made it increasingly easy to overcome Madison's carefully thought-out safeguards. What is at stake for American politics in the ability of the Internet to "revolutionize political organizing"? ∎

The old adage says there is safety in numbers, but more important in politics, there is also power in numbers. In *Federalist* No. 10, James Madison wasn't worried about the odd voter getting antsy and voting for a harebrained candidate or idea. He was concerned that large numbers of voters would come to define themselves as opposed to what he thought was good for the public and would vote for their particular interests. He was worried about the political power of *groups*.

And small wonder. Madison saw what happened under the Articles of Confederation, when individuals banded together to make claims on their government. Since then, we have seen innumerable examples of group power, everything from Republican attempts to restore the South after the Civil War, to the woman suffrage movement, to the National Rifle Association's efforts to limit gun control, to the insurance companies' and medical associations' effective campaign against national health care in 1993. For many Americans, this group action is the meaning of modern democracy. In fact, we saw in earlier chapters that while some people argue that the individual voter in America cannot make a difference, many others believe in **pluralist democracy,** the idea that individuals can only find their political strength in numbers, by joining with other like-minded people to get the representation they want.

pluralist democracy
a theory of democracy that holds that citizen membership in groups is the key to political power

In this chapter, we examine two central kinds of political groups that Americans form: parties and interest groups. Both types of groups form on the basis of common political ideas and goals. The key difference is that political parties seek to elect their members to office in order to control government, and interest groups seek only to influence what government does. Specifically, we look at

- the role of political parties in a democracy

- the American party system

- the various roles interest groups play and the types of interest groups in the U.S. political system

- how interest groups attempt to exert their political influence

- the resources that different interest groups bring to bear in influencing government decisions

The Role of Political Parties in a Democracy

Probably because Madison hoped that political parties would not thrive, parties—unlike Congress, the presidency, the Supreme Court, and even the free press—are not mentioned in the Constitution. As we will see in fact, many of the rules that determine the establishment and role of parties have been created by party members themselves. Although the founding documents of American politics are silent on the place of political parties, keen political observers have long appreciated the fundamental role that parties play in our system of government.[6] According to one scholar, "Political parties created democracy, and . . . democracy is unthinkable save in terms of parties."[7]

What Are Parties?

political party
a group of citizens united by ideology and seeking control of government in order to promote their ideas and policies

Political parties are organizations that seek, under a common banner, to promote their ideas and policies by gaining control of government through the nomination and election of candidates for office. In addition, parties provide support for democratic government in three crucial ways.

1. They provide a linkage between voters and elected officials, helping to tell voters what candidates stand for and providing a way for voters to hold their officials accountable for what they do in office, both individually and collectively.

2. They overcome some of the fragmentation in government that comes from separation of powers and federalism by linking members in all branches and levels of government.

3. They provide an articulate opposition to the ideas and policies of those elected to serve in government. Some citizens and critics may decry the **partisanship,** or taking of political sides, that sometimes seems to be motivated by the possibilities for party gain as much as by principle or public interest. Others, however, see partisanship as providing the necessary antagonistic relationship that keeps politicians honest and allows the best political ideas and policies to emerge.

partisanship loyalty to a political cause or party

To highlight the multiple tasks that parties perform to make democracy work and to make life easier for politicians, political scientists find it useful to divide political parties into three separate components: the party organization, the party-in-government, and the party-in-the-electorate.[8]

party organization the official structure that conducts the political business of parties

Party Organization   The **party organization** is what most people think of as a political party. It represents the system of central committees at the national, state, and local levels. At the top of the Democratic Party organization is the Democratic National Committee. Likewise, the Republican National Committee heads the Republican Party. Underneath these national committees are state-level party committees, and below them are county-level party committees, or county equivalents (see Figure 11.1). The party organization performs the central party function of electioneering. **Electioneering** involves recruiting and nominating candidates, defining policy agendas, and getting candidates elected.

electioneering the process of getting a person elected to public office

- *Candidate recruitment.* Each party's electioneering activities begin months before the general election. The first step is simply finding candidates to run. Fulfilling this responsibility is often difficult because in many instances, the organizations must recruit candidates to run against a current officeholder—the incumbent—and incumbents are hard to beat.

- *Nomination phase.* The nomination phase is a formal process through which the party chooses a candidate for each elective office to be contested that year. Today party primaries, or preliminary elections between members of the same party vying for the party's nomination, are the dominant means of choosing candidates for congressional, statewide, state legislative, and local offices. Some candidates are nominated at a convention. A **nominating convention** is a formal party gathering that is bound by a number of strict rules relating to the selection of voting participants, called *delegates,* and the nomination of candidates. The most prominent conventions are the national presidential nominating conventions for the Democratic and Republican Parties,[9] which are held the summer before the election, after the state presidential primaries. Usually, the presidential nominating convention merely rubber-stamps the primary victor.

nominating convention formal party gathering to choose candidates

- *Defining policy agendas.* After nominating its candidates, one of the main roles of a political party is to develop a policy agenda, which represents policies that a party's candidates agree to promote when campaigning and to pursue when governing. The development of such an agenda involves much politicking and gamesmanship as each faction of the party tries to get its views written into the party platform. Whoever wins control of the party platform has decisive input into how the campaign will proceed.

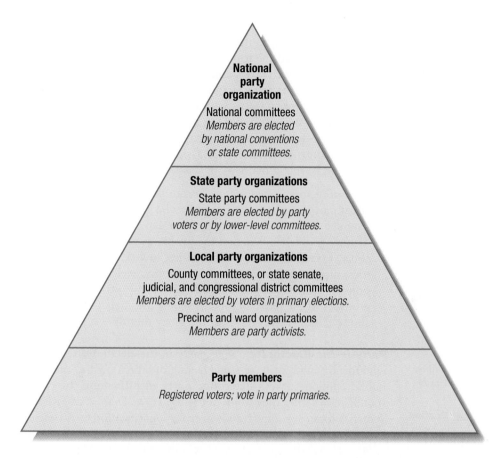

Figure 11.1 Organizational Structure of the Party System

Within the pyramid:

National party organization
National committees
Members are elected by national conventions or state committees.

State party organizations
State party committees
Members are elected by party voters or by lower-level committees.

Local party organizations
County committees, or state senate, judicial, and congressional district committees
Members are elected by voters in primary elections.
Precinct and ward organizations
Members are party activists.

Party members
Registered voters; vote in party primaries.

---

party-in-government members of the party who have been elected to serve in government

governing activities directed toward controlling the distribution of political resources by providing executive/legislative leadership, enacting agendas, mobilizing support, and building coalitions

- *General elections.* In the election phase, the role of the party changes from choosing among competing candidates within the party and developing policy agendas to getting its nominated candidates elected. Traditionally, the party's role here was to "organize and mobilize" voters, but increasingly parties also provide extensive services to candidates, including fundraising, training in campaign tactics, instruction in compliance with election laws, public opinion polling, and professional campaign assistance.[10]

Party-in-Government The **party-in-government** includes all the candidates for national, state, and local office who are elected. A key function of political parties is **governing,** or controlling government by organizing and providing leadership for the legislative and/or executive branches, enacting policy agendas, mobilizing support for party policy, and building coalitions.

- *Controlling government.* When a party "controls" government at the national level and in the states, it means that the party determines who occupies the leadership positions in the branch of government in which it has a majority. Thus when George W. Bush won the presidency in 2000, Bush, and by extension the Republicans, controlled the top leadership positions in the executive branch of government (cabinet secretaries and undersecretaries and the White House staff). When the Republicans won a majority of the U.S. House and Senate contests in 1994, their new majority status won them the right to organize their respective houses of Congress by occupying the major leadership roles. In the Senate and House, this meant selecting the majority leader in the Senate and the Speaker of the House, controlling committee assignments, selecting chairs of legislative committees, and having a majority of seats on each committee.

- *Executing policy agendas and accountability.* Of course, the ultimate goal of a political party is not only to choose who occupies the leadership positions in government but also to execute its policy agenda—the party's solutions to the nation's problems. Whether the problems concern affordable health care, welfare abuse, taxes, distressed communities, low-skill jobs moving to third world countries, illegal immigrants, or the economy, each party represents an alternative vision for how to approach and solve these problems. About two-thirds of the promises of the party that controls the presidency are implemented, compared to about half of the promises of the party that does not control the presidency.[11]

party-in-the-electorate ordinary citizens who identify with the party

party identification voter affiliation with a political party

Party-in-the-Electorate The **party-in-the-electorate** represents ordinary citizens who identify with or have some feeling of attachment to one of the political parties. Public opinion surveys determine **party identification,** or party ID, by asking respondents whether they think of themselves as Democrats, Republicans, or Independents. You can see some trends in party identification over time in Figure 11.2. Party ID declined in the 1960s and 1970s, and even though it rose somewhat in the mid-1990s, it has still not recovered its previous levels. Most voters who identify with one of the political parties "inherit" their party IDs from their parents, as we sug-

**Figure 11.2
Party Identification, 1947–1997**

Source: For 1947, National Opinion Research Center; for all other years, Center for Political Studies National Election Studies.

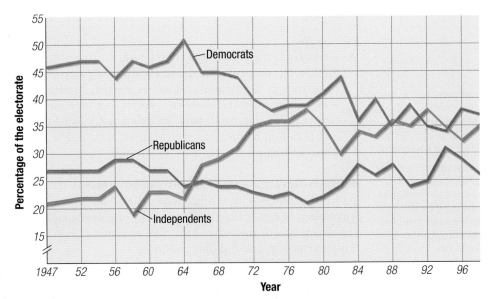

gested in our discussion of political socialization in Chapter 10.[12] Party identifiers generally support the party's basic ideology and policy principles. These principles usually relate to the party's stance on the use of government to solve various economic and social problems.

Although voters do not have a strong formal role to play in the party organization, parties use identifiers as a necessary base of support during elections. In the 2000 election, both George W. Bush and Al Gore won the votes of an overwhelming percentage of those who identified with their respective parties. Capturing one's **party base** is not sufficient to win a national election, however. Since neither party claims a majority of the nation's voters as supporters, successful candidates must reach out to voters who identify themselves as Independents. In 2000 Bush won slightly more support (2 percent) from Independents than did Gore. Keeping the base of the party-in-the-electorate happy is essential, but so is appealing to a broader audience. As we will see, this often puts politicians in the position of having to make tough choices, since these two groups of voters do not always want the same thing.

party base members of a political party who consistently vote for that party's candidates

The Responsible Party Model

responsible party model party government when four conditions are met: clear choice of ideologies, candidates pledged to implement ideas, party held accountable by voters, party control over members

Earlier we said that one of the democratic roles of parties is to provide a link between voters and elected officials, or, to use the terms we just introduced, between the party-in-the-electorate and the party-in-government. There are many ways in which parties can link voters and officials, but for the link to truly enhance democracy—that is, the control of leaders by citizens—certain conditions have to be met. Political scientists call the fulfillment of these conditions the **responsible party model**.[13] Under the responsible party model,

- each party should present a coherent set of programs to the voters, consistent with its ideology and clearly different from the other party's programs

Party Outreach
Although the Democratic and Republican Parties maintain formal organizations in Washington, D.C., and the state capitals, they need widespread support to win elections. Thus both parties reach out to the public with events such as this April 1999 town meeting in St. Louis, sponsored by the Republican National Committee and featuring Senate Majority Leader Trent Lott.

- the candidates for each party should pledge to support their party's platform and to implement their party's programs if elected

- voters should make their choices based on which party's programs most closely reflects their own ideas and hold the parties responsible for unkept promises by voting their members out of office

- each party should exercise control over its elected officials to ensure that party officials are promoting and voting for its programs, thereby providing accountability to voters

The responsible party model proposes that democracy is strengthened when voters are given clear alternatives and hold the parties responsible for keeping their promises. Voters can, of course, hold officials accountable without the assistance of parties, but it takes a good deal more of their time and attention. Furthermore, several political scientists have noted that although individuals can be held accountable for their own actions, many, if not most, government actions are the products of many officials. Political parties give us a way of holding officials accountable for what they do collectively as well as individually.[14]

The responsible party model reflects an ideal party system—one that the American two-party system rarely measures up to in reality (although other countries, notably Great Britain, do come close to the model). For example, even though voters theoretically make decisions based on each party's programs, as we will see in Chapter 13, a host of other factors, such as candidate image or evaluations of economic conditions, also influence voting behavior.[15] In addition, parties themselves do not always behave as the model dictates. For instance, American parties cannot always control candidates who refuse to support their programs. Despite these problems, the responsible party model is valuable because it underscores the importance of voters holding the parties accountable for governing. Even if the responsible party model is not an accurate description of party politics in America, it provides a useful yardstick for understanding the character of the American two-party system.

WHO, WHAT, HOW   Political parties play a crucial role in who gets what in American politics. Not only are they an important "who" themselves, but they are also crucial in making the rules (the "how") and determining "what" is at stake.

WHO are the actors?	WHAT do they want?	HOW do they get it?
Political parties	• Control of government • Promotion of ideas and policy	• Control of nominations, campaigns, and elections • Party-in-government
Politicians	• To win nominations • To win elections • To run government	• Party organization support • Nonparty support
Citizens	• Democratic government	• Political parties

The American Party System

For James Madison, parties were just an organized version of that potentially dangerous political association, the faction. He had hopes that their influence on American politics would be minimal, but scarcely was the ink dry on the Constitution before the founders were organizing themselves into groups to promote their political views. In this section, we look at the history of American parties, examine the question of what the parties stand for today and whether they offer voters a choice, and explore the specific characteristics of the American two-party system.

The History of Parties in America

In the 1790s, a host of disagreements among politicians led Alexander Hamilton and John Adams to organize the Federalists, a group of legislators who supported their views. Later, Thomas Jefferson and James Madison would do the same with the Democratic-Republicans. Over the course of the next decade, these organizations expanded beyond their legislative purposes to include recruiting candidates to run under their party label for both Congress and the presidency. The primary focus, however, was on the party-in-government and not on the voters.[16]

Early Party Organization

In 1828 Martin Van Buren and Andrew Jackson turned the Democratic Party away from a focus on the party-in-government, creating the country's first mass-based party and setting the stage for the development of the voter-oriented party machine. **Party machines** were tightly organized party systems at the state, city, and county levels that kept control of voters by getting them jobs, helping them out financially when necessary, and in fact becoming part of their lives and their communities. This mass organization was built around one principal goal: taking advantage of the expansion of voting rights to all white men (even those without property) to elect more Democratic candidates.[17]

The Jacksonian Democrats enacted a number of party and government reforms designed to enhance the control of party leaders, known as **party bosses,** over candidates, officeholders, and campaigns. During the nomination process, the party bosses would choose the party's candidates for the general election. Winning candidates were expected to hire only other party supporters for government positions and reward only party supporters with government contracts, expanding the range of people with a stake in the party's electoral success. This system of **patronage,** which we discussed in Chapter 8, rewarded faithful party supporters with public offices, jobs, and government contracts and ensured that the party's candidates were loyal to the party or at least to the party bosses.

Because the Democratic Party machine was so effective at getting votes and controlling government, the Whig Party (1830s through 1850s), and later the Republican Party (starting in the mid-1850s), used these same techniques to organize. Party bosses and their party machines were exceptionally strong in urban areas in the East and Midwest. These urban machines, designed to further the interests of the parties themselves, had the important democratic consequence of integrating into the political process the masses of new immigrants coming into the urban centers at the turn

party machine mass-based party system in which parties provided services and resources to voters in exchange for votes

party boss party leader, usually in an urban district, who exercised tight control over electioneering and patronage

patronage a system in which successful party candidates reward supporters with jobs or favors

of the twentieth century. Because parties were so effective at mobilizing voters, the average voter participation rate exceeded 80 percent in most U.S. elections prior to the 1900s.

Party Reform   The strength of these party machines was also their weakness. In many cases, parties would do almost anything to win, including buying votes, mobilizing new immigrants who could not speak English and were not U.S. citizens, and resurrecting dead people to vote. In addition, the whole system of patronage, based on doling out government jobs, contracts, and favors, came under attack by reformers in the early 1900s as representing favoritism and corruption. Political reforms such as **party primaries,** in which the party-in-the-electorate rather than the party bosses chose between competing party candidates for a party's nomination, and civil service reform, under which government jobs were filled on the basis of merit instead of party loyalty, did much to ensure that party machines went the way of the dinosaur.

Party Eras and Party Change   A striking feature of American history is that although we have not had a revolution since 1776, we have changed our political course several times and in rather dramatic ways. One of the many advantages of a democratic form of government is that dramatic changes in policy direction can be effected through the ballot box rather than through bloody revolution. Over the course of two centuries, the two-party system in the United States has been marked by twenty-five- to forty-year periods of relative stability, with one party tending to maintain a majority of congressional seats and controlling the presidency. These periods of stability are called **party eras.** Short periods of large-scale change—peaceful revolutions, as it were, signaled by one major **critical election** in which the majority of people shift their political allegiance from one party to another—mark the end of one party era and the beginning of another. Scholars call such shifts in party dominance a **realignment.** In these realignments, the coalitions of groups supporting the parties change. Although it is not always the case, realignments generally result in parallel changes in government policies, reflecting the policy agenda of each party's new coalition. Realignments have been precipitated by critical events like the Civil War and the Great Depression. The United States has gone through five party eras in its history (see Figure 11.3).

For much of the twentieth century, the United States was in the midst of the fifth party era, a period ushered in by Franklin Roosevelt's New Deal and marked by the congressional domination of the Democratic Party. Most analysts agree that the New Deal coalition supporting the fifth party era has changed, even though there has not been a defining critical election. The dramatic but slow nature of this change can be seen in how the geographic centers of the two parties have moved since the New Deal. We used to be able to talk about the "solid Democratic South," because the southern states, though conservative on many issues, voted Democratic so as not to support the "party of Lincoln." But today the southern states are reliably Republican in presidential elections, and the Democrats' geographic strength lies in the industrial Northeast and Midwest and on the Pacific Coast.

Although these realigning changes have undoubtedly taken place, some analysts believe that we are really in a period of **dealignment,** a dissolving of the old era of

party primary nomination of party candidates by registered party members rather than party bosses

party era extended period of relative political stability in which one party tends to control both the presidency and Congress

critical election an election signaling the significant change in popular allegiance from one party to another

realignment substantial and long-term shift in party allegiance by individuals and groups, usually resulting in a change in policy direction

dealignment a trend among voters to identify themselves as Independents rather than as members of a major party

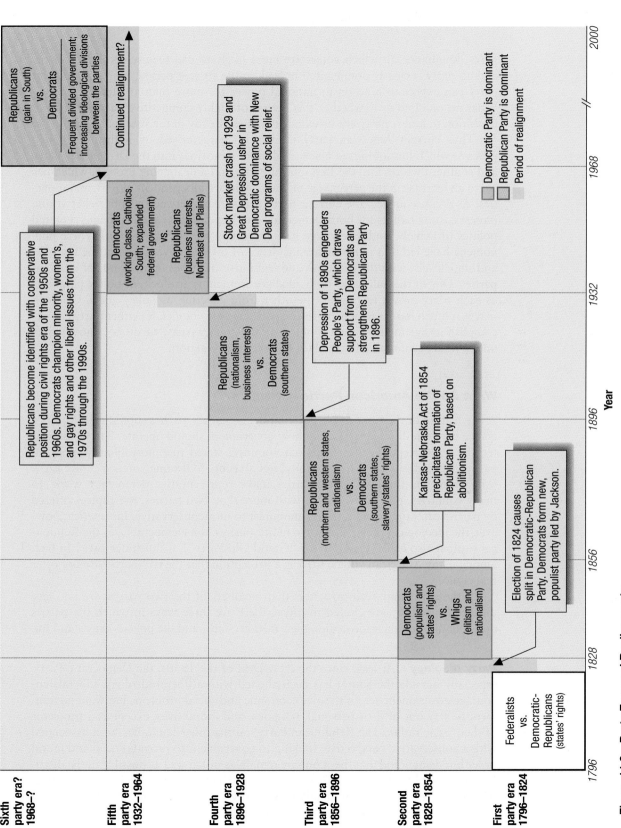

Figure 11.3 Party Eras and Realignments

First party era 1796–1824

Federalists vs. Democratic-Republicans (states' rights)

Election of 1824 causes split in Democratic-Republican Party. Democrats form new, populist party led by Jackson.

Second party era 1828–1854

Democrats (populism and states' rights) vs. Whigs (elitism and nationalism)

Kansas-Nebraska Act of 1854 precipitates formation of Republican Party, based on abolitionism.

Third party era 1856–1896

Republicans (northern and western states, nationalism) vs. Democrats (southern states, slavery/states' rights)

Depression of 1890s engenders People's Party, which draws support from Democrats and strengthens Republican Party in 1896.

Fourth party era 1896–1928

Republicans (nationalism, business interests) vs. Democrats (southern states)

Stock market crash of 1929 and Great Depression usher in Democratic dominance with New Deal programs of social relief.

Fifth party era 1932–1964

Democrats (working class, Catholics, South; expanded federal government) vs. Republicans (business interests, Northeast and Plains)

Republicans become identified with conservative position during civil rights era of the 1950s and 1960s. Democrats champion minority, women's, and gay rights and other liberal issues from the 1970s through the 1990s.

Sixth party era? 1968–?

Republicans (gain in South) vs. Democrats

Frequent divided government; increasing ideological divisions between the parties

Continued realignment?

Year

1796   1828   1856   1896   1932   1968   2000

Democratic Party is dominant

Republican Party is dominant

Period of realignment

party dominance, in which voters are more likely to call themselves Independents and no party is clearly dominant.[18] Indeed, in the current period, it appears that no party can expect to hold on to national power for more than an election or two. What no one knows is whether this period of highly competitive parties is one of transition to a new party era or whether we are already in the sixth party era.

Thus current American party politics is characterized by both a realigning process, which has mobilized blacks and other minorities into the Democratic Party and southern whites into the Republican Party, and a dealigning process, which has led to an increase in the percentage of voters who are independent of both major parties. As a consequence, the current party era is characterized by split-ticket voting (voters casting ballots for both Democrats and Republicans) and candidate-centered politics (in which candidate image is as important as party affiliation). These phenomena have led to a much higher incidence of divided government at the national and state levels, with the executive and legislative branches in the hands of different parties. One of the hallmarks of divided government is gridlock, or policy paralysis, as each party moves to prevent the other from enacting its policy goals. Gridlock makes it much harder to achieve the responsible party model. If neither party can accomplish its agenda because it is blocked by the other party, we do not know which one to hold accountable for the lack of government action.

What Do the American Parties Stand For?

A key feature of the responsible party model is that the parties should offer voters a choice between different visions of how government should operate. Barry Goldwater, the 1964 Republican presidential nominee, stated this more bluntly: political parties, he said, should offer "a choice, not an echo." Offering voters a choice is the primary means through which parties make representative democracy work. In many countries, particularly those with more than two parties, the choices offered by parties can range from radical communist to ultraconservative. In America, however, the ideological range of the two major parties, the Democrats and the Republicans (often also called the GOP for "Grand Old Party"), is much narrower. In fact, among many American voters, there is a perception that the two parties do not offer real choices.

Although it may seem to voters that members of the two parties are not very different once they are elected to office, there are three ways in which the parties are quite distinct: their ideologies, their memberships, and the policies they stand for.

Party Ideology   At least since the New Deal of the 1930s, the Democratic Party, especially outside the South, has been aligned with a liberal ideology. Liberals encourage government action to solve economic and social problems but want government to stay out of their personal, religious, and moral lives, except as a protector of their basic rights. The Republican Party, on the other hand, has been associated with a conservative perspective, looking to government to provide social and moral order but demanding that the economy remain as unfettered as possible in the distribution of material resources. This is not to say that all Democrats are equally liberal or that all Republicans are equally conservative. Each party has its more extreme

Table 11.1
Party Identification and Issue Positions, 1998

	Democrats	Independents	Republicans
Ideological Self-Identification			
Liberal	39%	23%	7%
Moderate	37	48	20
Conservative	21	29	73
Social Spending			
Percent preferring "more services" over "cutting government spending"	51	42	28
Affirmative Action			
Percent that "oppose strongly" the preferential hiring and promotion of blacks	48	64	71
Abortion			
Percent who say abortion should be allowed "in cases of need" or "woman's preference"	62	61	51
Environment			
Percent favoring "tougher regulations on business to protect the environment"	68	62	42
Schools			
Percent favoring a school voucher program that would allow parents to use tax funds to send their children to the school of their choice, even if it were a private school	43	50	58
The Clinton Impeachment			
Percent believing that Special Prosecutor Kenneth Starr's investigation was a partisan effort to damage President Clinton	89	74	42

Source: Calculated by the authors from the 1998 National Election Studies data. Ideological self-identification categories total 100 percent except for rounding error. Read down each column; i.e., 39 percent of all Democrats identified themselves as liberal. Similarly, 37 percent of all Democrats identified themselves as moderate.

members and its more moderate members. Democrats and Republicans who hold their ideologies only moderately might be quite similar in terms of what they believe and stand for. Table 11.1 shows how party ID matches up with a number of issue positions.

Since the 1960s, the parties have become more consistent internally with respect to their ideologies. The most conservative region in the country is the South, but because of lingering resentment of the Republican Party for its role in the Civil War, the South was for decades tightly tied to the Democratic Party. In the 1960s, however, conservative southern Democratic voters began to vote for the Republican Party, and formerly Democratic politicians were switching their allegiances as well. By the 1990s, the South had become predominantly Republican. This swing made the Democratic Party more consistently liberal and the Republicans more consistently conservative, and gave the party activist bases more power within each party, because they did not have to do battle with people of different ideological persuasions.

Table 11.2
Party ID by Group

Social Group	Democrats	Independents	Republicans	Party Difference
Religious Groups				
Protestants	39%	30%	31%	+8%
Catholics	41	32	27	+24
Jews	57	29	14	+43
No religious preference	32	50	19	+13
Sex				
Men	34	36	30	+ 4
Women	41	35	24	+17
Race/Ethnicity				
Whites	33	37	30	+ 3
Blacks	73	24	3	+70
Hispanics	55	31	15	+40
Education				
High school or less	42	38	20	+22
College or college graduate	34	34	32	+ 2

Source: Calculated by the authors from the 1998 National Election Studies data. Cell entries for party affiliation across the rows total 100 percent except for rounding error. Read across each row; i.e., 39 percent of the Protestants are Democrats, 30 percent are Independents, and 31 percent are Republicans.

Party Membership   Party ideologies attract and are reinforced by different coalitions of voters. This means that the Democrats' post–New Deal liberal ideology reflects the preferences of its coalition of working- and lower-class voters, including union members, minorities, women, the elderly, and urban dwellers. The Republicans' conservative ideology reflects the preferences of upper- and middle-class whites, those who belong to evangelical and Protestant religions, and suburban voters. Table 11.2 shows how each party's coalition differs based on group characteristics. There is nothing inevitable about these coalitions, and they are subject to change as the parties' stances on issues change and as the opposing party offers new alternatives. Union members, for instance, once stalwartly Democratic, have become less loyal to that party as issues of labor versus management have faded in importance and other issues, like concerns about the effects of affirmative action and crime, have become more relevant.

Policy Differences Between the Parties   When the parties run slates of candidates for office, those candidates run on a **party platform**—a list of policy positions the party endorses and pledges its elected officials to enact. A platform is the national party's campaign promises, usually made only in a presidential election year. If the parties are to make a difference politically, their platforms have to reflect substantial differences that are consistent with their ideologies. The responsible party model requires that the parties offer distinct platforms, that voters know about them and vote on the basis of them, and that the parties ensure that their elected officials follow through in implementing them. The two major parties' stated positions on some key

party platform
list of policy positions a party endorses and pledges its elected officials to enact

issues from their 2000 platforms appear in "Consider the Source: How to Be a Critical Reader of Political Party Platforms."

Forces Drawing the Parties Together and Pushing Them Apart   As we have seen, there are clear differences between the parties in terms of their ideologies, their members, and their platforms. That does not guarantee that the parties will really seem different to voters, however, especially when their candidates are running for national office. There are important electoral forces that draw the parties together, as well as internal forces that drive them apart. These forces are central to understanding electoral politics in America today.

On any policy or set of policies, voters' opinions range from very liberal to very conservative. In the American two-party system, however, most voters tend to be in the middle, holding a moderate position between the two ideological extremes (see Figure 11.4). The party that appeals best to the moderate voters usually wins most

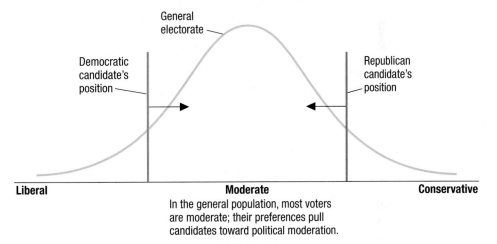

THE PULL TOWARD MODERATION

In the general population, most voters are moderate; their preferences pull candidates toward political moderation.

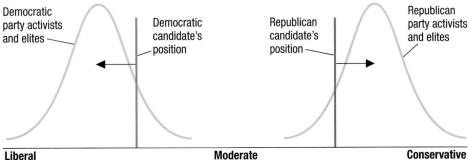

THE PULL TOWARD EXTREMISM

Figure 11.4 External and Internal Forces on the Parties

Democratic primary voters, party elites, and contributors are liberal, drawing Democratic candidates toward liberal positions.

Republican primary voters, party elites, and contributors are conservative, pulling Republican candidates toward conservative positions.

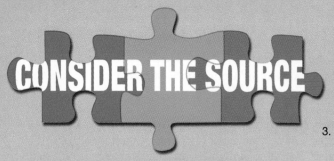

How to Be a Critical Reader of Political Party Platforms

Think of it as an invitation to a party—so to speak. In their platforms, political parties make a broad statement about who they are and what they stand for in the hope that you will decide to join them. The excerpts below from the Democratic and Republican platforms of 2000 show differing positions on several key issues. The full text of those platforms can be found on the web pages of the parties' national committees. Platforms of various third parties can also be found on the Web. Should you be interested enough to pursue your acquaintance with any or all of these parties, go armed with these questions:

1. **Whose platform is it, and what do you know about that party's basic political positions?** Understanding the basics will help you to interpret key phrases. For instance, how might the terms "family values" and "religious freedom" be defined differently in the Democratic and Republican platforms?

2. **Who is the audience?** Parties direct their platforms to two different groups—the party faithful and potential new supporters. For example, Democrats want to keep their traditional supporters, like union members, but they also want to broaden their appeal to the middle class and to small business owners. Republicans want to keep their base (including pro-life activists) happy but also want to attract more women in an effort to close the gender gap. How does this dual audience affect how parties portray themselves?

3. **Which statements reflect values, and which are statements of fact?** First, get clear about the values you are being asked to support. Parties tend to sprinkle their platforms liberally with phrases like "fundamental rights." Everybody is in favor of fundamental rights—which ones do they actually mean, and do *you* consider them fundamental rights? What are the costs and benefits of agreeing to their value claims? Then evaluate the facts. Are they accurate? Check out statistics. Do they seem reasonable? If not, look them up.

4. **Do you think the party can deliver on its policy proposals?** What resources (money, power, and so on) would it need? Can it get them? What if the party does enact the promised policies? Would they achieve what the party claims they would achieve? Who would be the winners, and who the losers?

5. **What is your reaction to the platform?** Could you support it? How does it fit with your personal values and political beliefs? Is the appeal of this platform emotional? Intellectual? Ideological? Moral? Remember that party platforms are not just statements of party principles and policy proposals; they are also advertisements. Read them with all the caution and suspicion you would bring to bear on any other ad that wants to convince you to buy, or buy into, something. *Caveat emptor!* (Let the buyer beware!)

Excerpts from 2000 National Party Platforms

Democratic Platform, 2000
Adopted by the Democratic National Convention, August 15, 2000

Affirmative Action and Civil Rights

(W)e need to end . . . racial profiling in America. . . . Hate crimes . . . based on gender, disability or sexual orientation . . . should be punished with extra force. . . . We recognize the importance of new battles against forms of discrimination . . . such as environmental injustices and predatory lending practices. And we will fight for full funding and full staffing of . . . civil rights enforcement agencies. . . .

Gay Rights

We support . . . efforts . . . to end workplace discrimination against gay men and lesbians, . . . support the full inclusion of gay and lesbian families in the life of the nation . . . (and) equitable alignment of benefits. Gore . . . believes all patriotic Americans [should] be allowed to serve their country without discrimination, persecution, and violence.

Republican Platform, 2000
Adopted by the Republican National Convention, August 31, 2000

Affirmative Action and Civil Rights

(R)ights inhere in individuals, not in groups. We will attain . . . equal opportunity without quotas or . . . preferential treatment. No one should be denied . . . because of their race or gender. Equal access . . . should guarantee every person a fair shot based on their potential and merit.

Gay Rights

We support the traditional definition of "marriage" as the legal union of one man and one woman. . . . That belief led Congress to enact the Defense of Marriage Act. . . . (W)e do not believe sexual preference should be given special legal protection or standing. . . . We affirm that homosexuality is incompatible with military service.

Democratic Platform, 2000

Abortion

The Democratic Party stands behind the right of every woman to choose . . . regardless of ability to pay. (I)t is a fundamental constitutional liberty. . . . (E)liminating a woman's right to choose is only one justice away. . . . We support contraceptive research, family planning. . . .

Education

(E)very teacher should pass a rigorous test. . . . Failing schools . . . should be quickly shut down and reopened with a new principal and new teachers. . . . We need . . . to put one million new . . . teachers . . . and start reducing class size. . . . The Democratic Party supports expansion of charter . . . and other nontraditional public school options . . . [and wants to] ensure that these . . . schools are fully accountable. . . . We should make a college education as universal as high school. . . .

Gun Control

We need mandatory child safety locks, to protect our children. We should require . . . a full background check and a gun safety test to buy a new handgun in America. We support more federal gun prosecutors, ATF agents and inspectors, and giving states and communities another 10,000 prosecutors to fight gun crime.

National Defense

(T)he Democratic Party will make sure that the military has the most advanced weaponry, sophisticated intelligence, and information systems. . . . (T)he Democratic Party support(s) the development of the technology for a limited national missile defense system . . . to defend the U.S. against . . . weapons of mass destruction . . . that . . . is compatible with the Anti-Ballistic Missile Treaty.

Budget

In the next 12 years, Democrats vow to wipe out the publicly-held national debt. . . . (W)e must . . . secure Social Security and Medicare for future generations . . . by using the savings from our current unprecedented prosperity. . . . (N)ew environmentally-friendly technologies can create new jobs. . . . (B)oth public and private investment . . . is crucial to sustaining our prosperity.

Taxes

Democrats want to give middle class . . . tax cuts that are specifically targeted . . . for college, [to] invest in their job skills and lifelong learning, pay for health insurance, afford child care, eliminate the marriage penalty for working families, care for elderly or disabled loved ones, invest in clean cars and clean homes, and build additional security for their retirement.

Source: http://www.democrats.org/hq/platform/#SEC

Republican Platform, 2000

Abortion

(T)he unborn child has a . . . right to life. We support a human life amendment to the Constitution. . . . We oppose using public revenues for abortion. . . . We support the appointment of judges who respect . . . the sanctity of innocent human life. . . .

Education

(W)e endorse . . . education reforms . . . which will . . . empower needy families to escape persistently failing schools by allowing federal dollars to follow their children to the school of their choice. . . . (W)e will encourage faith-based and community organizations to take leading roles in after-school programs. . . . (W)e defend the option for home schooling . . . and will continue to work for the return of voluntary school prayer to our schools. . . .

Gun Control

Because self-defense is a basic human right . . . a Republican administration will vigorously enforce current gun laws. . . . (W)e oppose federal licensing of law-abiding gun owners and national gun registration as a violation of the Second Amendment. . . . (W)e will hold criminals individually accountable for their actions by strong enforcement of federal and state firearm laws. . . .

National Defense

A Republican president . . . will . . . incorporate new technologies and new strategies . . . and . . . transform our military into a true twenty-first century force. We support the advancement of women in the military, support their exemption from ground combat units, and . . . recommend that co-ed basic training be ended. The new Republican president will deploy a national missile defense for reasons of national security.

Budget

Budget surpluses are the result of over-taxation of the American people. The Social Security surplus is off-limits. . . . We . . . are also determined to protect Medicare and to pay down the national debt. . . . (W)e reaffirm our support for a constitutional amendment to require a balanced budget. We call for full repeal of the death tax. . . .

Taxes

(W)e will return half a trillion dollars to the taxpayers. . . . (I)t's time to change the tax system, to make it simpler, flatter, and fairer. . . . We . . . endorse . . . (replacing) the five current tax brackets with four lower ones. . . . (W)e support legislation requiring a super-majority vote in both houses of Congress to raise taxes.

Source: http://www.rnc.org/2000/2000platformcontents

of the votes. Thus even though the ideologies of the parties are distinct, the pressures related to winning a majority of votes can lead both parties to campaign on the same issue positions, making them appear more alike to voters.[19] For instance, Republicans have moved from their initial opposition to join the majority of voters in supporting social security, Medicare, and Medicaid. Similarly, Democrats have dropped their resistance to a balanced federal budget and have become advocates of fiscal responsibility.

Although the need to appeal to the many moderate voters in the middle of the American political spectrum has drawn the two major parties together, powerful forces within the parties still keep them apart. These are the need to placate party activists and the need to raise money.

The main players in a political party are often called the "party faithful," or **party activists,** people who are especially committed to the values and policies of the party and who devote more of their resources, both time and money, to the party's cause. Although these activists are not an official organ of the party, they represent its lifeblood. Compared to the average voter, party activists tend to be more ideologically extreme (more conservative or more liberal even than the average party identifier) and to care more intensely about the party's issues. They can have a significant influence on the ideological character of the party.[20]

Party activists play a key role in keeping the parties ideologically distinct, because one of their primary purposes in being active in the party is to ensure that the party advocates their issue positions (see Figure 11.4). Because they tend to be concerned with keeping the party pure, they are reluctant to compromise on these issues, even if it means losing an election.[21] Liberal activists kept the Democratic Party to the left of most Americans during the 1970s and 1980s. The only Democratic candidate who won a presidential election during that time was Jimmy Carter, in the immediate aftermath of the Watergate scandal that drove Republican Richard Nixon from office. While the Democrats dealt with this problem by restructuring their internal politics and giving more weight to moderates like Bill Clinton and Al Gore, the Republicans got caught in the same trap of appearing to be as conservative as their most activist members in the religious right. The Democrats were consequently able to capture the presidency by appealing to the moderate middle—focusing on the economic problems of Americans in 1992 and appropriating and giving less extreme meaning to the label "family values" in 1996. The Republicans responded by moving to the middle in 2000, choosing a candidate in George W. Bush who could appeal to moderate voters.

The need to please party activists gives candidates a powerful incentive to remain true to the party's causes. Candidates who moderate too much or too often risk alienating the activists who are

party activists

the "party faithful"; the rank-and-file members who actually carry out the party's electioneering efforts

Presidential nominees must represent the various interests of their party while maintaining their appeal to the average voter— often easier said than done. This cartoon suggests that George W. Bush wants the religious right (wearing the Pilgrim hats) to relax a little bit.

a key component of their success. Thus, even though many nominees moderate their stances to win a majority of the voters, winning candidates, mindful of their bases, tend to return to their roots once in office.[22] This means that few politicians are willing to truly moderate and work with the other side. The 1980s and 1990s saw an increased partisanship in politics, which often led to gridlock and inaction.

Characteristics of the American Party System

Party systems vary tremendously around the world. The American party system is distinctive: it is predominantly a two-party system, it tends toward ideological moderation, it has decentralized party organizations, and its parties-in-government are undisciplined.

Two Parties   The United States has a two-party system. Throughout most of our history, in fact, the Democrats and the Republicans have been the only parties with a viable chance of winning the vast majority of elective offices. The most important reason the United States maintains a two-party system is that the rules of the system—in most cases designed by members of the two parties themselves—make it very difficult for third parties to do well on a permanent basis.[23] The U.S. Constitution prescribes a single-member-district electoral system for choosing members of Congress. This means that the candidate who receives the most votes in a defined district wins that seat and the loser gets nothing, except perhaps some campaign debt. This type of winner-take-all system creates strong incentives for voters to cast their ballots for one of the two established parties, because many voters believe that they are effectively throwing their votes away when they vote for a third-party candidate.

The United States has other legal barriers that reinforce the two-party system. In most states, state legislators from both parties have created state election laws that regulate each major party's activities, but these laws also protect the parties from competition. For example, state election laws ensure the place of both major parties on the ballot and make it difficult for third parties to gain ballot access. Many states require that potential Independent or third-party candidates gather a large number of signatures before their names can be placed on the ballot. Another common state law is that for a third party to conduct a primary to select its candidates, it must have earned some minimum percentage of the votes in the previous election.

As campaigns have become more dependent on money and television, both major parties have sought to limit third-party candidates' access to these vital resources. Thanks to 1974 campaign reforms, federal election laws now dictate the amount of campaign contributions that presidential candidates can receive from individuals and political action committees. These laws also provide dollar-for-dollar federal matching money for both major parties' nominees, if they agree to limit their spending to a predetermined amount. Third-party candidates cannot claim federal campaign funds until after the election is over, however, and even then their funds are limited by the percentage of past and current votes they received. In practice, they need to have gained about 5 percent or more of the national vote to be eligible for federal funds.[24] In 1992 billionaire Ross Perot funded his presidential campaign out of his own fortune, refusing the limits set by federal law and making himself ineligible to receive matching funds. This gesture, which few candidates can afford to make, enabled him to receive a large enough percentage of the votes that he qualified

Table 11.3
Third Party Movements in America

Third Party	Year Est.	Most Successful Candidate	History and Platform
National Republican Party	1824	John Quincy Adams	Split off from Democratic-Republicans to oppose Andrew Jackson's campaign for the presidency.
Anti-Masonic Party	1826	William Wirt	Held the first American party convention in 1831. Opposed elite organizations (the Masons in particular), charging they were antidemocratic.
Free-Soil Party	1848	Former president Martin Van Buren	Fought for cheap land and an end to slavery. The antislavery members eventually became supporters of Lincoln's Republican Party.
Know-Nothing Party	1849	Millard Fillmore	Promoted native-born Protestants' interests, claiming that Catholics were more loyal to the pope than to the United States.
Prohibition Party	1869	James Black	Advocated the prohibition of alcohol manufacture and use. The party continues to run candidates.
Populist Party	1891	James Weaver	Appealed to farmers during the depressed agricultural economy period by blaming railroads and eastern industrialists for unfair prices.
Socialist Party of America	1901	Eugene V. Debs	Fought for workers to control the means of production and for an end to the capitalist economic system in the United States. Debs ran in the 1900, 1904, 1908, and 1912 elections with limited success. When jailed for sedition in 1920, he ran for president from prison and received 3.4 percent of the popular vote.
Bull Moose Party (Progressive Party)	1912	Former president Teddy Roosevelt	As the most successful third-party candidate in American presidential election history, Roosevelt joined, then split, forces with progressive crusader Robert La Follette, hoping to defeat President Taft, whom he felt had led the Republican Party too conservatively. He received 27.4 percent of the vote.
States' Rights Party (Dixiecrats)	1948	Strom Thurmond (currently senator from South Carolina)	Split from the Democratic Party in 1948 because of President Truman's civil rights position; advocated segregation of races and used the Democratic Party infrastructure in southern states to gain 2.4 percent of the presidential vote.

Table 13.3 (*cont.*)
Third Party Movements in America

Third Party	Year Est.	Most Successful Candidate	History and Platform
American Independent Party	1968	George Wallace	Former Democrat George Wallace began his own party, which attacked civil rights legislation and Great Society programs. He received 13.5 percent of the presidential vote.
Libertarian Party	1971	Ed Clark	Fights for personal liberties and opposes all state welfare policies. Clark won 1.1 percent of the presidential vote in 1980.
Reform Party	1995	Ross Perot	Perot, who received 19 percent of the presidential vote as an Independent in 1992, began this party to formalize a third-party challenge. Perot won 8 percent of the vote in 1996, but took himself out of the running in 2000. Pat Buchanan ran on the Reform Party ticket instead, but failed to mobilize many voters.
Green Party	1984	Ralph Nadar	Nader ran for the presidency on the Green Party ticket in 2000 and won less than 3 percent of the popular vote.

for federal campaign funds in the 1996 election, when he did limit his spending. In addition, his party, the Reform Party, was eligible to receive such funds in 2000. Unfortunately for the Reform Party, its 2000 candidate, Pat Buchanan, did not enjoy similar success, and the party will not receive federal funds in 2004.

Just because the Democrats and the Republicans have dominated our party system does not mean that they have gone unchallenged. Over the years, numerous third parties have tried to alter the partisan makeup of American politics. These parties have usually arisen either to address specific issues that the major parties failed to address, like prohibition in 1869 or the environment in 1972, or to promote ideas that were not part of the ideological spectrum covered by the existing parties, like socialist parties or the Libertarian Party. In general, third parties have sprung up from the grassroots or have broken off from an existing party (the latter are referred to as **splinter parties**). In many cases they have had a strong leader who carried much of the burden of the party's success on his or her shoulders. Teddy Roosevelt's Bull Moose Party (1912) and Ross Perot's Reform Party (1992) are prime examples.

Although no third-party candidate has ever won the presidency, that should not be taken to mean that the impact of third parties on presidential elections is negligible. For example, if Ralph Nader had not run as a third-party candidate in 2000, Al Gore probably would have won the electoral college vote as well as the popular vote. When a third-party candidate changes the results of an election in such a way, he or she is said to have played the role of a *spoiler*. Table 11.3 lists some third parties that have made their mark on U.S. history.

splinter party
a third party that breaks off from one of the major political parties

Ideological Moderation   U.S. voters must select from a limited ideological menu: the moderately conservative Republican Party and the moderately liberal Democratic Party. Neither the Democrats nor the Republicans promote vast changes in the political and economic systems. Both parties support the Bill of Rights, the Constitution and its institutions (presidency, Congress, courts, and so on), the capitalist free-enterprise system, and even basic government policies like social security and the Federal Reserve System. This broad agreement between the two parties in major policy areas is a reflection of public opinion. Surveys show broad public support for the basic structure and foundations of the U.S. political and economic systems. Even though, as we saw earlier, the parties do offer a real choice, they do so within the confines of the basic American political culture we discussed in Chapter 1. No communist or fascist party has ever enjoyed major electoral success in this country.

Decentralized Party Organizations   In American political parties, local and state party organizations make their own decisions. They have affiliations to the national party organization, but no obligation to obey its dictates other than selecting delegates to the national convention. Decision-making is dispersed across the organization rather than centralized at the national level; power tends to move from the bottom up instead of from the top down. This means that local concerns and politics dominate the lower levels of the party, molding its structure, politics, and policy agendas. American parties are organized into several major divisions.

- Each party has a *national committee,* the Republican National Committee (RNC) and the Democratic National Committee (DNC), whose members come from every state. The national committees run the party business between conventions. The RNC and DNC expend enormous sums of money to get their candidates elected to office.

- The *congressional campaign committees* are formed by both parties for the sole purpose of raising and distributing campaign funds for party candidates in the House and the Senate.

- *State party committees* generally focus their efforts on statewide races and, to a lesser extent, state legislative contests.

- *Local party organizations* come together when an election approaches but are not permanently organized.

There are several reasons for the decentralized structure of American parties. One reason is that the federal electoral system makes it difficult for any national coordinating body to exercise control. Federalism also leads to decentralized parties because state laws have historically dictated the organizational structures and procedures of the state and local parties. In addition, U.S. parties lack strong organizational tools to exercise centralized control of candidates for office. In most cases, each party's candidates are chosen in direct primaries. Direct primaries, in which local party voters rather than party leaders control the nomination process, make strong centralized control an almost impossible task. When former Ku Klux Klan member David Duke ran for governor of Louisiana as a Republican in 1992, Republican leaders were outraged but powerless to stop him (he lost the election).

Undisciplined Parties-in-Government

Not only are American party organizations notable for their lack of a hierarchical (top-down) power structure, but the officials who have been elected to government from the two parties are equally unlikely to take their orders from the top. Although there have been exceptions, American parties are often noted for their undisciplined nature; that is, party leaders often have trouble getting their members to follow the party line, a necessary component of the responsible party model. Beginning in the 1980s, however, and perhaps best illustrated by Newt Gingrich's House Speakership (1994–1998), party loyalty began to play a much stronger role in legislative politics. Gingrich made party loyalty a condition for leadership positions in committees and for his support. Strong partisan voting patterns were very evident during the impeachment of President Bill Clinton, even after Gingrich had resigned as Speaker. Since Gingrich left office, however, Speaker Dennis Hastert has had difficulty holding the moderate and conservative wings of the party together.

WHO, WHAT, HOW   The actors in American politics—politicians, reformers, party activists, interest groups, politicians, and voters alike—all struggle within the rules (and attempt to create new rules) to get what they want from the American party system.

WHO are the actors?	WHAT do they want?	HOW do they get it?
Early party leaders	• Strong parties with powerful leaders	• Elite parties • Party machines
Reformers	• Accountable parties • Less boss power and patronage power	• Primary elections • Civil service reform
Party activists	• Control of party agenda	• Primary voting • Participation in nomination process and platform writing • Increased party discipline
Democrats and Republicans	• Electoral victory • Control of government • Limited competition from third parties	• Electioneering • Governing • Rules that discourage third-party success
Citizens	• Representation of ideas and issues not addressed by two major parties	• Formation of third parties

The Roles, Formation, and Types of Interest Groups

Americans have long been addicted not only to political parties but to membership in other groups as well. As the French observer Alexis de Tocqueville, traveling in America in the early 1830s, noted, "Americans of all ages, all conditions, and all dispositions, constantly form associations. They have not only commercial and manufacturing companies, in which all take part, but associations of a thousand other kinds,—religious, moral, serious, futile, general or restricted, enormous or diminutive."[25] Figure 11.5 shows that Americans are indeed among the top "joiners" in the world.

This tendency of Americans to form groups disturbed James Madison, who worried about the power of **factions,** or citizens united by some interest or passion that might be opposed to the common good. Most political scientists, however, have a different take on factions, which they call by the more neutral term *interest groups.* An **interest group** is an organization of individuals who share a common political goal and unite for the purpose of influencing public policy decisions.[26] We saw in Chapter 1 that interest groups play a central role in the pluralist theory of democracy, which argues that democracy is enhanced when citizens' interests are represented through group membership. Group interaction ensures that members' interests are represented, but also that no group can become too powerful.

faction a group of citizens united by some common passion or interest and opposed to the rights of other citizens or to the interests of the whole community

interest group an organization of individuals who share a common political goal and unite for the purpose of influencing government decisions

Roles of Interest Groups

Negative images of interest groups abound in American politics and the media. Republicans speak of the Democrats as "pandering" to special-interest groups like labor unions and trial lawyers, hoping to give the impression that the Democrats give special treatment to some groups at the expense of the public good. In turn, Demo-

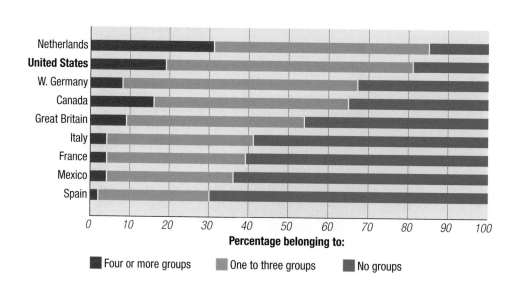

**Figure 11.5
Americans Like to Belong**

Source: Data from *The Public Perspective,* April/May 1995.

crats claim that the Republican Party has been captured by big business or the religious right, again suggesting that they do not have the national interest at heart but rather the specialized interests of small segments of society. In truth, interest groups have become an integral part of American politics, and neither party can afford to ignore them. In this section, we go beyond the negative stereotypes of interest groups to discuss six important roles they play in the American political system.[27]

- *Representation.* Interest groups help represent their members' views to Congress, the executive branch, and administrative agencies. Representation in this case is not geographic, as it is in Congress, but rather is based on common interests. Whether an interest group represents teachers, manufacturers of baby food, people concerned with the environment, or the elderly, it ensures that its members' concerns are adequately heard in the policymaking process. The activity of persuading policymakers to support an interest group's positions is called **lobbying.**

- *Participation.* Interest groups provide an avenue for citizen participation in politics that goes beyond voting in periodic elections. They are a mechanism for people sharing the same interests or pursuing the same policy goals to come together, pool their resources, and channel their efforts for collective action. Whereas individual political action might seem futile, participation in a group can be much more effective.

- *Education.* One of the more important functions of interest groups is to educate policymakers regarding issues that are important to the groups.

- *Agenda building.* Interest groups alert the proper government authorities about their issues, get the issues on the political agenda, and make those issues a high priority for action.

- *Provision of program alternatives.* Interest groups can be effective in supplying alternative suggestions for how issues should be dealt with once they have been put on the agenda. From this mix of proposals, political actors choose a solution.[28]

- *Program monitoring.* Once laws are enacted, interest groups keep tabs on their consequences, informing Congress and the regulatory agencies about the effects, both expected and unexpected, of federal policy.

lobbying interest group activities aimed at persuading policymakers to support the group's positions

Why Do Interest Groups Form?

Many of us can imagine public problems that we think need to be addressed. But despite our reputation as a nation of joiners, most of us never act, never organize a group, and never even join one. What makes the potential members of an interest group come together in the first place? There are several conditions that make organization easier. It helps if the potential members share a perception of a problem that needs to be solved or a threat to their interests that needs to be addressed. It also helps if the members have the resources—time, money, and leadership—to organize.

But even though external threats, financial resources, and effective leadership can all spur interest group formation, these factors are usually not enough to overcome what political scientists call the *problem of collective action.* Another name for this is the **free rider problem:** why should people join a group to solve a problem

free rider problem the difficulty groups face in recruiting when potential members can gain the benefits of the group's actions whether they join or not

when they can free ride—that is, reap the benefits of the group's actions—whether they join or not?[29] The free rider problem affects interest groups because most of the policies that these groups advocate involve the distribution of a collective good. A **collective good** is a good or benefit that, once provided, cannot be denied to others. Public safety, clean air, peace, and lower consumer prices are all examples of collective goods that can be enjoyed by anyone. When collective goods are involved, it is difficult to persuade people to join groups, because they are going to reap the benefits anyway. The larger the number of potential members involved, the more this holds true, because each member will have trouble seeing that his or her efforts will make a difference.

Many groups overcome the free rider problem by supplying **selective incentives**—benefits available to their members that are not available to the general population. There are three types of these incentives.[30]

- **Material benefits** are tangible rewards that members can use. One of the most common material benefits is information. For example, many groups publish a magazine or newsletter packed with information about issues important to the group and pending legislation relevant to the group's activities.

- **Solidary benefits** come from interaction and bonding among group members. For many individuals, politics is an enjoyable activity, and the social interactions occurring through group activities provide high levels of satisfaction and are a strong motivating force.

- **Expressive benefits** are those rewards that come from doing something that you strongly believe in—essentially from the expression of your values and interests.

It is important to note that group leaders often use a mixture of incentives to recruit and sustain members. Thus the National Rifle Association (NRA) recruits many of its members because they are committed to the cause of protecting an individual's right to bear arms. The NRA reinforces this expressive incentive with material incentives, such as its magazine, and solidary incentives resulting from group fellowship. The combination of all these incentives helps make the NRA one of the strongest interest groups in Washington.

collective good
a good or service that, by its very nature, cannot be denied to anyone who wants to consume it

selective incentive
a benefit that is available only to group members as an inducement to get them to join

material benefit
a selective incentive in the form of a tangible reward

solidary benefit
a selective incentive related to the interaction and bonding among group members

expressive benefit
a selective incentive that derives from the opportunity to express values and beliefs and to be committed to a greater cause

Types of Interest Groups

There are potentially as many interest groups in America as there are interests, which is to say the possibilities are endless. Therefore, it is

Guns
This woman is checking out a handgun at a National Rifle Association Convention. Besides providing such occasions for gun enthusiasts to get together, the NRA is one of the most active and effective lobbies in Washington, D.C.

helpful to divide these groups into different types, based on the kind of benefit they seek for their members. Here we distinguish between economic, equal opportunity, public, and government (both foreign and domestic) interest groups. Depending on the definitions they use, scholars have come up with different schemes for classifying interest groups, so don't be surprised if you come across these groups under other labels.

economic interest group   a group that organizes to influence government policy for the economic benefit of its members

Economic Interest Groups   **Economic interest groups** seek to influence government for the economic benefit of their members. Generally, these groups are players in the productive and professional activities of the nation. The economic benefits they seek may be higher wages, lower tax rates, bigger government subsidies, or more favorable regulations, for example. What all economic interest groups have in common is that they focus primarily on pocketbook issues. Such groups include corporations and business associations, unions and professional associations, and agricultural interest groups.

equal opportunity interest group   a group that organizes to promote the civil and economic rights of underrepresented or disadvantaged groups

Equal Opportunity Interest Groups   **Equal opportunity interest groups** organize to promote the civil rights of people who believe that their interests are not being adequately represented and protected in national politics through traditional means. Because in many cases these groups are economically disadvantaged or are afraid that they might become so, they also advocate economic rights. Equal opportunity groups believe that they are underrepresented not because of *what they do* but because of *who they are*. They may be the victims of discrimination or see themselves as threatened. These groups organize on the basis of age, race, ethnic group, gender, and sexual orientation. Membership is not limited to people who are part of the demographic group, because many people believe that promoting the interests and

March for Justice
Groups that seek to promote racial or ethnic equality rely on protest as a tactic of influence much more frequently than business interest groups do, since the resulting media coverage may reach a large, potentially sympathetic audience. American Indian Movement (AIM) activist Russell Means here leads a 1999 protest march from South Dakota's Pine Ridge Reservation to Whiteclay, Nebraska, to draw attention to treaty violations.

rights of various groups in society is in the broader interest of all. For this reason, some scholars classify these groups as public interest groups.

public interest group   a group that organizes to influence government to produce collective goods or services that benefit the general public

Public Interest Groups   A **public interest group** tries to influence government to produce noneconomic benefits that cannot be restricted to the interest group's members or denied to any member of the general public. The benefits of clean air, for instance, are available to all, not just the members of the environmental group that fights for them. In a way, all interest group benefits are collective goods that all members of the group can enjoy, but public interest groups seek collective goods that are open to all members of society or, in some cases, everyone in the world.

Public interest group members are usually motivated by a view of the world that they think everyone would be better off to adopt. They believe that the benefit they seek is good for everyone, even if individuals outside their groups disagree or even reject the benefit. Although few people would dispute the value of clean air, peace, and the protection of human rights internationally, there is no such consensus about protecting the right to an abortion, the right to carry a concealed weapon, or the right to smoke marijuana. Yet public interest groups are involved in procuring and enforcing these rights for all Americans.

Because public interest groups are involved in the production of collective goods for very large populations and the incentive to contribute on an individual basis may be particularly difficult to perceive, these groups are especially vulnerable to the free rider problem. That has not stopped them from organizing, however. There are more than twenty-five hundred public interest groups in the United States today.[31] People are drawn to a particular group because they support its values and goals; that is, expressive benefits are the primary membership draw. Although many members are initially attracted by expressive benefits, public interest groups seek to keep them active by offering material benefits and services, ranging from a free subscription to the group's magazine to discount insurance packages. Public interest groups include environmental groups, consumer groups, religious groups, Second Amendment groups, reproductive rights groups, and human rights groups.

Government Interest Groups   Both foreign and domestic governments lobby Congress and the president. Typically, some lobbyists' most lucrative contracts come from foreign governments seeking to influence foreign trade policies. In recent years, ethics rules have been initiated to prevent former government officials from working as foreign government lobbyists as soon as they leave office, but lobbying firms continue to hire them when they can because of their contacts and expertise.[32]

Domestic governments have become increasingly involved in the business of influencing federal policy. With the growing complexities of American federalism, state and local governments have an enormous stake in what the federal government does and often try to gain resources, limit the impact of policy, and otherwise alter the effects of federal law. All fifty states have government relations offices in Washington to attempt to influence federal policy directly.[33]

WHO, WHAT, HOW   Interest groups may have any number of goals and various kinds of members, but their primary goal is to influence policy.

WHO are the actors?	WHAT do they want?	HOW do they get it?
People with common interests	• Protection of group interests • Recruitment of group members • Prevention of free riders	• Formation of interest groups • Representation, participation, education, agenda setting, posing program alternatives, program monitoring • Material benefits • Purposive benefits • Solidary benefits
Economic actors	• Protection and improvement of economic status and interests	• Formation of economic interest groups
Members of threatened or disadvantaged groups	• Protection and improvement of legal rights and economic status	• Formation of equal opportunity groups
People ideologically committed to a view of the "good" society	• Social reform based on their vision of what is right	• Formation of public interest groups
Nations; state and local governments	• Protection and improvement of their relationship with the federal government	• Formation of government interest groups

Interest Group Politics

The term *lobbying* comes from seventeenth-century England, where representatives of special interests would meet members of the English House of Commons in the large anteroom, or lobby, outside the House floor to plead their cases.[34] Contemporary lobbying reaches far beyond the lobby of the House or Senate, however. Interest groups contact lawmakers directly, but they no longer confine their efforts to chance meetings in the legislative lobby—or to members of the legislature. Today they target all branches of government, and the American people as well. The ranks of those who work with lobbyists also have swelled. Beginning in the 1980s, interest groups, especially those representing corporate interests, have been turning to a diverse group of political consultants, including professional Washington lobbyists, campaign specialists, advertising and media experts, pollsters, and academics. Lobbying today is a big business in its own right.

There are two main types of lobbying strategy: **direct lobbying,** or interaction with actual decision-makers within government institutions, and **indirect lobbying,** or attempts to influence public opinion and mobilize interest group members or the general public to contact their elected representatives on an issue. Some groups have

direct lobbying
direct interaction with public officials for the purpose of influencing policy decisions

indirect lobbying
attempts to influence government policy-makers by encouraging the general public to put pressure on them

resorted to more confrontational indirect methods, using political protests (often developing into full-blown social movements) to make their demands heard by policymakers. Recently, corporations and other more traditional interest groups have been combining tactics—joining conventional lobbying methods with the use of e-mail, computerized databases, talk radio, and twenty-four-hour cable TV—to bring unprecedented pressure to bear on the voting public to influence members of government.

Direct Lobbying

Direct lobbying involves a face-to-face interaction between lobbyists and members of government. We tend to think of Congress as the typical recipient of lobbying efforts, but the president, the bureaucracy, and even the courts are also the focus of efforts to influence policy.

Lobbying Congress   When interest groups lobby Congress, they rarely concentrate on all 435 members of the House or all 100 members of the Senate. Rather, lobbyists focus their efforts on congressional committees, because that is where most bills are written and revised. Because the committee leadership is relatively stable from one Congress to the next (unless a different party wins a majority), lobbyists can develop long-term relationships with committee members and their staffs. These personal contacts are important because they represent a major means through which interest groups provide information to members of Congress. Following are some of the strategies used by those who lobby Congress.

- *Personal contacts.* Personal contacts, including appointments, banquets, parties, lunches, or simply casual meetings in the hallways of Congress, are the most common and the most effective form of lobbying.

- *Professional lobbyists.* Much of modern-day lobbying involves the use of "hired guns," or professional lobbyists, many of them former government officials, put on retainer by a client to lobby for that client's interests. Rotating into lobbying jobs from elected or other government positions is known as passing through the **revolving door,** a concept we will encounter again in Chapter 13. It refers to public officials who leave their posts to become interest group representatives (or media figures), parlaying the special knowledge and contacts they gathered in government into lucrative salaries in the private sector. Revolving-door activity is subject to occasional attempts at regulation and frequent ethical debate, because it raises questions about whether people should be able to convert public service into private profit, and whether such an incentive draws people into public office for motives other than serving the public interest.

revolving door
the tendency of public officials, journalists, and lobbyists to move between public and private sector (media, lobbying) jobs

- *Expert testimony.* Interest groups also lobby decision-makers by providing testimony and expertise, and sometimes they even draft legislation on the many issue areas that policymakers cannot take the time to become expert in.[35] Information is one of the most important resources lobbyists can bring to their effort to influence Congress.

- *Campaign contributions.* Giving money to candidates is another lobbying technique that helps interest groups gain access and a friendly ear. The 1974 Federal

political action committee
the fundraising arm of an interest group

Election Campaign Act, which was passed in an effort to curb campaign spending abuses, sought to regulate the amount of money an interest group can give to candidates for federal office by providing for **political action committees** (PACs), which serve as fundraisers for interest groups. PACs have strict limitations on how much money they can donate to a candidate, but a number of loopholes allow them to get around some of the restrictions.

- *Coalitions.* Interest groups also attempt to bolster their lobbying efforts by forming coalitions with other interest groups. These coalitions tend to be based on single issues, and building such coalitions has become an important strategy in lobbying Congress.

Many attempts have been made to regulate the tight relationships between lobbyists and lawmakers. The difficulty, of course, is that lawmakers benefit from their relationships with lobbyists in many ways and are not enthusiastic about curtailing their opportunities to get money and support. In 1995 Congress completed its first attempt in half a century to regulate lobbying when it passed the Lobbying Disclosure Act. The act requires lobbyists to report how much they are paid, by whom, and what issues they are promoting.[36] Also in 1995, both the Senate and House passed separate resolutions addressing gifts and travel opportunities given by interest groups to senators and representatives.[37] The House's ban is in some ways more restrictive than the Senate's.

These reforms have not closed the door on lavish spending by lobbyists, although initially the rule changes cast a definite chill on lobbyists' activities.[38] As lobbyists and members of Congress have learned where they can bend the rules, however, relations between them have returned to a more familiar footing.

Lobbying the President   Lobbyists also target the president and the White House staff to try to influence policy. As with Congress, personal contacts within the White House are extremely important, and the higher up the better. The official contact point between the White House and interest groups is the Office of Public Liaison. The basic purpose of this office is to foster good relations between the White House and interest groups in order to mobilize these groups to support the administration's policies.

Lobbying the Bureaucracy   Whereas opportunities for lobbying the president may be somewhat limited, opportunities for lobbying the rest of the executive branch abound. Interest groups know that winning the legislative battle is only the first step. The second, and sometimes more important, battle takes place in the bureaucracy, where Congress has delegated rule-making authority to federal agencies that implement the law.[39]

Interest groups often try to gain an advantage by developing strong relations with regulating agencies. Because many of the experts on a topic are employed by the interests being regulated, it is not unusual to find lobbyists being hired by government agencies, or vice versa, in an extension of the revolving-door situation we just discussed. The close relationships that exist between the regulated and regulators, along with the close relationships between lobbyists and congressional staffs, lead to the creation of iron triangles (see Chapter 8 and especially Figure 8.3).

Lobbying the Courts Interest groups try to influence government policy by challenging the legality of laws or administrative regulations in the courts. These legal tactics have been used by groups like the National Association for the Advancement of Colored People (anti-discrimination cases), the American Civil Liberties Union (freedom of speech, freedom of religion, and civil liberties cases), the Sierra Club (environmental enforcement), and Common Cause (ethics in government). Sometimes groups bring cases directly, and sometimes they file amicus curiae ("friend of the court") briefs asking the courts to rule in ways favoring their positions.

Indirect Lobbying

One of the most powerful and fastest-growing kinds of lobbying is indirect lobbying, in which lobbyists use public opinion to put pressure on politicians to do what the lobbyists want.[40] In this section, we examine the various ways in which interest groups use the public to lobby and influence government decision-makers.

Educating the Public Many interest group leaders are sure that the public will rally to their side once they know the "truth" about their causes. They conduct extensive research to make their cases and court media attention and hire public relations firms to get their ideas across.[41] An increasingly popular way for interest groups to promote their message is the use of **issue advocacy ads,** which encourage constituents to support or oppose a certain policy or candidate without directly telling them how to vote. As long as the ads do not specifically address a particular candidate, they are not subject to the limits on PAC contributions to political campaigns.

issue advocacy ads
advertisements that support issues or candidates without telling constituents how to vote

Mobilizing the Public The point of disseminating information, hiring public relations firms, and running issue advocacy ads is to motivate the public to lobby politicians themselves. As you might expect, groups like the American Association of Retired Persons, the Christian Coalition, and the NRA, which are blessed with large memberships, have an advantage, because they can mobilize a large contingent of citizens from all over the country to lobby representatives and senators. Generally, this mobilization involves encouraging members to write letters, send e-mail messages or faxes, or make phone calls to legislators about a pending issue.

social protest
public activities designed to bring attention to political causes, usually generated by those without access to conventional means of expressing their views

Using Social Protest Throughout our history, groups have turned to **social protest**—activities ranging from planned, orderly demonstrations, to strikes and boycotts, to acts of civil disobedience—when other techniques have failed to bring attention to their causes. Social protest provides a way for people to publicly express their disagreement with a government policy or action. At the same time, it often signals the strength of participants' feelings about an issue or their outrage over being closed off from more traditional avenues of political action. The media explosion of the modern age, especially the advent of the Internet, has given social protesters many more ways to find each other and organize. Social analysts also have observed that the Internet has facilitated the growth of groups like militias and white supremacist organizations that previously dwelled on the fringes of society.[42]

Napping for Trees
Citizens engage in political actions both conventional and unconventional. Here an Earth First! activist passes the time in a northern California forest, suspended from a tree he is trying to protect from being harvested.

"Astroturf" Political Campaigns and the State of Lobbying Today

grassroots lobbying
indirect lobbying efforts that spring from widespread public concern

astroturf lobbying
indirect lobbying efforts that manipulate or create public sentiment, "astroturf" being artificial grassroots

Lobbying the public is often called **grassroots lobbying,** meaning that it addresses people in their roles as ordinary citizens. It is the wielding of power from the bottom (roots) up, rather than from the top down. Most of what we refer to as grassroots lobbying, however, does not spring spontaneously from the people, but is orchestrated by elites, leading some people to call it **astroturf lobbying**—indicating that it is not genuine.

Often the line between real grassroots and astroturf lobbying is blurred, however. A movement may be partly spontaneous but partly orchestrated. Censure and Move On is an example of a group that started out as a spontaneous expression of the popular will to lobby Congress against the impeachment of President Clinton but that spread by "word of mouse" over the Internet. In response to the 1999 shooting deaths in Littleton, Colorado, the organizers of Censure and Move On began another "flash campaign," called "Gun Safety First," urging people to support gun control measures. This was less clearly a spontaneous popular movement, but it still involved mobilizing citizens to support a cause the group believed in.

At the astroturf extreme was the tobacco industry's 1998 effort to mobilize citizens against an increase in cigarette taxes. The industry spent $40 million on radio and television ads to assail antitobacco legislators for increasing taxes (on cigarettes only, but the ads did not make that clear) and asked citizens to call their legislators (via a toll-free number) to register their disgust.[43] Such a strategy is obviously an attempt to create an opinion that might not otherwise even exist, playing on popular sentiment about freedom of expression to achieve corporate ends.

Other corporate interests seeking to take advantage of astroturf techniques employ armies of lobbyists, media experts, and political strategists to conduct polls, craft multimedia advertising campaigns, and get the message out to "the people" through cable and radio talk shows, the Internet, outbound call centers, and/or fax machines. Astroturf campaigns are very expensive. The trade journal *Campaigns and Elections* estimated that in 1993 and 1994, more than $800 million was spent on these efforts.[44]

One media consultant has predicted that direct lobbying will become less important as indirect lobbying increases in effectiveness and popularity.[45] While indirect lobbying seems on its face to be more democratic, to the extent that it manipulates public opinion, it may in fact be less so. And as the multimedia campaigns get more and more expensive, the number of groups that can afford to participate will undoubtedly decline. Ironically, as lobbying moves away from the closed committee rooms of Congress and into the realm of what *appears* to be popular politics, it may not be any more democratic than it has traditionally been.

WHO, WHAT, HOW   Because of the complexity of American society, interest groups can realize their primary goal of influencing policy in a variety of ways.

WHO are the actors?	WHAT do they want?	HOW do they get it?
Lobbyists	• Influence on public policy	• Direct lobbying of three branches of government • Indirect lobbying of public • Astroturf lobbying
Citizens	• Placement of issues on the public agenda • Registering demands with government	• Grassroots action • Social protest

Interest Group Resources

Interest group success depends in large part on the resources a group can bring to the project of influencing government. The pluralist defense of interest groups is that all citizens have the opportunity to organize, and thus all can exercise equal power. But all interest groups are not created equal. Some have more money, more effective leadership, more members, or better information than others, and these resources can translate into real power differences. In this section, we examine the resources that interest groups can draw on to exert influence over policymaking: money, leadership, membership, and information.

Money

Interest groups need money to conduct the business of trying to influence government policymakers. Money can buy an interest group the ability to put together a well-trained staff, to hire outside professional assistance, and to make campaign contributions in the hopes of gaining access to government officials. Having money does not guarantee favorable policies, but not having money just about guarantees failure.

Staff   One of the reasons money is important is that it enables an interest group to hire a professional staff, usually an executive director, assistants, and other office support personnel. The main job of this professional staff is to take care of the day-to-day operations of the group, including pursuing policy initiatives, recruiting and maintaining membership, providing membership services, and, of course, getting more money through direct mailings, telemarketing, and organizational functions. Money is important for creating an organizational infrastructure that can in turn be used to raise additional support and resources.

Professional Assistance   Money also enables the interest group to hire the services of professionals, such as a high-powered lobbying firm. Such firms have invested heavily to ensure that they have connections to members of Congress.[46] A well-endowed group also can hire a public relations firm to help shape public opinion on a particular policy.

Figure 11.6 Increasing PAC Contributions for Congressional Campaigns, 1981–1998
Source: Data from U.S. Federal Election Commission, *FEC Reports on Financial Activity, Party and Non-Party Political Committees, Final Report,* biennial.

Campaign Contributions   Interest groups live by the axiom that to receive, one must give—and give a lot to important people. The maximum that any PAC can give to a congressional campaign is $5,000 for each separate election. In the 1997–1998 election cycle, PACs gave a total of $206.8 million to congressional candidates.[47] Figure 11.6 shows that this is an all-time high for PAC contributions. This figure represents more than 25 percent of all funds raised from all sources during that period. Although some PACs give millions to campaigns, most PACs give less than $50,000 to candidates for each election cycle, focusing their contributions on members of the committees responsible for drafting legislation important to their groups.[48] Early FEC data indicated that PAC contributions in 2000 increased by about 24 percent over the 1998 election cycle.

PAC spending is usually directed toward incumbents of both parties, with incumbents in the majority party, especially committee chairs, getting the greatest share. This means for the 1996 elections, about 78 percent of PAC contributions went to incumbent members of Congress, the bulk landing in Republican campaign coffers.[49] However, when the Democrats controlled Congress prior to 1994, they obtained the lion's share of PAC contributions. While most PACs want to curry favor with incumbents of either party, some tend to channel their money to one party. For instance, business interests, the American Medical Association, pro-life groups, Christian groups,

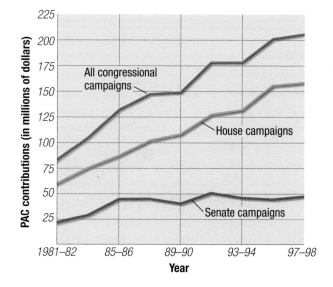

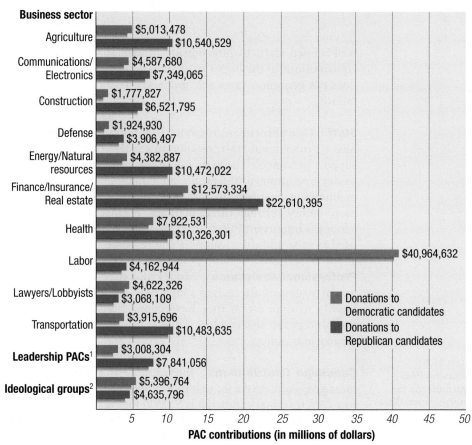

Business sector

1. Personal PACs allowing congressional leadership to raise money for other members' campaigns.
2. See chart below for the breakdown of PAC contributions by ideological groups.

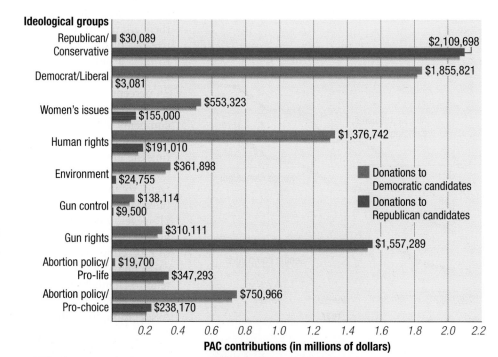

**Figure 11.7
How Interest
Groups Spend
Their Money**
These two figures
show the break-
down of contribu-
tions made to
Democratic and
Republican candi-
dates by interest
groups in different
sectors. The bottom
figure itemizes the
"ideological groups"
category even fur-
ther—according to
the focus of their
efforts.
Source: Data from
Center for Responsive
Politics.

and the NRA tend to support Republican candidates; labor groups, the Association of Trial Lawyers of America, the National Education Association, and environmental and pro-choice groups give primarily to Democrats. Figure 11.7 shows how the major types of interest groups divide their money among the Democratic and Republican Parties.

The ability to make sizable and strategically placed campaign contributions buys an interest group access to government officials.[50] Access gives the interest group the ability to talk to a representative and members of his or her staff and to present information relevant to the policies they seek to initiate, change, or protect. Access is important because representatives have any number of competing interests vying for their time. Money is meant to oil the door hinge of a representative's office so that it swings open for the interest group. For instance, a $175,000 donation to the Republican National Committee over four years yielded a three-day private event between the donors and the Republican leadership of Congress.[51] The Clinton administration was known in its early years for allowing major donors to stay in the Lincoln bedroom of the White House. The access bought by campaign contributions is usually less blatant, but officials know who has supported their campaigns, and they are unlikely to forget it when interest groups come knocking at their doors.

The relationship between money and political influence is extremely controversial. Many critics argue that this money buys more than just access; they say it buys votes. The circumstantial evidence for this contention is strong. For instance, in a Senate vote to allow the timber industry to harvest dead and dying trees from public lands, the fifty-four senators voting in favor of the policy had received almost $20,000 on average in campaign contributions from the timber industry. The forty-two who voted against it had received less than $3,000 on average.[52]

However, in the matter of vote buying, systematic studies of congressional voting patterns are mixed. These studies show that the influence of campaign contributions is strongest in committees, where most bills are drafted. Once a bill reaches the floor of the House or Senate, though, there is no consistent link between campaign contributions and roll call voting.[53] This suggests that campaign contributions influence the process of creating and shaping legislation, and thus defining the policy alternatives. Nonetheless, the final outcome of a bill is determined by political circumstances that go beyond the campaign contributions of interest groups.

Leadership

interest group entrepreneur an effective group leader, who is likely to have organized the group and can effectively promote its interests among members and the public

Leadership is an intangible element in the success or failure of an interest group. The strong effective leadership of what one scholar has called **interest group entrepreneurs** can help a group organize even if it lacks other resources.[54] Such a leader can keep a group going when it seems to lack support from other sources. Candy Lightner's role in Mothers Against Drunk Driving (MADD) is an excellent case in point (see the box on page 336).

Membership: Size and Intensity

The size of any interest group is an important resource. For instance, with more than 32 million members, the American Association of Retired Persons (AARP) can

Candy Lightner and MADD:
An Entrepreneur with a Real Agenda

The drunk driver who killed thirteen-year-old Cari Lightner as she walked on a city sidewalk was not likely to lose his license for long. This was true, despite the fact that Lightner's killer had been convicted of drunk driving twice already and, when he killed Cari, was out on bail from a hit-and-run under the influence of alcohol that had occurred just two days earlier. At the time, 1980, one in two highway deaths stemmed from drunken driving, and yet there was little government coordination to solve the problem. No uniform drinking age existed among the states, and permissible blood alcohol limits for drivers were relatively high. Moreover, Americans attached little significant social stigma to people who "tied one on" and then got behind the wheel of a car.

This would begin to change just four days after Cari Lightner's death, when Lightner's mother, Candy, her grandfather, and a family friend established Mothers Against Drunk Driving (MADD). The grassroots movement caught on quickly in California, and before long Candy Lightner was testifying before Congress about the evils of drunk driving. MADD quickly became a multifaceted organization that lobbied lawmakers, researched state drunk-driving laws and sentencing, and raised public awareness (especially among students) about the gravity of the problem. Within four years, Congress passed legislation mandating that all states raise their minimum drinking age to twenty-one in order to receive federal highway funds. President Reagan, who had been against the measure, quickly changed his view in the face of the groundswell of public support. With its hundreds of local chapters, MADD has also lobbied state legislatures to lower blood alcohol rates that define when a driver is considered intoxicated.

MADD's success has gone beyond its legal victories. First, it has given grief-stricken families a means of fighting back. Second, it has spawned similar movements—most prominently among students (Students Against Drunk Driving). Most important, however, it has fundamentally changed the public's attitude concerning alcohol and driving. Alcohol producers now run advertisements discouraging drinking and driving; the National Restaurant Association pushes members to train staff to cut off drunken patrons; other groups have worked with MADD to coordinate free taxi service on New Year's Eve. Thus, as the entrepreneur who pinpointed a timely societal concern, Candy Lightner has established an interest group that has accomplished the fundamental goals that all interest groups share: informing lawmakers, promoting successful changes in laws, and rallying the public to support such laws.

Sources: Frances D'Emilio, "Today's Topic: Working to Clear the Roads of Drunks," Associated Press, 26 February 1981; Tom Seppy, "Senate Panel Takes Testimony on Drunken Driving Issue," Associated Press, 4 March 1982; Thomas Murphy, "Ruling Sparks Outrage, Vows of Court Fight," Associated Press, 3 June 1983; Jay Mathews, "One California Mother's MADD Drive to Bar Highways to Drunken Killers: Loss of Her Daughter May Save Other Lives," *Washington Post*, 16 June 1984, A2; Carole Sugarman, "Restaurants Join the Fight Against Drunk Driving; On the Road Again," *Washington Post*, 25 March 1984, D1.

mobilize thousands of people in an attempt to influence elected officials' decisions regarding issues like mandatory retirement, social security, and Medicare. In addition, if an interest group's members are spread throughout the country, as are the AARP's, that group can exert its influence on almost every member of Congress.

The level of intensity that members exhibit in support of a group's causes also is critical. If a group's members are intensely dedicated to its causes, the group may be far stronger than its numbers would indicate. Members represent the lifeblood of an interest group, because they generally fund its activities and they can be mobilized to write letters, send e-mail messages, and engage in other forms of personal contact with legislators or administrative officials. For instance, despite the fact that a majority of Americans favor some form of gun control, they are outweighed in the political process by the intense feeling of the 2.8 million members of the NRA, who strongly oppose gun control.

Information

Information is one of the most powerful resources in an interest group's arsenal. Often the members of a group are the only sources of information on the potential or actual impact of a law or regulation. The long struggle to regulate tobacco is a case in point. While individuals witnessed their loved ones and friends suffering from lung disease, cancer, and heart problems, it took public health interest groups like the American Cancer Society, the Public Health Cancer Association, and the American Heart Association to conduct the studies, collect the data, and show the connection between these life-threatening illnesses and smoking. Of course, the tobacco industry and its interest group, the American Tobacco Institute, presented their own research to counter these claims. Not surprisingly, the tobacco industry's investigations showed "no causal relationship" between tobacco use and these illnesses.[55] Eventually, the volume of information showing a strong relationship overwhelmed industry research suggesting otherwise. In 1998 the tobacco industry reached a settlement with states to pay millions of dollars for the treatment of tobacco-related illnesses.

WHO, WHAT, HOW Some interest groups are more successful than others in getting what their members want from government. The rules of interest group politics reward some group characteristics and resources more than others.

WHO are the actors?	WHAT do they want?	HOW do they get it?
Interest groups	• Influence on policy	• Money • Effective leadership • Large and intense membership • Information

Citizenship and Political Groups

Defenders of pluralism believe that group formation helps give more power to more citizens, and we have seen that it certainly can enhance democratic life. Parties and interest groups offer channels for representation and participation, and they help to keep politicians accountable. Pluralists also believe that the system as a whole benefits from group politics. They argue that groups will compete with one another and ultimately must form coalitions to create a majority. In the process of forming coalitions, groups compromise on policy issues, leading to final policy outcomes that reflect the general will of the people, as opposed to the narrow interests of specific groups or individuals.[56] In this final section, we examine the claims of critics of who argue that the politics of groups skews democracy—gives more power to some people than to others—and particularly discriminates against segments of society that tend to be underrepresented in the first place (the poor and the young, for instance).

We have seen in this chapter that a variety of factors—money, leadership, information, intensity—can make a group successful. But this raises a red flag for American democracy. In American political culture, we value political equality, which is to say the principle of one person, one vote. And as far as voting goes, this is how we practice democracy. Anyone who attempts to visit the polls twice on election day is turned away, no matter how rich that person is, how intensely she feels about the election, or how eloquently he begs for another vote. But policy is not made only at the ballot box. It is also made in the halls and hearing rooms of Congress, the conference rooms of the bureaucracy, corporate boardrooms, private offices, restaurants, and bars. In these places, parties and interest groups speak loudly, and since some groups are vastly more successful than others, they have the equivalent of extra votes in the policymaking process.

We are not terribly uncomfortable with the idea that interest groups with large memberships should have more power. After all, democracy is usually about counting numbers. But when it comes to the idea that the wealthy, those who feel intensely, or those who have more information have an advantage, we balk. What about the rest of us? Should we have relatively less power over who gets what because we lack these resources?

It is true that the major parties and interest groups with money have the distinct advantages of organization and access. Many critics suggest that business interests represent a small, wealthy, and united set of elites who dominate the political process,[57] and there is much evidence to support the view that business interests maintain a special relationship with government and tend to unite behind basic conservative issues (less government spending and lower taxes). Other evidence, however, suggests that business interests are often divided regarding government policies and that other factors, such as membership, can counterbalance their superior monetary resources. While corporate money may buy access, politicians ultimately depend on votes. Groups with large memberships have more voters. When a group's membership is highly motivated and numerous, it can win despite the opposition's lavish resources.[58]

Points of Access

- Read the platforms of the two major parties and any third parties that appeal to you.
- Register to vote as a member of the party of your choice.
- Vote in the next election.
- Join the College Republicans, the College Democrats, or the campus branch of some other party.
- Campaign for candidates of your party in your dorm or local neighborhoods.
- Start a third party if none of the existing ones appeals to you. Write a platform.
- Contribute money to a political party or PAC.
- Attend a local party meeting.
- Become a party precinct chairperson.
- Join an interest group.
- Participate in a demonstration or boycott.
- Participate in a letter-writing campaign.

Thus what helps to equalize the position of powerful groups in American politics is the willingness on the part of citizens to fight fire with fire, politics with politics, organization with organization. It is, finally, the power of participation and democracy that can make pluralism fit the pluralists' hopes. For some groups, such as the poor, such advice may be nearly impossible to follow. Other groups left out of the system, such as the merely indifferent or young people who regard current issues as irrelevant, will pay the price of inattention and disorganization when the scorecards of interest group politics are finally tallied.

WHAT'S AT STAKE REVISITED

Technology has repeatedly opened doors to political participation that founder James Madison did not anticipate. The latest door to open, the Internet, has radically changed the costs and opportunities of organizing for the public. As we have noted, participation in politics can be costly in terms of time, energy, and money. But the Internet reduces the amount of time that is needed to register one's beliefs and join up with like-minded souls. Having learned something about how interest groups work, we can speculate about what is at stake in using the Internet as an organizing tool.

One founder of Censure and Move On says that the Internet allows people to be "five-minute activists" instead of having to devote considerable time to the enterprise of getting involved. In his opinion, this immediacy may overturn the conventional wisdom that only extreme ideologues and activists have the time and energy to participate in politics: "It could be a strong force for pulling the center back into the process . . . if we can allow people to be effective with a small investment of time."[59] Five-minute activists, once involved, might find that they are willing to make a larger investment. During the impeachment process, one Washington woman, who had not previously been politically active, used Censure and Move On's database to organize, on the Internet, a three-thousand-person anti-impeachment rally at a local shopping mall.

The Internet's impact on political organization has the potential to warm the hearts of participatory democrats as well as pluralists, and to bring alienated citizens back into the civic fold. It could indeed increase representation, at least among the computer-owning public, and give more weight to organizations in the center of the political spectrum. We should note, however, that it might just add another resource to the already active and involved people at the ideological extremes, allowing them to find each other and organize more effectively. There is already some evidence that various white supremacist and militia groups have been taking advantage of the Internet to organize and recruit new members.[60]

Critics could argue that the Internet allows the participation of precisely those people Madison wished to exclude—those who are unwilling to demonstrate their commitment to politics by going the extra mile and making the extra effort. Do we really want to reward those people who are willing to spend no more than five minutes on their civic lives? What will be the impact on politics if we make it easy for the less informed and less active to have a clearer say?

Some people do not think that the critics need to worry. They doubt that the five-minute activists have the staying power to hang in and make a political difference. Other analysts point out that politicians don't yet know how to respond to cyberpetitions. At least during the impeachment process, they seem to have decided that the cyberactivists would not follow through at the ballot box. It is not clear that, despite the enormous number of signatures and e-mail messages generated, Censure and Move On's drive changed any congressional votes.

Working against the likelihood of Censure and Move On's success, at least in this case, is the powerful incumbency advantage we noted in Chapter 6: citizens are very reluctant to vote their representatives out of office, and incumbents have a host of resources at their disposal to help them stay there. It is clearly too early to judge the impact of Internet organizing on interest group politics in America. What is at stake here depends on your perspective. Pluralists and participatory democrats will welcome the effects as promoting democracy; elitists are likely to fear that they will bring instability. In this sense, the debate echoes the concerns that kept Madison focused on the problem of factions so long ago. ■

key terms

astroturf lobbying   331
collective good   324
critical election   308
dealignment   308
direct lobbying   327
economic interest group   325
electioneering   302
equal opportunity interest
  group   325
expressive benefit   324
faction   322
free rider problem   323
governing   303
grassroots lobbying   331
indirect lobbying   327
interest group   322

interest group
  entrepreneur   335
issue advocacy ads   330
lobbying   323
material benefit   324
nominating convention   302
partisanship   302
party activists   316
party base   305
party boss   307
party era   308
party identification   304
party-in-government   303
party-in-the-electorate   304
party machine   307
party organization   302

party platform   312
party primary   308
patronage   307
pluralist democracy   301
political action committee   329
political party   301
public interest group   326
realignment   308
responsible party model   305
revolving door   328
selective incentive   324
social protest   330
solidary benefit   324
splinter party   319

summary

■ Political parties make a major contribution to American government by linking citizens and government, overcoming some of the fragmentation of government that separation of powers and federalism can produce, and creating an articulate opposition.

■ American history reveals at least five distinct party eras. These are periods of political stability when one party has a majority of congressional seats and controls the presidency. A realignment, or new era, occurs when a different party assumes control of government. Party politics today may be undergoing both a realignment and a dealignment, resulting in greater numbers of voters identifying themselves as Independents.

■ American political parties offer the average voter a choice in terms of ideology, membership, and policy positions (platform). The differences may not always be evident, however, because electoral forces create incentives for parties to take moderate positions, drawing the parties together. At the same time, party activists who are committed to the values and policies of a particular party play a key role in pushing the parties apart and keeping them ideologically distinct.

■ America's two-party system is relatively moderate, decentralized, and undisciplined. Although the rules are designed to make it hard for third parties to break in, numerous third-party movements have arisen at different times to challenge the two dominant parties.

■ People who want some influence on the way government policy decisions are made form interest groups. To accomplish their goals, interest groups lobby elected officials, rally public opinion, offer policy suggestions, and keep tabs on policies once enacted. Interest groups also must organize and convince others to join, often offering selective benefits to members.

■ Interest groups are of all different types. Economic groups such as business associations or trade unions want to protect and improve their status. Public interest groups advocate their vision of society, while equal opportunity groups organize to gain, or at least improve, economic status and civil rights. Governments form associations to improve relations among their ranks.

■ Lobbyists are the key players in interest groups. They influence public policy either by approaching the three branches of government (direct lobbying) or convincing the people to pressure the government (indirect lobbying).

■ The success of individual interest groups is often affected by factors like funding, quality of leadership, membership size and intensity, and access to information.

■ Critics of interest groups fear that the most powerful groups are simply those with the most money and that this poses a danger for American democracy. But interest group formation also may be seen as a way to give more power to more citizens, providing a mechanism to keep politicians accountable by offering additional channels for representation, participation, education, creation of policy solutions, and public agenda setting.

12

What's at Stake?

Exercising the Right to Vote in America
- Who Votes and Who Doesn't?
- Why Americans Don't Vote
- Does Nonvoting Matter?

How the Voter Decides
- Partisanship
- Issues and Policy
- The Candidates

Electing the President
- Getting Nominated
- The Electoral College
- The General Election Campaign
- Interpreting Elections

Citizenship and Elections

What's at Stake Revisited

Voting, Campaigns, and Elections

WHAT'S AT STAKE?

In the weeks before an election, nervous campaign officials fret about the possibility of an "October surprise," a last-minute event that could suddenly influence wavering voters. What neither George W. Bush nor Al Gore officials foresaw in the fall of 2000, however, was the possibility of a nearly unprecedented *November* surprise—an undecided presidential election on election night itself.

As election tracking polls had indicated before election day, the outcome was going to be a close one. Texas governor George W. Bush had had a very small lead in the polls in the weeks preceding the election, but immediately before the vote, Vice President Al Gore had edged ahead in some polls. On election night, the media first indicated that Gore might be winning the election after he had apparently captured Florida's twenty-five electoral college votes. Later that evening, however, the networks found errors in the Florida data and declared that state too close to call. Very early the next morning, the networks put Florida's votes in Bush's column and projected him the winner of the presidency. But when Bush's lead dwindled to a few hundred votes, the media changed their minds again and declared the entire race too close to call. After phoning the Texas governor to concede defeat, Gore, on his way to make a speech to disappointed supporters, got word that the election was still up in the air. The vice president called Bush back to retract his concession and returned to his hotel. By the time the sun rose on Wednesday, Gore was ahead in the popular vote by about 200,000 votes and also led in the electoral college. But with Florida still undecided, neither candidate had won the required 270 electoral votes.

What was the problem? Bush led at the end of the night in Florida by something less than 2,000 votes, triggering a Florida state law that requires an automatic electronic recount when the winning margin is less than one-half of 1 percent. At the end of the recount, several days later, Bush's lead had been cut to 300 votes, with up to 2,000 absentee ballots from overseas still to be counted. Adding to the sense of chaos was the impression that (amid other claims of voting irregularities in Florida) voting in Palm Beach County, a largely Democratic district, had gone awry. The format of the ballot (determined under Florida law by local officials) was confusing to some voters, perhaps leading many who wanted to vote for the Democratic ticket to vote instead for Reform Party candidate Pat Buchanan or to mistakenly vote for multiple candidates.

A political firestorm ensued. Newspaper editorials begged for caution and statesmanlike behavior from both sides. Bush held meetings to begin his transition to the White House, while Democrats accused him of trying to assume the mantle of the presidency without waiting for the official results. Private individuals in Florida filed lawsuits claiming that their right to vote had been denied, and citizens demonstrated in the streets, asking for a new vote in Palm Beach County. Democrats suggested that they might pursue legal recourse and in the meantime asked for a manual count of the ballots, a possibility allowed under Florida law to help determine the intention of the voters. At the same time, Republicans accused Gore of trying to steal the election and criticized the Democrats for bringing it into the courts.

Public opinion polls showed that Americans generally had cooler heads than their leaders, and more than half were reported to be willing to wait for a fair resolution. Two-thirds said that the federal government should move to make the ballot procedure consistent from state to state, and nearly as many said that the electoral college should be abolished. Foreign observers watched in disbelief as the electoral college, an institution that many had never heard of and fewer understood, seemed to stand in the way of a popularly elected president taking office.

A contested election was not unheard-of in the United States, but it hadn't happened since 1888. Was the United States in a constitutional crisis? Had the will of the people been thwarted? Could the new president, whoever he turned out to be, govern under such a cloud? Are elections a state matter, as the Constitution decrees, or should they be turned over to the federal government? And what about that seemingly arcane institution, the electoral college? Just what is at stake in a contested presidential election? ■

Today global commitment to democracy is on the rise. Americans and, increasingly, other citizens around the world believe that government with the consent of the governed is superior to government imposed on unwilling subjects and that political change is best accomplished through the ballot box rather than on the battlefield or in the streets. The mechanism that connects citizens with their governments, by which they signify their consent and through which they accomplish peaceful change, is elections. Looked at from this perspective, elections are an amazing innovation—they provide a method for the peaceful transfer of power that allows people to avoid violence. Quite radical political changes can take place without blood being shed—an accomplishment that would confound most of our political ancestors.

Although we pride ourselves on our democratic government, Americans seem to have a love-hate relationship with the idea of campaigns and voting. On the one hand, many citizens believe that elections do not accomplish anything, that elected officials ignore the wishes of the people, and that government is run for the interests of the elite rather than the many. Only about half of the eligible electorate have turned out to vote in recent presidential elections.

On the other hand, when it is necessary to choose a leader—whether it's the captain of a football team, the president of a dorm, or a local precinct chairperson—the first instinct of most Americans is to call an election. Even though there are other ways to choose leaders—picking the oldest, the wisest, or the strongest; holding a lottery; or asking for volunteers—Americans almost always prefer an election. We elect more than half a million public officials in America.[1] That means we have a lot of elections—more elections, more often, and for more officials than any other democracy.

In this chapter, we examine the complicated place of elections in American politics and American culture. We consider

- Americans' ambivalence about the vote and the reasons only about half of the citizenry even bothers to exercise what is supposed to be a precious right

- how voters go about making decisions, and how this in turn influences the character of presidential elections

- the organization and strategic aspects of running for the presidency

- reflections on what elections mean for citizens

Exercising the Right to Vote in America

We argued in Chapter 10 that even without being well informed and following campaigns closely, Americans can still cast intelligent votes reflecting their best interests. But what does it say about the American citizen that barely half of the adult population votes in presidential elections? In off-year congressional elections, in primaries, and in many state and local elections held at different times from the presidential contest, the rate of participation drops even lower.

Who Votes and Who Doesn't?

Many political observers, activists, politicians, and political scientists worry about the extent of nonvoting in the United States.[2] When people do not vote, they have no say in choosing their leaders, their policy preferences are not registered, and they do not develop as active citizens. Some observers fear that their abstention signals an alienation from the political process.

We know quite a lot about nonvoters in America in terms of their age, education, income, and racial and ethnic makeup.

- *Age.* Only 59 percent of those age eighteen to twenty-nine report voting. Turnout increases with age, so that among those forty and over, reported turnout runs above 80 percent.[3]

- *Income.* Turnout among the relatively wealthy (income above $50,000) is 89 percent and drops with income to the point that only 59 percent of the poor (income less than $10,000) report voting.

- *Race and ethnicity.* Blacks (68 percent) and Hispanics (64 percent) vote less frequently than whites (78 percent) and Asians (71 percent).

When we add these characteristics together, the differences are quite substantial. Wealthy, college-educated, older whites vote at a rate of 91 percent, whereas poor, young, minority group members who did not finish high school are estimated to vote at a rate of 22 percent.[4] The clear implication is that the successful white middle class is substantially overrepresented in the active electorate and their interests get a disproportionate amount of attention from politicians.

Why Americans Don't Vote

Not only do large numbers of Americans fail to vote, but the percentage of nonvoters has grown over time, despite overall increases in education, age of population, and income, which *should* increase the number of voters[5] (see Figure 12.1). As we have noted elsewhere, compared with other democratic nations, our turnout levels are low—almost at the bottom of the list (see Figure 10.2 on page 285). What accounts for turnout rates hovering around 50 percent in a country where 82 percent of adults say voting is important to democracy[6]—indeed, in a country that often prides itself on being one of the best and oldest examples of democracy in the world? The question of low and declining voter turnout in the United States poses a tremendous puzzle for political scientists, who have focused on six factors to try to explain this mystery.

Legal Obstacles   Voter turnout provides a dramatic illustration of our theme that rules make a difference in who wins and who loses in politics. The rules that govern

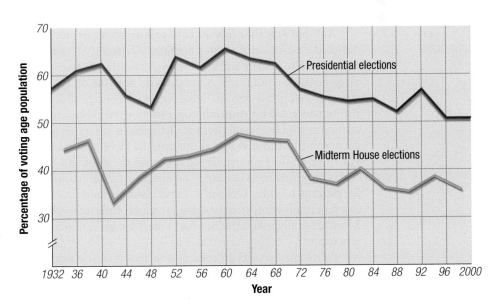

**Figure 12.1
Voter Turnout in
Presidential and
Midterm House
Elections,
1932–2000**

Source: Data from Harold W. Stanley and Richard G. Niemi, *Vital Statistics on American Politics, 1999–2000* (Washington, DC: Congressional Quarterly Press, 2000), 12–13.

elections vary in democracies around the world, yielding very different rates of turnout. Several election rules in the United States contribute to low turnout by making it more difficult for voters to exercise their right to vote. The low turnout may be an accidental consequence of laws intended for other purposes, but in some cases it is a deliberate goal of politicians who believe that high turnout will benefit the other party or be harmful to stable government.

One U.S. election law that lowers voter turnout is the requirement that citizens register before they vote. Usually, voters must register well before the campaign has even begun and before they are engaged enough in the issues or personalities to think they might want to vote. About a third of the electorate never registers and is therefore ineligible to vote on election day. In many other democracies, it is government, not the individual voter, that bears the responsibility of registering citizens, and if voters do not vote, it is not because they neglected to register months before. In a number of countries—Australia, Belgium, and Italy, for example—voting is actually required by law. Turnout rates in those countries are 94 percent, 85 percent, and 87 percent, respectively. The National Voter Registration Act of 1993, or the **Motor Voter Bill** as it is more commonly called, requires that the states take a more active role in registering voters, allowing them to register when they apply for a driver's license, welfare, or other state benefits. Since the passage of the bill, the number of registered voters has increased, but after a mild jump in 1992, turnout on election day has continued to decline. At best, Motor Voter seems only to have slowed the decline in turnout.[7]

Motor Voter Bill
legislation allowing citizens to register to vote at the same time they apply for a driver's license or other state benefit

Besides registration, other election regulations make voting in America more difficult than it typically is in European democracies. For one thing, U.S. laws allow for a lot of elections. We vote for president (and other offices) every four years. Two years later, we vote in midterm elections. There are also primary elections, which take place the spring before each November election. Most states hold local elections and vote on local issues or taxes, often in the spring of odd-numbered years. Thus citizens in the United States are asked to trek to the polls eight to twelve times over a four-year period. In contrast, most Europeans are asked to vote only two or three times. The evidence suggests that frequency of elections leads to voter fatigue.

Another law that lowers U.S. participation in elections is the requirement that national elections are always held on a Tuesday, typically a workday. Many people find it hard to get off work or to juggle waiting in line at the polls with their normal weekday tasks, and many Americans do not vote as a result. By contrast, a large majority of European nations have weekend voting, which contributes to their higher turnout levels. The research suggests that switching to weekend voting would increase turnout by 5 or 6 percent.[8] Moreover, voters seem to like the idea. In one poll, 59 percent of those who did not vote in 1998 said they would be "more likely" to vote if given the opportunity to do so on the weekend.[9]

In an effort to save money on electoral administration and also to make it easier for citizens to vote, Oregon is experimenting with voting by mail. One study indicated that allowing vote-by-mail increased turnout in the Beaver State by 6 percent. More generally, estimates are that vote-by-mail can increase participation by around 4 percent.[10]

Politicians have been reluctant to pass major electoral reforms because of fears about who the beneficiaries of such changes might be. The conventional wisdom is that Democrats would benefit from efforts to increase turnout because Republicans are already motivated enough to turn out under current laws, but this expectation (or fear) does not seem to have been borne out by our experience with the Motor Voter Bill. In the wake of the 2000 presidential election, calls for various sorts of reform are louder and more widespread than ever, and state legislators around the country are now grappling with the issue.

Attitude Changes   Political scientists have found that some of the decrease in voter turnout we noted in Figure 12.1 is accounted for by changes over time in psychological orientations or attitudes toward politics.[11] For one thing, if people feel that they do not or cannot make a difference and that government is not responsive to their wishes, they often don't bother to vote. Lower feelings of political efficacy lead to less participation.

A second orientation that has proved important in explaining low turnout is partisanship. There has been a distinct decline in Americans' attachments to the two major political parties in the 1960s and 1970s. With a drop in party identification came a drop in voting levels. This decline, however, has leveled off, and in recent years there has even been a slight increase in the percentage of citizens saying they identify as Democrats or Republicans. This slight increase in partisanship, however, has not been sufficient to offset the decline in turnout.

Attitudes, of course, do not change without some cause; they reflect citizens' reactions to what they see in the political world. Looking over the time period from the 1950s to the present, it is easy to understand why attitudes have changed. The Vietnam War; the Watergate scandal; the Carter years of pessimism and dismay; the Reagan administration's Iran-contra affair, which spilled over into the elder Bush years; and the numerous sex and financial scandals that haunted the Clinton administration have all yielded sustained negative information and images about the leadership of the national government. This is reflected in negative attitudes toward government (lower feelings of efficacy and government responsiveness) and a tendency to withdraw from politics (lower levels of party identification).

Lower Levels of Mobilization   Another factor that political scientists believe has led to lower turnout is a change in the strategies of the political parties. Parties in recent years have devoted much less energy to voter mobilization than they used to (although they increased their efforts in 2000). **Voter mobilization** is a party's efforts to inform supporters about the election and to persuade them to vote. It can take the form of phone calls, knocking on doors, or even supplying rides to the polls. Through the 1980s and 1990s, parties tended to concentrate on helping candidates, especially with campaign organization and television advertising, rather than mobilizing voters.[12] A reduction in mobilization efforts may account for a substantial portion of the decline in voting, especially among those lower on the socioeconomic scale, who are less likely to be involved in politics on their own.[13]

voter mobilization
a party's efforts to inform potential voters about issues and candidates and persuade them to vote

Decrease in Social Connectedness   Some of the decline in voter turnout is due to larger societal changes rather than to citizen reactions to parties and political leaders. **Social connectedness** refers to the number of organizations people participate in and how tightly knit their communities and families are—that is, how well integrated they are into the society in which they live. The evidence is that people are increasingly likely to live alone and to be single, new to their communities, and isolated from organizations. As individuals loosen or altogether lose their ties to the larger

social connectedness
citizens' involvement in groups and their relationships to their communities and families

community, they have less stake in participating in communal decisions—and less support for participatory activities. Lower levels of social connectedness have been an important factor in accounting for the declining turnout in national elections.[14]

Generational Changes   Another factor accounting for declining turnout is changes in political generations. Events occurring in the formative years of a generation continue to shape its members' orientation toward politics throughout their lives. This is different from the observation that people are more likely to vote as they get older. For instance, those age groups (cohorts) that came of age after the 1960s show much lower levels of attachment to politics, and they vote at lower levels than their parents or grandparents. Some research suggests that generational differences account for much or most of turnout decline. That is, people who once voted have not stopped voting; rather they are dying and are being replaced by younger, less politically engaged voters. The result is lower turnout overall.[15] The interesting question for the future is whether this lower level of civic involvement of recent generations will endure through their middle age and into retirement.

The Rational Nonvoter   A final explanation for the puzzle of low voter turnout in America considers that, for some people, not voting may be the rational choice. This suggests that the question to ask is not "Why don't people vote?" but rather "Why does anyone vote?" The definition of *rational* means that the benefits of an action outweigh the costs. It is rational for us to do those things from which we get more back than we put in. Voting demands our resources, time, and effort, which we can ill afford in our busy lives. Given those costs, if someone views voting primarily as a way to influence government and sees no other benefits from it, it becomes a largely irrational act. That is, no one individual's vote can change the course of an election unless the election would otherwise be a tie, and the probability of that happening in a presidential election is too small to calculate.

For many people, however, the benefits of voting go beyond the likelihood that they will affect the outcome of the election. In fact, studies have demonstrated that turnout decisions are not really based on our thinking that our votes will determine the outcome. Rather, we achieve other kinds of benefits from voting. It feels good to do what we think we are supposed to do or to help, however little, the side or the causes we believe in. Plus, we get social rewards from our politically involved friends for voting (and avoid sarcastic remarks for not voting). All of these benefits accrue no matter which side wins.

Does Nonvoting Matter?

What difference does it make that some people vote and others do not? There are two ways to tackle this question. One approach is to ask whether election outcomes would be different if nonvoters were to participate. The other approach is to ask whether higher levels of nonvoting indicate that democracy is not healthy. Both, of course, concern important potential consequences of low participation in our elections.

Consequences for Outcomes   Studies of the likely effects of nonvoting come up with contradictory answers. A traditional, and seemingly logical, approach is to note that nonvoters, being disproportionately poor and less educated, have social and economic characteristics that are more common among Democrats than among Republicans. Therefore were these people to vote, we could expect that Democratic candidates would do better. Some polling results from the 1998 elections support this thinking. Pollsters asked registered voters a number of questions to judge how likely it was that they would actually vote in elections for House members. When the voting intentions of all registered voters and the subset of likely voters were compared, the likely voters were distinctly more Republican. If this were to hold true generally, we could conclude that nonvoting works to the disadvantage of Democratic candidates. One political scholar found some evidence of this for the 1980 presidential election and concluded that a much higher turnout among nonvoters would have made the election closer and that Carter might even have won reelection.[16]

Undermining this interpretation are findings from most other presidential elections. There we find that nonvoters' preferences are quite responsive to short-term factors, so they go disproportionately for the winning candidate. Because they are less partisan and have less intensely held issue positions, they are moved more easily by the short-term campaign factors favoring one party or the other. In most presidential elections, nonvoters' participation would have increased the winner's margin only slightly or not changed things at all.[17] The potential effects of nonvoters being mobilized, therefore, are probably not as consistently pro-Democratic as popular commentary suggests.

Consequences for Democracy   Although low turnout might not affect who actually wins an election, we have made it clear that elections do more than simply select leaders. How might nonvoting affect the quality of democratic life in America? Nonvoting can influence the stability and legitimacy of democratic government. The victor in close presidential elections, for example, must govern the country, but as critics often point out, as little as 25 percent of the eligible electorate may have voted for the winner. When a majority of the electorate sits out an election, the entire governmental process may begin to lose legitimacy in society at large. Nonvoting can also have consequences for the nonvoter. As we have noted, failure to participate politically can aggravate already low feelings of efficacy and produce higher levels of political estrangement. To the extent that being a citizen is an activepursuit, unhappy, unfulfilled, and unconnected citizens seriously damage the quality of democratic life for themselves and for the country as a whole.

WHO, WHAT, HOW   All political actors are not equal on election day. Some reduce their power considerably by failing to turn out to vote.

WHO are the actors?	WHAT do they want?	HOW do they get it?
Citizens	• Electoral power • Representation of interests • Political stability and quality of democratic life	• Ability to overcome legal, attitudinal, party, and social obstacles to voting

How the Voter Decides

Putting an X next to a name on a ballot or pulling a lever on a voting machine to register a preference would seem like a pretty simple act. But although the action itself may be simple, the decision process behind the choice is anything but. A number of considerations go into our decision about how to vote, including our partisan identification, our stance on the issues, our evaluation of the job government has been doing generally, and our opinions of the candidates. In this section, we examine how these factors play out in the simple act of voting.

Partisanship

The single biggest factor accounting for how people decide to vote is *party identification,* a concept we discussed in Chapter 11. For most citizens, party ID is stable and long-term, carrying over from one election to the next in what one scholar has called "a standing decision."[18] Although party ID has declined slowly in recent decades, the majority of party identifiers remain loyal to their party.[19] In 2000, for example, 86 percent of those identifying with the Democratic Party voted for Al Gore, and 91 percent of those identifying with the Republican Party voted for George W. Bush. Moreover, most Americans consider themselves to be either Democrats or Republicans.

Under unusual circumstances, social group characteristics can exaggerate or override traditional partisan loyalties. The 1960 election, for instance, was cast in terms of whether the nation would elect its first Catholic president. In that context, religion was especially salient, and fully 82 percent of Roman Catholics supported Kennedy, compared to just 37 percent of Protestants—a difference of 45 percent. Compare that to 1976, when the Democrats ran a devout Baptist, Jimmy Carter, for president. The percentage of Catholics voting Democratic dropped to 58 percent, while Protestants voting Democratic increased to 46 percent. The difference shrank to just 12 percent.

In 2000 Al Gore chose Connecticut senator Joseph Lieberman, an orthodox Jew, as his running mate. Lieberman's run as the first Jew on a major-party ticket did not have as dramatic an effect on Democratic support as Kennedy's nomination did, since Jews already turn out for Democrats in large numbers.

Issues and Policy

An idealized view of elections would have highly attentive citizens paying careful attention to the different policy positions offered by the candidates and then, perhaps aided by informed policy analyses from the media, casting their ballots for the candidates who best represent their preferred policy solutions. In truth, as we know by now, American citizens are not "ideal," and the role played by issues is less obvious and more complicated than the ideal model would predict. The role of issues in electoral decision-making is limited by the following factors:

- People are busy and, in many cases, rely on party labels to tell them what they need to know about the candidates.[20]

- People know where they stand on "easy" issues like capital punishment or prayer in schools, but some issues, like economic policy or health care reform, are very complicated, and many citizens tend to tune them out.[21]

- The media do not generally cover issues in depth. Instead, they much prefer to focus on the horse race aspect of elections, looking at who is ahead in the polls rather than what substantive policy issues mean for the nation.[22]

- As we discussed in Chapter 10, people process a lot of policy-relevant information in terms of their impressions of candidates (on-line processing) rather than as policy information. They are certainly influenced by policy information, but they cannot necessarily articulate their opinions and preferences on policy.

prospective voting
basing voting decisions on well-informed opinions and consideration of the future consequences of a given vote

Although calculated policy decisions by voters are rare, policy considerations do have a real impact on voters' decisions. To see that, it is useful to distinguish between prospective and retrospective voting. The idealized model of policy voting with which we opened this section is **prospective voting,** in which voters base their decisions on what will happen in the future if they vote for a candidate—what policies will be enacted, what values will be emphasized in policy. Prospective voting requires a good deal of information that average voters, as we have seen, do not always have or even want. While all voters do some prospective voting and, by election time, are usually aware of the candidate's major issue positions, it is primarily party activists and political elites who engage in the full-scale policy analysis that prospective voting entails.

retrospective voting
basing voting decisions on reactions to past performance; approving the status quo or signaling a desire for change

Instead, most voters supplement their spotty policy information and interest with their evaluation of how they think the country is doing, how the economy is performing, and how well the incumbents are carrying out their jobs. They engage in **retrospective voting,** casting their votes as signs of approval or to signal their desire for change.[23] In presidential elections, this means that voters consistently look back at the state of the economy, at perceived successes or failures in foreign policy, and at domestic issues like education, gun control, or welfare reform. In 1980 the economy was suffering from a high rate of inflation. Ronald Reagan skillfully focused on voter frustration in the presidential debate by asking voters this question: "Next Tuesday, all of you will go to the polls, and stand there in the polling place and make a decision. I think when you make that decision it might be well if you would ask yourself, are you better off than you were four years ago?"[24]

Our idealized model has voters listening as candidates debate the issues through the campaign. More realistic is a model that views voters as perhaps listening to policy debates with one ear and getting information through their party or their friends and families (the opinion leaders we discussed in Chapter 10) but also evaluating the past performance of candidates, particularly as those performances have affected their lives. Thus voters decide partly on what candidates promise to do and partly on what incumbents have done.

The Candidates

When Americans vote, they are casting ballots for people. In addition to considerations of party and issues, voters also base their decisions on judgments about candidates as individuals. What goes into voters' images of candidates?

Some observers have claimed that voters view candidate characteristics much as they would a beauty or personality contest. There is little support, however, for the notion that voters are won over merely by good looks or movie star qualities. Consider, for example, that Richard Nixon almost won against John F. Kennedy, who had good looks, youth, and a quick wit in his favor. Then, in 1964, the awkward, gangly Lyndon Johnson defeated the much more handsome and articulate Barry Goldwater in a landslide. In contrast, there is ample evidence that voters form clear opinions about candidate qualities that are relevant to governing. These include trustworthiness, competence, experience, and sincerity. Citizens also make judgments about the ability of the candidates to lead the nation and to withstand the pressures of the presidency. Ronald Reagan, for example, was widely admired for his ability to stay above the fray of Washington politics and to see the humor in many situations. He appeared, to most Americans, to be in control. By contrast, his predecessor, Jimmy Carter, seemed overwhelmed by the job.

By the end of the 2000 campaign, voters had quite distinctive images of the candidates George W. Bush and Al Gore. According to Pew Research Center data, more people saw Bush as personally likable (48% to 39%), honest and truthful (43% to 32%), and willing to take an unpopular stand (49% to 35%). Gore was seen as more of a "typical politician" (51% to 29%) but more personally qualified to be president (45% to 38%). Not surprisingly, Gore campaigned hard on the issues and his qualifications for office, whereas Bush continually emphasized character and tried to tie Gore to the Clinton administration and partisan Washington politics.

WHO, WHAT, HOW Citizens have a strong interest in seeing that good and effective leaders are elected and that power transfers peacefully from losers to winners.

WHO are the actors?	WHAT do they want?	HOW do they get it?
Voters	• Ability to make decisions about how to vote	• Party identification • Social groups • Policy considerations • Candidate images

Electing the President

Being president of the United States is undoubtedly a difficult challenge, but so is getting the job in the first place. In this section, we examine the long, expensive, and grueling "road to the White House," as the media like to call it.

Getting Nominated

Each major party (and minor parties, too) needs to winnow down the long list of party members with ambitions to serve in the White House to a single viable candidate. How the candidate is chosen will determine the sort of candidate chosen. Remember, in politics the rules are always central to shaping the outcome. Since 1972 party nominees for the presidency have been chosen in primaries, taking the power away from the party elite and giving it to the activist members of the party who care enough to turn out and vote on election day.

The Pre-primary Season   It is hard to say when a candidate's presidential campaign actually begins. Potential candidates may begin planning and thinking about running for the presidency in childhood. At one time or another, many people in politics consider going for the big prize, but there are several crucial steps between wishful thinking and actually running for the nomination. Candidates vary somewhat in their approach to the process, but most of those considering a run for the White House go through the following stages.

- First, potential candidates usually test the waters unofficially. They talk to friends and fellow politicians to see just how much support they can count on, and they often leak news of their possible candidacy to the press to see how it is received in the media.

- If the first stage has positive results, candidates file with the Federal Elections Commission to set up a committee to receive funds so they can officially explore their prospects. The formation of an *exploratory committee* can be exploited as a media event by the candidate, using the occasion to get free publicity for the launching of the still-unannounced campaign.

- The third step is to acquire a substantial war chest to pay for the enormous expenses of running for the nomination.

- The potential candidate must also use the pre-primary season to position himself or herself as a credible prospect with the media. It is no coincidence that in the last seven elections, the parties' nominees have all held prominent government offices and have entered the field with some media credibility. Incumbents especially have a huge advantage here.

Putting out Feelers
One of the first steps candidates take in the pre-primary season is to test the political waters to see if they have enough support to run for office. George W. Bush's exploratory committee, formed in March 1999, consisted entirely of members of Congress and prominent Republicans.

- The final step of the pre-primary season is the official announcement of candidacy. Like the formation of the exploratory committee, this statement is actually part of the campaign itself. Promises are made to supporters, agendas are set, media attention is captured, and the process is under way.

Primaries and Caucuses   The actual fight for the nomination takes place in the state party caucuses and primaries in which delegates to the parties' national conventions are chosen. In a **party caucus,** grassroots members of the party in each community gather in selected locations to discuss the current candidates. They then vote for delegates from that locality who will be sent to the national convention, or who will go on to larger caucuses at the state level to choose the national delegates. Attending a caucus is time-consuming, and turnout percentages are frequently in the single digits. Even in an early state like Iowa, which is virtually bombarded with candidates and advertisements prior to the caucuses, only about 10 percent of Iowa's voters participated in 2000.[25] About a quarter of the states choose delegates by party caucus, accounting for less than 25 percent of the delegates at the national conventions.

party caucus local gathering of party members to choose convention delegates

The most common device for choosing delegates to the national conventions is the **presidential primary.** Primary voters cast ballots that send delegates committed to voting for a particular candidate to the conventions. Primaries can be open, blanket, or closed, depending on the rules the state party organizations adopt, and these can change from year to year.

presidential primary an election by which voters choose convention delegates committed to voting for a certain candidate

- *Open primary.* Any registered voter may vote in an open primary, regardless of party affiliation. At the polling place, the voter chooses the ballot of the party whose primary he or she wants to vote in.

- *Blanket primary.* These are also open to any registered voter. Separate ballots are not issued for individual parties, but rather all candidates of all parties are listed together by office. Neither party allows a blanket primary to choose presidential nominees.

- *Closed primary.* Only registered party members may vote in a closed primary. A subset of this is the independent primary, open only to registered party members and those not registered as members of another party.

Most primaries are closed. Democrats generally favor closed primaries, while Republican rules vary. Neither party cares very much for the blanket primary, as it dilutes the influence of party altogether by not requiring voters to make a party commitment. In addition to the delegates chosen by the state's preferred method, the Democrats also send elected state officials, including such people as Democratic members of Congress and governors, to their national conventions. Some of these officials are "superdelegates," able to vote as free agents, but the rest must reflect the state's primary vote.[26]

In addition to varying in terms of who may vote, primary rules also differ in how the delegates are to be distributed among the candidates running. The Democrats generally use a method of proportional representation, in which the candidates get the percentage of delegates equal to the percentage of the primary vote they win (provided they get at least 15 percent). Republican rules run from proportional representation, to winner take all (the candidate with the most votes gets all the delegates, even if he or she does not win an absolute majority), to direct voting for delegates (the delegates are not bound to vote for a particular candidate at the convention), to the absence of a formal system (caucus participants may decide how to distribute the delegates).

State primaries also vary in the times at which they are held, with various states engaged in **front-loading,** vying to hold their primaries first to gain maximum exposure in the media and power over the nomination. By tradition, the Iowa caucus and the New Hampshire primary are the first contests for delegates. Because of this, they get tremendous attention, both from candidates and from the media—much more than their contribution to the delegate count would justify. This is why other states have been moving their primaries earlier in the primary season. In 1988, eleven southern states, seeking to boost their clout, agreed to have their primaries on the second Tuesday in March, a day they called Super Tuesday. In an attempt to highlight his state's role in the process, Governor Pete Wilson signed a bill in the fall of 1998 moving his state's primary from the end of March to the first Tuesday in March.

The consequence of Super Tuesday, the early California primary, and other such front-loading is that candidates must have a full war chest and be prepared to campaign nationally from the beginning. Traditionally, winners of early primaries could use that success to raise more campaign funds to continue the battle. With the primaries stacked at the beginning, however, this becomes much harder. When the winner can be determined within weeks of the first primary, it is less likely that a dark horse, or unknown candidate, can emerge. The process favors well-known, well-connected, and especially well-funded candidates. Again, incumbents have an enormous advantage here.

Every candidate's goal is to develop **momentum,** the perception by the press, the public, and the other candidates in the field that one is on a roll and that polls, primary victories, endorsements, and funding are all coming one's way. A candidate with momentum is one whose showing is better than expected and who seems to be gaining strength. Developing momentum helps to distinguish one's candidacy in a crowded field and is typically established in the early primaries.

In most of the crowded primaries in recent years, there has been a clear **front-runner,** a person who many assume will win the nomination. While having momentum is good, there are some hazards attached to being perceived as a front-runner, notably that the growing expectations are increasingly hard to fulfill. The strategy for each of the other candidates is to simultaneously attack the front-runner so as to drive down his or her support, while maneuvering into position as the chief alternative. When the front-runner stumbles, as often happens, the attacking candidate hopes to emerge from the pack.

The Convention Since 1972 delegates attending the national conventions have not had to decide who the parties' nominees would be. However, there are still two official actions that continue to take place at the conventions. First, as we discussed in Chapter 11, the parties hammer out and approve their platforms, the documents in which parties set out their distinct issue positions. Second, the vice-presidential candidate is named. The choice of the vice president is up to the presidential nomi-

front-loading
the process of scheduling presidential primaries early in the primary season

momentum
the perception that a candidate is moving ahead of the rest of the field

front-runner
the leading candidate and expected winner of a nomination or an election

The Conventions
The national nominating conventions are carefully orches-trated for television to showcase the parties and their nomi-nees. The 2000 Republican gathering featured a display of racial diversity, which served to frame George W. Bush's campaign of inclusiveness and compassionate conservatism.

nee. Traditionally, the choice was made to balance the ticket (ideologically, regionally, or even, when Democrat Walter Mondale chose Geraldine Ferraro in 1984, by gender). Bill Clinton's choice of Al Gore was a departure from this practice, as he tapped a candidate much like himself—a Democratic moderate from a southern state. Gore returned to the balancing principle in 2000, choosing as his running mate Connecticut senator Joe Lieberman, a Jewish northeasterner. George W. Bush picked Dick Cheney, a man whose considerable experience in the federal government could be expected to offset Bush's relative lack of it. In any case, the evidence to date suggests that the vice-presidential choice does not have significant electoral consequences.

Although their actual party business is limited, the conventions still provide the nominee with a "convention bump" in the polls. The harmonious coverage, the enthusiasm of party supporters, and even the staged theatrics seem to have a positive impact on viewers. The result is that candidates have generally realized a noticeable rise in the polls immediately following the conventions, as both Bush and Gore did in the summer of 2000.

The Electoral College

Because our founders feared giving too much power to the volatile electorate, we do not actually vote for the president and vice president in presidential elections. Rather, we cast our votes in November for electors (members of the electoral college), who in turn actually vote for the president in December. The Constitution provides for each state to have as many electoral votes as it does senators and representatives in Congress. Thus Alaska has 3 electoral votes (1 for each of the state's U.S. senators and 1 for its sole member of the House of Representatives). California has 54 (2 senators and 52 representatives). In addition, the Twenty-third Amendment gave the District of Columbia 3 electoral votes. There are 538 electoral votes in all; 270 are needed to win the presidency. Figure 12.2 shows the distribution of electoral votes among the states today.

Electors are generally activist members of the party whose presidential candidate carried the state. In December, following the election, the electors meet and vote

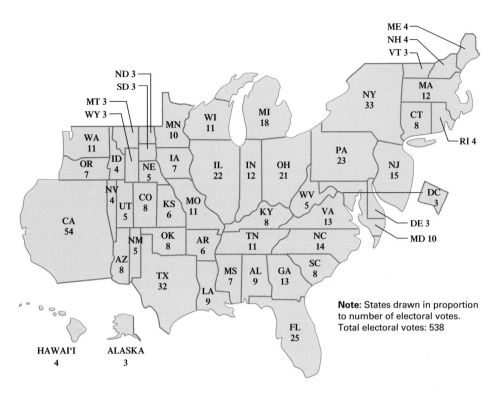

**Figure 12.2
Electoral College**
This distorted map, in which the states are sized according to their number of electoral votes, demonstrates the electoral power of the more populous states.

Note: States drawn in proportion to number of electoral votes. Total electoral votes: 538

in their state capitals. In the vast majority of cases, they vote as expected, but there are occasional "faithless electors" who vote for their own preferences. The results of the electors' choices in the states are then sent to the Senate, where the ballots are counted when the new session opens. If no candidate achieves a majority in the electoral college, the Constitution calls for the House of Representatives to choose from the top three electoral vote winners. In this process, each state has one vote. Whenever the vote goes to the House, the Senate decides on the vice president, with each senator having a vote. This has happened only twice (the last time was in 1824), although some observers of the 2000 election speculated that that election, too, could have been decided in the House of Representatives if Florida's electoral votes had not been decided and neither Bush nor Gore had obtained a majority.

The importance of the electoral college is that all the states but Maine and Nebraska operate on a winner-take-all basis. Thus the winner in California, even if he or she has less than a majority of the popular vote, wins all of the state's 54 electoral votes. The loser in California may have won 49 percent of the popular vote, but he or she gets nothing in the electoral college. It is possible, then, for the popular vote winner to lose in the electoral college. This has happened only three times in our history, most recently in 2000, when Bush received an electoral college majority even though Gore won the popular vote by more than half a million votes. Usually, however, the opposite happens: the electoral college exaggerates the candidate's apparent majority. In 1992 and 1996, Bill Clinton received only 43.2 and 49 percent of the popular vote, but his electoral majorities were 69 and 70 percent. This exaggeration of the winning margin has the effect of legitimizing the winner's victory and allowing him to claim that he has a *mandate*—a broad popular endorsement—even if he won by a small margin of the popular vote.

The winner-take-all provision for allocating the states' electors influences how candidates campaign. The swing voters who will help the candidate win a large state, and hence the full pot of the state's electoral votes, become much more important to a candidate than all the voters in a small state. Thus small states receive very few campaign visits from presidential candidates. Similarly, voters in competitive states (where the race is tight) are much more important to the candidates than the voters in a state where the winner can be safely predicted. The state of Indiana, for instance, almost always votes Republican. Consequently, Hoosiers are rarely visited by presidential campaigns, and candidates do not bother to spend their advertising dollars there. It is not worthwhile for the Democrats to go to Indiana, and the Republicans don't need to bother. The fact that large, diverse states like Michigan, Florida, and California are usually the most competitive reinforces candidates' tendencies to spend the lion's share of their time, resources, and media efforts in those states. The consequence of this aspect of the electoral college is that not all citizens experience the same political campaign.

Hundreds of bills have been introduced in Congress to reform or abolish the electoral college, and many more can be expected in the wake of the 2000 election.[27] Major criticisms include the following:

● The electoral college is undemocratic because it is possible for the popular winner not to get a majority of the electoral votes.

● In a very close contest, the popular outcome could be dictated by a few "faithless electors" who vote their consciences rather than the will of the people of their states.

● The electoral college distorts candidates' campaign strategies. The winner-take-all provision in all but two states puts a premium on a few large competitive states, which get a disproportionate share of the candidates' attention.

Few people deny the truth of these charges, and hardly anyone believes that if we were to start all over, the current electoral college would be chosen as the best way to elect a president. Nevertheless, all the proposed alternatives also have problems, or at least serious criticisms. And the large states, which have the most to gain in keeping the current system, have the clout in Congress to prevent reforms from passing. See "What's at Stake Revisited" at the end of this chapter for a discussion of whether the 2000 election is likely to finish off the electoral college.

The General Election Campaign

After the candidates are nominated in August, there is a short break, at least for the public, before the traditional official campaign kickoff after Labor Day. The goal of each campaign is to convince supporters to turn out and to get undecided voters to choose its candidate. There is little doubt about whom most voters, the party identifiers, prefer, but they need to be motivated by the campaign to turn out and cast their ballots. Most of the battle in a presidential campaign is for the **swing voters,** the one-

swing voters
the approximately one-third of the electorate who are undecided at the start of a campaign

third or so of the electorate who have not made up their minds at the start of the campaign and who are open to persuasion by either side. Each seeks to get its message across, to define the choice in terms that give its candidate the advantage. This massive effort to influence the information citizens are exposed to requires a clear overall strategy that incorporates the projected image of the candidate (and his or her opponent), the issues, the media, and money. All these components of the campaign strategy are masterminded, for better or worse, by a professional campaign staff.

Who Runs the Campaign?   Running a modern presidential campaign has become a highly specialized profession. Most presidential campaigns are led by an "amateur," a nationally prestigious chairperson who may serve as an adviser and assist in fundraising. However, the real work of the campaign is done by the professional staff the candidate hires. These may be people the candidate knows well and trusts, or they may be professionals who sign on for the duration of the campaign and then move on to another. Campaign work at the beginning of the twenty-first century is big business.

The jobs include not only the well-known ones of campaign manager and strategist but also more specialized components tailored to the modern campaign's emphasis on information and money. For instance, candidates need to hire research teams to prepare position papers on issues so that the candidate can answer any question posed by potential supporters and the media. But researchers also engage in the controversial but necessary task of **oppo research**—delving into the background and vulnerabilities of the opposing candidate with an eye to exploiting his or her weaknesses. Central to the modern campaign's efforts to get and control the flow of information are pollsters and focus group administrators, who are critical for testing the public's reactions to issues and strategies. Media consultants try to get free coverage of the campaign whenever possible and to make the best use of the campaign's advertising dollars by designing commercials and print advertisements.

Candidates also need advance teams to plan and prepare their travel agendas, to arrange for crowds (and the signs they wave) to greet the candidates at airports, and even to reserve accommodations for the press. Fundraisers are essential to ensure the constant flow of money necessary to grease the wheels of any presidential campaign. They work with big donors and engage in direct-mail campaigns to solicit money from targeted groups. Finally, of course, candidates need to hire a legal team to keep their campaigns in compliance with the regulations of the Federal Elections Commission and to file the required reports. In general, campaign consultants are able to provide specialized technical services that the parties' political committees cannot.[28]

Presenting the Candidate   An effective campaign begins with a clear understanding of how the strengths of the candidate fit with the context of the times and the mood of the voters. As a campaign struggles to control the flow of information about its candidate, it often also tries to influence how voters see the opposition. This is where the oppo research mentioned earlier comes into play, sometimes complete with focus groups and poll testing. In fact, oppo research has become a central component in all elections, leading to the negative campaigning so prevalent in recent years.[29] Research on one's opponent, however, cannot compensate for the fail-

oppo research
investigation of an opponent's background for the purpose of exploiting weaknesses or undermining credibility

ure to define oneself in clear and attractive terms. In 2000 Al Gore's failure to define himself clearly to voters left the field wide-open for the Bush campaign to create the impression that Gore was dishonest, even though he had previously had a reputation as a squeaky-clean "boy scout."

The Issues   Earlier we indicated that voters do take issues into consideration in making up their minds about how to vote, both prospectively and retrospectively. This means that issues must be central to the candidate's strategy for getting elected. From the candidate's point of view, there are two kinds of issues to consider when planning a strategy: valence issues and position issues.

valence issue
an issue on which most voters and candidates share the same position

Valence issues are policy matters on which the voters and the candidates all share the same preference. These are what we might call "motherhood and apple pie" issues, because no one opposes them. Everyone is for a strong, prosperous economy, for America having a respected leadership role in the world, for thrift in government, and for a clean environment. Similarly, everyone opposes crime and drug abuse, government waste, political corruption, and immorality.

position issue
an issue on which the parties differ in their perspectives and proposed solutions

Position issues have two sides. On abortion, there are those who are pro-life and those who are pro-choice. On Vietnam, there were the hawks who favored pursuing a military victory and the doves who favored just getting out. Many of the hardest decisions for candidates are on position issues, because, while a clear stand means that they will gain some friends, it also guarantees that they will make some enemies. Realistic candidates, who want to win as many votes as possible, try to avoid being clearly identified with the losing side of important position issues. One example is abortion. Activists in the Republican Party fought to keep their strong pro-life plank in the party platform in 2000. However, because a majority of the electorate are opposed to the strong pro-life position, George W. Bush seldom mentioned the issue during the campaign, even though one of his first acts as president was to cut federal funding to overseas groups that provide abortions or abortion counseling.

wedge issue
a controversial issue that one party uses to split the voters in the other party

When a candidate or party does take a stand on a difficult position issue, the other side often uses it against them as a wedge issue. A **wedge issue** is a position issue on which the parties differ and that proves controversial within the ranks of a particular party. For a Republican, an anti–affirmative action position is not dangerous, since few Republicans actively support affirmative action. For a Democrat, though, it is a very dicey issue, because liberal party members endorse it but more moderate members do not. An astute strategy for a Republican candidate is to raise the issue in a campaign, hoping to drive a wedge between the Democrats and to recruit the Democratic opponents of affirmative action to his or her side.

issue ownership
the tendency of one party to be seen as more competent in a specific policy area

The idea of **issue ownership** helps to clarify the role of policy issues in presidential campaigns. Because of their past stands and performance, each of the parties is widely perceived as better able to handle certain kinds of problems. The voter's decision is not so much based on evaluating positions on education and crime, but rather on deciding which problem is more important. From the candidate's point of view, the trick is to convince voters that the election is about the issues that your party "owns."

An example of how issue ownership operated in the 2000 presidential election can be seen in the exit poll data. Voters were asked which of seven issues was most important in their vote decision. Table 12.1 shows that four of those issues (Medicare/prescription drugs, health care, economy/jobs, and social security) clearly

Table 12.1
Issue Ownership in the 2000 Election

"Which issue mattered most in how you voted for president?"	Percentage Naming the Issue	Voted for Gore	Voted for Bush
Gore's Issues			
Medicare/prescription drugs	7%	60%	39%
Health care	8	64	33
Economy/jobs	18	59	37
Social security	14	58	40
Total concerned about Gore's issues	47		
Bush's Issues			
World affairs	12	40	54
Taxes	14	17	80
Total concerned about Bush's issues	26		
Claimed by Both Candidates			
Education	15	52	44

Source: Voter News Service 2000 exit poll.

worked to the benefit of Al Gore. Among those most concerned with those issues, Gore received between 58 and 64 percent of the vote. George W. Bush had the edge on only two of the seven issues, with a modest advantage on world affairs and a whopping 80 percent of the vote among those saying taxes were most important to them. Sometimes a party will try to take an issue that is "owned" by the other party and redefine it in order to claim ownership of it. Bush's effort to appropriate the education issue in the 2000 election is a case in point. Education has traditionally been favored by Democrats, but Bush made it a centerpiece of his campaign. As a result, what had been a big vote winner for the Democrats in 1996 was almost an even split in 2000. Bush successfully nullified the Democrats' advantage on this issue.

Because valence issues are relatively safe, candidates stress them at every opportunity. They also focus on the position issues that their parties "own" or on which they have majority support. What this suggests is that the real campaign is not about debating positions on issues—how to reduce the deficit or whether to restrict abortion—but about which issues should be considered. Issue campaigning is to a large extent about setting the agenda.

The Media   It is impossible to understand the modern political campaign without appreciating the pervasive role of the media. Even though many voters tend to ignore campaign ads—or at least they tell survey interviewers that they do—we know that campaign advertising matters. It has increased dramatically with the rise of television as people's information source of choice. Studies show that advertising provides usable information for voters. Political ads can heighten the loyalty of existing supporters, and they can educate the public about what candidates stand for and what issues candidates believe are most important. Ads also can be effective in establishing the criteria on which voters decide between candidates. And while **negative advertising** tends to turn voters off and increase their perception that politics is an unpleasant business, it does work to create a negative image of a political opponent.

negative advertising
campaign advertising that emphasizes the negative characteristics of opponents rather than one's own strengths

Lincoln. People remember it better than they do positive advertising; tracking polls show that after a voter has seen a negative ad eight times, he or she begins to move away from the attacked candidate.[3] Some candidates claim that their advertising is not really negative but rather "comparative," and indeed a candidate often needs to compare her record with another's in order to make the case that she is the superior choice. Negative

Interpreting Campaign Advertising

"Sticks and stones may break my bones," goes the old childhood rhyme, "but words can never hurt me." Try telling that to the innumerable targets of negative advertising, sloganeering that emphasizes the negative characteristics of one's opponents rather than one's own strengths. Negative advertising has characterized American election campaigns since the days of George Washington. George Washington? His opponents called him a "dictator" who would "debauch the nation."[1] Thomas Jefferson was accused of having an affair with a slave, a controversy that has outlived any of the people involved; Abraham Lincoln was claimed to have had an illegitimate child; and Grover Cleveland, who admitted to fathering a child out of wedlock, was taunted with the words, "Ma, Ma, where's my Pa?"[2] (His supporters had the last laugh, however: "Gone to the White House, ha, ha, ha.")

Like it or not (and most Americans say they do not), the truth is that negative campaign advertising works, and in the television age it is far more prevalent than anything that plagued Washington, Jefferson, or

Is Negative Necessarily "Dirty" in Campaigns?
In this 1996 ad, presidential candidate Bob Dole is labeled as antagonistic toward family leave policies based on his roll call voting on such measures while he served as a senator. It is often difficult to draw the line between legitimate policy comparisons and distortions of the opponent's record. Ultimately, what is "dirty" is up to the voters—but a critical eye can lead to more informed judgments.

Because paid media coverage is so expensive, a campaign's goal is to maximize opportunities for free coverage. The major parties' presidential candidates are accompanied by a substantial entourage of reporters who need to file stories on a regular basis. As a result, daily campaign events are planned more for the press and the demands of the evening news than for the personal audiences, who often seem to function primarily as a backdrop for the candidates' efforts to get favorable airtime each day. Although the candidates want the regular exposure, they do not like the norms of broadcast news, which they see as "horse race journalism."[30] The exhausting nature of campaigns, and the mistakes and gaffes that follow, are a source of constant concern because of the media's tendency to zero in on them. The relationship between the campaigns and the media is testy. They need each other, but the candidates want to control the message, and the media want stories that are "news"—controversies, changes in the candidates' standings, or stories of goofs and

advertising is nonetheless unpopular with voters, who often see it as nasty, unfair, and false. In fact, advertising that is proved to be false can frequently backfire on the person doing the advertising. But how is a savvy media consumer to know what to believe? Be careful, be critical, and be fair in how you interpret campaign ads. Here are some tips. Ask yourself these questions.

1. **Who is running the ad?** What do they have to gain by it? Look to see who has paid for the ad. Is it the opponent's campaign? An interest group? A Political Action Committee (PAC)? What do they have at stake, and how might that affect their charges? If the ad's sponsors do not identify themselves, what might that tell you about the source of the information? About the information itself?

2. **Are the accusations relevant to the campaign or the office in question?** If character is a legitimate issue, questions of adultery or drug use might have bearing on the election. If not, they might just be personal details used to smear this candidate's reputation. Ask yourself, What kind of person should hold the job? What kinds of qualities are important?

3. **Is the accusation or attack timely?** If a person is accused of youthful experimentation with drugs or indiscreet behavior in his twenties, but has been an upstanding lawyer and public servant for twenty-five years, do the accusations have bearing on how the candidate will do the job?

4. **Does the ad convey a fair charge that can be answered, or does it evoke unarticulated fears and emotions?** A 1964 ad for Lyndon Johnson's presidential campaign showed a little girl counting as she plucked petals from a daisy. An adult male voice gradually replaced hers, counting down to an explosion of a mushroom cloud that obliterated the picture. The daisy commercial never even mentioned Johnson's opponent, Barry Goldwater, though the clear implication was that the conservative, promilitary Goldwater was likely to lead the nation to a nuclear war. Amid cries of "Foul!" from Goldwater's Republican supporters, the ad was aired only once, but it became a classic example of the sort of ad that seeks to play on the fears of its viewers.

5. **Is the ad true?** Often media outlets like the *New York Times* will run "ad watches" to help viewers determine if the information in an advertisement is true. If it is not (and sometimes even if it is), you can usually count on hearing a response from the attacked candidate rebutting the charges. Occasionally, candidates have chosen not to respond, claiming to take the high road, but as Michael Dukakis's dismal performance in the 1988 election showed, false attacks left unanswered can be devastating. Try to conduct your own "ad watch." Study the campaign ads and evaluate their truthfulness.

[1]Alexandra Marks, "Backlash Grows Against Negative Political Ads," *Christian Science Monitor,* 28 September 1995, p. 1.

[2]Roger Stone, "Positively Negative," *New York Times,* 26 February 1996, 13.

[3]Stone, 13.

scandals. We discuss the complex relationship between the media and the candidates at greater length in Chapter 13.

Traditionally, most citizens got information from "hard news" sources like the television networks' evening newscasts. Candidates in recent elections, however, have turned increasingly to "soft news" and entertainment programming to get their messages across. *Larry King Live* was the site where third-party presidential hopeful Ross Perot announced his candidacy in 1992 and 1996. Bill Clinton did a stint on MTV to appeal to younger voters and played his sax on *The Arsenio Hall Show.* Following this example, both Bush and Gore hit the talk show circuit in 2000, with appearances on *The Oprah Winfrey Show, Late Show with David Letterman, The Tonight Show with Jay Leno,* MTV, and *Saturday Night Live,* among many others. Such appearances give the candidates more unedited airtime and allow them to evade the hard news tendency to interpret all events in horse race terms.

Image and Visuals Count
Campaigns are run for television. In the 2000 campaign, Al Gore's appearance at this town hall meeting in Clayton, Missouri, with loosened tie and rolled up shirt sleeves as he talked with "real people" about "real problems" (in this case the costs of prescription drugs), was intended to reinforce visually his campaign theme of the candidate who would fight for the people.

Since 1976 the presidential debates have become one of the major focal points of the campaign. The first televised debate was held in 1960 between Senator John Kennedy and Vice President Richard Nixon. The younger and more photogenic Kennedy came out on top in those televised debates, but interestingly, those who heard the debates on radio thought that Nixon did a better job.[31] In general, leading candidates find it less in their interest to participate in debates because they have more to lose and less to win, and so for years debates took place on a sporadic basis.

In the past twenty-five years, however, media and public pressure have all but guaranteed that at least the major-party candidates will participate in debates, although the number, timing, and format of the debates are renegotiated for each presidential election season. Recent elections have generated two or three debates, with a debate among the vice-presidential contenders worked in as well. Third-party candidates, who have the most to gain from the free media exposure and the legitimacy that debate participation confers on a campaign, lobby to be included but rarely are. Ross Perot was invited in 1992 because both George Bush and Bill Clinton hoped to woo his supporters. Ralph Nader and Pat Buchanan were shut out of all three debates in 2000.

Do the debates matter? Detailed statistical studies show, not surprisingly, that many of the debates have been standoffs. However, some of the debates, especially those identified with significant candidate errors or positive performances, have moved vote intentions 2 to 4 percent, which in a close race could be significant.[32] George W. Bush took a slight lead after his first debate with Al Gore in 2000 and maintained it for most of the remainder of the campaign. In addition, there is a good deal of evidence that citizens actually learn about the candidates and their issue positions from the debates.[33] Interest in the debates varies with how much suspense surrounds the outcome of the election. With an open seat and the candidates less

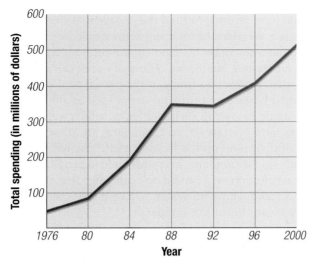

**Figure 12.3
Increase in Total
Spending on
Presidential Campaigns, 1976–1996**
Source: Data from Federal
Elections Commission and
Center for Responsible
Politics.

Note: Estimates of money spent by all presidential candidates in the primaries and general election. Does not include "soft money" or issue advocacy expenditures.

well known in 1992, more people watched the presidential debates and found them helpful than in the 1996 contest.[34]

Money Winning—or even losing—a presidential campaign involves serious money. All of the presidential candidates in 2000, together with their parties, spent more than $500 million, and as Figure 12.3 shows, this is part of an upward trend that is likely to continue until meaningful campaign finance reforms are enacted.

This torrent of cash is used to cover the costs of all the activities just discussed: campaign professionals, polling, travel for the candidates and often their wives (along with the accompanying staff and media), and the production and purchase of media advertising. The campaign costs for all federal offices in 2000 came in at about $3 billion, or almost $11 for every man, woman, and child in the country.

Where does all this money come from? To make sense of the changing world of election campaign finances, we need to start by defining two different kinds of campaign contributions, each with different sources and regulations.

hard money
campaign funds
donated directly to
candidates; amounts are
limited by federal
election laws

- **Hard money** consists of the funds given *directly* to candidates by individuals, political action committees (PACs), the political parties, and the government. The spending of hard money is under the control of the candidates, but its collection is governed by the rules of the Federal Elections Commission Act (FECA) of 1972, 1974, and its various amendments. This act established the Federal Elections Commission (FEC) and was intended to stop the flow of money from, and the influence of, large contributors by outlawing contributions by corporations and unions and by restricting contributions from individuals ($1,000 per candidate per election) and PACs ($5,000 per candidate per election). The parties are also allowed to contribute to their candidates' campaigns directly (the limit was $13.7 million for presidential candidates in 2000). For the presidential candidates, the law also provides for matching funds in the primaries and the general election ($57.7 million in 2000). These matching funds are public money, derived from taxpayers, who have the option of checking a box on their tax returns that sends $3 ($6 on joint returns) to fund the presidential election campaigns. The idea behind the law was that the full campaigns would be paid by public funds, allowing the candidates to concentrate on communicating with the public, ensuring a fair contest, and taking big-money influence out of the campaigns.

To receive matching funds in the presidential primaries, candidates have to show broad-based support by raising at least $5,000 in each of twenty states and agree to abide by overall spending limits, which were about $45 million in 2000, as well as state-by-state limits. Candidates are allowed to spend an additional 20 percent of their total on fundraising itself.[35] In addition, each party was allowed to provide smaller amounts in coordinated expenditures, which is money spent in the general election on a candidate's campaign, but the money is controlled by the parties. A candidate who wants to avoid any spending limits cannot take any public funds for his or her campaign.

The limit on the parties' hard money contributions to candidates was held to be unconstitutional in a 1999 Colorado federal district court decision. The judge's logic in this case is interesting. He stated that the law is supposed to prevent corruption, but that, by definition, a party cannot corrupt its own candidates. If that ruling is upheld by the Supreme Court, it could mean that the parties could make unlimited hard money contributions to congressional and presidential candidates.[36] The limitations on hard money, however, have been greatly watered down by the increased influence of "soft money."

soft money
unregulated campaign contributions by individuals, groups, or parties that promote general election activities but do not directly support individual candidates

● **Soft money** is money spent by individuals, organizations, or parties on campaign or election activities that are independent of a specific candidate. As long as this money is not spent for efforts that tell people how to vote or is not coordinated with a particular campaign, it is not regulated by the FEC. Soft money is spent to promote issue positions or to support general party-building activities like registration drives, get-out-the-vote efforts, and general party image-building campaigns. In practice, a good deal of the soft money is closely coordinated and targeted to help the election of the presidential contenders. Soft money has grown greatly in recent campaigns because it is not regulated and is thus a loophole through which parties (and contributors) can legally get extra money to candidates. It cannot be given directly to candidates, but it can be spent on their behalf. Individuals, corporations, and groups can donate as much as they want to the parties' soft money accounts. In 2000 more than $480 million raised by the major parties was used for everything from polls to registration drives to aiding state party organizations. This is more than an 85 percent increase over the amount raised in 2000.[37] (see Figure 12.4).

issue advocacy ads
advertisements paid for by soft money, and thus not regulated, that promote certain issue positions but do not endorse specific candidates

Issue advocacy ads are the newest and seemingly fastest-growing area of campaign expenditures. The Supreme Court has held (*Buckley* v. *Valeo*, 1976) that individuals and organizations cannot be stopped from spending money to express their opinions about issues or even candidates. Such opinions, even when voiced via television advertising during election campaigns, are protected free speech. The only restriction on such ads is that they cannot explicitly tell viewers how to vote. Otherwise, they look and sound like regular campaign advertisements, paid for by groups that do not necessarily have to identify themselves. This "loophole in the law" or "exercise of free speech" (depending on your point of

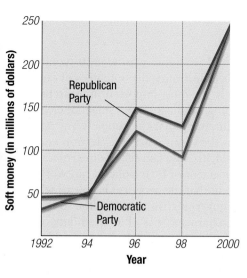

**Figure 12.4
Increases in Soft
Money Raised by
the Political Parties**
Source: Data from Federal
Elections Commission and
Center for Responsible
Politics (http: www.
opensecrets.org).

view) was used by unions, the political parties, industry groups, and religious and environmental groups in 2000 to the tune of at least $300 million in television advertisements, more than twice the amount spent in 1996.[38] The parties alone spent more than $20 million on issue advocacy ads in 1996—far exceeding what they were permitted to give to the candidates directly under FEC regulations. Like contributions to the parties' soft money kitties, issue advocacy costs are not regulated. What is attractive about these unregulated sources of campaign funds is that money can be raised in large chunks. The Center for Responsive Politics labels issue ads "the Hot New Thing in electioneering" and predicts that they "will undoubtedly grow in importance . . . as major donors invest in them as a way to influence elections without leaving any financial fingerprints."[39] Issue advocacy ads essentially allow candidates and their contributors to get around the FEC regulations completely.

It is interesting that the loopholes of soft money and issue advocacy ads have not reduced the amount of FEC-regulated hard money that the candidates spend. As the costs of elections continue to rise, candidates do all they can within the FEC rules to raise smaller amounts by mass mailings and traditional fundraising dinners and speeches, since these sources account for the bulk of the funds for presidential campaigns. The avalanche of soft money and issue advocacy spending is just piled on top of the regulated hard money that the candidates control. These newer forms of spending have largely undermined the goals of the FEC to hold campaign spending down and to check the apparent influence of the infamous "fat cats."

The development of the soft money loophole has brought considerable pressure to fix the campaign finance laws. Groups such as Common Cause, Public Campaign, and the Center for Responsive Politics have formed to publicize abuses of the system and to help build public awareness of the need for change.[40] Reform is difficult, however, because changing the campaign finance laws means changing the rules by which those in office got where they are, and many politicians are reluctant to pass laws that may lead to their own political demise. This is the case even though most members of Congress hate having to spend so much of their time raising money, and some even leave Congress because of the pressure.[41]

In the 105th Congress (1997–1998), Senators John McCain (R-AZ) and Russell Feingold (D-WI) made a major effort to pass a bill that would have banned unregulated soft money contributions to the national parties and prohibited issue advocacy ads during the campaign season. The bill had majority support in the Senate, mostly from Democrats and moderate Republicans, but it was killed by a Republican filibuster led by Senate Majority Leader Trent Lott and Senator Mitch McConnell (R-KY), who was serving as the chair of the National Republican Senatorial Committee (which helps to finance Republican Senate campaigns).[42] Senator McConnell, one of the most avid opponents of campaign finance reform, has an unusual perspective on the meaning of big money in politics: "If you are able to raise a lot of money, it means you have a lot of support, and I think that should be applauded, not condemned."[43] A similar bill failed to pass in 1999, but McCain had plans to reintroduce it early in 2001. Getting a bill that members of Congress can live with and that the Supreme Court will uphold will not be easy.

Interpreting Elections

After the election is over, the votes are counted, and we know who won, it would seem that the whole election season is finally finished. In reality, the outcomes of our collective decisions cry for interpretation. Probably the most important interpretation is the one articulated by the victor. The winning candidate in presidential elections inevitably claims an **electoral mandate,** maintaining that the people want the president to do the things he campaigned on. Thus the winner casts the election as a preference for his leadership and his policies. Presidents who can sell the interpretation that their election to office is a ringing endorsement of their policies can work with Congress from a favored position. To the extent that the president is able to sell his interpretation, he will be more successful in governing. In contrast, the losing party will try to argue that its loss was due to the characteristics of its candidate or specific campaign mistakes. Party members will, predictably, resist the interpretation that the voters rejected their message and their vision for the nation. As we indicate in "What's at Stake Revisited," George W. Bush may have a particularly hard time claiming a mandate in the wake of the close 2000 election.

The media also offer their interpretations. In fact, research shows that of the many possible explanations that are available, the media quickly—in just a matter of weeks—hone in on an agreed-upon standard explanation of the election.[44] Thus in 1992 Bill Clinton was said to have won because of George Bush's ineffectual dealing with the recession, while the 1996 election was interpreted in terms of Clinton's superior appeal to "soccer moms" and his challenger Bob Dole's inability to expand effectively from his conservative base. In 2000 the media, in explaining the closeness of the race, focused on how much more likable voters found George W. Bush, despite the majority's agreement with Al Gore on the issues, and on what they claimed to be Gore's badly run campaign.

electoral mandate
the perception that an election victory signals broad support for the winner's proposed policies

WHO, WHAT, HOW In the matter of choosing a president, the parties and the candidates all have something vital at stake.

WHO are the actors?	WHAT do they want?	HOW do they get it?
Party activists	• Control of party platform • Control of nomination • Advancement of ideological and issue agenda	• Primary system • Campaign activity
Candidates	• Nomination • National victory	• Pleasing activists as well as moderates • Geographic strategy • Professional staff • Strategic positions on issues • Effective use of media • Money

Citizenship and Elections

Points of Access

- Register to vote.
- Join a political party.
- Join the League of Women Voters, a non-partisan political organization that is open to any person—male or female—of voting age. Call 1-800-249-VOTE or log on at http://www.lwv.org to contact your state chapter.
- Organize a campaign rally at your school for a candidate you support.
- Become informed about the candidates and issues in an upcoming election.
- Apply for an internship with Project Vote Smart (http://www.vote-smart.org).
- Join a voter registration drive or "get-out-the-vote" campaign through your town or city government.
- Organize a debate or forum at your school for candidates campaigning for local or state office.
- Volunteer to work at a voting station in your town or city.
- Vote!

At the beginning of this chapter, we acknowledged that the American citizen does not bear a strong resemblance to the ideal citizen of classic democratic theory. Nothing we have learned here leads us to think otherwise, but that does not mean that Americans are doomed to an undemocratic future. Scholars who conducted the earliest studies of voting based on survey research were surprised at the low levels of interest most citizens showed in presidential election campaigns. These studies of the 1944 and 1948 presidential elections found that most citizens had their minds made up before the campaigns began and that opinions changed only slightly in response to the efforts of the parties and candidates. Instead of people relying on new information coming from the campaigns, these studies found that people voted according to the groups they belonged to. Income, occupation, religion, and similar factors structured whom people talked to, what they learned, and how they voted. The authors concluded that democracy is probably safer without a single type of citizen who matches the civics ideal of high levels of participation, knowledge, and commitment.[45]

In this view, such high levels of involvement would indicate a citizenry wrought with conflict. Intense participation comes with intense commitment and strongly held positions, which make for an unwillingness to compromise. This revision of the call for classic "good citizens" holds that our democratic polity is actually better off when it has lots of different types of citizens: some who care deeply, are highly informed, and participate intensely; many more who care moderately, are a bit informed, and participate as much out of duty to the process as commitment to one party or candidate; and some who are less aware of politics until some great issue or controversy awakens their political slumber.

The virtue of modern democracy in this *political specialization view* is that citizens play different roles and that together these combine to form an electoral system that has the attributes we prefer: it is reasonably stable; it responds to changes of issues and candidates, but not too much; and the electorate as a whole cares, but not so intensely that any significant portion of the citizenry will challenge the results of an election. Its most obvious flaw is that it is biased against the interests of those who are least likely to be activist or pluralist citizens—the young, the poor, the uneducated, and minorities.

WHAT'S AT STAKE REVISITED

As we all know by now, George W. Bush won the presidency in 2000 with the eleventh-hour intervention of the Supreme Court, and much of the heat of the weeks following the election has been forgotten. But the issues generated by this messy election still remain. Commentators and scholars have suggested a number of things that might be at stake in a contested presidential election.

Many have direly hinted, with vague references to a "constitutional crisis," that the very Constitution is at stake. It is quite true, as we discussed in Chapter 1, that when governments are perceived as illegitimate, they lose their authority. Peaceful transitions of power require that people trust the system and accept the results of that system as legitimate. But there is no evidence that in 2000 Americans were rejecting either their constitutional system or its results. In the immediate aftermath of the election, 82 percent of Americans polled told Gallup that they would accept Gore as a legitimate president, and 79 percent said that they would accept Bush. Although there were calls for a constitutional amendment, for lawsuits, for recounts, and even for new elections, these were all potential remedies *within* the constitutional framework. No one called for revolution, for a military coup, or for any of the other radical remedies that would signal a constitutional crisis. In fact, the U.S. Constitution allows for different winners of the popular vote and the electoral college vote, and state laws contain provisions for close elections precisely because they do happen, and happen often. The rarity of these circumstances coinciding shouldn't confuse us into thinking that they are necessarily unacceptable.

Still other observers suggest that the presidency of the winner of a contested election is at stake—that no one can lead who is believed to have "squeaked through" with a victory or who may not have won a majority of the popular votes cast. As we said in Chapter 7, presidents need to convincingly claim a mandate to lead in order to gather popular and congressional support for their proposals. History suggests that strong leadership may be hard to achieve after a contested election. Previous presidents who have won the electoral college but lost the popular vote have found governing difficult and have lasted only one term.

We also should consider that federalism is at issue here. The Constitution gives states the power to conduct elections. Appeals to federal courts to settle election disputes within states, particularly before state courts have been allowed to resolve the issues, seriously challenge the balance of power between nation and states. Similarly, appeals for a national ballot and a uniform system of voting would require a federal law to override the Constitution, and such a law would be challenged in the courts as unconstitutional. At the same time, the Fifteenth, Nineteenth, Twenty-fourth, and Twenty-sixth Amendments put limits on how states conduct elections and determine eligible voters, and the Fourteenth Amendment says that no state can deny its citizens the equal protection of the laws. Challenges to state election laws on these grounds are constitutional.

Clearly at stake in this contested election is the future of the electoral college. Although, as we have seen, there have been many calls for reform of this institution over the years, the public may only now be truly aware of the institution and what they see as its potentially negative consequences—namely a divergence between the popular vote winner and the electoral college winner. Senator Hillary Rodham Clinton, for instance, lost no time after her own election in 2000 in declaring that the electoral college should be abolished. To weigh in on the other side of this issue, we ask that you consider what havoc would be visited on the nation in an election this close *without* an electoral college. In addition to the results in Florida—or New Mexico, Wisconsin, Iowa, or Oregon—the entire national vote would likely be contested. A recount on that scale would take months and would leave the nation in limbo for a far longer time than a recount in a few states. Furthermore, the electoral college goes to the heart of the federalism issue, giving states as well as citizens a role in electing the president. We should consider the benefits of that arrangement before we rush to dismantle it.

The fate of third parties, if not actually at stake, is certainly questionable after an election this close. People who voted for Ralph Nader in 2000 are divided between those who are satisfied at having thrown the system into a tailspin and those who regret having contributed to the confusion. What does seem clear is that the old maxim that voting for a third party is just throwing a vote away has been proved to be untrue. No one can argue that Nader voters did not make a difference in 2000—although perhaps not the type of difference they had hoped to make.

A number of observers, both foreign and domestic, argue that America's standing in the world is at stake in this close election—that we who have been telling the world how to run a democratic government run the risk of looking like a fledgling third world democracy ourselves, with people denied the right to vote and demonstrating in the streets. On the heels of the Yugoslavian election, in which Slobodan Milosević refused to acknowledge the results of a popular vote and the electorate rioted in the streets to throw him out, it is understandable that the scenes of demonstrators in Palm Beach might give the world pause. Probably only time will allay this worry. The world will see that, far from revealing a weakness in American democracy, the resolution of this election shows that the system works as well as ever. Citizens express their views vocally, courts handle legal challenges, the politicians negotiate compromises, and the Constitution provides a framework of stability, just as the founders intended.

Finally, we need to think about what is at stake for American political culture in this unusual election. We noted in Chapter 1 that the United States is more committed to procedural than to substantive values—that is, we are committed more to following the rules and trusting the outcome of those rules than to evaluating the outcome by independent criteria. Although to the rest of the world, it may seem insane that a candidate preferred by a majority of voters can lose to a candidate who wins the electoral college, Americans have less difficulty accepting that outcome. Many Americans, however, do chafe at the notion, and this contested election shows the cracks in consensus on national political norms. Another aspect of our political culture that is at stake is our desire to believe that democracy is a neat and tidy form of government. As we discussed in Chapter 6, democracy is notoriously messy, something many Americans find objectionable. Contested elections put our distaste for partisanship and political disagreement on the line. ■

key terms

electoral mandate   368

front-loading   355

front-runner   355

hard money   365

issue advocacy ads   366

issue ownership   360

momentum   355

Motor Voter Bill   346

negative advertising   361

oppo research   359

party caucus   354

position issue   360

presidential primary   354

prospective voting   351

retrospective voting   351

social connectedness   347

soft money   366

swing voters   358

valence issue   360

voter mobilization   347

wedge issue   360

summary

■ Voting enhances the quality of democratic life by legitimizing the outcomes of elections. However, American voter turnout levels are among the lowest in the world and may endanger American democracy. Factors such as age, race, education, and income affect whether a person is likely to vote or not.

■ Candidates and the media often blur issue positions, and voters realistically cannot investigate policy proposals on their own. Therefore voters make a decision by considering peer viewpoints, party identification, prominent issues, and campaign images.

■ The "road to the White House" is long, expensive, and grueling. It begins with planning and early fundraising in the pre-primary phase and develops into more active campaigning during the primary phase, which ends with each party's choice of a candidate, announced at the party conventions. During the general election, the major-party candidates are pitted against each other in a process that relies increasingly on money and media. Much of the battle at this stage is focused on attracting those voters who have not yet made up their minds.

■ The electoral college demonstrates well the founders' desire to insulate government from public whims. Citizens do not vote directly for president or vice president, but rather for electors from their state who have already pledged to vote for that particular candidate. The candidate with the majority of votes in a state wins all the electoral votes in that state.

■ In spite of the fact that American citizens do not fit the mythical ideal of the democratic citizen, elections still seem to work in representing the people in terms of citizen policy preferences.

13

The Media

What's at Stake?

What Media?
- *Newspapers and Magazines*
- *Radio*
- *Television*
- *The Internet*
- *Where Do Americans Get Their News?*

History of the American Media
- *The Early American Press: Dependence on Government*
- *Growing Media Independence*
- *The Media Today: Concentrated Corporate Power*
- *Regulation of the Broadcast Media*

Who Are the Journalists?
- *Who Chooses Journalism?*
- *What Journalists Believe: Is There a Liberal Bias in the Media?*
- *The Growth of the Washington Press Corps*

The Media and Politics
- *The Shaping of Public Opinion*
- *The Reduction of Politics to Conflict and Image*
- *Politics as Public Relations*
- *A Reduction in Political Accountability*

Citizenship and the Media

What's at Stake Revisited

WHAT'S AT STAKE?

Once upon a time, television news came on for only an hour in the evening. If you wanted to watch the evening news, you sat down to watch it at six o'clock with the rest of the nation, and when it was over, it was over. A late-night news show might pick up the slack at eleven o'clock, and occasionally a major event, like John Glenn's first trip into space or the assassination of President John Kennedy, gave rise to extended coverage. But for the most part, watching TV news was a part-time occupation. Americans hung on the words of trusted news anchors like Walter Cronkite, so valued by his viewers that some referred to him as "Uncle Walter" and suggested that he should run for president. It was a golden age of TV news.

Sound like misty-eyed nostalgia? Welcome to the modern world of cable TV and all news, all the time. Networks like CNN, C-SPAN, MSNBC, and the Fox News Channel allow us to sit down and watch the news whenever we please, for as long as we please. Not only do we get immediate coverage of breaking events—such as the bombing of a foreign country, the unfolding of a natural disaster, or the funeral of a world leader—but we get endless coverage of everything else. Individual media figures do not enjoy the status Walter Cronkite once did. Today giant staffs with multiple anchors and battalions of news analysts and experts present more extensive, but also more anonymous, coverage of events. Twenty-four-hour television news outlets have altered the rules of American journalism in dramatic ways, and that in turn has changed not only how Americans view the news itself but also how they view politics, the subject of much of the news we get. What's at stake for American politics in the adoption of the twenty-four-hour news cycle? ■

It's hard to imagine today, but most of those who voted for George Washington for president, or for Abraham Lincoln, never heard the voice of the candidate they chose. While photographs of Lincoln were available, only portraits, sketches, or cartoons of Washington could reach voters. And while Franklin Roosevelt's voice reached millions in his radio "fireside chats" and his face was widely familiar to Americans from newspaper and magazine photographs, his video image was restricted to newsreels that had to be viewed in movie theaters. Not until the advent of television in the mid-twentieth century were presidents, congressional representatives, and senators beamed into the living rooms of Americans and their smiling, moving images made part of the modern culture of American politics.

Today we cannot picture politics without the accompanying brouhaha of the electronic media. Campaign commercials, State of the Union addresses, nightly sound bites, talk shows, and endless commentary help shape our political perceptions. C-SPAN even allows us to watch politics on television around the clock. Indeed, the advent of television has shaped American politics in distinctive ways. But that fact should not obscure the truth that modern democracy itself would not be possible without some form of mass communication. Nor should the speed with which technology cranks out ever new ways of communicating overshadow the fact that, in terms of making democracy possible, the most marvelous technological development of all may have been the printing press, which for the first time made communication affordable on a broad scale.

Democracy demands that citizens be informed about their government and that they be able to criticize it, deliberate about it, and change it if it doesn't do their will. Information, in a very real sense, is power. Information must be available, and it must be widely disseminated. This was fairly easy to accomplish in the direct democracy of ancient Athens, where the small number of citizens were able to meet together and debate the political issues of the day. Because their democracy was direct and they were, in effect, the government, there was no need for anything to mediate between them and the government, to keep them informed, to publicize candidates for office, to identify issues, or to act as a watchdog for their democracy.

But today our democratic political community is harder to achieve. We don't know many of our fellow citizens, we cannot directly discover the issues ourselves, and we have no idea what actions our government takes to deal with issues unless the media tell us. The mass media create a political community, connecting us to our government and creating the only real space we have for public deliberation of issues. Increasing technological developments make possible ever new forms of political community. Ross Perot, third-party presidential candidate in 1992 and 1996, talked of the day when we would all vote electronically on individual issues from our home computers. If we have not yet arrived at that day of direct democratic decision-making, we can certainly meet like-minded citizens and share our political views on the Internet, which is revolutionizing the possibilities of democracy, much as the printing press and television both did earlier, bringing us closer to the Athenian ideal of political community in cyberspace, if not in real space.

In this chapter, we examine this powerful entity called the media by focusing on

- the definition of *media* and the various forms the media have taken through time

- the historical development of the ownership of the American media and its implications for the political news we get

- the role of journalists themselves—who they are and what they believe

- the link between the media and politics

- the relationship of citizens to the media

What Media?

Media is the plural of *medium*, meaning in this case an agency through which communication between two different entities can take place. Just as a medium can be a person who claims to transmit messages from the spiritual world to earthbound souls, so today's media convey information from the upper reaches of the political world to everyday citizens. And, just as important in a democratic society, the media help carry information from citizens to the politicians who lead, or seek to lead, them. **Mass media** refers to those forms of communication that reach large public audiences. The modern media take many forms, from the "hard copy" of the printed word to electronic signals that are translated by radio, television, and computer.

Thousands of years of civilization passed before the advent of the printing press provided human beings with the means to print multiple copies of documents using movable type. In the one thousand years since the first printing presses were invented in Asia, at around A.D. 1000, technology has surpassed all expectations, and almost all of the truly amazing innovations—telegraph, telephone, photography, radio, television, computer, fax machine, and Internet—have been developed in the past two hundred years. Most of them have come into common use only in the past fifty.

What that means is that our technological capabilities sometimes outrun our sophistication about how that technology ought to be used. We do not always know what the sociological, political, or ethical consequences of using new forms of media are before we plunge headlong into their use. The Internet provides an excellent example of this, with its easy access to pornography, its proliferation of chatrooms

mass media

means of conveying information to large public audiences cheaply and efficiently

Jeff Stahler, reprinted by permission of Newspaper Enterprise Association, Inc.

where people can meet others who share their interests (no matter how far from the mainstream these may be), and the vast amounts of unsifted, often unverified, and frequently false "information" that regularly flood users.

Even less "exotic" forms of communication, like television, have transformed our world in ways we are only now beginning to understand and grapple with. New forms of communication alter the "old" media, as newsgathering, production, and delivery capabilities are all dramatically "improved" by technology. In this section, we sort out the various forms of the modern mass media that have changed and continue to change the social, political, and ethical lives we lead.

Newspapers and Magazines

newspaper
a printed publication that is issued regularly, is directed to a general audience, and offers timely news

A modern **newspaper** is a publication that is issued regularly, either daily or weekly, is directed to a general audience, and offers "timely" news.[1] Beginning as early as 1704, American newspapers grew in number and readership steadily until the 1930s, when, in the midst of the Depression, the number of papers began to decline. Readership, however, continued to grow until the 1960s, when it slowly began to fall.[2] Not only is American newspaper readership currently at a historical low, but as Figure 13.1 shows, it is also lower than in most other industrialized nations.[3]

Today fewer than thirty cities have more than one daily paper, although the *Wall Street Journal, USA Today,* the *New York Times,* the *Christian Science Monitor,* the *Washington Post,* and the *Los Angeles Times* are available in many U.S. cities, providing Americans with something they have never had but that is common in many smaller countries: a national press. Those major papers gather their own news, and some smaller papers that cannot afford to station correspondents around the world

**Figure 13.1
U.S. Newspaper Circulation Compared to Other Countries**
Source: Data from UNESCO, Statistical Yearbook, 1998. UNESCO Publishing and Bernan Press, 7-47–7-50.

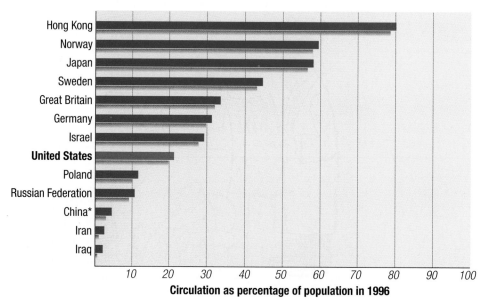

Circulation as percentage of population in 1996

*1990 data

can subscribe to their news services. Practically speaking, this means that most of the news that Americans read on a daily basis comes from very few sources—these outlets or wire services like the Associated Press (AP) and Reuters.

Newspapers cover political news, of course, but many other subjects also compete with advertising for space in a newspaper's pages. Business, sports, entertainment (movies and TV), religion, weather, book reviews, comics, crossword puzzles, advice columns, classified ads, and travel information are only some of the kinds of content that most newspapers provide in an effort to woo readers.

Magazines can often be more specialized than newspapers. Although the standard weekly news magazines *(Newsweek, Time,* and *U.S. News and World Report)* carry the same eclectic mix of subjects as the major newspapers, they offer more comprehensive news coverage because they do not need to meet daily deadlines, giving them more time to develop each story. These popular news magazines tend to be middle-of-the-road in their ideological outlooks. Other magazines appeal specifically to liberals *(The New Republic* and *The Nation)* or conservatives (the *National Review* and *The American Spectator).*

Radio

One reason the number of newspapers started to decline around the 1930s, of course, may have been that they began to face competition from radio. The first voice broadcast over telegraph wire occurred in 1906, and by the 1920s, Americans had a new way to get news and entertainment. Although radios were expensive at first, by 1926 one in six American families owned one,[4] and radio became a central part of American life. Radio made the news in general and politics in particular more personal and more immediate. For example, Franklin Delano Roosevelt used his "fireside chats" to sell his New Deal policies directly to the public, without having to go through the reporters he viewed as hostile to his ideas.[5] Today more than eleven thousand radio stations offer entertainment, news shows, and that curious hybrid, interactive call-in talk shows, through commercial networks, their local affiliates, and the nation's two noncommercial networks, National Public Radio and Public Radio International.

Television

The impact of radio on the American public, however dramatic initially, could not compare with the effects of television. American ownership of TVs snowballed from 9 percent of households in 1950 to 98 percent in 1975, a statistic that continues to hold true. In fact, 40 percent of American households today own three or more TV sets, and two-thirds receive cable transmission. Politicians were quick to realize that, like radio, TV allowed them to reach a broad audience without having to deal with print reporters and their adversarial questions. The Kennedy administration was the first to make real use of television, which might have been made for the young, telegenic president. In fact, it was partly Kennedy's adroit use of TV in the first televised presidential debate with Richard Nixon that helped him win the 1960 election. And it was television, three years later, that brought the nation together in a community of grief when Kennedy was assassinated. Television brought the Vietnam

24-Hour News
With the advent of CNN's twenty-four-hour news programming, today's news comes from many sources, including the Internet, providing information around the clock.

War (along with its protesters) and the civil rights movement into Americans' homes, and the images that it created helped build popular support to end the war abroad and the segregation at home. Television can create global as well as national communities, as worldwide broadcasts of the Persian Gulf War in 1991 and Princess Diana's funeral in 1997 showed.

There are many TV shows whose primary subject is politics. CNN and C-SPAN, sometimes called "America's Town Hall," offer news around the clock, although not all the news concerns politics. Weekend shows like *Meet the Press, Washington Week in Review,* and *Face the Nation* highlight the week's coverage of politics, and shows like *The Capital Gang, Crossfire,* and *The McLaughlin Group* showcase debates between liberals and conservatives on current issues. Some networks, such as the music channel MTV, direct their political shows to a specific age group (young people), and others, like America's Voice, appeal to those holding particular ideologies (conservatism). Like radio, TV has its call-in talk shows, the most prominent being CNN's *Larry King Live,* on which third-party candidate Ross Perot twice announced his candidacy for president (in 1992 and 1996). And politics is often the subject of jokes on shows such as *Late Night with David Letterman, The Tonight Show with Jay Leno,* and *Saturday Night Live.*

In the 1992 presidential campaign, Bill Clinton appeared on *The Arsenio Hall Show* playing his saxophone, showing that astute politicians understand the changing nature of the medium. In 2000 both George W. Bush and Al Gore appeared on these and other entertainment shows.

The Internet

The most recent medium to revolutionize the way we learn political news is the Internet, or Web (for World Wide Web). Telephone lines connect home and business computer subscribers to a global network of sites that provide printed, audio, and visual information on any topic you can imagine. In 2000 half of all Americans over age eighteen went on-line to access the Internet.[6] Considering the fact that computers are much more expensive than radios and TVs and that some technical knowledge is required to access news on-line, this is an astonishing number.

All the major newspapers and the Associated Press have web sites where consumers can read all or most of the news published in their print versions, usually for free (see Table 13.1). Many magazines and journals are also available on-line. By searching for the topics we want and connecting to links with related sites, we can customize our web news. Politics buffs can bypass nonpolitical news and vice versa.

In addition to traditional media outlets that provide on-line versions, there are

Table 13.1
Web Site Addresses for National News Organizations

ABC News	http://www.abcnews.com
Associated Press Wire	http://wire.ap.org/
CBS News	http://www.cbsnews.com
CNN	http://www.cnn.com (http://www.allpolitics.com is the CNN site devoted to *political* news)
Fox News	http://www.foxnews.com
Los Angeles Times	http://www.latimes.com
MSNBC	http://www.msnbc.com
National Public Radio	http://www.npr.org
The NewsHour with Jim Lehrer	http://www.pbs.org/newshour/
Newsweek	http://www.newsweek.com
New York Times	http://www.nytimes.com
Slate	http://www.slate.com
Time	http://www.time.com
USA Today	http://www.usatoday.com
U.S. News and World Report	http://www.usnews.com
Wall Street Journal	http://www.wsj.com
Washington Post	http://www.washingtonpost.com

myriad other web sources of information. On-line magazines like Slate, Salon, and the Drudge Report exist solely on the Internet and may or may not adopt the conventions, practices, and standards of the more traditional media. The federal government makes enormous amounts of information available, for instance at its www.whitehouse.gov and www.senate.gov sites. In fact, anyone can put up a web page and distribute information on any topic. This makes the task of using the information on the Web very challenging. Although the Internet gives us access to more information than ever before, the task of sorting and evaluating that information is solely our own responsibility (see "Consider the Source: How to Be a Savvy Web Surfer" on page 102).

Not only does the World Wide Web provide information, but it is interactive to a degree that far surpasses talk radio or TV. Many web sites have chatrooms or discussion opportunities where all sorts of information can be shared, topics debated, and people met. While this can allow the formation of communities based on specialized interests or similar views, it also can have the disadvantage of making it very easy for people with fringe or extremist views to find each other and organize.[7] And although the Internet has the potential to increase the direct participation of citizens in political communities and political decisions, the fact that not all Americans have access to the Web means that multiple classes of citizenship could form.

Where Do Americans Get Their News?

With all these media outlets available to them, where do Americans get their news? In 2000 the largest percentage of Americans, 75 percent, identified themselves as regular watchers of TV news programs, 63 percent said they were regular readers of a daily newspaper, and 46 percent said they listened to the radio regularly.[8] Many other people reported using these news sources less frequently. Twenty percent of the public (32 percent of those under age thirty) said they learned something new about politics from late-night shows such as Jay Leno's and David Letterman's. Clearly, these numbers tell us that many people use multiple news sources, although the number doing so is slipping. Young people and computer users especially are watching less TV news. Whether these people are getting their news off the Web is unclear, but the number of people who say they are getting their news on-line is growing rapidly. In 1998, 20 percent of Americans said that they got some news off the Web.[9] In 2000, 18 percent of all Americans and 28 percent of voters said that they got some information about the presidential election off the Web.[10]

Despite the fact that three-quarters of the American public are exposed to some news, and some people are exposed to quite a lot of it, levels of political information in this country are not high. In one study, an average of only 43 percent of the public answered questions about news events and public figures correctly.[11] These politically informed people are not evenly distributed throughout the population. In the study, young people were less likely than older people to answer the questions correctly, and women were less likely than men to get them right. Men were more likely than women to give the correct answers to questions dealing with domestic policy, public figures, and international news. This reflects the fact that women say they pay more attention to news about disasters, court rulings, crime, and celebrity scandals, whereas men focus on the military, international politics, the economy, and sports.

WHO, WHAT, HOW From the earliest newspapers through the advent of radio, television, and, most recently, the Internet, Americans have moved eagerly to embrace the new forms of technology that entertain them and provide new ways of communicating information.

WHO are the actors?	WHAT do they want?	HOW do they get it?
Citizens	• Entertainment • More information without expending scarce resources (time, effort, money) to get it	• Newspapers, magazines, radio, television, Internet

History of the American Media

Most media professionals in the United States take great pride in being "objective"—that is, in not adopting or pushing a particular point of view, but in looking at all sides of political issues and leaving readers to evaluate those issues on their own. This effort to be objective, which we see as a journalistic virtue today, has not always characterized the American media, and it has not come about as a result of ethical debate about how to cover the news. Instead, objectivity was the result of the economic imperative of selling newspapers to large numbers of people who did not share the same political views. In this section, we look at the historical development of the American media and the ways in which ownership has changed the kind of news we get.

The Early American Press: Dependence on Government

In its earliest days, the press in America was dependent on government officials for its financial, and sometimes its political, survival. Under those circumstances, the press could hardly perform either the watchdog function of checking up on government or the democratic function of empowering citizens. It primarily served to empower government or, during the American Revolution, the patriots who seized control of many of the colonial presses.

Andrew Jackson, elected in 1828, carried government support of the press to new lengths. Like his predecessors, he offered friendly papers the opportunity to print government documents and the authority to print the laws, but he denied this opportunity to his critics. Yet Jackson came to power in an age of mass democracy. Voter turnout doubled between 1824 and 1828.[12] People were reading newspapers in unheard-of numbers, and those papers were catering to their new mass audiences with a blunter and less elite style than they had used in the past. The lack of deference toward public officials, and the fact that journalists often spent some time as public officials themselves (at least 10 percent of Jackson's first political appointees were journalists[13]), contributed to a leveling of the differences between the press and the politicians, giving more power to the former and less to the latter.

Growing Media Independence

The newspapers after Jackson's day were characterized by larger circulations, which drew more advertising and increased their financial independence. Although journalists continued to move in and out of government positions, their stance toward politicians was more evenhanded.

The Penny Press   Prior to 1833, newspapers were expensive; a year's subscription cost more than the average weekly wages of a skilled worker.[14] But that year, the *New York Sun* was sold for only a penny a copy. Its subject matter was not an intellectual treatment of complex political and economic topics, but rather a more superficial mix of crime, human interest stories, humor, and advertising. As papers began to appeal to mass audiences rather than partisan supporters, they left behind their opinionated reporting and strove for a more objective, "fair" treatment of their subjects that would be less likely to alienate readers and the advertisers on whom they depended. This isn't to say that newspaper editors stayed out of politics, but they were no longer seen as being in the pocket of one or the other of the political parties. In 1848 the Associated Press was organized as a wire service to collect foreign news and distribute it to member papers in the states. This underscored the need for objectivity in political reporting so that the news would be acceptable to a variety of papers.[15]

After the Civil War, *yellow journalism*, the effort to lure readers with sensational reporting on topics like sex, crime, and gossip, proved extremely profitable. Newspapers became big business in the United States. The irony, of course, is that although yellow journalism allowed papers to achieve greater independence from political parties and politicians by attracting more readers and thus becoming more profitable, it also lowered journalistic standards.

The Media Today: Concentrated Corporate Power

Today the media continue to be big business, but on a scale undreamed-of by early journalistic entrepreneurs. No longer does a single figure dominate a paper's editorial policy; rather all but one of the major newspapers in this country (the *Christian Science Monitor*), as well as the national radio and television stations, are owned by large conglomerates. Often editorial decisions are matters of corporate policy, not individual judgment, and profit is the overriding concern. Interestingly, journalists freed themselves from the political masters who controlled them in the early years of this country, only to find themselves just as thoroughly dominated by the corporate bottom line.

Media Monopoly   The modern media get five times as much of their revenue from advertising as from circulation. Logic dictates that advertisers will want to spend their money where they can get the biggest bang for their buck: the papers with the most readers, the stations with the largest audiences. Since advertisers go after the most popular media outlets, competition is fierce, and those outlets that cannot promise advertisers wide enough exposure fail to get the advertising dollars and go out of business. Competition drives out the weaker outlets, corporations seeking to maximize market share gobble up smaller outlets, and to retain viewers, they all stick to the formulas that are known to produce success. What this means for the media world today is that there are fewer and fewer outlets, they are owned by fewer and fewer corporations, and the content they offer is more and more the same.[16]

In fact, ten corporations—Time Warner, Disney, Viacom, News Corporation, Sony, Tele-Communications Inc., Seagram, Westinghouse, Gannett, and General Electric—own the major national newspapers, the leading news magazines, and the national television networks (including CNN and other cable networks), as well as publishing houses, movie studios, and telephone, entertainment, and other multimedia operations. Most of these corporations are also involved in other businesses, as their familiar names attest. These ten corporations controlled more than $80 billion in 1996.[17] Media critic Ben Bagdikian has called these media giants a "new communications cartel within the United States," with the "power to surround every man, woman, and child in the country with controlled images and words, to socialize each new generation of Americans, to alter the political agenda of the country."[18] What troubles him and other critics is that many Americans don't know that most of their news and entertainment come from just a few corporate sources.

commercial bias
the tendency of the media to make coverage and programming decisions based on what will attract a large audience and maximize profits

Implications of Corporate Ownership for the News We Get   What does the concentrated corporate ownership of the media mean to us as consumers of the news? There are at least five major consequences that we should be aware of.

- There is a **commercial bias** in the media today toward what will increase advertising revenue and audience share. Stories like the O. J. Simpson murder trial and President Bill Clinton's affair with Monica Lewinsky, both media-consuming scandals of the 1990s, appear relentlessly on the front pages of every newspaper in the country, from the gossip-hungry tabloids to the more sober *New York Times, Christian Science Monitor,* and *Wall Street Journal.* This may not be because an editor has decided that the American people need to know the latest developments, but because papers that don't publish those developments may be passed over by consumers for other that do. Journalistic judgment and ethics are often at odds with the imperative to turn a profit.

- The effort to get and keep large audiences, and to make way for increased advertising, means that there is a reduced emphasis on political news in the modern media.

- The content of the news we get is lightened up and dramatized to keep audiences tuned in.[19] As in the days of yellow journalism, market forces encourage sensational coverage of the news. Sensational newscasts focus our attention on scandalous or tragic events rather than the nitty-gritty political news that democratic theory argues citizens need.

- The corporate ownership of today's media also means that the media outlets frequently face conflicts of interest in deciding which news to cover and how to cover it. One critic asks, how can NBC's Tom Brokaw report critically on nuclear power without crossing the network's corporate parent, General Electric, or ABC give fair treatment to Disney's business practices?[20] In fact, 33 percent of newspaper editors in America said that they would not feel free to publish news that might harm their parent companies,[21] a statistic that should make us question what is being left out of the news we receive.

- Finally, the corporate nature of the American media means that, to a far greater extent than before, publishers let their advertisers dictate the content of the news. Note as one example the media's slowness to pick up on stories critical of the tobacco industry, a major advertiser.[22]

Alternatives to the Corporate Media   The corporate media monopoly affects the news we get in serious ways. Citizens have some alternative news options, but none is truly satisfactory as a remedy, and all require more work than switching on the TV in the evening. One alternative is public radio and television. Americans tend to assume that media wholly owned or controlled by the government serve the interests of the government, rather than the citizens. This was certainly true in our early history, and it is true in totalitarian countries such as the former Soviet Union or China. But as we have seen, privately owned media are not necessarily free either, and the experiences of Great Britain and other European countries attest to the fact that government-controlled media are not necessarily repressive.

Another choice for citizens is the "alternative press." Born of the counterculture and antiwar movement of the 1970s, these local weekly papers, including *The Village Voice* (New York) and *SF Weekly* (San Francisco), were intended to offer a radical alternative to the mainstream media. But today these papers, usually free and dependent on advertising, have lost their radical edge and have become so profitable that, in an ironic turn of events, they are getting bought up by chains like New Times.[23] Rejecting the alternative press as too conventional, an "alternative to the alternative press," aimed at a younger audience and coveted by advertisers, is now available. Cynical and critical, but not in general political, these outlets do not offer a real alternative for political news.[24]

A final alternative to the mainstream corporate media is the Internet. Certainly, the Internet offers myriad sources of political news, but it takes time and effort to figure out which sources are accurate and trustworthy. In addition, in many cases the news options on the Web are dominated by the same corporate interests as are the rest of the media. Using the Web is inexpensive for those who own a computer, but that still excludes a large portion of Americans. And it may not be long before corporate America figures out a way to charge for access to individual media sites on the Web. It is too soon to tell whether the Web will offer a truly democratic, practical, and "free" alternative to the corporate-produced news we now receive.

Regulation of the Broadcast Media

The media in America are almost entirely privately owned, but they do not operate without some regulation. Although the principle of freedom of the press keeps the print media almost free of restriction (see Chapter 4), the broadcast media have been treated differently. In the early days of radio, great public enthusiasm for the new medium resulted in so many radio stations that signal interference threatened to damage the industry. Broadcasters asked the government to impose some order, which it did with the passage of the Federal Communications Act, creating the Federal Communications Commission (FCC), an independent regulatory agency, in 1934.

Because access to the airwaves was considered a scarce resource, the government acted to ensure that radio and television serve the public interest by representing a variety of viewpoints. Accordingly, the 1934 bill contained three provisions designed to ensure fairness in broadcasting.

- *Equal time provision.* The equal time rule means that if a station allows a candidate for office to buy or use airtime outside of regular news broadcasts, it must allow all candidates the same opportunity. On its face, this provision seems to give the public a chance to hear from candidates of all ideologies and political parties, but it often has the reverse effect. Confronted with the prospect of allowing every candidate to speak, no matter how slight the chance of his or her victory and how small an audience is likely to tune in, many stations instead opt to allow none to speak. This rule has been suspended for purposes of televising political debates. Minor-party candidates may be excluded and may appeal to the FCC if they think they have been unfairly left out.

- *Fairness doctrine.* The fairness doctrine extended beyond election broadcasts. It required that stations give free airtime to issues that concerned the public and to opposing sides when controversial issues were covered. Like the equal time rule, this had the effect of encouraging stations to avoid controversial topics. The FCC ended the rule in the 1980s, and when Congress tried to revive it in 1987, President Ronald Reagan vetoed the bill, claiming it led to "bland" programming.[25]

- *Right of rebuttal.* The right of rebuttal says that individuals whose reputations are damaged on the air have a right to respond. This rule is not strictly enforced by the FCC and the courts, however, for fear that it will quell controversial broadcasts, as the other two rules have done.

All of these rules remain somewhat controversial. Politicians would, of course, like to have them enforced because they help them to air their views publicly. Theoretically, the rules should benefit the public, but as we have seen, they often do not. Media owners see these rules as forcing them to air unpopular speakers that damage their ratings and as limiting their ability to decide station policy. They argue that given all the cable and satellite outlets, access to broadcast time is no longer such a scarce resource and that the broadcast media should be subject to the same legal protections as the print media.

WHO, WHAT, HOW   Democratic theory and American political tradition tell us that democracy requires a free press to which all citizens have access. While we say we have a free press in this country, we also have a free market, and the press has largely been the loser in the clash between the two.

WHO are the actors?	WHAT do they want?	HOW do they get it?
Citizens	• Political information necessary for democracy	• Political rules of a free press • Consumer freedom of choice
Media-owning corporations	• Profit	• Economic rules of a free market • Sensationalist stories that draw readers and viewers

Who Are the Journalists?

journalist a person who discovers, reports, writes, edits, and/or publishes the news

gatekeeping
the function of determining which news stories are covered and which are not

Corporate ownership does not tell the whole story of modern journalism. Although the mass media are no longer owned primarily by individuals, individuals continue to be the eyes, ears, nose, and legs of the business. **Journalists** are people who discover, report, edit, and publish the news in newspapers and magazines and on radio, television, and the Internet. They decide, in large part, the details about what news gets covered and how. This journalistic function is called **gatekeeping.** Not all journalists share this enormous power equally. Managers of the wire services, which determine which news gets sent on to their members; editors, who decide which stories should be covered or which parts of a story should be cut; and even reporters, who decide how to pitch a story, are all gatekeepers, though to varying degrees. To understand the powerful influence the media exert on American politics, we need to move beyond the ownership structure to the question of who American journalists are and how they do their jobs.

Who Chooses Journalism?

In 1996 journalism professors David Weaver and Cleveland Wilhoit estimated the number of people working in the mainstream media in the United States to be 122,015. Of those, the vast majority (just over two-thirds) worked in the print media, and about one-third worked in broadcast journalism. Weaver and Wilhoit found that although journalists lived throughout the country, those with more high-powered jobs tended to be concentrated in the Northeast. They also found that 82 percent of journalists had college degrees.[26]

Table 13.2 reflects the age, gender, ethnic backgrounds, and religious affiliations of American journalists. According to Weaver and Wilhoit, in 1996, 74 percent of journalists were between the ages of twenty-five and forty-four, 66 percent were male, 92 percent were white, and 54 percent were Protestant. Only in religious affiliation were journalists in sync with the rest of the American population. For instance, whereas 66 percent of journalists were male and 34 percent female, in the general labor force those percentages were 55 and 45 percent, respectively. The researchers found more women in entry-level jobs than in higher positions, perhaps reflecting a recent effort by news organizations to hire more women.

Does this demographic profile of journalism make any difference? Does a population need to get its news from a group of reporters who mirror its own age, gender,

Table 13.2
Who Are the Journalists?

		Journalists in Age Group	U.S. Civilian Labor Force in Age Group
	Under 20	0%	6.4%
	20–24	4.1	11.4
	25–34	37.2	29.0
Age	35–44	36.7	24.7
	45–54	13.9	16.1
	55–64	6.6	9.6
	65+	1.5	2.8
		Gender of Journalists	**Gender of U.S. Civilian Labor Force**
	Male	66.0%	54.8%
Gender	Female	34.0	45.2
		Ethnic Origins of Journalists	**Ethnic Origins of U.S. Population, 1990**
	African American	3.7%	12.1%
	Hispanic	2.2	9.0
Race	Asian American	1.0	2.9
	Native American	0.6	0.8
	White and other*	92.5	75.2
		Journalists' Religions	**Religions of U.S. Adult Population**
	Protestant	54.4%	55%
	Catholic	29.9	26
Religion	Jewish	5.4	1
	Other or none	10.2	18

*Includes "Jewish" category from Weaver and Wilhoit.

Source: Data are from David H. Weaver and G. Cleveland Wilhoit, *The American Journalist in the 1990s: U.S. News People at the End of an Era* (Mahwah, NJ: Lawrence Erlbaum, 1996), 1–8.

ethnic, and religious characteristics in order to get an accurate picture of what is going on? Not surprisingly, this question generates controversy among journalists. While some insist that the personal profile of a journalist is irrelevant to the quality of his or her news coverage, others cite evidence suggesting that the life experiences of journalists do influence their reporting. For instance, most mainstream media focus on issues of concern to white, middle-class America and reflect the values of that population, at the expense of issues of more concern to minorities and the poor. General reporting also emphasizes urban rather than rural issues and concentrates on male-dominated topics such as sports. Women journalists, however, tend to report more on social issues that are of more concern to women.[27]

What Journalists Believe: Is There a Liberal Bias in the Media?

It is not the demographic profile of journalists, but their ideological profile—that is, the political views they hold—that concerns many observers. Political scientists know that the more educated people are, the more liberal their views tend to be, and journalists are a well-educated lot on the whole. But even so, their views tend to be more liberal, particularly on social issues, than the average educated American's,[28] raising the question of whether those views in turn slant the news that Americans get in a liberal direction.

There is no question that members of the media are more liberal than the rest of America. Table 13.3 shows how the political leanings of journalists compare with those of the U.S. adult population. This ideological gap is mirrored by party membership. Journalists are more likely to be Democrats than are average Americans. This is especially true of women and minority journalists (see Table 13.4).[29]

Table 13.3
Political Leanings of U.S. Journalists Compared with U.S. Adult Population

Political Leanings	Journalists			U.S. Adult Population	
	1971[a]	1982–1983[b]	1992	1982[c]	1992[d]
Pretty far to left	7.5%	3.8%	11.6%	—	—
A little to left	30.5	18.3	35.7	21%	18%
Middle-of-the-road	38.5	57.5	30.0	37	41
A little to right	15.6	16.3	17.0	32	34
Pretty far to right	3.4	1.6	4.7	—	—
Don't know/refused	4.5	2.5	1.0	10	7
Total	100.0	100.0	100.0	100	100

[a]From Johnstone, Slawski, and Bowman, *The News People*, 93.
[b]From Weaver and Wilhoit, *The American Journalist*, 26.
[c]From George H. Gallup, *The Gallup Poll: Public Opinion, 1983* (Wilmington, DE: Scholarly Resources, 1984), 82.
[d]From Gallup Organization national telephone surveys of 1,307 U.S. adults, July 6–8, 1992, and 955 U.S. adults, July 17, 1992.

Source: David H. Weaver and G. Cleveland Wilhoit, *The American Journalist in the 1990s: U.S. News People at the End of an Era* (Mahwah, NJ: Lawrence Erlbaum, 1996), 1–8.

Table 13.4
Political Party Identification of U.S. Journalists Compared with U.S. Adult Population

Party	Journalists			U.S. Adult Population		
	1971[a]	1982–1983[b]	1992	1972[c]	1982–1983[d]	1992[e]
Democrat	35.5%	38.5%	44.1%	43%	45%	34%
Republican	25.7	18.8	16.4	28	25	33
Independent	32.5	39.1	34.4	29	30	31
Other	5.8	1.6	3.5	—[f]	—	1
Don't know/refused	0.5	2.1	1.6	—	—	2
Total	100.0	100.1[g]	100.0	100	100	101[g]

[a]From Johnstone, Slawski, and Bowman, *The News People,* 92.
[b]From Weaver and Wilhoit, *The American Journalist,* 29.
[c]From George H. Gallup, *The Gallup Poll: Public Opinion, 1983* (Wilmington, DE: Scholarly Resources, 1984), 43.
[d]From Gallup, 42.
[e]Gallup Organization national telephone survey of 1,307 U.S. adults, July 6–8, 1992. Data provided by the Roper Center, University of Connecticut.
[f]Not reported by Gallup.
[g]Does not total 100 percent because of rounding.

Source: David H. Weaver and G. Cleveland Wilhoit, *The American Journalist in the 1990s: U.S. News People at the End of an Era* (Mahwah, NJ: Lawrence Erlbaum, 1996), 1–8.

Figure 13.2
Newspaper Endorsements of Presidential Candidates, 1932–1996
Source: Harold W. Stanley and Richard G. Niemi, *Vital Statistics on American Politics, 1997–1998* (Washington, DC: Congressional Quarterly Press, 1998), 190. Reprinted by permission.

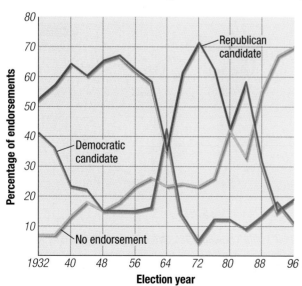

What influence does this have on the news we get? Most journalists, aware that their values are more liberal than the average American's, try hard to keep their coverage balanced. Some Democratic candidates for president have even accused the press of being harder on them to compensate for their personal preferences.[30] In addition to this sort of self-restraint, the liberal tendencies of many journalists are tempered by the undoubtedly conservative nature of news ownership and management we have already discussed. The editorial tone of many papers is conservative; for instance, far more papers endorse Republican candidates for president than Democrats (see Figure 13.2).

Do Americans on the whole think that the political reporting they get is biased? In a 1985 *Los Angeles Times* study, Americans reported that they do not feel indoctrinated by the press, and their perception of the press's stand on many issues reflected public opinion on those issues, not the more liberal view we might attribute to journalists.[31] In other words, what people see in the media largely mirrors their own values. As we will see later in this chapter, media audiences have special defenses that help to cancel out any ideological bias.

The Growth of the Washington Press Corps

beat a specific area (for example, police, the White House, business) covered by a journalist, who becomes familiar with the territory and its news sources

From a newsgathering perspective, America is organized into **beats,** identifiable areas covered by reporters who become familiar with their territories, get to know the sources of their stories, and otherwise institutionalize their official bits of journalistic "turf." Typical beats include police, politics, business, education, and sports, and these can be broken down into even more specialized areas, such as the White House, Congress, and the Supreme Court.

The beat system is well entrenched in American journalism, and the top echelon of American journalists are those who cover the national political beat in Washington. National politics takes place in our nation's capital and includes not just the interactions of Congress, the president, and the courts, but also the internal workings of political parties and the rival lobbying of interest groups such as states, major corporations, and other national organizations. For a political reporter, Washington is the place to be.

As the political reporter David Broder has pointed out, however, the concentration of politics, politicians, and reporters in Washington leads to "a complex but cozy relationship between journalists and public officials."[32] Washington journalists share an interest in politics with politicians, they have similar educations, they often make about the same amount of money, and they are in many ways natural colleagues and friends. So much do journalists and politicians have in common that they often exchange jobs with ease. Broder calls this practice the revolving door.

revolving door the tendency of public officials, journalists, and lobbyists to move between public and private sector (media, lobbying) jobs

The **revolving door,** as we discussed in Chapter 11, refers to the practice of journalists who take positions in government and then return to journalism, perhaps several times over. Among the prominent journalists who have gone through the revolving door are such notables as William Safire, former Nixon speechwriter and now columnist for the *New York Times;* Pat Buchanan, Republican presidential speechwriter (Nixon and Reagan), candidate for president himself, and syndicated columnist; and David Gergen, adviser to presidents from Nixon to Clinton, editor and columnist for *U.S. News and World Report,* and commentator on *The News-Hour with Jim Lehrer,* to name just a few.[33]

These journalists' insider status is both the greatest strength and the greatest weakness of the revolving door. On the plus side, having worked in government gives a journalist much greater knowledge of how the system works and who works it. The contacts made in government can pay off in increased access to official sources, gossip, background information, and the ever present government "leak," or secretly and anonymously provided confidential information. On the negative side, the revolving door can result in a lack of objectivity on the part of the journalist. Those about whom he or she is now reporting were colleagues and friends not long ago. How neutral and dispassionate can the journalist be?

WHO, WHAT, HOW American journalists do not mirror American society, and many members of the elite Washington press corps rotate in and out of government positions. Both of these characteristics of the American media are warning signals that citizens should heed when engaging in a more critical evaluation of the news.

WHO are the actors?	WHAT do they want?	HOW do they get it?
Journalists	• Prestige, professional honor, money, fame	• Unchecked power • Access to politicians • Freedom of the press • Revolving door
Citizens	• Better, uncompromised political coverage	• Critical scrutiny of the media

The Media and Politics

As we have seen, the American media are an amazingly complex institution. Once primarily a nation of print journalism, the United States is now in the grip of the electronic media. Television has changed the American political landscape, and now the Internet promises, or threatens, to do the same. Privately owned, the media have a tendency to represent the corporate interest, but that influence is countered to some extent by the professional concerns of journalists. Still, some of those at the upper levels of the profession—those who tend to report on national politics—have very close links with the political world they cover, and this also influences the news we get. What is the effect of all this on American politics? In this section, we look at four major areas of media influence on politics: the shaping of public opinion, the emphasis on conflict and image, politics as public relations, and the reduction in political accountability.

The Shaping of Public Opinion

We have already looked at the question of bias in the media and concluded that although there is probably no strong ideological bias in today's media, there is certainly a corporate or commercial bias. Political scientists conclude that it isn't so much that the media tell us *what* to think as that they tell us what to think *about*. These scholars have documented four kinds of media effects on our thinking: agenda setting, priming, framing, and persuasion by professional communicators.[34]

Agenda Setting   Most of us get most of our news from television, but television is limited in which of the many daily political events it can cover. As political scientists Shanto Iyengar and Donald Kinder have said, television news is "news that matters,"[35] which means that television reporters perform the function of agenda setting. When television reporters choose to cover an event, they are telling us that out of all the events happening, this one is important, and we should pay attention. A classic example of agenda setting in television news concerns the famine in Ethiopia that hit the American airwaves in 1984 in the form of a freelance film that NBC's Tom Brokaw insisted on showing on the *Nightly News*. Although the famine had been going on for more than a decade, it became news only after NBC chose to make it news, and it was a major concern of the American public for almost a year. U.S. government food aid rose from $23 million in 1984 to $98 million after the NBC broadcast.[36]

The agenda-setting role of the media is not the last word, however. When Americans lost interest in the famine, the network coverage ceased, even though the famine itself continued. Often the media will be fascinated by an event that simply fails to resonate with the public. Despite extensive media coverage of President Clinton's alleged sex scandals in 1998, for example, public opinion polls continued to show that the public did not think it was an issue worthy of the time the media spent on it.

Priming Priming is closely related to agenda setting. Priming refers to the media's influence on how people and events should be evaluated. The theory of priming says that if the media are constantly emphasizing crime, then politicians, and particularly the president, will be evaluated on how well they deal with crime. If the media emphasize the environment, that will become the relevant yardstick for evaluation. In effect, according to this concept, the media not only tell us what to think about but also how to think about those things. In the 1992 presidential campaign, the media echoed the message of the Clinton campaign—"It's the economy, stupid"—and much of the election coverage was focused on that issue. According to the idea of priming, this encouraged Americans to evaluate the two candidates in terms of how they did or would handle the economy, which benefited Clinton and hurt his opponent, President George Bush. Presumably, had the media continued its emphasis on military prowess from the Persian Gulf War the year before, Clinton would have fared poorly compared with Bush. The existence of priming has been supported by empirical evidence,[37] although it is clearly not in effect all the time on all the issues.

Framing A third media effect is called framing. The same painting can look very different depending on its frame: a heavy, gold, baroque frame gives a painting weight and tradition, whereas a thin metal frame makes it look more stark and modern. The painting doesn't change, but how we see it does. This same phenomenon applies to how the media present, or frame, the news. For example, people view news of a disaster differently depending on whether a report highlights the number of dead or the number of survivors.

Persuasion by Professional Communicators Finally, some political scientists argue that the media affect public opinion by actually causing people to change their minds about the policies and issues they cover. The mechanism for change here is the use of trusted newscasters and expert sources—professional communicators whose considerable authority on a particular issue seems so solid that viewers, who don't have the time or background to research the issues themselves, change their minds to agree with the experts.[38] Familiar with this phenomenon, President Lyndon Johnson knew that there would be little support for continuing the Vietnam War when he heard the popular CBS news anchor Walter Cronkite take a stand against the war. Johnson told an aide that it was "all over," predicting that the public would follow the lead of one of the most trusted figures in America. Often, however, the professional communicators on whom the media rely are not revered figures like "Uncle Walter," but people who regularly pass through the revolving door and whose objectivity cannot be taken for granted.

Do Media Effects Matter?   The effects of agenda setting, priming, framing, and expert persuasion should not be taken to mean that we are all unwitting dupes of the media. In the first place, these are not ironclad rules; they are tendencies that scholars have discovered and confirmed with experimentation and public opinion surveys. That means that they hold true for many but not all people. Agenda setting is less important for members of the two major political parties, for instance, than for Independents, perhaps because they do not have a party to rely on to tell them what is important.[39]

Second, we bring our own armor to the barrage of media effects we face regularly. We all bring ideas, values, and distinct perspectives to our news watching that influence what we get from it. Scholars who emphasize that audiences are active, not passive, consumers of the media say that people counter the effects of the media by setting their own agendas. That is, viewers, readers, and listeners practice **selective perception**—they select the news items they will pay attention to, the items they will remember, and the items they will forget.[40] In fact, researchers have found that there is a gap between what the media focus on in the news and what people say are the important issues in their lives.[41] If people do not seem to be well informed on the issues emphasized by the media, it may be that they do not see them as having an effect on their lives. As consumers, we do more than passively absorb the messages and values provided by the media.

selective perception
the phenomenon of filtering incoming information through personal values and interests and deciding what to pay attention to

The Reduction of Politics to Conflict and Image

In addition to shaping public opinion, the media also affect politics by their tendency to reduce complex and substantive political issues to questions of personal image and contests between individuals. Rather than examining the details and nuances of policy differences, the media tend to focus on image and to play up personalities and conflicts, even when their readers and viewers say they want something quite different. The effect of this, according to some researchers, is to make politics seem negative and to increase popular cynicism.

horse race journalism
the media's focus on the competitive aspects of politics rather than on actual policy proposals and political decisions

'...Political campaigns have become so simplistic and superficial... In the 20 seconds we have left, could you explain why?..

Horse Race Journalism   Horse race **journalism** refers to the media's tendency to see politics as competition between individuals. Rather than report on the policy differences between politicians or the effects their proposals will have on ordinary Americans, today's media tend to report on politics as if it were a battle between individual gladiators or a game of strategy and wit but not substance. This sort of journalism not only shows politics in the most negative light, as if politicians cared only about scoring victories over one another in a never-ending fight to promote their own self-interests, but it also ignores the concerns that citizens have about politics. As journalist James Fallows points out, when citizens are given a chance to ask questions of politicians, they focus on all the elements of politics that touch their lives: taxes, wars, social security, student loans, education, and welfare.[42] But journalists focus on questions of strategy, popularity, and relative positioning vis-à-vis real or imagined rivals. The obsession with who is winning makes the coverage of campaigns, partisan battles in Congress, or disputes between president and Congress far more trivial than they need to be and far less educational to the American public. "Consider the Source: Becoming a Savvy Media Consumer" will help you get beyond the horse race coverage in much of today's media.

The Emphasis on Image   Television is primarily an entertainment medium and, by its nature, one that focuses on image: what people look like, what they sound like, and how an event is staged and presented. Television, and to some extent its competitors in the print media, concentrates on doing what it does well—giving us pictures of politics instead of delving beneath the surface. This has the effect of leading us to value the more superficial aspects of politics, even if only subconsciously. An early and telling example was the 1960 presidential debate between Richard Nixon and John Kennedy, when the young and telegenic Kennedy presented a more presidential image than the swarthy and sweating Nixon and won both the debate and the election. Combine this emphasis on image with horse race journalism, and the result is a preoccupation with appearance and strategy at the cost of substance.

sound bite a brief, snappy excerpt from a public figure's speech that is easy to repeat on the news

The words of politicians are being similarly reduced to the audio equivalent of a snapshot—the sound bite. A **sound bite** is a short block of speech that is used on the news. Sound bites are often played repetitively and can drown out the substance of the message a politician wishes to convey. Occasionally, they can come back to haunt a politician, as did Vice President George Bush's famous 1988 campaign promise, "Read my lips, no new taxes," broken in 1992 when he supported a tax hike as president. The amount of time the electronic media devote to the words politicians utter has shrunk. In 1968 the average sound bite accompanying a film clip of a candidate was forty-two seconds; by 1988 and 1992, it was down to ten seconds. The extra time is used by journalists to interpret what was said and often to put it into the horse race metaphor we just discussed.[43]

feeding frenzy excessive press coverage of an embarrassing or scandalous subject

Scandal Watching   Reporters also tend to concentrate on developing scandals to the exclusion of other, possibly more relevant, news events. The 1998 revelations about President Clinton's affair with White House intern Monica Lewinsky are a case in point. During the period of daily revelations, allegations, and investigations, almost nothing else Clinton did got media attention. Even when visiting British prime minister Tony Blair held a joint press conference with Clinton, many of the questions asked by the media focused on Lewinsky. Political scientist Larry Sabato refers to this behavior as a **feeding frenzy**[44]—"the press coverage attending any political event or circumstance where a critical mass of journalists leap to cover the same embarrassing or scandalous subject and pursue it intensely, often excessively, and sometimes uncontrollably." Many feeding frenzies have been over scandals that

CONSIDER THE SOURCE

Becoming a Savvy Media Consumer

As we have seen in this chapter, many forces are working to make the citizen's job difficult when it comes to getting, following, and interpreting the news. But forewarned is forearmed, and the knowledge you have gained can turn you into the savviest of media consumers. Journalist Carlin Romano says, "*What* the press covers matters less in the end than *how* the public reads. Effective reading of the news requires not just a key—a Rosetta stone by which to decipher current cliches—but an activity, a regimen."* When you read the paper, watch the news, listen to the radio, or surf the Net, try to remember to ask yourself the following questions. This will be a lot more work than just letting the words wash over you or pass before your eyes, but as a payoff you will know more and be less cynical about politics; you will be less likely to be manipulated, either by the media or by more knowledgeable friends and family; and, as a bonus, you will be a more effective, sophisticated, and satisfied citizen. Here are the questions. Keep a copy in your wallet.

1. **Who owns this media source?** Look at the page in newspapers and magazines that lists the publisher and editors. Take note of radio and TV call letters. Look to see who takes credit for a web site. What could be this owner's agenda? Is it corporate, political, ideological? How might it affect the news?

2. **Who is this journalist (reporter, anchorperson, webmaster, etc.)?** Does he or she share the characteristics of the average American or of the media elite? How might that affect his or her perspective on the news? Has he or she been in politics? In what role? How might that affect how he or she sees current political events? Some of this information might be hard to find at first, but if a particular journalist appears to have a special agenda, it might be worth the extra research to find out.

3. **What is the news of the day?** How do the news stories covered by your source (radio, TV, newspaper, magazine, or Web) compare to the stories covered elsewhere? Why are these stories covered and not others? Who makes the decisions? How are the stories framed? Are positive or negative aspects emphasized? What standards do the journalists suggest you should use to evaluate the story—that is, what standards do they seem to focus on?

4. **What issues are involved?** Can you get beyond the "horse race"? For instance, if reporters are focusing on the delivery of a politician's speech and her opponent's reactions to it, try to get a copy of the speech to read for yourself. Check the Web or a source like the *New York Times.* Similarly, when

have proved to be untrue or that have seemed insignificant with the passing of time, and yet the media have treated them with the seriousness of a world crisis. Reputations have been shredded, justly or unjustly, but once a frenzy begins, it is difficult to bring rational judgment to bear on the case. After such attacks, the media frequently indulge in introspection and remorse—until the next scandal starts to brew.

Growing Negativism, Increased Cynicism Political scientist Thomas Patterson attributes the phenomenon of the feeding frenzy to an increased cynicism among members of the media. He argues that it is not a liberal or a conservative bias among reporters that we ought to worry about. Rather, it is their antigovernment views, focusing on the adversarial and negative aspects of politics to the exclusion of its positive achievements, that foster a cynical view of politics among the general public. Most presidents and presidential candidates are treated by the press as fundamentally untrustworthy, when in fact most do precisely what they say they are going to

the media emphasize conflict, ask yourself what underlying issues are involved. Look for primary (original) sources whenever possible, ones that have not been processed by the media for you. If conflicts are presented as a choice between two sides, ask yourself if there are other sides that might be relevant.

5. **Who are the story's sources?** Are they "official" sources? Whose point of view do they represent? Are their remarks attributed to them, or are they speaking "on background" (anonymously)? Such sources frequently show up as "highly placed administration officials" or "sources close to the Senator." Why would people not want their names disclosed? How should that affect how we interpret what they say? Do you see the same sources appearing in many stories in different types of media? Have these sources been through the "revolving door"? Are they pundits? What audience are they addressing?

6. **Is someone putting a spin on this story?** Is there visible news management? Is the main source the politician's press office? Is the story based on a leak? If so, can you make a guess at the motivation of the leaker? What evidence supports your guess? What is the spin? That is, what do the politician's handlers want you to think about the issue or event?

7. **Who are the advertisers?** How might that affect the coverage of the news? What sorts of stories might be affected by the advertisers' presence? Are there potential stories that might hurt the advertiser?

8. **What are the media doing to get your attention?** Is the coverage of a news event detailed and thorough, or is it "lightened up" to make it faster and easier for you to process? If so, what are you missing? What is on the cover of the newspaper or magazine? What is the lead story on the network? How do the media's efforts to get your attention affect the news you get? Would you have read/listened to the story if the media had not worked at getting your attention?

9. **What values and beliefs do you bring to the news?** What are your biases? Are you liberal? Conservative? Do you think government is too big, captured by special interests, always ineffective, or totally irrelevant to your life? Do you have any pet peeves that direct your attention? How do your current life experiences affect your political views or priorities? How do these values, beliefs, and ideas affect how you see the news, what you pay attention to, and what you skip? List all the articles or stories you tuned out, and ask yourself why you did this.

10. **Can you find a news source that you usually disagree with, that you think is biased or always wrong?** Read it now and again. It will help you keep your perspective and ensure that you get a mix of views that will keep you thinking critically. We are not challenged by ideas we agree with but by those that we find flawed. Stay an active media consumer.

*Carlin Romano, "What? The Grisly Truth About Bare Facts," in Robert Karl Manoff and Michael Schudson, eds., *Reading the News* (New York: Pantheon Books, 1986), 78.

do. Since it takes time and energy to systematically investigate all the claims that a president or a candidate makes, the media substitute statements from political opponents for their own careful scrutiny. This makes politics appear endlessly adversarial and, as Patterson says, replaces investigative journalism with attack journalism.[45]

Consequences of the Emphasis on Conflict and Image   Two scholars argue that the "conflict-driven sound-bite oriented discourse of politicians," in conjunction with the "conflict-saturated strategy-oriented structure of press coverage," creates a mutually reinforcing lack of confidence in the system that they call the "spiral of cynicism."[46] But as we argued at the start of this chapter, the media have a legitimate role to play in a democracy—in disseminating information, checking government, and creating political community. If people cease to trust the media, the media become less effective in playing their legitimate role, and democracy becomes more difficult to sustain.

Another consequence of this emphasis, and one that may somewhat alleviate the first, is that new forms of media are opening up to supplement or even replace older ones. Television talk shows, radio call-in shows, and other outlets that involve public input and bypass the adversarial questions and negative comments of the traditional media allow the public, in some ways, to set the agenda. In fact, a study of the 1992 election showed that television talk shows focused more on substantive policy issues and presented more balanced and positive images of the candidates than the mainstream media did.[47]

Politics as Public Relations

There is no doubt that the media portray politics in a negative light and that news reporting emphasizes personality, superficial image, and conflict over substantive policy issues. Some media figures argue, however, that this is not the media's fault but the result of politicians and their press officers being so obsessed with their own images on television that they limit access to the media, speak only in prearranged sound bites, and present themselves to the public in carefully orchestrated "media events."[48] Media events are designed to limit the ability of reporters to put their own interpretation on an occasion. The rules of American politics mean that politicians have to try to get maximum exposure for their ideas and accomplishments, while limiting the damage the media can do with their intense scrutiny, probing investigations, and critical perspectives.

news management the efforts of a politician's staff to control news about the politician

News Management   **News management** describes the efforts of a politician's staff—his or her media consultants, press secretaries, pollsters, campaign strategists, and general advisers—to control the news about the politician. Staff members want to put their own issues on the agenda, determine for themselves the standards by which the politician will be evaluated, frame the issues, and supply the sources for reporters who will put their client, the politician, in the best possible light. In contemporary political jargon, they want to put a **spin,** or an interpretation, on the news that will be most flattering to the politician whose image is in their care. To some extent, modern American politics has become a battle between the press and the politicians, as well as among the politicians themselves, to control the agenda and the images that reach the public. It has become a battle of the "spin doctors."

spin   an interpretation of a politician's words or actions designed to present a favorable image

The classic example of news management is the rehabilitation of the image of Richard Nixon after he lost the 1960 election to the more media savvy John F. Kennedy. Inspired by the way the Kennedy campaign had managed the image of Kennedy as war hero, patriot, devoted father, and faithful husband, when at least one of those characterizations wasn't true, Nixon speechwriter Ray Price saw his mission clearly. Noting that Nixon was personally unpopular with the public, he wrote in a 1967 memo,

> We have to be very clear on this point: that the response is to the image, not to the man, since 99 percent of the voters have no contact with the man. It's not what's there that counts, it's what's projected—and it's not what he projects but rather what the voter receives. It's not the man we have to change, but rather the received impression.[49]

With the help of an advertising executive and a television producer, among others, Nixon was repackaged and sold to voters as the "New Nixon." He won election as president in 1968 and 1972. That he had to resign in 1974 is perhaps less a failure of his image-makers than the inevitable revelation of the "real" Nixon underneath.

News Management Techniques   The techniques developed by the Nixon handlers for managing his image have become part of the basic repertoire of political staffs, particularly in the White House but also to some extent among holders of lesser offices. They can include any or all of the following:[50]

- Tight control of information

- Tight control of access to the politician

- Elaborate communications bureaucracy, beginning with the White House press secretary

- A concerted effort to bypass the White House press corps and go directly to the public

- Prepackaging the news in sound bite–size pieces

- **Leaking,** or secretly revealing confidential information to the press

leaking   secretly revealing confidential information to the press

Not all presidential administrations are equally accomplished at using these techniques of news management, of course. Nixon's was successful, at least in his first administration, and Ronald Reagan's has been referred to as a model of public relations.[51] Bill Clinton's staff, on the other hand, did not manage the media effectively in the early years of his first administration, and he was consequently at the mercy of a frustrated and annoyed press corps. Within a couple of years, however, the Clinton staff had become much more skilled and, by his second administration, was adeptly handling scandals that would have daunted more seasoned public relations experts. The George W. Bush administration began with the same sure handling of the press that had characterized his presidential campaign.

We should note that there is a real cost to the transformation of politics into public relations. Politicians must spend time and energy on image considerations that do not really help them serve the public, and the people who are skilled enough at managing the press to get elected to office have not necessarily demonstrated any leadership skills. The skills required by an actor and a statesperson are not the same. The current system may encourage voters to choose the wrong leaders for the wrong reasons and may discourage the right people from running at all.

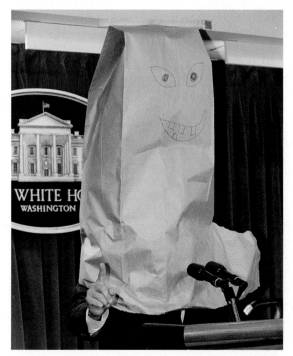

An Unnamed White House Source
White House press secretary Mike McCurry is pictured here making fun of the Washington institution of the "anonymous" leak, with a bag over his head to symbolize its widespread use.

A Reduction in Political Accountability

A final political effect of the media, according to some scholars, is a reduction in political accountability. To hold someone politically accountable is to make him or her acknowledge and bear the consequences of his or her actions. Political accountability is the very hallmark of a democracy: if our leaders do something we do not like, we can hold them accountable by voting them out of office. The threat of being voted out of office is supposed to encourage elected officials to do what we want in the first place.

Some political scientists, however, argue that the coming of television has weakened political accountability and thus democracy itself.[52] Their arguments are complex, but compelling.

- First, they say that television has come to reduce the influence of political parties, since it allows politicians to take their messages directly to the people. Parties are no longer absolutely necessary to mediate politics—that is, to provide a link between leaders and the people—but parties have, in American politics, traditionally been a way to keep politicians accountable.

- Second, television covers politicians as individuals, and as individuals, they have incentives to take credit for what the public likes and to blame others for what the public doesn't like. In addition, because they are covered as individuals, they have little reason to form coalitions to work together.

- Third, television, by emphasizing image and style, allows politicians to avoid taking stances on substantive policy issues. The public often does not know where they stand and cannot hold them accountable.

- Finally, the episodic way in which the media frame political events makes it difficult for people to discern what has really happened politically and whose responsibility it is.

The result is that the modern media, and especially television, have changed the rules of politics. Today it is harder for citizens to know who is responsible for laws, policies, and political actions, and thus harder for us to make our politicians behave responsibly.

WHO, WHAT, HOW   At the intersection of the political and media worlds, many actors have something serious at stake.

WHO are the actors?	WHAT do they want?	HOW do they get it?
Journalists	• Professional acclaim • Power to set the agenda	• Rules of media coverage: emphasis on immediacy, image, and keeping viewers' attention
Politicians	• Ability to communicate with the public • Power to set the agenda	• Changing rules of media access to politicians • Principles of public relations
Citizens	• Trust and confidence in government and the media • Democratic accountability	• Critical scrutiny of the media

Citizenship and the Media

We have been unable to talk about the media in this chapter without talking about citizenship. Citizens have been a constant "who" in our analysis because the media exist, by definition, to give information to citizens and to mediate their relationship to government. But if we evaluate the traditional role of the media with respect to the public, the relationship that emerges is not a particularly responsive one. Almost from the beginning, control of the American media has been in the hands of an elite group, whether party leaders, politicians, wealthy entrepreneurs, or corporate owners. Financial concerns have meant that the media in the United States have been driven more by profit than by public interest. Not only is ownership and control of the media far removed from the hands of everyday Americans, but the reporting of national news is done mostly by reporters who do not fit the profile of the "average" citizen and whose concerns often do not reflect the concerns of their audience.

Citizens' access to the media is correspondingly remote. The primary role available to them is passive—that of reader, listener, or watcher. The power they wield is the power of switching newspapers or changing channels—essentially choosing among competing elites—but this is not an active participatory role. Although freedom of the press is a right technically held by all citizens, there is no right of *access* to the press. Citizens have difficulty making their voices heard, and, of course, most do not even try. Members of the media holler long and loud about their right to publish what they want, but only sporadically and briefly do they consider their obligations to the public to provide the sort of information that can sustain a democracy. If an active democracy requires a political community in which the public can deliberate about important issues, it would seem that the American media are failing miserably at creating that community.

Two developments in the American media offer some hope that they can be made to serve the public interest more effectively. One development concerns new technology that offers competition to the traditional media, and the second, perhaps prompted by the first, involves reforms from within the media.

The term "new media" refers to the variety of high-tech outlets that have sprung up to compete with traditional newspapers, magazines, and network news. Some of these, such as cable news, specialized television programs, and Internet news, allow citizens to get fast-breaking reports of events as they occur, and even to customize the news that they get. Talk radio and call-in television shows—new uses of the "old media"—allow citizen interaction, as do Internet chatrooms and other on-line forums. Many web sites allow users to give their opinions of issues in unscientific "straw polls." Some analysts speculate that it is only a matter of time until we can all vote on issues from our home computers. The one thing that these new forms of media have in common is that they bypass the old, making the corporate journalistic establishment less powerful than it was, but perhaps giving rise to new elites and raising new questions about participation and how much access we really want citizens to have.

A second noteworthy development in the American media has emerged from a crisis of conscience on the part of some journalists. These reformers, drawn by increasing levels of public cynicism about the press and politics and by relentless criticism of the

civic journalism
a movement among journalists to be responsive to citizen input in determining what news stories to cover

media to reconsider the principles that guide their profession, advocate **civic journalism,** a journalistic movement to be responsive to citizen input in determining what news to cover. Under the banner of civic journalism, a wide range of projects and experiments focused on bringing citizens' concerns and proposed solutions into the reporting process have been carried out. If civic journalism catches on in America, citizens will have a potentially transforming role to play in media and politics.

WHAT'S AT STAKE REVISITED

Obviously, many more changes have transformed the American media in the past two decades than just the adoption of the twenty-four-hour, all-news format on cable news networks like CNN. But the rule changes stemming from the nonstop news cycle have had critical consequences for American politics. On the positive side, the infrastructure that supports networks like CNN also allows for the nearly instantaneous transmission of events happening around the world. We said earlier in this chapter that television brought the Vietnam War into American living rooms. Cable TV transported Americans to the rooftops of Baghdad in the Persian Gulf War in 1990. Americans watched as tracers lit the night sky and shuddered as bombs exploded. Such immediacy and presence have helped Americans form a sort of electronic community, as they rallied to support the American cause in the Persian Gulf or grieved together over the bombing of the Alfred P. Murrah Federal Building in Oklahoma City in 1995.

But there are also negative consequences of twenty-four-hour news, and these may have a more lasting impact on politics. Even though the free dissemination of information is essential to the health of a democracy, it may be possible to have too much of a good thing. First, having to fill twenty-four hours with news means that round-the-clock news outlets must elaborate and expand the news they have, often dwelling on insignificant details to make an ongoing story look new. More and more expert analysts are interviewed, and their pronouncements on events themselves become part of the news.

Not only does twenty-four-hour news require the continual coverage and even creation of news, but it requires the *dramatization* of news. No one is going to watch hours of coverage unless it grips the imagination and creates some suspense. Consequently, news anchors cast their coverage in life-or-death terms, exaggerating and sensationalizing events or statements that often cannot live up to their headlines. For example, CNN's wall-to-wall coverage of the Clinton impeachment hearings and trial in 1998–1999, which it called "Investigating the President," revealed very little investigation and a good deal of reporting of news leaks and regurgitation of the day's legal pronouncements.

Nonetheless, the existence of at least one all-news cable TV station has spawned the creation of others. As we have seen throughout this chapter, commercial interests are the driving force in the organization of the media. In an effort to compete, media outlets imitate each other's innovations and merge with each other and larger corporations to try to stay ahead of the game. The creation of CNN meant reduced ratings for the network news and scrambling among the networks for a way to compete. When CNBC was founded and caused CNN's market share to decline, CNN and CBS discussed the possibility of a merger to recapture CNN's viewers and stop the decline in CBS's audience.

Points of Access

- Read a daily newspaper.
- Watch television network news or cable news on a regular basis.
- Join an on-line political news chat group.
- Place a call to a talk radio show.
- Write a letter to the editor of your student or local newspaper.
- Write a commentary piece for your local paper (or try to get one published in the *New York Times*).
- Start your own web page.
- Intern at a local newspaper or radio or TV station.
- Find out how to air a program on the local cable access station.
- Start an alternative newspaper.

All the audience-seeking, merger-forming, drama-creating forces that control the twenty-four-hour news cycle have distinctive effects on politics. Politicians, always ready to deliver a sound bite, are given plenty of play on stations with plenty of airtime. During the Clinton impeachment trial, senators, the House managers prosecuting the case, and White House spokespersons would rush to the microphones to deliver a rebuttal, add information, or float a trial balloon at every break in the proceedings. The constant TV camera presence became part of the political process, as participants, limited by Senate rules or inclination from talking directly to one another, did their politicking through the medium of television.

The unceasing media attention to politics seems only to decrease public confidence in both the media and politicians. At the peak of the Clinton scandal, the American people were disappointed in both parties in Congress, but they also blamed the media for dragging out a scandal they thought had been given too much attention for too long. This was not solely the responsibility of cable news, of course, but it was cable that hung in there with its coverage long after the networks had gone back to their regularly scheduled sporting events and soap operas. Apparently, the public is well able to see through the media hype designed to keep them riveted to their screens, and there is some evidence that this hype only increases their cynicism. Gone are the days of "Uncle Walter" Cronkite, whose emotions people shared and whose views they respected. Today Americans seem to be feeling besieged by the very institutions that should be arming them with information to provide a check on government. ■

key terms

beat   389
civic journalism   400
commercial bias   382
feeding frenzy   393
gatekeeping   385

horse race journalism   392
journalist   385
leaking   397
mass media   375
news management   396

newspaper   376
revolving door   389
selective perception   392
sound bite   393
spin   396

summary

■ Mass media are forms of communication—such as television, radio, the Internet, newspapers, and magazines—that reach large public audiences. More media outlets and more information mean that Americans must devote ever-increasing time, effort, and money to sort out what is relevant to them.

■ Media ownership can influence the kind of news we get. Early political parties and candidates created newspapers to advocate their issues. Later, newspaper owners used sensationalist reporting to sell more newspapers and gain independence from political interests. Today's media, still profit driven, are owned by a few large corporate interests.

- The 1934 Federal Communications Act, which created the Federal Communications Commission, imposed order on multiple media outlets and attempted to serve the public interest through three provisions: the equal time provision, the fairness doctrine, and the right of rebuttal.

- Public skepticism of the media has increased in recent decades. Some critics believe that the homogeneous background of journalists—mostly male, white, well-educated, and concentrated in the Northeast—biases the media, as does their predominantly liberal ideology. Others claim that the revolving door—the practice of journalists who take government positions but later return to reporting—damages objectivity.

- Citizen access to the media has been primarily passive, but the rise of new, interactive media and the growth of civic journalism may help to transform citizens into more active media participants.

14

Domestic and Foreign Policy

What's at Stake?

Making Public Policy
- Solving Social Problems
- Difficulties in Solving Social Problems
- Types of Public Policy
- Who Makes Policy?
- Steps in the Policymaking Process

Foreign Policy
- Understanding Foreign Policy
- The Post–Cold War Setting of American Foreign Policy
- Types of Foreign Policy
- Who Makes Foreign Policy?
- How Do We Define a Foreign Policy Problem?

Citizenship and Policy

What's at Stake Revisited

WHAT'S AT STAKE?

If tough on crime is good, is tougher better? Those making criminal justice policy in the United States certainly seem to think so. Since 1984 forty states have passed "truth in sentencing laws" that require prison inmates to serve a substantial portion of their sentences before being released. Fifteen states have eliminated parole boards.[1] In addition, a number of states and the federal government have passed "three strikes and you're out" laws that put offenders in jail for life after they commit a third felony. Depending on the state, three strikes laws may apply just to violent criminals or to any who commit felonies, including drug offenders.[2] Along with mandatory sentencing laws for drug offenses, these sentencing changes have increased the U.S. incarceration rate since 1985 by 130 percent, putting the United States well ahead of all other countries in the world except Russia in terms of the percentage of its population living in prison.[3]

Can this be the same United States that in the 1970s and 1980s was accused by conservative politicians of being soft on crime? Of being a nation where those accused of crimes were more likely than their victims to be the focus of social concern? Indeed it is. Philosophies on crime and the policies to enforce them have come full circle in the United States. Public sentiment is largely behind the shift toward getting "tough on crime" over the past three decades. Politicians of both parties have taken pride in their commitment to making the streets safe, and citizens like to feel that their homes and their neighborhoods are free from danger. And to a considerable extent, they are. In the last seven years of the 1990s, the crime rate dropped rather than rose, as it had been doing throughout the 1980s. Are tougher sentencing laws the perfect policy solution to a grievous social problem? Not necessarily. In fact, like many public policies, tightening up sentencing laws has had many unforeseen and certainly unintended consequences that make the policies much more costly than expected. What is really at stake in getting tough on crime? ■

Thighis is disgraceful," we say as we look at the total we owe on our federal tax returns. "Someone ought to do something about this."

"It's intolerable that homeless people are allowed to sleep in the public library. Why doesn't somebody do something?"

"How tragic that so many young children don't have health care. Can't anyone do anything about it?"

When we utter such cries of disgust, frustration, or compassion, we are not calling on the heavens to visit us with divine intervention. Usually, the general somebody/anybody we call on for action is our government, and what government does or doesn't do is called public policy. In fact, public policy has been a focus of discussion throughout this book. When we ask what's at stake, as we do at the beginning of each chapter, or pause within a chapter to reflect on who, what, and how, the "what" is almost always a government action or policy. The study of public policy is inseparable from the study of American politics.

In this chapter, we focus on policy, both domestic and foreign, and how the parts of government we have studied come together to create it. But government is not something "out there," something external to us. We have seen in this book that in many ways, American government is very responsive to us, either individually as voters or collectively as interest groups. While we do not dictate the details of American public policy, the broad outlines of that policy are largely what we say they should be. In some policy areas, such as social welfare reform and crime, politicians have responded to public opinion by limiting welfare and getting tough on criminals. In other areas, notably social security and health care, they have responded to the powerful demands of organized interest groups. In still other areas, primarily economic policy and foreign policy, some of the political decisions have been taken out of the hands of elected officials precisely because they tend to respond to what voters and interest groups want. Thus in this chapter, we look at

- domestic policy and how it is made

- profiles of important domestic policies, such as social security, welfare, health care, and economic policy

- foreign policy and how it is made

- the responsiveness of public policy to citizens' wishes

Making Public Policy

Our lives are regulated by policies that influence nearly everything we do. For example, many stores have a "no return" policy on sale merchandise. Restaurant owners alert customers to their policy toward underdressed diners with the sign "No shirt, no shoes, no service." Your college or university may have a policy requiring a minimum grade point average for continued enrollment.

These are private, nongovernmental policies, adopted by individuals, businesses, or organizations to solve problems and to advance individual or group interests.

Stores want to sell their new merchandise, not last season's leftovers; restaurant owners want a certain clientele to dine in their establishments; and institutions of higher education want to maintain standards and give students an incentive to excel. The problems of the clothing store, the restaurant, and the university are straightforward. Addressing these problems with specific policies is pretty easy. Creating public policies, however, is more difficult than creating policies on merchandise returns, dining attire, and acceptable grades.

public policy
a government plan of action to solve a social problem

Public policy is a government plan of action to solve a social problem. That is not to say that the intended problem is always solved or that the plan might not create more and even worse problems. Sometimes government's plan of action is to do nothing. That is, it may be a plan of *inaction,* with the expectation (or hope) that the problem will go away on its own or in the belief that it is not or should not be government's business to solve it. Some issues may be so controversial that policymakers would rather leave them alone, confining the scope of a policy debate to relatively "safe" issues.[4] But by and large, we can understand public policy as a purposeful course of action intended by public officials to solve a social problem.[5] When that problem occurs here in the United States, we say that the government response is domestic policy. When it concerns our relations with other nations, we call it foreign policy, a topic we will discuss later in this chapter.

Solving Social Problems

Public policies differ from the restaurant's "No shirt, no shoes, no service" policy because they are designed to solve common social problems, not to address the concerns of a single business or institution. We think of problems as social when they cannot be handled by individuals, groups, businesses, or other actors privately, or when they directly or indirectly affect many citizens. Social problems might include the need for public goods that individuals alone cannot or will not produce, such as highways, schools, and welfare. Social problems can include harm caused to citizens by the environment, foreign countries, dangerous products, or each other. Sometimes the very question of whether a problem is social or not becomes the subject of political debate. When people suggest that government ought to do something about violent crime, drug use, or poor school quality, they are suggesting that government should create a public policy to address a social problem.

Government can address social problems directly, by building schools, prisons, or highways, but a great deal of public problem solving entails offering incentives to individuals or groups to get them to behave the way government wants them to behave. In other words, public policy can encourage or discourage behaviors in order to solve a problem that already exists or to avoid creating a future problem. For instance, government has an interest in having well-educated, property-owning citizens, since the conventional wisdom is that such people are more stable and more likely to obey the laws—in short, to be good citizens. Consequently, government policy encourages students to go to college by offering low-interest college loans and generous tax credits. It encourages home ownership in the same way. These various forms of federal assistance provide incentives for us to behave in a certain way to avoid creating the problem of an uneducated, rootless society.

Difficulties in Solving Social Problems

Despite the good intentions of policymakers, however, public problems can be difficult to solve. First, as we have already suggested, people have different ideas about what constitutes a problem in the first place. The definition of a social problem is not something that can be looked up in a book. It is the product of the values and beliefs of political actors and, consequently, is frequently the subject of passionate debate. Even something as seemingly problematic as poverty can be controversial. To people who believe that poverty is an inevitable though unfortunate part of life, or to those who feel that poor people should take responsibility for themselves, poverty may not be a problem requiring a public solution.

A second reason solving public problems can be hard is that solutions cost money—often a lot of money. Finding the money to address a new problem usually requires shifting it out of existing programs or raising taxes. With an eye toward the next election, politicians are reluctant to spend tax dollars to support new initiatives. This is especially true when these new initiatives are not widely supported by citizens, which is often the case with policies that take money from some citizens to benefit others, such as welfare policy.

Public problems also can be difficult to solve because often their solutions generate new problems. Government is a powerful actor; when it steps in to solve a problem, it can inadvertently set off a chain reaction of further problems. Policies that are tough on crime, for example, can jam up the courts and slow the criminal justice system. Policies to help the poor can create dependence on government among the disadvantaged. And environmental policies can impair business's ability to compete. Often the problems caused by policies require new policies to solve the problems.

A final reason problems can be hard to solve has to do with their complexity. Seldom are there easy answers to any public dilemma. Even when policymakers can agree on a goal, they often lack sufficient knowledge about how to get there. Competing solutions may be proposed, with no one knowing definitively which will best solve the problem. And some social problems may in reality be multiple problems with multiple causes—further muddying the effort to find adequate solutions. Policymaking in the American context is made even more complex by the federal system. Whose responsibility is it to solve a given problem—the federal, state, or local government's?

Types of Public Policy

In an effort to make sense of all the policies in contemporary politics, some political scientists divide them into three types: redistributive, distributive, and regulatory policy, depending on who benefits and who pays, what the policy tries to accomplish, and how it is made.[6] This classification, summarized in Table 14.1, is not perfect (it turns out, for instance, that sometimes a policy can fit into more than one category), but it does help us to think about policy in a coherent way.

redistributive policy
a policy that shifts resources from the "haves" to the "have-nots"

Redistributive policies attempt to shift wealth, income, and other resources from the "haves" to the "have-nots." Like Robin Hood, government, acting through redistributive policies, seeks to help its poor citizens. Government's policy to tax the

Table 14.1
Types of Policy

Type of Policy	Policy Goal	Who Promotes This Policy?	Who Benefits? (Wins)	Who Pays? (Loses)	Examples
Redistributive	To help the have-nots in society	Public interest groups and officials motivated by values	Disadvantaged citizens	Middle- and upper-class taxpayers	Medicaid Food stamps
Distributive	To meet the needs of various groups	Legislators and interest groups	Representatives of interest groups and the legislators they support	All taxpayers	Homeowner tax deductions Veterans' benefits Anticrime policies Education reform
Regulatory	To limit or control the actions of individuals or groups	Public interest groups	Public	Targeted groups	Environmental policy

income of its citizens is redistributive because it is based on a progressive tax rate. People who earn more pay a higher percentage of their incomes to the federal government in taxes. (The progressivity of the income tax, however, is tempered by other elements of the U.S. tax code.) Programs such as Medicaid or food stamps are redistributive social welfare policies because they shift dollars away from people with relatively larger incomes to people with smaller or no incomes. As we will see later in this chapter, U.S. welfare policy is largely redistributive. Health care policy in the United States also is redistributive—at least so far—since the government, through taxation, provides for the cost of health care for those who cannot afford it.

One key characteristic of the politics of redistributive policies is that they are difficult to put in place. Redistributive policies take resources away from the affluent segments of society. Affluent citizens are more likely to be politically active, to vote regularly, and to contribute to political campaigns and interest groups. These attentive constituents individually or collectively contact their congressional representatives to express their views. In contrast, the recipients of redistributive policies, who are often alienated from politics, tend to vote less often and lack the resources to donate to political campaigns or form interest groups. Their causes may be taken up by public interest groups, professional organizations representing social workers, or legislators who believe that it is government's job to help the needy. In the battle of who gets what in politics, policies that redistribute wealth are relatively rare because the people who must pay for the policies (the more affluent) are better equipped than the poor to fight political battles.

Distributive policies are much easier to make, because the costs are not perceived to be borne by any particular segment of the population. Tax deductions for interest on home mortgage payments, agriculture price supports, interstate highway policies, federal grants for higher education, even programs that provide for parks and recreation are examples of distributive policies. The common feature of **distributive policies** is that while they provide benefits to a recognizable group (such as homeowners or the families of college students), the costs are widely distributed. In other words, all taxpayers foot the bill.

distributive policy
a policy funded by the whole taxpayer base that addresses the needs of particular groups

regulatory policy
a policy designed to restrict or change the behavior of certain groups or individuals

Regulatory policies differ from redistributive and distributive policies in that they are designed to restrict or change the behavior of certain groups or individuals. Whereas redistributive and distributive policies work to increase assistance to particular groups, regulatory policies tend to do just the opposite. They limit the actions of the regulatory target group—the group whose behavior government seeks to control. Most environmental policies, for example, are regulatory in nature. Business owners face myriad air emission limitations and permit requirements that must be met in order to avoid government sanctions, including the possibility of a civil fine or a criminal trial. Since the groups being regulated frequently have greater resources at their disposal than the groups seeking the regulation (often public interest groups), the battle to regulate business can be lopsided.

The politics surrounding the creation of regulatory policies are highly confrontational. The "loser" in a regulatory policy is often the target group. Business doesn't want to pay for environmental controls, nor do manufacturers want to be monitored for compliance by government. By contrast, interest groups representing the beneficiaries of the policy argue just as strongly for the need for regulatory control. To continue our environmental policy example, the Environmental Defense Fund and the American Lung Association are repeat players in policy developments under the Clean Air Act. These groups have frequently sued the U.S. Environmental Protection Agency to compel it to lower the acceptable levels of airborne pollutants.[7]

Who Makes Policy?

All the political actors we have studied in this book have a hand in the policymaking process. Government actors inside the system—members of Congress, the president, the courts, and bureaucrats—are involved, as are actors outside the system—interest groups, the media, and the public.

Policies are usually created by members of Congress as one or more new laws. Sometimes what we think of as a single policy is really a bundle of several laws or amendments to laws. Environmental policy and social welfare policy are prime examples of bundles of programs and laws. National environmental policy is included in more than a dozen laws, among them the Clean Air Act, the Clean Water Act, and the Safe Drinking Water Act. Social welfare policy consists of more than direct financial assistance to poor families. Also included are programs that subsidize food purchases, supply daycare for children, and provide job training and education for parents.

The role of Congress in creating and legitimating policy through its laws is critically important to understanding national public policy. As we saw in Chapter 6, members of Congress are often most attentive to what their constituencies and the interest groups who support their campaigns want. Nonetheless, many members of Congress also follow their own values and consciences when making difficult political decisions.

Back from the Brink
Once considered close to extinction, the American bald eagle, living symbol of the United States since 1782, was pronounced safe to come off the "endangered" list by President Bill Clinton in a July 1999 White House ceremony. The passage of the Endangered Species Act in 1973 and the 1972 banning of the use of the pesticide DDT contributed greatly to the eagle's recovery. Today more than 5,800 breeding pairs exist in the United States, compared to only 417 in 1963.

The president may also create policy, perhaps by putting an issue on the public agenda, by including it (or not) in his budget proposal, by vetoing a law made by Congress, or by issuing an executive order that establishes a new policy or augments an existing one. Executive orders sometimes make profound changes in policy. One such order created affirmative action. When Congress passed the Civil Rights Act in 1964 banning employment discrimination against women and minorities, the law did not require that employers actively seek to employ persons within these protected classes. Arguing that America must seek "equality as a fact and equality as a result," President Lyndon Johnson issued Executive Orders 11246 and 11375 requiring federal contractors to develop affirmative action programs to promote the hiring and advancement of minorities and women.

Government bureaucracies at the federal, state, and local levels may create or enhance policy through their power to regulate. Administrative agencies are crucial to the policymaking process, helping to propose laws, lobbying for their passage, making laws of their own under authority delegated by Congress, and implementing laws. Agencies also have enormous control over policies simply by how they enforce the policies.

Finally, the courts are policymakers. We saw clearly in Chapter 9 that the Supreme Court has been responsible for some of the major changes in policy direction in this country with respect to business regulation, civil rights, and civil liberties, to name just a few areas. When the courts rule about what the government can or cannot do and should or should not do, they are clearly taking an active policymaking role. In addition, they are often asked to rule on the implementation of policy decisions made elsewhere in the government—on affirmative action, welfare policy, or education, for example.

Usually, national policies are best thought of as packages made by several actors. Congress passes a law that establishes a policy. In turn, federal and/or state agencies respond by writing regulations and working with individuals who are affected by the policy. The president may want to emphasize (or deemphasize) a policy in several ways. He may publicize the new policy through public statements—most notably the State of the Union address. He may issue formal instructions (executive orders) or informal directions to agencies that highlight policy goals. So, although a law may initially establish a plan of action for a public problem, a policy tends to evolve over time and contain many elements from all branches of government. These various

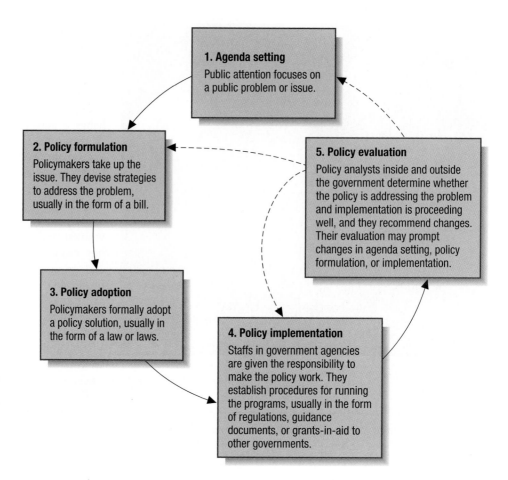

**Figure 14.1
The Policymaking
Process**
Policymaking begins
with agenda setting
and ends with policy
evaluation, which
often cycles back to
the creation of new
policy initiatives.

components (laws, regulations, executive orders, agency actions, and so on), taken as a whole, form the government's policy.

In addition to the actual representatives of government, many other actors get involved in the policymaking process, as we have seen throughout this book. Political parties, interest groups, the media, and the public, through the influence of polls and participatory behavior like letter writing, all play significant roles in the battle over what government should do.

Steps in the Policymaking Process

Political scientists have isolated five steps that most policymakers follow in trying to solve a social problem. Figure 14.1 illustrates the policymaking process.

Agenda Setting   The first step in creating policy is agenda setting. Agenda setting occurs when problems come to the attention of people who can address them (usually members of Congress). These problems can be brought to Congress's attention by individual members, by the president, by interest groups, by the media, or by public opinion polls.

Setting the Agenda
The president can create policy by putting an issue on the public agenda. Soon after he took office, George W. Bush focused attention on his education agenda by making visits to schools and calling for greater accountability from schools and teachers.

Policy Formulation   The second step in the policymaking process is called policy formulation. In this phase, several competing solutions to the policy problem or objective are developed and debated in Congress. These alternative strategies often take the form of bills, perhaps proposed by the president or an administrative agency, that are introduced into Congress and sent to committees for deliberation.

Policy Adoption   If a preferred policy alternative emerges from the policy formulation stage, it must be legitimized through formal government action. Usually, this means that Congress enacts legislation. However, it may also mean that the president issues an executive order, that an agency creates a regulation, or that a court makes a ruling.

Policy Implementation   Once policies are adopted, they must be put into practice. During the implementation phase of the policymaking process, federal and/or state agencies interpret the policy by writing regulations, creating guidance documents, or drafting memoranda of agreement with other agencies. Agency staff meet with the beneficiaries of the policy, staff in other departments, citizens, and interest groups in an attempt to devise a workable plan for putting the policy into action. Implementation of public policy is neither easy nor guaranteed, however; those charged with implementing it can often derail the policy by not enforcing it.

Policy Evaluation   The last step in the policymaking process is to evaluate the policy. Policy evaluation requires the policy analyst to ask several fundamental questions: Does the policy, as currently constructed, address the initial public problem?

Does it represent a reasonable use of public resources? Would other strategies be more effective? Has it produced any undesirable effects?

Policy evaluation is conducted inside government by agencies such as the General Accounting Office, the Congressional Budget Office, the Office of Technology Assessment, the Office of Management and Budget, and the Congressional Research Service. Congress also conducts oversight hearings in which agencies that implement programs report their progress toward policy goals. Groups outside government also evaluate policy to determine whether the desired outcomes are being achieved. Some of these groups are nonpartisan and are funded by philanthropic organizations.

WHO, WHAT, HOW   Public policies are government's strategies for addressing public problems or changing behaviors.

WHO are the actors?	WHAT do they want?	HOW do they get it?
Government actors: Congress, the president, bureaucrats, courts	• Solutions to social problems	• Setting an agenda • Forming policy • Adopting policy • Implementing policy • Evaluating policy
Nongovernment actors: parties, interest groups, media	• Solutions to social problems	• Participation in the system, lobbying, reporting
Citizens	• Solutions to social problems	• Voting for candidates responsive to their concerns

Policy Profile: Middle-Class and Corporate Welfare

Major Problem Being Addressed: Encouraging individual behaviors the national government considers "healthy" for the country as a whole

Policy Type: Distributive

Background: Social welfare policies do not only include what we typically think of as welfare—programs to assist the poor—but also programs that increase the quality of life for the middle class. For instance, a number of distributive policies benefit workers, middle-class homeowners, students, and members of the military—that is, they benefit a particular group in society at the expense of all taxpayers. Some of these policies are designed to encourage certain behaviors that policymakers value (such as homeownership and going to college), but they have long since fallen into the category of benefits to which groups feel entitled. It would be a brave congressperson, for instance, who decided to incur the wrath of middle-class home buyers by removing the income tax deduction for mortgage interest.

Major Programs in Place

Education Subsidies. The government sometimes uses a subsidy to encourage production of a particular good or a certain type of behavior. Farm subsidies or price supports are an essential part of the government's agricultural policy, for example. Education subsidies provide funds to local school systems for certain types of educational programs but allow the school districts themselves to manage the programs. The federal government also provides direct student loans and guarantees loans made to students by private lenders such as banks and credit unions. One of the newer government incentives to help citizens with the cost of higher education is the Hope Scholarship credit (first made available in 1999 for higher-education expenses incurred in 1998). This program provides some relief to families with dependents in college by allowing taxpayers a credit of up to $1,500 on their income taxes as long as their adjusted gross incomes are below a certain amount (for 1998 that limit was $50,000 for single taxpayers and $100,000 for married taxpayers filing jointly).

Homeowning Subsidies. Homeowning is encouraged through the mortgage interest tax deduction, which allows homeowners to deduct the cost of their mortgage interest payments from their taxable income. Because homeowners must meet a certain income level to receive this tax break, the policy in effect helps only the taxpayers in the middle- and upper-income brackets. A similar government program provides student and home mortgage loans to veterans and those currently serving in the military.

Corporate "Welfare" Subsidies. U.S. corporations are also beneficiaries of social subsidies. According to some analysts, an estimated $150 billion is funneled to American corporations through direct federal subsidies and tax breaks.[1] Many subsidies are linked to efforts to create jobs. However, there is little oversight for many of these programs, and there are many instances of subsidies going to companies that are downsizing or—in the case of many high-tech companies—moving jobs overseas. Business leaders also claim that subsidies for research and development are needed to keep American companies afloat in the global marketplace. Business is heavily subsidized in some countries, and business lobbyists claim that U.S. subsidies are essential to the development of new technology. But others say that corporate America has become too dependent on federal handouts. The biggest winners are agribusiness, the oil industry, and energy plants. States have also gotten into the corporate welfare business, handing out millions of dollars to fund corporations that stay within their borders in the defense, high-tech, and science and medical industries.

---

[1]Charles M. Sennott, "$150 Billion 'Welfare Recipients?' U.S. Corporations," *Boston Globe*, 7 July 1996, 1.

Policy Profile: Welfare Policy

Major Problem Being Addressed: Poverty among children (1 in 5 children lives in poverty in the United States)

Policy Type: Redistributive

Background: It was not until the Great Depression of 1929 forced large numbers of previously successful working- and middle-class people into poverty that the public view shifted from the idea that poverty was the result of individual failings and citizens demanded that government step in. Government responded with President Franklin Roosevelt's New Deal, a period of the most extensive economic security policy this country had ever seen. The New Deal included (1) social welfare programs, a variety of policies designed to deal with the immediate economic crisis by getting people back to work and caring for their needs until jobs could be found; and (2) social insurance, or programs that would offer benefits in exchange for contributions made by the workers to offset future economic need. The first type of intervention was designed to be temporary, and the second to cover longer-range needs.

Aid to Families with Dependent Children

Established by the Social Security Act of 1935, Aid to Dependent Children (later renamed Aid to Families with Dependent Children, or AFDC) formed the mainstay of America's social welfare "safety net" for many years. AFDC provided cash welfare payments for needy children whose parents were unable to support them. The federal government contributed more than half the AFDC payments, and the states supplied the balance, managed the program, and determined who was eligible and how much they received. By 1996 more than 4 million families received an average monthly payment of $377. According to government statistics, the majority of AFDC recipients in the 1990s were young un-

married mothers (ages nineteen to thirty) who were unemployed and resided in central cities.[1]

AFDC was designed to raise above the poverty line those families hurt by economic downturns. It was a means-tested program—that is, to receive benefits, recipients had to prove that they lacked the necessary means to provide for themselves, according to the government's definitions of eligibility. President Roosevelt and the New Deal architects believed that the government should provide some temporary support when the economy slumped. Yet the explosive growth of the program, particularly from 1970 to 1995, prompted many policymakers to question its success. During that time, enrollment increased by more than 50 percent, from 1.9 million to 4.9 million families. In fiscal year 1994, enrollment and benefits rose to an all-time high, with a monthly average of 14.2 million persons receiving benefits totaling $22.8 billion. Studies also indicated that many families were moving on and off AFDC rolls over longer periods of time.[2] Opponents of AFDC posed the question, How long is "temporary"?

Major Program in Place

AFDC was criticized because it contained no work requirements and set no time limits for remaining on welfare. Also, many states provided additional cash assistance for each additional child, leading some critics to claim that the program encouraged irresponsible childbearing, especially among unwed mothers, and fostered a culture of dependence in which people came to believe that they had a right to welfare as a way of life. Public opinion polls showed that many Americans believed that welfare recipients were unwilling to work, living off the generosity of hard-working taxpayers. Reports of fraud gave rise to stereotypes of the "welfare queen" driving a Cadillac to the post office to pick up her welfare check. Since lower-income people are less likely to organize for political purposes, welfare recipients put up no coordinated defense of their benefits. Although Republicans had traditionally been more critical of welfare policy, even some Democrats began to heed the calls of their constituents for welfare reform, arguing that the welfare system created disincentives for recipients to become productive members of society. On August 22, 1996, President Clinton signed the Personal Responsibility and Work Opportunity Reconciliation Act, fulfilling his promise to "end welfare as we know it."

AFDC was replaced by the Temporary Assistance to Needy Families (TANF) block grant to state governments. This reform gives states greater control over how they spend their money but caps the amount the federal government will pay for welfare. The new law requires work in exchange for time-limited benefits. Most recipients must find a job within two years of going on welfare and cannot stay on the welfare rolls for more than a total of five years or less, depending on the state. By the year 2002, 50 percent of single-parent and 90 percent of two-parent families must be working. Moreover, many states cap family benefits when an additional child is born to a family on welfare.

It's too soon to know whether the new welfare program will more effectively keep people out of poverty than its predecessor. One thing is clear: the new system has lowered welfare caseloads. In June 1998, the Department of Health and Human Services reported that just over 3 million families were receiving welfare benefits, a drop of 31 percent since August 1996.[3] By July 31, 1998, the Clinton administration was able to report that 35 percent of all adult welfare recipients were working and all fifty states plus the District of Columbia had met the basic work requirements of the 1996 reform. As of March 1999, just 2.7 percent of the population (7.3 million Americans) were on welfare, the lowest percentage since 1967.[4]

It is not known, however, how many of these former welfare recipients have moved from welfare into jobs that pay enough to support their families. There is evidence that additional burdens have been placed on extended families, particularly grandmothers, to fill in when mothers with small children have lost their benefits but have been unable to hold down a job or care for their children. Nationwide, about 1.4 million children are living in "skip-generation" households, which represents a 52 percent increase since 1990.[5] In addition, some analysts have argued that the reform's success may have more to do with the country's economic growth than with its inherent merits. A study by the Urban Institute predicts that the new welfare program will actually increase the number of children living in poverty by 20 percent.[6]

[1]U.S. Census Bureau, Statistical Brief, "Mothers Who Receive AFDC Payments: Fertility and Socioeconomic Characteristics," March 1995.
[2]1996 Green Book, Ways and Means Committee Print WMCP: 104-14, Section 8. Aid to Families with Dependent Children and Related Programs (Title IV-A), U.S. Government Printing Office Online via GPO Access.
[3]U.S. Department of Health and Human Services, Administration for Children and Families, "Change in Welfare Caseloads Since Enactment of the New Welfare Law" (August 1998), 1 (http://www.acf.dhhs.gov/news/aug-jun.htm).
[4]Robert Pear, "Clinton Hears Success Stories of Ex-Welfare Recipients," New York Times, 4 August 1999, A12; Robert Pear, "White House Releases New Figures on Welfare," New York Times, 1 August 1999, 16.
[5]Jason DeParle, "As Welfare Rolls Shrink, Burden on Relatives Grows," New York Times on the Web, 21 February 1999.
[6]David A. Super, Sharon Parrott, Susan Steinmetz, and Cindy Mann, "The New Welfare Law: A Summary, Center on Budget and Policy Priorities," 13 August 1996, 3 (http://www.cbpp.org/wcnsum.htm).

Policy Profile: Social Security

Major Problem Being Addressed: Poverty among the elderly

Policy Type: Redistributive

Background: When extended families lived together and grown children took care of their aging parents, care for the elderly wasn't considered to be a social problem. But in modern society, with its mobile populations and splintered families, people often do not live in the same state as their parents, let alone in the same town or house. And although people are living longer and longer, American society no longer emphasizes the responsibility of each generation to care for the previous one. Because individuals are often unwilling or unable to make financial provision for their old age, President Franklin Roosevelt's 1935 Social Security Act inaugurated a program to provide what is essentially forced savings for retirement. President Lyndon Johnson's amendment to the act added health care benefits for the elderly in the form of Medicare. (For more on health care policy in the United States, see "Policy Profile: Health Care.")

Major Program in Place

Social Security is a social insurance program—that is, people contribute to social security during their working lives in order to receive benefits when they retire. Consequently, most people do not view social security in the same negative light—people getting something for nothing—as they do welfare. Unlike welfare, social security is not means tested, which means that workers who pay into social security are entitled to receive benefits, no matter what their income.

On its face, social security looks very different the government's welfare program, Temporary Assistance to Needy Families (TANF). Recipients contribute a portion of their incomes, matched by their employers, directly into a fund

for social security. If you receive a paycheck, your social security contribution appears as a withholding called FICA (Federal Insurance Contributions Act). Workers contribute 6.2 percent of the first $72,600 (in 1999) of their salaries in FICA taxes, and their employers match that amount, for a total of 12.4 percent. In 1998, the average monthly payment for all retired workers was $765, and the maximum monthly benefit was $1,342.[1] When workers retire at age sixty-five, they receive 100 percent of the benefit they are entitled to, based on the total payroll tax contributions they and their employers made during their working lives. Workers may retire early (at age sixty-two) and receive 80 percent of their benefit. Benefits are authorized not only for retired workers but also for their spouses; survivors' benefits are available to the minor children of workers who have died.

But social security is more similar to the welfare program we discussed in "Policy Profile: Welfare Policy" than is first apparent. The average social security recipient gets back what he or she put into the program within the first seven years of receiving benefits.[2] Everything received after that is a direct subsidy from younger taxpayers—a form of government assistance in the guise of a social insurance program. And since there is no means test for social security, not only poor recipients but also billionaires can continue to collect this direct subsidy from taxpayers long after they have gotten back what they put in. In addition, since billionaires and other wealthy people are taxed only on the first $72,600 of their income, they do not even contribute proportionately. Although we tend to think of social security as social insurance, it is a distributive policy, since everyone pays for the benefit of a particular group (even though it is a group to which most of us expect to belong).

According to the Social Security Administration, 41 percent of senior citizens would be living in poverty without social security.[3] Many

Americans continue to need the economic insurance that social security provides. However, policymakers in 1935 could not have predicted how politics and demographics would jeopardize the future of this social insurance program. Social security beneficiaries have steadily increased in the past fifty years because people now live longer than they used to. But the program also has grown because retired people, organized into the American Association of Retired Persons, form a powerful lobby that jealously guards their benefits. And since elderly people are far more likely to vote than younger citizens, elected officials dare not cross them. Today social security is the government's largest program, paying $365 billion in benefits, or about 23 percent of the federal budget in 1997.

The Future of Social Security

Our current social security program is probably unsustainable for several reasons. First, although beneficiaries must pay into the Social Security Trust Fund while they are working, they don't just recover what they've contributed. They collect benefits as long as they live. As life expectancies increase, people receive more in social security benefits than they pay in FICA taxes.

Second, the baby-boom generation will retire in the next two decades. By 2027, nearly 20 percent of all Americans will be over sixty-five. That would not be so bad if there were enough workers to cover the retirement costs of these new retirees. However, as illustrated by the accompaying figure, projections are that the ratio of workers to retirees will decline from 5:1 in 1960 to 2:1 in 2030. To put it another way, between 2010 and 2030, the number of Americans over sixty-five will increase 72 percent, while the number of working-age Americans (those between 20 and 64) will increase only 4 percent.[4] In short, fewer workers will have to pay for more retirees.

Given these changing demographics and the political barriers that exist to cutting, limiting, or means-testing benefits, the government should act quickly. The Social Security Trust Fund now receives more in FICA taxes than is paid out in benefits, but that situation will reverse around the year 2030. Plans to reform or in some cases "rescue" social security have been put forth by both the president and members of Congress over the past few years and were the subject of much debate in the 2000 presidential election. Most plans include a provision to "lock up" surplus payroll tax revenues so that they will be available to fund the baby boomers' benefits in the coming decades, and some, such as President George W. Bush's controversial preference, include turning some social security funds over to the control of individuals themselves.

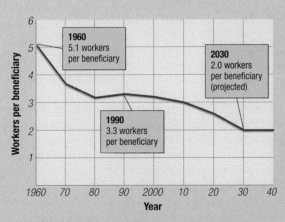

The Worker-per-Retiree Ratio
In 1960 there were over five workers contributing payroll taxes for every one social security beneficiary. That ratio dropped sharply between 1960 and 1980, and it is expected to continue to decrease, so that by 2030 there will be only two workers supporting each beneficiary, through ever larger payroll deductions.
Source: Concord Coalition and Social Security Trustees.

[1] Americans Discuss Social Security, "Social Security and You," 2 (http://www. americansdiscuss.org).
[2] Congressional Research Service, "Social Security: Brief Facts and Statistics," CRS Report for Congress, updated 1 May 1998.
[3] Social Security Administration, *Income of the Aged, Chart Book for 1996,* (Washington, DC: Government Printing Office, 1998).
[4] Concord Coalition, http://www. concordcoalition.org.

Major Problem Being Addressed: Health care for those who can't afford it

Policy Type: Redistributive

Background: The United States is the only industrialized nation not to have a universal health care system. Yet it also spends the most on health care: 10.8 percent of gross domestic product in 1996, compared to Germany's 10.4 percent and Switzerland's and France's 9.8 percent. In the meantime, most Americans support some form of health care reform. According to a recent survey, 58 percent of all adults see a role for government in expanding health insurance coverage.[1]

Major Programs in Place

Medicare. Medicare is the federal government's hospital insurance program for people who are over age sixty-five, disabled, or have permanent kidney failure. Signed into law by President Lyndon Johnson in 1965 as part of the amendments to the Social Security Act, Medicare extended health care coverage to virtually all Americans over age sixty-five. Collected as a payroll tax like FICA (see "Policy Profile: Social Security"), Medicare was created to protect retired persons from huge medical bills. Workers would pay a small Medicare tax while they were healthy in order to receive medical health insurance when they retired.

Medicare has two parts. Part A provides hospital insurance, limited stays at skilled nursing facilities, home health services, and hospice care. Part B helps pay for doctors' services, outpatient hospital services (including emergency room visits), ambulance transportation, diagnostic tests, laboratory services, and a variety of other health services. Part B requires that beneficiaries pay a monthly premium, which was $43.80 in 1998.[2]

In 1997 nearly 40 million aged and disabled people were on Medicare.[3] At a cost of $209 billion in 1998, Medicare is the nation's fourth most expensive program, with costs averaging about $5,500 per enrollee. The Social Security Administration Trustees project that costs per enrollee will double in ten years.[4] Many politicians have called for a portion of the federal budget surplus to be allocated to maintaining Medicare. Others

are skeptical about the government's ability to continue to fund Medicare, given escalating medical costs and the aging of the U.S. population. The Concord Coalition, a bipartisan advocacy group for entitlement reform, argues that real per-beneficiary Medicare spending has grown at the rate of 5 percent per year since 1970. If this rate continues, Medicare would cost over 40 percent of payroll by the year 2040.[5]

Medicaid. Medicaid was enacted as an amendment to the Social Security Act in 1965, as part of President Johnson's Great Society program. A federally sponsored program that provides free medical care to the poor, Medicaid is jointly funded by the national and state governments. Prior to the passage of welfare reform, needy people who were eligible for Medicaid were already receiving some kind of cash assistance—either as welfare or Supplemental Social Security payments. Currently, families who are not eligible under the new welfare program, Temporary Assistance to Needy Families (TANF), may still qualify for Medicaid if they meet previous program requirements. Moreover, since part of the new welfare law requires that recipients get a job, families who move from welfare to work are eligible for transitional Medicaid assistance for six to twelve months. Another program established under the welfare reform package is the Children's Health Insurance Program, which allows states to expand family eligibility for Medicaid to those who earn up to 200 percent of the poverty line established by the government.

States can establish more generous eligibility requirements for Medicaid if they wish. For example, states can choose to increase income and personal asset limits, thereby insuring more families. In most states, families with young children who have incomes equal to or less than 133 percent of the poverty line are eligible. States can choose to disregard personal assets, such as the family car, in calculating eligibility. In this sense, it's possible for poor families to receive medical care without receiving welfare. This is a tremendous advantage over the former system, in which medical benefits depended on qualification for welfare and welfare recipients would lose their children's health coverage if they took a job, giving them a disincentive to get off the welfare rolls.

Medicaid coverage includes hospitalization, prescription drugs, doctor visits, and long-term nursing care. Rising medical costs are a concern to state and national policymakers, however, who worry about the states' ability to continue to fund Medicaid, a program that costs states around one-fourth of their budgets. An equal concern is the fact that not all poor people are covered by Medicaid. Estimates are that only about one-third of poor people have medical insurance.[6]

Health Care Policy Issues on the Horizon: A National Health Care System?

U.S. policymakers have consistently hesitated to create a national health care system to serve all Americans. Fears of excessive government control, large costs, and inefficient services have doomed reform efforts. This may have something to do with the two sides of our uniquely American political culture, something we discussed in Chapter 1. Recall that we described Americans as both procedural and individualistic; in other words, Americans value rules over results and individual choice over the collective good. President Bill Clinton's 1993–1994 health care reform effort is a good example of how our political culture can make social policy very difficult to formulate.

In September 1993, President Clinton presented his "Health Security" plan to give every citizen at least some basic health care services. He wanted all Americans to have the ability to purchase health care at a reasonable price without fear of losing their coverage if they changed jobs or developed a serious medical condition. Also, in keeping with his deficit reduction goals, he aimed to slow the rate of growth in health care expenditures, specifically Medicare and Medicaid. Despite Democratic control of the presidency and both houses of Congress, the reform effort never took hold in Congress.

Reaction to the Clinton reform effort demonstrates the uneasy feelings concerning health care shared by both Americans and special-interest groups (such as physicians, hospitals, HMOs, and pharmaceutical companies). The principal beliefs supporting the American system are that the free market and the ability to choose our physicians and hospitals will provide the best health care.

Certainly, the United States has the most advanced health care services in the world, but many Americans still lack access to health insurance coverage because of differences in education, income, gender, and race. An estimated 43.4 million Americans, or 16 percent of the population, were without coverage in 1997.[7] In addition, Medicaid failed to cover nearly one-third of those classified as poor by the government. Why do Americans tolerate the neglect of basic health services for so many?

Proponents of universal health care find it difficult to eliminate the perception that government control will harm the quality and raise the cost of health care services. The rise of HMOs (health maintenance organizations) in the 1990s raised hopes that the phenomenal costs could be controlled and health care standards maintained. However, doctors now frequently lament the loss of autonomy, while patients complain of diminishing quality of care.

During the 2000 elections, both Republicans and Democrats introduced proposals aimed at protecting the rights of patients in managed care plans. The plans considered, dubbed *patient's bills of rights*, would not apply to all plans, but would offer consumer protections, including appeal processes for the denial of coverage and a ban on physician gag rules. Many interest groups representing various professional organizations have weighed in on these proposals. Some, like the National Education Association, have recommended that any bill passed should leave "medical decisions in the hands of physicians, not insurance companies; give access to specialty care; and promote continuity of the doctor-patient relationship."[8]

[1]"America Unplugged: Citizens and Their Government," Peter Hart and Robert Teeter public opinion poll on behalf of the Council for Excellence in Government between 21 May and 1 June 1999 (http://www.excelgov.org/excel/usunplugged.htm).
[2]Health Care Finance Administration, U.S. Department of Health and Human Services, http://www.hcfa.gov/medicare.
[3]Concord Coalition, "Facing Facts Alert: Medicare's Long Fiscal Shadow," *The Truth About Entitlements and the Budget*, 21 January 1999.
[4]Ibid.
[5]Ibid.
[6]Robert Bennefield, "Health Insurance Coverage 1997," Current Population Reports, September 1998, 60–202.
[7]Ibid.
[8]National Education Association, "Congressional Issues, Overview, Managed Health Care," June 1999. NEA Government Relations 202/822-7300 (web version).

Policy Profile: Economic Policy

Major Problems Being Addressed: Economic prosperity for all of society; evening out the dramatic cycles of inflation and recession without undermining the vitality and productivity of a market-driven economy

Policy Type: Regulatory, redistributive

Background: For much of our history, policymakers have felt that government should pursue a hands-off policy of doing very little to regulate the economy, in effect letting the market take care of itself, guided only by the laws of supply and demand.[1] The Great Depression of the 1930s, however, changed the way government policymakers viewed the economy. The challenge for government is to achieve a balance of steady growth—growth that is not so rapid that it causes inflation, nor so sluggish that the economy slides into a recession or depression. Its intervention can take one of two forms: fiscal policy, which enables government to regulate the economy through its powers to tax and spend, or monetary policy, which allows government to manage the economy by controlling the money supply through the regulation of interest rates. Each of these strategies has different political advantages and different costs, and both play an important role in contemporary economic policy.

The strategy of increasing government spending during recessionary periods and cutting back during expansionary periods gradually became the primary tool of economic policy between 1930 and the 1970s. President Franklin Roosevelt used it to lead the country out of the Depression in the 1930s. His New Deal created federal agencies to help business recover, jobs programs to put people to work, and social programs to restore the buying power of consumers. Subsequent presidents made fiscal policy the foundation of their economic programs until the late 1970s, when the economy took a turn that fiscal policy seemed unable to manage, combining both inflation and unemployment. Taxing and spending, as redistributive policies, can be politically tricky for elected officials who want to maximize their chances of reelection. The temptation is to lower taxes and increase spending, which can result in a sizable national debt and loses sight of the goal of leveling out the cycles of a market economy.

Many people looking at the high inflation and growing unemployment of the 1970s began to turn to monetary policy as a way to manage the economy. Monetary policy controls the money supply (the sum of all currency on hand in the country plus the amount held in checking accounts) as a way of regulating the economy. The monetarists believed that the high inflation of the 1970s was caused by too much money in the economy, and they advocated cutting back on the supply. By raising and lowering interest rates, government can regulate the amount of money in society, and thus the cycles of the market economy, just as it does by taxing and spending. As a tool of economic policy, however, monetary policy can be somewhat hard to control. Small changes can have big effects. Reducing the money supply might lower inflation, but too great a reduction can also cause a recession, which is what happened in the early 1980s. Changes need to be made in narrow increments rather than in broad sweeps.

Major Programs in Place

Today policymakers use a combination of fiscal and monetary policy to achieve economic goals. As the accompanying figure shows, since the 1940s, when the federal government made a full commitment to regulate the gyrations of the business cycle, the highs and lows of boom and bust have been greatly tempered. There are still fluctuations in inflation, unemployment, and gross domestic product (GDP), but they lack the punishing ferocity of the earlier period under laissez-faire.

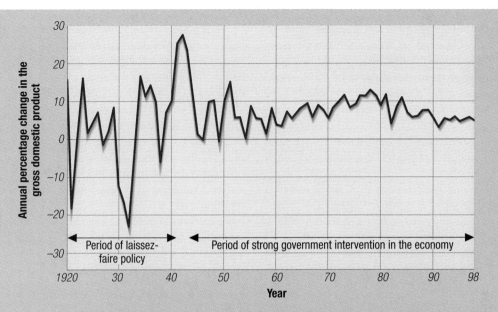

Government: A Steadying Influence on Gross Domestic Product
The zero line in this figure represents no economic growth (and no decline). The ideal for economic prosperity is steady, positive economic growth, or a change in the gross domestic product just a few percentage points above the zero line. Notice here that with strong government intervention in the economy beginning in the late 1930s, the radical swings between growth and decline were substantially diminished.
Source: U.S. Department of Commerce, *Historical Statistics of the United States, Colonial Times to 1970* and *Statistical Abstract of the United States, 1998,* CD-ROM version.

As we have indicated, the two kinds of policy are not equally easy for government to employ. Most significantly, the instruments of monetary policy are removed from the political arena and are wielded by actors who are not subject to electoral pressures, namely the Federal Reserve System, known as the Fed, currently headed by Alan Greenspan. The Fed controls the supply of money by controlling the interest rates at which banks borrow money, by limiting the amount the banks have to hold in reserve, and by buying government securities. When banks have a lot of money to loan, interest rates tend to drop and people borrow more, thus increasing levels of economic activity, which includes everything from buying a new car to investing in an automobile manufacturing plant. When lending institutions have less to loan (smaller reserves), they charge more for their money (higher interest rates), and, at every level of demand for money, economic activity slows down.

By contrast, fiscal policy is very much at the center of enduring political struggles. Fiscal policy is actually made by Congress and the president through the budget process. Budgets may seem tedious and boring, reminding us of our own efforts at financial responsibility. But government budgets are where we find the clearest indications, in black and white, of politics—who gets what and who pays for it. The government budget process also exemplifies the conflict we discussed in Chapter 6 between the needs of lawmaking and the electoral imperatives of representation. Members of Congress and the president, as lawmakers, have an interest in maintaining a healthy economy and should be able to agree on appropriate levels of taxing and spending to see that the economy stays in good shape. But as elected leaders, they are also accountable to constituencies and committed to ideological or partisan goals. From a representative's perspective, the budget is a pie to be divided and fought over.

When the government uses fiscal policy to stimulate a slow economy, it generally runs a deficit for a few years (as it does anytime it spends more than it brings in). As the shortfalls accumulate, the government amasses a national debt, which is the total of the nation's unpaid deficits, or simply the sum total of what the national government owes. The national debt grew during the New Deal period as the federal government attempted to use fiscal policy, especially massive spending on domestic programs such as the Works Project Administration and the Civilian Conservation Corps, to stimulate the economy out of the Great Depression. It continued to rise as the government borrowed heavily to finance U.S. participation in World War II. By the time the war was over, the economy was moving again, and the growing economy generated additional revenues, permitting the government to pay down a portion of the national debt. Budget deficits started rising again in the 1980s, and by the mid-1990s, the national debt had climbed to more than $5 trillion, more than $20,000 per citizen. Just like citizens who carry a credit card balance or borrow money to buy a car, the government pays interest on the national debt. In 1998, 14.6 percent of Americans' taxes went to pay the interest on the national debt.

The 1980s and 1990s became known as the era of deficit politics.[2] All federal program decisions were made in light of their impact on the deficit. This changed the character of the politics involved and helped to increase the power of the congressional leadership, particularly in the House of Representatives. Dealing with the deficit called for more coordination and discipline. Congress then developed a dizzying array of informal mechanisms in an effort to streamline the budgetary process.[3] After all the tinkering, however, Congress still has been unable to balance the demands of lawmaking and representation, nor is it likely to reconcile the strong and ideologically divergent goals that exist among the main actors in the national budget process. As a consequence, the budget is not very effective as a tool of fiscal policy.

Given all of the difficulties involved in making economic policy and our history of boom and bust, the sustained and moderate growth of the U.S. economy for most of the postwar era is quite an accomplishment. Some say that the most recent expansionary period, which has lasted for more than eight years, is certain to be followed by a recession—and one that may introduce some new wrinkles to the practice of monetary and fiscal policy.[4]

---

[1]Adam Smith, *The Wealth of Nations* (London: Strahan and Cadell, 1776).

[2]Daniel Wirls, "Busted: Government and Elections in the Era of Deficit Politics," in Benjamin Ginsberg and Alan Stone, eds., *Do Elections Matter?* 3rd ed. (Armonk, NY: M. E. Sharpe, 1996), 65–85.

[3]Barbara Sinclair, "Party Leaders and the New Legislative Process," in Lawrence C. Dodd and Bruce I. Oppenheimer, eds., *Congress Reconsidered*, 6th ed. (Washington, DC: Congressional Quarterly Press, 1997), 229–245.

[4]Louis Uchitelle, "Who You Gonna Call After the Next Bust?" *New York Times*, 22 August 1999, sect. 4, p. 5.

Policy Profile: Tax Policy

Major Problems Being Addressed: Need for government services; alleviation of poverty; remedy for economic slowdown or recession

Policy Type: Distributive, redistributive

Major Programs in Place

The U.S. government takes in a lot of money in taxes every year, now well over $1.6 trillion. The largest single source is individual federal income taxes. The next largest is social insurance, and by far the biggest component of this is social security, with funds coming equally from workers' paychecks and employers. The smallest category is excise taxes—taxes levied on specific items like cigarettes and alcohol—but that still represents $55 billion.

One of the features of the U.S. tax code is that some money is earmarked for particular purposes, whereas other money goes into the general fund. Thus social security taxes cannot be used to purchase new jets for the air force, and the highway trust funds cannot be used to supplement Medicare costs. An apparent exception to this is when the government borrows money from itself with a promise to pay it back. This was the practice in recent years when the Social Security Trust Fund was running large surpluses. The national government borrowed money from the trust fund to pay for other things, vowing to reimburse social security in the future out of general fund revenues.

Personal income taxes in the United States are progressive taxes, which means that those with higher incomes not only pay more taxes but also pay at a higher rate. Taxes are paid on all the income an individual or household receives, including wage and salary income, interest and dividends, rent on property owned, and royalties. The amount owed depends on the tax rate and the amount of taxable income, which is total income minus certain exemptions and deductions. Deductions can include interest payments on a home mortgage or charitable contributions that an individual or household can deduct from their income. Single taxpayers are allowed a standard deduction of $4,000, married couples $6,700. Everyone is subject to the same rate of taxation for some base amount, and incomes over that amount are subject to increasingly high rates. The range of taxable income in each tax bracket determines the marginal tax rate. For instance, if you are in a 35 percent tax bracket, that does not mean you pay 35 percent of all your income in taxes, but that you pay 35 percent on everything you make above the tax bracket beneath you and a lower percentage on the income made under that base amount.

Other taxes are called regressive taxes, even if they are fixed percentages, because they take a higher proportion of a poor person's income than that of someone who is well-off. Sales taxes are often said to be regressive, particularly when they are levied on necessities like food and electricity. If a poor person and a rich person each buy an air conditioner for $200, with a sales tax of 5 percent, the resulting $10 tax is a bigger chunk of the poor person's income than it is of the rich person's. Furthermore, poor people spend a higher portion of their incomes on consumables that are subject to the sales tax. By contrast, the wealthy spend a significant portion of their incomes on investments, stocks, and education for their children, which are not subject to sales taxes.

The major political parties differ in their approaches to tax policy, particularly on the issue of the progressivity of taxes—who should bear the brunt of the tax burden, and whose tax loads should be relieved. In general, Democrats focus on easing the tax burden on lower-income groups in the name of fairness and equity. As a matter of fiscal policy, they tend to want to put money into the hands of workers and the working poor on the assumption that this will translate quickly into consumer spending, which increases demand and stimulates the whole economy. This is the "trickle-up" strategy: give benefits to those with less and let the effects percolate upward, throughout the economic system.

Republicans focus more on lowering the high rates of taxation on those with higher incomes. Their sentiments are motivated by a different view of fairness: those who make more money should be able to keep it. Republicans argue that the wealthy are more likely to save or invest money resulting from a tax break, thus providing businesses with the capital they need to expand. Not only do they believe that the rate of taxation in the top tax brackets should be reduced, but they argue for a reduction in the capital gains tax—the tax levied on the returns people earn from capital investments, like the profits from the sale of stocks or a home. The notion here is that if wealthy people are taxed at lower rates, they will invest and spend more, the economy will prosper, and the benefits will "trickle down" to the rest of society. The debate between proponents of the trickle-up and trickle-down theories of taxation is one of the major partisan battles in Congress. It not only reveals deep ideological divisions between the parties but also demonstrates the very real differences in the constituencies they represent.

Prospects for Reform

There's no doubt about it—America's current income tax system is extremely complicated. Many people believe that it is unfair as well. Countless taxpayers rely on sophisticated computer programs or expensive tax consultants for help in understanding the convoluted bureaucratese of the tax return form. The American urge for simplicity and evenhandedness has resulted in numerous calls for tax reform.

Many politicians have argued for a flat tax system, in which one tax rate is levied across the board on all personal income. In its simplest form, there are no deductions (that is, no tax reductions for having children or owning a home, circumstances that currently allow citizens to lower the amount of income on which they pay taxes), no loopholes (unintended results of tax laws that allow some wealthy individuals and businesses to escape paying taxes they would normally owe), and no progressivity (everyone pays the same percentage of his or her income to the government.)[1] An April 1999 Gallup/*USA Today* poll found that 58 percent of Americans would prefer the flat tax to the current system of progressive taxation with complicated deductions. In addition, a poll of state legislative candidates found that more than half of those with an opinion would opt for a flat tax for their states over their current income tax systems.[2] Accountants, who depend on a complicated tax code to make a living, oppose such a reform, as do advocates for the poor, who claim that a flat tax would unfairly burden them.

Many politicians who propose a flat tax end up "unflattening" it as they build back in deductions for things that are popular with voters, like home ownership. For instance, House Majority Leader Dick Armey once sponsored a flat tax bill that would tax all individuals and businesses at the same rate but would allow a generous personal deduction for each member of a family.

A second tax reform supported by many people is the value-added tax (VAT). The VAT is a consumption tax that, according to its proponents, could largely take the place of our federal income tax. The VAT is standard across most of Europe and works much like our state and city sales taxes. There are three important differences, however: (1) the VAT is a national tax, not limited to a particular state or local jurisdiction; (2) the VAT is calculated at each stage of the production process, not just on the final sale; and (3) the price of the VAT is built into the good—some say concealed—rather than added onto the posted price at the cash register.[3] A hat that costs 20 pounds in England, for example, includes a 17.5 percent VAT in the purchase price. The pretax price of the hat, which you never see, would be just over 17 pounds.

Advantages of the VAT tax are that it is easy to collect and is more or less hidden from view.

Also, revenues grow with the economy, generating more income as incomes go up. It is different from an income tax because it taxes consumption, not the production of income. The VAT thus provides an incentive to make money but also to save or invest. In contrast, the income tax can be seen as a disincentive to save because one is taxed on income and, if it is invested and not spent, one is taxed again on the interest or dividends, even if these do no more than keep pace with inflation.

Will the flat tax or the VAT—or some combination of these plans—ever be adopted in the United States? Although both have their supporters, the plans represent a substantial change, which means many new winners and losers—and the likely losers will fight hard against them. Change is possible, of course. When President Ronald Reagan spearheaded the Tax Reform of 1986, tax rates were cut in half, and dozens of loopholes and exemptions were eliminated. Filing taxes became easier for individuals and businesses, and the reform was acclaimed as a huge improvement. But it did not last, as citizens and groups pushed for laws that would give them a financial advantage at tax time.[4] Thus it is likely to take some kind of a crisis, combined with effective leadership, to overcome the inertia that keeps the current complex, loophole-ridden, and highly unpopular system in place.

[1]Marc Levinson and Rich Thomas, "One Tax Fits All," *Newsweek*, 15 January 1996, 36.
[2]Gallup/CNN/*USA Today* poll, 15 April 1999. Data on state legislative candidates were collected by Project Vote Smart and calculated by the authors.
[3]Marc Levinson, "Once Again, Tiptoeing Around the T Word," *Newsweek*, 26 April 1993, 46.
[4]David E. Rosenbaum, "Never Mind: Reform Taxes? Give Us a Break!" *New York Times*, 26 December 1994, sect. 4, p. 1.

Foreign Policy

foreign policy
a country's official positions, practices, and procedures for dealing with actors outside its borders

In this section, we discuss **foreign policy**—official U.S. policy designed to solve problems that take place between the United States and actors outside its borders. Foreign policy is crucial to domestic tranquillity, for without a strong and effective foreign policy, the complacency we feel as a rich, secure, insulated country could be destroyed in a heartbeat. Our foreign policy is almost always carried out for the good of American citizens or in the interest of national security. Even foreign aid, which may seem like giving away American taxpayers' hard-earned money to people who have done nothing to deserve it, is part of a foreign policy to stabilize the world, to help strengthen international partnerships and alliances, and to keep Americans safe. Similarly, humanitarian intervention, like the NATO (North Atlantic Treaty Organization) military action in Kosovo in 1999, is ultimately conducted to support our values and the quality of life we think other nations ought to provide for their citizens.

isolationism
a foreign policy view that nations should stay out of international political alliances and activities and focus instead on domestic matters

Many politicians have tried to encourage Americans to turn their backs on the rest of the world, promoting a foreign policy called **isolationism,** which holds that Americans should put themselves and their problems first and not interfere in global events. The United States has tried to pursue an isolationist policy before, perhaps most notably after World War I, but this experiment was largely seen as a failure. In a world increasingly interconnected, it is hard for politicians to argue convincingly that what is happening "over there" is unrelated to what is happening at home.

Foreign policy takes place to support American interests, but determining what American interests are can be very difficult. In crisis situations, as we will see, foreign policy decisions are very often made in secret, hidden from public view. When situations are not critical, however, foreign policy decisions are made in the usual hubbub of American politics. Here, as we know, many actors with competing interests struggle to make their voices heard and to get policies to benefit them. Foreign policy, like domestic policy, is about who gets what and how they get it. The difference is that the stakes can be a matter of life and death, and we have far less control over the other actors involved.

Understanding Foreign Policy

Foreign policy focuses on U.S. government goals and actions directed toward actors outside our country's borders. This outward focus separates foreign policy from domestic policy, although sometimes the distinction between "foreign" and "domestic" is not so clear. Consider, for example, how environmental policy in America can have foreign repercussions. American industries located on the border with Canada have been the source of some tensions between the two countries because pollution from U.S. factories is carried into Canada by prevailing winds. This pollution can damage forests and increase the acidity of lakes, killing fish and harming other wildlife. Environmental regulations are largely a domestic matter, but because pollution is not confined to the geography of the United States, the issue takes on unintended international importance. In this section, we focus on actions that are intentionally directed at external actors and the forces that shape these actions. External actors include the following:

- Other countries—sovereign bodies with governments and territories, like China or the Republic of Ireland

intergovernmental organization
a body such as the United Nations whose members are countries

- **Intergovernmental organizations**—bodies that have countries as members, such as the United Nations (UN), which has 185 member countries; NATO, which has 19 members from North America and Europe; and the Organization of Petroleum Exporting Countries (OPEC), which has 11 members from Africa, Asia, the Middle East, and Latin America

nongovernmental organization
an organization comprising individuals or interest groups from around the world focused on a special issue

- **Nongovernmental organizations**—organizations that focus on specific issues and whose members are private individuals or groups from around the world; examples include Greenpeace (environmental), Amnesty International (human rights), International Committee of the Red Cross (humanitarian relief), and Doctors Without Borders (medical care)

multinational corporation a large company that does business in multiple countries

- **Multinational corporations**—large companies, like Nike and General Motors, that do business in multiple countries and that often wield tremendous economic power

- Miscellaneous actors, including those that have a government but no territory, such as the Palestinians in the Middle East and the Irish Republican Army

The Post–Cold War Setting of American Foreign Policy

Before we can hope to have a clear understanding of contemporary American foreign policy, a historical note is in order. At the end of World War II, when the common purpose of fighting Adolf Hitler and ending German fascism no longer held the

United States and the Soviet Union in an awkward alliance, the tensions that existed between the two largest and strongest superpowers in global politics began to bubble to the surface. Nearly all of Europe was divided between allies of the Soviets and allies of the United States, a division most graphically seen in the splitting of postwar Germany into a communist East and a capitalist West.

For nearly fifty years following World War II, tensions between the two superpowers shaped U.S. foreign policy and gave it a predictable order. The **Cold War,** waged between the United States and the Soviet Union from 1945 to 1989, was a bitter global competition between democracy and authoritarianism, capitalism and communism. It never erupted into a "hot" war of military action due in large part to the deterrent effect provided by a policy of "mutual assured destruction." Each side spent tremendous sums of money on nuclear weapons to make sure it had the ability to wipe out the other side. During this era, American foreign policy makers pursued a policy of **containment,** in which the United States tried to prevent the Soviet Union from expanding its influence, especially in Europe.

But as dangerous as the world was during the Cold War, it seemed easy to understand, casting complicated issues into simple choices of black and white. Countries were either with us or against us: they were free societies or closed ones, had capitalist or communist economies, were good or bad. Although the world was hardly that simple, it seemed that way to many people, and much of the complexity of world politics was glossed over—or perhaps bottled up—only to explode upon the end of the Cold War in 1989.[8]

In 1991 the Soviet Union finally fell apart, to be replaced by more than a dozen independent states. Although most Westerners hailed the fall of the Soviet Union as an end to the tensions that kept the Cold War alive, Russia (one of the states of the former USSR) still holds the Soviet nuclear arsenal, and its citizens still project considerable fear and hostility toward the United States. Recently, anti-American sentiment has grown there, especially as efforts at Russian economic reform have been accompanied by suffering, deprivation, and economic humiliation, and as the Western military alliance, NATO, has enlarged by absorbing members of the former Soviet alliance.

This "new world order," or post–Cold War era, has eluded easy description in terms of global organization and threats to the United States.[9] Who is likely to be our most dangerous adversary? Russia? Iraq? China? Or perhaps international terrorists, who call no country home? Neither is it at all clear what is required of U.S. foreign policy. What threats must we prepare for? How much should we spend on military preparedness? What role should we play vis-à-vis other nations? Are we the world's policeman, a global banker, or a humanitarian protector? We have experimented with all of these roles in the past decade. In this confusing new global setting, U.S. policymakers—who cut their teeth on the Cold War—try to navigate the ship of state. The waters are not as dangerous as before, but there are few good markers and no clear destination.[10]

Cold War   the half century of competition and conflict after World War II between the United States and the Soviet Union (and their allies)

containment
the U.S. Cold War policy of preventing the spread of communism

Types of Foreign Policy

We can more easily understand what American foreign policy is if we break it down into three specific types.[11]

crisis policy   foreign policy, usually made quickly and secretly, that responds to an emergency threat

strategic policy foreign policy that lays out a country's basic stance toward international actors or problems

structural defense policy   foreign policy dealing with defense spending, military bases, and weapons procurement

- **Crisis policy** deals with emergency threats to our national interests or values. Such situations often come as a surprise, and the use of force is one way to respond.[12]

- **Strategic policy** lays out the basic U.S. stance toward another country or a particular problem. Containment, for example, was the key strategy for dealing with the Soviets during the Cold War—the plan was to prevent communism from spreading to other countries.

- **Structural defense policy** focuses largely on the policies and programs that deal with defense spending and military bases. These policies usually focus on, for example, buying new aircraft for the air force and navy or deciding which military bases to consolidate or close down.

Who Makes Foreign Policy?

Consider the following headlines: "U.S. Opens Relations with China" and "U.S. Demands Libyan Terrorists Be Brought to Justice." These headlines make it sound as if a single actor—the United States—makes foreign policy. Even as a figure of speech, this is misleading in two important ways. First, the image of the United States as a single actor suggests that the country acts with a single, united mind, diverting our attention from the political reality of conflict, bargaining, and cooperation that takes place within the government over foreign policy.[13] Second, it implies that all foreign policies are essentially the same—having the same goals and made by the same actors and processes. Our earlier description of the three different policy types indicates that this is not so. In fact, as we will see, each type of policy is made by different actors in different political contexts.

The political dynamics behind crisis policy, for instance, are dominated by the president and the small group of advisers around the Oval Office. Congress tends not to be much engaged in crisis policy, but often watches with the rest of the public (and the world) as presidents and their advisers decide how to respond to international crises.

Strategic policy tends to be formulated in the executive branch, but usually deep in the bureaucracy rather than at the top levels. This gives interest groups and concerned members of Congress opportunities to lobby for certain policies. The public usually learns about these policies (and responds to and evaluates them) once they are announced by the president. The U.S. policy of containment of communism in the 1940s, for example, was developed largely in the State Department and was then approved by President Harry Truman.[14]

Finally, structural defense policy, which often starts in the executive branch, is largely crafted in Congress, where members tend to have their fingers on the pulses of their constituents, with much input from the bureaucracy and interest groups. When a plan to build and deploy a new fighter jet is developed, for example, it is made with close coordination between Congress and the Defense Department—usually with members of Congress keeping an eye on how their states and districts will fare from the projects.

Clearly, a variety of actors are involved in making different types of foreign policy. What they all have in common is that they are officially acting on behalf of the federal government. It is not official foreign policy when New York City and San Francisco impose economic sanctions on Burma, or when private citizens like former president Jimmy Carter or the Reverend Jesse Jackson attempt to help resolve conflicts in Africa or Serbia.[15]

The President and the Executive Branch As we saw in Chapter 7, the president is the chief foreign policy maker. The president is more likely to set the foreign policy agenda than other actors in American politics because of his constitutional powers, the informal powers that come with this high-profile job, and the chief executive's opportunities to communicate directly with the public.

The president sits at the top of a large pyramid of executive agencies and departments that assist him in making foreign policy (see Figure 14.2). If he does not take time to manage the agencies, other individuals may seize the opportunity to interpret foreign policy in terms of their own interests and goals. In a sense, the president provides a check on the power of the executive agencies, and without his leadership, foreign policy can drift. President Ronald Reagan didn't pay a lot of attention to foreign affairs, and so staff members in the National Security Council began to make foreign policy themselves. The result was the Iran-contra affair in the mid-1980s.

National Security Council organization within the Executive Office of the President that provides foreign policy advice to the president

The **National Security Council** (NSC) is part of the president's inner circle, the Executive Office of the President. It was created in 1947 by the National Security Act to advise the president on matters of foreign policy and is coordinated by the national security adviser. By law, the NSC includes the president, vice president, secretary of state, and secretary of defense. Additionally, the director of central intelligence (who is also the head of the Central Intelligence Agency) and the chairman of the Joint Chiefs of Staff (the head of the commanders of the military services)

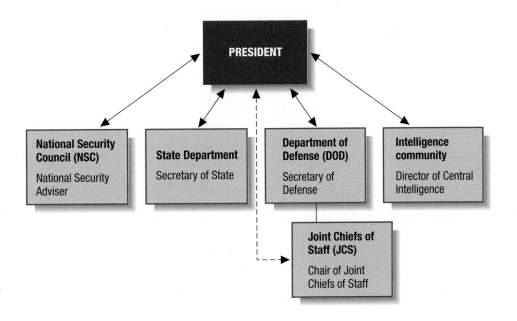

**Figure 14.2
Key Foreign Policy
Agencies**

Traveling the World for Peace
Former U.S. secretary of state Madeleine Albright emerges from a meeting with Russian foreign minister Igor Ivanov in Moscow. The meeting was one of many held between Albright and other world leaders in the winter and spring of 1999 to discuss a solution to the Kosovo crisis, a topic about which the United States and Russia largely disagreed.

Department of State the executive department charged with managing foreign affairs

Department of Defense the executive department charged with managing the country's military personnel, equipment, and operations

Joint Chiefs of Staff the senior military officers from the four branches of the U.S. armed forces

intelligence community the agencies and bureaus responsible for obtaining and interpreting information for the government

sit as advisers to the NSC. Beyond this, the president has wide discretion to decide what the NSC will look like and how he will use it by appointing other members and deciding how the council will function.

In addition to the NSC, several executive departments and agencies play a critical role in foreign policy making. The **Department of State** is charged with managing foreign affairs. It is often considered to be "first among equals" in its position relative to the other departments because it was the first department established by the Constitution in 1789. The State Department is headed by the secretary of state, who is part of the president's cabinet and fulfills a variety of foreign policy roles, including maintaining diplomatic and consular posts around the world, sending delegates and missions (groups of government officials) to a variety of international organization meetings, and negotiating treaties and executive agreements with other countries. Among the employees of the State Department are the foreign service officers, the most senior of which are the U.S. ambassadors.

The second major department involved in foreign policy is the **Department of Defense,** headquartered in the Pentagon. The main job of this department is to manage American soldiers and their equipment in order to protect the United States. The Defense Department is headed by the secretary of defense, whose job in part is to advise the president on defense matters and who, it is important to note, is a civilian.

The **Joint Chiefs of Staff** (JCS) is part of the Defense Department. This group consists of the senior military officers of the armed forces: the army and navy chiefs of staff, the chief of naval operations, and the commandant of the marine corps. The chairman is selected by the president. The JCS advises the secretary of defense, although the chair also may offer advice directly to the president and is responsible for managing the armed forces of the United States.

Another executive actor in foreign policy making is the **intelligence community,** which comprises several government agencies and bureaus. This community's job is to collect, organize, and analyze information. Information can be gathered in a number of ways, from the mundane (such as reading foreign newspapers) to the more clandestine (for instance, spying both by human beings and through surveillance satellites). The community is coordinated by the director of central intelligence, who is also the head of the **Central Intelligence Agency (CIA).**

Central Intelligence Agency
the government organization that oversees foreign intelligence-gathering and related classified activities

In addition to the State Department, the Defense Department, and the intelligence community, a variety of other departments play various roles in foreign policy. For instance, the Treasury Department and the Commerce Department are concerned with America's foreign economic policy, and the Department of Agriculture is interested in promoting American agricultural products abroad.

Congress   As we saw in Chapter 6, Congress has a variety of constitutional roles in making foreign policy, including the power to make treaties, to declare war, and to appropriate money, to name just a few. But Congress faces obstacles in its efforts to play an active role in foreign policy. It must deal with the considerable powers of the president, for instance, and it is more oriented toward domestic than foreign affairs, given the ever present imperative of reelection. Congressional organization also can hamper Congress's role in foreign policy. The fragmentation of Congress, the slow speed of deliberation, and the complex nature of many foreign issues can make it difficult for Congress to play a big role, particularly in fast-moving foreign events.

The foreign policy tension between president and Congress is illustrated by the complex issues surrounding the use of military force. The president is in charge of the armed forces, but only Congress can declare war. Presidents try to get around the power of Congress by committing troops to military actions that do not have the official status of a war, but this can infuriate legislators. Presidents have sent troops abroad without a formal declaration of war on a number of occasions—for example, in Korea (1950), Vietnam (1965), Lebanon (1982), the Dominican Republic (1965), Grenada (1983), Panama (1989), and the Persian Gulf (1990). As the United States became more involved in the Vietnam War, however, Congress became increasingly unhappy with the president's role. When, in the early 1970s, public opinion against the war became increasingly vocal, Congress turned on the commander-in-chief, passing the War Powers Act of 1973 over President Richard Nixon's veto. The act includes the following provisions:

1. The president must inform Congress of the introduction of forces into hostilities or situations where imminent involvement in hostilities is clearly indicated by the circumstances.

2. Troop commitments by the president cannot extend past sixty days without specific congressional authorization.

3. Anytime American forces become engaged in hostilities without a declaration of war or specific congressional authorization, Congress can direct the president to disengage such troops by a concurrent resolution of the two houses of Congress.

The War Powers Act has not stopped presidents from using force abroad, however. Chief executives have largely sidestepped the act through a simple loophole: they don't make their reports to Congress exactly as the act requires, and therefore they never trigger the sixty-day clock. They generally report "consistent with but not pursuant to" the act, a technicality that allows them to satisfy Congress's interest in being informed without tying their hands by starting the clock.

Despite its difficulties in enforcing the War Powers Act, Congress has tried to play a fairly active role in foreign policy making, sometimes working with the president and sometimes at odds with him. The calculation for Congress is fairly straightforward: Let the president pursue risky military strategies. If he succeeds, take credit for staying out of his way. If he fails, blame him for not consulting and for being "imperial." Either way, Congress wins.

How Do We Define a Foreign Policy Problem?

The actors we have just discussed work in a very distinctive political environment that helps them decide when a foreign situation constitutes a problem and when it should be acted on. Most foreign policy is either action to correct something we don't like in the world or reaction to world events. America could try to meddle in almost any country's affairs and could react to almost anything that happens in the world. How do policymakers in Washington, members of the media, and average Americans decide what is sufficiently important to Americans and American interests to require a foreign policy? What makes the United States act or react?

The answer is complex. First, a distinctive American approach to foreign policy has developed over the years that reflects America's view of its global role, its values, and its political goals. For instance, American foreign policy makers are divided about what the United States' role in the world should be: should it be an interventionist actor, or should it focus on problems closer to home and leave the global community to solve its own problems? A second tension comes from the question of whether U.S. foreign policy should be driven by moral concerns (doing what is right—for instance, with respect to human rights) or practical concerns (ignoring what is right in favor of what is expedient—for instance, ensuring U.S. access to foreign oil or other natural resources). A final tension arises from the conflict between the United States' desire to promote its own national security and economic growth and its desire to promote the spread of democracy in the world. Because of inherent tensions among these roles, values, and goals, our country's approach to defining foreign policy problems is not always consistent.

Foreign policy also is shaped by politics. The political context in which American foreign policy is forged involves the actors we have just met, in combination with pressures both global and domestic. Global pressures involve the actions of other nations, over which we have no control other than brute force, and international organizations, like the UN and NATO. Other global pressures concern economic issues. In an increasingly interdependent global economy, ups and downs in one country tend to reverberate throughout the world. Foreign policy makers are influenced by these international forces, but also by domestic pressures. Just as in domestic policy, the media, public opinion, and interest groups weigh in and try to influence what policymakers do. To the extent that the policymakers are elected officials, these domestic actors can carry considerable weight.

WHO, WHAT, HOW   In foreign policy, government actors seek to solve problems outside the United States.

WHO are the actors?	WHAT do they want?	HOW do they get it?
United States	• To solve problems outside the United States and to define America's post–Cold War global role	• Crisis, strategic, and structural policymaking
The president, executive departments and agencies, Congress	• To realize foreign policy goals • To use power and influence	• Constitutional rules • Existing legislation • Creation of new laws
All foreign policy makers	• To determine what constitutes a foreign policy problem requiring action	• Culture of American foreign policy • Global pressures • Domestic pressures

Citizenship and Policy

In this book, we have discussed elite, pluralist, and participatory theories of democracy. This chapter has shown that each theory explains some aspect of policymaking in the United States. Clearly, some foreign policy and domestic policy are the products of a closely guarded elite policymaking process that could not be less democratic at its core. Foreign policy, especially when dealing with crisis situations, takes place in secrecy, with the details kept even from other policymakers at the elite level. Monetary policy is specifically designed to protect the economy from the forces of democracy—from the short-term preferences of citizens and the eagerness of elected officials to give citizens what they want. Other policy areas, like social security policy, are very pluralistic. Even though society as a whole might be better off with more stringent rules concerning who gets what from social security, older Americans, in the guise of the American Association of Retired Persons, have successfully lobbied to maintain the generous and universal benefits that make social security so expensive. But the power of political groups does not negate the power of citizens. Individual Americans, in their roles as voters and participants in public opinion polls, have a decisive influence on policymaking, both domestic and foreign. Although they may not participate in the sense of getting deeply involved in the process themselves, there is no doubt that politicians respond to their preferences in creating public policy.

As we saw in Chapter 10, public opinion matters in politics. State legislators, for instance, vote in accordance with the ideological preferences of their citizens.[16] States with more liberal citizens, such as New York, Massachusetts, and California, have more liberal policies, and more conservative states, like those in the South and the Rocky Mountains, have more conservative state policies. Other studies have found a similar pattern in national elections.[17] What these findings tell us is that for

Points of Access

- Submit a policy idea to your congressional representative.
- Attend an open hearing or committee meeting about a public policy under review.
- Intern at the U.S. Department of State.
- Join the Peace Corps.
- Travel or study abroad and ask about other people's perceptions of the United States.
- Organize a collection of food and supplies to send to a nation in need.
- Join a foreign policy interest group such as Amnesty International, Human Rights Watch, or a country-specific group.
- If your city or town participates in Sister City International (an organization devoted to promoting global tolerance), find out how you can join or contribute to its activities.
- Express your support for (or opposition to) government action abroad by phoning, writing, or demonstrating.

all the cynicism in politics today, when it comes to who gets what when and how, American democracy works to a remarkable degree.

WHAT'S AT STAKE REVISITED

We have seen in this chapter that many public policies have consequences that politicians did not anticipate. Getting tough on crime is an excellent case in point. The primary result of the sentencing reform discussed at the beginning of the chapter is that prisons are becoming severely overcrowded, necessitating the building of more prisons, funded by taxpayers. In 1999, 1.8 million inmates were under state or federal jurisdiction.[18] The United States now leads the world in the percentage of its population in prison or jail or on probation (2.8 percent).[19] At current incarceration rates, the United States needs 1,143 new prison beds each week.[20] One author estimates that a new prison is built every week, on average, to keep up with the increasing demand on the system.[21] While this no doubt pleases prison guards and prison contractors, whose professional associations lobby for policies that require more prisons, it does not please many taxpayers or those officials whose job it is to squeeze from the budgets enough money to pay for other social costs.

Building and operating prisons is expensive. Tough sentencing policies create huge budgetary sinkholes, and costs will only rise as the prison population ages and requires more expensive geriatric care. Since 1996 California has spent more money on corrections than it has on its universities and colleges. In 1999 Wisconsin's corrections budget of more than $1.5 billion rivaled its $1.9 billion budget for the University of Wisconsin system.[22] Other states are likely to follow suit, as their corrections costs escalate at two or three times the rate of those of other public programs. Ironically, the more money that is spent keeping people in prison, the less that can be spent on prevention—keeping them out of prison in the first place.

Making the growing jail population even more problematic is the fact that many people sent to and kept in jail under the new laws are nonviolent offenders who have been convicted under tough new laws regulating the possession or distribution of illicit drugs. Sixty percent of the people in federal penitentiaries have been convicted of nonviolent drug offenses; about half of state prison inmates are serving time for nonviolent crimes.[23] Drug offenders, often young people facing jail for the first time, can be given a variety of alternative sentences, including community service, intensive probation, and electronic detention (at home and at work), that would drastically cut the costs of long-term mandatory incarceration and might aid in these individuals' rehabilitation as well.[24]

What's at stake in tougher sentencing laws may seem straightforward on its face. If crime is a problem, put the people who commit the crimes in jail and keep them there. But the matter is obviously far more complex than this. Crime rates have fallen, but there is little consensus among experts that this is due to tighter sentencing practices.[25] Politicians did not adequately take into account the additional costs of new prisons and lost human capital when devising the new laws. As we have seen in this chapter, and indeed throughout this book, one of the hazards of policymaking is that one might actually create new problems on the way to solving old ones. ∎

key terms

Central Intelligence Agency 431
Cold War 427
containment 427
crisis policy 428
Department of Defense 430
Department of State 430
distributive policy 408

foreign policy 425
intelligence community 430
intergovernmental organization 426
isolationism 425
Joint Chiefs of Staff 430
multinational corporation 426
National Security Council 429

nongovernmental organization 426
public policy 405
redistributive policy 406
regulatory policy 408
strategic policy 428
structural defense policy 428

summary

- Public policy is a government plan of action to solve a common social problem. Social problems may affect many citizens and require government action because individuals, groups, businesses, or other private actors either cannot handle these problems or have no incentive to address them.

- Public policy is generally one of three types: redistributive, distributive, or regulatory. Redistributive policies attempt to shift wealth, income, and other resources from the "haves" to the "have-nots." Distributive policies address the particular needs of an identifiable group, and the costs are shared among all taxpayers. Regulatory policies limit the actions of a specific, targeted group.

- Creating public policy involves many steps (agenda setting, formulation, adoption, implementation, and evaluation) and a multitude of groups (including Congress, the president, the courts, the bureaucracy, special interests, and the public).

- Foreign policy refers to a government's goals and actions toward actors outside its territory. These foreign actors may include other countries, multinational corporations, intergovernmental organizations, nongovernmental organizations, or groups that fall outside these categories.

- There are three types of American foreign policy, each dominated by different actors. Crisis policy requires immediate decision-making and is controlled by the president and his national security advisers. Strategic policy (long-range) tends to be formulated within the executive branch. Structural defense policy, which deals primarily with defense spending and military bases, is most often crafted by the Defense Department and Congress, which has the ultimate authority when it comes to spending.

- Americans as a whole may not get deeply involved in the process of policymaking, but they play an important role in influencing policymakers by voting and voicing their opinions about specific policies.

Appendix

The Declaration of Independence

The Constitution of the United States

Federalist No. 10

Federalist No. 51

Presidents of the United States

Twentieth-Century Justices of the Supreme Court

Party Control of the Presidency, Senate, and House of Representatives, 1901–2001

The Declaration of Independence

In Congress, July 4, 1776

The Unanimous Declaration of the Thirteen United States of America

When, in the course of human events, it becomes necessary for one people to dissolve the political bands which have connected them with another, and to assume, among the powers of the earth, the separate and equal station to which the laws of nature and of nature's God entitle them, a decent respect to the opinions of mankind requires that they should declare the causes which impel them to the separation.

We hold these truths to be self-evident: That all men are created equal; that they are endowed by their Creator with certain unalienable rights; that among these are life, liberty, and the pursuit of happiness; that, to secure these rights, governments are instituted among men, deriving their just powers from the consent of the governed; that whenever any form of government becomes destructive of these ends, it is the right of the people to alter or to abolish it, and to institute new government, laying its foundation on such principles, and organizing its powers in such form, as to them shall seem most likely to effect their safety and happiness. Prudence, indeed, will dictate that governments long established should not be changed for light and transient causes; and accordingly all experience hath shown that mankind are more disposed to suffer, while evils are sufferable, than to right themselves by abolishing the forms to which they are accustomed. But when a long train of abuses and usurpations, pursuing invariably the same object, evinces a design to reduce them under absolute despotism, it is their right, it is their duty, to throw off such government, and to provide new guards for their future security. Such has been the patient sufferance of these colonies; and such is now the necessity which constrains them to alter their former systems of government. The history of the present King of Great Britain is a history of repeated injuries and usurpations, all having in direct object the establishment of an absolute tyranny over these states. To prove this, let facts be submitted to a candid world.

He has refused to assent to laws, the most wholesome and necessary for the public good.

He has forbidden his governors to pass laws of immediate and pressing importance, unless suspended in their operation till his assent should be obtained; and, when so suspended, he has utterly neglected to attend to them.

He has refused to pass other laws for the accommodation of large districts of people, unless those people would relinquish the right of representation in the legislature, a right inestimable to them, and formidable to tyrants only.

He has called together legislative bodies at places unusual, uncomfortable, and distant from the depository of their public records, for the sole purpose of fatiguing them into compliance with his measures.

He has dissolved representative houses repeatedly, for opposing, with manly firmness, his invasions on the rights of the people.

He has refused for a long time, after such dissolutions, to cause others to be elected; whereby the legislative powers, incapable of annihilation, have returned to the people at large for their exercise; the state remaining, in the mean time, exposed to all dangers of invasions from without and convulsions within.

He has endeavored to prevent the population of these states; for that purpose obstructing the laws for naturalization of foreigners; refusing to pass others to encourage their migration hither, and raising the conditions of new appropriations of lands.

He has obstructed the administration of justice, by refusing his assent to laws for establishing judiciary powers.

He has made judges dependent on his will alone, for the tenure of their offices, and the amount and payment of their salaries.

He has erected a multitude of new offices, and sent hither swarms of officers to harass our people, and eat out their substance.

He has kept among us, in times of peace, standing armies, without the consent of our legislatures.

He has affected to render the military independent of, and superior to, the civil power.

He has combined with others to subject us to a jurisdiction foreign to our constitution, and unacknowledged by our laws, giving his assent to their acts of pretended legislation:

For quartering large bodies of armed troops among us:

For protecting them, by a mock trial, from punishment for any murders which they should commit on the inhabitants of these states;

For cutting off our trade with all parts of the world;

For imposing taxes on us without our consent;

For depriving us, in many cases, of the benefits of trial by jury;

For transporting us beyond seas, to be tried for pretended offenses;

For abolishing the free system of English laws in a neighboring province, establishing therein an arbitrary government, and enlarging its boundaries, so as to render it at once an example and fit instrument for introducing the same absolute rule into these colonies;

For taking away our charters, abolishing our most valuable laws, and altering fundamentally the forms of our governments;

For suspending our own legislatures, and declaring themselves invested with power to legislate for us in all cases whatsoever.

He has abdicated government here, by declaring us out of his protection and waging war against us.

He has plundered our seas, ravaged our coasts, burned our towns, and destroyed the lives of our people.

He is at this time transporting large armies of foreign mercenaries to complete the works of death, desolation, and tyranny already begun with circumstances of cruelty and perfidy scarcely paralleled in the most barbarous ages, and totally unworthy the head of a civilized nation.

He has constrained our fellow-citizens, taken captive on the high seas, to bear arms against their country, to become the executioners of their friends and brethren, or to fall themselves by their hands.

He has excited domestic insurrections among us, and has endeavored to bring on the inhabitants of our frontiers the merciless Indian savages, whose known rule of warfare is an undistinguished destruction of all ages, sexes, and conditions.

In every stage of these oppressions we have petitioned for redress in the most humble terms; our repeated petitions have been answered only by repeated injury. A prince, whose character is thus marked by every act which may define a tyrant, is unfit to be the ruler of a free people.

Nor have we been wanting in our attentions to our British brethren. We have warned them, from time to time, of attempts by their Legislature to extend an unwarrantable jurisdiction over us. We have reminded them of the circumstances of our emigration and settlement here. We have appealed to their native justice and magnanimity; and we have conjured them, by the ties of our common kindred, to disavow these usurpations, which would inevitably interrupt our connections and correspondence. They, too, have been deaf to the voice of justice and of consanguinity. We must, therefore, acquiesce in the necessity which denounces our separation, and hold them, as we hold the rest of mankind, enemies in war, in peace friends.

We, therefore, the representatives of the United States of America, in General Congress assembled, appealing to the Supreme Judge of the world for the rectitude of our intentions, do, in the name and by the authority of the good people of these colonies, solemnly publish and declare, that these United Colonies are, and of right ought to be, FREE AND INDEPENDENT STATES; that they are absolved from all allegiance to the British crown, and that all political connection between them and the state of Great Britain is, and ought to be, totally dissolved; and that, as free and independent states, they have full power to levy war, conclude peace, contract alliances, establish commerce, and do all other acts and things which independent states may of right do. And for the support of this declaration, with a firm reliance on the protection of Divine Providence, we mutually pledge to each other our lives, our fortunes, and our sacred honor.

JOHN HANCOCK [*President*]
[*and fifty-five others*]

The Constitution of the United States

We the People of the United States, in Order to form a more perfect Union, establish Justice, insure domestic Tranquility, provide for the common defence, promote the general Welfare, and secure the Blessings of Liberty to ourselves and our Posterity, do ordain and establish this Constitution for the United States of America.

ARTICLE I.

Section 1.   All legislative Powers herein granted shall be vested in a Congress of the United States, which shall consist of a Senate and House of Representatives.

Section 2.   The House of Representatives shall be composed of Members chosen every second Year by the People of the several States, and the Electors in each State shall have the Qualifications requisite for Electors of the most numerous Branch of the State Legislature.

No person shall be a Representative who shall not have attained to the age of twenty five Years, and been seven Years a Citizen of the United States, and who shall not, when elected, be an Inhabitant of that State in which he shall be chosen.

Representatives and direct Taxes shall be apportioned among the several States which may be included within this Union, according to their respective Numbers, which shall be determined by adding to the whole Number of free Persons, including those bound to Service for a Term of Years, and excluding Indians not taxed, three

fifths of all other Persons.[1] The actual Enumeration shall be made within three Years after the first Meeting of the Congress of the United States, and within every subsequent Term of ten Years, in such Manner as they shall by Law direct. The Number of Representatives shall not exceed one for every thirty Thousand, but each State shall have at Least one Representative; and until such enumeration shall be made, the State of New Hampshire shall be entitled to chuse three, Massachusetts eight, Rhode-Island and Providence Plantations one, Connecticut five, New-York six, New Jersey four, Pennsylvania eight, Delaware one, Maryland six, Virginia ten, North Carolina five, South Carolina five, and Georgia three.

When vacancies happen in the Representation from any State, the Executive Authority thereof shall issue Writs of Election to fill such Vacancies.

The House of Representatives shall chuse their Speaker and other Officers; and shall have the sole Power of Impeachment.

Section 3.   The Senate of the United States shall be composed of two Senators from each State, *chosen by the Legislature thereof,*[2] *for six Years; and each Senator shall have one Vote.*

Immediately after they shall be assembled in Consequence of the first Election, they shall be divided as equally as may be into three Classes. The Seats of the Senators of the first class shall be vacated at the Expiration of the second Year, of the second Class at the Expi-

Note: Those portions set in italic type have been superseded or changed by later amendments.

1. Changed by the Fourteenth Amendment, section 2.
2. Changed by the Seventeenth Amendment.

ration of the fourth Year, and of the third Class at the Expiration of the sixth Year, so that one third may be chosen every second Year; *and if Vacancies happen by Resignation, or otherwise, during the Recess of the Legislature of any State, the Executive thereof may make temporary Appointments until the next Meeting of the Legislature, which shall then fill such Vacancies.*[3]

No Person shall be a Senator who shall not have attained to the Age of thirty Years, and been nine Years a Citizen of the United States, and who shall not, when elected, be an Inhabitant of that State for which he shall be chosen.

The Vice President of the United States shall be President of the Senate, but shall have no Vote, unless they be equally divided.

The Senate shall chuse their other Officers, and also a President pro tempore, in the Absence of the Vice President, or when he shall exercise the Office of President of the United States.

The Senate shall have the sole Power to try all Impeachments. When sitting for that Purpose, they shall be on Oath or Affirmation. When the President of the United States is tried the Chief Justice shall preside: And no Person shall be convicted without the Concurrence of two thirds of the Members present.

Judgment in Cases of Impeachment shall not extend further than to removal from Office, and disqualification to hold and enjoy any Office of honor, Trust or Profit under the United States: but the Party convicted shall nevertheless be liable and subject to Indictment, Trial, Judgment and Punishment, according to Law.

Section 4.   The Times, Places and Manner of holding Elections for Senators and Representatives, shall be prescribed in each State by the Legislature thereof; but the Congress may at any time by Law make or alter such Regulations, except as to the Places of chusing Senators.

The Congress shall assemble at least once in every Year, and such Meeting shall be on the *first Monday in December, unless they shall by Law appoint a different Day.*[4]

Section 5.   Each House shall be the Judge of the Elections, Returns and Qualifications of its own Members, and a Majority of each shall constitute a Quorum to do Business; but a smaller number may adjourn from day to day, and may be authorized to compel the Attendance of absent Members, in such Manner, and under such Penalties as each House may provide.

3. Changed by the Seventeenth Amendment.
4. Changed by the Twentieth Amendment, section 2.

Each House may determine the Rules of its Proceedings, punish its Members for disorderly Behaviour, and, with the Concurrence of two thirds, expel a Member.

Each House shall keep a Journal of its Proceedings, and from time to time publish the same, excepting such Parts as may in their Judgment require Secrecy; and the Yeas and Nays of the Members of either House on any question shall, at the Desire of one fifth of those Present, be entered on the Journal.

Neither House, during the Session of Congress, shall, without the Consent of the other, adjourn for more than three days, nor to any other Place than that in which the two Houses shall be sitting.

Section 6.   The Senators and Representatives shall receive a Compensation for their Services, to be ascertained by Law, and paid out of the Treasury of the United States. They shall in all Cases, except Treason, Felony and Breach of the Peace, be privileged from Arrest during their Attendance at the Session of their respective Houses, and in going to and returning from the same; and for any Speech or Debate in either House, they shall not be questioned in any other Place.

No Senator or Representative shall, during the Time for which he was elected, be appointed to any civil Office under the Authority of the United States, which shall have been created, or the Emoluments whereof shall have been encreased during such time; and no Person holding any Office under the United States, shall be a Member of either House during his Continuance in Office.

Section 7.   All Bills for raising Revenue shall originate in the House of Representatives; but the Senate may propose or concur with Amendments as on other Bills.

Every Bill which shall have passed the House of Representatives and the Senate, shall, before it become a Law, be presented to the President of the United States; If he approve he shall sign it, but if not he shall return it, with his Objections to that House in which it shall have originated, who shall enter the Objections at large on their Journal, and proceed to reconsider it. If after such Reconsideration two thirds of that House shall agree to pass the Bill, it shall be sent, together with the Objections, to the other House, by which it shall likewise be reconsidered, and if approved by two thirds of that House, it shall become a Law. But in all such Cases the Votes of both Houses shall be determined by yeas and Nays, and the Names of the Persons voting for and against the Bill shall be entered on the Journal of each House respectively. If any Bill shall not be returned by the President within ten Days (Sundays excepted) after it shall have been presented to him, the Same shall be a Law, in like Manner, as if he had signed it, unless the Congress by their Adjournment prevent its Return, in which Case it shall not be a Law.

Every Order, Resolution, or Vote to which the Concurrence of the Senate and House of Representatives may be necessary (except on a question of Adjournment) shall be presented to the President of the United States; and before the Same shall take Effect, shall be approved by him, or being disapproved by him, shall be repassed by two thirds of the Senate and House of Representatives, according to the Rules and Limitations prescribed in the Case of a Bill.

Section 8. The Congress shall have Power To lay and Collect Taxes, Duties, Imposts and Excises, to pay the Debts and provide for the common Defence and general Welfare of the United States; but all Duties, Imposts and Excises shall be uniform throughout the United States.

To borrow Money on the credit of the United States;

To regulate Commerce with foreign Nations, and among the several States, and with the Indian Tribes;

To establish an uniform Rule of Naturalization, and uniform Laws on the subject of Bankruptcies throughout the United States;

To coin Money, regulate the Value thereof, and of foreign Coin, and fix the Standard of Weights and Measures;

To provide for the Punishment of counterfeiting the Securities and current Coin of the United States;

To establish Post Offices and post Roads;

To promote the Progress of Science and useful Arts, by securing for limited Times to Authors and Inventors the exclusive Right to their respective Writings and Discoveries;

To constitute Tribunals inferior to the Supreme Court;

To define and punish Piracies and Felonies committed on the high Seas, and Offences against the Law of Nations;

To declare War, grant Letters of Marque and Reprisal, and make Rules concerning Captures on Land and Water;

To raise and support Armies, but no Appropriation of Money to that Use shall be for a longer Term than two Years;

To provide and maintain a Navy;

To make Rules for the Government and Regulation of the land and naval Forces;

To provide for calling forth the Militia to execute the Laws of the Union, suppress Insurrections and repel Invasions;

To provide for organizing, arming, and disciplining, the Militia, and for governing such Part of them as may be employed in the Service of the United States, reserving to the States respectively, the Appointment of the Officers, and the Authority of training the Militia according to the discipline prescribed by Congress;

To exercise exclusive Legislation in all Cases whatsoever, over such District (not exceeding ten Miles square) as may, by Cession of Particular States, and the Acceptance of Congress, become the Seat of the Government of the United States, and to exercise like Authority over all Places purchased by the Consent of the Legislature of the State in which the Same shall be, for the Erection of Forts, Magazines, Arsenals, dock-Yards and other needful Buildings;—And

To make all Laws which shall be necessary and proper for carrying into Execution the foregoing Powers, and all other Powers vested by this Constitution in the Government of the United States, or in any Department or Officer thereof.

Section 9. The Migration or Importation of such Persons as any of the States now existing shall think proper to admit, shall not be prohibited by the Congress prior to the Year one thousand eight hundred and eight, but a Tax or duty may be imposed on such Importation, not exceeding ten dollars for each Person.

The Privilege of the Writ of Habeas Corpus shall not be suspended, unless when in Cases of Rebellion or Invasion the public Safety may require it.

No bill of Attainder or ex post facto Law shall be passed.

No Capitation, or other direct, Tax shall be laid, *unless in Proportion to the Census or Enumeration herein before directed to be taken.*[5]

No Tax or Duty shall be laid on Articles exported from any State.

No Preference shall be given by any Regulation of Commerce or Revenue to the Ports of one State over those of another; nor shall Vessels bound to, or from, one State, be obliged to enter, clear or pay Duties in another.

No Money shall be drawn from the Treasury, but in Consequence of Appropriations made by Law; and a regular Statement and Account of the Receipts and Expenditures of all public Money shall be published from time to time.

No Title of Nobility shall be granted by the United States: And no Person holding any Office of Profit or Trust under them, shall, without the Consent of the Congress,

---

5. Changed by the Sixteenth Amendment.

accept of any present, Emolument, Office, or Title, of any kind whatever, from any King, Prince, or foreign State.

Section 10.   No State shall enter into any Treaty, Alliance, or Confederation; grant Letters of Marque and Reprisal; coin Money; emit Bills of Credit; make any Thing but gold and silver Coin a Tender in Payment of Debts; pass any Bill of Attainder, ex post facto Law, or Law impairing the Obligation of Contracts, or grant any Title of Nobility.

No State shall, without the Consent of the Congress, lay any Imposts or Duties on Imports or Exports, except what may be absolutely necessary for executing its inspection Laws; and the net Produce of all Duties and Imposts, laid by any State on Imports or Exports, shall be for the Use of the Treasury of the United States; and all such Laws shall be subject to the Revision and Controul of the Congress.

No State shall, without the Consent of Congress, lay any Duty of Tonnage, keep Troops, or Ships of War in time of Peace, enter into any Agreement or Compact with another State, or with a foreign Power, or engage in War, unless actually invaded, or in such imminent Danger as will not admit of delay.

ARTICLE II.

Section 1.   The executive Power shall be vested in a President of the United States of America. He shall hold his Office during the Term of four Years, and, together with the Vice President, chosen for the same Term, be elected, as follows:

Each State shall appoint, in such Manner as the Legislature thereof may direct, a Number of Electors, equal to the whole Number of Senators and Representatives to which the State may be entitled in the Congress: but no Senator or Representative, or Person holding an Office of Trust or Profit under the United States, shall be appointed an Elector.

The Electors shall meet in their respective States, and vote by Ballot for two Persons, of whom one at least shall not be an Inhabitant of the same State with themselves. And they shall make a List of all the Persons voted for, and of the Number of Votes for each; which List they shall sign and certify, and transmit sealed to the Seat of the Government of the United States, directed to the President of the Senate. The President of the Senate shall, in the Presence of the Senate and House of Representatives, open all the Certificates, and the Votes shall then be counted. The Person having the greatest Number of Votes

shall be the President, if such Number be a Majority of the whole Number of Electors appointed; and if there be more than one who have such Majority, and have an equal Number of Votes, then the House of Representatives shall immediately chuse by Ballot one of them for President; and if no Person have a Majority, then from the five highest on the List the said House shall in like Manner chuse the President. But in chusing the President, the Votes shall be taken by States, the Representation from each State having one Vote; a quorum for this Purpose shall consist of a Member or Members from two thirds of the States, and a Majority of all the States shall be necessary to a Choice. In every Case, after the Choice of the President, the Person having the greatest Number of Votes of the Electors shall be the Vice President. But if there should remain two or more who have equal Votes, the Senate shall chuse from them by Ballot the Vice President.[6]

The Congress may determine the Time of chusing the Electors, and the Day on which they shall give their Votes, which Day shall be the same throughout the United States.

No Person except a natural born Citizen, or a Citizen of the United States, at the time of the Adoption of this Constitution, shall be eligible to the Office of President; neither shall any person be eligible to that Office who shall not have attained to the Age of thirty five Years, and been fourteen Years a Resident within the United States.

In Case of the Removal of the President from Office, or of his Death, Resignation, or Inability to discharge the Powers and Duties of the said Office, the Same shall devolve on the Vice President, and the Congress may by Law provide for the Case of Removal, Death, Resignation or Inability, both of the President and Vice President, declaring what Officer shall then act as President, and such Officer shall accordingly, until the Disability be removed, or a President shall be elected.[7]

The President shall, at stated Times, receive for his Services, a Compensation, which shall neither be increased nor diminished during the Period for which he shall have been elected, and he shall not receive within that Period any other Emolument from the United States, or any of them.

Before he enter on the Execution of his Office, he shall take the following Oath or Affirmation:—"I do solemnly swear (or affirm) that I will faithfully execute the Office of President of the United States, and will to the best of my Ability preserve, protect and defend the Constitution of the United States."

6. Superseded by the Twelfth Amendment.
7. Modified by the Twenty-fifth Amendment.

Section 2. The President shall be Commander in Chief of the Army and Navy of the United States, and of the Militia of the several States, when called into the actual Service of the United States; he may require the Opinion, in writing, of the principal Officer in each of the executive Departments, upon any Subject relating to the Duties of their respective Offices, and he shall have Power to grant Reprieves and Pardons for Offences against the United States, except in Cases of Impeachment.

He shall have Power, by and with the Advice and Consent of the Senate, to make Treaties, provided two thirds of the Senators present concur; and he shall nominate, and by and with the Advice and Consent of the Senate, shall appoint Ambassadors, other public Ministers and Consuls, Judges of the supreme Court, and all other Officers of the United States, whose Appointments are not herein otherwise provided for, and which shall be established by Law: but the Congress may by Law vest the Appointment of such inferior Officers, as they think proper, in the President alone, in the Courts of Law, or in the Heads of Departments.

The President shall have Power to fill up all Vacancies that may happen during the Recess of the Senate, by granting Commissions which shall expire at the End of their next Session.

Section 3. He shall from time to time give to the Congress Information of the State of the Union, and recommend to their Consideration such Measures as he shall judge necessary and expedient; he may, on extraordinary Occasions, convene both Houses, or either of them, and in Case of Disagreement between them, with Respect to the Time of Adjournment, he may adjourn them to such Time as he shall think proper; he shall receive Ambassadors and other public Ministers; he shall take Care that the Laws be faithfully executed, and shall Commission all the Officers of the United States.

Section 4. The President, Vice President and all civil Officers of the United States, shall be removed from Office on Impeachment for, and Conviction of, Treason, Bribery, or other high Crimes and Misdemeanors.

ARTICLE III.

Section 1. The judicial Power of the United States, shall be vested in one supreme Court, and in such inferior Courts as the Congress may from time to time ordain and establish. The Judges, both of the supreme and inferior Courts, shall hold their Offices during good Be-

haviour, and shall, at stated Times, receive for their Services, a Compensation, which shall not be diminished during their Continuance in Office.

Section 2. The judicial Power shall extend to all Cases, in Law and Equity, arising under this Constitution, the Laws of the United States, and Treaties made, or which shall be made, under their Authority;—to all Cases affecting Ambassadors, other public Ministers and Consuls;—to all Cases of admiralty and maritime Jurisdiction;—to Controversies to which the United States shall be a Party;—to Controversies between two or more States;—*between a State and Citizens of another State;*[8]—between Citizens of different States;—between Citizens of the same State claiming Lands under Grants of different States, and between a State, or the Citizens thereof, and foreign States, Citizens or Subjects.

In all Cases affecting Ambassadors, other public Ministers and Consuls, and those in which a State shall be Party, the supreme Court shall have original Jurisdiction. In all the other Cases before mentioned, the supreme Court shall have appellate Jurisdiction, both as to Law and Fact, with such Exceptions, and under such Regulations as the Congress shall make.

The Trial of all Crimes, except in Cases of Impeachment, shall be by Jury; and such Trial shall be held in the State where the said Crimes shall have been committed; but when not committed within any State, the Trial shall be at such Place or Places as the Congress may by Law have directed.

Section 3. Treason against the United States, shall consist only in levying War against them, or in adhering to their Enemies, giving them Aid and Comfort. No Person shall be convicted of Treason unless on the Testimony of two Witnesses to the same overt Act, or on Confession in open Court.

The Congress shall have Power to declare the Punishment of Treason, but no Attainder of Treason shall work Corruption of Blood, or Forfeiture except during the Life of the Person attainted.

ARTICLE IV.

Section 1. Full Faith and Credit shall be given in each State to the public Acts, Records, and judicial Proceedings of every other State. And the Congress may by general Laws prescribe the Manner in which such Acts, Records

8. Modified by the Eleventh Amendment.

and Proceedings shall be proved, and the Effect thereof.

Section 2.   The Citizens of each State shall be entitled to all Privileges and Immunities of Citizens in the several States.

A person charged in any State with Treason, Felony, or other Crime, who shall flee from Justice, and be found in another State, shall on Demand of the executive Authority of the State from which he fled, be delivered up, to be removed to the State having Jurisdiction of the Crime.

No Person held to Service or Labour in one State, under the Laws thereof, escaping into another, shall, in Consequence of any Law or Regulation therein, be discharged from such Service or Labour, but shall be delivered up on Claim of the Party to whom such Service or Labour may be due.[9]

Section 3.   New States may be admitted by the Congress into this Union; but no new State shall be formed or erected within the Jurisdiction of any other State; nor any State be formed by the Junction of two or more States, or Parts of States, without the Consent of the Legislatures of the States concerned as well as of the Congress.

The Congress shall have Power to dispose of and make all needful Rules and Regulations respecting the Territory or other Property belonging to the United States; and nothing in this Constitution shall be so construed as to Prejudice any Claims of the United States, or of any particular State.

Section 4.   The United States shall guarantee to every State in this Union a Republican Form of Government, and shall protect each of them against Invasion; and on Application of the Legislature, or of the Executive (when the Legislature cannot be convened) against domestic Violence.

ARTICLE V.

The Congress, whenever two thirds of both Houses shall deem it necessary, shall propose Amendments to this Constitution, or, on the Application of the Legislatures of two thirds of the several States, shall call a Convention for proposing Amendments, which, in either Case, shall be valid to all Intents and Purposes, as Part of this Constitution, when ratified by the Legislatures of three fourths of the several States, or by Conventions in three fourths thereof, as the one or the other Mode of Ratification may be proposed by the Congress; Provided that no

9. Changed by the Thirteenth Amendment.

Amendment which may be made prior to the Year One thousand eight hundred and eight shall in any Manner after the first and fourth Clauses in the Ninth Section of the first Article; and that no State, without its Consent, shall be deprived of its equal Suffrage in the Senate.

ARTICLE VI.

All Debts contracted and Engagements entered into, before the Adoption of this Constitution, shall be as valid against the United States under this Constitution, as under the Confederation.

This Constitution, and the Laws of the United States which shall be made in Pursuance thereof; and all Treaties made, or which shall be made, under the Authority of the United States, shall be the Supreme Law of the Land; and the Judges in every State shall be bound thereby, any Thing in the Constitution or Laws of any State to the Contrary notwithstanding.

The Senators and Representatives before mentioned, and the Members of the several State Legislatures, and all executive and judicial Officers, both of the United States and of the several States, shall be bound by Oath or Affirmation, to support this Constitution; but no religious Test shall ever be required as a Qualification to any Office or public Trust under the United States.

ARTICLE VII.

The Ratification of the Conventions of nine States, shall be sufficient for the Establishment of this Constitution between the States so ratifying the Same.

Done in Convention by the Unanimous Consent of the States present the Seventeenth Day of September in the Year of our Lord one thousand seven hundred and Eighty seven and of the Independence of the United States of America the Twelfth In witness whereof We have hereunto subscribed our Names,

George Washington
[*and thirty-seven others*]

[*The first ten amendments, known as the "Bill of Rights," were ratified in 1791.*]

AMENDMENT I.

Congress shall make no law respecting an establishment of religion, or prohibiting the free exercise thereof, or abridging the freedom of speech, or of the press; or the right of the people peaceably to assemble, and to petition the Government for a redress of grievances.

AMENDMENT II.

A well regulated Militia, being necessary to the security of a free State, the right of the people to keep and bear Arms, shall not be infringed.

AMENDMENT III.

No Soldier shall, in time of peace be quartered in any house, without the consent of the Owner, nor in time of war, but in a manner to be prescribed by law.

AMENDMENT IV.

The right of the people to be secure in their persons, houses, papers, and effects, against unreasonable searches and seizures, shall not be violated, and no Warrants shall issue, but upon probable cause, supported by Oath or affirmation, and particularly describing the place to be searched, and the persons or things to be seized.

AMENDMENT V.

No person shall be held to answer for a capital, or otherwise infamous crime, unless on a presentment or indictment of a Grand Jury, except in cases arising in the land or naval forces, or in the Militia, when in actual service in time of War or public danger; nor shall any person be subject for the same offence to be twice put in jeopardy of life or limb; nor shall be compelled in any criminal case to be a witness against himself, nor be deprived of life, liberty, or property, without due process of law, nor shall private property be taken for public use, without just compensation.

AMENDMENT VI.

In all criminal prosecutions, the accused shall enjoy the right to a speedy and public trial, by an impartial jury of the State and district wherein the crime shall have been committed, which district shall have been previously ascertained by law, and to be informed of the nature and cause of the accusation; to be confronted with the witnesses against him; to have compulsory process for obtaining witnesses in his favor, and to have the Assistance of Counsel for his defence.

AMENDMENT VII.

In Suits at common law, where the value in controversy shall exceed twenty dollars, the right of trial by jury shall be preserved, and no fact tried by a jury, shall be otherwise reexamined in any Court of the United States, than according to the rules of the common law.

AMENDMENT VIII.

Excessive bail shall not be required, nor excessive fines imposed, nor cruel and unusual punishments inflicted.

AMENDMENT IX.

The enumeration in the Constitution, of certain rights, shall not be construed to deny or disparage others retained by the people.

AMENDMENT X.

The powers not delegated to the United States by the Constitution, nor prohibited by it to the States, are reserved to the States respectively, or to the people.

AMENDMENT XI.
[*Ratified in 1795.*]

The Judicial power of the United States shall not be construed to extend to any suit in law or equity, commenced or prosecuted against one of the United States by Citizens of another State, or by Citizens or Subjects of any Foreign State.

AMENDMENT XII.
[*Ratified in 1804.*]

The Electors shall meet in their respective states and vote by ballot for President and Vice President, one of whom, at least, shall not be an inhabitant of the same state with themselves; they shall name in their ballots the person voted for as President, and in distinct ballots the person voted for as Vice President, and they shall make distinct lists of all persons voted for as President, and of all persons voted for as Vice President, and of the number of votes for each, which lists they shall sign and certify, and transmit sealed to the seat of the government of the United States, directed to the President of the Senate;—The President of the Senate shall, in the presence of the Senate and House of Representatives, open all the certificates and the votes shall then be counted;—The person having the greatest number of votes for President, shall be the President, if such number be a majority of the whole number of Electors appointed; and if no person have such majority, then from the persons having the highest numbers not exceeding three on the list of those voted for as President, the House of Representatives shall choose immediately, by ballot, the President. But in choosing the President, the votes shall be taken by states, the representation from each state having one vote; a quorum for this purpose shall consist of a member or members from two-thirds of the states, and a majority of all the states shall be necessary to a choice. *And if the House of Representatives shall not choose a President whenever the right of choice shall devolve upon them, before the fourth day of March next following, then the Vice President shall act as President, as in the case of the death or other constitutional disability of the President.*—[10] The person having the greatest number of votes as Vice President, shall be the Vice President, if such number be a majority of the whole number of Electors appointed, and if no person have a majority, then from the two highest numbers on the list, the Senate shall choose the Vice President; a quorum for the purpose shall consist of two-thirds of the whole number of Senators, and a majority of the whole number shall be necessary to a choice. But no person constitutionally ineligible to the office of President shall be eligible to that of Vice President of the United States.

AMENDMENT XIII.
[*Ratified in 1865.*]

Section 1.   Neither slavery nor involuntary servitude, except as a punishment for crime whereof the party shall have been duly convicted, shall exist within the United States, or any place subject to their jurisdiction.

Section 2.   Congress shall have power to enforce this article by appropriate legislation.

AMENDMENT XIV.
[*Ratified in 1868.*]

Section 1.   All persons born or naturalized in the United States and subject to the jurisdiction thereof, are citizens of the United States and of the State wherein they reside. No State shall make or enforce any law which shall abridge the privileges or immunities of citizens of the United States; nor shall any State deprive any person of life, liberty, or property, without due process of

law; nor deny to any person within its jurisdiction the equal protection of the laws.

Section 2.   Representatives shall be apportioned among the several States according to their respective numbers, counting the whole number of persons in each State, excluding Indians not taxed. But when the right to vote at any election for the choice of electors for President and Vice President of the United States, Representatives in Congress, the Executive and Judicial officers of a State, or the members of the Legislature thereof, is denied to any of the male inhabitants of such State, being *twenty-one*[11] years of age, and citizens of the United States, or in any way abridged, except for participation in rebellion, or other crime, the basis of representation therein shall be reduced in the proportion which the number of such male citizens shall bear to the whole number of male citizens twenty-one years of age in such State.

Section 3.   No person shall be a Senator or Representative in Congress, or elector of President and Vice President, or hold any office, civil or military, under the United States, or under any State, who, having previously taken an oath, as a member of Congress, or as an officer of the United States, or as a member of any State legislature, or as an executive or judicial officer of any State, to support the Constitution of the United States, shall have engaged in insurrection or rebellion against the same, or given aid or comfort to the enemies thereof. But Congress may by a vote of two-thirds of each House, remove such disability.

Section 4.   The validity of the public debt of the United States, authorized by law, including debts incurred for payment of pensions and bounties for services in suppressing insurrection or rebellion, shall not be questioned. But neither the United States nor any State shall assume or pay any debt or obligation incurred in aid of insurrection or rebellion against the United States, or any claim for the loss or emancipation of any slave; but all such debts, obligations and claims shall be held illegal and void.

Section 5.   The Congress shall have power to enforce, by appropriate legislation, the provisions of this article.

AMENDMENT XV.
[*Ratified in 1870.*]

Section 1.   The right of citizens of the United States to vote shall not be denied or abridged by the United States

---

10. Changed by the Twentieth Amendment, section 3.

11. Changed by the Twenty-sixth Amendment.

or by any State on account of race, color, or previous condition of servitude.

Section 2.   The Congress shall have power to enforce this article by appropriate legislation.

AMENDMENT XVI.
[*Ratified in 1913.*]

The Congress shall have power to lay and collect taxes on incomes, from whatever source derived, without apportionment among the several States, and without regard to any census or enumeration.

AMENDMENT XVII.
[*Ratified in 1913.*]

The Senate of the United States shall be composed of two Senators from each State, elected by the people thereof, for six years; and each Senator shall have one vote. The electors in each State shall have the qualifications requisite for electors of the most numerous branch of the State legislatures.

When vacancies happen in the representation of any State in the Senate, the executive authority of such State shall issue writs of election to fill such vacancies: Provided, That the legislature of any State may empower the executive thereof to make temporary appointments until the people fill the vacancies by election as the legislature may direct.

This amendment shall not be so construed as to affect the election or term of any Senator chosen before it becomes valid as part of the Constitution.

AMENDMENT XVIII.
[*Ratified in 1919.*]

Section 1.   *After one year from the ratification of this article the manufacture, sale, or transportation of intoxicating liquors within, the importation thereof into, or the exportation thereof from the United States and all territory subject to the jurisdiction thereof for beverage purposes is hereby prohibited.*

Section 2.   *The Congress and the several States shall have concurrent power to enforce this article by appropriate legislation.*

Section 3.   *This article shall be inoperative unless it shall have been ratified as an amendment to the Constitution by the legislatures of the several States, as provided in the*

Constitution, within seven years from the date of the submission hereof to the States by the Congress.[12]

AMENDMENT XIX.
[*Ratified in 1920.*]

The right of citizens of the United States to vote shall not be denied or abridged by the United States or by any State on account of sex.

Congress shall have power to enforce this article by appropriate legislation.

AMENDMENT XX.
[*Ratified in 1933.*]

Section 1.   The terms of the President and Vice President shall end at noon on the 20th day of January, and the terms of Senators and Representatives at noon on the 3d day of January, of the years in which such terms would have ended if this article had not been ratified; and the terms of their successors shall then begin.

Section 2.   The Congress shall assemble at least once in every year, and such meeting shall begin at noon on the 3d day of January, unless they shall by law appoint a different day.

Section 3.   If, at the time fixed for the beginning of the term of the President, the President elect shall have died, the Vice President elect shall become President. If a President shall not have been chosen before the time fixed for the beginning of his term, or if the President elect shall have failed to qualify, then the Vice President elect shall act as President until a President shall have qualified; and the Congress may by law provide for the case wherein neither a President elect nor a Vice President elect shall have qualified, declaring who shall then act as President, or the manner in which one who is to act shall be selected, and such person shall act accordingly until a President or Vice President shall have qualified.

Section 4.   The Congress may by law provide for the case of the death of any of the persons from whom the House of Representatives may choose a President whenever the right of choice shall have devolved upon them, and for the case of the death of any of the persons from whom the Senate may choose a Vice President whenever the right of choice shall have devolved upon them.

Section 5.   Sections 1 and 2 shall take effect on the 15th day of October following the ratification of this article.

12. Repealed by the Twenty-first Amendment.

Section 6.   This article shall be inoperative unless it shall have been ratified as an amendment to the Constitution by the legislatures of three-fourths of the several States within seven years from the date of its submission.

AMENDMENT XXI.
[*Ratified in 1933.*]

Section 1.   The eighteenth article of amendment to the Constitution of the United States is hereby repealed.

Section 2.   The transportation or importation into any State, Territory, or possession of the United States for delivery or use therein of intoxicating liquors, in violation of the laws thereof, is hereby prohibited.

Section 3.   This article shall be inoperative unless it shall have been ratified as an amendment to the Constitution by conventions in the several States, as provided in the Constitution, within seven years from the date of submission hereof to the States by the Congress.

AMENDMENT XXII.
[*Ratified in 1951.*]

Section 1.   No person shall be elected to the office of the President more than twice, and no person who has held the office of President, or acted as President, for more than two years of a term to which some other person was elected President shall be elected to the office of President more than once. But this Article shall not apply to any person holding the office of President when this Article was proposed by the Congress, and shall not prevent any person who may be holding the office of President, or acting as President, during the term within which this Article becomes operative from holding the office of President or acting as President during the remainder of such term.

Section 2.   This Article shall be inoperative unless it shall have been ratified as an amendment to the Constitution by the legislatures of three-fourths of the several States within seven years from the date of its submission to the States by the Congress.

AMENDMENT XXIII.
[*Ratified in 1961.*]

Section 1.   The District constituting the seat of Government of the United States shall appoint in such manner as the Congress may direct:

A number of electors of President and Vice President equal to the whole number of Senators and Representatives in Congress to which the District would be entitled if it were a State, but in no event more than the least populous State; they shall be in addition to those appointed by the States, but they shall be considered, for the purposes of the election of President and Vice President, to be electors appointed by a State; and they shall meet in the District and perform such duties as provided by the twelfth article of amendment.

Section 2.   The Congress shall have power to enforce this article by appropriate legislation.

AMENDMENT XXIV.
[*Ratified in 1964.*]

Section 1.   The right of citizens of the United States to vote in any primary or other election for President or Vice President, for electors for President or Vice President, or for Senator or Representative in Congress, shall not be denied or abridged by the United States or any State by reason of failure to pay any poll tax or other tax.

Section 2.   The Congress shall have power to enforce this article by appropriate legislation.

AMENDMENT XXV.
[*Ratified in 1967.*]

Section 1.   In case of the removal of the President from office or of his death or resignation, the Vice President shall become President.

Section 2.   Whenever there is a vacancy in the office of the Vice President, the President shall nominate a Vice President who shall take office upon confirmation by a majority vote of both Houses of Congress.

Section 3.   Whenever the President transmits to the President pro tempore of the Senate and the Speaker of the House of Representatives his written declaration that he is unable to discharge the powers and duties of his office, and until he transmits to them a written declaration to the contrary, such powers and duties shall be discharged by the Vice President as Acting President.

Section 4.   Whenever the Vice President and a majority of either the principal officers of the executive departments or of such other body as Congress may by law provide, transmit to the President pro tempore of the Senate and the Speaker of the House of Representatives their written declaration that the President is unable to discharge the powers and duties of his office, the Vice President shall immediately assume the powers and duties of the office as Acting President.

Thereafter, when the President transmits to the President pro tempore of the Senate and the Speaker of the House of Representatives his written declaration that no inability exists, he shall resume the powers and duties of his office unless the Vice President and a majority of either the principal officers of the executive department[s] or of such other body as Congress may by law provide, transmit within four days to the President pro tempore of the Senate and the Speaker of the House of Representatives their written declaration that the President is unable to discharge the powers and duties of his office. Thereupon Congress shall decide the issue, assembling within forty-eight hours for that purpose if not in session. If the Congress, within twenty-one days after receipt of the latter written declaration, or, if Congress is not in session, within twenty-one days after Congress is required to assemble, determines by two-thirds vote of both Houses that the President is unable to discharge the powers and duties of his office, the Vice President shall continue to discharge the same as Acting President; otherwise, the President shall resume the powers and duties of his office.

AMENDMENT XXVI.
[*Ratified in 1971.*]

Section 1.   The right of citizens of the United States, who are eighteen years of age or older, to vote shall not be denied or abridged by the United States or by any State on account of age.

Section 2.   The Congress shall have power to enforce this article by appropriate legislation.

AMENDMENT XXVII.
[*Ratified in 1992.*]

No law varying the compensation for the services of the Senators and Representatives shall take effect, until an election of Representatives shall have intervened.

Federalist No. 10

November 22, 1787

James Madison

TO THE PEOPLE OF THE STATE OF NEW YORK:

Among the numerous advantages promised by a well constructed Union, none deserves to be more accurately developed than its tendency to break and control the violence of faction. The friend of popular governments, never finds himself so much alarmed for their character and fate, as when he contemplates their propensity to this dangerous vice. He will not fail therefore to set a due value on any plan which, without violating the principles to which he is attached, provides a proper cure for it. The instability, injustice and confusion introduced into the public councils, have in truth been the mortal diseases under which popular governments have every where perished; as they continue to be the favorite and fruitful topics from which the adversaries to liberty derive their most specious declamations. The valuable improvements made by the American Constitutions on the popular models, both ancient and modern, cannot certainly be too much admired; but it would be an unwarrantable partiality, to contend that they have as effectually obviated the danger on this side as was wished and expected. Complaints are every where heard from our most considerate and virtuous citizens, equally the friends of public and private faith, and of public and personal liberty; that our governments are too unstable; that the public good is disregarded in the conflicts of rival parties; and that measures are too often decided, not according to the rules of justice, and the rights of the minor party; but by the superior force of an interested and over-bearing majority. However anxiously we may wish that these complaints had no foundation, the evidence of known facts will not permit us to deny that they are in some degree true. It will be found indeed, on a candid review of our situation, that some of the distresses under which we labor, have been erroneously charged on the operation of our governments; but it will be found, at the same time, that other causes will not alone account for many of our heaviest misfortunes; and particularly, for that prevailing and increasing distrust of public engagements, and alarm for private rights, which are echoed from one end of the continent to the other. These must be chiefly, if not wholly, effects of the unsteadiness and injustice, with which a factious spirit has tainted our public administrations.

By a faction I understand a number of citizens, whether amounting to a majority or minority of the whole, who are united and actuated by some common impulse of passion, or of interest, adverse to the rights of other citizens, or to the permanent and aggregate interests of the community.

There are two methods of curing the mischiefs of faction: the one, by removing its causes; the other, by controlling its effects.

There are again two methods of removing the causes of faction: the one by destroying the liberty which is essential to its existence; the other, by giving to every citizen the same opinions, the same passions, and the same interests.

It could never be more truly said than of the first remedy, that it is worse than the disease. Liberty is to faction, what air is to fire, an aliment without which it instantly expires. But it could not be a less folly to abolish liberty, which is essential to political life, because it nourishes faction, than it would be to wish the annihilation of air, which is essential to animal life, because it imparts to fire its destructive agency.

The second expedient is as impracticable, as the first would be unwise. As long as the reason of man continues fallible, and he is at liberty to exercise it, different opinions will be formed. As long as the connection subsists between his reason and his self-love, his opinions and his passions will have a reciprocal influence on each other; and the former will be objects to which the latter will attach themselves. The diversity in the faculties of men from which the rights of property originate, is not less an insuperable obstacle to a uniformity of interests. The protection of these faculties is the first object of Government. From the protection of different and unequal faculties of acquiring property, the possession of different degrees and kinds of property immediately results: and from the influence of these on the sentiments and views of the respective proprietors, ensues a division of the society into different interests and parties.

The latent causes of faction are thus sown in the nature of man; and we see them every where brought into different degrees of activity, according to the different circumstances of civil society. A zeal for different opinions concerning religion, concerning Government and many other points, as well of speculation as of practice; an attachment to different leaders ambitiously contending for pre-eminence and power; or to persons of other descriptions whose fortunes have been interesting to the human passions, have in turn divided mankind into parties, inflamed them with mutual animosity, and rendered them much more disposed to vex and oppress each other, than to cooperate for their common good. So strong is this propensity of mankind to fall into mutual animosities, that where no substantial occasion presents itself, the most frivolous and fanciful distinctions have been sufficient to kindle their unfriendly passions, and excite their most violent conflicts. But the most common and durable source of factions, has been the various and unequal distribution of property. Those who hold, and those who are without property, have ever formed distinct interests in society. Those who are creditors, and those who are debtors, fall under a like discrimination. A landed interest, a manufacturing interest, a mercantile interest, a monied interest, with many lesser interests, grow up of necessity in civilized nations, and divide them into different classes, actuated by different sentiments and views. The regulation of these various and interfering interests forms the principal task of modern Legislation, and involves the spirit of party and faction in the necessary and ordinary operations of Government.

No man is allowed to be judge in his own cause; because his interest would certainly bias his judgment, and, not improbably, corrupt his integrity. With equal, nay with greater reason, a body of men, are unfit to be judges and parties, at the same time; yet, what are many of the most important acts of legislation, but so many judicial determinations, not indeed concerning the rights of single persons, but concerning the rights of large bodies of citizens, and what are the different classes of legislators, but advocates and parties to the causes which they determine? Is a law proposed concerning private debts? It is a question to which the creditors are parties on one side, and the debtors on the other. Justice ought to hold the balance between them. Yet the parties are and must be themselves the judges; and the most numerous party, or, in other words, the most powerful faction must be expected to prevail. Shall domestic manufactures be encouraged, and in what degree, by restrictions on foreign manufactures? are questions which would be differently decided by the landed and the manufacturing classes; and probably by neither, with a sole regard to justice and the public good. The apportionment of taxes on the various descriptions of property, is an act which seems to require the most exact impartiality; yet, there is perhaps no legislative act in which greater opportunity and temptation are given to a predominant party, to trample on the rules of justice. Every shilling with which they overburden the inferior number, is a shilling saved to their own pockets.

It is in vain to say, that enlightened statesmen will be able to adjust these clashing interests, and render them all subservient to the public good. Enlightened statesmen will not always be at the helm: Nor, in many cases, can such an adjustment be made at all, without taking into view indirect and remote considerations, which will rarely prevail over the immediate interest which one party may find in disregarding the rights of another, or the good of the whole.

The inference to which we are brought, is, that the *causes* of faction cannot be removed; and that relief is only to be sought in the means of controlling its *effects*.

If a faction consists of less than a majority, relief is supplied by the republican principle, which enables the majority to defeat its sinister views by regular vote: It may clog the administration, it may convulse the society; but it will be unable to execute and mask its violence under the forms of the Constitution. When a majority is included in a faction, the form of popular government on the other hand enables it to sacrifice to its ruling passion or interest, both the public good and the rights of other citizens. To secure the public good, and private rights, against the danger of such a faction, and at the same time to preserve the spirit and the form of popular government, is then the great object to which our inquiries are directed: Let me add that it is the great desideratum, by which alone this form of government can be rescued from the opprobrium under which it has so long labored, and be recommended to the esteem and adoption of mankind.

By what means is this object attainable? Evidently by one of two only. Either the existence of the same passion or interest in a majority at the same time, must be prevented; or the majority, having such co-existent passion or interest, must be rendered, by their number and local situation, unable to concert and carry into effect schemes of oppression. If the impulse and the opportu-

nity be suffered to coincide, we well know that neither moral nor religious motives can be relied on as an adequate control. They are not found to be such on the injustice and violence of individuals, and lose their efficacy in proportion to the number combined together; that is, in proportion as their efficacy becomes needful.

From this view of the subject, it may be concluded, that a pure Democracy, by which I mean, a Society, consisting of a small number of citizens, who assemble and administer the Government in person, can admit of no cure for the mischiefs of faction. A common passion or interest will, in almost every case, be felt by a majority of the whole; a communication and concert results from the form of Government itself; and there is nothing to check the inducements to sacrifice the weaker party, or an obnoxious individual. Hence it is, that such Democracies have ever been spectacles of turbulence and contention; have ever been found incompatible with personal security, or the rights of property; and have in general been as short in their lives, as they have been violent in their deaths. Theoretic politicians, who have patronized this species of Government, have erroneously supposed, that by reducing mankind to a perfect equality in their political rights, they would, at the same time, be perfectly equalized and assimilated in their possessions, their opinions, and their passions.

A republic, by which I mean a government in which the scheme of representation takes place, opens a different prospect, and promises the cure for which we are seeking. Let us examine the points in which it varies from pure democracy, and we shall comprehend both the nature of the cure and the efficacy which it must derive from the union.

The two great points of difference, between a democracy and a republic, are, first, the delegation of the government, in the latter, to a small number of citizens, elected by the rest; secondly, the greater number of citizens, and greater sphere of country, over which the latter may be extended.

The effect of the first difference is, on the one hand, to refine and enlarge the public views, by passing them through the medium of a chosen body of citizens, whose wisdom may best discern the true interest of their country, and whose patriotism and love of justice, will be least likely to sacrifice it to temporary or partial considerations. Under such a regulation, it may well happen, that the public voice, pronounced by the representatives of the people, will be more consonant to the public good, than if pronounced by the people themselves, convened for the purpose. On the other hand the effect may be inverted. Men of factious tempers, of local prejudices, or of sinister designs, may by intrigue, by corruption, or by other means, first obtain the suffrages, and then betray the interest of the people. The question resulting is, whether small or extensive republics are most favorable to the election of proper guardians of the public weal, and it is clearly decided in favor of the latter by two obvious considerations.

In the first place, it is to be remarked that, however small the republic may be, the representatives must be raised to a certain number, in order to guard against the cabals of a few; and that however large it may be, they must be limited to a certain number, in order to guard against the confusion of a multitude. Hence, the number of representatives in the two cases not being in proportion to that of the constituents, and being proportionally greatest in the small republic, it follows, that if the proportion of fit characters be not less in the large than in the small republic, the former will present a greater option, and consequently a greater probability of a fit choice.

In the next place, as each Representative will be chosen by a greater number of citizens in the large than in the small Republic, it will be more difficult for unworthy candidates to practise with success the vicious arts, by which elections are too often carried; and the suffrages of the people being more free, will be more likely to center on men who possess the most attractive merit, and the most diffusive and established characters.

It must be confessed, that in this, as in most other cases, there is a mean, on both sides of which inconveniences will be found to lie. By enlarging too much the number of electors, you render the representatives too little acquainted with all their local circumstances and lesser interests; as by reducing it too much, you render him unduly attached to these, and too little fit to comprehend and pursue great and national objects. The Federal Constitution forms a happy combination in this respect; the great and aggregate interests being referred to the national, the local and particular, to the state legislatures.

The other point of difference is, the greater number of citizens and extent of territory which may be brought within the compass of Republican, than of Democratic Government; and it is this circumstance principally which renders factious combinations less to be dreaded in the former, than in the latter. The smaller the society, the fewer probably will be the distinct parties and interests composing it; the fewer the distinct parties and interests, the more frequently will a majority be found of the same party; and the smaller the number of individuals composing a majority, and the smaller the compass within which

they are placed, the more easily they will concert and execute their plans of oppression. Extend the sphere, and you take in a greater variety of parties and interests; you make it less probable that a majority of the whole will have a common motive to invade the rights of other citizens; or if such a common motive exists, it will be more difficult for all who feel it to discover their own strength, and to act in unison with each other. Besides other impediments, it may be remarked, that where there is a consciousness of unjust or dishonorable purposes, communication is always checked by distrust, in proportion to the number whose concurrence is necessary.

Hence it clearly appears, that the same advantage, which a Republic has over a Democracy, in controlling the effects of factions, is enjoyed by a large over a small Republic—is enjoyed by the Union over the States composing it. Does this advantage consist in the substitution of Representatives, whose enlightened views and virtuous sentiments render them superior to local prejudices, and to schemes of injustice? It will not be denied, that the Representation of the Union will be most likely to possess these requisite endowments. Does it consist in the greater security afforded by a greater variety of parties, against the event of any one party being able to outnumber and oppress the rest? In an equal degree does the increase variety of parties, comprised within the Union, increase this security? Does it, in fine, consist in the greater obstacles opposed to the concert and accomplishment of the secret wishes of an unjust and interested majority? Here, again, the extent of the Union gives it the most palpable advantage.

The influence of factious leaders may kindle a flame within their particular States, but will be unable to spread a general conflagration through the other States: a religious sect, may degenerate into a political faction in a part of the Confederacy but the variety of sects dispersed over the entire face of it, must secure the national Councils against any danger from that source: a rage for paper money, for an abolition of debts, for an equal division of property, or for any other improper or wicked project, will be less apt to pervade the whole body of the Union, than a particular member of it; in the same proportion as such a malady is more likely to taint a particular county or district, than an entire State.

In the extent and proper structure of the Union, therefore, we behold a Republican remedy for the diseases most incident to Republican Government. And according to the degree of pleasure and pride, we feel in being Republicans, ought to be our zeal in cherishing the spirit, and supporting the character of Federalists.

PUBLIUS

Federalist No. 51

February 6, 1788

James Madison

TO THE PEOPLE OF THE STATE OF NEW YORK:

To what expedient then shall we finally resort for maintaining in practice the necessary partition of power among the several departments, as laid down in the constitution? The only answer that can be given is, that as all these exterior provisions are found to be inadequate, the defect must be supplied, by so contriving the interior structure of the government, as that its several constituent parts may, by their mutual relations, be the means of keeping each other in their proper places. Without presuming to undertake a full development of this important idea, I will hazard a few general observations, which may perhaps place it in a clearer light, and enable us to form a more correct judgment of the principles and structure of the government planned by the convention.

In order to lay a due foundation for that separate and distinct exercise of the different powers of government, which to a certain extent, is admitted on all hands to be essential to the preservation of liberty, it is evident that each department should have a will of its own; and consequently should be so constituted, that the members of each should have as little agency as possible in the appointment of the members of the others. Were this principle rigorously adhered to, it would require that all the appointments for the supreme executive, legislative, and judiciary magistracies, should be drawn from the same fountain of authority, the people, through channels, having no communication whatever with one another. Perhaps such a plan of constructing the several departments would be less difficult in practice than in it may in contemplation appear. Some difficulties however, and some additional expense, would attend the execution of it. Some deviations therefore from the principle must be admitted. In the constitution of the judiciary department in particular, it might be inexpedient to insist rigorously on the principle; first, because peculiar qualifications being essential in the members, the primary consideration ought to be to select that mode of choice, which best secures these qualifications; secondly, because the permanent tenure by which the appointments are held in that department, must soon destroy all sense of dependence on the authority conferring them.

It is equally evident that the members of each department should be as little dependent as possible on those of the others, for the emoluments annexed to their offices. Were the executive magistrate, or the judges, not independent of the legislature in this particular, their independence in every other would be merely nominal.

But the great security against a gradual concentration of the several powers in the same department, consists in giving to those who administer each department, the necessary constitutional means, and personal motives, to resist encroachments of the others. The provision for defense must in this, as in all other cases, be made commensurate to the danger of attack. Ambition must be made to counteract ambition. The interest of the man must be connected with the constitutional right of the place. It may be a reflection on human nature, that such devices should be necessary to control the abuses of government. But what is government itself but the greatest of all reflections on human nature? If men were angels, no government would be necessary. If angels were to govern men, neither external nor internal controls on government would be necessary. In framing a government which is to be administered by men over men, the great difficulty lies in this: You must first enable the government to control the governed; and in the next place, oblige it to control itself. A dependence on the people is no doubt the primary control on the government; but experience has taught mankind the necessity of auxiliary precautions.

This policy of supplying by opposite and rival interests, the defect of better motives, might be traced through the whole system of human affairs, private as well as public. We see it particularly displayed in all the subordinate distributions of power; where the constant aim is to divide and arrange the several offices in such a manner as that each may be a check on the other; that the private interest of every individual, may be a sentinel over the public rights. These inventions of prudence cannot be less requisite in the distribution of the supreme powers of the state.

But it is not possible to give each department an equal power of self defense. In republican government the legislative authority, necessarily, predominates. The remedy for this inconvenience is, to divide the legislative into different branches; and to render them by different modes of election, and different principles of action, as little connected with each other, as the nature of their common functions, and their common dependence on the society, will admit. It may even be necessary to guard against dangerous encroachments by still further precautions. As the weight of the legislative authority requires that it should be thus divided, the weakness of the executive may require, on the other hand, that it should be fortified. An absolute negative, on the legislature, appears at first view to be the natural defense with which the executive magistrate should be armed. But perhaps it would be neither altogether safe, nor alone sufficient. On ordinary occasions, it might not be exerted with the requisite firmness, and on extraordinary occasions, it might be prefidiously abused. May not this defect of an absolute negative be supplied, by some qualified connection between this weaker department, and the weaker branch of the stronger department, by which the latter may be led to support the constitutional rights of the former, without being too much detached from the rights of its own department?

If the principles on which these observations are founded be just, as I persuade myself they are, and they be applied as a criterion, to the several state constitutions, and to the federal constitution, it will be found, that if the latter does not perfectly correspond with them, the former are infinitely less able to bear such a test.

There are moreover two considerations particularly applicable to the federal system of America, which place the system in a very interesting point of view.

First. In a single republic, all the power surrendered by the people, is submitted to the administration of a single government; and usurpations are guarded against by a division of the government into distinct and separate departments. In the compound republic of America, the power surrendered by the people, is first divided between two distinct governments, and then the portion allotted to each, subdivided among distinct and separate departments. Hence a double security arises to the rights of the people. The different governments will control each other; at the same time that each will be controlled by itself.

Second. It is of great importance in a republic, not only to guard the society against the oppression of its rulers; but to guard one part of the society against the injustice of the other part. Different interests necessarily exist in different classes of citizens. If a majority be united by a common interest, the rights of the minority will be insecure. There are but two methods of providing against this evil: The one by creating a will in the community independent of the majority, that is, of the society itself, the other by comprehending in the society so many separate descriptions of citizens, as will render an unjust combination of a majority of the whole, very improbable, if not impracticable. The first method prevails in all governments possessing an hereditary or self appointed authority. This at best is but a precarious security; because a power independent of the society may as well espouse the unjust views of the major, as the rightful interests, of the minor party, and may possibly be turned against both parties. The second method will be exemplified in the federal republic of the United States. While all authority in it will be derived from and dependent on the society, the society itself will be broken into so many parts, interests and classes of citizens, that the rights of individuals or of the minority, will be in little danger from interested combinations of the majority. In a free government, the security for civil rights must be the same as for religious rights. It consists in the one case in the multiplicity of interests, and in the other, in the multiplicity of sects. The degree of security in both cases will depend on the number of interests and sects; and this may be presumed to depend on the extent of country and number of people comprehended under the same government. This view of the subject must particularly recommend a proper federal system to all the sincere and considerate friends of republican government: Since it shows that in exact proportion as the territory of the union may be formed into more circumscribed confederacies or states, oppressive combinations of a majority will be facilitated, the best security under the republican form, for the rights of every class of citizens, will be diminished; and consequently, the stability and independence of some member of the government, the only other security, must be proportionally increased. Justice is the end of government. It is the end of civil society. It ever has been, and ever will be pursued, until it be obtained, or until liberty be lost in the pursuit. In a society under the forms of which the stronger faction can readily unite and oppress the weaker, anarchy may as truly be said to reign, as in a state of nature where the weaker individual is not secured against the violence of the stronger: And as in the latter state even the stronger individuals are prompted by the uncertainty of their condition, to submit to a government which may protect the weak as well as themselves: So in the former state, will the more powerful factions or parties be gradually induced by a like motive, to wish for a government which will protect all parties, the weaker as well as the more powerful. It can be little doubted, that if the state of Rhode Island was separated from the confederacy, and left to itself, the insecurity of rights under the popular form of government within such narrow limits, would be displayed by such reiterated oppressions of factious majorities, that some power altogether independent of the people would soon be called for by the voice of the very factions whose misrule had proved the necessity of it. In the extended republic of the United States, and among the great variety of interests, parties and sects which it embraces, a coalition of a majority of the whole society could seldom take place on any other principles than those of justice and the general good; and there being thus less danger to a minor from the will of the major party, there must be less pretext also, to provide for the security of the former, by introducing into the government a will not dependent on the latter; or in other words, a will independent of the society itself. It is no less certain than it is important, notwithstanding the contrary opinions which have been entertained, that the larger the society, provided it lie within a practicable sphere, the more duly capable it will be of self government. And happily for the *republican cause,* the practicable sphere may be carried to a very great extent, by a judicious modification and mixture of the *federal principle.*

PUBLIUS

Presidents of the United States

President	Party	Term
1. George Washington (1732–1799)	Federalist	1789–1797
2. John Adams (1734–1826)	Federalist	1797–1801
3. Thomas Jefferson (1743–1826)	Democratic-Republican	1801–1809
4. James Madison (1751–1836)	Democratic-Republican	1809–1817
5. James Monroe (1758–1831)	Democratic-Republican	1817–1825
6. John Quincy Adams (1767–1848)	Democratic-Republican	1825–1829
7. Andrew Jackson (1767–1845)	Democratic	1829–1837
8. Martin Van Buren (1782–1862)	Democratic	1837–1841
9. William Henry Harrison (1773–1841)	Whig	1841
10. John Tyler (1790–1862)	Whig	1841–1845
11. James K. Polk (1795–1849)	Democratic	1845–1849
12. Zachary Taylor (1784–1850)	Whig	1849–1850
13. Millard Fillmore (1800–1874)	Whig	1850–1853
14. Franklin Pierce (1804–1869)	Democratic	1853–1857
15. James Buchanan (1791–1868)	Democratic	1857–1861
16. Abraham Lincoln (1809–1865)	Republican	1861–1865
17. Andrew Johnson (1808–1875)	Union	1865–1869
18. Ulysses S. Grant (1822–1885)	Republican	1869–1877
19. Rutherford B. Hayes (1822–1893)	Republican	1877–1881
20. James A. Garfield (1831–1881)	Republican	1881
21. Chester A. Arthur (1830–1886)	Republican	1881–1885
22. Grover Cleveland (1837–1908)	Democratic	1885–1889
23. Benjamin Harrison (1833–1901)	Republican	1889–1893
24. Grover Cleveland (1837–1908)	Democratic	1893–1897
25. William McKinley (1843–1901)	Republican	1897–1901
26. Theodore Roosevelt (1858–1919)	Republican	1901–1909
27. William Howard Taft (1857–1930)	Republican	1909–1913
28. Woodrow Wilson (1856–1924)	Democratic	1913–1921
29. Warren G. Harding (1865–1923)	Republican	1921–1923
30. Calvin Coolidge (1871–1933)	Republican	1923–1929
31. Herbert Hoover (1874–1964)	Republican	1929–1933
32. Franklin Delano Roosevelt (1882–1945)	Democratic	1933–1945
33. Harry S Truman (1884–1972)	Democratic	1945–1953
34. Dwight D. Eisenhower (1890–1969)	Republican	1953–1961
35. John F. Kennedy (1917–1963)	Democratic	1961–1963
36. Lyndon B. Johnson (1908–1973)	Democratic	1963–1969
37. Richard M. Nixon (1913–1994)	Republican	1969–1974
38. Gerald R. Ford (b. 1913)	Republican	1974–1977
39. Jimmy Carter (b. 1924)	Democratic	1977–1981
40. Ronald Reagan (b. 1911)	Republican	1981–1989
41. George Bush (b. 1924)	Republican	1989–1993
42. Bill Clinton (b. 1946)	Democratic	1993–2001
43. George W. Bush (b. 1946)	Republican	2001–

Twentieth-Century Justices of the Supreme Court

Justice*	Term of Service	Years of Service	Life Span	Justice*	Term of Service	Years of Service	Life Span
Oliver W. Holmes	1902–1932	30	1841–1935	Wiley B. Rutledge	1943–1949	6	1894–1949
William R. Day	1903–1922	19	1849–1923	Harold H. Burton	1945–1958	13	1888–1964
William H. Moody	1906–1910	3	1853–1917	Fred M. Vinson	1946–1953	7	1890–1953
Horace H. Lurton	1910–1914	4	1844–1914	Tom C. Clark	1949–1967	18	1899–1977
Charles E. Hughes	1910–1916	5	1862–1948	Sherman Minton	1949–1956	7	1890–1965
Willis Van Devanter	1911–1937	26	1859–1941	Earl Warren	1953–1969	16	1891–1974
Joseph R. Lamar	1911–1916	5	1857–1916	John Marshall Harlan	1955–1971	16	1899–1971
Edward D. White	1910–1921	11	1845–1921	William J. Brennan, Jr.	1956–1990	34	1906–1997
Mahlon Pitney	1912–1922	10	1858–1924	Charles E. Whittaker	1957–1962	5	1901–1973
James C. McReynolds	1914–1941	26	1862–1946	Potter Stewart	1958–1981	23	1915–1985
Louis D. Brandeis	1916–1939	22	1856–1941	Byron R. White	1962–1993	31	1917–
John H. Clarke	1916–1922	6	1857–1930	Arthur J. Goldberg	1962–1965	3	1908–1990
William H. Taft	1921–1930	8	1857–1945	Abe Fortas	1965–1969	4	1910–1982
George Sutherland	1922–1938	15	1862–1942	Thurgood Marshall	1967–1991	24	1908–1993
Pierce Butler	1922–1939	16	1866–1939	Warren E. Burger	1969–1986	17	1907–1995
Edward T. Sandford	1923–1930	7	1865–1930	Harry A. Blackmun	1970–1994	24	1908–1999
Harlan F. Stone	1925–1941	16	1872–1946	Lewis F. Powell, Jr.	1972–1987	15	1907–1998
Charles E. Hughes	1930–1941	11	1862–1948	William H. Rehnquist	1972–1986	14	1924–
Owen J. Roberts	1930–1945	15	1875–1955	John P. Stevens	1975–	—	1920–
Benjamin N. Cardozo	1932–1938	6	1870–1938	Sandra Day O'Connor	1981–	—	1930–
Hugo L. Black	1937–1971	34	1886–1971	William H. Rehnquist	1986–	—	1924–
Stanley F. Reed	1938–1957	19	1884–1980	Antonin Scalia	1986–	—	1936–
Felix Frankfurter	1939–1962	23	1882–1965	Anthony M. Kennedy	1988–	—	1936–
William O. Douglas	1939–1975	36	1898–1980	David H. Souter	1990–	—	1939–
Frank Murphy	1940–1949	9	1890–1949	Clarence Thomas	1991–	—	1948–
Harlan F. Stone	1941–1946	5	1872–1946	Ruth Bader Ginsburg	1993–	—	1933–
James F. Byrnes	1941–1942	1	1879–1972	Stephen G. Breyer	1994–	—	1938–
Robert H. Jackson	1941–1954	13	1892–1954				

*The names of chief justices are printed in italic type.

Party Control of the Presidency, Senate, and House of Representatives, 1901–2001

Congress	Years	President	Senate D	Senate R	Senate Other*	House D	House R	House Other*
57th	1901–1903	McKinley T. Roosevelt	31	55	4	151	197	9
58th	1903–1905	T. Roosevelt	33	57	—	178	208	—
59th	1905–1907	T. Roosevelt	33	57	—	136	250	—
60th	1907–1909	T. Roosevelt	31	61	—	164	222	—
61st	1909–1911	Taft	32	61	—	172	219	—
62d	1911–1913	Taft	41	51	—	228	161	1
63d	1913–1915	Wilson	51	44	1	291	127	17

Sources: Department of Commerce, Bureau of the Census, *Statistical Abstract of the United States* (Washington, DC: U. S. Government Printing Office, 1980), p. 509, and *Members of Congress Since 1789*, 2d ed. (Washington, DC: Congressional Quarterly Press, 1981), pp. 176–177. Adapted from Barbara Hinckley, *Congressional Elections* (Washington, DC: Congressional Quarterly Press, 1981), pp. 144–145.

*Excludes vacancies at beginning of each session.

Party Control of the Presidency, Senate, and House of Representatives, 1901–2001 (*continued*)

Congress	Years	President	Senate D	R	Other*	House D	R	Other*
64th	1915–1917	Wilson	56	40	—	230	196	9
65th	1917–1919	Wilson	53	42	—	216	10	6
66th	1919–1921	Wilson	47	49	—	190	240	3
67th	1921–1923	Harding	37	59	—	131	301	1
68th	1923–1925	Coolidge	43	51	2	205	225	5
69th	1925–1927	Coolidge	39	56	1	183	247	4
70th	1927–1929	Coolidge	46	49	1	195	237	3
71st	1929–1931	Hoover	39	56	1	167	267	1
72d	1931–1933	Hoover	47	48	1	220	214	1
73d	1933–1935	F. Roosevelt	60	35	1	319	117	5
74th	1935–1937	F. Roosevelt	69	25	2	319	103	10
75th	1937–1939	F. Roosevelt	76	16	4	331	89	13
76th	1939–1941	F. Roosevelt	69	23	4	261	164	4
77th	1941–1943	F. Roosevelt	66	28	2	268	162	5
78th	1943–1945	F. Roosevelt	58	37	1	218	208	4
79th	1945–1947	Truman	56	38	1	242	190	2
80th	1947–1949	Truman	45	51	—	188	245	1
81st	1949–1951	Truman	54	42	—	263	171	1
82d	1951–1953	Truman	49	47	—	234	199	1
83d	1953–1955	Eisenhower	47	48	1	211	221	—
84th	1955–1957	Eisenhower	48	47	1	232	203	—
85th	1957–1959	Eisenhower	49	47	—	233	200	—
86th**	1959–1961	Eisenhower	65	35	—	284	153	—
87th**	1961–1963	Kennedy	65	35	—	263	174	—
88th	1963–1965	Kennedy Johnson	67	33	—	258	177	—
89th	1965–1967	Johnson	68	32	—	295	140	—
90th	1967–1969	Johnson	64	36	—	247	187	—
91st	1969–1971	Nixon	57	43	—	243	192	—
92d	1971–1973	Nixon	54	44	2	254	180	—
93d	1973–1975	Nixon Ford	56	42	2	239	192	1
94th	1975–1977	Ford	60	37	2	291	144	—
95th	1977–1979	Carter	61	38	1	292	143	—
96th	1979–1981	Carter	58	41	1	276	157	—
97th	1981–1983	Reagan	46	53	1	243	192	—
98th	1983–1985	Reagan	45	55	—	267	168	—
99th	1985–1987	Reagan	47	53	—	252	183	—
100th	1987–1989	Reagan	54	46	—	257	178	—
101st	1989–1991	Bush	55	45	—	262	173	—
102d	1991–1993	Bush	56	44	—	276	167	—
103d	1993–1995	Clinton	56	44	—	256	178	1
104th	1995–1997	Clinton	47	53	—	204	230	1
105th	1997–1999	Clinton	45	55	—	206	228	—
106th	1999–2001	Clinton	46	54	—	210	223	2
107th	2001–	G. W. Bush	50	50	—	212	221	2

**The 437 members of the House in the 86th and 87th Congresses is attributable to the at-large representative given to both Alaska (January 3, 1959) and Hawaii (August 2, 1959) prior to redistricting in 1962.

Glossary

accommodationists   supporters of government nonpreferential accommodation of religions (4)

accountability   the principle that bureaucratic employees should be answerable for their performance to supervisors, all the way up the chain of command (8)

administrative law   law established by the bureaucracy, on behalf of Congress (9)

affirmative action   a policy of creating opportunities for members of certain groups as a substantive remedy for past discrimination (5)

allocative representation   congressional work to secure projects, services, and funds for the represented district (6)

amendability   the provision for the Constitution to be changed so as to adapt to new circumstances (2)

amicus curiae brief   a "friend of the court" document filed by interested parties to encourage the court to grant or deny certiorari or to urge it to decide a case in a particular way (9)

Anti-Federalists   opponents of the Constitution (2)

appeal   a rehearing of a case because the losing party in the original trial argues that a point of law was not applied properly (9)

appellate jurisdiction   the authority of a court to review decisions made by lower courts (9)

Articles of Confederation   the first constitution of the United States (1777), creating an association of states with a weak central government (2)

astroturf lobbying   indirect lobbying efforts that manipulate or create public sentiment, "astroturf" being artificial grassroots (11)

asylum   protection or sanctuary, especially from political persecution (1)

authoritarian government   a system in which the state holds all power (1)

authority   power that is recognized as legitimate (1)

beat   a specific area (for example, police, the White House, business) covered by a journalist, who becomes familiar with the territory and its news sources (13)

bicameral legislature   a legislature with two chambers (2, 6)

Bill of Rights   a summary of citizen rights guaranteed and protected by a government; added to the Constitution as its first ten amendments in order to achieve ratification (2)

bills of attainder   laws under which persons or groups are detained and sentenced without trial (4)

black codes   a series of laws in the post–Civil War South designed to restrict the rights of former slaves before the passage of the Fourteenth and Fifteenth Amendments (5)

block grant   federal funds provided for a broad purpose, unrestricted by detailed requirements and regulations (3)

boycott   the refusal to buy certain goods or services as a way to protest policy or force political reform (5)

bureaucracy   an organization characterized by hierarchical structure, worker specialization, explicit rules, and advancement by merit (8)

bureaucratese   the often unintelligible language used by bureaucrats to avoid controversy and lend weight to their words (8)

bureaucratic culture   the accepted values and procedures of an organization (8)

bureaucratic discretion   top bureaucrats' authority to use their own judgment in interpreting and carrying out the laws of Congress (8)

busing   achieving racial balance by transporting students to schools across neighborhood boundaries (5)

cabinet   a presidential advisory group selected by the president and made up of the vice president, the heads of the fourteen federal executive departments, and other high officials to whom the president elects to give cabinet status (7)

capitalist economy   an economic system in which the market determines production, distribution, and price decisions and property is privately owned (1)

casework   legislative work on behalf of individual constituents to solve their problems with government agencies and programs (6)

categorical grant   federal funds provided for a specific purpose, restricted by detailed instructions, regulations, and compliance standards (3)

Central Intelligence Agency   the government organization that oversees foreign intelligence-gathering and related classified activities (14)

checks and balances   the principle that each branch of government guards against the abuse of power by the others (2)

chief administrator   the president's executive role as the head of federal agencies and the person responsible for the implementation of national policy (7)

chief foreign policy maker   the president's executive role as the primary shaper of relations with other nations (7)

chief of staff   the person who oversees the operations of all White House staff and controls access to the president (7)

citizen advisory council   a citizen group that considers the policy decisions of an agency; a way to make the bureaucracy responsive to the general public (8)

citizens   members of a political community having both rights and responsibilities (1)

civic journalism   a movement among journalists to be responsive to citizen input in determining what news stories to cover (13)

civil law   law regulating interactions between individuals; a violation of a civil law is called a tort (9)

civil law tradition   a legal system based on a detailed, comprehensive legal code, usually created by the legislature (9)

civil liberties   individual freedoms guaranteed to the people primarily by the Bill of Rights (4)

civil rights   citizenship rights guaranteed to the people (primarily in the Thirteenth, Fourteenth, Fifteenth, and Nineteenth Amendments) and protected by government (4, 5)

civil service   nonmilitary employees of the government who are appointed through the merit system (8)

clear and present danger test   rule used by the court in which language can be regulated only if it presents an immediate and urgent danger (4)

clientele groups   groups of citizens whose interests are affected by an agency or department and who work to influence its policies (8)

cloture   a vote to end a Senate filibuster; requires a three-fifths majority, or sixty votes (6)

coattail effect   the added votes received by congressional candidates of a winning presidential party (6)

Cold War   the half century of competition and conflict after World War II, between the United States and the Soviet Union (and their allies) (14)

collective good   a good or service that, by its very nature, cannot be denied to anyone who wants to consume it (11)

commander-in-chief   the president's role as the top officer of the country's military establishment (7)

commercial bias   the tendency of the media to make coverage and programming decisions based on what will attract a large audience and maximize profits (13)

common law tradition   a legal system based on the accumulated rulings of judges over time, applied uniformly—judge-made law (9)

communist economy   an economic system in which the state determines production, distribution, and price decisions and property is government owned (1)

compelling state interest   a fundamental state purpose, which must be shown before the law can limit some freedoms or treat some groups of people differently (4)

concurrent powers   powers that are shared by both the federal and state governments (3)

concurring opinions   documents written by justices expressing agreement with the majority ruling but describing different or additional reasons for the ruling (9)

confederal system   government in which local units hold all the power (3)

confederation   a government in which independent states unite for common purposes but retain their own sovereignty (2)

conference committee   a temporary committee formed to reconcile differences in the House and Senate versions of a bill (6)

conservative   generally favoring limited government and cautious about change (1)

constituency   the voters in a state or district (6)

constitution   the rules that establish a government (2)

Constitutional Convention   the assembly of fifty-five delegates in the summer of 1787 to recast the Articles of Confederation; the result was the U.S. Constitution (2)

constitutional law   law stated in the Constitution and the body of judicial decisions about the meaning of the Constitution (9)

containment   the U.S. Cold War policy of preventing the spread of communism (14)

cooperative federalism   the federal system under which the national and state governments share responsibility for most domestic policy areas (3)

Council of Economic Advisers   organization within the Executive Office of the President that advises the president on economic matters (7)

courts   institutions that sit as neutral third parties to resolve conflicts according to the law (9)

criminal law   law prohibiting behavior the government has determined is harmful to society; a violation of criminal law is called a crime (9)

crisis policy   foreign policy, usually made quickly and secretly, that responds to an emergency threat (14)

critical election an election signaling the significant change in popular allegiance from one party to another (11)

critical thinking analysis and evaluation of ideas and arguments based on reason and evidence (1)

cycle effect the predictable rise and fall of a president's popularity at different stages of a term in office (7)

dealignment a trend among voters to identify themselves as Independents rather than as members of a major party (11)

Declaration of Independence the political document that dissolved the colonial ties between the United States and Britain (2)

de facto discrimination discrimination that is not the result of the law but rather of tradition and habit (5)

de jure discrimination discrimination arising from or supported by the law (5)

democracy government that vests power in the people (1)

department one of fourteen major subdivisions of the federal government, represented in the president's cabinet (8)

Department of Defense the executive department charged with managing the country's military personnel, equipment, and operations (14)

Department of State the executive department charged with managing foreign affairs (14)

devolution the transfer of powers and responsibilities from the federal government to the states (3)

direct lobbying direct interaction with public officials for the purpose of influencing policy decisions (11)

dissenting opinions documents written by justices expressing disagreement with the majority ruling (9)

distributive policy a policy funded by the whole taxpayer base that addresses the needs of particular groups (14)

divided government political rule split between two parties, one controlling the White House and the other controlling one or both houses of Congress (7)

dual federalism the federal system under which the national and state governments were responsible for separate policy areas (3)

due process of the law guarantee that laws will be fair and reasonable and that citizens suspected of breaking the law will be fairly treated (4)

economic interest group a group that organizes to influence government policy for the economic benefit of its members (11)

economics the production and distribution of a society's goods and services (1)

electioneering the process of getting a person elected to public office (11)

electoral college an intermediary body that elects the president (2)

electoral mandate the perception that an election victory signals broad support for the winner's proposed policies (12)

elite democracy a theory of democracy that limits the citizens' role to choosing among competing leaders (1)

enumerated powers of Congress congressional powers specifically named in the Constitution (Article I, Section 8) (3)

equal opportunity interest group a group that organizes to promote the civil and economic rights of underrepresented or disadvantaged groups (11)

Equal Rights Amendment constitutional amendment, passed by Congress but never ratified, that would have banned discrimination on the basis of gender (5)

establishment clause the First Amendment guarantee that the government will not create and support an official state church (4)

exclusionary rule rule created by the Supreme Court holding that evidence illegally seized may not be used to obtain a conviction (4)

executive the branch of government responsible for putting laws into effect (2)

executive agreement a presidential arrangement with another country that creates foreign policy without the need for Senate approval (7)

Executive Office of the President collection of nine organizations that help the president with his policy and political objectives (7)

executive order a clarification of congressional policy issued by the president and having the full force of law (7, 9)

exit poll election-related questions asked of voters right after they vote (10)

ex post facto laws laws that criminalize an action after it occurs (4)

expressive benefit a selective incentive that derives from the opportunity to express values and beliefs and to be committed to a greater cause (11)

faction a group of citizens united by some common passion or interest and opposed to the rights of other citizens or to the interests of the whole community (2, 11)

fascist government an authoritarian government in which policy is made for the ultimate glory of the state (1)

federalism a political system in which power is divided between the central and regional units (2)

The Federalist Papers a series of essays written in support of the Constitution to encourage its ratification (2)

Federalists   supporters of the Constitution (2)

Federal Register   publication containing all federal regulations and notifications of regulatory agency hearings (8)

feeding frenzy   excessive press coverage of an embarrassing or scandalous subject (13)

fighting words   speech intended to incite violence (4)

filibuster   the practice of unlimited debate in the Senate to prevent or delay a vote on a bill (6)

foreign policy   a country's official positions, practices, and procedures for dealing with actors outside its borders (14)

franking   the privilege of free mail service provided to members of Congress (6)

freedom of assembly   the right of people to gather peacefully and to petition government (4)

Freedom of Information Act   a 1966 law that allows citizens to obtain copies of most public records (8)

free exercise clause   the First Amendment guarantee that citizens may freely engage in the religious activities of their choice (4)

free rider problem   the difficulty groups face in recruiting when potential members can gain the benefits of the group's actions whether they join or not (11)

French and Indian War   a war fought between France and England, and allied Indians, from 1754 to 1763; resulted in France's expulsion from the New World (2)

front-loading   the process of scheduling presidential primaries early in the primary season (12)

front-runner   the leading candidate and expected winner of an election (12)

gatekeeping   the function of determining which news stories are covered and which are not (13)

gender gap   the tendency of men and women to differ in their political views on some issues (10)

gerrymandering   redistricting to benefit a particular group (6)

Gibbons v. Ogden   Supreme Court ruling (1824) establishing national authority over interstate business (3)

going public   a president's strategy of appealing to the public on an issue, expecting that public pressure will be brought to bear on other political actors (7)

governing   activities directed toward controlling the distribution of resources by providing executive/legislative leadership, enacting agendas, mobilizing support, and building coalitions (11)

government   a system or organization for exercising authority over a body of people (1)

government corporation   a company created by Congress to provide a good or service to the public that private enterprise cannot or will not profitably provide (8)

grandfather clause   a provision exempting from voting restrictions the descendants of those able to vote in 1867 (5)

grassroots lobbying   indirect lobbying efforts that spring from widespread public concern (11)

Great Compromise   the constitutional solution to congressional representation: equal representation in the Senate; representation by population in the House (2)

habeas corpus   the right of an accused person to be brought before a judge and informed of the charges and evidence against him or her (4)

hard money   campaign funds donated directly to candidates; amounts are limited by federal election laws (12)

Hatch Act   a 1939 law limiting the political involvement of civil servants to protect them from political pressure and keep politics out of the bureaucracy (8)

head of government   the political role of the president as leader of a political party and chief arbiter of who gets what resources (7)

head of state   the apolitical, unifying role of the president as symbolic representative of the whole country (7)

honeymoon period   the time following an election when a president's popularity is high and congressional relations are likely to be productive (7)

horse race journalism   the media's focus on the competitive aspect of politics rather than on actual policy proposals and political decisions (13)

House Rules Committee   the committee that determines how and when debate on a bill will take place (6)

ideologies   sets of beliefs about politics and society that help people make sense of their world (1)

immigrants   citizens or subjects of other countries who come to the United States to live or work (1)

incorporation   Supreme Court action making the protections of the Bill of Rights applicable to the states (4)

incumbency advantage   the electoral edge afforded to those already in office (6)

independent agency   a government organization independent of the departments but with a narrower policy focus (8)

independent regulatory boards and commissions   government organizations that regulate various businesses, industries, or economic sectors (8)

indirect lobbying   attempts to influence government policymakers by encouraging the general public to put pressure on them (11)

individualistic   believing that what is good for society derives from what is good for the individual (1)

inherent powers   presidential powers implied but not explicitly stated in the Constitution (7)

institutions   organizations where governmental power is exercised (1)

intelligence community   the agencies and bureaus responsible for obtaining and interpreting information for the government (14)

interest group   an organization of individuals who share a common political goal and unite for the purpose of influencing government decisions (11)

interest group entrepreneur   an effective group leader, who is likely to have organized the group and can effectively promote its interests among members and the public (11)

intergovernmental organization   a body such as the United Nations whose members are countries (14)

intermediate standard of review   standard of review used by the Supreme Court to evaluate laws that make a quasi-suspect classification (5)

iron triangle   the phenomenon of a clientele group, congressional committee, and bureaucratic agency cooperating to make mutually beneficial policy (8)

isolationism   a foreign policy view that nations should stay out of international political alliances and activities and focus instead on domestic matters (14)

issue advocacy ads   advertisements that support issues or candidates without telling constituents how to vote (11, 12)

issue ownership   the tendency of one party to be seen as more competent in a specific policy area (12)

Jim Crow laws   southern laws designed to circumvent the Thirteenth, Fourteenth, and Fifteenth Amendments and to deny blacks rights on bases other than race (5)

Joint Chiefs of Staff   the senior military officers from the four branches of the U.S. armed forces (14)

joint committee   a combined House-Senate committee formed to coordinate activities and expedite legislation in a certain area (6)

journalist   a person who discovers, reports, writes, edits, and/or publishes the news (13)

judicial activism   view that the courts should be lawmaking, policymaking bodies (9)

judicial interpretivism   a judicial approach holding that the Constitution is a living document and that judges should interpret it according to changing times and values (9)

judicial power   the power to interpret laws and judge whether a law has been broken (2)

judicial restraint   view that the courts should reject any active lawmaking functions and stick to judicial interpretations of the past (9)

judicial review   the power of the Supreme Court to rule on the constitutionality of laws (2, 9)

jurisdiction   a court's authority to hear certain cases (9)

lawmaking   the creation of policy to address national problems (6)

leaking   secretly revealing confidential information to the press (13)

legislative agenda   the slate of proposals and issues that representatives think it worthwhile to consider and act on (6)

legislative liaison   executive personnel who work with members of Congress to secure their support in getting a president's legislation passed (7)

legislative oversight   a committee's investigation of government agencies to ensure they are acting as Congress intends (6)

legislature   the body of government that makes laws (2)

legitimate   accepted as "right" or proper (1)

***Lemon* test**   three-pronged rule used by the courts to determine whether the establishment clause has been violated (4)

libel   written defamation of character (4)

liberal   generally favoring government action and viewing change as progress (1)

line-item veto   presidential authority to strike out individual spending provisions in a budget; passed by Congress but ruled unconstitutional by the Supreme Court (6)

literacy test   the requirement of reading or comprehension skills as a qualification for voting (5)

lobbying   interest group activities aimed at persuading policymakers to support the group's positions (11)

majority party   the party with the most seats in a house of Congress (6)

malapportionment   the unequal distribution of population among districts (6)

marriage gap   the tendency for married people to hold different political opinions than people who have never been married (10)

mass media   means of conveying information to large public audiences cheaply and efficiently (13)

material benefit   a selective incentive in the form of a tangible reward (11)

McCulloch* v. *Maryland   Supreme Court ruling (1819) confirming the supremacy of national over state government (3)

midterm loss   the tendency for the presidential party to lose congressional seats in off-year elections (6)

Miller **test**   rule used by the courts in which the definition of *obscenity* must be based on local standards (4)

minimum rationality test   standard of review used by the Supreme Court to evaluate laws that make a nonsuspect classification (5)

momentum   the perception that a candidate is moving ahead of the rest of the field and gaining strength (12)

monarchy   an authoritarian government with power vested in a king or queen (1)

Motor Voter Bill   legislation allowing citizens to register to vote at the same time they apply for a driver's license or other state benefit (12)

multinational corporation   a large company that does business in multiple countries (14)

National Association for the Advancement of Colored People   an interest group founded in 1910 to promote civil rights for African Americans (5)

National Security Council   organization within the Executive Office of the President that provides foreign policy advice to the president (7, 14)

naturalization   the legal process of acquiring citizenship for someone who has not acquired it by birth (1)

necessary and proper clause   constitutional authorization for Congress to make any law required to carry out its powers (3)

negative advertising   campaign advertising that emphasizes the negative characteristics of opponents rather than one's own strengths (12)

neutral competence   the principle that bureaucracy should be depoliticized by making it more professional (8)

New Jersey Plan   a proposal at the Constitutional Convention that congressional representation be equal, thus favoring the small states (2)

news management   the efforts of a politician's staff to control news about the politician (13)

newspaper   a printed publication that is issued regularly, is directed to a general audience, and offers timely news (13)

nominating convention   formal party gathering to choose candidates (11)

nongovernmental organization   an organization comprising individuals or interest groups from around the world focused on a special issue (14)

norms   informal rules that govern behavior in Congress (6)

nullification   declaration by a state that a federal law is void within its borders (3)

Office of Management and Budget   organization within the Executive Office of the President that oversees the budgets of departments and agencies (7)

oligarchy   rule by a small group of elites (1)

on-line processing   the ability to receive and evaluate information as events happen, allowing us to remember our evaluation even if we have forgotten the specific events that caused it (10)

opinion   written decision of the court that states the judgment of the majority (9)

opinion leaders   people who know more about certain topics than we do and whose advice we trust, seek out, and follow (10)

oppo research   investigation of an opponent's background for the purpose of exploiting weaknesses or undermining credibility (12)

original jurisdiction   the authority of a court to hear a case first (9)

pardoning power   the president's authority to release or excuse a person from the legal penalties of a crime (7)

participatory democracy   a theory of democracy that holds that citizens should actively and directly control all aspects of their lives (1)

partisanship   loyalty to a political cause or party (11)

party activists   the "party faithful"; the rank-and-file members who actually carry out the party's electioneering efforts (11)

party base   members of a political party who consistently vote for that party's candidates (11)

party boss   party leader, usually in an urban district, who exercised tight control over electioneering and patronage (11)

party caucuses   party groupings in each legislative chamber (6)

party era   extended period of relative political stability in which one party tends to control both the presidency and Congress (11)

party identification   voter affiliation with a political party (11)

party-in-government   members of the party who have been elected to serve in government (11)

party-in-the-electorate   ordinary citizens who identify with the party (11)

party machine   mass-based party system in which parties provided services and resources to voters in exchange for votes (11)

party organization   the official structure that conducts the political business of parties (11)

party platform   list of policy positions a party endorses and pledges its elected officials to enact (11)

party primary   nomination of party candidates by registered party members rather than party bosses (11)

patronage   a system in which successful party candidates reward supporters with jobs or favors (8, 11)

Pendleton Act civil service reform (1883) that required the hiring and promoting of civil servants to be based on merit, not patronage (8)

pluralist democracy a theory of democracy that holds that citizen membership in groups is the key to political power (1, 11)

pocket veto presidential authority to kill a bill submitted within ten days of the end of a legislative session by not signing it (6)

police power the ability of a government to protect its citizens and maintain social order (4)

policy entrepreneurship the practice of legislators becoming experts and taking leadership roles in specific policy areas (6)

policy representation congressional work to advance the issues and ideological preferences of constituents (6)

political action committee the fundraising arm of an interest group (11)

political correctness the idea that language shapes behavior and therefore should be regulated to control its social effects (4)

political culture the broad pattern of ideas, beliefs, and values about citizens and government held by a population (1)

political party a group of citizens united by ideology and seeking control of government in order to promote their ideas and policies (11)

political socialization the process by which we learn our political orientations and allegiances (10)

politics who gets what, when, and how; a process of determining how power and resources are distributed in a society without recourse to violence (1)

poll tax a tax levied as a qualification for voting (5)

popular sovereignty the concept that the citizens are the ultimate source of political power (1)

popular tyranny the unrestrained power of the people (2)

pork barrel public works projects and grants for specific districts paid for by general revenues (6)

position issue an issue on which the parties differ in their perspectives and proposed solutions (12)

power the ability to get other people to do what you want (1)

power to persuade a president's ability to convince Congress, other political actors, and the public to cooperate with the administration's agenda (7)

precedent a previous decision or ruling that, in common law tradition, is binding on subsequent decisions (9)

presidential primary an election by which voters choose convention delegates committed to voting for a certain candidate (12)

presidential veto a president's authority to reject a bill passed by Congress; may be overridden only by a two-thirds majority in both houses (7)

prior restraint punishment for expression of ideas before the ideas are spoken or printed (4)

Privacy Act of 1974 a law that gives citizens access to the government's files on them (8)

procedural relating to the rules of operation, not the outcomes (1)

procedural due process procedural laws that protect the rights of individuals who must deal with the legal system (9)

procedural law law that establishes how laws are applied and enforced—how legal proceedings take place (9)

progressive tax a tax whose rate increases with income level (14)

prospective voting basing voting decisions on well-informed opinions and consideration of the future consequences of a given vote (12)

public interest group a group that organizes to influence government to produce collective goods or services that benefit the general public (11)

public opinion the collective attitudes and beliefs of individuals on one or more issues (10)

public opinion polls scientific efforts to estimate what an entire group thinks about an issue by asking a smaller sample of the group for its opinion (10)

public policy a government plan of action to solve a social problem (14)

push poll a poll that asks for reactions to hypothetical, often false, information in order to manipulate public opinion (10)

racial gerrymandering redistricting to enhance or reduce the chances that a racial or ethnic group will elect members to the legislature (6)

ratified formally approved and adopted by vote (2)

rational ignorance the state of being uninformed about politics because of the cost in time and energy (10)

realignment substantial and long-term shift in party allegiance by individuals and groups, usually resulting in a change in policy direction (11)

reapportionment a reallocation of congressional seats among the states every ten years, following the census (6)

Reconstruction the period following the Civil War during which the federal government took action to rebuild the South (5)

redistributive policy a policy that shifts resources from the "haves" to the "have-nots" (14)

redistricting the process of dividing states into legislative districts (6)

red tape the complex procedures and regulations surrounding bureaucratic activity (8)

refugees individuals who flee an area or country because of persecution on the basis of race, nationality, religion, group membership, or political opinion (1)

regressive tax a tax that, even if a fixed rate, takes a higher proportion of lower incomes (14)

regulations limitations or restrictions on the activities of a business or individual (8)

regulatory policy a policy designed to restrict or change the behavior of certain groups or individuals (14)

representation the efforts of elected officials to look out for the interests of those who elect them (6)

republic a government in which decisions are made through representatives of the people (1)

responsible party model party government when four conditions are met: clear choice of ideologies, candidates pledged to implement ideas, party held accountable by voters, party control over members (11)

retrospective voting basing voting decisions on reactions to past performance; approving the status quo or signaling a desire for change (12)

revolving door the tendency of public officials, journalists, and lobbyists to move between public and private sector (media, lobbying) jobs (11, 13)

roll call voting publicly recorded votes on bills and amendments on the floor of the House or Senate (6)

Rule of Four requirement that four Supreme Court justices must agree to grant a case certiorari in order for the case to be heard (9)

rules directives that specify how resources will be distributed or what procedures will govern collective activity (1)

sample the portion of the population that is selected to participate in a poll (10)

sample bias the effect of having a sample that does not represent all segments of the population (10)

sampling error a number that indicates within what range the results of a poll are accurate (10)

sedition speech that criticizes the government (4)

segregation the practice and policy of separating races (5)

select committee a committee appointed to deal with an issue or problem not suited to a standing committee (6)

selective incentive a benefit that is available only to group members as an inducement to get them to join (11)

selective incorporation incorporation of rights on a case-by-case basis (4)

selective perception the phenomenon of filtering incoming information through personal values and interests and deciding what to pay attention to (13)

senatorial courtesy the tradition of granting senior senators of the president's party considerable power over federal judicial appointments in their home states (7, 9)

seniority system the accumulation of power and authority in conjunction with the length of time spent in office (6)

separationists supporters of a "wall of separation" between church and state (4)

separation of powers a safeguard calling for legislative, executive, and judicial powers to be exercised by different people (2)

Shays's Rebellion a grassroots uprising (1787) by armed Massachusetts farmers protesting foreclosures (2)

social connectedness citizens' involvement in groups and their relationships to their communities and families (12)

social contract the notion that society is based on an agreement between government and the governed in which people agree to give up some rights in exchange for the protection of others (1)

social democracy a hybrid system combining a capitalist economy and a government that supports equality (1)

social protest public activities designed to bring attention to political causes, usually generated by those without access to conventional means of expressing their views (11)

soft money unregulated campaign contributions by individuals, groups, or parties that promote general election activities but do not directly support individual candidates (12)

solicitor general the Justice Department officer who argues the government's cases before the Supreme Court (7, 9)

solidary benefit a selective incentive related to the interaction and bonding among group members (11)

sound bite a brief, snappy excerpt from a public figure's speech that is easy to repeat on the news (13)

Speaker of the House the leader of the majority party, who serves as the presiding officer of the House of Representatives (6)

spin an interpretation of a politician's words or actions designed to present a favorable image (13)

splinter party a third party that breaks off from one of the major political parties (11)

spoils system the nineteenth-century practice of rewarding political supporters with public office (8)

standing committee a permanent committee responsible for legislation in a particular policy area (6)

State of the Union address a speech given annually by the president to a joint session of Congress and to the nation announcing the president's agenda (7)

statutory law   law passed by a state or the federal legislature (9)

strategic policy   foreign policy that lays out a country's basic stance toward international actors or problems (14)

strategic politician   an office seeker who bases the decision to run on a rational calculation that he or she will be successful (6)

strict constructionism   a judicial approach holding that the Constitution should be read literally with the framers' intentions uppermost in mind (9)

strict scrutiny   a heightened standard of review used by the Supreme Court to assess the constitutionality of laws that limit some freedoms or that make a suspect classification (5)

structural defense policy   foreign policy dealing with defense spending, military bases, and weapons procurement (14)

subjects   individuals who are obliged to submit to a government authority against which they have no rights (1)

substantive law   law whose content, or substance, defines what we can or cannot do (9)

sunshine laws   legislation opening the process of bureaucratic policymaking to the public (8)

supremacy clause   constitutional declaration (Article VI) that the Constitution and laws made under its provisions are the supreme law of the land (3)

suspect classification   classification, such as race, for which any discriminatory law must be justified by a compelling state interest (5)

swing voters   the approximately one-third of the electorate who are undecided at the start of a campaign (12)

symbolic representation   the efforts of members of Congress to stand for American ideals or to identify with common constituency values (6)

theocracy   an authoritarian government that claims to draw its power from divine or religious authority (1)

Three-fifths Compromise   the formula for counting five slaves as three people for purposes of representation; reconciled northern and southern factions at the Constitutional Convention (2)

totalitarian government   a system in which absolute power is exercised over every aspect of life (1)

tracking poll   an ongoing series of surveys that follow changes in public opinion over time (10)

treaties   formal agreements with other countries; negotiated by the president and requiring two-thirds Senate approval (7)

two-step flow of information   the process by which citizens take their political cues from more well-informed opinion leaders (10)

unfunded mandate   a federal order that states operate and pay for a program created at the national level (3)

unitary system   government in which all power is centralized (3)

valence issue   an issue on which most voters and candidates share the same position (12)

values   central ideas, principles, or standards that most people agree are important (1)

veto override   the reversal of a presidential veto by a two-thirds vote in both houses of Congress (6)

Virginia Plan   a proposal at the Constitutional Convention that congressional representation be based on population, thus favoring the large states (2)

voter mobilization   a party's efforts to inform potential voters about issues and candidates and persuade them to vote (12)

wedge issue   a controversial issue that one party uses to split the voters in the other party (12)

whistle blowers   individuals who publicize instances of fraud, corruption, or other wrongdoing in the bureaucracy (8)

White House Office   the approximately five hundred employees within the Executive Office of the President who work most closely and directly with the president (7)

writ of certiorari   formal request by the U.S. Supreme Court to call up the lower court case it decides to hear on appeal (9)

References

Chapter 1

1. Karen Thomas, "'We the People' or www? For Teens, Pop Culture Tops Constitution," *USA Today,* 3 September 1998, 3D.

2. Harold D. Lasswell, *Politics: Who Gets What, When, How* (New York: McGraw-Hill, 1938).

3. Joseph A. Schumpeter, *Capitalism, Socialism, and Democracy,* 3rd ed. (New York: Harper Colophon Books, 1950), 269–296.

4. Robert A. Dahl, *Pluralist Democracy in the United States* (Chicago: Rand McNally, 1967).

5. Carole Pateman, *Participation and Democratic Theory* (New York: Cambridge University Press, 1970).

6. For an explanation of this view, see, for example, Russell L. Hanson, *The Democratic Imagination in America: Conversations with Our Past* (Princeton: Princeton University Press, 1985), 55–91; and Gordon Wood, *The Creation of the American Republic, 1776–1787* (New York: Norton, 1969).

7. E. J. Dionne, Jr., *Why Americans Hate Politics* (New York: Simon and Schuster, 1991), 354, 355.

8. *Graham v. Richardson,* 403 U.S. 532 (1971).

9. See, for instance, Nicole Cusano, "Amherst Mulls Giving Non-Citizens Right to Vote," *Boston Globe,* 26 October 1998, B1; "Casual Citizenship?" editorial, *Boston Globe,* 31 October 1998, A18.

Chapter 2

1. There are many good illustrations of this point of view. See, for example, Gordon Wood, *The Creation of the American Republic, 1776–1787* (New York: Norton, 1969); Lawrence Henry Gipson, *The Coming of the Revolution, 1763–1775* (New York: Harper Torchbooks, 1962); Bernard Bailyn, *The Ideological Origins of the American Revolution* (Cambridge,

MA: Belknap, 1967); and Jack P. Greene, ed., *The Reinterpretation of the American Revolution, 1763–1789* (New York: Harper and Row, 1968).

2. Cited in John L. Moore, *Speaking of Washington* (Washington, DC: Congressional Quarterly Press, 1993), 102–103.

3. John Locke, *Second Treatise of Government,* C. B. Macpherson, ed. (Indianapolis: Hackett, 1980), 31.

4. Donald R. Wright, *African Americans in the Colonial Era* (Arlington Heights, IL: Harlan Davidson, 1990), 122.

5. Ibid., 152.

6. Mary Beth Norton, et al., *A People and a Nation* (Boston: Houghton Mifflin, 1994), 159.

7. Robert Darcy, Susan Welch, and Janet Clark, *Women, Elections, and Representation* (Lincoln: University of Nebraska Press, 1994), 8.

8. See, for example, Sally Smith Booth, *The Women of '76* (New York: Hastings House, 1973); and Charles E. Claghorn, *Women Patriots of the American Revolution: A Biographical Dictionary* (Metuchen, NJ: Scarecrow Press, 1991).

9. Carl Holliday, *Woman's Life in Colonial Days* (Boston: Cornhill, 1922), 143.

10. Wood, 398–399.

11. Ibid., 404.

12. Alexander Hamilton, James Madison, and John Jay, *The Federalist Papers,* Clinton Rossiter, ed. (New York: New American Library, 1961), 84.

13. James Madison, *Notes of Debates in the Federal Convention of 1787* (New York: Norton, 1969), 86.

14. Baron de Montesquieu, *The Spirit of the Laws,* Thomas Nugent, trans. (New York: Hafner Press, 1949), 152.

15. There are many collections of Anti-Federalist writings. See, for example, W. B. Allen and Gordon Lloyd, eds., *The Essential Antifederalist* (Lanham, MD: University Press of America, 1985); Cecilia Kenyon, ed., *The Antifederalists* (Indianapolis: Bobbs Merrill, 1966); and

Ralph Ketcham, *The Anti-Federalist Papers and the Constitutional Convention Debates* (New York: New American Library, 1986).

16. Rossiter, "Introduction," in Hamilton, Madison, and Jay, vii.

17. Hamilton, Madison, and Jay, 322.

18. Ketcham, 14.

Chapter 3

1. For a full explanation of the bakery metaphors, see Morton Grodzins, *The American System* (Chicago: Rand McNally, 1966). A more updated discussion of federalism can be found in Joseph Zimmerman, *Contemporary American Federalism: The Growth of National Power* (New York: Praeger, 1992).

2. Thomas Bodenheimer, "The Oregon Health Plan: Lessons for the Nation (First of Two Parts)," *New England Journal of Medicine,* 337, no. 9, 28 August 1997: 651–655; "The Oregon Health Plan: Lessons for the Nation (Second of Two Parts)," *New England Journal of Medicine,* 337, no. 10, 4 September 1997: 720–723.

3. *McCulloch v. Maryland,* 4 Wheat. 316 (1819).

4. *Gibbons v. Ogden,* 9 Wheat. 1 (1824).

5. *Cooley v. Board of Wardens of Port of Philadelphia,* 53 U.S. (12 How.) 299 (1851).

6. *Dred Scott v. Sanford,* 60 U.S. 393 (1857).

7. *Pollock v. Farmer's Loan and Trust Company,* 1157 U.S. 429 (1895).

8. *Lochner v. New York,* 198 U.S. 45 (1905).

9. *Hammer v. Dagenhart,* 247 U.S. 251 (1918).

10. *Garcia v. San Antonio Metropolitan Transit Authority,* 469 U.S. 528 (1985).

11. U.S. Advisory Commission on Intergovernmental Relations, *Federal Regulation of State and Local Governments: The Mixed Record of the 1980s* (Washington, DC: Government Printing Office, July 1993), 3.

12. *United States* v. *Lopez,* 514 U.S. 549 (1995).

13. *Printz* v. *United States,* 521 U.S. 898 (1997).

14. Theodore Lowi, *The End of Liberalism* (New York: Norton, 1969).

15. Morris Fiorina, *Congress: Keystone of the Washington Establishment,* 2nd ed. (New Haven: Yale University Press, 1989); John E. Chubb, "Federalism and the Bias for Centralization," in John E. Chubb and Paul E. Peterson, eds., *The New Directions in American Politics* (Washington, DC: Brookings Institution, 1985), 273–306.

16. Harold W. Stanley and Richard G. Niemi, *Vital Statistics on American Politics,* 5th ed. (Washington DC: Congressional Quarterly Press, 1995), table 10-5, 299.

17. David Walker, *The Rebirth of Federalism* (Chatham, NJ: Chatham House, 1995), 139, 224.

18. Quote from Rochelle L. Stanfield, "Holding the Bag," *National Journal,* 9 September 1995, 2206.

19. Walker, 232–234.

20. Martha Derthick, "Madison's Middle Ground in the 1980s," *Public Administration Review,* January–February 1987, 66–74.

21. Advisory Commission on Intergovernmental Relations, *Federal Mandate Relief for State, Local, and Tribal Governments* (Washington, DC: Government Printing Office, January 1995), 18.

22. *South Dakota* v. *Dole,* 483 U.S. 203 (1987).

23. *Federal Regulation of State and Local Governments.*

24. John Maggs, "Hizzoner, the Pizza Man," *National Journal,* 21 November 1998, 2796–2798.

25. Garry Wills, "The War Between the States . . . and Washington," *New York Times Magazine,* 5 July 1998, 26. Lexis Nexis version.

Chapter 4

1. Alan Charles Kors and Harvey A. Silverglate, *The Shadow University: The Betrayal of Liberty on America's Campuses* (New York: Free Press, 1998), 9.

2. Ibid., 11.

3. Ann Bowman and Richard Kearney, *State and Local Government,* 3rd ed. (Boston: Houghton Mifflin, 1996), 39.

4. David M. O'Brien, *Constitutional Law and Politics,* vol. 2 (New York: Norton, 1995), 300.

5. *Barron* v. *The Mayor and City Council of Baltimore,* 7 Peters 243 (1833).

6. *Chicago, Burlington & Quincy Railroad Co.* v. *Chicago,* 166 U.S. 226 (1897).

7. *Gitlow* v. *New York* 268 U.S. 652 (1920), cited in David M. O'Brien, *Constitutional Law and Politics,* vol. 2 (New York: Norton, 1995), 304.

8. Peter Irons, *Brennan vs. Rehnquist: The Battle for the Constitution* (New York: Knopf, 1994), 116.

9. O'Brien, 646.

10. Irons, 137.

11. *Abington School District* v. *Schempp,* 374 U.S. 203, 83 S.Ct. 1560 (1963).

12. Cited in O'Brien, 679.

13. *Murray* v. *Curlett,* 374 U.S. 203, 83 S.Ct. 1560 (1963).

14. *Engel* v. *Vitale,* 370 U.S. 421, 82 S.Ct. 1261 (1962).

15. *Epperson* v. *Arkansas,* 393 U.S. 97 (1968).

16. *Lemon* v. *Kurtzman,* 403 U.S. 602, 91 S.Ct. 2105 (1971).

17. *Lynch* v. *Donnelly,* 465 U.S. 668 (1984); *Wallace* v. *Jaffree,* 472 U.S. 38 (1985); *Edwards* v. *Aguillard,* 482 U.S. 578 (1987); *Board of Education of Westside Community Schools* v. *Mergens,* 496 U.S. 226; *Lee* v. *Weisman,* 112 S.Ct. 2649 (1992).

18. *Cantwell* v. *Connecticut,* 310 U.S. 296 (1940).

19. *Minersville School District* v. *Gobitis,* 310 U.S. 586 (1940).

20. *West Virginia State Board of Education* v. *Barnette,* 319 U.S. 624 (1943).

21. *McGowan* v. *Maryland,* 36 U.S. 420 (year); *Two Guys from Harrison-Allentown, Inc.,* v. *McGinley,* 366 U.S. 582 (year); *Gallagher* v. *Crown Kosher Super Market of Massachusetts,* 366 U.S. 617 (year); *Braunfield* v. *Brown,* 366 U.S. 599 (1961).

22. *Sherbert* v. *Verner,* 374 U.S. 398 (1963).

23. 494 U.S. 872 (1990).

24. *City of Boerne* v. *Flores,* 521 U.S. 507 (1997).

25. John L. Sullivan, James Piereson, and George Marcus, *Political Tolerance and American Democracy* (Chicago: University of Chicago Press, 1982), 203.

26. O'Brien, 373; Samuel Walker, *In Defense of American Liberties: A History of the ACLU* (New York: Oxford University Press, 1990), 14.

27. *Schenck* v. *United States,* 249 U.S. 47 (1919); *Debs* v. *United States,* 249 U.S. 211 (1919); *Frowerk* v. *United States,* 249 U.S. 204 (1919); *Abrams* v. *United States,* 250 U.S. 616 (1919).

28. *Brandenburg* v. *Ohio,* 395 U.S. 444 (1969).

29. *United States* v. *O'Brien,* 391 U.S. 367 (1968).

30. *Tinker* v. *Des Moines,* 393 U.S. 503 (1969).

31. *Street* v. *New York,* 394 U.S. 576 (1969).

32. *Texas* v. *Johnson,* 491 U.S. 397 (1989).

33. *United States* v. *Eichman,* 110 S.Ct. 2404 (1990).

34. *National Association for the Advancement of Colored People* v. *Alabama,* 357 U.S. 449 (1958).

35. *Sheldon* v. *Tucker,* 364 U.S. 516 (1960).

36. *Heart of Atlanta Motel* v. *United States,* 379 U.S. 241 (1964).

37. *Roberts* v. *United States Jaycees,* 468 U.S. 609 (1984).

38. *Jacobellis* v. *Ohio,* 378 U.S. 476 (1964).

39. *Miller* v. *California,* 413 U.S. 15 (1973).

40. *Cohen* v. *California,* 403 U.S. 15 (1971).

41. *Chaplinsky* v. *New Hampshire,* 315 U.S. 568 (1942).

42. *Terminello* v. *Chicago,* 337 U.S. 1 (1949).

43. *Cohen* v. *California,* 403 U.S. 15 (1971).

44. *Doe* v. *University of Michigan,* 721 F.Supp. 852 (E.D. Mich. 1989); *UMW Post* v. *Board of Regents of the University of Wisconsin,* 774 F.Supp. 1163, 1167, 1179 (E.D. Wis. 1991).

45. *R.A.V.* v. *City of St. Paul,* 60 LW 4667 (1992).

46. *Near* v. *Minnesota,* 283 U.S. 697 (1930).

47. *New York Times Company* v. *United States,* 403 U.S. 670 (1971).

48. *New York Times* v. *Sullivan,* 376 U.S. 254 (1964).

49. *Sheppard* v. *Maxwell,* 385 U.S. 333 (1966).

50. *Nebraska Press Association* v. *Stuart,* 427 U.S. 539 (1976).

51. *Reno v. ACLU,* 521 U.S. 1113 (1997).

52. *United States v. Lopez,* 514 U.S. 549 (1995); *Printz v. United States,* 521 U.S. 898 (1997).

53. Robert J. Spitzer, *The Politics of Gun Control* (Chatham, NJ: Chatham House, 1995), 47, 49.

54. *United States v. Cruikshank,* 92 U.S. 542 (1876); *Presser v. Illinois,* 116 U.S. 252 (1886); *Miller v. Texas,* 153 U.S. 535 (1894); *United States v. Miller,* 307 U.S. 174 (1939).

55. *Printz v. United States.*

56. *Katz v. United States,* 389 U.S. 347 (1967).

57. *Skinner v. Railway Labor Executive Association,* 489 U.S. 602 (1989).

58. *Veronia School District v. Acton,* 515 U.S. 646 (1995).

59. *Weeks v. United States,* 232 U.S. 383 (1914).

60. *United States v. Calandra,* 414 U.S. 338 (1974).

61. *United States v. Janis,* 428 U.S. 433 (1976).

62. *Massachusetts v. Sheppard,* 468 U.S. 981 (1984); *United States v. Leon,* 468 U.S. 897 (1984); *Illinois v. Krull,* 480 U.S. 340 (1987).

63. *Dickerson v. United States,* 530 U.S. 428, 120 S.Ct. 2326; 2000 U.S. LEXIS 4305.

64. *Gideon v. Wainwright,* 372 U.S. 335 (1963).

65. *Ross v. Moffitt,* 417 U.S. 600 (1974); *Murray v. Giarratano,* 492 U.S. 1 (1989).

66. *Furman v. Georgia, Jackson v. Georgia, Branch v. Texas,* 408 U.S. 238 (1972).

67. *Gregg v. Georgia,* 428 U.S. 153 (1976); *Woodson v. North Carolina,* 428 U.S. 280 (1976); *Roberts v. Louisiana,* 428 U.S. 325 (1976).

68. *McClesky v. Kemp,* 481 U.S. 279 (1987).

69. *Griswold v. Connecticut,* 391 U.S. 145 (1965).

70. *Eisenstadt v. Baird,* 405 U.S. 438 (1972).

71. *Roe v. Wade,* 410 U.S. 113 (1973).

72. See, for example, *Webster v. Reproductive Health Services,* 492 U.S. 4090 (1989); and *Rust v. Sullivan,* 111 S.Ct. 1759 (1991).

73. *Romer v. Evans,* 517 U.S. 620 (1996).

74. *Cruzan by Cruzan v. Director, Missouri Department of Health,* 497 U.S. 261 (1990).

75. *Washington v. Glucksberg,* 521 U.S. 702 (1997); *Vacco v. Quill,* 521 U.S. 793 (1997).

Chapter 5

1. Marjorie Coeyman, "Backing Busing," *Christian Science Monitor,* 29 September 1998, B1.

2. Nat Hentoff, "Celebrating Atlanta's Dream Does Not Include Protecting Human Rights," *Bloomington Herald Times,* 22 July 1996.

3. David M. O'Brien, *Constitutional Law and Politics,* vol. 2 (New York: Norton, 1995), 1265.

4. Roberto Suro, "Felonies to Bar 1.4 Million Black Men from Voting, Study Says," *Washington Post,* Friday, 23 October 1998, A12.

5. Donald G. Nieman, *Promises to Keep: African-Americans and the Constitutional Order, 1776 to the Present* (New York: Oxford University Press, 1991), 55. Scholars are divided about Lincoln's motives in issuing the Emancipation Proclamation. Whether he genuinely desired to end slavery or merely used political means to shorten the war is hard to tell at this distance.

6. Nieman, 107.

7. *Plessy v. Ferguson,* 163 U.S. 537 (1896).

8. *Brown v. Board of Education of Topeka (I),* 347 U.S. 483 (1954).

9. *Brown v. Board of Education of Topeka (II),* 349 U.S. 294 (1955).

10. *Gayle v. Browder,* 352 U.S. 903 (1956).

11. *Heart of Atlanta Motel, Inc. v. United States,* 379 U.S. 241 (1964); *Katzenbach v. McClung,* 379 U.S. 294 (1964).

12. *Harper v. Virginia Board of Elections,* 383 U.S. 663 (1966).

13. Nieman, 179.

14. Ibid., 180.

15. *Swann v. Charlotte-Mecklenberg Board of Education,* 402 U.S. 1 (1971).

16. *Milliken v. Bradley,* 418 U.S. 717 (1974).

17. Nieman, 200.

18. *Regents of the University of California v. Bakke,* 438 U.S. 265 (1978).

19. *Patterson v. McLean Credit Union,* 491 U.S. 164 (1989).

20. *Wards Cove Packing, Inc., v. Atonio,* 490 U.S. 642 (1989).

21. *City of Richmond v. J. A. Croson,* 488 U.S. 469 (1989).

22. Jonathan D. Glater, "Racial Gap in Pay Gets a Degree Sharper, A Study Finds," *Washington Post,* 2 November 1995, 13.

23. Suzi Parker, "For Blacks, a Degree of Equality," *Christian Science Monitor,* 30 June 1998, 1, 2. Web version.

24. Voter News Service 1996 exit poll.

25. "Despite Prayers, a Navajo-Mormon Culture Clash," *New York Times,* 24 July 1996, A8.

26. Jon Magnuson, "Casino Wars: Ethics and Economics in Indian Country," *Christian Century,* 16 February 1994, 169.

27. Mark Falcoff, "Our Language Needs No Law," *New York Times,* 5 August 1996.

28. Christine Nifong, "Hispanics and Asians Change the Face of the South," *Christian Science Monitor,* 6 August 1996.

29. *Hirabayashi v. United States,* 320 U.S. 81 (1943); *Korematsu v. United States,* 323 U.S. 214 (1944).

30. http://vpf-web.harvard.edu/factbook/99-00/page7.html/; http://www.stanford.edu/dept/new/htmlstudents/html; http://osr4.berkeley.edu/public/student.data/f00.eth.

31. Lena H. Sun, "Getting Out the Ethnic Vote," *Washington Post,* 7 October 1996, B5; K. Connie Kang, "Asian Americans Slow to Flex Their Political Muscle," *Los Angeles Times,* 31 October 1996, A18.

32. Sun, B5; Kang, A18.

33. William Booth, "California Race Could Signal New Cohesion for Asian Voters," *Washington Post,* 3 November 1998, 1. Web version.

34. "Asian Americans' Political Mark," *Los Angeles Times,* 25 November 1996, B4.

35. William Booth, "California Race Could Signal New Cohesion for Asian Voters," *Washington Post,* 3 November 1998, 3 (web version); Public Policy Institute of California, http://www.ppic.org/facts/analysis.nov00.pdf.

36. Sun, B5.

37. Paul Van Slambrouck, "Asian-Americans' Politics Evolving," *Christian Science Monitor,* 8 September 1998, 2. Web version.

38. Eleanor Flexner, *Century of Struggle: The Woman's Rights Movement in the United States* (New York: Atheneum, 1973), 148–149.

39. Nancy E. McGlen and Karen O'Connor, *Women's Rights: The Struggle for Equality in the 19th and 20th Centuries* (New York: Praeger, 1983), 272–273.

40. Flexner, 296.

41. Jane Mansbridge, *Why We Lost the ERA* (Chicago: Chicago University Press, 1986), 13.

42. *Reed v. Reed,* 404 U.S. 71 (1971); *Craig v. Boren,* 429 U.S. 190 (1976).

43. Shelley Donald Coolidge, "Flat Tire on the Road to Pay Equity," *Christian Science Monitor,* 11 April 1997, 9.

44. Barbara Noble, "At Work: And Now the Sticky Floor," *New York Times,* 22 November 1992, 23.

45. Kenneth Gray, "The Gender Gap in Yearly Earnings: Can Vocational Education Help?" Office of Special Populations' Brief, University of California, Berkeley, vol. 5, no. 2.

46. *Bowers v. Hardwick,* 478 U.S. 186 (1986).

47. *Romer v. Evans,* 115 S.Ct. 1092 (1996).

48. "Gay-targeted Marketing Shows the Restaurateur Is Being Savvy," *Restaurant Business,* 20 March 1995, 46.

49. Alexandra Marks, "Efforts to Curb Gay Rights Deepen an American Divide," *Christian Science Monitor,* 23 July 1998, 2. Web version.

50. *Massachusetts Board of Retirement v. Murgia,* 427 U.S. 307 (1976).

51. Ibid.; *Vance v. Bradley,* 440 U.S. 93 (1979); *Gregory v. Ashcroft,* 501 U.S. 452 (1991).

52. Coeyman.

Chapter 6

1. Bill Turque, "The Class of '92," *Newsweek,* 29 November 1993, 9. Web version.

2. Ibid.

3. Florence King, review of *A Woman's Place: The Freshmen Women Who Changed the Face of Congress,* by Marjorie Margolies-Mezvinsky with Barbara Feinman, *The American Spectator,* June 1994, 3. Web version.

4. R. W. Apple, Jr., "The 1994 Campaign: In Pennsylvania, Feeling the Consequences of One Vote," *New York Times,* 27 September 1994, A22.

5. John R. Hibbing and Elizabeth Theiss-Morse, *Congress as Public Enemy* (New York: Cambridge University Press, 1995), chs. 2, 3.

6. Glenn R. Parker and Roger H. Davidson, "Why Do Americans Love Their Congressmen So Much More Than Their Congress?" *Legislative Studies Quarterly,* 4 (February 1979): 52–61.

7. Heinz Eulau and Paul D. Karps, "The Puzzle of Representation: Specifying Components of Responsiveness," *Legislative Studies Quarterly,* 2 (May 1977): 233–254.

8. Ross K. Baker, *House and Senate* (New York: Norton, 1989).

9. Charles Cameron, Albert Cover, and Jeffrey Segal, "Senate Voting on Supreme Court Nominations," *American Political Science Review,* 84 (June 1990): 525–534.

10. *Baker v. Carr,* 396 U.S. 186 (1962); *Westberry v. Sanders,* 376 U.S. 1 (1964).

11. Roger H. Davidson and Walter J. Oleszek, *Congress and Its Members,* 6th ed. (Washington, DC: Congressional Quarterly Press, 1997), 25.

12. Charles Cameron, David Epstein, and Sharyn O'Halloran, "Do Majority-Minority Districts Maximize Substantive Black Representation in Congress?" *American Political Science Review,* 90 (December 1996): 794–812; Kevin Hill, "Does the Creation of Majority Black Districts Aid Republicans? An Analysis of the 1992 Congressional Election in Eight Southern States," *Journal of Politics,* 57 (May 1995): 384–401.

13. Holly Idelson, "Court Takes a Hard Line on Minority Voting Blocs," *C Q Weekly Report,* 1 July 1995, 4, 5. Web version.

14. *Shaw v. Reno,* 509 U.S. 630 (1993); *Miller v. Johnson,* 115 S.Ct. 2475 (1995).

15. *Shaw v. Hunt,* 116 S.Ct. 1894 (1996); *Bush v. Vera,* 116 S.Ct. 1941 (1996).

16. Ornstein, Mann, and Malbin, *Vital Statistics on Congress, 1997–1998* (1998), tables 1-16 to 1-18; *Statistical Abstract of the United States, 1997,* tables 13 and 24.

17. Harold W. Stanley and Richard G. Niemi, *Vital Statistics on American Politics,* 5th ed. (Washington, DC: Congressional Quarterly Press, 1995).

18. Edward R. Tufte, *Political Control of the Economy* (Princeton: Princeton University Press, 1978); Robert S. Erikson, "The Puzzle of the Midterm Loss," *Journal of Politics,* 50 (November 1988): 1011–1029; Robert S. Erikson and Gerald C. Wright, "Voters, Candidates, and Issues in Congressional Elections," in Lawrence Dodd and Bruce Oppenheimer, eds., *Congress Reconsidered,* 6th ed. (Washington, DC: Congressional Quarterly Press, 1997), 132–140.

19. Glenn Parker, *Characteristics of Congress: Patterns in Congressional Behavior* (Englewood Cliffs, NJ: Prentice Hall, 1989), 17–18, ch. 9.

20. Leroy Rieselbach, *Congressional Reform in the Seventies* (Morristown, NJ: General Learning Press, 1977); Leroy Rieselbach, *Congressional Reform* (Washington, DC: Congressional Quarterly Press, 1986).

21. Ed Gillespie and Bob Schellhas, eds., *Contract with America: The Bold Plan by Rep. Newt Gingrich, Rep. Dick Armey and the House Republicans to Change the Nation* (New York: Random House, 1994); James G. Gimpel, *Legislating the Revolution* (Boston: Allyn and Bacon, 1996).

22. David S. Broder, "Nice Guy in the Hot Seat," *Washington Post,* 19 May 1999, A23; Timothy J. Burger, "Hastert Can't Cut It, Some Republicans Say," *New York Daily News,* 7 May 1999, 44.

23. *New York Times,* 13 May 1986, A24, quoted in Roger H. Davidson and Walter J. Oleszek, *Congress and Its Members,* 4th ed. (Washington, DC: Congressional Quarterly Press, 1993), 203.

24. Matthew McCubbins and Thomas Schwartz, "Congressional Oversight Overlooked: Police Patrols Versus Fire Alarms," *American Journal of Political Science,* 28 (February 1984): 165–179.

25. Barbara Sinclair, "Party Leaders and the New Legislative Process," in Lawrence Dodd and Bruce Oppenheimer, eds., *Congress Reconsidered,* 6th ed. (Washington, DC: Congressional Quarterly Press, 1997), 229–245.

26. Davidson and Oleszek, 215.

27. Steven Smith and Eric Lawrence, "Party Control of Committees in the Republican Congress," in Lawrence Dodd and Bruce Oppenheimer, eds., *Congress Reconsidered,* 6th ed. (Washington, DC:

Congressional Quarterly Press, 1997), 163–192.

28. Davidson and Oleszek, 229–231.

29. Barbara Sinclair, *The Transformation of the U.S. Senate* (Baltimore: Johns Hopkins University Press, 1989).

30. John Stewart. "A Chronology of the Civil Rights Act of 1964," in Robert Loevy, ed., *The Civil Rights Act of 1964: The Passage of the Law That Ended Racial Segregation* (Albany: SUNY Press, 1997), 358.

31. Ibid., 358–360.

32. Clifford Krauss, "Clinton's Woes on Capitol Hill Spur Sharp Criticism of His Top Lobbyist," *New York Times,* 25 May 1993, A20, quoted in Davidson and Oleszek, 246.

33. Richard S. Dunham, "Power to the President—Courtesy of the GOP," *Business Week,* 20 October 1997, 51.

34. Donald R. Matthews and James A. Stimson, *Yeas and Nays* (New York: Wiley, 1975).

35. Richard Smith, "Interest Group Influence in the U.S. Congress," *Legislative Studies Quarterly,* 20 (February 1995): 89–140.

36. Parker and Davidson; Richard F. Fenno, Jr., "If, as Ralph Nader Says, Congress Is 'the Broken Branch,' How Come We Love Our Congressmen So Much?" in Norman J. Ornstein, ed., *Congress in Change* (New York: Praeger, 1975), 277–287.

37. Hibbing and Theiss-Morse.

38. John R. Hibbing and Elizabeth Theiss-Morse, "Civics Is Not Enough: Teaching Barbarics in K–12," *Political Science & Politics,* 29 (1996): 157.

39. Turque, 11.

40. Apple, 1.

Chapter 7

1. Bruce Miroff, "Monopolizing the Public Space: The President as a Problem for Democratic Politics," in Bruce Miroff, Raymond Seidelman, and Todd Swanstrom, eds., *Debating Democracy* (Boston: Houghton Mifflin, 1997), 294–303.

2. James P. Pfiffner, *The Modern Presidency* (New York: St. Martin's Press, 1994), ch. 1; Jeffrey K. Tulis, "The Two Constitutional Presidencies," in Michael Nelson, ed., *The Presidency and the Political System* (Washington, DC: Congressional Quarterly Press, 1995), 91–123.

3. D. Roderick Kiewiet and Matthew D. McCubbins, "Presidential Influence on Congressional Appropriations Decisions," *American Journal of Political Science,* 32 (August 1988): 713–736.

4. Charles C. Moskos and John Sibley Butler, *All That We Can Be: Black Leadership and Racial Integration the Army Way* (New York: Basic Books, 1996), 30.

5. Gerald Boyd, "White House Hunts for a Justice, Hoping to Tip Ideological Scales," *New York Times,* June 30, 1987, sec. 1, p. 1; Alan I. Abramowitz and Jeffrey A. Segal, *Senate Elections* (Ann Arbor: University of Michigan Press, 1992), 1–6.

6. David Plotz, "Advise and Consent (Also, Obstruct, Delay, and Stymie): What's Still Wrong with the Appointments Process," Slate, 19 March 1999 (<http:// *www.slate.com/StrangeBedfellow/99-03-19/StrangeBedfellow.asp*>).

7. *In re Neagle,* 135 U.S. 546 (1890); *In re Debs,* 158 U.S. 564 (1895); *United States v. Curtiss-Wright Export Corp.,* 299 U.S. 304, 57 S.Ct. 216 (1936); *Youngstown Sheet & Tube v. Sawyer,* 343 U.S. 579 (1952).

8. Lyn Ragsdale, *Presidential Politics* (Boston: Houghton Mifflin, 1993), 55.

9. *Historical Statistics of the United States: Colonial Times to 1970* (Washington, DC: Government Printing Office, 1975).

10. *Inaugural Addresses of the United States* (Washington, DC: Government Printing Office, 1982), quoted in Ragsdale, 71.

11. Jeffrey Tulis, *The Rhetorical Presidency* (Princeton: Princeton University Press, 1987).

12. Richard E. Neustadt, *Presidential Power and the Modern Presidents* (New York: Free Press, 1990), 10.

13. Samuel Kernell, *Going Public: New Strategies of Presidential Leadership,* 2nd ed. (Washington, DC: Congressional Quarterly Press, 1996).

14. Barbara Hinckley, *The Symbolic Presidency* (London: Routledge, 1990), ch. 2.

15. See Hedrick Smith, *The Power Game: How Washington Works* (New York: Random House, 1988), 405–406, for similar reports on the Nixon and Reagan administrations.

16. Lee Sigelman, "Gauging the Public Response to Presidential Leadership," *Presidential Studies Quarterly,* 10 (Summer 1980): 427–433; James A. Stimson, "Public Support for American Presidents: A Cyclical Model," *Public Opinion Quarterly,* 40 (Spring 1976): 1–21; Michael MacKuen, "Political Drama, Economic Conditions, and the Dynamics of Presidential Popularity," *American Journal of Political Science,* 27 (February 1983): 165–192.

17. Gerald Pomper, "The Presidential Election," in Gerald Pomper, ed., *The Election of 1992* (Chatham, NJ: Chatham House, 1993), 144–150; Richard L. Berke, "Poll Finds Most Give Clinton Credit for Strong Economy," *New York Times,* 6 September 1996, A1.

18. John E. Mueller, *Policy and Opinion in the Gulf War* (Chicago: University of Chicago Press, 1994).

19. John R. Hibbing and Elizabeth Theiss-Morse, *Congress as Public Enemy* (New York: Cambridge University Press, 1995), demonstrates the public intolerance for controversy in Congress; the same reaction is undoubtedly true for the presidency.

20. Paul Brace and Barbara Hinckley, *Follow the Leader: Opinion Polls and the Modern Presidents* (New York: Basic Books, 1992), chs. 4, 5.

21. Ibid., ch. 6.

22. Neustadt, 50–72.

23. James L. Sundquist, "Needed: A Political Theory for a New Era of Coalition Government in the United States," *Political Science Quarterly,* 103 (Winter 1988–1989): 613–635.

24. *CQ Weekly Report,* 21 December 1996, 3455.

25. David Mayhew, *Divided We Govern: Party Control, Lawmaking, and Investigations, 1946–1990* (New Haven: Yale University Press, 1991).

26. The President's Committee on Administrative Management, *Report of the Committee* (Washington, DC: Government Printing Office, 1937).

27. Pfiffner, 91.

28. Harold Relyea, "Growth and Development of the President's Office," in David Kozak and Kenneth Ciboski, *The American Presidency* (Chicago: Nelson Hall, 1985), 135; Pfiffner, 122.

29. Sid Frank and Arden Davis Melick, *The Presidents: Tidbits and Trivia* (Maplewood, NJ: Hammond, 1986), 103.

30. Timothy Walch, ed., *At the President's Side: The Vice-Presidency in the Twentieth Century* (Columbia: University of Missouri Press, 1997), 45.

31. Barbara Bush, *Barbara Bush: A Memoir* (New York: Charles Scribner's Sons, 1994).

32. *USA Today*, "Laura Bush Ties Her Speech to Kids, Points Out Education as Her Issue," 1 August 2000, p. 59.

33. James MacGregor Burns, "Our Super-Government—Can We Control It?" *New York Times*, 24 April 1949, 32.

34. Robert K. Murray and Tim H. Blessing, "The Presidential Performance Study: A Progress Report," *Journal of American History*, 70 (December 1983): 535–555.

35. James David Barber, *The Presidential Character*, 4th ed. (Englewood Cliffs, NJ: Prentice Hall, 1992).

36. See Michael Nelson, "James David Barber and the Psychological Presidency," in David Pederson, ed., *The "Barberian" Presidency: Theoretical and Empirical Readings* (New York: Peter Lang, 1989), 93–110; Alexander George, "Assessing Presidential Character," *World Politics*, January 1974, 234–283; Jeffrey Tulis, "On Presidential Character," in Jeffrey Tulis and Joseph Bessette, eds., *Presidency and the Constitutional Order* (Baton Rouge: Louisiana State University Press, 1981).

37. Alexander Hamilton, James Madison, and John Jay, *The Federalist Papers*, Clinton Rossiter, ed. (New York: New American Library, 1961), 84.

Chapter 8

1. "Organic Standards Regrown: New USDA Guidelines," *Better Homes and Gardens*, August 1998, 80.

2. Dann Denny, "Defining 'Organic,'" *Bloomington Herald Times*, 16 April 1998, D1.

3. Marian Burros, "Eating Well: U.S. Proposal on Organic Food Gets a Grass-Roots Review," *New York Times*, 25 March 1998, F10.

4. Gene Kahn, "National Organic Standard Will Aid Consumers," *Frozen Food Age*, September 1998, 18.

5. Burros, 10.

6. H. H. Gerth and C. Wright Mills, eds., *From Max Weber* (New York: Oxford University Press, 1946), 196–199.

7. Herbert Kaufman, "Emerging Conflicts in the Doctrines of Public Administration," *American Political Science Review*, 50 (December 1956): 1057–1073.

8. Morris P. Fiorina, *Congress: Keystone of the Washington Establishment* (New Haven: Yale University Press, 1977).

9. *Federal Civilian Workforce Statistics: Employment and Trends as of July 1994* (Washington, DC: U.S. Office of Personnel Management, March 31, 1994), table 2.

10. Kenneth J. Meier, *Politics and the Bureaucracy: Policymaking in the Fourth Branch of Government* (Pacific Grove, CA: Brooks/Cole, 1993), 18.

11. Ibid., 18–24.

12. David Nachmias and David H. Rosenbloom, *Bureaucratic Government: USA* (New York: St. Martin's Press, 1980).

13. Dennis D. Riley, *Controlling the Federal Bureaucracy* (Philadelphia: Temple University Press, 1987), 139–142.

14. Meier, 84–85.

15. *U.S. News and World Report*, 11 February 1980, 64.

16. Meier, 205–208.

17. Malcolm McConnell, *Challenger: A Major Malfunction* (Garden City, NY: Doubleday, 1987), 187, cited in James Q. Wilson, *Bureaucracy* (New York: Basic Books, 1989), 62, 104.

18. Richard J. Stillman II, *The American Bureaucracy* (Chicago: Nelson-Hall, 1987).

19. Eugene B. MacGregor, "Politics and Career Mobility of Civil Servants," *American Political Science Review*, 68 (March 1974): 22–24.

20. Francis E. Rourke, *Bureaucracy, Politics and Public Policy*, 3rd ed. (Boston: Little, Brown, 1984), 106.

21. Albert B. Crenshaw, "Cash Flow," *Washington Post*, 28 June 1998, H1.

22. Anthony E. Brown, *The Politics of Airline Regulation* (Knoxville: University of Tennessee Press, 1987).

23. Riley, ch. 2.

24. Harold Seidman and Robert Gilmour, *Politics, Position, and Power: From the Positive to the Regulatory State*, 4th ed. (New York: Oxford University Press, 1986), 3.

25. Elaine Kamarck, *Insight on the News*, 15 June 1998, 1, 3. Web version.

26. Quoted in Riley, 43.

27. Hugh Heclo, "Issue Networks and the Executive Establishment," in Anthony King, ed., *The New American Political System* (Washington, DC: American Enterprise Institute, 1978), 87–124.

28. Matthew Crenson and Francis E. Rourke, "By Way of Conclusion: American Bureaucracy Since World War II," in Louis Galambois, ed., *The New American State: Bureaucracies and Policies Since World War II* (Baltimore: Johns Hopkins University Press, 1987), 137–177.

Chapter 9

1. *A.L.A. Schechter Poultry Corp.* v. *United States*, 295 U.S. 495 (1935).

2. Walter F. Murray and C. Herman Pritchett, *Courts, Judges, and Politics*, 4th ed. (New York: Random House, 1986), 311–312.

3. This list is based loosely on the discussion of the functions of law in James V. Calvi and Susan Coleman, *American Law and Legal Systems* (Upper Saddle River, NJ: Prentice Hall, 1997), 2–4; Steven Vago, *Law and Society* (Upper Saddle River, NJ: Prentice Hall, 1997), 16–20; and Lawrence Baum, *American Courts*, 4th ed. (Boston: Houghton Mifflin, 1998), 4–5.

4. Alexander Hamilton, James Madison, and John Jay, *The Federalist Papers*, Clinton Rossiter, ed. (New York: New American Library, 1961), 84.

5. *Marbury* v. *Madison*, 5 U.S. (1 Cranch) 137 (1803).

6. *Dred Scott* v. *Sanford*, 60 U.S. 393 (1857).

7. Baum, 22–24.

8. Joan Biskupic, "Making a Mark on the Bench," *Washington Post National Weekly Edition*, 2–8 December 1996, 31.

9. Ibid.

10. Ibid.

11. Robert Marquand, "Why America Puts Its Supreme Court on a Lofty Pedestal," *Christian Science Monitor*, 25 June 1997, 1, 4.

12. Although there is no official "list" of criteria a president considers, scholars are mostly agreed on these factors. See, for instance, Henry J. Abraham, *The Judiciary* (New York: New York University Press, 1996), 65–69; Baum, 105–106; Philip

Cooper and Howard Ball, *The United States Supreme Court: From the Inside Out* (Upper Saddle River, NJ: Prentice Hall, 1996), 49–60; and Thomas G. Walker and Lee Epstein, *The Supreme Court of the United States* (New York: St. Martin's Press, 1993), 34–40.

13. Baum, 105.

14. From *This Honorable Court* (Washington, DC: Greater Washington Educational Telecommunications Association, 1988, program 1), filmstrip.

15. Ibid.

16. Baum, 105.

17. Walker and Epstein, 40.

18. Cooper and Ball, 102.

19. Ibid., 120.

20. Ibid., 104.

21. Walker and Epstein, 90.

22. Ibid., 129–130.

23. Ibid., 126–130.

24. What follows is drawn from the excellent discussion in Walker and Epstein, 131–139.

25. Ibid., 134.

26. *Webster v. Reproductive Services*, 492 U.S. 490 (1989).

27. Philip J. Cooper, *Battles on the Bench: Conflict Inside the Supreme Court* (Lawrence: University Press of Kansas, 1995), 42–46.

28. For a provocative argument that the Court does not, in fact, successfully produce significant social reform and actually damaged the civil rights struggles in this country, see Gerald N. Rosenberg, *The Hollow Hope: Can Courts Bring About Social Change?* (Chicago: University of Chicago Press, 1991).

29. *Marbury v. Madison* (1803).

30. *Martin v. Hunter's Lessee* (1816).

31. *McCulloch v. Maryland* (1819).

32. *Gibbons v. Ogden* (1824).

33. *Lochner v. New York* (1905).

34. *Hammer v. Dagenhart* (1918).

35. *Adkins v. Children's Hospital* (1923).

36. *Dred Scott v. Sanford* (1857).

37. *Plessy v. Ferguson* (1896).

38. *Brown v. Board of Education* (1954).

39. For example, *Mapp v. Ohio* (1961), *Gideon v. Wainwright* (1963), and *Miranda v. Arizona* (1965).

40. *Baker v. Carr* (1962).

41. *Roe v. Wade* (1973).

42. Maria Puente, "Poll: Blacks' Confidence in Police Plummets," *USA Today*,

21 March 1995, 3A; "One Verdict, Clashing Voices," *Newsweek*, 16 October 1995, 46; Michael Tonry, "Racial Politics, Racial Disparities, and the War on Crime," *Crime and Delinquency*, 40, no. 4 (1994): 475–494.

43. John H. Langbein, "Money Talks, Clients Walk," *Newsweek*, 17 April 1995, 32.

Chapter 10

1. Mike Gravel, "Philadelphia II: National Initiatives," *Campaigns and Elections*, December 1995/January 1996, 25.

2. According to a September 1994 Roper poll, 76 percent favor a national referendum.

3. Adam Nagourney, "Behind Impeachment," *New York Times*, 20 December 1999, 1. Web version.

4. V. O. Key, Jr., *Public Opinion and American Democracy* (New York: Knopf, 1961), 7.

5. John Kingdon, *Congressmen's Voting Decisions*, 2nd ed. (New York: Harper and Row, 1981), ch. 2.

6. This used to be called Voter Research and Surveys and in 1998 included the following member organizations—all of which make use of the exit poll data in their election coverage: CBS News/*New York Times*; NBC News/*Wall Street Journal*; ABC News/*Washington Post*; CNN/*USA Today*.

7. "Pollsters Seek AAPC Action," *Campaigns and Elections*, July 1996, 55.

8. Robert S. Erikson and Kent Tedin, *American Public Opinion*, 5th ed. (Boston: Allyn and Bacon, 1995), 42–47.

9. Many works repeat this theme of the uninformed and ignorant citizen. See, for example, Bernard Berelson, Paul F. Lazarsfeld, and William N. McPhee, *Voting* (Chicago: University of Chicago Press, 1954); Angus Campbell, Philip E. Converse, Warren E. Miller, and Donald E. Stokes, *The American Voter* (New York: Wiley, 1960); W. Russell Neuman, *The Paradox of Mass Politics* (Cambridge, MA: Harvard University Press, 1986); and Michael X. Delli Carpini and Scott Keeter, *What Americans Know About Politics and Why It Matters* (New Haven: Yale University Press, 1996).

10. These data come from Carpini and Keeter, 70–75.

11. The changes in ideological self-identification are based on the collected CBS News/*New York Times* polls. Results calculated by the authors.

12. 1996 National Election Studies codebook.

13. Philip Converse, "The Nature of Belief Systems in Mass Publics," in David Apter, ed., *Ideology and Discontent* (Glencoe, IL: Free Press, 1964); Erikson and Tedin, 74–77.

14. Herbert McClosky and Alida Brill, *Dimensions of Tolerance* (New York: Russell Sage Foundation, 1983), 250.

15. Ibid., 250.

16. Sidney Verba, Norman Nie, and J. O. Kim, *Modes of Democratic Participation* (Beverly Hills, CA: Sage, 1971); Russell Dalton, *Citizen Politics*, 2nd ed. (Chatham, NJ: Chatham House, 1996), 57–58; Raymond Wolfinger and Steven Rosenstone, *Who Votes?* (New Haven: Yale University Press, 1980).

17. M. Kent Jennings and Richard G. Niemi, *The Political Character of Adolescence* (Princeton: Princeton University Press, 1974); Robert C. Luskin, John P. McIver, and Edward Carmines, "Issues and the Transmission of Partisanship," *American Journal of Political Science*, 33 (May 1989): 440–458; Erikson and Tedin, 127–128.

18. Jennings and Niemi, 41.

19. Shirley Engle and Anna Ochoa, *Education for Democratic Citizenship: Decision Making in the Social Studies* (New York: Teacher's College of Columbia University, 1988).

20. Robert Huckfeldt, Eric Plutzer, and John Sprague, "Alternative Contexts of Political Behavior: Churches, Neighborhoods, and Individuals," *Journal of Politics*, 55 (May 1993): 365; Ted G. Jelen, "Political Christianity: A Contextual Analysis," *American Journal of Political Science*, 36 (August 1992): 692; Kenneth D. Wald, Dennis E. Owen, and Samuel S. Hill, Jr., "Political Cohesion in Churches," *Journal of Politics*, 52 (February 1990): 197.

21. Paul R. Abramson and Ada W. Finifter, "On the Meaning of Political Trust: New Evidence from Items Introduced in 1978," *American Journal of Political Science*, 25 (May 1981): 295–306; Arthur H. Miller, "Political Issues and

Trust in Government," *American Political Science Review,* 68 (September 1974): 944–961.

22. Norman H. Nie, Jane Junn, and Kenneth Stehlik-Barry, *Education and Democratic Citizenship in America* (Chicago: University of Chicago Press, 1996).

23. For more on the effects of education, see Delli Carpini and Keeter, 188–189; and Herbert H. Hyman, Charles R. Wright, and John Shelton Reed, *The Enduring Effects of Education* (Chicago: University of Chicago Press, 1975). But for a dissenting view that formal education is just a mask for intelligence and native cognitive ability, see Robert Luskin, "Explaining Political Sophistication," *Political Behavior,* 12 (1990): 3298–3409.

24. Christine L. Day, *What Older Americans Think: Interest Groups and Aging Policy* (Princeton: Princeton University Press, 1990).

25. Erikson and Tedin, 208–212.

26. Based on the 1996 Voter News Service election day exit polls.

27. Lee Sigelman and Susan Welch, *Black Americans' Views of Racial Equality— The Dream Deferred* (Cambridge, UK: Cambridge University Press, 1991).

28. Katherine Tate, "Black Political Participation in the 1984 and 1988 Presidential Elections," *American Political Science Review,* 85 (December 1991): 1159–1176.

29. Robert S. Erikson, Gerald C. Wright, and John P. McIver, *Statehouse Democracy* (New York: Cambridge University Press, 1993), 18.

30. Milton Lodge, Kathleen McGraw, and Patrick Stroh, "An Impression-Driven Model of Candidate Evaluation," *American Political Science Review,* 82 (June 1989): 399–419.

31. Bernard R. Berelson, Paul F. Lazarsfeld, and William N. McPhee, *Voting: A Study of Opinion Formation in a Presidential Campaign* (Chicago: University of Chicago Press, 1954), 109–115.

32. Gerald C. Wright, "Level of Analysis Effects on Explanations of Voting," *British Journal of Political Science,* 18 (July 1989): 381–398; Samuel Popkin, *The Reasoning Voter* (Chicago: University of Chicago Press, 1991); Benjamin Page and Robert Shapiro, *The Rational Public* (Chicago: University of Chicago Press, 1993).

33. Erikson, Wright, and McIver.

34. Michael B. MacKuen, Robert S. Erikson, and James A. Stimson, "Macropartisanship," *American Political Science Review,* 89 (December 1989): 1125–1142.

35. Jean Bethke Elshtain, "A Parody of True Democracy," *Christian Science Monitor,* 13 August 1992, 18.

Chapter 11

1. Censure and Move On, news release, 15 October 1998 (http://www.moveon.org).

2. Katharine Q. Seelye, "Public Is Flooding Capitol with Impeachment Views," New York Times on the Web, 15 December 1998, 2.

3. "We Will Remember," Censure and Move On, 22 December 1998 (http://www.moveon.org/pledge.htm).

4. Chris Carr, "On-Line Call Against Impeachment Is on Fire; $13 Million Pledged to Grass-Roots Campaign Urging Senate to Censure, 'Move On,'" *Washington Post,* 1 February 1999, A10.

5. Censure and Move On, news release, 15 October 1998 (http://www.moveon.org).

6. See, for example, Jame Bryce, *The American Commonwealth,* vol. 2 (Chicago: Sergel, 1891), pt. 3.

7. E. E. Schattschneider, *Party Government* (New York: Holt, Rinehart and Winston, 1942), 1.

8. This definition and the following discussion are based on Frank Sorauf, *Party Politics in America* (Boston: Little, Brown, 1964), ch. 1; and V. O. Key, *Politics, Parties, and Pressure Groups,* 5th ed. (New York: Corwell, 1964).

9. The discussion of national conventions is based on David Price, *Bring Back the Parties* (Washington, DC: Congressional Quarterly Press, 1984), chs. 6 and 7; and Leon D. Epstein, *Political Parties in the American Mold* (Madison: University of Wisconsin Press, 1986), ch. 4.

10. C. P. Cotter, J. L. Gibson, J. F. Bibby, and R. J. Huckshorn, *Party Organizations in American Politics* (New York: Praeger, 1984); John J. Coleman, "Resurgent or Just Busy? Party Organizations in Contemporary America," in John Green and Daniel Shea, eds., *The State of the Parties,* 2nd ed. (Lanham, MD: Rowman and Littlefield, 1996), ch. 2.

11. Gerald Pomper with Susan Lederman, *Elections in America,* 2nd ed. (New York: Longman, 1980), 145–150, 167–173.

12. Richard G. Niemi and M. Kent Jennings, "Issues of Inheritance in the Formation of Party Identification," *American Journal of Political Science,* 35 (November 1991): 970–988.

13. The discussion of the responsible party model is based on Austin Ranney, *The Doctrine of the Responsible Party Government* (Urbana: University of Illinois Press, 1962), chs. 1 and 2; Frank J. Sorauf and Paul Allen Beck, *Party Politics in America,* 6th ed. (Glenview, IL: Scott, Foresman, 1988), ch. 16.

14. Morris P. Fiorina, "The Decline of Collective Responsibility in American Politics," *Daedalus,* 109 (Summer 1980): 25–45; John H. Aldrich, *Why Parties: The Origin and Transformation of Party Politics in America* (Chicago: University of Chicago Press, 1995), 3.

15. Sorauf and Beck, 454.

16. Aldrich, 69.

17. This discussion of the Jacksonian Democrats and machine politics and patronage is based on Aldrich, ch. 4; Epstein, 134–143; and Sorauf and Beck, 83–91.

18. William H. Flanigan and Nancy H. Zingale, *Political Behavior of the American Electorate,* 9th ed. (Washington, DC: Congressional Quarterly Press, 1998), 59–66.

19. Anthony Downs, *An Economic Theory of Democracy* (New York: Harper and Row, 1957).

20. James L. Gibson and Susan E. Scarrow, "State Organizations in American Politics," in Eric M. Uslaner, ed., *American Political Parties: A Reader* (Itasca, IL: Peacock, 1993), 234.

21. James Q. Wilson, *The Amateur Democrat: Club Politics in Three Cities* (Chicago: University of Chicago Press, 1965).

22. Gerald C. Wright and Michael B. Berkman, "Candidates and Policy in U.S. Senatorial Elections," *American Political Science Review,* 80 (June 1986): 576–590.

23. This section is based on Alan Ware, *Political Parties and Party Systems* (Oxford, UK: Oxford University Press, 1996).

24. L. Sandy Maisel, *Parties and Elections in America,* 2nd ed. (New York: McGraw-Hill, 1993), ch 10; Price, 284.

25. Alexis de Tocqueville, *Democracy in America,* Richard D. Heffner, ed. (New York: New American Library, 1956), 198.

26. This definition is based on Jeffrey M. Berry, *The Interest Group Society,* 3rd ed. (New York: Longman, 1997); and David Truman, *The Governmental Process,* 2nd ed. (New York: Knopf, 1971).

27. Berry, 6–8; John W. Kingdon, *Agendas, Alternatives, and Public Policy* (Boston: Little, Brown, 1984).

28. Kingdon.

29. Mancur Olson, Jr., *The Logic of Collective Action* (New York: Schocken, 1971).

30. The idea of selective incentives is Mancur Olson's (1971, 51). This discussion comes from the work of Peter B. Clark and James Q. Wilson, "Incentive Systems: A Theory of Organizations," *Administrative Science Quarterly,* 6 (1961): 129–166, as interpreted in Robert H. Salisbury, "An Exchange Theory of Interest Groups," *Midwest Journal of Political Science,* 13 (February 1969): 1–32. Clark and Wilson use the terms "material, solidary, and purposive" benefits, while Salisbury prefers "material, solidary, and expressive." We follow Salisbury's interpretation and usage here.

31. Allan J. Cigler and Anthony J. Nowns, "Public Interest Entrepreneurs and Group Patrons," in Allan J. Cigler and Burdett A. Loomis, eds., *Interest Group Politics,* 4th ed. (Washington, DC: Congressional Quarterly Press, 1995), 77–78.

32. Pamela Fessler, "Ethics Standards Announced," *Congressional Quarterly Weekly Report,* 50, no. 49, 12 December 1992, 3792; Allison Mitchell, "A New Form of Lobbying Puts Public Face on Private Interests," New York Times on the Web, 30 September 1998.

33. Beverly A. Cigler, "Not Just Another Special Interest: Intergovernmental Representation," in Allan J. Cigler and Burdett A. Loomis, eds., *Interest Group Politics,* 4th ed. (Washington, DC: Congressional Quarterly Press, 1995), 134–135.

34. William Safire, *Safire's New Political Dictionary* (New York: Random House, 1993), 417–418.

35. See Diana M. Evans, "Lobbying the Committee: Interest Groups and the House Public Works and Transportation Committee," in Allan J. Cigler and Burdett A. Loomis, eds., *Interest Group Politics,* 3rd ed. (Washington, DC: Congressional Quarterly Press, 1991), 264–265. For a graphic example of this practice, see Michael Weisskopf and David Maraniss, "Forging an Alliance for Deregulation; Rep. DeLay Makes Companies Full Partners in the Movement," *Washington Post,* 12 March 1995, A1.

36. Adam Clymer, "Congress Passes Bill to Disclose Lobbyists' Roles," *New York Times,* 30 November 1995, 1.

37. Adam Clymer, "Senate, 98–0, Sets Tough Restriction on Lobbyist Gifts," *New York Times,* 29 July 1995, 1; "House Approves Rule to Prohibit Lobbyists' Gifts," *New York Times,* 17 November 1995, 1.

38. David S. Cloud, "Three-Month-Old Gift Ban Having Ripple Effect," *Congressional Quarterly,* 23 March 1996, 777–778.

39. See Douglas Yates, *Bureaucratic Democracy* (Cambridge, MA: Harvard University Press, 1982), ch. 4.

40. Samuel Kernell, *Going Public: New Strategies of Presidential Leadership* (Washington, DC: Congressional Quarterly Press, 1986), 34.

41. Berry, 121–122.

42. Susan Dodge and Becky Beaupre, "Internet Blamed in Spread of Hate," *Chicago Sun-Times,* 6 July 1999, 3; Jennifer Oldham, "Wiesenthal Center Compiles List of Hate-Based Web Sites," *Los Angeles Times,* 18 December 1999, A1; Victor Volland, "Group Warns of Hate on Internet," *St. Louis Post-Dispatch,* 22 October 1997, 8A; Becky Beaupre, "Internet Pumps Up the Volume of Hatred," *USA Today,* 18 February 1997, 6A.

43. Jill Abramson, "The Business of Persuasion Thrives in Nation's Capital," New York Times on the Web, 29 September 1998.

44. Robert Pear, "Getting Even with Harry and Louise, Or, Republicans Get a Taste of Their Own Medicine," *New York Times,* 10 July 1994, sect. 4, p. 2.

45. Mike Murphy, quoted in Alison Mitchell, "A New Form of Lobbying Puts Public Face on Private Interest," *New York Times,* 30 September 1998, A1.

46. Bill McAllister, "Rainmakers Making a Splash," *Washington Post,* 4 December 1997, A21.

47. Federal Elections Commission, "18-Month Summary on Political Action Committees," 27 September 2000 (web version), http://www.fec.gov/press/pac1800 text.htm .

48. Federal Elections Commission, "PAC Activity Increases in 1995–96 Election Cycle," 23 January 1996.

49. Harold Stanley and Richard G. Niemi, eds., *Vital Statistics on Congress, 1995–1996* (Washington, DC: Congressional Quarterly Press, 1996).

50. Andrew Bard Schmookler, "When Money Talks, Is It Free Speech?" *Christian Science Monitor,* 11 November 1997, 15; Nelson W. Polsby, "Money Gains Access. So What?" *New York Times,* 13 August 1997, A19.

51. Sara Fritz, "Citizen Lobby's Call to Arms," *International Herald-Tribune,* 4–5 January 1997; Katharine Q. Seelye, "G.O.P.'s Reward for Top Donors: 3 Days with Party Leaders," *New York Times,* 20 February 1997, A6.

52. Leslie Wayne, "Lobbyists' Gifts to Politicians Reap Benefits, Study Shows," *New York Times,* 23 January 1997.

53. See John R. Wright, *Interest Groups and Congress* (Boston: Allyn and Bacon, 1996), 136–145; "Contributions, Lobbying, and Committee Voting in the U.S. House of Representatives," *American Political Science Review,* 84 (June 1990): 417–438; Richard L. Hall and Frank W. Wayman, "Buying Time: Money Interests and the Mobilization of Bias in Congressional Committees," *American Political Science Review,* 84 (September 1990): 797–820.

54. Robert Salisbury, "An Exchange Theory of Interest Groups," *Midwest Journal of Political Science,* 13 (1969): 1–32.

55. A. Lee Fritscheler and James M. Hoefler, *Smoking and Politics,* 5th ed. (Upper Saddle River, NJ: Prentice Hall, 1996), 20–35.

56. Truman, 519.

57. See C. Wright Mills, *The Power Elite* (New York: Oxford University Press, 1956); G. William Domhoff, *The Powers That Be* (New York: Vintage, 1979).

58. The problem is that there are a relatively small number of groups with large memberships. Labor unions, some environmental groups like the Sierra Club, some social movements revolving around

abortion and women's rights, and the National Rifle Association (NRA) currently have large memberships spread across a number of congressional districts.

59. Melissa Healy, "Grass-Roots Organizing Effort Gets a Big Boost from Internet," *Los Angeles Times,* 13 January 1999, A15.

60. Dodge and Beaupre, 3; Oldham, A1; Volland, 8A; Beaupre, 6A.

Chapter 12

1. Gerald Pomper, *Elections in America* (New York: Dodd, Mead, 1970), 1.

2. Steven J. Rosenstone and John Mark Hansen, *Mobilization, Participation, and Democracy in America* (New York: Macmillan, 1993); Ruy A. Teixeira, *The Disappearing American Voter* (Washington, DC: Brookings Institution, 1992); Raymond E. Wolfinger and Steven J. Rosenstone, *Who Votes?* (New Haven: Yale University Press, 1980); Richard J. Timpone, "Structure, Behavior, and Voter Turnout in the United States," *American Political Science Review,* 92 (March 1998): 145–158.

3. Cumulative National Election Studies, 1996. These figures are for the 1992 and 1996 elections combined. Note that in surveys such as this, "reported turnout" always runs higher than actual turnout for two reasons: the homeless and institutionalized are not sampled and seldom vote, and some nonvoters give what they see as the socially desirable response and say they voted.

4. Calculated by the authors for the 1992 and 1996 elections using the Cumulative National Election Studies, 1996 data file.

5. Richard Brody, "The Puzzle of Political Participation in America," in Anthony King, *The New American Political System* (Washington, DC: American Enterprise Institute, 1978), 287–324.

6. "Report on the 1996 Survey of American Political Culture," *The Public Perspective,* 8 (February/March 1997): 12.

7. Stephen Knack, "Drivers Wanted: Motor Voter and the Election of 1996," paper, School of Public Affairs, American University, n.d.

8. Mark N. Franklin, "Electoral Participation," in Laurence LeDuc, Richard G. Niemi, and Pippa Norris, eds., *Comparing Democracies: Elections and Voting in Global Perspective* (Thousand Oaks, CA: Sage, 1996), 226–230.

9. "Getting Voters to Vote," *USA Today,* 4 December 1998, 1A.

10. The Oregon analysis is by Michael Traugott and Robert Mason and is reported in David Broder, "What Works," *Washington Post Magazine,* 11 October 1998, W9. The general analysis is reported in Franklin.

11. Teixeira, ch. 2; Paul R. Abramson, John H. Aldrich, and David W. Rohde, *Change and Continuity in the 1998 Elections* (Washington, DC: Congressional Quarterly Press, 1999).

12. Paul Herrnson, *Congressional Elections,* 2nd ed. (Washington, DC: Congressional Quarterly Press, 1998).

13. Rosenstone and Hansen.

14. Teixeira, 36–50; Robert Putnam, "Bowling Alone: America's Declining Social Capital," *Current,* June 1995, 3–32.

15. Warren E. Miller and Merrill J. Shanks, *The New American Voter* (Cambridge, MA: Harvard University Press, 1996); Kevin Chen, *Political Alienation and Voting Turnout in the United States, 1969–1988* (Pittsburgh: Mellon Research University Press, 1992).

16. John Petrocik, "Voter Turnout and Electoral Preference: The Anomalous Reagan Elections," in Kay Lehman Schlozman, ed., *Election in America* (Boston: Allyn and Unwin, 1987), 239–260.

17. Petrocik, 243–251; Stephen Earl Bennett and David Resnick, "The Implications of Nonvoting for Democracy in the United States," *American Journal of Political Science,* 34 (August 1990): 795.

18. V. O. Key, Jr., *The Responsible Electorate: Rationality in Presidential Voting, 1936–1960* (Cambridge, MA: Harvard University Press, 1966).

19. Miller and Shanks.

20. Anthony Downs, *An Economic Theory of Democracy* (New York: Harper and Row, 1957).

21. Edward Carmines and James Stimson, "Two Faces of Issue Voting," *American Political Science Review,* 74 (March 1980): 78–91.

22. James Fallows, "Why Americans Hate the Media," *Atlantic Monthly,* February 1996, 45–64.

23. Morris P. Fiorina, *Retrospective Voting in American National Elections* (New Haven: Yale University Press, 1981).

24. "The Candidates' Confrontation: Excerpts from the Debate," *Washington Post,* 30 October 1980, A14.

25. T. Christian Miller, "Despite the Fuss, Majority of Iowans Avoid Caucuses," *Chicago Sun-Times,* 24 January 2000, p. 20.

26. Rhodes Cook, "Steps to the Nomination: Earlier Voting in 1996 Forecasts Fast and Furious Campaigns," *Congressional Quarterly Weekly Report,* 19 August 1995, 24487.

27. Sholomo Slonim, "The Electoral College at Philadelphia," *Journal of American History,* 73 (June 1986): 35.

28. Robin Kolodny and Angela Logan, "Political Consultants and the Extension of Party Goals," *PS,* June 1998, 155–159.

29. Ruth Shalit, "The Oppo Boom," *The New Republic,* 3 January 1994, 16–21; Adam Nagourney, "Researching the Enemy: An Old Political Tool Resurfaces in a New Election," *New York Times,* 3 April 1996, D20.

30. Thomas Patterson, *Out of Order* (New York: Knopf, 1993); Fallows, 45–64.

31. Elihu Katz and Jacob Feldman, "The Debates in Light of Research," in Sidney Kraus, ed., *The Great Debates* (Bloomington: Indiana University Press, 1962), 173–223.

32. Thomas Holbrook, "Campaigns, National Conditions, and U.S. Presidential Elections," *American Journal of Political Science,* 38 (November 1994): 986–992; John Geer, "The Effects of Presidential Debates on the Electorate's Preferences for Candidates," *American Politics Quarterly,* 16 (1988): 486–501; David Lanoue, "The 'Turning Point': Viewers' Reactions to the Second 1988 Presidential Debate," *American Politics Quarterly,* 19 (1991): 80–89.

33. David Lanoue, "One That Made a Difference: Cognitive Consistency, Political Knowledge, and the 1980 Presidential Debate," *Public Opinion Quarterly,* 56 (Summer 1992): 168–184; Carol Winkler and Catherine Black, "Assessing the 1992 Presidential and Vice Presidential Debates: The Public Rationale," *Argumentation and Advocacy,* 30 (Fall 1993): 77–87; Lori McKinnon, John Tedesco, and Lynda

Kaid, "The Third 1992 Presidential Debate: Channel and Commentary Effects," *Argumentation and Advocacy*, 30 (Fall 1993): 106–118; Mike Yawn, Kevin Ellsworth, and Kim Fridkin Kahn, "How a Presidential Primary Debate Changed Attitudes of Audience Members," *Political Behavior*, 20 (July 1998): 155–164.

34. Scott Keeter, "Public Opinion and the Election," in Gerald Pomper, ed., *The Election of 1996* (Chatham, NJ: Chatham House, 1997), 127; drawn from polls done by the Pew Research Center and the Times Mirror Center.

35. Federal Elections Commission, "Public Funding of Presidential Elections," August 1996 (http://www.fec.gov/pages/citnlist.htm); Anthony Corrado, "Financing the 1996 Election," in Pomper (1997), 137.

36. Susan Glasser, "Court's Ruling in Colorado Case May Reshape Campaign Finance; Limits on Political Parties' 'Hard Money' Spending Nullified," *Washington Post*, 28 March 1999, A6.

37. Jennifer Keen and John Daly, "Beyond the Limits: Soft Money in the 1996 Elections," Center for Responsive Politics (http://www.opensecrets.org/parties).

38. Richard Berke, "The 1998 Campaign: Issue Advertisements—Making of an Issue" *New York Times*, 21 October 1998, A12.

39. Center for Responsive Politics, "The Big Picture: Where the Money Came From in the 1996 Elections" (http://www.crp.org/pubs/bigpicture/overview/bpoverview.htm).

40. The web sites for these organizations provide an enormous amount of information regarding campaign finance: http://www.commoncause.org/; http://www.publiccampaign.org/; http://www.crp.org/. In addition, the Federal Elections Commission site has links to both general studies and reports as well as individual candidate campaign finance reports: http://www.fec.gov/.

41. Press conference, 18 February 1999, quoted in "People Are Talking," Public Campaign (http://www.publiccampaign.org/quotesmain.html).

42. Helen Dewar, "Campaign Finance Bill Dies in Senate," *Washington Post*, 27 February 1998, A1.

43. Newhouse News Service/Ann Arbor News, 28 April 1997, quoted in "People Are Talking," Public Campaign (http://www.publiccampaign.org/quotesmain.html).

44. Marjorie Hershey, "The Constructed Explanation: Interpreting Election Results in the 1984 Presidential Race," *Journal of Politics*, 54 (November 1992): 943–976.

45. Bernard Berelson, Paul Lazarsfeld, and William N. McPhee, *Voting* (Chicago: University of Chicago Press, 1954), ch. 10.

Chapter 13

1. Michael Emery and Edwin Emery, *The Press and America* (Englewood Cliffs, NJ: Prentice Hall, 1988), 7.

2. Harold W. Stanley and Richard G. Niemi, *Vital Statistics on American Politics 1997–1998* (Washington, DC: Congressional Quarterly Press, 1998), 163–164.

3. Ben H. Bagdikian, *The Media Monopoly*, 5th ed. (Boston: Beacon Press, 1997), 203.

4. Richard Davis, *The Press and American Politics: The New Mediator* (Upper Saddle River, NJ: Prentice Hall, 1996), 60.

5. Ibid., 67.

6. Mediamark Research, "Cyberstats, 2000" (http://www.mediamark.com).

7. Robert Marquand, "Hate Groups Market to the Mainstream," *Christian Science Monitor*, 6 March 1998, 4.

8. Pew Research Center for the People and the Press, "Investors Now Go Online for Quotes, Advice: Internet Sapping Broadcast News Audience," 11 June 2000 (http://www.people-press.org).

9. Pew Research Center for the People and the Press, "Event-Driven News Audiences: Internet News Takes Off," 8 June 1998 (http://www.people-press.org).

10. Pew Research Center for the People and the Press, "Youth Vote Influenced by Online Information: Internet Election News Audience Seeks Convenience, Familiar Names," 3 December 2000, (http://www.people-press.org).

11. Pew Research Center for the People and the Press, "The Times Mirror News Interest Index: 1989–1995," 28 December 1995 (http://www.people-press.org).

12. Davis, 27.

13. Ibid., 29.

14. Emery and Emery, 115.

15. David Broder, *Behind the Front Page* (New York: Simon and Schuster, 1987), 134–135.

16. Bagdikian, xv.

17. Jonathan Tasini, "The Tele-Barons: Media Moguls Rewrite the Law and Rewire the Country," *Washington Post*, 4 February 1996, CO1.

18. Bagdikian, ix.

19. Walter Goodman, "Where's Edward R. Murrow When You Need Him?" *New York Times*, 30 December 1997, E2.

20. Mark Crispin Miller, "Free the Media," *The Nation*, 3 June 1996, 9–14.

21. Bagdikian, 217.

22. Miller, 2.

23. David Armstrong, "Alternative, Inc.," *In These Times*, 21 August 1995, 14–18.

24. Jeff Gremillion, "Showdown at Generation Gap," *Columbia Journalism Review*, 34, no. 2 (July/August 1995): 34–38.

25. Doris Graber, *Mass Media and American Politics*, 5th ed. (Washington, DC: Congressional Quarterly Press, 1997), 62.

26. David H. Weaver and G. Cleveland Wilhoit, *The American Journalist in the 1990s* (Mahwah, NJ: Lawrence Erlbaum, 1996).

27. Doris A. Graber, Mass Media and American Politics (Washington, DC: Congressional Quarterly Press, 1997), 95–96.

28. William Schneider and I. A. Lewis, "Views on the News," *Public Opinion*, August/September 1985, 6.

29. David H. Weaver and G. Cleveland Wilhoit, *The American Journalist in the 1990s* (Mahwah, NJ: Lawrence Erlbaum, 1996), 15–19.

30. Mark Hertsgaard, *On Bended Knee: The Press and the Reagan Presidency* (New York: Farrar, Straus and Giroux, 1988), 3.

31. Schneider and Lewis, 8.

32. Broder, 148.

33. Dom Bonafede, "Crossing Over," *National Journal*, 14 January 1989, 102; Michael Kelly, "David Gergen, Master of the Game," *New York Times Magazine*, 31 October 1993, 64ff; Jonathan Alter, "Lost in the Big Blur," *Newsweek*, 9 June 1997, 43.

34. Shanto Iyengar, *Is Anyone Responsible?* (Chicago: University of Chicago Press, 1991), 2.

35. Shanto Iyengar and Donald R. Kinder, *News That Matters* (Chicago: University of Chicago Press, 1987).

36. Stephen Hess, *News and Newsmaking* (Washington, DC: Brookings Institution, 1996), 91–92.

37. Iyengar and Kinder, 72.

38. Benjamin I. Page, Robert Y. Shapiro, and Glenn R. Dempsey, "What Moves Public Opinion?" *American Political Science Review,* 81 (March 1987): 23–43. The term "professional communicator" is used by Benjamin Page, *Who Deliberates? Mass Media in Modern Democracy* (Chicago: University of Chicago Press, 1996): 106–109.

39. Iyengar and Kinder, 93.

40. W. Russell Neuman, Marion R. Just, and Ann N. Crigler, *Common Knowledge: News and the Construction of Political Meaning* (Chicago: University of Chicago Press, 1992), 119.

41. Ibid., 110.

42. James Fallows, "Why Americans Hate the Media," *Atlantic Monthly,* February 1996, 16. Web version.

43. Thomas E. Patterson, *Out of Order* (New York: Vintage Books, 1994), 74.

44. Larry J. Sabato, *Feeding Frenzy: How Attack Journalism Has Transformed American Politics* (New York: Free Press, 1991).

45. Patterson, 245.

46. Joseph N. Cappella and Kathleen Hall Jamieson, *Spiral of Cynicism: The Press and the Public Good* (New York: Oxford University Press, 1997), 9–10.

47. S. Robert Lichter and Richard E. Noyes, *Good Intentions Make Bad News: Why Americans Hate Campaign Journalism* (Lanham, MD: Rowman and Littlefield, 1995), xix.

48. Walter Cronkite, "Reporting Political Campaigns: A Reporter's View," in Doris Graber, Denis McQuail, and Pippa Norris, eds., *The Politics of News, The News of Politics* (Washington, DC: Congressional Quarterly Press, 1998), 57–69.

49. Kelly, 7. Web version.

50. Ibid., 7–10.

51. Hertsgaard, 6.

52. Stephen Ansolabehere, Roy Beyr, and Shanto Iyengar, *The Media Game: American Politics in the Television Age* (New York: Macmillan, 1993); Iyengar, *Is Anyone Responsible?*

Chapter 14

1. Fox Butterfield, "Inmates Serving More Time, Justice Department Reports," *New York Times,* 11 January 1999, 10.

2. Franklin Zimring, "'Three Strikes' Law Is Fool's Gold," *Christian Science Monitor,* 11 April 1994, 23.

3. Timothy Egan, "War on Crack Retreats, Still Taking Prisoners," *New York Times,* 28 February 1999, 1.

4. Peter Bachrach and Morton S. Baratz, "The Two Faces of Power," *American Political Science Review,* 56 (December 1962): 948.

5. This definition is based on the one offered by James E. Anderson, *Public Policymaking: An Introduction* (Boston: Houghton Mifflin, 1997), 9.

6. Theodore Lowi, "American Business, Public Policy Case Studies, and Political Theory," *World Politics,* 16, no. 4 (1964): 677–715.

7. For a discussion of the effect of lawsuits on air emission standards, see Robert Percival, Alan Miller, Christopher Schroeder, and James Leape, *Environmental Regulation: Law, Science and Policy,* 2nd ed. (Boston: Little, Brown, 1996).

8. See John Lewis Gaddis, *Strategies of Containment* (New York: Oxford University Press, 1982).

9. John Lewis Gaddis, *The United States and the End of the Cold War* (New York: Oxford University Press, 1992); Richard Ned Lebow and Thomas Risse-Kappen, eds., *International Relations Theory and the End of the Cold War* (New York: Columbia University Press, 1995).

10. See, for example, Richard N. Haass, *The Reluctant Sheriff: The United States After the Cold War* (New York: Council on Foreign Relations Press, 1997).

11. Randall B. Ripley and Grace A. Franklin, *Congress, the Bureaucracy, and Public Policy,* 5th ed. (Belmont, CA: Wadsworth, 1991).

12. See Charles F. Hermann, *Crises in Foreign Policy* (Indianapolis: Bobbs-Merrill, 1969); Michael Brecher, "A Theoretical Approach to International Crisis Behavior," *Jerusalem Journal of International Relations,* 3, no. 2–3 (1978): 5–24.

13. See Graham Allison, *Essence of Decision* (New York: HarperCollins, 1971); Helen V. Milner, *Interest, Institutions, and Information: Domestic Politics and International Relations* (Princeton: Princeton University Press, 1997).

14. See X (George F. Kennan), "The Sources of Soviet Conduct," *Foreign Affairs,* 25 (July 1947): 566–582.

15. See, for example, Michael H. Shuman, "Dateline Main Street: Local Foreign Policies," *Foreign Policy,* 65 (Winter 1986/1987): 154–174.

16. Robert S. Erikson, Gerald C. Wright, and John P. McIver, *Statehouse Democracy* (New York: Cambridge University Press, 1993).

17. Michael B. MacKuen, Robert S. Erikson, and James A. Stimson, "Macropartisanship," *American Political Science Review,* 89 (December 1989): 1125–1142.

18. Butterfield, 10.

19. U.S. Department of Justice, Bureau of Justice Statistics, "Corrections Statistics: Summary Findings," 11 December 1998 (http://www.ojp.usdoj.gov/bjs/correct.htm).

20. David B. Koepl, "Prison Blues: How America's Foolish Sentencing Policies Endanger Public Safety," *Policy Analysis,* 208 (1994): 3.

21. Timothy Egan, "War on Crack Retreats, Still Taking Prisoners," *New York Times,* 28 February 1999, 1.

22. Richard P. Jones, "Corrections Secretary Completes Long Voyage," *Milwaukee Journal Sentinel,* 10 January 1999, B-1.

23. U.S. Department of Justice.

24. David Holmstrom, "More Prisons Not a Cure to Crime, Experts Say," *Christian Science Monitor,* 23 February 1994, 7.

25. Butterfield, 10; Fox Butterfield, "Number of Inmates Reaches Record 1.8 Million," *New York Times,* 15 March 1999, 14.

Credits

Index

Note: Numbers in boldface indicate the page on which a key term is defined.

Abolitionist movement, 37, 140
Abortion: party identification and position on, 311; 2000 party platforms on, 315; privacy rights and, 111–112
Abrams v. *United States,* 96
Accommodationists, **91**–92
Accountability, **223**–224; interest groups in, 323; media and, 397–398; political parties and, 304, 306
Activist presidency, 200–201
Adams, John, 36; Federalists and, 307; judicial appointments by, 253–254
Adams, John Quincy, 40, 318
Adams, Sam, 35, 36
Administration, bureaucracy's role in, 230
Administrative law, **252**
Administrative Procedures Act (1946), 242, 243
Advertising: issue advocacy, **330,** 366–367; media reliability and, 395; media revenue from, 382; negative, **361**–363
Affirmative action, **129**–130; Johnson and, 252, 409; party identification and position on, 311; 2000 party platforms on, 314
African Americans: American Revolution and, 37; in the civil service, 231–232; in Congress, 162, 163; in contemporary politics, 130–131; death penalty and, 109–110; de facto discrimination against, 128–130; de jure discrimination against, 126–128; Democratic Party and, 291, 310; life expectancy of, 119; racial gerrymandering and, **161**–162; socioeconomic status of, 130; on the

Supreme Court, 264; voting rights of, 20
Age: public opinion and, 290; voter turnout and, 146, 344
Age discrimination, 145–146
Agenda: legislative, 175, 176
Agenda building, 323
Agendas: defining party, 302–303; political parties and, 304
Agenda setting: media role in, 390–391; in public policymaking, 410–411
Agricultural Adjustment Act, 246
AIDS, 146
Aid to Families with Dependent Children (AFDC), 60, 77, 414–415
Albright, Madeleine, 430
Alcohol use testing, 107
Alien and Sedition Act (1798), 96
Allocative representation, **153**
The Almanac of American Politics, 155
Alternative press, 383–384
Ambassadors, 196
Amendability, **52**–53
American Association of Political Consultants, 281
American Association of Retired Persons (AARP), 146; membership of, 335, 337; public mobilization by, 330; social security and, 417
American Bar Association, 262; on the death penalty, 109–110
American Cancer Society, 337
American Civil Liberties Union, 114; on the death penalty, 109–110; lobbying of courts by, 330
American Heart Association, 337
American Independent Party, 319
American Indian Civil Rights Council, 133

American Indian Movement (AIM), 133, 325
American Lung Association, 241, 408
American Revolution, 35–36, 381; African Americans and, 37; Native Americans and, 37–38
Americans with Disabilities Act (ADA), 146
America's Voice, 378
AMERIND, 133
Amicus curiae briefs, 199, **266,** 267, 330
Ammiano, Tom, 87
Amnesty International, 102, 119, 426
Amtrak, 229–230
Analytical thinking. *See* Critical thinking
Anarchy, 8, 21
Anti-Federalists, **42**; Bill of Rights and, 88; in ratification process, 54
Anti-Masonic Party, 318
Anti-Semitic groups, 32
Antiterrorism bill, 32
Apathy, 12
Appeal, **256**
Appellate jurisdiction, **256**
Appointments: presidential, 48, 238; presidential vs. career civil service, 235–236; Senate confirmation of, 158; senatorial courtesy and, **199, 260**–261
Approval ratings: of Clinton, 215–216, 275; of Congress, 183; of the Supreme Court, 261
Arafat, Yasser, 196
Arguments: evaluating, 24–26; parts of, 25
Aristotle, 3
Armey, Dick, 424
The Arsenio Hall Show, 363, 378

Article I (legislative branch), 46–47, A3–A6; checks and balances in, 50; necessary and proper clause, **62**–63; state powers in, 63–64

Article II (executive branch), 48, A6–A7; checks and balances in, 50; qualifications and conditions of office, 194–195

Article III (judicial branch), 48–50, A7; checks and balances in, 50; court system established in, 253

Article IV, A7–A8

Article V, A8

Article V (amendability), 53

Article VI, 63, A8

Article VII, A8

Articles of Confederation, **39**–41; executive power in, 47, 194; factions and, 301; federalism in, 64, 65

Ashcroft, John, 166

Asian Americans, 119, 136–138; diversity of, 136–137; socioeconomic status of, 137–138

Assimilation, 132

Assisted suicide, 113

Associated Press (AP), 377

Assumptions, 25

Astroturf lobbying, **331**–332

Asylum, **16**

Attack journalism, 395

Attitude changes, 347

Attorney general, 227

Attucks, Crispus, 35

Authoritarian governments, **8**–9; citizenship in, 10

Authority, **4**, 74

Baby-boom generation, 417

Bagdikian, Ben, 382

Baker v. *Carr,* 263

Balanced Budget Act (1997), 180

Barber, James David, 214

Barnum, P. T., 102

Beats, **389**

Benton v. *Maryland,* 89

Bernasconi, Socorro Hernandez, 14

Bicameral legislature, **46**–47, **156**

Big government, 69

Bill of Rights, 19; extension of, 52–53; government limitations in,

63; Hamilton on, **55**–56; importance of, 88; states under, 88–90

Bills (legislative). *See also* Law: agenda setting and, 176; legislative process for, 176–180; overcoming obstacles to, 180–181

Bills of attainder, **88**

Birth control, 111–112

Black, James, 318

Black codes, **123**–124

Black Muslims, 128

Black Panthers, 128

Black power, 128

Blades, Joan, 299–300

Blair, Tony, 393

Blanket primaries, 354

Block grants, **76**–78

Blue Law Cases, 93

Boerne v. *Flores,* 94

Bonneville Power Administration, 229

Bork, Robert, 198, 262–263, 264

Boss rule, 170

Boston Massacre, 35, 36

Boston Tea Party, 35, 36

Bowers v. *Hardwick,* 112–113, 144–145

Boycott, **126**

Boyd, Wes, 299–300

Brady bill, 73, 105

Branch Davidians, 58

Brandeis, Louis, 79

Broder, David, 389

Brokaw, Tom, 390

Brown v. *Board of Education,* 117–118, 125–126

Bryant, Ed, 275

Buchanan, Pat, 319, 389; presidential debates and, 364

Budgets: Congressional Budget Office and, 173–174; fiscal policy in, 421–422; House of Representatives in, 157; Office of Management and Budget in, 238–239; 2000 party platforms on, 315

Bull Moose Party, 318, 319

Bureaucracy, 219–246; accountability and rules in, 223–224; appointees vs. civil service in, 235–236; citizen access to, 244;

citizenship and, 243–244; communications, 397; Congress and, 240–242; congressional, 173–174; courts and, 242; culture in, 232–235; definition of, **221**–224; democracy and, 222–223; federal, 224–232; iron triangles and, **240**–242; lobbying, 329; politics inside, 232–236; politics outside, 236–243; president and, 238–240; presidential, 195; public policy-making by, 409; reforms of, 243–244; spoils system and, **221**–222; stereotypes of, 220

Bureaucratese, **233**

Bureaucratic culture, **232**–235; advantages and disadvantages of, 234–235

Bureaucratic discretion, **230**

Bureau of Engraving and Printing, 225

Bureau of Indian Affairs (BIA), 132

Burger, Warren, 112, 263

Bush, Barbara, 212

Bush, George: economy under, 204; judicial appointments by, 198, 259, 264; media access by, 202; media interpretations of election of, 368; Persian Gulf War and, 204; in presidential debates, 364; on religious rights, 92; sound bites by, 393; veto use by, 197–198; as vice president, 211

Bush, George W.: on abortion, 112, 360; agenda setting by, 411; cabinet diversity of, 131, 135, 208; Cheney and, 210, 211, 356; 2000 election, 342–343; exploratory committee of, 353; honeymoon period of, 204; judicial appointments by, 198; mandate of, 368, 369–371; media access by, 191; media management by, 397; moderate voters and, 316; personality of, 214; presidential debates and, 364; on religious rights, 92; Republican Party and, 304; social security under, 417; television appearances of, 363; voter image of, 352; working with Congress by, 205

Bush, Laura, 212
Busing, 117–118, 129, 130, 147–148

Cabinet, **195,** 208; makeup of, 227–228; succession to presidency by secretaries, 194–195; White House staff and, 210
Campaign contributions: by interest groups, 328–329; PACs and, 333–335
Campaign finance reform, 182, 183, 367; third parties and, 317, 319
Campaign managers, 359
Campaign polls, 280–281
Campaigns, spending on, 365–367
Campaigns and Elections, 332
Candidate recruitment, 302–303
Candidates, voter images of, 351–352
Cannon, Joe, 170
Cantwell v. *Connecticut,* 89
The Capital Gang, 378
Capitalism, 4–6
Capitalist economy, **4**
Capital punishment, 109–110, 119
CapWeb, 154
Cardozo, Benjamin, 90
Carnahan, Jean, 166
Carnahan, Mel, 166
Carter, Jimmy, 199, 211, 316, 350; foreign policy and, 429; judicial appointments by, 259–260; voter image of, 352
Carter, Rosalynn, 212
Case-work, **153**
Categorical grants, **75**–76
Caucuses, 354–355
Censorship, 95; of cartoons, 192; Internet, 101–103
Censure and Move On, 299–300, 331, 339–340
Center for Responsive Politics, 367
Central Intelligence Agency (CIA), **431**
Challenger disaster, 234
Chavez, Cesar, 135
Checks and balances, **50**–52; on Congress, 156, 158–159; Madison on, 55
Cheney, Dick, 204, 210, 211, 356

Chicago, Burlington & Quincy v. *Chicago,* 89
Chief administrator, **195**
Chief executive officer (CEO), 195
Chief foreign policy maker, **196**
Chief of staff, **209**
Child Labor Amendment, 52
Children's Health Insurance Program, 418
Christian Coalition, 92, 112; public mobilization by, 330
Christian Right, 112; gay rights and, 145
Christian Science Monitor, 376, 382, 383
Circuit courts, 258–259
Citizen advisory councils, **243**
Citizens, **10;** beliefs of American, 17–22; compared with subjects, 57; educating, 330; ideal democratic, 276; ideologies of, 284; moderate position by, 313, 316; participation by, 286–287; parties as link to officials for, 305–306; points of access for, 26; political knowledge of, 283–284; power of president of, 215; refugees, 16; roles of in democracy, 10, 276; tolerance of, 284–286
Citizenship, 8–12; in America, 12–17; in authoritarian systems, 10; in democracy, 10–12; dual, 15; duties of, 114; exclusions from, 11; involvement and, 27–29; as legal status, 14–16
Civic journalism, **400**
Civil Aeronautics Board, 237
Civilian Conservation Corps, 422
Civil justice system, 270–271
Civil laws, **251**
Civil law tradition, **250**
Civil liberties, 19, 83–116; citizenship and, 114; citizen support of, 285–286; definition of, **85**
Civil rights, 70, **85, 119;** Supreme Court in, 269
Civil Rights Act (1964), 177–179, 409
Civil Rights Act (1991), 143
Civil Rights Bill (1964), 128
Civil Rights Bill (1991), 130

Civil rights movement, 126
Civil service, 220, **222.** *See also* Bureaucracy; Federal bureaucracy
Civil Service Commission, 222
Civil Service Reform Act (1883), 222
Civil War, 70; African Americans after, 123–125; Reconstruction and, 124–125; Republican Party and, 311
Clarity, in arguments, 25
Clark, Ed, 319
Clean Air Act, 408
Clean Water Act, 408
Clear and present danger test, **96,** 97, 120
Cleveland, Grover, 362
Clientele groups, **225**
Clinton, Bill: access to, 335; antiterrorism bill, 32; approval ratings of, 215–216, 275; budget of, 150–151; cabinet diversity of, 135; citizen perceptions of, 28–29; economy under, 204; effects of divided government on, 206; electoral college and, 357–358; Gore and, 356; health care policy of, 419; honeymoon period of, 204; impeachment, media coverage of, 400–401; impeachment, party identification and position on, 311, 321; impeachment of, 1, 157, 187, 195, 215–216, 275; judicial appointments by, 259–260; line-item veto by, 180; media coverage of, 391; media interpretations of election of, 368; media management by, 397; moderate voters and, 316; Monica Lewinsky and, 299–300, 382, 393; National Performance Review, 239–240; Native Americans under, 133; pardons by, 199; peace talks, 196; personality of, 214; in presidential debates, 364; scandals surrounding, 347; television appearances of, 363; two terms of, 166, 190; Unfunded Mandate Act, 78; veto use by, 198; welfare reform, 60–61, 77, 415; White House staff of, 210; Whitewater investigation, 172; women voters and, 291

Clinton, Hillary Rodham: electoral college and, 370; as first lady, 212; run for the Senate, 162, 166; Whitewater investigation, 172

Clintonomics, 150–151

Closed primaries, 354

Cloture, **177**

CNBC, 400

CNN, 373, 378, 400

Coalitions, 329

Coalition to Stop Gun Violence, 105

Coattail effect, 164–**165**

Coercive Acts (1774), 35, 36

Cold War, **427**; Congress during, 182; foreign policy since, 426–427

Collective action, problem of, 323–324

Collective good, **324**

College loans, 405

College speech codes, 83–84, 99–100, 114–115

Commander-in-chief, 48, **195**–196

Commercial bias, **382**–383

Committee system, 170–173; bill consideration in, 176–177; chairs in, 173; committee types in, 171–172; conference committees, 172; getting on the right committees in, 172–173; iron triangles and, **240**–242; joint committees, 172; select committees, 172; staff of, 173; standing committees, 171–172

Common Cause, 330, 367

Common law tradition, **249**–250

Communications Decency Act (CDA), 101

Communism, 6; containment policy and, **427**

Communist economy, **6**

Communities Organized for Public Service (COPS), 136

Community formation, 379

Compelling state interest, **93**–94

Compensatory damages, 251

Competence, neutral, **221**

Conclusions, in arguments, 25

Concord Coalition, 418

Concurrent powers, **64**

Concurring opinions, **268**

Confederal systems, **65**–66

Confederation, **39**

Conference committees, **172**

Confidentiality, 243

Conflict resolution, 249

Congress, 150–186; agenda setting in, 176; under the Articles of Confederation, 39; Bill of Rights on, 89; bureaucracy and, 223, 240–242; checks and balances in, 158–159; committees in, 170–173; Constitutional Congress and, 42–44; constitutional powers of, 46–47; deciding to run for, 162–165; decision-making in, 181; districts of, 160–162; distrust of, 151–152; divided government and, 205–206; effectiveness of, 182–183; elections to, 159–167; 2000 elections to, 166–167; enumerated powers of, 156; evaluating critically, 154–155; foreign policymaking by, 431–432; fragmentation of, 175; lawmaking by, 153–154; leadership of, 168–170; lobbying, 328–329; majority party in, **167**; media coverage of, 183; necessary and proper clause and, **62**–63; norms of, **175**; organization of, 167–174; oversight hearings, 412; partisanship in, 166–167, 179–180; party control in, 165, A21–A22; powers and responsibilities of, 156–159; power to convene, 197; presidential goals and, 204–205; presidential vetoes and, 198; process and politics in, 174–183; public approval of, 183; in public policy making, 408–409; qualifications for, 162; reforms of, 183–184; representation in, 152–153; role of party in, 167; staff and bureaucracy of, 173–174; state policy influenced by, 74–78; 107th, 165–167

Congressional Budget and Impoundment Act (1974), 182

Congressional Budget Office (CBO), 173–174, 412

Congressional campaign committees, 320

Congressional Quarterly Weekly, 155

Congressional Record, 154–155

Congressional Research Service (CRS), 173, 412

Connerly, Ward, 291

Conservative ideology, **20**–22; of citizens, 284; marriage gap and, 291; Republican Party and, 310–311

Constituency, **152**–153; building, 237–238; president's vs. Congress', 158, 205; roll call voting and, 181

Constitution, 46–53, A3–A13. *See also specific amendments; specific articles*; amendability of, 52–53; as bill of rights, 88; checks and balances in, 50–52; distribution of powers in, 44; executive branch in, 47–48; judicial branch in, 48–50, 252–254; legislative branch in, 46–47; ratification of, 53–57; separation of powers in, 50–52; on slavery, 45; state powers in, 63–64

Constitution, **39**

Constitutional Convention, **41**–46

Constitutional law, **251**

Containment, **427**, 428

Contract with America, 170

Convention bumps, 356

Conventions, national, 355–356

Cooley v. Board of Wardens of Port of Philadelphia, 69–70

Cooperative federalism, **64**

Corporate welfare policy, 413

Corruption: free expression as limit to, 95

Council of Economic Advisers, **209**

Court-packing, 246–247, 271–272

Courts, 246–273. *See also* Judicial branch; bureaucracy and, 242; citizenship and, 270–271; conflict resolution by, **249**; constitutional provisions on, 252–254; dual system of, 255–261; federal, 257–261; judicial review and, 253–254; jurisdiction of, 255–256; legal system and, 249–252; lobbying, 330; as public policymakers,

409; state, 256–257; Supreme Court and politics, 261–269

Crawford, Michelle, 79

Crime Control and Safe Streets Act (1968), 108

Criminal defendants rights, 106–110

Criminal justice policy, 403

Criminal justice system, 270–271

Criminal laws, **250**–251

Crisis policy, **428**

Critical elections, **308**

Critical thinking, **27**; about campaign advertising, 362–363; about Congress, 154–155; about party platforms, 314–315; about political cartoons, 192–193; about politics, 24–26; about polls, 282; about the media, 394–395; steps in, 25

Cronkite, Walter, 373, 391

Crossfire, 378

Cruel and unusual punishment, 89, 107, 109–110

Cruzan, Nancy, 113

C-SPAN, 373, 378

Cuban Americans, 135

Culture: bureaucratic, 232–235; of entitlement, 61; political, 17–20

Cycle effect, **203**–204

Cynicism, 392, 394–395; spiral of, 395–396

Damages, legal, 251

Dance of Legislation (Redman), 181

Daughters of Liberty, 38

Davis, Gray, 136

Dealignment, **308**, 310

Death penalty, 109–110, 119

Debates, 364–365

Debs, Eugene V., 318

Decentralization, 239–240; of party organization, 320

Decision-making: bureaucratic, 222–223; Supreme Court, 264–268; voter, 350–352

Declaration of Independence, **36**–38, 86, A1–A3

De facto discrimination, **127**, 128–130

Deficit, national, 157, 422; unfunded mandates and, 78

Dejanews.com, 103

DeJonge v. *Oregon*, 89

De jure discrimination, **126**–127

Delegates, 302

Deliberation, 14, 296–297

Demand, 5–6

Democracy, **9**–10; in America, 12–17; bureaucracy in, 222–223; citizenship in, 10–12; dangers of, 12; direct, 274, 296–297; elite, **9**; globalization of, 343; low voter turnout and, 349; meaning of in America, 19; participatory, **10**; pluralist, **10**; rights in, 86–87; role of law in, 249

Democratic National Committee, 302, 320

Democratic Party, 73; African Americans and, 291; African Americans in, 138; Asian Americans in, 138; geographic strength of, 308; ideology of, 310–311; interest groups and, 334–335; Jackson and, 307; journalists in, 387–388; membership of, 312; moderating influences on, 313, 316–317; party machines in, **307**–308; platform of, 312–313, 314–315; tax policy of, 423–424; voter turnout and, 349

Department of Commerce, 225, 226, 227, 431

Department of Defense, 224, 227, **430**; containment policy of, 428

Department of Education, 225, 226, 227

Department of Energy, 227

Department of Health and Human Services, 227, 229

Department of Housing and Urban Development, 225, 227

Department of Justice, 227

Department of Labor, 225, 226, 227

Department of State, 224, 227, **430**

Department of the Interior, 225, 227, 242

Department of the Treasury, 224–225, 227, 431

Department of Transportation, 227

Department of Veterans Affairs, 225, 226, 227, 242

Department of War, 224

Departments, federal, 227–228

Deregulation, 239–240

Devolution, **61**, 78–80

Diana, Princess of Wales, 378

Dionne, E. J., 14

Direct lobbying, **327**–330

Direct primaries, 320

Disability, 146

Discrimination: age, 145–146; against Asian Americans, 137; de facto, **127**, 128–130; de jure, **126**–127; against disabled persons, 146; gender-based, 139–144

Discuss List, 266

Dissenting opinions, **268**

Distributive policies, 407–**408**

District courts, 257, 258

Districts, congressional, 160–162; selecting, 164

Divided government, **205**–206, 310

Dixiecrats, 318

Doctors Without Borders, 426

Dole, Robert, 291, 368

Double jeopardy, 89

Douglas, William O., 97

Draft card burning, 97

Dred Scott v. *Sanford*, 70, 271

Drinking age, minimum, 62, 78

Drudge Report, 379

Drug offenses, 434

Drugs, legalization of, 22

Drug testing, 107

Dual federalism, **64**, 74

Due process of the law, **106**–107; procedural, 250; Supreme Court on, 269

Duke, David, 320

Duncan v. *Louisiana*, 89

Earth First!, 331

Economic freedom, 19; race and, 118–119

Economic interest groups, **325**

Economic policy, 420–422

Economics, 4–6; capitalism, 4–6; communism, 6; definition of, **4**; social democracy, 6–7

Economies of scale, 66

Economy, state of, 204

Education: affirmative action in, 129–130; Asian Americans and, 137–138; government participation and, 286–287; influence of on political opinions, 289–290; interest groups in, 323, 330; party identification and amount of, 312; party identification and position on, 311; 2000 party platforms on, 315; political socialization in, 288; school choice in, 148; segregation in, 125–130; state vs. national influence in, 74–78; subsidies, 413; tolerance and, 286
Education Amendments, 142, 143
Efficacy, feelings of, 349
Eighteenth Amendment, A11
Eighth Amendment, A9; applied to states, 89; cruel and unusual punishment in, 109–110
Eisenhower, Dwight, 126, 201; judicial appointments by, 262
Electioneering, 302–303
Elections, 342–372; campaign contributions, 328–329, 333–335; citizen interest in, 369; electoral college in, 356–358; general election campaign in, 358–367; interpreting, 368; pre-primary season, 353–354; presidential, 352–368; presidential debates in, 364–365; primaries and caucuses in, 354–355; reforms, 346–347; voter turnout and, 344–348
Elections, congressional, 159–167; 2000, 165–167; campaign spending in, 164; congressional districts and, 160–162; deciding to run, 162–165; reasons to run, 162–163; strategy in, 164–165
Electoral college, **48**, 194, 356–358; 2000 election and, 370–371; reforms, 358
Electoral mandates, **368**
Electors, 356–357
Eleventh Amendment, A9
Elite democracy, **9**; as protectors of values, 286; on public opinion, 276
Emancipation Proclamation, 123
Employment discrimination, 130;

age and, 145–146; against women, 143
Employment Division, Department of Human Resources v. *Smith*, 93–94
En banc, 259
Endangered Species Act, 242, 409
England, American split from, 33–38
Entitlement, culture of, 61
Enumerated powers of Congress, **62**–63
Environment: party identification and position on, 311; policy, foreign repercussions of, 426; public policy on, 408
Environmental Defense Fund, 408
Environmental Protection Agency, 228, 408
Equal Employment Opportunity Commission (EEOC), 128, 146
Equality: citizen support of, 285–286; in the Declaration of Independence, 36–38; before the law, 270–271; meaning of in America, 19–20; procedural, 122; property laws and, 40; substantive, 122
Equal opportunity interest groups, **325**–326
Equal Rights Amendment, 52, **142**
Equal time provision, 384
Espionage Act (1917), 96
Establishment clause, **91**–92
Ethiopia, famine in, 390–391
European Union, 66
Everson v. *Board of Education*, 89
Evidence, in arguments, 25
Excise taxes, 423
Exclusionary rule, 89, **107**–108
Executive, **47**
Executive agreement, **196**
Executive branch, 47–48; foreign policy and, 429–431
Executive Office of the President, 208, **209**, 429
Executive Order 9381, 198
Executive Order 11246, 129, 409
Executive Order 11375, 409
Executive orders, 198, **252**
Exit polls, **280**–281

Expertise, 233–234; interest groups and, 328
Expert testimony, 328
Exploratory committees, 353
Ex post facto laws, **88**
Expressive benefits, **324**
Extremist groups, 285

Face the Nation, 378
Factions, **322**; Madison on, 12, **55**, 57
Fair Deal, 201
Fairness doctrine, 384
Fallows, James, 393
Family values, 21–22, 284, 316
Fascist governments, **9**
Faubus, Orval, 126
Federal bureaucracy, 224–232. *See also* Bureaucracy; demographics of personnel in, 231–232; departments in, 227–228; evolution of, 224–225; government corporations in, 229–230; independent agencies in, 228; independent regulatory boards and commissions in, 228–229; organization of, 225–230; roles of, 230–231
Federal Bureau of Investigation (FBI), 262
Federal Communications Act (1934), 384–385
Federal Communications Commission (FCC), 384
Federal courts, 255, 257–261
Federal Election Campaign Act (1974), 328–329
Federal Elections Commission, 228, 359, 365
Federal Elections Commission Act (1972, 1974), 365
Federalism, **42**, 60–82; alternatives to, 64–66; balance of power in, 68–69; changes in American, 67–71; citizenship and, 80–81; Constitution on, 62–64; cooperative, 64; current American, 72–80; decentralized parties in, 320; definition of, 62–67; dual, 64, 74; effects of, 66; 2000 election and, 370, 371; state innovations and, 79

The Federalist Papers, **54**–56, 57; on judicial review, 48–49; No. 10, A13–A16; No. 51, A17–A19

Federalists, **42,** 307; Bill of Rights and, 88; in ratification process, 54

Federal Judiciary Act (1789), 255

Federal Register, **231,** 243, 244

Federal Reserve System, 225, 320, 421

Federal Trade Commission, 225

Feeding frenzy, **393**–394

Feingold, Russell, 367

Felonies, 251

Feminism, 99

Ferraro, Geraldine, 356

FICA (Federal Insurance Contributions Act), 416

Fifteenth Amendment, A10–A11; civil rights in, 85; voting rights in, 124

Fifth Amendment, A9; applied to states, 89; self-incrimination and, 108

Fighting words, **99**–100

Filibuster, **177**–180

Fillmore, Millard, 318

Fireside chats, 373, 377

First Amendment, 91–94, A8–A9; applied to states, 89; establishment clause, 91–92; freedom of expression, 95–104; freedom of the press, 100–101; free exercise clause, 93–94

First Continental Congress, 36

First lady, 211–212

Fiscal policy, 420–422, 421–422

Fiske v. *Kansas,* 89

Flag burning, 97–98

Flag Protection Act (1989), 98

Flat tax system, 424

Food and Drug Administration, 229

Ford, Gerald: block grants under, 77; judicial appointments by, 259; pardon of Nixon by, 199; popularity of, 204

Foreign Affairs Committee, 172

Foreign policy, **425**–433; after the Cold War, 426–427; citizenship and, 433–434; Congress in, 431–432; crisis, **428;** defining problems in, 432; makers of,

428–432; president as chief maker of, 196, 429–431; strategic, **428;** structural defense, **428;** types of, 427–428

Fortas, Abe, 263

Fort Wayne, Indiana, busing in, 117–118, 147–148

Fourteenth Amendment, 71, A10; applicability of to states, 89–90; civil rights in, 85; gay rights and, 113; privacy rights and, 111; racial harassment and, 130; state powers in, 64

Fourth Amendment, A9; applied to states, 89; exclusionary rule and, **107**–108; on unreasonable search and seizure, 107–108

Fox, Jon D., 184

Fox News Channel, 373

Fragmentation: of Congress, 175; political parties and, 302

Framing, 391

Franking, **163**

Franklin, Benjamin, 2, 192

Freedom: Locke on, 11–12; meaning of in America, 19

Freedom of assembly, 89, **98**

Freedom of conscience, 91

Freedom of expression, 95–104; fighting words/offensive speech and, 99–100; importance of, 95; obscenity and pornography and, 98–99; sedition and, 96–97; symbolic speech, 97–98

Freedom of Information Act (1966), **243**

Freedom of religion, 89, 91–94; citizen support of, 285–286

Freedom of speech, 89; citizen support of, 285–286; college speech codes and, 83–84; fighting words/offensive speech and, 99–100; obscenity and pornography and, 98–99; sedition and, 96–97; symbolic speech and, 97–98

Freedom of the press, 89, 100–101; libel and, **100**–101; prior restraint and, **100;** trial coverage and, 101

Free exercise, 89

Free exercise clause, **93**–94

Free rider problem, **323**–324

Free-Soil Party, 318

French and Indian War, **34**–35

Front-loading, **355**

Front-runners, **355**

Funding: block grants, **76**–78; campaign, 365–367; campaign finance reform and, 182, 183, 317, 319, 367; categorical grants, **75**–76; federalism and, 74–78; by interest groups, 328–329; PACs and, 333–335; unfunded mandates, **78**

Furman v. *Georgia,* 110

Gallup, George, 279

Gallup polls, 202–203, 424

Garcia v. *San Antonio Metropolitan Transit Authority,* 72

Gardner, John, 240

Garner, John Nance, 211

Gatekeeping, **385**

Gay rights, 22, 66, 112–113; legal discrimination and, 144–145; 2000 party platforms on, 314; suspect class status and, 122

Gender: party identification by, 312; public opinion and, 290–291; as suspect class, 121–122

Gender gap, **290**–291

General Accounting Office, 412

General Revenue Sharing (GRS), 77

Generational changes, 348

Geographic region, political beliefs and, 292–293, 308

George III (England), 36, 194

Gergen, David, 210, 389

Gerry, Elbridge, 47

Gerrymandering, **161**–162

G.I. Bill of Rights, 182

Gibbons v. *Ogden,* **69**–70

Gideon, Clarence Earl, 109

Gideon v. *Wainwright,* 89, 109

Gilbert v. *Minnesota,* 89

Gilmore, Gary, 110

Gingrich, Newt, 1, 170, 321

Gitlow v. *New York,* 89, 90

Glass ceiling, 143

Glass Ceiling Commission, 143

Glenn, John, 5, 373

Glickman, Dan, 220

Going public, **202**–204, 215

Goldwater, Barry, 310, 363; voter image of, 352

Good faith exception, 108

Gore, Al, 1, 166; 2000 election, 342–343; moderate voters and, 316; National Performance Review and, 239–240; presidential debates and, 364; television appearances of, 363; as vice president, 210, 211, 356; voter image of, 352, 360

Governing, **303**–304

Government: Articles of Confederation and, 39–41; attitudes toward, 347; Constitutional Convention and, 41–46; definition of, **4**; growth of American, 68–69; interest groups of, 326; public trust in, 1–2; rights against, 83–116; rules and institutions of, 7–8; speech criticizing, 96–97

Government Accounting Office (GAO), 173

Government corporations, **229**–230

Government interest groups, 326

Grandfather clauses, **124**

Grassroots lobbying, **331**

Gravel, Mike, 274

Great Compromise, **43**–44, 160

Great Depression, 21, 70; Congress during, 182; economic policy and, 420; presidential power during, 200–201

Great Society, 201, 418

Green Party, 319

Greenpeace, 426

Greenspan, Alan, 421

Gridlock, 310

Griswold v. *Connecticut*, 111–112, 263

Gross domestic product (GDP), 420–421

Gross national product (GNP), 200

Group behavior, 294–295

Gun control, 331; libertarians on, 22; militia groups and, 31–32, 57–58; 2000 party platforms on, 315; right to bear arms and,

104–106; school shootings and, 176

Gun Safety First, 331

Habeas corpus, **88**

Hamilton, Alexander: *Federalist Papers*, 54, 55–56, 253; Federalists and, 307

Hamilton v. *Regents of California*, 89

Hammer v. *Dagenhart*, 70

Hancock, John, 36

Handgun Control, 105

Hard money, **365**–366, 367

Hardwick, Michael, 112–113

Harlan, John Marshall, 99

Hastert, Dennis, 170, 321

Hatch Act (1939), **222**

Hate crime laws, 99–100

Head of government, **190**–191

Head of state, **190**–191

Health care. *See also* Medicaid; Medicare: national, 419; Oregon program of, 66; policy, 407, 418–419

Hearings: oversight, 412; subcommittee, 177

Henry, Patrick, 56, 84

Hierarchy: in bureaucracy, 221, 233; in political parties, 321

The Hill, 155

Hispanic Americans, 119, 133–136; in the civil service, 231–232; in Congress, 162, 163; diversity of, 133–135

Hitler, Adolf, 9, 426

HMOs (health maintenance organizations), 419

Hobbes, Thomas, 3, 11, 248

Holmes, Oliver Wendell, 96

Home ownership, 405, 413

Homosexuals. *See* Gay rights

Honeymoon period, **203**–204

Hoover, Herbert, 200

Hope Scholarship credit, 413

Hopper, 176

Horizon Organic Dairy, 220

Horse race journalism, 362, 363, **392**–393

Horse race polls, 277

Hotline, 155

House of Lords, 47

House of Representatives, 12; Article I on, 47; basis of representation in, 43–44, 160; differences between Senate and, 156–158; leadership of, 168–170; majority leader, 168; organization of, 175; Speaker of the, **168**; term length in, 156

House Rules Committee, **172**, 173, 177

House Un-American Activities Committee, 96–97

House Ways and Means Committee, 172

Huerta, Dolores, 136

Humanitarian interventions, 425

Human nature, views of, 54–56, 248

Humphrey, Hubert, 177–178

Hussein, King, 196

Hussein, Saddam, 287

Hypothesis, 25

Ideas, traffic of, 95

Ideologies, **20**–22; of citizens, 284; conservative, 20–22; liberal, 20–22; moderation of party, 320; political parties, 310–311

Illegal immigrants, 16–17; Hispanic, 135

Illegal Immigration Reform and Immigrant Responsibility Act (1996), 17

Image, emphasis on, 393, 395–396

Immigrants, **15**; Asian, 137; illegal, 16–17; Mexican, 135; naturalization of, 15–16

Immigration, backlash against, 135

Impeachment: of Clinton, 1, 187; Congress in, 157–158; Constitution on, 48; of judges, 259; process of, 195; stakes involved in, 216–217

Imperial presidency, 182

Important interest test, 120

Inaction, as public policy, 405

Income: equality before the law and, 270–271; voter turnout and, 345

Income taxes, 423–424

Incorporation, **90**

Incumbency advantage, **164,** 302, 340

Independent agencies, **228**

Independent and Montgomery Transcript, 184

Independent regulatory boards and commissions, **228**–229, 237

Independents, 310, 317

Indian Land Rights Association, 133

Indirect lobbying, **327**–328, 330

Individualistic, **18**

Individualistic political culture, 18–20

Influence, money and, 335

In forma pauperis, 266

Information: congressional sources of, 278; interest groups and, 337; levels of political, 380; media sources of, 363; two-step flow of, **294**

Inherent powers, **200**

In re *Oliver,* 89

Institutions, **7**–8

Insurrection, 58

Intelligence community, **430**–431

Interest group entrepreneurs, **335**

Interest groups, 62, 322–327; block grants and, 77–78; campaign finance and, 182; clientele groups and, **225;** definition of, **322;** economic, 325; equal opportunity, 325–326; government, 326; information resources of, 337; iron triangles and, **240**–242; lobbying by, 327–332; membership of, 335, 337; politics of, 327–332; public, 326; reasons for formation of, 323–324; resources of, 332–337; roles of, 322–323; roll call voting and, 181; in Supreme Court cases, 267–268; types of, 324–326

Intergovernmental organizations, **426**

Intermediate standard of review, **120,** 122

Internal Revenue Service, 225, 231, 237

Internet: as alternative to corporate media, 384; censorship on, 101–103; Censure and Move On,

299–300; congressional, 154; effects of, 375–376; evaluating sources on, 102–103; as news medium, 378–379; political organizing via, 299–300, 339–340; polls via, 281

Interstate Commerce Commission, 225

Investigative journalism, 395

Iran-contra affair, 347, 429

Iron triangle, **240**–242, 329

Isolationism, **425**

Issue advocacy ads, **330, 366**–367

Issue networks, 241

Issue ownership, **360**–361

Issues: avoidance of stances on, 398; campaigning on, 360–362; ownership of, **360**–361; position, **360;** valence, **360,** 361; in voter decision-making, 350–351; wedge, **360**

Ivanov, Igor, 430

Iyengar, Shanto, 390

Jackson, Andrew, 200; Democratic Party and, 307; spoils system under, 222; support of the press by, 381

Jackson, Jesse, 429

Jacobowitz, Eden, 83–84, 114–115

Japanese Americans, detention of, 137

Jay, John, 54

Jefferson, Thomas: on a bill of rights, 88; campaign advertising and, 362; Declaration of Independence, 36, 86; Democratic-Republicans and, 307; on freedom of conscience, 91; Marbury and, 254; presidential power under, 200; on public opinion, 276; on women's place, 38

Jim Crow laws, **124**–125

Johnson, Andrew, 123; impeachment of, 157, 187, 195

Johnson, Lady Bird, 212

Johnson, Lyndon: affirmative action and, **129**–130, 252, 409; campaign advertising by, 363; civil rights and, 128; congressional

politics of, 181; Great Society, 201; judicial appointments by, 263; Medicaid under, 418; Medicare under, 416; popularity of, 204; Vietnam War and, 196; voter image of, 352; welfare under, 60

Johnson v. *Zerbst,* 109

Joint Chiefs of Staff, 429–430, **430**

Joint committees, **172**

Journalism, 385–390; attack vs. investigative, 395; civic, **400;** horse race, 362, **392**–393; investigative, 100–101; liberal bias in, 387–388; Washington press corps, 389; yellow, 381–382

Journalists, **385;** demographic makeup of, 385–387; reform among, 399–400; revolving door and, **389**

Judges. *See also* Court system; Judicial branch; Justices: in common law tradition, 250; nomination of, 198–199; selection of federal, 259–261; state supreme court, 257

Judicial activism, **267**

Judicial branch, 48–50; Congress checks and balances with, 158–159; presidential power in, 198–199

Judicial interpretivism, **263**

Judicial power, **48**

Judicial restraint, **267**

Judicial review, 48–49, **49;** definition of, **253;** Marshall and, **253**–254

Judicial revolution, 198

Judiciary Act (1789), 254

Jurisdiction, **255**–256, 259

Jurisprudence, 252

Jury trials, 49–50, 89; as duty of citizenship, 114

Jus sanguinis, 15

Jus soli, 15

Just compensation, 89

Justice Department, 199

Justices. *See also* Courts; Judges; Judicial branch; Supreme Court: influences on, 267–268; state, 257; Supreme Court, 261–264

Kelly, Tina, 103
Kennedy, Anthony, 92
Kennedy, Jacqueline, 211–212
Kennedy, John F., 13–14, 36; assassination of, 373, 377; bureaucracy and, 238; Catholic support of, 350; civil rights and, 128; debates with Nixon, 364, 377, 393; judicial appointments by, 263; media image of, 396; New Frontier, 201; Peace Corps, 236; personality of, 214; voter image of, 352
Kessler, David, 241
Key, V. I., Kr., 276
Kinder, Donald, 390
King, Martin Luther, Jr., 127
Klopfer v. *North Carolina*, 89
Know-Nothing Party, 318
Koop, C. Everett, 241
Ku Klux Klan, 124, 284

Laissez-faire, 5, 69
Langbein, John H., 270
Larry King Live, 363, 378
Lasswell, Harold, 3, 23
Late Night with David Letterman, 363, 378
Latinos. *See* Hispanic Americans
Latino Vote USA, 136
Law: American legal tradition, 249–250; discrimination in, 119–120; equality before the, 20; executive orders, 198; ex post facto, **88**; how bills become laws, 175–181; kinds of, 250–252; philosophy of, 252; procedural equality under, 122; role of in democratic societies, 249; statutory, 256; substantive equality under, 122; suspect classifications under, **120**–122; women's status under, 139–140
Lawmaking, **153**–154
Leadership, 26; of Congress, 168–170; House of Representatives, 168–170; interest group, 335; Senate, 168–170
League of United Latin American Citizens (LULAC), 135
League of Women Voters, 369
Leaking, **397**

Legal aid programs, 271
Legal Services Corporation (LSC), 271
Legislative agenda, 175; setting, **176**
Legislative branch: constitution on, 46–47; presidential power in, 197–198
Legislative liaison, **205**
Legislative oversight, **171**
Legislative Reorganization Act (1946), 171
Legislative Reorganization Act (1970), 171
Legislature, **46**; bicameral, **46**–47, **156**
Legitimate, **3**
Lemon test, **92**, 120
Lemon v. *Kurtzman*, 92
Lewinsky, Monica, 299–300, 382, 393
Libel, **100**–101
Liberal ideology, **20**–22; of citizens, 284; Democratic Party and, 310–311; gender gap and, 290–291
Libertarian Party, 319
Libertarians, 22
Library of Congress, 173
Lieberman, Joseph, 350, 356
Life expectancy, 119
Lightner, Candy, 335, 336
Lincoln, Abraham, 123, 200, 276, 373; campaign advertising and, 362
Line-item veto, **180**, 198
Literacy tests, **124**
Littleton, Colorado, shooting, 104
Livingston, Robert, 217
Lobbying, **323**, 327–332; astroturf, **331**–332; direct, **327**–328; grassroots, **331**; indirect, **327**–328, 330; reforms on, 328–329; spending by, 334; staff for, 333
Lobbying Disclosure Act (1995), 329
Lobbyists, professional, 328, 333
Local party organizations, 320
Lochner v. *New York,* 70
Locke, Gary, 138
Locke, John, 11, 86, 248; Declaration of Independence influenced

by, 36; *A Second Treatise on Government,* 37
Log Cabin Republicans, 145
Logic, 25
Los Angeles Times, 376, 388
Lott, Trent, 305, 367

MacNelly, Jeff, 192
Madison, James, 1, 41; on a bill of rights, 88; on citizens, 12–13; on democracy, 12; Democratic-Republicans and, 307; on factions, 300–301, 322; *Federalist No. 10*, A13–A16; *Federalist No. 51*, A17–A19; *Federalist Papers*, 54, 55; on freedom of conscience, 91; Marbury and, 254; on political parties, 307; Virginia Plan, **43**
Magazines, 377
Magnet schools, 148
Majority minority districts, 161–162
Majority party, **167**
Majority rule, 9
Majority tyranny, 296
Malapportionment, **160**–162
Malcolm X, 128
Malloy v. *Hogan*, 89
Mandates, 358, 368
Mandatory retirement, 145–146
Mapp v. *Ohio*, 89
Marbury v. *Madison*, 49, 50, 72–73, 253–254
Margin of error, 279
Margolies-Mezvinsky, Marjorie, 150–151, 184–185
Markets, 5
Markup, 177
Marriage gap, **291**
Marshall, John, 49, 69–70, 253–254; power of the court under, 269
Marshall, Thomas, 211
Marshall, Thurgood, 264, 267
Marx, Karl, 6
Mason, George, 56
Massachusetts Bay Company, 34
Mass media, **375**. *See also* Media
Material benefits, **324**
McCain, John, 367
McCarran Act (1950), 96, 97
McCarthy, Joseph, 96

McClesky v. *Kemp,* 110
McConnell, Mitch, 367
McCulloch v. *Maryland,* **69**
The McLaughlin Group, 378
Means, Russell, 325
Media, 373–402; accountability and, 397–398; alternative press, 383–384; campaigns and, 361–365; citizen access to, 399–400; corporate ownership of, 382–384; coverage of Congress by, 183; coverage of issues by, 351; critical thinking about, 394–395; cynicism of, 394–395; definition of, 375–380; dramatization of news in, 400; history of American, 380–385; Internet, 378–379; interpretations of elections by, 368; liberal bias in, 387–388; negative advertising in, **361**–363; newspapers and magazines, 376–377; news sources on, 379–380; objectivity, 380–381; perceived role of, 28–29; politics as conflict and image in, 392–396; politics as public relations in, 396–397; presidency and, 202–204; presidential candidate positioning for, 353; public opinion and, 276–277, 390–392; radio, 377; regulation of, 384–385; Spanish-language, 135; television, 377–378; trial coverage by, 101
Medicaid, 418–419; federalism and, 72; Oregon program of, 66, 79
Medicare, 146, 416, 418
Meet the Press, 378
Megabills, 172
Merit, 221, 262
Merrill, Bruce, 300
Mexican American Legal Defense and Education Fund (MALDEF), 135
Mexican Americans, 135
Midterm loss, **165**
Military: commander-in-chief of, **195**–196; turf guarding in, 238
Military service: as duty of citizenship, 114
Militias, 31–32, 57–58; Internet

and, 339; Second Amendment and, 104–106
Mill, John Stuart, 95
Miller test, **98**
Milosević, Slobodan, 371
Minersville School District v. *Gobitis,* 93
Minimum rationality test, **120**–122
Minimum wage, 72
Minorities: excluded from citizenship, 11; majority rule and rights of, 9
Miranda v. *Arizona,* 108
Misdemeanors, 251
Missouri Compromise, 254
Mobility, 80–81
Momentum, **355**
Monarchy, **8**
Mondale, Walter, 211, 356
Monetary policy, 420–422, 433
Money supply, 420, 421
Montesquieu, Baron de, 50
Montgomery bus boycott, 126, 127
Morality, 21–22
Moral Majority, 92
Mothers Against Drunk Driving (MADD), 335, 336
Motor Voter Bill, **346,** 347
MSNBC, 373
MTV, 378
Multinational corporations, **426**
Mussolini, Benito, 9

Nader, Ralph, 319, 371; presidential debates and, 364
Nast, Thomas, 192
National Aeronautics and Space Administration, 225; *Challenger* disaster and, 234–235
National Association for the Advancement of Colored People (NAACP), 98, **125**; on the death penalty, 109–110; lobbying of courts by, 330; work against segregation, 125–130
National Committee on Pay Equity, 143
National conventions, 355–356
National defense: 2000 party platforms on, 315
National Education Association, 419

National Indian Youth Council, 133
National Industrial Recovery Act (NIRA), 246–247
National initiatives, 274, 296–297
National Journal, 155
National Park Service, 230
National Partnership for Reinventing Government, 239–240
National Performance Review, 211, 239–240
National polls, 280
National Public Radio, 377
National Railroad Passenger Corporation, 229–230
National referendum, 274, 296–297
National Republican Party, 318
National Republican Senatorial Committee, 367
National Restaurant Association, 336
National Rifle Association (NRA), 104, 105, 176; benefits of, 324; public mobilization by, 330
National Science Foundation, 225
National security, 200, 432
National Security Council (NSC), **209, 429**–430
National Voter Registration Act (1993), 346, 347
Native Americans, 119, 132–133; American Revolution and, 37–38
Naturalization, **15**
Naturalization Act (1790), 137
Near, Jay, 100
Near v. *Minnesota,* 89, 100
Necessary and proper clause, **62**–63
Negative advertising, **361**–363
Netanyahu, Benjamin, 196
Neutral competence, **221**
New Deal, 6, 21, 71; economic policy of, 420; increase in federal power from, 70; national debt and, 422; party era of, 308; presidential power under, 200–201
New Frontier, 201
New Jersey Plan, **43,** 44
News magazines, 377
News management, **396**–397
Newspapers, **376**–377, 379–380; presidential endorsements in, 388; web sites of, 379

News programs, 379–380

New York Sun, 381

New York Times, 376, 383

New York Times Company v. *United States*, 100

New York Times v. *Sullivan*, 100–101

Nineteenth Amendment, 141, A11; civil rights in, 85

Ninth Amendment, A9

Nixon, Richard: block grants under, 77; debates with Kennedy, 364, 393; federalism under, 71; judicial appointments by, 92; media image of, 396–397; Pentagon Papers, 100; personality of, 214; pornography and, **98**; resignation of, 187, 288; Vietnam War and, 196; voter image of, 352; Watergate scandal, 1

Nominating convention, **302**

Nongovernmental organizations, **426**

Nonviolent resistance movement, 127–128

Normative concepts, 14

Norms, **175**

North Atlantic Treaty Organization (NATO), 425, 426

Northwest Ordinance (1787), 123

Norton, Gale, 208

Objectivity, 380–381

Obscenity and pornography, 98–99

O'Connor, Sandra Day, 263

Offensive speech, **99**–100

Office of Economic Opportunity, 225

Office of Management and Budget (OMB), **209**; in budget process, 238–239; interagency politics and, 237; policy evaluation by, 412

Office of Public Liaison, 329

Office of Technology Assessment, 412

Oligarchy, **9**

Olympic Games (1996), 118–119

On-line processing, **294,** 351

OPEC (Organization of Petroleum Exporting Countries), 426

Open primaries, 354

Open rule, 177

Opinion leaders, **294,** 295–296

Opinions, **268**

Opinion studies, 281

Oppo research, **359**

The Oprah Winfrey Show, 363

Oregon health care program, 66

Organic foods, 219–220, 244

Organization of Petroleum Exporting Countries (OPEC), 426

Original jurisdiction, **256**

Panetta, Leon, 210

Pardoning power, **199**

Parker v. *Gladden,* 89

Parks, Rosa, 126, 127

Parliamentary systems, 216–217

Participation, citizen, 286–287

Participatory democracy, **10**; on public opinion, 276

Partisan gerrymandering, 161–162

Partisanship, **302**; in Congress, 166–167, 179–180; undisciplined parties-in-government and, 321; in voter decision-making, 350

Party activists, **316**–317

Party base, **305**

Party bosses, **307**

Party caucus, **354**

Party caucuses, **168**

Party eras, **308**

Party faithful, 316–317

Party identification, **304**–305; in voter decision-making, 350

Party-in-government, **303**–304; undisciplined, 321

Party-in-the-electorate, **304**–305

Party machines, **307**–308

Party organization, **302**–303

Party platforms, **312**–313, 314–315

Party primaries, **308**

Party whips, 168

Paterson, William, 43

Patient's bills of rights, 419

Patronage, **222**; party machines and, **307**; reform of, 308

Patterson, Thomas, 394–395

Peace Corps, 236

Peer groups, 288

Pendleton Act (1883), **222**

Penny press, 381–382

Pentagon Papers, 100

People for the American Way, 300

Perot, Ross, 317, 319, 363, 364; media access and, 374

Persian Gulf War, 204, 378, 391

Personal contacts, 328

Personality, presidential, 213–215

Personal Responsibility and Work Opportunity Reconciliation Act (1996), 60–61, 81, 206, 415

Persuasion, power of, 240; media, 391–392

Plebiscites, national, 274

Plessy, Homer, 125

Plessy v. *Ferguson,* 125

Pluralism, 147; interest groups and, 338–339

Pluralist democracy, **10, 301**; civil rights and, 147; on public opinion, 276

Pocket veto, **180**

Police power, **93**

Policy adoption, 411

Policy commitment, 233

Policy entrepreneurship, **176**

Policy evaluation, 411–412

Policy formulation, 411

Policy implementation, 411

Policy paralysis, 310

Policy representation, **153**

Political action committee (PAC), **329**; campaign contributions by, 333–335, 365–366; congressional campaign donations by, 164

Political cartoons, 192–193

Political correctness, **99**–100

Political culture, **17**–20; individualistic, 18–20; procedural, 18–19

Political equality, 20, 117–149; African Americans and, 123–131; age and, 145–146; Asian Americans and, 136–138; definition of, 119–122; disability and, 146; Hispanic Americans and, 133–136; interest groups and, 338–339; Native Americans and, 132–133; sexual orientation and, 144–145; women and, 139–144

Political knowledge, 283–284, 294

Political parties, 301–306. *See also* Democratic Party; Republican

Party; accountability and, 398; American system of, 307–312; coattail effect and, 164–165; congressional control by, 179–180; decentralized organization of, 320; definition of, **301**–305; electioneering by, 302–303; eras and change in, 308–310; ideologies of, 310–317; national conventions, 355–356; organization of, **302**–303; party-in-government, **303**–304, 321; party-in-the-electorate, **304**–305; policies of, 167; president as head of, 190; reform of, 308; responsible party model of, **305**–306; role of in Congress, 167; roll call voting and, 181; television's effects on, 398; third, 318–319; two-party system of, 317, 319; voter mobilization by, **347**

Political socialization, **287**–288

Political specialization, 369

Political systems, 8–12; authoritarian, 8–9; democratic, 9–10; meanings of citizenship in, 10–12

Politics: blacks in, 130–131; compared to government, 4; as conflict and image, 392–396; definition of, **3**–8; economics and, 4–6; external bureaucratic, 236–243; inside the bureaucracy, 232–236; interagency, 237–238; interest group, 327–332; involvement in, 27–29; media roles in, 390–398; presidential, 201–207; as public relations, 396–397; Supreme Court and, 261–269; thinking critically about, 24–26

Politics in America, 155

Pollock v. *Farmer's Loan and Trust Co.,* 70

Polls, 202–204; straw, 399

Poll taxes, **124**, 128

Popular sovereignty, **9**

Popular tyranny, **40**

Popular vote, 357

Populist Party, 318

Pork barrel, **153**

Pornography, 98–99

Position issues, **360**

Powell, Colin, 131, 208

Powell, Lewis, 113

Powell v. *Alabama,* 89

Power. *See also* Federalism: in Articles of Confederation, 39–41; Constitutional Convention and, 42–44; definition of, **3**; in democratic theory, 10; media access and, 374; rights as, 86; state vs. central government, 39–41, 42–44

Power to persuade, 201–**202**

Prayer in school, 92

Precedent, **250**

Premises, 25

President, 187–218; appointment power of, 238; budget power of, 238–239; bureaucracy and, 223, 238–240; character and, 213–215; citizenship and, 215–216; conflicting roles of, 190–191; conflict with Congress and, 158; constitutional powers of, 47–48, 188, 195–199; electing, 352–368; evolution of office of, 194–201; executive powers of, 195–196; expectations of, 188–193; foreign policy and, 429–431; going public by, 202–204; judicial powers of, 198–199; legislative powers of, 197–198; list of, A20; lobbying, 329; modern presidency, 200–201; nominating process, 352–356; politics and, 201–207; popularity of, 202–204; powers of, 189–190; in public policy making, 409; qualifications for, 194–195; roll call voting and, 181; staff of, 207–213; State of the Union address, 48; term limits on, 189; traditional presidency, 199–200; veto power of, 180, 239; working with Congress, 204–207

Presidential debates, 364–365

Presidential primary, **354**

Presidential Succession Act (1947), 194–195

Presidential veto, **197**–198

President pro tempore, 168; succession to presidency by, 194–195

Presidents: public opinion and, 276–277

Primaries, 354–355

Priming, 391

Printing press, 375

Printz v. *United States,* 73

Prior restraint, **100**

Privacy, right to, 111–114; gay rights and, 112–113; public officials and, 217; right to die and, 113

Privacy Act of 1974, **243**

Privatization, 6

Problem of collective action, 323–324

Procedural, **18**

Procedural due process, **250**

Procedural equality, 122

Procedural laws, **250**

Procedural political culture, 18–19

Progressive Party, 318

Progressive taxes, 423

Prohibition Party, 318

Project Vote Smart (PVS), 154

Property: as citizenship prerequisite, 11–12; redistribution of, 40

Prospective voting, **351**

Public Campaign, 367

Public expectations, 188–189, 201–202

Public Health Cancer Association, 337

Public interest groups, **326**

Public mobilization, 330

Public opinion, 274–298; citizenship and, 293–296; citizen values and, 283–287; definition of, **275**; influences on, 287–293; measuring, 277–283; media shaping of, 390–392; role of in democracy, 275–277; sources of divisions in, 288–293; toward politics, 347

Public opinion polls, **275,** 277–283; accuracy of, 281; campaign, 280–281; critical thinking about, 282; horse race, 277; national, 280; push, 281; quality of, 278–280; questions used in, 279–280; sampling in, 278, 279; types of, 280–281

Public policy, 403–435; definition of, **405**; distributive, **407**–408; economic, 420–422; health care, 418–419; impact of federalism on, 66; makers of, 408–410; making, 404–425; middle-class and corporate welfare, 413; process of making, 410–412; redistributive, **406**–408; regulatory, **408**; social problems and, 405–406; social security, 416–417; tax, 423–425; types of, 406–408; in voter decision-making, 350–351; welfare, 414–415

Public Radio International, 377

Public relations, politics as, 396–397

Puerto Rican Legal Defense and Education Fund, 135

Puerto Ricans, 135

Punitive damages, 251

Push polls, **281**

Quality of life, 21–22

Race: equality before the law and, 270–271; influence of on public opinion, 291; party identification by, 312; political inequality and, 118–119, 122; as suspect class, 121, 162; voter turnout and, 135–136, 138, 345

Racial gerrymandering, **161**–162

Racism, 123

Radio, 377, 380, 399

Ratification, 53–57; of Thirteenth Amendment, 123

Ratified, **53**

Ratings, 202–203

Rational electorate, 294–296

Rational ignorance, **293**–294

Rational nonvoters, 348

Reagan, Nancy, 212

Reagan, Ronald: affirmative action under, 130; block grants under, 77; communication skills of, 214, 397; fairness doctrine and, 384; federalism under, 71; Iran-contra affair, 429; judicial appointments by, 92, 112, 198, 259, 263; legal aid programs under, 271; on religious rights, 92; retrospective

voting and, **351**; tax reform of, 425; two terms of, 190; vice president under, 211; voter image of, 352

Realignment, **308**–310

Reapportionment, **160**

Reconstruction, **124**–125

Redistributive policies, **406**–407

Redistricting, **160**–161

Redman, Eric, 181

Red tape, **223**–224

Reform Party, 319

Refugees, **16**, 135

Regressive taxes, 423

Regulation, 6; of broadcast media, 384–385; of business, 69–70, 73; of organic foods, 219–220; Supreme Court on, 269; waivers from, 79

Regulations, **228**

Regulatory policies, 407, **408**

Rehnquist, William, 1, 110, 112

Religion: influence of on public opinion, 291–292; party identification by, 312; protection of American Indian religious sites, 133; in voter decision-making, 350; as voting qualification, 34

Religious freedom. See Freedom of religion

Religious Freedom Restoration Act (RFRA), 94

Reorganization, government, 239–240

Representation, **152**–153; allocative, **153**; balancing constituency and national, 184–185; interest groups in, 323; policy, **153**; Supreme Court justices and, 263–264; symbolic, **153**

Reproductive rights, 111–112

Republican National Committee, 302, 320

Republican Party: abortion and, 112; African Americans in, 138; Asian Americans in, 138; Christian Right and, 112; Congress controlled by, 158, 165; gays in, 145; ideology of, 310–311; interest groups and, 334–335; membership of, 312; moderating influences on, 313,

316–317; organization of, 307–308; platform of, 312–313, 314–315; tax policy of, 424; voter turnout and, 349

Republican Revolution, 158

Republican virtue, 13–14

Republics, **12**; Madison on, 55

Resources, 3; of interest groups, 332–337; law as distribution of, 249

Response rates, 282

Responsible party model, **305**–306, 310

Restrictive rule, 177

Retrospective voting, **351**

Reuters, 377

Revere, Paul, 36, 192

Revolution, 58

Revolving door, **328**, **389**

Riders, 177

Right of blood, 15

Right of rebuttal, 384

Right of the soil, 15

Rights, 83–116; to bear arms, 104–106; citizen power and, 86; conflicting, 87; of criminal defendants, 106–110; in a democracy, 86–87; freedom of assembly, 98; freedom of expression, 95–104; freedom of religion, 91–94; government size and, 68–69; of illegal immigrants, 17; Locke on, 11–12; majority vs. minority, 296–297; to privacy, 111–114; reproductive, 111–112

Right to a fair trial, 101

Right to bear arms, 104–106; importance of, 104–105; judicial decisions on, 105

Right to counsel, 89, 109

Right to die, 113

Right to know, 101

Robinson v. *California*, 89

Roe v. *Wade*, 112, 142, 267

Roll Call, 155

Roll call voting, **181**; campaign contributions and, 335

Rolling Stone, 28

Romano, Carlin, 394

Roosevelt, Franklin D.: economic intervention by, 6; economic pol-

icy of, 420; Executive Office of the President and, **209**; fireside chats, 373–374, 377; G.I. Bill of Rights and, 182; growth of government under, 70; judicial appointments by, 263, 271–272; New Deal, 71; party era of, 308; personality of, 214; presidential power under, 200–201; public expectations and, 189; Supreme Court and, 246–247; welfare under, 60
Roosevelt, Teddy, 318, 319
Rule of Four, **266**
Rule of unanimity, 9
Rules, **7**–8; bureaucratic, 221, 223–224, 230–231
Rumsfeld, Donald, 208
Russia, 427

Sabato, Larry, 393
Safe Drinking Water Act, 408
Safire, William, 389
Sales taxes, 423
Salon magazine, 379
Sample bias, **278**
Samples, **278**, 282
Sampling error, **279**
Sanford, Edward, 90
Saturday Night Live, 363, 378
Saturday Press, 100
Scalia, Antonin, 112
Scandal watching, 393–394
Scandinavia, 18; as social democracy, 6–7
Schechter Poulter Corporation v. *United States*, 246–247
Schenck v. *United States*, 96
School choice, 148
School desegregation, 117–118, 125–126, 128–129, 147–148
Scott, Dred, 271
Search and seizure, unreasonable, 89, 107–108
Second Amendment, 90, A9; right to bear arms and, 31–32, 104–106
A Second Treatise on Government (Locke), 37
Secretaries, department, 227–228
Secular intent, 92
Securities and Exchange Commission, 229

Security, law as, 249
Sedition, **96**–97
Segregation, 66, 117–118, **124**–130; educational, 128–130; Jim Crow laws and, **124**–125
Select committee, **172**
Selective incentives, **324**
Selective incorporation, **90**
Selective perception, **392**
Self-incrimination, 108
Self-interest, 13–14, 276; public opinion divisiveness from, 288
Senate: approval of appointments by, 198; Article I on, 47; basis of representation in, 43–44; confirmation of justices by, 264; differences between House and, 156–158; leadership of, 168–170; qualifications for, 47; term length in, 156
Senate Appropriations Committee, 173
Senate Armed Services Committee, 173
Senate Finance Committee, 172
Senate Foreign Relations Committee, 173
Senate Judiciary Committee, 264
Senate Select Committee on Whitewater, 172
Senatorial courtesy, **199, 260**–261
Seneca Falls convention, 140
Seniority system, **170**, 173
Sensationalism, 383
Sentencing laws, 403, 434
Separate but equal, 125–126
Separationists, **91**–92
Separation of church and state, 91–92
Separation of powers, **50**–52; Madison on, 55
Seventeenth Amendment, A11
Seventh Amendment, A9
SF Weekly, 383
Shays, Daniel, 40
Shays's Rebellion, **40**–41
Shepard, Matthew, 22
Sherbert v. *Verner*, 93
Sierra Club, lobbying of courts by, 330
Simpson, O. J., 382

Sisters of Perpetual Indulgence, 87
Sit-ins, 127–128
Sixteenth Amendment, A11
Sixth Amendment, A9; applied to states, 89; media coverage of trials and, 101; right to counsel in, 109
Skip-generation households, 415
Slander, 100
SLAPS test, 98
Slate magazine, 379
Slavery: American Revolution and, 37; Article V on, 53; Constitution on, 45; ended, 123; Three-fifths Compromise and, **45**
Smith, Will, 1
Smith Act (1940), 96, 97
Social connectedness, **347**–348
Social contract, **11**
Social democracy, **6–7**
Socialism, 6
Socialist Party of America, 318
Socialization, 287–288
Social problems, 405–406. *See also* Public policy
Social protest, **330**
Social security, 70, 146; future of, 417; income taxes and, 423; policy, 416–417, 433
Social Security Act (1935), 225, 416–417
Social Security Act (1965), 418
Social Security Administration, 225
Social Security Trust Fund, 423
Social spending, 311
Soft money, **366**–367
Solicitor general, **199, 266**
Solidary benefits, **324**
Sons of Liberty, 31, 35, 36
Sound bites, **393**
Southern Christian Leadership Conference (SCLC), 127–128
Southwest Voter Registration Project (SWVRP), 136
Soviet Union, 427; as oligarchy, 9
Speaker of the House, **168**, 170; power of, 177; succession to presidency by, 194–195
Special Committee on the Year 2000 Technology Problem, 172
Special interests: campaign finance and, 182; Madison on, 55

Specialization, 221, 233–234, 369

Speech codes, 83–84, 99–100, 114–115

Spin, 395, **396**–397

Spiral of cynicism, 395–396

The Spirit of the Laws (Montesquieu), 50

Splinter parties, **319**

Split-ticket voting, 310

Spoilers, 319

Spoils system, **221**–222

Staff: of committee system, 173; congressional, 173–174; of president, 207–213; White House, 208, **209**–210

Stamp Act (1765), 35

Standards of review, 120–122

Standing committees, **171–172**

Stare decisis, 250, 267

State courts, 255, 256–257

State of the Union address, 48, 158, **197**

State party committees, 320

State primaries, 355

States: Constitutional Convention and, 42–44; constitutional powers of, 63–64; innovations by, 79; welfare powers of, 60–61; woman suffrage in, 140–142

States' Rights Party, 318

Statutory laws, **251**–252, 256

Stereotypes of bureaucracy, 220

Stewart, Potter, 98

Stonewall riots, 145

Strategic policy, **428**

Strategic politicians, **164**

Straw polls, 399

Strict constructionism, **262**–263

Strict scrutiny, **120**

Structural defense policy, **428**

Student Nonviolent Coordinating Committee (SNCC), 128

Subcommittees, 177

Subjects, **10,** 57

Substantive equality, 122

Substantive laws, **250**

Sugar Act (1764), 35

Sunshine laws, **243**–244

Super Tuesday, 355

Supply, 5–6

Supremacy clause, **63**

Supreme Court: case selection by, 265–266; constitutional powers of, 48–50; as court of appeals, 256; Court packing, 246–247, 271–272; decision-making by, 264–268; establishment of, 253; on federalism, 72–80; on Fourteenth Amendment, 71; on freedom of religion, 92–94; on gun rights, 105; incorporation by, 89–90; interpretive powers of, 67–68, 253–254; justices listed, A21; opinions, **268**; political effects of decisions by, 268–269; Roosevelt and, 246–247, 271–272; selection of justices to, 261–264; on supremacy clause, 64

Susan B. Anthony Amendment, 140

Suspect classifications, **120**–122

Sweden, 18–19

Swing voters, **358**–359

Symbolic representation, **153**

Symbolic speech, 97–98

Tammany Hall, 192, 193

Taxes: as duty of citizenship, 114; English colonial, 34–35; 2000 party platforms on, 315; policy on, 423–425; public opinion toward, 289; reforms, 424–425

Taxpayer Relief Act (1997), 180

Tea Act (1773), 35

Television. *See* Media

Temporary Assistance to Needy Families (TANF), 60, 77, 415; Medicaid and, 418

Tennessee Valley Authority, 229

Tenth Amendment, A9

Term limits, 182, 183–184, 189; presidential, 194

Terrorism, 58

Thatcher, Margaret, 65

Theocracy, **8**

Thesis, 25

Third Amendment, A9

Third parties, 317, 319, 371

Thirteenth Amendment, 45, A10; civil rights in, 85; ratification of, 123

Thomas, Clarence, 264, 291

Thompson, Tommy G., 79

Three-fifths Compromise, **45**

Thurmond, Strom, 318

Title IX, 142, 143

Tobacco industry: astroturf lobbying by, 331; interest groups and, 337; iron triangle, 240–241

Tobacco Institute, 241, 337

Tocqueville, Alexis de, 119, 322

Tolerance: of citizens, 284–286; freedom of expression and, 95

The Tonight Show with Jay Leno, 363, 378

Torts, 251

Totalitarian governments, **8,** 21

Townshend Acts (1767), 35

Tracking polls, **280**

Treaties, **196**

Trial courts, 256

Trickle-down strategy, 424

Trickle-up strategy, 423–424

Truman, Harry, 198, 213; containment policy of, 428; executive orders of, 252; Fair Deal, 201; judicial appointments by, 263; popularity of, 204

Trust in government: Congress and, 151–152; since Watergate, 1–2

Truth in sentencing laws, 403, 434

Turf guarding, 238

Tweed, "Boss," 192

Twelfth Amendment, A9–A10

Twentieth Amendment, A11–A12

Twenty-fifth Amendment, A12–A13

Twenty-first Amendment, A12

Twenty-fourth Amendment, 128, A12

Twenty-second Amendment, A12

Twenty-sixth Amendment, A13; civil rights in, 85

Twenty-third Amendment, A12

2000 election, 342–343; Asian American vote in, 138; congressional, 165–167; electoral college in, 357; issue ownership in, 360–361; mandate of, 368, 369–371; Nader in, 319; party base in, 305, 350; party platforms, 314–315; Supreme Court ruling on, 261; voter images of candidates in, 352, 360

Two-party system, 317, 319

Unanimity, rule of, 9
Unfunded Mandate Act (1995), 78
Unfunded mandates, **78**
Unitary systems, **65**
United Farm Workers of America, 136
United Kingdom, unitary system in, 65
United Nations, 32, 65–66, 426
United States, founding of, 31–59
United States v. *Eichman*, 98
United States v. *O'Brien*, 97–98
Unreasonable search and seizure, 89, 107–108
Urban Institute, 415
U.S. courts of appeals, 257, 258–259
U.S. Department of Agriculture (USDA), 225, 226, 227; organic food regulations, 219–220, 244; tobacco iron triangle and, 240–241
U.S. Forest Service, 242
U.S. Immigration and Naturalization Service (INS), 15, 16; Illegal Immigration Reform and Immigrant Responsibility Act and, 17
U.S. Postal Service, 5, 229
USA Today, 1, 376

Valence issues, **360**, 361
Value-added taxes (VAT), 424–425
Values: American, 17–20; in arguments, 25; citizen, 283–287; conservative, 21; definition of, **17**–18; family, 21–22; law as conformity to, 249; liberal, 21; in the media, 395
Van Buren, Martin, 307, 318
Veto override, **180**
Veto power, 50, 197–198; bureaucracy and, 239
Vice president: candidate selection, 355–356; Senate leadership of, 168; succession to presidency by, 194–195; working with the president, 210–211
Vietnam War, 182, 196, 347, 391;

television and, 377–378; War Powers Act and, 431
Village Voice, 383
Virginia Plan, **43**, 44
Voter mobilization, **347**
Voter News Service (VNS), 280
Voters: candidate images among, 351–352; decision-making by, 350–352; swing, **358**–359
Voter turnout, 12, 286, 344–349; age and, 146, 344; among Asian Americans, 138; among Hispanic Americans, 135–136; consequences of, 348–349; education and, 289; income and, 345; Jackson and, 381; legal obstacles to, 345–347; party roles in, 303; race and ethnicity and, 135–136, 138, 345; reasons for low, 345–348
Voting, 26; African Americans excluded from, 123–125; benefits of, 348; colonial requirements for, 34; as duty of citizenship, 114; felons loss of right to, 120; prospective, **351**; registration for, 345–347; retrospective, **351**; woman suffrage and, 20, 38, 140–142
Voting Rights Act (1965), 128
Voting Rights Act (1982), 161

Waivers, 79
Walker, Robert S., 180
Wallace, George, 319
Wall Street Journal, 376, 383
War, power to declare, 195–196
War Powers Act (1973), 182, 196, 431–432
Warren, Earl, 97, 126, 262
Washington, George, 200, 207–208, 362, 373
Washington Post, 100, 376
Washington press corps, 389
Washington Week in Review, 378
Watergate scandal, 1, 182, 288, 347
Waxman, Henry, 241
Weaver, David, 385–386
Weaver, James, 318

Webster v. *Reproductive Services*, 267–268
Wedge issues, **360**
Weeks v. *United States*, **107**–108
Welfare: middle-class and corporate, 413; policy, 414–415; public opinion toward, 289; redistributive policies of, 407; reforms, 60–61, 77, 81, 414–415; in social democracies, 7
Welfare states, 7
West Virginia State Board of Education v. *Barnette*, 93
Whig Party, 307
Whips, 168. *See also* Lobbying
Whistleblower Protection Act (1989), 235
Whistle blowers, **235**
White, Byron, 263
White House staff, 208, **209**–210
White supremacists, 32, 339
Widener University Wolfgram Memorial Library, 103
Wilhoit, Cleveland, 385–386
Wilson, Pete, 355
Wilson, Woodrow, 141
Wire services, 377, 385
Wirt, William, 318
Wolf v. *Colorado*, 89
Woman suffrage, 20, 38, 140–142
Women: American Revolution and, 38; in the civil service, 231; in Congress, 162, 163; in journalism, 387; liberalism of, 290–291; pornography and, 99
Women's rights movement, 140
Working Assets, 300
Works Project Administration, 422
World War II, 422, 426–427
World Wide Web: censorship of, 101–103; Censure and Move On, 299–300; evaluating sources on, 102–103
Writs of certiorari, **266**

Yellow journalism, 381–382

Zone of privacy, 111